Classics
— of —
Public
Policy

Jay M. Shafritz
University of Pittsburgh

Karen S. Layne
University of Nevada at Las Vegas

Christopher P. Borick
Muhlenberg College

PEARSON
Longman

New York   San Francisco   Boston
London   Toronto   Sydney   Tokyo   Singapore   Madrid
Mexico City   Munich   Paris   Cape Town   Hong Kong   Montreal

Executive Editor: Eric Stano
Senior Marketing Manager: Elizabeth Fogarty
Production Manager: Denise Phillip
Project Coordination, Text Design,
   and Electronic Page Makeup: WestWords, Inc.
Cover Design Manager: John Callahan
Cover Designer: Maria Ilardi
CoverPhoto: Courtesy PhotoDisc Inc.
Manufacturing Manager: Mary Fischer

For permission to use copyrighted material, grateful acknowledgment is
made to the copyright holders on pp. 1, 5, 9, 18, 26, 41, 51, 62, 77, 83, 88,
100, 107, 128, 137, 148, 167, 170, 180, 185, 189, 199, 201, 209, 223, 230,
234, 248, 285, 291, 297, 300, 302, 310, 320, 327, 335, 342, 365, 369, 375,
396, 409, and 415 which are hereby made part of this copyright page.

Library of Congress Cataloging-in-Publication Data

Classics of public policy / [edited by] Jay M. Shafritz, Karen S. Layne,
Christopher P. Borick.
       p. cm.
     ISBN 0-321-08989-8 (pbk.)
     1. Public policy. I. Shafritz, Jay M. II. Layne, Karen S.
     III. Borick, Christopher P.
    H97.C54 2005
    320.6–dc22

                                      2004020799

Please visit our website at http://www.ablongman.com

ISBN 0-321-08989-8

Contents

Preface

The examination of public policy issues goes back as far as we can trace civilization. Policy issues can be found in the Old Testament, Genesis 4:9 ("Am I my brother's keeper?"); in the New Testament, Matthew 22:21 ("Render therefore unto Caesar the things which are Caesar's. . . ."); in Homer's The Iliad ("It is not unseemly for a man to die fighting in defense of his country."); in Aesop's fable of "The Cat and the Mice" ("Who shall bell the cat?"); and in the works of countless other ancient storytellers, philosophers and historians. Indeed, the only really new thing about public policy is the self-conscious study of it.

All fields of endeavor have landmarks as they progress. Sometimes they are literal and physical. Thus the landmarks of ancient architecture and engineering can still be seen in the pyramids of Egypt and the roads of Rome. Sometimes they are procedures as in military drills and techniques for weaving rugs. Our concern is the intellectual landmarks of public policy. Just as the arch perfected by the ancient Romans must be studied anew by each generation of architects, so must those who would understand and advance public policy study their classic concepts. All this volume seeks to do is to compile a grouping of many of the most recognized of these classic writings in one convenient place.

It is often said in relation to real estate that three things are critical in arriving at a sale price: location, location, and location. Of course other factors also enter into consideration. But none comes even close to location in importance. It is often the same with the location of public policy studies. Few things are more important in determining the nature of a public policy study or proposal than its source of origin.

This phenomenon is commonly known as Miles Law after a manager in the Bureau of the Budget (now the Office of Management and Budget) who first observed: "Where you stand depends on where you sit." Rufus E. Miles, Jr. wrote the history of his law in a 1978 Public Administration Review article after it had been folk wisdom among federal bureaucrats for many years. While admitting that his "concept was as old as Plato," the "phraseology" evolved from a specific sequence of events that occurred when Miles was supervising a group of budget examiners. One of the examiners was offered a higher paying job as a budget analyst at one of the agencies he had been reviewing. Since he had been particularly critical of this agency in his capacity as a reviewing budget examiner, he told Miles (his boss) that he would prefer to stay in his present job if his salary could be raised. Miles, ever concerned about federal expenditure levels, refused to support a raise of his subordinate's salary. So the subordinate resigned to accept the job with an agency he felt was not very efficient.

Miles then remarked to the remaining workers under his supervision that soon the former employee would be defending the new budget policies that he had so vociferously criticized. His fellow budget examiners found this unbelievable. After all, the exiting analyst was a man of strongly felt judgments and integrity. But Miles insisted, and was proven correct by events, that as his law states: "Where you stand depends upon where you sit." Since the former employee was sitting elsewhere, his views would naturally evolve to reflect his new position. It wasn't a matter of ethics so much as it was a matter of perspective. In effect, no employee can be separated from the perspective of the particular responsibilities of their current position. Revised stances on issues and policies can be, and often are, the opposite of those previously held. This is not so much hypocrisy as it is loyalty to one's new employer.

Miles's Law has never been repealed. Stances on policy issues still tend to reflect their source—the organizations that promulgate them—far more so than any ideals of objectivity. It is not that these sources are necessarily corrupt or dishonest, they just look at policy issues through nonobjective lenses. They are often like the person whose only tool is a hammer; to that individual every problem looks very much like a nail. This is why to a lawyer all public policy issues look like legal problems. Economists have a well-known proclivity to apply econometrics to policy questions. Each academic discipline has its own biased bag of tricks with which to view the public policy world.

These so called "bags of tricks," the approaches to problems taken by the various disciplines (as well as the specializations within them) constitute their doctrines—their core beliefs about how public policy problems are to be viewed. How viewed? Why through their doctrinal lenses. They don't see the policy world so much through rose colored glasses as through professional, organizational, and methodological bias. However, this bias is not a negative unreasoning prejudice; it is how their occupational socialization has taught them to see public policy problems.

Consequently, there is no consensus on how to study public policy—nor is there likely to be any unanimity in the foreseeable future. Anyone studying public policy is free to accept the discipline and doctrinal approaches of his or her choice. But before casting your lot with one approach to the exclusion of others, consider the options. Examine each approach's strengths and weaknesses. See if its philosophy and doctrines are in harmony with your already established beliefs, assumptions, and predispositions. You may find that no single perspective deserves your loyalty, that each contains important information and insights that are useful in differing circumstances. Remember the disciplines exist only as intellectual constructs to organize education for students and to serve as mutual support networks for scholars.

Policy science refers to a problem-solving orientation that cuts across all disciplines to deal with important societal decisions. It sought to integrate the policy related aspects of relevant disciplines into a unified whole. It began as a post-World War II effort to distinguish between (1) an objective conception of social science (which rejected public purposes and goals) and (2) the pragmatic approach of policy practitioners (who insisted on application as the sole basis for education and research). Harold D. Lasswell, in his *Preview of the Policy Sciences* (1971) held that policy science studies "the process of deciding or choosing and evaluating the relevance of available knowledge for the solution of particular problems."

While the policy sciences are alive and well, policy science as an independent integrating academic discipline has not done well. Its subject matter has been subsumed into policy studies programs that are most often located in political science, public administration, and economics departments. Lasswell's call for a new discipline was simply not heeded. The great contribution of the concept of policy science was to call attention to the inherently interdisciplinary nature of public policy research.

And each of these traditional academic disciplines was able to say—with a relatively straight face—that they could be as interdisciplinary as the next guy (or department). Nevertheless, location still rules here. Thus Stuart S. Nagel, a preeminent historian of policy studies as a discipline, is able to write in his "Policy Studies" article for the *International Encyclopedia of Public Policy and Administration* (1998) that "the most distinguishing characteristic of various programs . . . is whether they emphasize a political science approach, as in the Berkeley Graduate School of Public Policy; an economics approach, as in the Harvard Kennedy School; or a social psychology approach as in Northwestern's Evaluation Research Program."

Overall, policy studies is an extremely broad term which is used to describe a vast variety of interdisciplinary academic programs that focus on aspects of public policy. Furthermore, policy studies as a program emphasis or as a specific research effort can be broken down into two broad categories:

1. The normative which critiques public policymaking and makes recommendations on how the process may be made more efficient, more equitable and more democratic; and
2. The analytic which uses policy analysis to develop models and explanations for policy outcomes.

Policy studies began a significant self-conscious expansion of programs and research in the 1960s. This was the same time that public administration enjoyed explosive growth. But while the growth in public administration leveled off by the early 1980s, policy studies has continued to expand. Why? Because it is so much easier to identify with a field that, unlike public administration, is so broad and amorphous that, like a gas, it will fill any space it occupies. Biologists and chemists, who once hid in their laboratories, have now come out as environmental policy experts. Civil engineers and city planners are now urban policy experts. Municipal bond analysts and government accountants are now fiscal policy experts. Social psychologists with interest in how people are motivated to act in the public interest become social policy experts. And it goes on and on. Every discipline has its only policy niche. And in the interdisciplinary field of policy studies each cries out for a place setting at the research grant dispensing table.

Typologies, commonly used in the study of public policy, have a long historical tradition. They create neatness out of chaos, make it easier to remember the essence of complex intellectual arguments and offer the happy illusion that a matter has been settled by our betters and therefore beyond question. For example, German sociologist Max Weber (1864–1920) wrote that there were three pure types of legitimate authority: charismatic (in which the personal qualities of a leader command obedience); traditional (in which custom and culture yield acquiescence); and legal (in which people obey laws enacted by what they perceive to be appropriate authorities).

The study of public policy offers enormous scope for the creation of typologies. Textbooks and scholarly monographs sag with lists, categories, and classifications of public policies and ways to analyze them. The study of public policy is a chaotic world that cries out for organization, for definitive classification, and for a unified approach. But this is a cry that will not be heeded. Chaos rules because there is no power—neither American president nor university president—that can tell the scholars of those academic disciplines concerned with public policy (political science, public administration, economics, international relations, etc.) how to ply their trade. Textbooks in science (biology, chemistry, physics, etc.) at least agree on the subject matter they cover. Public policy texts, in contrast, are far less agreeable. True, there is considerable overlap; but it is minimal compared to the sciences. This is largely because the disciplines that study public policy have such different traditions and approaches.

The table of contents for this book is a typology. We have classified our classic selections into eleven categories or chapters. This has been a necessarily arbitrary exercise. If we simply organized them by date in chronological order, it would not have been a very useful means of organizing a course of instruction. And this is, after all, a textbook. So we arranged our selections into chapters that we hoped would reflect how public policy courses are taught. Before you criticize our typology reflect for a moment on the sign often found in nineteenth-century western saloons: "Please don't shoot the piano player. He is doing the best he can."

We start with the overall context of public policy; then look at decision making in support of policymaking, examine the influence of interest groups, and review how policies arrive on governmental agendas. Next we put this into the context of the overall political economy. Then we examine how policy is dealt with by the three branches of government: the legislative, the executive, and the judiciary. Finally we examine foreign policy, public policy as public relations, and offer an overview of policy analysis.

With the world so chock full of writings on public policy issues, we had to develop extremely restrictive criteria for inclusion. First we looked for readings with enduring value. After all, classics of whatever kind are classics in the first place because they offer something of value from the past that will continue to be of value in the future. Second, there had to be a broad consensus that a selection was important—directly relevant to the core public policy concerns of today. An "unrecognized classic" seems to us to be a contradiction. Thus, we asked ourselves: "Should a student of public affairs, broadly defined, be expected to identify this author and his or her basic themes?" If the answer was yes, it was so because such a contribution has long been recognized as an important theme by a significant writer. While one might fairly criticize the exclusion of a particular author or item, one would find it difficult to honestly criticize us for our inclusions—because they are among the most widely quoted and reprinted analyses of public policy. Our final criterion for inclusion was readability. We sought selections that would be read and appreciated by people with no background in public policy literature. To accommodate this last criterion we severely edited many selections to enhance their readability.

Each chapter begins with an introduction to the topic and discussions of the selections. This material is designed to "set up" the selected reading and briefly synopsize its content. Review questions follow at the end of each chapter.

Chapter 1

The Context of
Public Policy

Public policy is always contextual in that it necessarily comes out of a time and place. The three selections in this chapter examine the context of public policy from three different perspectives: utility, system, and change. They will ask, in turn, what is the usefulness of a policy, where does a policy fit within the overall political system and how does policy evolve or change?

The ancient Greek philosophers and the political analysts that they inspired over the next two millennia were concerned with grand theories of the state and governance, of war and peace, and of power and politics. But someone had to start thinking about the relatively small issues; less about war and peace and more about how best to collect taxes, build sewers, and design prisons. This is where Jeremy Bentham (1748–1832) comes in. He was a one-man think tank for a great many of the comparatively petty details of governance. In consequence he is considered one of the founders of the practice, indeed the science, of policy analysis.

Bentham started his professional life as a lawyer. But instead of practicing law, he decided to devote his life to reforming it. By it he meant both the established doctrines of the law as well as the laws themselves. While the life of a reformer seldom pays well, he didn't worry—especially after his father died and left him independently wealthy.

Bentham is best known as the British philosopher who held that self-interest was the prime motivator and that a government should strive to do the greatest good for the greatest number. He wanted institutions to justify themselves on the practical grounds of the level of useful welfare achieved. He was thereby the prophet of the movement called Utilitarianism, which held that an action is right if and only if its performance will be more productive of pleasure than pain, more productive of happiness than unhappiness—than of available alternatives.

By using the principle of utility to explain all human motivation, Bentham felt he had found the key to a science of human welfare. The overall welfare of a society would be measured by how well off each of its members were. Thus governments, through their policies, should strive to achieve the "greatest happiness for the greatest number." This was not an attitude that endeared him to the British aristocracy who, as a class, were determined to keep themselves happy at the direct expense of the lower social classes.

The difference between Bentham and other would-be reformers was that Bentham sought to develop techniques to deal with policy questions—techniques that others could use to apply to yet unknown problems. In effect, Bentham's patrimony is so great because he was the first methodologist in policy analysis. He showed the way to find a way.

Bentham admittedly did not originate the principle of utility which can be traced back to the ancient Greeks. However, he was the first to rigorously and mathematically apply the principle to current and proposed public policies. Bentham was the first to empirically examine public policy problems, to use the investigation of social facts as a justification for reforming the law on a matter. A hundred years later this would be called a Brandeis brief, a legal argument that takes into account not only the law but the technical data from social or scientific research that have economic and sociological implications for the law as well as society. This kind of legal argument was pioneered by Louis D. Brandeis (1856–1941), who later served on the U.S. Supreme Court (1916–1939). It was a Brandeis brief, for example, that helped win the 1954 *Brown v. Board of Education* case when, with testimony from psychologists about the effects of segregation on black children, the lawyers for Brown proved that separate education facilities were inherently unequal. "Bentham brief" would be the more intellectually honest phrase.

Bentham demanded that all laws and policies answer the question "who benefits?" And if the proposal didn't meet his test of the "greatest happiness for the greatest number," then it was not deserving of enactment. Above all, Bentham urged practical, pragmatic solutions to the problems of crime, education, welfare, and public health among others. He urged that legislators be guided not by their party but by his principle of utility. To do otherwise is to be dishonorably immoral. That is why his most influential work is called *An Introduction to the Principles of Morals and Legislation*. After all, the whole point of legislation is to do the moral, the ethical thing. Isn't it? Excerpts from Bentham's *Principles* are reprinted here.

A system is any organized collection of parts that are united by prescribed interactions; it is designed for the accomplishment of a special goal or a general purpose. A systems approach is any analytical framework that views situations as systems. While they didn't use the phrase, the ancient big three of the Greek philosophers were fully aware of the utility of how a systems approach could enhance understanding. For example, Socrates, according to an account by Xenophon (430–355 B.C.E.), understood the universality of management systems—that the same skills are needed whether you are managing a business, a government or an army. Plato presented a complete political system in his *Republic*. And Aristotle in his *Politics* systematically explains all of the elements of a political community; that it is best when "formed by citizens of the middle class" and "exists for the sake of noble actions, not of mere companionship."

Perhaps the best poetic description of the human social system is that of English poet John Donne (1572–1631). When he wrote that: "No man is an island, entire of itself; every man is a piece of the continent, a part of the main;" he provided the preamble for modern social science. When he concluded that "any man's death diminishes me, because I am involved in mankind; and therefore never send to know for whom the bell tolls; it tolls for thee," he explained why everyone had to understand the doctrines of systems theory.

Since World War II, the social sciences have increasingly used systems theory to examine their assertions about human behavior. Systems theory views social organizations—whether they are as small as a family or as large as a state—as a complex set of dynamically intertwined and interconnected elements. Every system includes inputs, processes, outputs, feedback loops, and the environment in which it operates and with which it continuously interacts. Any change in any element of the system causes changes in other elements. The interconnections tend to be complex, dynamic (constantly changing), and often unknown. For example, consider a beehive. If the drone worker bees ventured forth one day and most of them never came back (because they inadvertently flew into a mist of insecticide), the whole hive would have to change. Honey production would have to be curtailed so that more drones could be raised until the hive, the system, was back in a state of equilibrium. Similarly, when policymakers make decisions involving one element of the system, unanticipated impacts may occur throughout the system. Systems theorists study these interconnections in order to anticipate what was once unanticipated.

Systems thinking is critically important because the whole world, in essence, is a collection of interrelated systems. Nothing happens in isolation. An open system is any organism or organization that interacts with its environment, as opposed to a closed system which does not. A closed system is mainly a theoretical concept since even the most isolated mechanical system will eventually be impacted by its environment. So for all practical purposes all systems theory—especially in the social sciences—is open systems theory. Because all social organizations are adaptive (and open) systems that are integral parts of their environments, they must adjust to changes in their environment if they are to survive. In turn, virtually all of their decisions and actions affect their environment.

The systems approach while always there, only became self-conscious after biologist Ludwig von Bertalanffy (1901–1972) in the mid-twentieth century sought to organize scientific knowledge into a unified system. This, in turn, influenced David

Easton (1917–) who first applied the approach to modern political analysis. Any review of a policy that seeks to put it in the context of a larger system is using a systems approach.

Easton emphasized the need for political systems to adapt to environmental and technological changes in order to maintain stability. While Easton first applied the systems approach to politics in his 1963 *The Political System*, reprinted here is his analysis of "The Political System Under Stress," from his 1965 *A Systems Analysis of Political Life*.

While Easton addressed how political systems had to adapt to change, Thomas S. Kuhn (1922–1996) looked at the more fundamental question of how change occurs in the first place. In his landmark book, *The Structure of Scientific Revolutions*, Kuhn explained that as the natural sciences progressed, they amassed a body of ever-changing theory. Scientific advances were not based on the accumulation of knowledge and facts; but rather on a dominant paradigm (or model) used in any specific period to explain the phenomena under study. Rather than refuting previous theories, each paradigm would build upon the body of relevant knowledge and theories. Once a paradigm was accepted by consensus among current scholars, it would last as long as it remained useful. Ultimately it would be displaced by a more relevant and useful paradigm; this process of replacement was Kuhn's "scientific revolution."

Kuhn first discovered his paradigms when he, as a graduate student in physics at Harvard, was asked to teach a course on the history of science for undergraduates. He realized that he had "never read an old document in science." After reviewing Aristotle's "Physics" he was startled to find how unlike it was to Isaac Newton's concepts of physics. Aristotle offered not an earlier version of Newton but an entirely different way of looking at the fundamentals of mass, speed and gravity. This led Kuhn to conclude that science is not a steady, step by step, ever upward accumulation of knowledge. Rather, it is "a series of peaceful interludes punctuated by intellectually violent revolutions." And when those revolutions occur, "one conceptual world view is replaced by another." The individuals who create such breakthroughs by inventing a new paradigm are "almost always . . . either very young or very new to the field whose paradigm they change. . . . These are the men [and women] who, being little committed by prior practice to the traditional rules of normal science, are particularly likely to see that those rules no longer define a playable game and to conceive another set that can replace them." This is why the physics of Newton is so radically different from that of Aristotle. Newton's ideas didn't expand upon those of Aristotle. Newton supplanted them with totally new ideas.

While paradigms have their own time frames and contents, they overlap both in time and content because they are constantly evolving. In a parallel sense doctrinal development in public policy and administration has been inherently cyclical. A successful innovation by reformers is followed by a period of increased effectiveness, at least until competing societies or organizations adopt similar reforms. But over time advancing technologies and changing environments allow the innovation to deteriorate relative to other arrangements, first to become less competent, then to become

incompetent. After an innovative change remedies the problem, the cycle of competence and incompetence repeats. This "time lag" phenomenon is similar to the traditional boom and bust business cycle with incompetence occurring when the cycle is
in recession. Thus maintaining organizational competence is a never-ending struggle.
And an understanding of this cycle is the key to understanding the ebb and flow of
public policies. Reprinted here is Kuhn's explanation of "The Nature and Necessity
of Scientific Revolutions."

1

Of the Principle of Utility (1780)

Jeremy Bentham

1. Nature has placed mankind under the governance of two sovereign masters, *pain* and *pleasure*. It is for them alone to point out what we ought to do,
as well as to determine what we shall do. On the one hand the standard of
right and wrong, on the other the chain of causes and effects, are fastened to
their throne. They govern us in all we do, in all we say, in all we think: every
effort we can make to throw off our subjection, will serve but to demonstrate
and confirm it. In words a man may pretend to abjure their empire: but in reality he will remain subject to it all the while. The *principle of utility* recognises
this subjection, and assumes it for the foundation of that system, the object of
which is to rear the fabric of felicity by the hands of reason and of law. Systems
which attempt to question it, deal in sounds instead of sense, in caprice
instead of reason, in darkness instead of light.

But enough of metaphor and declamation: it is not by such means that
moral science is to be improved.

2. The principle of utility is the foundation of the present work: it will be
proper therefore at the outset to give an explicit and determinate account of
what is meant by it. By the principle of utility is meant that principle which

---

Source: Jeremy Bentham, *An Introduction to the Principles and Morals of Legislation,* 1780.

approves or disapproves of every action whatsoever, according to the tendency which it appears to have to augment or diminish the happiness of the party whose interest is in question: or, what is the same thing in other words, to promote or to oppose that happiness. I say of every action whatsoever; and therefore not only of every action of a private individual, but of every measure of government.

3. By utility is meant that property in any object, whereby it tends to produce benefit, advantage, pleasure, good, or happiness, (all this in the present case comes to the same thing) or (what comes again to the same thing) to prevent the happening of mischief, pain, evil, or unhappiness to the party whose interest is considered: if that party be the community in general, then the happiness of the community: if a particular individual, then the happiness of that individual.

4. The interest of the community is one of the most general expressions that can occur in the phraseology of morals: no wonder that the meaning of it is often lost. When it has a meaning, it is this. The community is a fictitious *body,* composed of the individual persons who are considered as constituting as it were its *members.* The interest of the community then is, what?—the sum of the interests of the several members who compose it.

5. It is in vain to talk of the interest of the community, without understanding what is the interest of the individual. A thing is said to promote the interest, or to be *for* the interest, of an individual, when it tends to add to the sum total of his pleasures: or, what comes to the same thing, to diminish the sum total of his pains.

6. An action then may be said to be conformable to the principle of utility, or, for shortness sake, to utility, (meaning with respect to the community at large) when the tendency it has to augment the happiness of the community is greater than any it has to diminish it.

7. A measure of government (which is but a particular kind of action, performed by a particular person or persons) may be said to be conformable to or dictated by the principle of utility, when in like manner the tendency which it has to augment the happiness of the community is greater than any which it has to diminish it.

8. When an action, or in particular a measure of government, is supposed by a man to be conformable to the principle of utility, it may be convenient, for the purposes of discourse, to imagine a kind of law or dictate, called a law or dictate of utility: and to speak of the action in question, as being conformable to such law or dictate.

9. A man may be said to be a partisan of the principle of utility, when the approbation or disapprobation he annexes to any action, or to any measure, is determined by, and proportioned to the tendency which he conceives it to have to augment or to diminish the happiness of the community: or in other words, to its conformity or unconformity to the laws or dictates of utility.

10. Of an action that is conformable to the principle of utility, one may always say either that it is one that ought to be done, or at least that it is not one that ought not to be done. One may say also, that it is right it should be done; at least that it is not wrong it should be done: that it is a right action; at

least that it is not a wrong action. When thus interpreted, the words *ought,* and *right* and *wrong,* and others of that stamp, have a meaning: when otherwise, they have none.

11. Has the rectitude of this principle been ever formally contested? It should seem that it had, by those who have not known what they have been meaning. Is it susceptible of any direct proof? it should seem not: for that which is used to prove every thing else, cannot itself be proved: a chain of proofs must have their commencement somewhere. To give such proof is as impossible as it is needless.

12. Not that there is or ever has been that human creature breathing, however stupid or perverse, who has not on many, perhaps on most occasions of his life, deferred to it. By the natural constitution of the human frame, on most occasions of their lives men in general embrace this principle, without thinking of it: if not for the ordering of their own actions, yet for the trying of their own actions, as well as of those of other men. There have been, at the same time, not many, perhaps, even of the most intelligent, who have been disposed to embrace it purely and without reserve. There are even few who have not taken some occasion or other to quarrel with it, either on account of their not understanding always how to apply it, or on account of some prejudice or other which they were afraid to examine into, or could not bear to part with. For such is the stuff that man is made of: in principle and in practice, in a right track and in a wrong one, the rarest of all human qualities is consistency.

13. When a man attempts to combat the principle of utility, it is with reasons drawn, without his being aware of it, from that very principle itself. His arguments, if they prove any thing, prove not that the principle is *wrong,* but that, according to the applications he supposes to be made of it, it is *misapplied.* Is it possible for a man to move the earth? Yes; but he must first find out another earth to stand upon.

14. To disprove the propriety of it by arguments is impossible; but, from the causes that have been mentioned, or from some confused or partial view of it, a man may happen to be disposed not to relish it. Where this is the case, if he thinks the settling of his opinions on such a subject worth the trouble, let him take the following steps, and at length, perhaps, he may come to reconcile himself to it.

1. Let him settle with himself, whether he would wish to discard this principle altogether; if so, let him consider what it is that all his reasonings (in matters of politics especially) can amount to?
2. If he would, let him settle with himself, whether he would judge and act without any principle, or whether there is any other he would judge and act by?
3. If there be, let him examine and satisfy himself whether the principle he thinks he has found is really any separate intelligible principle; or whether it be not a mere principle in words, a kind of phrase, which at bottom expresses neither more nor less than the mere averment of his own unfounded sentiments; that is, what in another person he might be apt to call *caprice?*

4. If he is inclined to think that his own approbation or disapprobation, annexed to the idea of an act, without any regard to its consequences, is a sufficient foundation for him to judge and act upon, let him ask himself whether his sentiment is to be a standard of right and wrong, with respect to every other man, or whether every man's sentiment has the same privilege of being a standard to itself?

5. In the first case, let him ask himself whether his principle is not despotical, and hostile to all the rest of human race?

6. In the second case, whether it is not anarchical, and whether at this rate there are not as many different standards of right and wrong as there are men? and whether even to the same man, the same thing, which is right today, may not (without the least change in its nature) be wrong to-morrow? and whether the same thing is not right and wrong in the same place at the same time? and in either case, whether all argument is not at an end? and whether, when two men have said, 'I like this', and 'I don't like it', they can (upon such a principle) have any thing more to say?

7. If he should have said to himself, No: for that the sentiment which he proposes as a standard must be grounded on reflection, let him say on what particulars the reflection is to turn? if on particulars having relation to the utility of the act, then let him say whether this is not deserting his own principle, and borrowing assistance from that very one in opposition to which he sets it up: or if not on those particulars, on what other particulars?

8. If he should be for compounding the matter, and adopting his own principle in part, and the principle of utility in part, let him say how far he will adopt it?

9. When he has settled with himself where he will stop, then let him ask himself how he justifies to himself the adopting it so far? and why he will not adopt it any farther?

10. Admitting any other principle than the principle of utility to be a right principle, a principle that it is right for a man to pursue; admitting (what is not true) that the word *right* can have a meaning without reference to utility, let him say whether there is any such thing as a *motive* that a man can have to pursue the dictates of it: if there is, let him say what that motive is, and how it is to be distinguished from those which enforce the dictates of utility: if not, then lastly let him say what it is this other principle can be good for?

2

The Political System
Under Stress (1965)

David Easton

Even if we drop the assumption that change is taking place in the environment and turn to systems whose environments have been relatively stable (an exception in the modern world but frequent in the past and undoubtedly possible episodically in the future), we continue to face the problem of how to deal economically and systematically with influences on a system that come from the environment. Whether a system is imbedded in a constantly changing environment or in a stable one, the elements of the environment continue to exert an effect upon the operations of the system. The analysis of the effect of the stable environment on a system poses the same theoretical problems as in the case of rapidly changing ones, even though the rate of change may have important additional consequences.

Although social science has recently and suddenly become enamored of problems of change and a tidal wave of theories of change threatens to engulf us, it has at least opened our eyes to the fact that any general theory, if it is even minimally adequate, must be able to handle change as easily as it does stability.[1] But the truth is that in the elaboration of the initial fundamental categories of an analysis, there is no need for special concepts to study change. Indeed to introduce them would be a sign of weakness and a disjunction in the theory, not one of strength and integration.

Stability is only a special example of change, not a genetically different one. There is never a social situation in which the patterns of interaction are

---

Source: David Easton, from *A Framework for Political Analysis.* Copyright © 1965. Reprinted by permission of the author.

[1] I am here using the concept "change" in the usual loose sense of social science. The fact is that stability is not related to change or its antithesis. For the difference between static as against changing conditions on the one hand and stability on the other, see my previously cited article "Limits of the Equilibrium Model in Social Research."

absolutely unchanging. If stability is to have any sensible meaning, it must represent a condition in which the rate of change is slow enough to create no special problems due to change. But some change there always is. Hence, the study of stable systems involves a special case of change, one where the rate is slow. Similarly, so-called change draws attention to another special case in which the rate is high enough to create special consequences of which it is necessary to take note, both analytically and empirically.

Any general theory or conceptual framework, however, should be able to take both special cases simultaneously in its stride. The vital objective at the outset is not to create a special set of categories to examine special cases but, rather, to develop a set that will be useful for identifying the major variables involved in the functioning of the system, regardless for the moment of the rate of change. Whether a system is changing imperceptibly and is, therefore, said to be stable or whether it is changing rapidly and is, therefore, characterized as unstable or in transition does not alter the nature of the fundamental variables that need to be examined. It may add to them, but it cannot detract from them. The categories presented below are designed to be of this generic character.

Environmental Disturbances Under Conditions of Stability

Even under conditions of stability, where the rate of change is low, interaction between the environment and a system continues to occur. Hence, even if a special theory of change were required, it could not eliminate the similarity between change and nonchange with respect to the continuing presence of exchanges between a political system and its environment.

To illustrate, let us assume that we were interested in tracing out the consequences of social stratification upon the political structure. At one point, where a change had taken place in the social structure, we might discover that the realignment of social classes had modified the distribution of power in society in such a way that a new political elite had displaced the old one. The French and Russian Revolutions both led to consequences such as these. But once these effects on the political system had been produced, this did not lead to the elimination of the effects of the new class structure on the society, even if the new class relationship remained absolutely static. Once a change is introduced and stabilized, it may continue to exert its influence on other aspects of society. It is not like a bolt of lightning that does its damage and disappears to leave a single deposit of effects. Rather, it constitutes a continuing pressure on the political system.

The new status and class structure of the society would exert its continuing pressure on the political structure in many ways. It might affect the kind of persons recruited to political positions, the variety of issues raised for discussion, and the kind of decisions actually adopted and implemented. The absence of change implies not that politics escapes the influence of its parameters, but the stabilization of these influences. In other words, the exchanges between an environment and the political system imbedded in it continue, but without important modification.

It is vital to realize this fact. Even under the unreal state of absolutely static conditions in the environment of a political system, transactions between the two would still take place. If it were otherwise, we could never understand how a system could experience stress even if its conditions of existence did not change. If the conditions themselves have always been stressful, a system could be destroyed, not as a result of new kinds of stress occurring, but as a consequence of the failure of the members of the system at some point to handle the old and stable kinds as adequately as their predecessors.

The Linkage Variables Between System and Environment

Two things are clear from the preceding discussion. First, there is an enormous variety of influences coming from the environment of a political system capable of disturbing the way in which the system performs its tasks. Second, these influences are there whether the environment is relatively stable or fluctuating wildly. Environmental change which draws so much attention today, and appropriately so, does not create entirely new theoretical problems in the construction of a general structure of analysis. It simply aggravates an analytic problem that is already present, namely: How are we to systematize our understanding of the way in which the disturbances or influences from the environment are transferred to a political system? Do we have to treat each change or disturbance as a particular or general type, as the case may be, and simply work out its specific effects in each instance? If so, because of the obviously enormous variety of influences at work, the problems for systematic analysis are virtually insurmountable. But if we can discover a way of generalizing our method for handling the impact of the environment on a system, there would be some hope for reducing the enormous variety of influences into a relatively few and, therefore, relatively manageable number of indicators or variables. This is precisely what I shall seek to do.

Transactions Across System Boundaries

Since we have been conceiving of a political system as analytically separable from all other social systems, and frequently empirically differentiated as well through an independent political structure, it is useful to treat the disturbances or influences occurring from behavior in the environmental systems as *exchanges or transactions* that cross the boundaries of the political system. None of the broad social systems into which I have classified the environment stands completely independent of the other; complex interpenetration occurs. That is, each is coupled to the other in some way, however slight it may be. Exchanges can be used when we wish to refer to the mutuality of the relationship, that is, where each has a reciprocal influence on the other. Transaction may be used when we wish to emphasize the movement of an effect in one direction, simply across the boundary from one system to another.[2]

However scientifically important it may be to point this out, by itself the statement is so obvious as to have little interest. What can and will carry recognition of this coupling beyond a mere truism is the invention of a way to trace out the complex exchanges so that we can readily reduce the immense variety of interactions to theoretically and empirically manageable proportions.

In order to accomplish this, I propose to reduce the major and significant environmental influences to a few indicators. Through the examination of these we should be able to appraise and follow through the potential impact of environmental events on the system. With this objective in mind, I shall designate the effects that are transmitted across the boundary of a system toward some other system as the *outputs* of the first system and, hence, as the *inputs* of the second system, the one that they influence. A transaction between systems will therefore be viewed as a linkage between them in the form of an input-output relationship.

If we now apply this general conceptualization of the points of linkage between systems to a political system and its environmental systems, it offers us a rudimentary model of the type illustrated in Diagram 2. This is, of course, a gargantuan oversimplification both of reality and of my developing conceptual scheme itself. But the task of analysis is at least to begin by stripping away all incidental relationships in order to lay bare the essential framework. These are the very minimal commitments if we inquire into political life as a system of behavior. In a succeeding volume the objective will be to add complicating relationships of various sorts so that the model will offer a somewhat closer approximation to the relationships in phenomenal systems. Here the analysis will remain macroscopic in intent. We shall be observing political systems from a considerable distance, as through a telescope rather than a microscope. This is in the nature of the case, given the present state of theoretical analysis in political research. Although we have much empirical detail, we have tended to lose sight of the need to see the outlines of the over-all picture.

---

[2]Exchange is sometimes used to suggest some kind of mutually beneficial relationship such as a settlement or contractual tie in which each of the parties feels there is something to be gained. I presume that Talcott Parsons typically uses the concept in this or in a closely related sense. See his use of the term in *The Social System* (New York: Free Press of Glencoe, Inc., 1951), especially at pp. 122 ff and in a volume with N. J. Smelser, *Economy and Society* (New York: Free Press of Glencoe, Inc., 1956), pp. 105 and 184. Here, however, I shall confine the term to a neutral meaning, one that denotes only that events in two or more systems have reciprocal effects on the systems involved and that these effects are not unrelated to each other. Interaction might well have been used to describe the relationship except that it has been customary to restrict this concept to the actions and reactions among social roles rather than among systems.

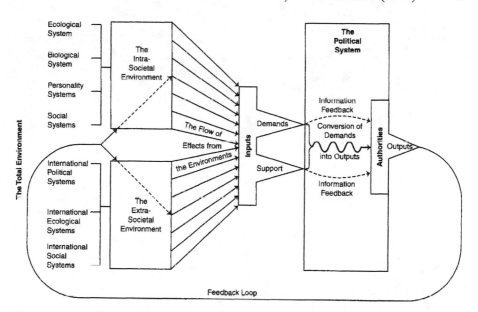

Diagram 2   *A Dynamic Response Model of a Political System*

A Flow Model of the Political System

Broadly, this diagramatic representation of the functioning of a political system suggests that what is happening in the environment affects the political system through the kinds of influences that flow into the system. Through its structures and processes the system then acts on these intakes in such a way that they are converted into outputs. These are the authoritative decisions and their implementation. The outputs return to the systems in the environment, or, in many cases, they may turn directly and without intermediaries back upon the system itself. In Diagram 2 at the top of the page, the arrows from the environments portray the vast variety of transactions between them and the political system. Here, though, the arrows have only single heads, and they are shown in such a way that they are fed into the system in summary form as demands and support. The exchange or reciprocity of the relationship between the system and its environments, previously depicted as double-headed arrows, is now indicated by arrows that show the direction of flow of the outputs toward the environmental systems. This clearly demonstrates that the inputs of the environment are really just the outputs of the political system. The broken lines in the environmental systems reflect the dynamics of the relationship. They indicate that there is a continuous flow of influences or outputs from the political system into and through the environments. By modifying the environments, political outputs thereby influence the next round of effects that move from the environment back to the political system. In this way we can identify a continuous feedback loop. The meaning of the other lines and designations on the diagram will become apparent as our discussion proceeds.

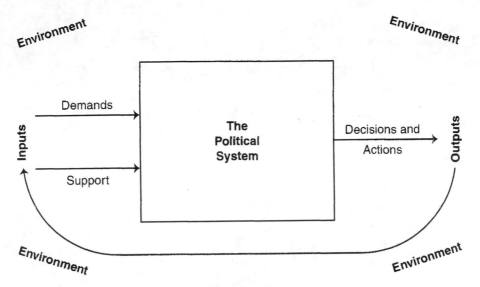

Diagram 3   *A Simplified Model of a Political System*

As detailed as the diagram is, much is omitted, as we would expect. First, many other environmental systems could be added even to take into account the few that were identified in an earlier chapter. Second, the interrelationships among environmental systems themselves are completely omitted since they would have so cluttered the diagram as to leave it virtually indecipherable. Finally, the structures and processes through which a political system converts its inputs into outputs are represented only by the serpentine line within the system. It does suggest, however, that the various inputs from the external system are worked upon and converted into outputs that return to one or another of the external systems as inputs for them.

Diagram 3 goes even further in stripping the rich and complex political processes down to their bare bones. It depicts in their simplest guise the dynamic relationships among the processes of a political system. It serves to dramatize an image to which we shall return; it reveals that, after all, in its elemental form a political system is just a means whereby certain kinds of inputs are converted into outputs. At least, this is a highly useful starting point from which to begin plugging in the complexities of political life.

The Input Variables

Demands and Support as Input Indicators

The value of inputs as a concept is that through its use we shall find it possible to capture the effect of the enormous variety of events and conditions in the environment as they pertain to the persistence of a political system. Without the inputs it would be difficult to delineate in any precise operational way how behavior in the various sectors of society affects what happens in the political sector. Inputs will serve as summary variables that concentrate and reflect everything in the environment which is relevant to political stress. Because it is possible to use inputs in this manner, the concept can serve as a powerful analytic tool.

Whether or not we use inputs as summary variables will depend upon how we define them. We might conceive of them in their broadest sense. Then we would interpret them as including any event external to the system— confining ourselves momentarily to environmental inputs—that alters, modifies, or affects the system in any way. If inputs are used in such a broad sense, we could never exhaust the list of those that leave an impact on the political system. The double-headed arrows coupling environmental systems to the political system could be multiplied a thousandfold, and we would not have begun to skim the surface of the number and variety of influences flowing among these systems.

Let us take only a minute number of illustrations. The effect of the economy on creating and sustaining powerful economic classes, urbanization, interest group segmentation, fluctuations in the business cycle, and the like would constitute inputs, broadly interpreted, that shape the character of the political structure, the distribution of power therein, and the goals of political controversy. The general culture helps to mold the constraints within which political discussion and competition take place (if it is permitted at all), lends color to the style of political life, and signalizes the kinds of issues that will be considered important by the members of the system. Motivational patterns found in modal personality types or in elite personalities within a society will contribute to the availability of personnel to fill the political roles, to the incentives for political participation, and to the types that achieve leadership status and to their perception of policy. We could enlarge this list indefinitely. For each sector of the environment introduced we would need a separate partial theory to explain the effect which its inputs might have. The only unifying element in it all would be that we were seeking to trace out and interrelate the inputs (that is, the general and specific effects) of each of these parameters on a common object—the political system.

However, we can simplify enormously the task of analyzing the impact of the environment on the political systems if we adopt more narrowly defined inputs and use them as indicators that will sum up most of the important effects that cross the boundary between these systems. This conceptualization would relieve us of the need to deal with and trace out the effect on a system of every different type of environmental event separately.

As the analytic tool for this purpose, it is helpful to view the major parameters as focusing their effects on two major inputs: demands and support. Through them a vast range of changes in the environment may be channeled, reflected, and summarized. For this reason they can be used as the key indicators of the way in which environmental events and conditions modify and affect the operations of the political system. On Diagram 2, page 13, the multiple transactions are collapsed into two major inputs, and these alone are conceived as flowing into and affecting the political system.

It will matter little whether we consider these inputs as internal or external to the political system. They stand on the border, bridging and linking the political system with all other intra- and extrasocietal systems. Depending upon the requirements of our analysis, they may be equally conceived to lie within the system or outside it, as long as we recognize that they remain in the neighborhood of the boundary.

"Withinputs" as Intrasystem Indicators

At times I have been writing as though all the influences or disturbances that had to be considered in understanding how a system manages to persist occurred in the environment of a system. As we know from what has already been said, many of these influences may occur within a system itself. Insofar as things happening within a system shape its destinies as a system of interactions, it will be possible to take them into account as they are reflected through the inputs of the members of a system. It does not seem reasonable to speak of these events as inputs since they already occur within the system rather than outside. For the sake of logical consistency we might call them "withinputs." All that would be meant by this neologism is that we have decided to treat, in a unified way, the effects that events and conditions both within and without a system may have upon its persistence. Hence, unless the context requires otherwise, in writing of inputs I shall include "withinputs" in the same category.

We need to take the trouble to make the distinction because recognition of the two categories sensitizes us to the value of looking within the system as well as the environment to find the major influences that may lead to stress. Just as a human body may fail because of an infection received from the outside or from the attrition, through old age, of some organ such as the heart, a political system may suffer stress from disturbances in the environment or from failures that can be attributed directly to processes or structural arrangements within the system itself. For example, members of the American political system have from time to time felt that the whole regime has been threatened by the difficulties that the separation of powers has aggravated with regard to the passage of legislation. This is traditionally brought out in discussions of a responsible two-party system for the United States. To signalize the fact that the disturbance has occurred within the system and that the stressing input has been shaped by internal events, the concept "withinputs" can be used.

Illustrations of the Summary Function of Inputs

It will be helpful to have some brief indication of what demands and support comprise and how they could be used, although a full analysis of their role as summary variables through which stress is transmitted will have to await a later work. To take a specific example, let us assume that we are interested in a developing nation which is undergoing a transition from a tribal form of organization based upon village headmen, lineage elders, and a lineage-determined paramount chief with minimal power, toward a national political leadership based upon secular party organization, a legislature, an efficiency-oriented bureaucracy, and a dominant leadership. Presumably the modifications of the old tribal system have been brought about in part through contact with Western ideals of democracy and administration, buttressed by the needs of a changing economy and social structure.

In accordance with current procedures of political research, we might specify the aspect of political change that seems to be important. Normally we would use as the criteria of relevance those changes in the direction of or away from Western democratic institutions. We might then seek to account for the direction, rate, and outcome of these changes by considering all of the external changes that can then be shown to be relevant to the political changes which we have already selected as important according to these criteria.

From the perspectives of our analysis the environmental changes are considered to be disturbances on the existing tribal system because of the stress they impose upon it, leading ultimately to its transformation. In response to the stress the system either becomes extinct and is absorbed by some other society, or it responds and adapts by adopting modernized political structures in the shape of parties, legislatures, rationalized bureaucracy, and a generalized leadership (rather than a lineage, tribal, or ethnically based leadership).

The critical questions for us do not relate to the way in which environmental disturbances modify the particular form of the internal structures or processes of the system. Such changes may take place without any discernible effect upon the capacity of some kind of system to persist, or they may not be fundamentally related to this capacity. That is to say, whether the adopted modernized structure happens to be modeled after the British parliamentary system or the American presidential type may or may not have relevance to the capacity of some kind of system to persist. What is important is that the traditional political forms have given way to at least a semblance of the bureaucratized types. For us the critical questions are: To what extent did the disturbances constitute stress on the pre-existing system? Precisely how did this stress manifest and communicate itself? How did the system cope with this stress, if at all?

A useful way of answering such questions lies in exploring the impact that contacts with the West, both ideological and economical, have upon the inputs. Briefly, exposure to the kind of life possible under Western forms of social organization, together with the emergence of the material means through transition from a subsistence to a cash and wage economy, has unleashed a vast increase in the volume of demands which members of the system now seek to satisfy through political action. This in itself imposes such a severe burden on the old tribal forms of political organization that they could not possibly cope with them.

Further, the changes in the environment serve to broaden the types of demands for which satisfaction is now sought through the political system. Such new demands, at their most inclusive level, are typically capsulated into programs for national freedom and political unity among divergent groups, linked usually to policies advocating a rapid rate of economic development. The kinds of commitments required from the members of the system for the fulfillment of these types of demands are dramatically different from those required under the prior traditional systems. The novelty of the demands themselves create severe crises in the developing nations.

Changes in volume and variety of demands represent a major and fundamentally neglected type of stress that environmental changes may be interpreted as bringing to bear upon a political system. In this way a vast host of different kinds of changes such as these may be drawn together and observed through a single kind of variable, that is, as they influence the volume and variety of demands.

3

The Nature and Necessity of Scientific Revolutions (1970)

Thomas S. Kuhn

These remarks permit us at last to consider the problems that provide this essay with its title. What are scientific revolutions, and what is their function in scientific development? Much of the answer to these questions has been anticipated in earlier sections. In particular, the preceding discussion has indicated that scientific revolutions are here taken to be those non-cumulative developmental episodes in which an older paradigm is replaced in whole or in part by an incompatible new one. There is more to be said, however, and an essential part of it can be introduced by asking one further question. Why should a

Source: Thomas Kuhn, from *The Structure of Scientific Revolutions,* 2nd Edition. Coypright © 1962, 1970 by The University of Chicago. Reprinted by permission of the University of Chicago Press.

change of paradigm be called a revolution? In the face of the vast and essential differences between political and scientific development, what parallelism can justify the metaphor that finds revolutions in both?

One aspect of the parallelism must already be apparent. Political revolutions are inaugurated by a growing sense, often restricted to a segment of the political community, that existing institutions have ceased adequately to meet the problems posed by an environment that they have in part created. In much the same way, scientific revolutions are inaugurated by a growing sense, again often restricted to a narrow subdivision of the scientific community, that an existing paradigm has ceased to function adequately in the exploration of an aspect of nature to which that paradigm itself had previously led the way. In both political and scientific development the sense of malfunction that can lead to crisis is prerequisite to revolution. Furthermore, though it admittedly strains the metaphor, that parallelism holds not only for the major paradigm changes, like those attributable to Copernicus and Lavoisier, but also for the far smaller ones associated with the assimilation of a new sort of phenomenon, like oxygen or X-rays. Scientific revolutions . . . need seem revolutionary only to those whose paradigms are affected by them. To outsiders they may, like the Balkan revolutions of the early twentieth century, seem normal parts of the developmental process. Astronomers, for example, could accept X-rays as a mere addition to knowledge, for their paradigms were unaffected by the existence of the new radiation. But for men like Kelvin, Crookes, and Roentgen, whose research dealt with radiation theory or with cathode ray tubes, the emergence of X-rays necessarily violated one paradigm as it created another. That is why these rays could be discovered only through something's first going wrong with normal research.

This genetic aspect of the parallel between political and scientific development should no longer be open to doubt. The parallel has, however, a second and more profound aspect upon which the significance of the first depends. Political revolutions aim to change political institutions in ways that those institutions themselves prohibit. Their success therefore necessitates the partial relinquishment of one set of institutions in favor of another, and in the interim, society is not fully governed by institutions at all. Initially it is crisis alone that attenuates the role of political institutions as we have already seen it attenuate the role of paradigms. In increasing numbers individuals become increasingly estranged from political life and behave more and more eccentrically within it. Then, as the crisis deepens, many of these individuals commit themselves to some concrete proposal for the reconstruction of society in a new institutional framework. At that point the society is divided into competing camps or parties, one seeking to defend the old institutional constellation, the others seeking to institute some new one. And, once that polarization has occurred, *political recourse fails.* Because they differ about the institutional matrix within which political change is to be achieved and evaluated, because they acknowledge no supra-institutional framework for the adjudication of revolutionary difference, the parties to a revolutionary conflict must finally resort to the techniques of mass persuasion, often including force. Though revolutions have had a vital role in the evolution of political institutions, that role depends upon their being partially extrapolitical or extrainstitutional events.

The remainder of this essay aims to demonstrate that the historical study of paradigm change reveals very similar characteristics in the evolution of the sciences. Like the choice between competing political institutions, that between competing paradigms proves to be a choice between incompatible modes of community life. Because it has that character, the choice is not and cannot be determined merely by the evaluative procedures characteristic of normal science, for these depend in part upon a particular paradigm, and that paradigm is at issue. When paradigms enter, as they must, into a debate about paradigm choice, their role is necessarily circular. Each group uses its own paradigm to argue in that paradigm's defense.

The resulting circularity does not, of course, make the arguments wrong or even ineffectual. The man who premises a paradigm when arguing in its defense can nonetheless provide a clear exhibit of what scientific practice will be like for those who adopt the new view of nature. That exhibit can be immensely persuasive, often compellingly so. Yet, whatever its force, the status of the circular argument is only that of persuasion. It cannot be made logically or even probabilistically compelling for those who refuse to step into the circle. The premises and values shared by the two parties to a debate over paradigms are not sufficiently extensive for that. As in political revolutions, so in paradigm choice—there is no standard higher than the assent of the relevant community. To discover how scientific revolutions are effected, we shall therefore have to examine not only the impact of nature and of logic, but also the techniques of persuasive argumentation effective within the quite special groups that constitute the community of scientists.

To discover why this issue of paradigm choice can never be unequivocally settled by logic and experiment alone, we must shortly examine the nature of the differences that separate the proponents of a traditional paradigm from their revolutionary successors. That examination is the principal object of this section and the next. We have, however, already noted numerous examples of such differences, and no one will doubt that history can supply many others. What is more likely to be doubted than their existence—and what must therefore be considered first—is that such examples provide essential information about the nature of science. Granting that paradigm rejection has been a historic fact, does it illuminate more than human credulity and confusion? Are there intrinsic reasons why the assimilation of either a new sort of phenomenon or a new scientific theory must demand the rejection of an older paradigm?

First notice that if there are such reasons, they do not derive from the logical structure of scientific knowledge. In principle, a new phenomenon might emerge without reflecting destructively upon any part of past scientific practice. Though discovering life on the moon would today be destructive of existing paradigms (these tell us things about the moon that seem incompatible with life's existence there), discovering life in some less well-known part of the galaxy would not. By the same token, a new theory does not have to conflict with any of its predecessors. It might deal exclusively with phenomena not previously known, as the quantum theory deals (but, significantly, not exclusively) with subatomic phenomena unknown before the twentieth century. Or again, the new theory might be simply a higher level theory than those known before, one that linked together a whole group of lower level theories without substantially changing any. Today, the theory of energy conservation provides just such links between dynamics, chemistry, electricity, optics, thermal theory, and so on. Still other compatible relationships between old and new theories can be conceived. Any and all of them might be exemplified by the historical process through which science has developed. If they were, scientific development would be genuinely cumulative. New sorts of phenomena would simply disclose order in an aspect of nature where none had been seen before. In the evolution of science new knowledge would replace ignorance rather than replace knowledge of another and incompatible sort.

Of course, science (or some other enterprise, perhaps less effective) might have developed in that fully cumulative manner. Many people have believed that it did so, and most still seem to suppose that cumulation is at least the ideal that historical development would display if only it had not so often been distorted by human idiosyncrasy. . . . Normal research, which *is* cumulative, owes its success to the ability of scientists regularly to select problems that can be solved with conceptual and instrumental techniques close to those already in existence. (That is why an excessive concern with useful problems, regardless of their relation to existing knowledge and technique, can so easily inhibit scientific development.) The man who is striving to solve a problem defined by existing knowledge and technique is not, however, just looking around. He knows what he wants to achieve, and he designs his instruments and directs his thoughts accordingly. Unanticipated novelty, the new discovery, can emerge only to the extent that his anticipations about nature and his instruments prove wrong. Often the importance of the resulting discovery will itself be proportional to the extent and stubbornness of the anomaly that foreshadowed it. Obviously, then, there must be a conflict between the paradigm that discloses anomaly and the one that later renders the anomaly law-like. The examples of discovery through paradigm destruction . . . did not confront us with mere historical accident. There is no other effective way in which discoveries might be generated.

The same argument applies even more clearly to the invention of new theories. There are, in principle, only three types of phenomena about which a new theory might be developed. The first consists of phenomena already well explained by existing paradigms, and these seldom provide either motive or point of departure for theory construction. . . . A second class of phenomena consists of those whose nature is indicated by existing paradigms but whose details can be understood only through further theory articulation. These are the phenomena to which scientists direct their research much of the time, but that research aims at the articulation of existing paradigms rather than at the invention of new ones. Only when these attempts at articulation fail do scientists encounter the third type of phenomena, the recognized anomalies whose characteristic feature is their stubborn refusal to be assimilated to existing paradigms. This type alone gives rise to new theories. Paradigms provide all phenomena except anomalies with a theory-determined place in the scientist's field of vision.

But if new theories are called forth to resolve anomalies in the relation of an existing theory to nature, then the successful new theory must somewhere permit predictions that are different from those derived from its predecessor. That difference could not occur if the two were logically compatible. In the process of being assimilated, the second must displace the first.

Review Questions

1. What is Jeremy Bentham's principle of utility? Why is Bentham considered one of the founders of the field of public policy analysis?

2. What are the basic elements common to all political, indeed all social, systems? According to David Easton how does a political system respond or adapt to new forces in its environment?

3. Why does Thomas Kuhn believe that scientific revolutions, as opposed to evolution, have been so crucial in the development of new knowledge? How does Kuhn's concept of scientific revolution apply to understanding developments in public policy?

Chapter 2

Public
Policymaking

Public policymaking is the totality of the decisional processes by which a government decides to deal or not to deal with a particular problem or concern. It is a never-ending process. Nineteenth-century British statesman Lord Salisbury (1830–1903) is usually credited with first remarking: "There is no such thing as a fixed policy, because policy like all organic entities is always in the making."

There are two distinct and opposite theories seeking to explain the mechanisms that produce policy decisions or nondecisions. The first might be called the rational decision-making approach and it generally has been attributed to political scientist Harold D. Lasswell (1901–1978). In his book *The Future of Political Science* (1963), he posited seven significant phases for every decision:

1. The intelligence phase, involving an influx of information;

2. The promoting or recommending phase, involving activities designed to influence the outcome;

3. The prescribing phase, involving the articulation of norms;

4. The invoking phase, involving establishing correspondence between prescriptions and concrete circumstances;

5. The application phase, in which the prescription is executed;

6. The appraisal phase, assessing intent in relation to effect, and

7. The terminating phase, treating expectations (rights) established while the prescription was in force.

Of course there is an immediate problem with this and every other such list. It is impossible to do. No matter how rational we would hope to be there is no way anyone can gather *all* the facts and take into account *every* consideration. Therefore, decision makers exercise what the Nobel Prize winning economist Herbert Simon (1916–2001) in *Administrative Behavior* (1947) called "bounded rationality." The "bounds" are what people put on their decisions. Simon asserts that: "It is impossible for the behavior of a single, isolated individual to reach any high degree of rationality. The number of alternatives he must explore is so great, the information he would need to evaluate them so vast that even an approximation to objective rationality is hard to conceive." Consequently, humans make decisions on satisfactory as opposed to optimal information. Inventing a new word, Simon said that decision makers "satisfice" when they accept a satisfactory and sufficient amount of information upon which to base a decision. Thus in the real world we are forced to reject the "rational comprehensive" approach and "satisfice" rather than "maximize."

A rejection of this approach was urged by Charles E. Lindblom, (1917–) the leading proponent of the second theory of policy decision making—the incremental approach. In his most famous article, "The Science of 'Muddling Through'," *Public Administration Review* (1959), reprinted here, Lindblom took a hard look at the rational models of the decisional processes of government. He rejected the notion that most decisions are made by rational (total information) processes. Instead, he saw such decisions—indeed, the whole policy-making process—as dependent upon small incremental decisions that tend to be made in response to short-term political conditions. Lindblom's thesis essentially held that decision making was controlled infinitely more by events and circumstances than by the will of those in policy-making positions. Disjointed incrementalism as a policy course was in reality the only truly feasible route, since incrementalism "concentrated the policymaker's analysis on familiar, better-known experiences, sharply reduced the number of different alternative policies to be explored, and sharply reduced the number and complexity of factors to be analyzed." Moreover, Lindblom argued that incrementalism was more consistent with the pluralistic nature of American democracy where individuals are free to combine to pursue common interests, whose contention "often can assure a more comprehensive regard for the values of the whole society than any attempt at intellectual comprehensiveness."

The rational and incremental models, useful intellectual tools for conceptualizing the decision-making process, have encouraged much subsequent modeling. For example, there is the "split the difference" compromise model that combines the two. Mixed scanning is the decision making model put forth by sociologist Amitai Etzioni (1929–) in "Mixed Scanning: 'Third' Approach to Decision Making," reprinted here. This calls for seeking short term solutions to problems by using both incrementalism and rational-comprehensive approaches to problem solving. For example, a foreign policy analyst responsible for reviewing political developments in Europe might superficially scan all recent developments (the comprehensive approach) but focus only on those political problems that have changed since the last scanning (the incremental approach). In this way the analyst saves time by dealing in detail only with those situations that truly demand attention.

But in reality all such models may be not much more than mind games for policy wonks. The real world of political executives and harried legislators is not an intellectual arena so much as it is a bare knuckles political arena. Decisions in the political arena are influenced far more by the perception of a situation than by any rational concept of objective reality. It is far more than the difference between a pessimist seeing a glass half empty while the optimist sees the same glass as half full. One actor in the decisional drama may view a program as absolutely essential for the national interest while another actor is equally certain that it is nothing more than an example of petty bureaucrats wasting the taxpayers' money.

Policymakers bring two kinds of intelligence to bear on their thinking. First is their mental ability to cope with complicated problems. Second is the information they have on and the experience they have with the issue at hand. Both kinds of intelligence are then filtered through their ideological predispositions and personal biases before an attitude toward any given problem is set. Thus political decisions are seldom made on the objective merits of a case because a case only has merit in the eyes of a political decision maker if he or she is intelligent enough to see it and, equally important, was ideologically and politically predisposed to support it.

Policy is hierarchical. The broadest, most overarching policy is made at the top. Then increasingly more focused policies must be made at every level on down. For example, the president of the United States sits at the top of the foreign policy-making pyramid. Dozens of layers below him sit thousands of clerks in the visa sections of hundreds of embassies and consulates making policy—that is, making decisions—on who may legally enter the United States. To be sure, policy at the bottom is heavily impacted by laws and regulations. But to the extent that these low-level officials, what Michael Lipsky calls street-level bureaucrats, have any discretion at all, they are making policy. And if you are on the receiving end of that policy, whether as a visa applicant or a motorist receiving a traffic citation from a police officer, the policy is as real to you as if it were coming from higher levels in the policy-making hierarchy. Lipsky's analysis of "Street-Level Bureaucrats as Policy Makers" is reprinted here.

Policy analysts have long been critical of the "either/or" nature of the rational versus the incremental approaches to decision making. A model advocated by Deborah Stone holds that the political community, the polis, is better able to deal with the ambiguity of less than perfect information—information often "spun" by "spin doctors"—than with the look at hard facts approach of the rational model. While rational analysis does not lend itself to the inconsistencies of real life, the polis model assumes it. In *Policy Paradox* (first chapter reprinted here) Stone contends that political communities constantly and inherently struggle over ideas and exchange meanings that are not mutually exclusive. While the rational model assumes that there are objective facts that can be applied, Stone finds that "behind every policy issue lurks a contest over conflicting, though equally plausible, conceptions of the same abstract goal or value."

4

The Science of "Muddling Through" (1959)

Charles E. Lindblom

Suppose an administrator is given responsibility for formulating policy with respect to inflation. He might start by trying to list all related values in order of importance, e.g., full employment, reasonable business profit, protection of small savings, prevention of a stock market crash. Then all possible policy outcomes could be rated as more or less efficient in attaining a maximum of these values. This would of course require a prodigious inquiry into values held by members of society and an equally prodigious set of calculations on how much of each value is equal to how much of each other value. He could then proceed to outline all possible policy alternatives. In a third step, he would undertake systematic comparison of his multitude of alternatives to determine which attains the greatest amount of values.

In comparing policies, he would take advantage of any theory available that generalized about classes of policies. In considering inflation, for example, he would compare all policies in the light of the theory of prices. Since no alternatives are beyond his investigation, he would consider strict central control and the abolition of all prices and markets on the one hand and elimination of all public controls with reliance completely on the free market on the other, both in the light of whatever theoretical generalizations he could find on such hypothetical economies.

Finally, he would try to make the choice that would in fact maximize his values.

An alternative line of attack would be to set as his principal objective, either explicitly or without conscious thought, the relatively simple goal of keeping prices level. This objective might be compromised or complicated by only a few other goals, such as full employment. He would in fact disregard most other social values as beyond his present interest, and he would

Source: Charles E. Lindblom, "The Science of Muddling Through," *Public Administration Review,* Spring 1959. Reprinted by permission of Blackwell Publishing Ltd.

for the moment not even attempt to rank the few values that he regarded as immediately relevant. Were he pressed, he would quickly admit that he was ignoring many related values and many possible important consequences of his policies.

As a second step, he would outline those relatively few policy alternatives that occurred to him. He would then compare them. In comparing his limited number of alternatives, most of them familiar from past controversies, he would not ordinarily find a body of theory precise enough to carry him through a comparison of their respective consequences. Instead he would rely heavily on the record of past experience with small policy steps to predict the consequences of similar steps extended into the future.

Moreover, he would find that the policy alternatives combined objectives or values in different ways. For example, one policy might offer price level stability at the cost of some risk of unemployment; another might offer less price stability but also less risk of unemployment. Hence, the next step in his approach—the final selection—would combine into one the choice among values and the choice among instruments for reaching values. It would not, as in the first method of policymaking, approximate a more mechanical process of choosing the means that best satisfied goals that were previously clarified and ranked. Because practitioners of the second approach expect to achieve their goals only partially, they would expect to repeat endlessly the sequence just described, as conditions and aspirations changed and as accuracy of prediction improved.

By Root or by Branch

For complex problems, the first of these two approaches is of course impossible. Although such an approach can be described, it cannot be practiced except for relatively simple problems and even then only in a somewhat modified form. It assumes intellectual capacities and sources of information that men simply do not possess, and it is even more absurd as an approach to policy when the time and money that can be allocated to a policy problem is limited, as is always the case. Of particular importance to public administrators is the fact that public agencies are in effect usually instructed not to practice the first method. That is to say, their prescribed functions and constraints—the politically or legally possible—restrict their attention to relatively few values and relatively few alternative policies among the countless alternatives that might be imagined. It is the second method that is practiced.

Curiously, however, the literatures of decision-making, policy formulation, planning, and public administration formalize the first approach rather than the second, leaving public administrators who handle complex decisions in the position of practicing what few preach. For emphasis I run some risk of overstatement. True enough, the literature is well aware of limits on man's capacities and of the inevitability that policies will be approached in some such style as the second. But attempts to formalize rational policy formulation—to lay out explicitly the necessary steps in the process—usually describe the first approach and not the second.[1]

The common tendency to describe policy formulation even for complex problems as though it followed the first approach has been strengthened by the attention given to, and successes enjoyed by, operations research, statistical decision theory, and systems analysis. The hallmarks of these procedures, typical of the first approach, are clarity of objective, explicitness of evaluation, a high degree of comprehensiveness of overview, and, wherever possible, quantification of values for mathematical analysis. But these advanced procedures remain largely the appropriate techniques of relatively small-scale problem-solving where the total number of variables to be considered is small and value problems restricted. Charles Hitch, head of the Economics Division of RAND Corporation, one of the leading centers for application of these techniques, has written:

> I would make the empirical generalization from my experience at RAND and elsewhere that operations research is the art of sub-optimizing, i.e., of solving some lower-level problems, and that difficulties increase and our special competence diminishes by an order of magnitude with every level of decision making we attempt to ascend. The sort of simple explicit model which operations researchers are so proficient in using can certainly reflect most of the significant factors influencing traffic control on the George Washington Bridge, but the proportion of the relevant reality which we can represent by any such model or models in studying, say, a major foreign-policy decision, appears to be almost trivial.[2]

Accordingly, I propose in this paper to clarify and formalize the second method, much neglected in the literature. This might be described as the method of *successive limited comparisons.* I will contrast it with the first approach, which might be called the rational-comprehensive method.[3] More impressionistically and briefly—and therefore generally used in this article— they could be characterized as the branch method and root method, the former continually building out from the current situation, step-by-step and by

---

[1] James G. March and Herbert A. Simon similarly characterize the literature. They also take some important steps, as have Simon's recent articles, to describe a less heroic model of policy-making. See *Organizations* (John Wiley and Sons, 1958), p. 137.

[2] "Operations Research and National Planning—A Dissent," 5 *Operations Research* 718 (October, 1957). Hitch's dissent is from particular points made in the article to which his paper is a reply; his claim that operations research is for low-level problems is widely accepted.

For examples of the kind of problems to which operations research is applied, see C. W. Churchman, R. L. Ackoff and E. L. Arnoff, *Introduction to Operations Research* (John Wiley and Sons, 1957); and J. F. McCloskey and J. M. Coppinger (eds.), *Operations Research for Management,* Vol. II, (The Johns Hopkins Press, 1956).

[3] I am assuming that administrators often make policy and advise in the making of policy and am treating decision-making and policy-making as synonymous for purposes of this paper.

small degrees; the latter starting from fundamentals anew each time, building on the past only as experience is embodied in a theory, and always prepared to start completely from the ground up.

Let us put the characteristics of the two methods side by side in simplest terms.

Assuming that the root method is familiar and understandable, we proceed directly to clarification of its alternative by contrast. In explaining the second, we shall be describing how most administrators do in fact approach complex questions, for the root method, the "best" way as a blueprint or model, is in fact not workable for complex policy questions, and administrators are forced to use the method of successive limited comparisons.

Intertwining Evaluation and Empirical Analysis (Ib)

The quickest way to understand how values are handled in the method of successive limited comparisons is to see how the root method often breaks down in *its* handling of values or objectives. The idea that values should be clarified,

Rational-Comprehensive (Root)	Successive Limited Comparisons (Branch)
1a. Clarification of values or objectives distinct from and usually prerequisite to empirical analysis of alternative policies.	1b. Selection of value goals and empirical analysis of the needed action are not distinct from one another but are closely intertwined.
2a. Policy-formulation is therefore approached through means-end analysis: First the ends are isolated, then the means to achieve them are sought.	2b. Since means and ends are not distinct, means-end analysis is often inappropriate or limited.
3a. The test of a "good" policy is that it can be shown to be the most appropriate means to desired ends.	3b. The test of a "good" policy is typically that various analysts find themselves directly agreeing on a policy (without their agreeing that it is the most appropriate means to an agreed objective).
4a. Analysis is comprehensive; every important relevant factor is taken into account.	4b. Analysis is drastically limited: i) Important possible outcomes are neglected. ii) Important alternative potential policies are neglected. iii) Important affected values are neglected.
5a. Theory is often heavily relied upon.	5b. A succession of comparisons greatly reduces or eliminates reliance on theory.

and in advance of the examination of alternative policies, is appealing. But what happens when we attempt it for complex social problems? The first difficulty is that on many critical values or objectives, citizens disagree, congressmen disagree, and public administrators disagree. Even where a fairly specific objective is prescribed for the administrator, there remains considerable room for disagreement on sub-objectives. Consider, for example, the conflict with respect to locating public housing, described in Meyerson and Banfield's study of the Chicago Housing Authority[4]—disagreement which occurred despite the clear objective of providing a certain number of public housing units in the city. Similarly conflicting are objectives in highway location, traffic control, minimum wage administration, development of tourist facilities in national parks, or insect control.

Administrators cannot escape these conflicts by ascertaining the majority's preference, for preferences have not been registered on most issues; indeed, there often *are* no preferences in the absence of public discussion sufficient to bring an issue to the attention of the electorate. Furthermore, there is a question of whether intensity of feeling should be considered as well as the number of persons preferring each alternative. By the impossibility of doing otherwise, administrators often are reduced to deciding policy without clarifying objectives first.

Even when an administrator resolves to follow his own values as a criterion for decisions, he often will not know how to rank them when they conflict with one another, as they usually do. Suppose, for example, that an administrator must relocate tenants living in tenements scheduled for destruction. One objective is to empty the buildings fairly promptly, another is to find suitable accommodation for persons displaced, another is to avoid friction with residents in other areas in which a large influx would be unwelcome, another is to deal with all concerned through persuasion if possible, and so on.

How does one state even to himself the relative importance of these partially conflicting values? A simple ranking of them is not enough; one needs ideally to know how much of one value is worth sacrificing for some of another value. The answer is that typically the administrator chooses—and must choose—directly among policies in which these values are combined in different ways. He cannot first clarify his values and then choose among policies.

A more subtle third point underlies both the first two. Social objectives do not always have the same relative values. One objective may be highly prized in one circumstance, another in another circumstance. If, for example, an administrator values highly both the dispatch with which his agency can carry through its projects *and* good public relations, it matters little which of the two possibly conflicting values he favors in some abstract or general sense. Policy questions arise in forms which put to administrators such a question as: Given the degree to which we are or are not already achieving the values of dispatch and the values of good public relations, is it worth sacrificing a little

---

[4]Martin Meyerson and Edward C. Banfield, *Politics, Planning and the Public Interest* (The Free Press, 1955).

speed for a happier clientele, or is it better to risk offending the clientele so that we can get on with our work? The answer to such a question varies with circumstances.

The value problem is, as the example shows, always a problem of adjustments at a margin. But there is no practicable way to state marginal objectives or values except in terms of particular policies. That one value is preferred to another in one decision situation does not mean that it will be preferred in another decision situation in which it can be had only at great sacrifice of another value. Attempts to rank or order values in general and abstract terms so that they do not shift from decision to decision end up by ignoring the relevant marginal preferences. The significance of this third point thus goes very far. Even if all administrators had at hand an agreed set of values, objectives, and constraints, and an agreed ranking of these values, objectives, and constraints, their marginal values in actual choice situations would be impossible to formulate.

Unable consequently to formulate the relevant values first and then choose among policies to achieve them, administrators must choose directly among alternative policies that offer different marginal combinations of values. Somewhat paradoxically, the only practicable way to disclose one's relevant marginal values even to oneself is to describe the policy one chooses to achieve them. Except roughly and vaguely, I know of no way to describe—or even to understand—what my relative evaluations are for, say, freedom and security, speed and accuracy in governmental decisions, or low taxes and better schools than to describe my preferences among specific policy choices that might be made between the alternatives in each of the pairs.

In summary, two aspects of the process by which values are actually handled can be distinguished. The first is clear: evaluation and empirical analysis are intertwined; that is, one chooses among values and among policies at one and the same time. Put a little more elaborately, one simultaneously chooses a policy to attain certain objectives and chooses the objectives themselves. The second aspect is related but distinct: the administrator focuses his attention on marginal or incremental values. Whether he is aware of it or not, he does not find general formulations of objectives very helpful and in fact makes specific marginal or incremental comparisons. Two policies, X and Y, confront him. Both promise the same degree of attainment of objectives a, b, c, d, and e. But X promises him somewhat more of f than does Y, while Y promises him somewhat more of g than does X. In choosing between them, he is in fact offered the alternative of a marginal or incremental amount of f at the expense of a marginal or incremental amount of g. The only values that are relevant to his choice are these increments by which the two policies differ; and, when he finally chooses between the two marginal values, he does so by making a choice between policies.[5]

As to whether the attempt to clarify objectives in advance of policy selection is more or less rational than the close intertwining of marginal evaluation

---

[5]The line of argument is, of course, an extension of the theory of market choice, especially the theory of consumer choice, to public policy choices.

and empirical analysis, the principal difference established is that for complex problems the first is impossible and irrelevant, and the second is both possible and relevant. The second is possible because the administrator need not try to analyze any values except the values by which alternative policies differ and need not be concerned with them except as they differ marginally. His need for information on values or objectives is drastically reduced as compared with the root method; and his capacity for grasping, comprehending, and relating values to one another is not strained beyond the breaking point.

Relations Between Means and Ends (2b)

Decision-making is ordinarily formalized as a means-ends relationship: means are conceived to be evaluated and chosen in the light of ends finally selected independently of and prior to the choice of means. This is the means-ends relationship of the root method. But it follows from all that has just been said that such a means-ends relationship is possible only to the extent that values are agreed upon, are reconcilable, and are stable at the margin. Typically, therefore, such a means-ends relationship is absent from the branch method, where means and ends are simultaneously chosen.

Yet any departure from the means-ends relationship of the root method will strike some readers as inconceivable. For it will appear to them that only in such a relationship is it possible to determine whether one policy choice is better or worse than another. How can an administrator know whether he has made a wise or foolish decision if he is without prior values or objectives by which to judge his decisions? The answer to this question calls up the third distinctive difference between root and branch methods: how to decide the best policy.

The Test of "Good" Policy (3b)

In the root method, a decision is "correct," "good," or "rational" if it can be shown to attain some specified objective, where the objective can be specified without simply describing the decision itself. Where objectives are defined only through the marginal or incremental approach to values described above, it is still sometimes possible to test whether a policy does in fact attain the desired objectives; but a precise statement of the objectives takes the form of a description of the policy chosen or some alternative to it. To show that a policy is mistaken one cannot offer an abstract argument that important objectives are not achieved; one must instead argue that another policy is more to be preferred.

So far, the departure from customary ways of looking at problem-solving is not troublesome, for many administrators will be quick to agree that the most effective discussion of the correctness of policy does take the form of comparison with other policies that might have been chosen. But what of the situation in which administrators cannot agree on values or objectives, either abstractly or in marginal terms? What then is the test of "good" policy? For the root method, there is no test. Agreement on objectives failing, there is no standard of "correctness." For the method of successive limited comparisons, the test is agreement on policy itself, which remains possible even when agreement on values is not.

It has been suggested that continuing agreement in Congress on the desirability of extending old age insurance stems from liberal desires to strengthen the welfare programs of the federal government and from conservative desires to reduce union demands for private pension plans. If so, this is an excellent demonstration of the ease with which individuals of different ideologies often can agree on concrete policy. Labor mediators report a similar phenomenon: the contestants cannot agree on criteria for settling their disputes but can agree on specific proposals. Similarly, when one administrator's objective turns out to be another's means, they often can agree on policy.

Agreement on policy thus becomes the only practicable test of the policy's correctness. And for one administrator to seek to win the other over to agreement on ends as well would accomplish nothing and create quite unnecessary controversy.

If agreement directly on policy as a test for "best" policy seems a poor substitute for testing the policy against its objectives, it ought to be remembered that objectives themselves have no ultimate validity other than they are agreed upon. Hence agreement is the test of "best" policy in both methods. But where the root method requires agreement on what elements in the decision constitute objectives and on which of these objectives should be sought, the branch method falls back on agreement wherever it can be found.

In an important sense, therefore, it is not irrational for an administrator to defend a policy as good without being able to specify what it is good for.

Non-Comprehensive Analysis (4b)

Ideally, rational-comprehensive analysis leaves out nothing important. But it is impossible to take everything important into consideration unless "important" is so narrowly defined that analysis is in fact quite limited. Limits on human intellectual capacities and on available information set definite limits to man's capacity to be comprehensive. In actual fact, therefore, no one can practice the rational-comprehensive method for really complex problems, and every administrator faced with a sufficiently complex problem must find ways drastically to simplify.

An administrator assisting in the formulation of agricultural economic policy cannot in the first place be competent on all possible policies. He cannot even comprehend one policy entirely. In planning a soil bank program, he cannot successfully anticipate the impact of higher or lower farm income on, say, urbanization—the possible consequent loosening of family ties, possible consequent eventual need for revisions in social security and further implications for tax problems arising out of new federal responsibilities for social security and municipal responsibilities for urban services. Nor, to follow another line of repercussions, can he work through the soil bank program's effects on prices for agricultural products in foreign markets and consequent implications for foreign relations, including those arising out of economic rivalry between the United States and the USSR.

In the method of successive limited comparisons, simplification is systematically achieved in two principal ways. First, it is achieved through limitation of policy comparisons to those policies that differ in relatively small degree from policies presently in effect. Such a limitation immediately reduces the number of alternatives to be investigated and also drastically simplifies the character of the investigation of each. For it is not necessary to undertake fundamental inquiry into an alternative and its consequences; it is necessary only to study those respects in which the proposed alternative and its consequences differ from the status quo. The empirical comparison of marginal differences among alternative policies that differ only marginally is, of course, a counterpart to the incremental or marginal comparison of values discussed above.[6]

Relevance as Well as Realism

It is a matter of common observation that in Western democracies public administrators and policy analysts in general do largely limit their analyses to incremental or marginal differences in policies that are chosen to differ only incrementally. They do not do so, however, solely because they desperately need some way to simplify their problems; they also do so in order to be relevant. Democracies change their policies almost entirely through incremental adjustments. Policy does not move in leaps and bounds.

The incremental character of political change in the United States has often been remarked. The two major political parties agree on fundamentals; they offer alternative policies to the voters only on relatively small points of difference. Both parties favor full employment, but they define it somewhat differently; both favor the development of water power resources, but in slightly different ways; and both favor unemployment compensation, but not the same level of benefits. Similarly, shifts of policy within a party take place largely through a series of relatively small changes, as can be seen in their only gradual acceptance of the idea of governmental responsibility for support of the unemployed, a change in party positions beginning in the early 30's and culminating in a sense in the Employment Act of 1946.

Party behavior is in turn rooted in public attitudes, and political theorists cannot conceive of democracy's surviving in the United States in the absence of fundamental agreement on potentially disruptive issues, with consequent limitation of policy debates to relatively small differences in policy.

Since the policies ignored by the administrator are politically impossible and so irrelevant, the simplification of analysis achieved by concentrating on policies that differ only incrementally is not a capricious kind of simplification. In addition, it can be argued that, given the limits on knowledge within which

---

[6]A more precise definition of incremental policies and a discussion of whether a change that appears "small" to one observer might be seen differently by another is to be found in my "Policy Analysis," 48 *American Economic Review* 298 (June, 1958).

policy-makers are confined, simplifying by limiting the focus to small variations from present policy makes the most of available knowledge. Because
policies being considered are like present and past policies, the administrator
can obtain information and claim some insight. Non-incremental policy proposals are therefore typically not only politically irrelevant but also unpredictable in their consequences.

The second method of simplification of analysis is the practice of ignoring
important possible consequences of possible policies, as well as the values
attached to the neglected consequences. If this appears to disclose a shocking
shortcoming of successive limited comparisons, it can be replied that, even if
the exclusions are random, policies may nevertheless be more intelligently formulated than through futile attempts to achieve a comprehensiveness beyond
human capacity. Actually, however, the exclusions, seeming arbitrary or random from one point of view, need be neither.

Achieving a Degree of Comprehensiveness

Suppose that each value neglected by one policy-making agency were a major
concern of at least one other agency. In that case, a helpful division of labor
would be achieved, and no agency need find its task beyond its capacities. The
shortcomings of such a system would be that one agency might destroy a value
either before another agency could be activated to safeguard it or in spite of
another agency's efforts. But the possibility that important values may be lost is
present in any form of organization, even where agencies attempt to comprehend in planning more than is humanly possible.

The virtue of such a hypothetical division of labor is that every important
interest or value has its watchdog. And these watchdogs can protect the interests in their jurisdiction in two quite different ways: first, by redressing dam-
ages done by other agencies; and, second, by anticipating and heading off
injury before it occurs.

In a society like that of the United States in which individuals are free to
combine to pursue almost any possible common interest they might have
and in which government agencies are sensitive to the pressures of these
groups, the system described is approximated. Almost every interest has its
watchdog. Without claiming that every interest has a sufficiently powerful
watchdog, it can be argued that our system often can assure a more comprehensive regard for the values of the whole society than any attempt at intellectual comprehensiveness.

In the United States, for example, no part of government attempts a comprehensive overview of policy on income distribution. A policy nevertheless
evolves, and one responding to a wide variety of interests. A process of mutual
adjustment among farm groups, labor unions, municipalities and school
boards, tax authorities, and government agencies with responsibilities in the
fields of housing, health, highways, national parks, fire, and police accom-
plishes a distribution of income in which particular income problems
neglected at one point in the decision processes become central at another
point.

Mutual adjustment is more pervasive than the explicit forms it takes in negotiation between groups; it persists through the mutual impacts of groups upon each other even where they are not in communication. For all the imperfections and latent dangers in this ubiquitous process of mutual adjustment, it will often accomplish an adaptation of policies to a wider range of interests than could be done by one group centrally.

Note, too, how the incremental pattern of policy-making fits with the multiple pressure pattern. For when decisions are only incremental—closely related to known policies, it is easier for one group to anticipate the kind of moves another might make and easier too for it to make correction for injury already accomplished.[7]

Even partisanship and narrowness, to use pejorative terms, will sometimes be assets to rational decision-making, for they can doubly insure that what one agency neglects, another will not; they specialize personnel to distinct points of view. The claim is valid that effective rational coordination of the federal administration, if possible to achieve at all, would require an agreed set of values[8]—if "rational" is defined as the practice of the root method of decision-making. But a high degree of administrative coordination occurs as each agency adjusts its policies to the concerns of the other agencies in the process of fragmented decision-making I have just described.

For all the apparent shortcomings of the incremental approach to policy alternatives with its arbitrary exclusion coupled with fragmentation, when compared to the root method, the branch method often looks far superior. In the root method, the inevitable exclusion of factors is accidental, unsystematic, and not defensible by any argument so far developed, while in the branch method the exclusions are deliberate, systematic, and defensible. Ideally, of course, the root method does not exclude; in practice it must.

Nor does the branch method necessarily neglect long-run considerations and objectives. It is clear that important values must be omitted in considering policy, and sometimes the only way long-run objectives can be given adequate attention is through the neglect of short-run considerations. But the values omitted can be either long-run or short-run.

Succession of Comparisons (5b)

The final distinctive element in the branch method is that the comparisons, together with the policy choice, proceed in a chronological series. Policy is not made once and for all; it is made and re-made endlessly. Policy-making is a process of successive approximation to some desired objectives in which what is desired itself continues to change under reconsideration.

---

[7]The link between the practice of the method of successive limited comparisons and mutual adjustment of interests in a highly fragmented decision-making process adds a new facet to pluralist theories of government and administration.

[8]Herbert Simon, Donald W. Smithburg, and Victor A. Thompson, *Public Administration* (Alfred A. Knopf, 1950), p. 434.

Making policy is at best a very rough process. Neither social scientists, nor politicians, nor public administrators yet know enough about the social world to avoid repeated error in predicting the consequences of policy moves. A wise policy-maker consequently expects that his policies will achieve only part of what he hopes and at the same time will produce unanticipated consequences he would have preferred to avoid. If he proceeds through a *succession* of incremental changes, he avoids serious lasting mistakes in several ways.

In the first place, past sequences of policy steps have given him knowledge about the probable consequences of further similar steps. Second, he need not attempt big jumps toward his goals that would require predictions beyond his or anyone else's knowledge, because he never expects his policy to be a final resolution of a problem. His decision is only one step, one that if successful can quickly be followed by another. Third, he is in effect able to test his previous predictions as he moves on to each further step. Lastly, he often can remedy a past error fairly quickly—more quickly than if policy proceeded through more distinct steps widely spaced in time.

Compare this comparative analysis of incremental changes with the aspiration to employ theory in the root method. Man cannot think without classifying, without subsuming one experience under a more general category of experiences. The attempt to push categorization as far as possible and to find general propositions which can be applied to specific situations is what I refer to with the word "theory." Where root analysis often leans heavily on theory in this sense, the branch method does not.

The assumption of root analysts is that theory is the most systematic and economical way to bring relevant knowledge to bear on a specific problem. Granting the assumption, an unhappy fact is that we do not have adequate theory to apply to problems in any policy area, although theory is more adequate in some areas—monetary policy, for example—than in others. Comparative analysis, as in the branch method, is sometimes a systematic alternative to theory.

Suppose an administrator must choose among a small group of policies that differ only incrementally from each other and from present policy. He might aspire to "understand" each of the alternatives—for example, to know all the consequences of each aspect of each policy. If so, he would indeed require theory. In fact, however, he would usually decide that, *for policy-making purposes,* he need know, as explained above, only the consequences of each of those aspects of the policies in which they differed from one another. For this much more modest aspiration, he requires no theory (although it might be helpful, if available), for he can proceed to isolate probable differences by examining the differences in consequences associated with past differences in policies, a feasible program because he can take his observations from a long sequence of incremental changes.

For example, without a more comprehensive social theory about juvenile delinquency than scholars have yet produced, one cannot possibly understand the ways in which a variety of public policies—say on education, housing, recreation, employment, race relations, and policing—might encourage or discourage delinquency. And one needs such an understanding if he undertakes the comprehensive overview of the problem prescribed in the models of the root method. If, however, one merely wants to mobilize knowledge sufficient to assist in a choice among a small group of similar policies—alternative policies on juvenile court procedures, for example—he can do so by comparative analysis of the results of similar past policy moves.

Theorists and Practitioners

This difference explains—in some cases at least—why the administrator often feels that the outside expert or academic problem-solver is sometimes not helpful and why they in turn often urge more theory on him. And it explains why an administrator often feels more confident when "flying by the seat of his pants" than when following the advice of theorists. Theorists often ask the administrator to go the long way round to the solution of his problems, in effect ask him to follow the best canons of the scientific method, when the administrator knows that the best available theory will work less well than more modest incremental comparisons. Theorists do not realize that the administrator is often in fact practicing a systematic method. It would be foolish to push this explanation too far, for sometimes practical decision-makers are pursuing neither a theoretical approach nor successive comparisons, nor any other systematic method.

It may be worth emphasizing that theory is sometimes of extremely limited helpfulness in policy-making for at least two rather different reasons. It is greedy for facts; it can be constructed only through a great collection of observations. And it is typically insufficiently precise for application to a policy process that moves through small changes. In contrast, the comparative method both economizes on the need for facts and directs the analyst's attention to just those facts that are relevant to the fine choices faced by the decision-maker.

With respect to precision of theory, economic theory serves as an example. It predicts that an economy without money or prices would in certain specified ways misallocate resources, but this finding pertains to an alternative far removed from the kind of policies on which administrators need help. On the other hand, it is not precise enough to predict the consequences of policies restricting business mergers, and this is the kind of issue on which the administrators need help. Only in relatively restricted areas does economic theory achieve sufficient precision to go far in resolving policy questions; its helpfulness in policy-making is always so limited that it requires supplementation through comparative analysis.

Successive Comparison as a System

Successive limited comparisons is, then, indeed a method or system; it is not a failure of method for which administrators ought to apologize. None the less, its imperfections, which have not been explored in this paper, are many. For example, the method is without a built-in safeguard for all relevant values, and it also may lead the decision-maker to overlook excellent policies for no other reason than that they are not suggested by the chain of successive policy steps leading up to the present. Hence, it ought to be said that under this method, as well as under some of the most sophisticated variants of the root method— operations research, for example—policies will continue to be as foolish as they are wise.

Why then bother to describe the method in all the above detail? Because it is in fact a common method of policy formulation, and is, for complex problems, the principal reliance of administrators as well as of other policy analysts.[9] And because it will be superior to any other decision-making method available for complex problems in many circumstances, certainly superior to a futile attempt at superhuman comprehensiveness. The reaction of the public administrator to the exposition of method doubtless will be less a discovery of a new method than a better acquaintance with an old. But by becoming more conscious of their practice of this method, administrators might practice it with more skill and know when to extend or constrict its use. (That they sometimes practice it effectively and sometimes not may explain the extremes of opinion on "muddling through," which is both praised as a highly sophisticated form of problem-solving and denounced as no method at all. For I suspect that in so far as there is a system in what is known as "muddling through," this method is it.)

One of the noteworthy incidental consequences of clarification of the method is the light it throws on the suspicion an administrator sometimes entertains that a consultant or adviser is not speaking relevantly and responsibly when in fact by all ordinary objective evidence he is. The trouble lies in the fact that most of us approach policy problems within a framework given by our view of a chain of successive policy choices made up to the present. One's thinking about appropriate policies with respect, say, to urban traffic control is greatly influenced by one's knowledge of the incremental steps taken up to the present. An administrator enjoys an intimate knowledge of his past sequences that "outsiders" do not share, and his thinking and that of the "outsider" will consequently be different in ways that may puzzle both. Both may appear to

---

[9]Elsewhere I have explored this same method of policy formulation as practiced by academic analysts of policy ("Policy Analysis," 48 *American Economic Review* 298 [June, 1958]). Although it has been here presented as a method for public administrators, it is no less necessary to analysts more removed from immediate policy questions, despite their tendencies to describe their own analytical efforts as though they were the rational-comprehensive method with an especially heavy use of theory. Similarly, this same method is inevitably resorted to in personal problem-solving, where means and ends are sometimes impossible to separate, where aspirations or objectives undergo constant development, and where drastic simplification of the complexity of the real world is urgent if problems are to be solved in the time that can be given to them. To an economist accustomed to dealing with the marginal or incremental concept in market processes, the central idea in the method is that both evaluation and empirical analysis are incremental. Accordingly I have referred to the method elsewhere as "the incremental method."

be talking intelligently, yet each may find the other unsatisfactory. The relevance of the policy chain of succession is even more clear when an American tries to discuss, say, antitrust policy with a Swiss, for the chains of policy in the two countries are strikingly different and the two individuals consequently have organized their knowledge in quite different ways.

If this phenomenon is a barrier to communication, an understanding of it promises an enrichment of intellectual interaction in policy formulation. Once the source of difference is understood, it will sometimes be stimulating for an administrator to seek out a policy analyst whose recent experience is with a policy chain different from his own.

This raises again a question only briefly discussed above on the merits of like-mindedness among government administrators. While much of organization theory argues the virtues of common values and agreed organizational objectives, for complex problems in which the root method is inapplicable, agencies will want among their own personnel two types of diversification: administrators whose thinking is organized by reference to policy chains other than those familiar to most members of the organization and, even more commonly, administrators whose professional or personal values or interests create diversity of view (perhaps coming from different specialties, social classes, geographical areas) so that, even within a single agency, decision-making can be fragmented and parts of the agency can serve as watchdogs for other parts.

5

Mixed Scanning: A "Third" Approach to Decision Making (1967)

Amitai Etzioni

In the concept of social decision-making, vague commitments of a normative and political nature are translated into specific commitments to one or more specific courses of action. Since decision-making includes an element of choice, it is the most deliberate and voluntaristic aspect of social conduct. As such, it raises the question: To what extent can social actors decide what their course will be, and to what extent are they compelled to follow a course set by forces beyond their control? Three conceptions of decision-making are considered here with assumptions that give varying weights to the conscious choice of the decision-makers.

Rationalistic models tend to posit a high degree of control over the decision-making situation on the part of the decision-maker. The incrementalist approach presents an alternative model, referred to as the art of "muddling through," which assumes much less command over the environment. Finally, the article outlines a third approach to social decision-making which, in combining elements of both earlier approaches, is neither as utopian in its assumptions as the first model nor as conservative as the second. For reasons which will become evident, this third approach is referred to as mixed-scanning.

Source: Amitai Etzioni, "Mixed Scanning: 'Third' Approach to Decision Making." *Public Administration Review,* December 1967. Reprinted by permission of Blackwell Publishing Ltd.

—Editor's Note: In working on this article, Professor Etzioni benefited from a Social Science Research Council fellowship for 1967–1968. A much more detailed discussion of societal decision-making is included in chapters 11 and 12 of the author's *The Active Society: A Theory of Societal and Political Processes,* to be published by The Free Press early in 1968.

The Rationalistic Approach

Rationalistic models are widely held conceptions about how decisions are and ought to be made. An actor becomes aware of a problem, posits a goal, carefully weighs alternative means, and chooses among them according to his estimates of their respective merit, with reference to the state of affairs he prefers. Incrementalists' criticism of this approach focuses on the disparity between the requirements of the model and the capacities of decision-makers.[1] Social decision-making centers, it is pointed out, frequently do not have a specific, agreed upon set of values that could provide the criteria for evaluating alternatives. Values, rather, are fluid and are affected by, as well as affect, the decisions made. Moreover, in actual practice, the rationalistic assumption that values and facts, means and ends, can be clearly distinguished seems inapplicable:

> . . . Public controversy . . . has surrounded the proposal to construct a branch of the Cook County Hospital on the South Side in or near the Negro area. Several questions of policy are involved in the matter, but the ones which have caused one of the few *public* debates of an issue in the Negro community concern whether, or to what extent, building such a branch would result in an all-Negro or "Jim Crow" hospital and whether such a hospital is desirable as a means of providing added medical facilities for Negro patients. Involved are both an issue of *fact* (whether the hospital would be segregated, intentionally or unintentionally, as a result of the character of the neighborhood in which it would be located) and an issue of *value* (whether even an all-Negro hospital would be preferable to no hospital at all in the area). In reality, however, the factions have aligned themselves in such a way and the debate has proceeded in such a manner that the fact issue and the value issue have been collapsed into the single question of whether to build or not to build. Those in favor of the proposal will argue that the facts do not bear out the charge of "Jim Crowism"— "the proposed site . . . is not considered to be placed in a segregated area for the exclusive use of one racial or minority group"; or "no responsible officials would try to develop a new hospital to further segregation"; or "establishing a branch hospital for the . . . more adequate care of the indigent patient load, from the facts thus presented, does not represent Jim Crowism." At the same time, these proponents argue that whatever the facts, the factual issue is secondary to the overriding consideration that "there is a here-and-now need for more hospital beds. . . . Integration may be the long-run goal, but in the short-run we need more facilities."[2]

In addition, information about consequences is, at best, fractional. Decision-makers have neither the assets nor the time to collect the information required

---

[1] See David Braybrooke and Charles E. Lindblom, *A Strategy of Decision* (New York: Free Press, 1963), pp. 48–50 and pp. 111–143; Charles E. Lindblom, *The Intelligence of Democracy* (New York: Free Press, 1965), pp. 137–139. See also Jerome S. Bruner, Jacqueline J. Goodnow, and George A. Austin, *A Study of Thinking* (New York: John Wiley, 1956) chapters 4–5.

[2] James Q. Wilson, *Negro Politics* (New York: Free Press, 1960), p. 189.

for rational choice. While knowledge technology, especially computers, does aid in the collection and processing of information, it cannot provide for the computation required by the rationalist model. (This holds even for chess playing, let alone "real-life" decisions.) Finally, rather than being confronted with a limited universe of relevant consequences, decision-makers face an open system of variables, a world in which all consequences cannot be surveyed.[3] A decision-maker, attempting to adhere to the tenets of a rationalistic model, will become frustrated, exhaust his resources without coming to a decision, and remain without an effective decision-making model to guide him. Rationalistic models are thus rejected as being at once unrealistic and undesirable.

The Incrementalist Approach

A less demanding model of decision-making has been outlined in the strategy of "disjointed incrementalism" advanced by Charles E. Lindblom and others.[4] Disjointed incrementalism seeks to adapt decision-making strategies to the limited cognitive capacities of decision-makers and to reduce the scope and cost of information collection and computation. Lindblom summarized the six primary requirements of the model in this way:[5]

1. Rather than attempting a comprehensive survey and evaluation of all alternatives, the decision-maker focuses only on those policies which differ incrementally from existing policies.
2. Only a relatively small number of policy alternatives are considered.
3. For each policy alternative, only a restricted number of "important" consequences are evaluated.
4. The problem confronting the decision-maker is continually redefined: Incrementalism allows for countless ends-means and means-ends adjustments which, in effect, make the problem more manageable.
5. Thus, there is no one decision or "right" solution but a "never-ending series of attacks" on the issues at hand through serial analyses and evaluation.
6. As such, incremental decision-making is described as remedial, geared more to the alleviation of present, concrete social imperfections than to the promotion of future social goals.

---

[3]See review of A Strategy of Decision by Kenneth J. Arrow in Political Science Quarterly, Vol. 79 (1964), p. 585. See also Herbert A. Simon, Models of Man (New York: Wiley, 1957), p. 198, and Aaron Wildavsky, The Politics of the Budgetary Process (Boston: Little, Brown and Co., 1964), pp. 147–152.

[4]Charles E. Lindblom, "The Science of 'Muddling Through'," Public Administration Review, Vol. 19 (1959), pp. 79–99; Robert A. Dahl and Charles E. Lindblom, Politics, Economics and Welfare (New York: Harper and Brothers, 1953); Strategy of Decision, op. cit.; and The Intelligence of Democracy, op. cit.

[5]Lindblom, The Intelligence of Democracy, op. cit., pp. 144–148.

Morphological Assumptions of the Incremental Approach

Beyond a model and a strategy of decision-making, disjointed incrementalism also posits a structure model; it is presented as the typical decision-making process of pluralistic societies, as contrasted with the master planning of total-itarian societies. Influenced by the free competition model of economics, incrementalists reject the notion that policies can guided in terms of central institutions of a society expressing the collective "good." Policies, rather, are the outcome of a give-and-take among numerous societal "partisans." The measure of a good decision is the decision makers' agreement about it. Poor decisions are those which exclude actors capable of affecting the projected course of action; decisions of this type tend to be blocked or modified later.

Partisan "mutual-adjustment" is held to provide for a measure of coordina-tion of decisions among a multiplicity of decision-makers and, in effect, to compensate on the societal level for the inadequacies of the individual incre-mental decision-maker and for the society's inability to make decisions effec-tively from one center. Incremental decision-making is claimed to be both a realistic account of how the American polity and other modern democracies decide and the most effective approach to societal decision-making, i.e., both a descriptive and a normative model.

A Critique of the Incremental Approach as a Normative Model

Decisions by consent among partisans without a societywide regulatory center and guiding institutions should not be viewed as the preferred approach to decision-making. In the first place, decisions so reached would, of necessity, reflect the interests of the most powerful, since partisans invariably differ in their respective power positions; demands of the underprivileged and politi-cally unorganized would be underrepresented.

Secondly, incrementalism would tend to neglect *basic* societal innova-tions, as it focuses on the short run and seeks no more than limited variations from past policies. While an accumulation of small steps could lead to a sig-nificant change, there is nothing in this approach to guide the accumulation; the steps may be circular—leading back to where they started, or dispersed—leading in many directions at once but leading nowhere. Boulding comments that, according to this approach, "we do stagger through history like a drunk putting one disjointed incremental foot after another."[6]

In addition, incrementalists seem to underestimate *their* impact on the decision-makers. As Dror put it, "Although Lindblom's thesis includes a num-ber of reservations, these are insufficient to alter its main impact as an ideolog-ical reinforcement of the pro-inertia and anti-innovation forces."[7]

---

[6]Kenneth E. Boulding in a review of *A Strategy of Decision* in the *American Socio-logical Review,* Vol. 29 (1964), p. 931.

[7]Yehezkel Dror, "Muddling Through—'Science' or Inertia?" *Public Administration Review,* Vol. 24 (1964), p. 155.

A Conceptual and Empirical Critique of Incrementalism

Incrementalist strategy clearly recognizes one subset of situations to which it does not apply—namely, "large" or fundamental decisions,[8] such as a declaration of war. While incremental decisions greatly outnumber fundamental ones, the latter's significance for societal decision-making is not commensurate with their number; it is thus a mistake to relegate nonincremental decisions to the category of exceptions. Moreover, it is often the fundamental decisions which set the context for the numerous incremental ones. Although fundamental decisions are frequently "prepared" by incremental ones in order that the final decision will initiate a less abrupt change, these decisions may still be considered relatively fundamental. The incremental steps which follow cannot be understood without them, and the preceding steps are useless unless they lead to fundamental decisions.

Thus, while the incrementalists hold that decision-making involves a choice between the two kinds of decision-making models, it should be noted that (a) *most incremental decisions specify or anticipate fundamental decisions, and* (b) *the cumulative value of the incremental decisions is greatly affected by the related fundamental decisions.*

Thus, it is not enough to show, as Fenno did, that Congress makes primarily marginal changes in the federal budget (a comparison of one year's budget for a federal agency with that of the preceding year showed on many occasions only a 10 per cent difference[9]), or that for long periods the defense budget does not change much in terms of its percentage of the federal budget, or that the federal budget changes little each year in terms of its percentage of the Gross National Product.[10] These incremental changes are often the unfolding of trends initiated at critical turning points at which fundamental decisions were made. The American defense budget jumped at the beginning of the Korean War in 1950 from 5 per cent of the GNP to 10.3 per cent in 1951. The fact that it stayed at about this level, ranging between 9 and 11.3 per cent of the GNP after the war ended (1954–1960), did reflect incremental decisions, but these were made within the context of the decision to engage in the Korean War.[11] Fenno's own figures show almost an equal number of changes above the 20 per cent level as below it; seven changes represented an increase of 100 per cent or more and 24 changes increased 50 per cent or more.[12]

It is clear that, while Congress or other societal decision-making bodies do make some cumulative incremental decisions without facing the fundamental

---

[8]Braybrooke and Lindblom, *A Strategy of Decision, op. cit.,* pp. 66–69.

[9]Richard Fenno, Jr., *The Power of the Purse* (Boston: Little, Brown and Co., 1966), pp. 266ff. See also Otto A. Davis, M. A. H. Dempster, and Aaron Wildavsky, "A Theory of the Budgetary Process," *American Political Science Review,* Vol. 60 (1966), esp. pp. 530–531.

[10]Samuel P. Huntington, quoted by Nelson E. Polsby, *Congress and the Presidency* (Englewood Cliffs, N. J.: Prentice-Hall, 1964), p. 86.

[11]*Ibid.*

[12]Fenno, *The Power of the Purse, Loc. cit.*

one implied, many other decisions which appear to be a series of incremental ones are, in effect, the implementation or elaboration of a fundamental decision. For example, after Congress set up a national space agency in 1958 and consented to back President Kennedy's space goals, it made "incremental" additional commitments for several years. Initially, however, a fundamental decision had been made. Congress in 1958, drawing on past experiences and on an understanding of the dynamics of incremental processes, could not have been unaware that once a fundamental commitment is made it is difficult to reverse it. While the initial space budget was relatively small, the very act of setting up a space agency amounted to subscribing to additional budget increments in future years.[13]

Incrementalists argue that incremental decisions tend to be remedial; small steps are taken in the "right" direction, or, when it is evident the direction is "wrong," the course is altered. But if the decision-maker evaluates his incremental decisions and small steps, which he must do if he is to decide whether or not the direction is right, his judgment will be greatly affected by the evaluative criteria he applies. Here, again, we have to go outside the incrementalist model to ascertain the ways in which these criteria are set.

Thus, while actors make both kinds of decisions, the number and role of fundamental decisions are significantly greater than incrementalists state, and when the fundamental ones are missing, incremental decision-making amounts to drifting—action without direction. A more active approach to societal decision-making requires two sets of mechanisms: (a) high-order, fundamental policy-making processes which set basic directions and (b) incremental processes which prepare for fundamental decisions and work them out after they have been reached. This is provided by mixed-scanning.

The Mixed-Scanning Approach

Mixed-scanning provides both a realistic description of the strategy used by actors in a large variety of fields and the strategy for effective actors to follow. Let us first illustrate this approach in a simple situation and then explore its societal dimensions. Assume we are about to set up a worldwide weather observation system using weather satellites. The rationalistic approach would seek an exhaustive survey of weather conditions by using cameras capable of detailed observations and by scheduling reviews of the entire sky as often as possible. This would yield an avalanche of details, costly to analyze and likely to overwhelm our action capacities (e.g., "seeding" cloud formations that could develop into hurricanes or bring rain to arid areas). Incrementalism would focus on those areas in which similar patterns developed in the recent

---

[13]For an example involving the Supreme Court's decision on desegregation, see Martin Shapiro, "Stability and Change in Judicial Decision-Making: Incrementalism or Stare Decisis," Law in Transition Quarterly, Vol. 2 (1965), pp. 134–157. See also a commentary by Bruce L. R. Smith, American Political Science Review, Vol. 61 (1967), esp. p. 151.

past and, perhaps, on a few nearby regions; it would thus ignore all formations which might deserve attention if they arose in unexpected areas.

A mixed-scanning strategy would include elements of both approaches by employing two cameras: a broad-angle camera that would cover all parts of the sky but not in great detail, and a second one which would zero in on those areas revealed by the first camera to require a more in-depth examination. While mixed-scanning might miss areas in which only a detailed camera could reveal trouble, it is less likely than incrementalism to miss obvious trouble spots in unfamiliar areas.

From an abstract viewpoint mixed-scanning provides a particular procedure for the collection of information (e.g., the surveying or "scanning" of weather conditions), a strategy about the allocation of resources (e.g., "seeding"), and—we shall see—guidelines for the relations between the two. The strategy combines a detailed ("rationalistic") examination of some sectors—which, unlike the exhaustive examination of the entire area, is feasible—with a "truncated" review of other sectors. The relative investment in the two kinds of scanning—full detail and truncated—as well as in the very act of scanning, depends on how costly it would be to miss, for example, one hurricane; the cost of additional scanning; and the amount of time it would take.

Scanning may be divided into more than two levels; there can be several levels with varying degrees of detail and coverage, though it seems most effective to include an all-encompassing level (so that no major option will be left uncovered) and a highly detailed level (so that the option selected can be explored as fully as is feasible).

The decision on how the investment of assets and time it takes to be allocated among the levels of scanning is, in fact, part of the strategy. The actual amount of assets and time spent depends on the total amount available and on experimentation with various inter-level combinations. Also, the amount spent is best changed over time. Effective decision-making requires that sporadically, or at set intervals, investment in encompassing (high-coverage) scanning be increased to check for far removed but "obvious" dangers and to search for better lines of approach. Annual budget reviews and the State of the Union messages provide, in principle, such occasions.

An increase in investment of this type is also effective when the actor realizes that the environment radically changes or when he sees that the early chain of increments brings no improvement in the situation or brings even a "worsening." If, at this point, the actor decides to drop the course of action, the effectiveness of his decision-making is reduced, since, through some high-coverage scanning, he may discover that a continuation of the "loss" is about to lead to a solution. (An obvious example is the selling of a declining stock if a further review reveals that the corporation is expected to improve its earning next year, after several years of decline.) Reality cannot be assumed to be structured in straight lines where each step towards a goal leads directly to another and where the accumulation of small steps in effect solves the problem. Often what from an incremental viewpoint is a step away from the goal ("worsening") may from a broader perspective be a step in the right direction, as when the temperature of a patient is allowed to rise because this will hasten his recovery. Thus mixed-scanning not only combines various levels of scanning but also provides a set of criteria for situations in which one level or another is to be emphasized.

In the exploration of mixed-scanning, it is essential to differentiate fundamental decisions from incremental ones. Fundamental decisions are made by exploring the main alternatives the actor sees in view of his conception of his goals, but—unlike what rationalism would indicate—details and specification are omitted so that an overview is feasible. Incremental decisions are made but within the contexts set by fundamental decisions (and fundamental reviews). Thus, each of the two elements in mixed-scanning helps to reduce the effects of the particular shortcomings of the other; incrementalism reduces the unrealistic aspects of rationalism by limiting the details required in fundamental decisions, and contextuating rationalism helps to overcome the conservative slant of incrementalism by exploring longer-run alternatives. Together, empirical tests and comparative study of decision-makers would show that these elements make for a third approach which is at once more realistic and more effective than its components.

Can Decisions Be Evaluated?

The preceding discussion assumes that both the observer and the actor have a capacity to evaluate decision-making strategies and to determine which is the more effective. Incrementalists, however, argue that since values cannot be scaled and summarized, "good" decisions cannot be defined and, hence, evaluation is not possible. In contrast, it is reasonable to expect that the decision-makers, as well as the observers, can summarize their values and rank them, at least in an ordinal scale.

For example, many societal projects have one primary goal such as increasing birth control, economically desalting sea water, or reducing price inflation by one-half over a two-year period. Other goals which are also served are secondary, e.g., increasing the country's R & D sector by investing in desalting. The actor, hence, may deal with the degree to which the *primary* goal was realized and make this the central evaluative measure for a "good" policy, while noting its effects on secondary goals. When he compares projects in these terms, he, in effect, weighs the primary goal as several times as important as all the secondary goals combined. This procedure amounts to saying, "As I care very much about one goal and little about the others, if the project does not serve the first goal, it is no good and I do not have to worry about measuring and totaling up whatever other gains it may be providing for my secondary values."

When there are two or even three primary goals (e.g., teaching, therapy, and research in a university hospital), the actor can still compare projects in terms of the extent to which they realize each primary goal. He can establish that project X is good for research but not for teaching while project Y is very good for teaching but not as good for research, etc., without having to raise the additional difficulties of combining the effectiveness measures into one numerical index. In effect, he proceeds as if they had identical weights.

Finally, an informal scaling of values is not as difficult as the incrementalists imagine. Most actors are able to rank their goals to some extent (e.g., faculty is more concerned about the quality of research than the quality of teaching).

> One of the most imaginative attempts to evaluate the effectiveness of programs with hard-to-assess objectives is a method devised by David Osborn, Deputy Assistant Secretary of State for Educational and Cultural Affairs. . . . Osborn recommends a scheme of cross-multiplying the costs of the activities with a number representing the rank of its objectives on a scale. For instance, the exchange of Fulbright professors may contribute to "cultural prestige and mutual respect," "educational development," and gaining "entrée," which might be given scale numbers such as 8, 6, and 5, respectively. These numbers are then multiplied with the costs of the program, and the resulting figure is in turn multiplied with an ingenious figure called a "country number." The latter is an attempt to get a rough measure of the importance to the U.S. of the countries with which we have cultural relations. It is arrived at by putting together in complicated ways certain key data, weighed to reflect cultural and educational matters, such as the country's population, Gross National Product, number of college students, rate of illiteracy, and so forth. The resulting numbers are then revised in the light of working experience, as when, because of its high per capita income, a certain tiny middle-eastern country turns out to be more important to the U.S. than a large eastern European one. At this point, country numbers are revised on the basis of judgment and experience, as are other numbers at other points. But those who make such revisions have a basic framework to start with, a set of numbers arranged on the basis of many factors, rather than single arbitrary guesses.[14]

Thus, in evaluation as in decision-making itself, while full detailed rationalism may well be impossible, truncated reviews are feasible, and this approach may be expected to be more effective in terms of the actors' goals than "muddling through."

Morphological Factors

The structures within which interactions among actors take place become more significant the more we recognize that the bases of decisions neither are nor can be a fully ordered set of values and an exhaustive examination of reality. In part, the strategy followed is determined neither by values nor by information but by the positions of and power relations among the decision-makers. For example, the extent to which one element of mixed-scanning is stressed as against the other is affected by the relationship between higher and lower organizational ranks. In some situations, the higher in rank, concerned only with the overall picture, are impatient with details, while lower ranks—especially experts—are more likely to focus on details. In other situations, the higher ranks, to avoid facing the overall picture, seek to bury themselves, their administration, and the public in details.

---

[14]Virginia Held, "PPBS Comes to Washington," *The Public Interest*, No. 4 (Summer 1966), pp. 102–115, quotation from pp. 112–113.

Next, the environment should be taken into account. For instance, a highly incremental approach would perhaps be adequate if the situation were more stable and the decisions made were effective from the start. This approach is expected to be less appropriate when conditions are rapidly changing and when the initial course was wrong. Thus, there seems to be no one effective decision-making strategy in the abstract, apart from the societal environment into which it is introduced. Mixed-scanning is flexible; changes in the relative investment in scanning in general as well as among the various levels of scanning permit it to adapt to the specific situation. For example, more encompassing scanning is called for when the environment is more malleable.

Another major consideration here is the capacities of the actor. This is illustrated with regard to interagency relations by the following statement: ". . . the State Department was hopelessly behind. Its cryptographic equipment was obsolescent, which slowed communications, and it had no central situation room at all."[15] The author goes on to show how as a consequence the State Department was less able to act than was the Defense Department.

An actor with a low capacity to mobilize power to implement his decisions may do better to rely less on encompassing scanning; even if remote outcomes are anticipated, he will be able to do little about them. More generally, the greater a unit's control capacities the more encompassing scanning it can undertake, and the more such scanning, the more effective its decision-making. This points to an interesting paradox: The developing nations, with much lower control capacities than the modern ones, tend to favor much more planning, although they may have to make do with a relatively high degree of incrementalism. Yet modern pluralistic societies—which are much more able to scan and, at least in some dimensions, are much more able to control—tend to plan less.

Two different factors are involved which highlight the difference in this regard among modern societies. While all have a higher capacity to scan and some control advantages as compared to nonmodern societies, they differ sharply in their capacity to build consensus. Democracies must accept a relatively high degree of incrementalism (though not as high as developing nations) because of their greater need to gain support for new decisions from many and conflicting subsocieties, a need which reduces their capacity to follow a long-run plan. It is easier to reach consensus under noncrisis situations, on increments similar to existing policies, than to gain support for a new policy. However, the role of crises is significant; in relatively less passive democracies, crises serve to build consensus for major changes of direction which are overdue (e.g., desegregation).

Totalitarian societies, more centralist and relying on powers which are less dependent on consensus, can plan more but they tend to overshoot the mark. Unlike democracies which first seek to build up a consensus and then proceed, often doing less than necessary later than necessary, totalitarian societies, lacking the capacity for consensus-building or even for assessing the various resis-

---

[15]Roger Hilsman, To Move a Nation: The Politics of Foreign Policy in the Administration of John F. Kennedy (Garden City, N.Y.: Doubleday & Co., 1967), p. 27.

tances, usually try for too much too early. They are then forced to adjust their plans after initiation, with the revised policies often scaled down and involving more "consensus" than the original one. While totalitarian gross misplanning constitutes a large waste of resources, some initial overplanning and later down-scaling is as much a decision-making strategy as is disjointed incrementalism, and is the one for which totalitarian societies may be best suited.

A society more able to effectively handle its problems (one referred to elsewhere as an *active society*)[16] would require:

1. A higher capacity to build consensus than even democracies command.
2. More effective though not necessarily more numerous means of control than totalitarian societies employ (which new knowledge technology and better analysis through the social sciences may make feasible).
3. A mixed-scanning strategy which is not as rationalistic as that which the totalitarian societies attempt to pursue and not as incremental as the strategy democracies advocate.

---

[16]Amitai Etzioni, *The Active Society: A Theory of Societal and Political Processes* (New York: Free Press, 1968).

6

Street-Level Bureaucrats as Policy Makers (1980)

Michael Lipsky

Public service workers currently occupy a critical position in American society. Although they are normally regarded as low-level employees, the actions of most public service workers actually constitute the services "delivered" by

---

government. Moreover, when taken together the individual decisions of these workers become, or add up to, agency policy. Whether government policy is to deliver "goods"—such as welfare or public housing—or to confer status—such as "criminal" or "mentally ill"—the discretionary actions of public employees are the benefits and sanctions of government programs or determine access to government rights and benefits.

Most citizens encounter government (if they encounter it at all) not through letters to congressmen or by attendance at school board meetings but through their teachers and their children's teachers and through the policeman on the corner or in the patrol car. Each encounter of this kind represents an instance of policy delivery.

Public service workers who interact directly with citizens in the course of their jobs, and who have substantial discretion in the execution of their work are called *street-level bureaucrats* in this study. Public service agencies that employ a significant number of street-level bureaucrats in proportion to their work force are called *street-level bureaucracies.* Typical street-level bureaucrats are teachers, police officers and other law enforcement personnel, social workers, judges, public lawyers and other court officers, health workers, and many other public employees who grant access to government programs and provide services with them. People who work in these jobs tend to have much in common because they experience analytically similar work conditions.[1]

The way in which street-level bureaucrats deliver benefits and sanctions structure and delimit people's lives and opportunities. These ways orient and provide the social (and political) contexts in which people act. Thus every extension of service benefits is accompanied by an extension of state influence and control. As providers of public benefits and keepers of public order, street-level bureaucrats are the focus of political controversy. They are constantly torn by the demands of service recipients to improve effectiveness and responsiveness and by the demands of citizen groups to improve the efficacy and efficiency of government services. Since the salaries of street-level bureaucrats comprise a significant proportion of nondefense governmental expenditures, any doubts about the size of government budgets quickly translate into concerns for the scope and content of these public services. Moreover, public service workers have expanded and increasingly consolidated their collective strength so that in disputes over the scope of public services they have become a substantial independent force in the resolution of controversy affecting their status and position.

Street-level bureaucrats dominate political controversies over public services for two general reasons. First, debates about the proper scope and focus of governmental services are essentially debates over the scope and function of these public employees. Second, street-level bureaucrats have considerable impact on people's lives. This impact may be of several kinds. They socialize citizens to expectations of government services and a place in the political community. They determine the eligibility of citizens for government benefits and sanctions. They oversee the treatment (the service) citizens receive in those programs. Thus, in a sense street-level bureaucrats implicitly mediate aspects of the constitutional relationship of citizens to the state. In short, they hold the keys to a dimension of citizenship.

Conflict over the Scope and Substance of Public Services

In the world of experience we perceive teachers, welfare workers, and police officers as members of separately organized and motivated public agencies. And so they are from many points of view. But if we divide public employees according to whether they interact with citizens directly and have discretion over significant aspects of citizens' lives, we see that a high proportion and enormous number of public workers share these job characteristics. They comprise a great portion of all public employees working in domestic affairs. State and local governments employ approximately 3.7 million in local schools, more than 500,000 people in police operations, and over 300,000 people in public welfare. Public school employees represent more than half of all workers employed in local governments. Instructional jobs represent about two-thirds of the educational personnel, and many of the rest are former teachers engaged in administration, or social workers, psychologists, and librarians who provide direct services in the schools. Of the 3.2 million local government public employees not engaged in education, approximately 14 percent work as police officers. One of every sixteen jobs in state and local government outside of education is held by a public welfare worker.[2] In this and other areas the majority of jobs are held by people with responsibility for involvement with citizens.

Other street-level bureaucrats comprise an important part of the remainder of local government personnel rolls. Although the U.S. Census Bureau does not provide breakdowns of other job classifications suitable for our purposes, we can assume that many of the 1.1 million health workers,[3] most of the 5,000 public service lawyers,[4] many of the employees of the various court systems, and other public employees also perform as street-level bureaucrats. Some of the nation's larger cities employ a staggering number of street-level bureaucrats. For example, the 26,680 school teachers in Chicago are more numerous than the populations of many of the Chicago suburbs.[5]

Another measure of the significance of street-level bureaucrats in public sector employment is the amount of public funds allocated to pay them. Of all local government salaries, more than half went to public education in 1973. Almost 80 percent of these monies was used to pay instructional personnel. Police salaries comprised approximately one-sixth of local public salaries not assigned to education.[6]

Much of the growth in public employment in the past 25 years has occurred in the ranks of street-level bureaucrats. From 1955 to 1975 government employment more than doubled, largely because the baby boom of the postwar years and the growing number of elderly, dependent citizens increased state and local activity in education, health, and public welfare.[7]

Street-level bureaucracies are labor-intensive in the extreme. Their business is providing service through people, and the operating costs of such agencies reflect their dependence upon salaried workers. Thus most of whatever is spent by government on education, police, or other social services (aside, of course, from income maintenance, or in the case of jails and prisons, inmate upkeep) goes directly to pay street-level bureaucrats. For example, in large cities over 90 percent of police expenditures is used to pay for salaries.[8]

Not only do the salaries of street-level bureaucrats constitute a major portion of the cost of public services, but also the scope of public services employing street-level bureaucrats has increased over time. Charity was once the responsibility of private agencies. The federal government now provides for the income needs of the poor. The public sector has absorbed responsibilities previously discharged by private organizations in such diverse and critical areas as policing, education, and health. Moreover, in all these fields government not only has supplanted private organizations but also has expanded the scope of responsibility of public ones. This is evident in increased public expectations for security and public safety, the extension of responsibilities in the schools to concerns with infant as well as postadolescent development, and public demands for affordable health care services.[9]

Public safety, public health, and public education *may* still be elusive social objectives, but in the past century they have been transformed into areas for which there is active governmental responsibility. The transformation of public responsibility in the area of social welfare has led some to recognize that what people "have" in modern American society often may consist primarily of their claims on government "largesse," and that claims to this "new property" should be protected as a right of citizens.[10] Street-level bureaucrats play a critical role in these citizen entitlements. Either they directly provide public benefits through services, or they mediate between citizens and their new but by no means secure estates.

The poorer people are, the greater the influence street-level bureaucrats tend to have over them. Indeed, these public workers are so situated that they may well be taken to be part of the problem of being poor. Consider the welfare recipient who lives in public housing and seeks the assistance of a legal services lawyer in order to reinstate her son in school. He has been suspended because of frequent encounters with the police. She is caught in a net of street-level bureaucrats with conflicting orientations toward her, all acting in what they call her "interest" and "the public interest."[11]

People who are not able to purchase services in the private sector must seek them from government if they are to receive them at all. Indeed, it is taken as a sign of social progress that poor people are granted access to services if they are too poor to pay for them.

Thus, when social reformers seek to ameliorate the problems of the poor, they often end up discussing the status of street-level bureaucrats. Welfare reformers move to separate service provision from decisions about support payments, or they design a negative income tax system that would eliminate social workers in allocating welfare. Problems of backlog in the courts are met with proposals to increase the number of judges. Recognition that early-childhood development largely established the potential for later achievement results in the development of new programs (such as Head Start) in and out of established institutions, to provide enriched early-childhood experiences.

In the 1960s and early 1970s the model governmental response to social problems was to commission a corps of street-level bureaucrats to attend to them. Are poor people deprived of equal access to the courts? Provide them with lawyers. Equal access to health care? Establish neighborhood clinics. Educational opportunity? Develop preschool enrichment programs. It is far easier and less disruptive to develop employment for street-level bureaucrats than to reduce income inequalities.

In recent years public employees have benefited considerably from the growth of public spending on street-level bureaucracies.[12] Salaries have increased from inadequate to respectable and even desirable. Meanwhile, public employees, with street-level bureaucrats in the lead, have secured unprecedented control over their work environments through the development of unions and union-like associations.[13] For example, teachers and other instructional personnel have often been able to maintain their positions and even increase in number, although schools are more frequently under attack for their cost to taxpayers. The ratio of instructional personnel in schools has continued to rise despite the decline in the number of school-age children.[14] This development supplements general public support for the view that some street-level bureaucrats, such as teachers and police officers, are necessary for a healthy society.[15]

The fiscal crisis that has affected many cities, notably New York and more recently Cleveland and Newark, has provided an opportunity to assess the capacity of public service workers to hold onto their jobs in the face of enormous pressures. Since so much of municipal budgets consists of inflexible, mandated costs—for debt service, pension plans and other personnel benefits, contractually obligated salary increases, capital expenditure commitments, energy purchases, and so on—the place to find "fat" to eliminate from municipal budgets is in the service sector, where most expenditures tend to be for salaries. While many public employees have been fired during this crisis period, it is significant that public service workers often have been able to lobby, bargain, and cajole to minimize this attrition.[16] They are supported in their claims by a public fearful of a reduced police force on the street and resentful of dirtier streets resulting from fewer garbage pickups. They are supported by families whose children will receive less instruction from fewer specialists than in the past if teachers are fired. And it does not hurt their arguments that many public employees and their relatives vote in the city considering force reductions.[17]

The growth of the service sector represents the furthest reaches of the welfare state. The service sector penetrates every area of human needs as they are recognized and defined, and it grows within each recognized area. This is not to say that the need is met, but only that the service state breaches the barriers between public responsibility and private affairs.

The fiscal crisis of the cities focuses on the service sector, fundamentally challenging the priorities of the service state under current perceptions of scarcity. Liberals have now joined fiscal conservatives in challenging service provision. They do not do so directly, by questioning whether public services and responsibilities developed in this century are appropriate. Instead, they do it backhandedly, arguing that the accretion of public employees and their apparently irreversible demands upon revenues threaten the autonomy, flexibility, and prosperity of the political order. Debates over the proper scope of services face the threat of being overwhelmed by challenges to the entire social service structure as seen from the perspective of unbalanced public budgets.

Conflict over Interactions with Citizens

I have argued that street-level bureaucrats engender controversy because they must be dealt with if policy is to change. A second reason street-level bureaucrats tend to be the focus of public controversy is the immediacy of their interactions with citizens and their impact on people's lives. The policy delivered by street-level bureaucrats is most often immediate and personal. They usually make decisions on the spot (although sometimes they try not to) and their determinations are focused entirely on the individual. In contrast, an urban renewal program might destroy a neighborhood and replace and substitute new housing and different people, but the policy was prolonged, had many different stages, and was usually played out in arenas far removed from the daily life of neighborhood residents.

The decisions of street-level bureaucrats tend to be redistributive as well as allocative. By determining eligibility for benefits they enhance the claims of some citizens to governmental goods and services at the expense of general taxpayers and those whose claims are denied. By increasing or decreasing benefits availability to low-income recipient populations they implicitly regulate the degree of redistribution that will be paid for by more affluent sectors.

In another sense, in delivering policy street-level bureaucrats make decisions about people that affect their life chances. To designate or treat someone as a welfare recipient, a juvenile delinquent, or a high achiever affects the relationships of others to that person and also affects the person's self-evaluation. Thus begins (or continues) the social process that we infer accounts for so many self-fulfilling prophecies. The child judged to be a juvenile delinquent develops such a self-image and is grouped with other "delinquents," increasing the chances that he or she will adopt the behavior thought to have been incipient in the first place. Children thought by their teacher to be richly endowed in learning ability learn more than peers of equal intelligence who were not thought to be superior.[18] Welfare recipients find or accept housing inferior to those with equal disposable incomes who are not recipients.[19]

A defining facet of the working environment of street-level bureaucrats is that they must deal with clients' personal reactions to their decisions, however they cope with their implications. To say that people's self-evaluation is affected by the actions of street-level bureaucrats is to say that people are reactive to the policy. This is not exclusively confined to subconscious processes. Clients of street-level bureaucracies respond angrily to real or perceived injustices, develop strategies to ingratiate themselves with workers, act grateful and elated or sullen and passive in reaction to street-level bureaucrats' decisions. It is one thing to be treated neglectfully and routinely by the telephone company, the motor vehicle bureau, or other government agencies whose agents know nothing of the personal circumstances surrounding a claim or request. It is quite another thing to be shuffled, categorized, and treated "bureaucratically" (in the pejorative sense), by someone to whom one is directly talking and from whom one expects at least an open and sympathetic hearing. In short, the reality of the work of street-level bureaucrats could hardly be farther from the bureaucratic ideal of impersonal detachment in decision making.[20] On the contrary, in street-level bureaucracies the objects of critical decisions—*people*—actually change as a result of the decisions.

Street-level bureaucrats are also the focus of citizen reactions because their discretion opens up the possibility that they will respond favorably on behalf of people. Their general and diffuse obligation to the "public interest" permits hope to flourish that the individual worker will adopt a benign or favorable orientation toward the client. Thus, in a world of large and impersonal agencies that apparently hold the keys to important benefits, sanctions, and opportunities, the ambiguity of work definitions sustains hope for a friend in court.

This discussion helps explain continued controversy over street-level bureaucracies at the level of individual service provision. At the same time, the peculiar nature of government service delivery through street-level bureaucrats helps explain why street-level bureaucracies are apparently the primary focus of community conflict in the current period, and why they are likely to remain the focus of such conflict in the foreseeable future. It is no accident that the most heated community conflicts since 1964 have focused on schools and police departments, and on the responsiveness of health and welfare agencies and institutions.[21] These are the sites of the provision of public benefits and sanctions. They are the locus of individual decisions about and treatment of citizens, and thus are primary targets of protest. As Frances Fox Piven and Richard Cloward explain:

> . . . people experience deprivation and oppression within a concrete setting, not as the end product of large and abstract processes, and it is the concrete experience that molds their discontent into specific grievances against specific targets. . . . People on relief [for example] experience the shabby waiting rooms, the overseer or caseworker, and the dole. They do not experience American social welfare policy. . . . In other words, it is the daily experience of people that shapes their grievances, establishes the measure of their demands, and points out the targets of their anger.[22]

While people may experience these bureaucracies as individuals, schools, precinct houses, or neighborhood clinics are places where policy about individuals is organized collectively. These administrative arrangements suggest to citizens the possibility that controlling, or at least affecting, their structures will influence the quality of individual treatment. Thus we have two preconditions for successful community organization efforts: the hope and plausibility that individual benefits may accrue to those taking part in group action and a visible, accessible, and blamable collective target.[23]

Community action focused on street-level bureaucracies is also apparently motivated by concerns for community character. The dominant institutions in communities help shape community identity. They may be responsive to the dominant community group (this has been the traditional role of high schools in Boston) or they may be unresponsive and opposed to conceptions of community and identity favored by residents, as in the case of schools that neglect the Spanish heritage of a significant minority. Whether people are motivated by specific grievances or more diffuse concerns that become directed at community institutions, their focus in protesting the actions of street-level bureaucracies may be attributed to the familiarity of the agency, its critical role in community welfare, and a perception at some level that these institutions are not sufficiently accountable to the people they serve.

Finally, street-level bureaucrats play a critical role in regulating the degree of contemporary conflict by virtue of their role as agents of social control. Citizens who receive public benefits interact with public agents who require certain behaviors of them. They must anticipate the requirements of these public agents and claimants must tailor their actions and develop "suitable" attitudes both toward the services they receive and toward the street-level bureaucrats themselves. Teachers convey and enforce expectations of proper attitudes toward schooling, self, and efficacy in other interactions. Policemen convey expectations about public behavior and authority. Social workers convey expectations about public benefits and the status of recipients.

The social control function of street-level bureaucrats requires comment in a discussion of the place of public service workers in the larger society. The public service sector plays a critical part in softening the impact of the economic system on those who are not its primary beneficiaries and inducing people to accept the neglect or inadequacy of primary economic and social institutions. Police, courts, and prisons obviously play such a role in processing the junkies, petty thieves, muggers, and others whose behavior toward society is associated with their economic position. It is a role equally played by schools in socializing the population to the economic order and the likely opportunities for different strata of the population. Public support and employment programs expand to ameliorate the impact of unemployment or reduce the incidence of discontent; they contract when employment opportunities improve. Moreover, they are designed and implemented to convey the message that welfare status is to be avoided and that work, however poorly rewarded, is preferable to public assistance. One can also see the two edges of public policy in the "war on poverty" where the public benefits of social service and community action invested neighborhood institutions with benefits for which potential dissidents could compete and ordinary citizens could develop dependency.[24]

What to some are the highest reaches of the welfare state are to others the furthest extension of social control. Street-level bureaucrats are partly the focus of controversy because they play this dual role. Welfare reform founders on disagreements over whether to eliminate close scrutiny of welfare applications in order to reduce administrative costs and harassment of recipients, or to increase the scrutiny in the name of controlling abuses and preventing welfare recipients from taking advantage. Juvenile corrections and mental health policy founder on disputes over the desirability of dismantling large institutions in the name of cost effectiveness and rehabilitation, or retaining close supervision in an effort to avoid the costs of letting unreconstructed "deviants" loose. In short, street-level bureaucrats are also at the center of controversy because a divided public perceives that social control in the name of public order and acceptance of the status quo are social objectives with which proposals to reduce the role of street-level bureaucrats (eliminating welfare checkups, reducing parole personnel, decriminalizing marijuana) would interfere.

Public controversy also focuses on the proper kind of social control. Current debates in corrections policy, concerning automatic sentencing and a "hard-nosed" view of punishment or more rehabilitative orientations, reflect conflict over the degree of harshness in managing prison populations. In educational practice the public is also divided as to the advisability of liberal disciplinary policies and more flexible instruction or punitive discipline and more rigid, traditional approaches. The "medicalization" of deviance, in which disruptive behavior is presumed cause for intervention by a doctor rather than a disciplinarian, is another area in which there is controversy over the appropriate kind of social control.

From the citizen's viewpoint, the roles of street-level bureaucrats are as extensive as the functions of government and intensively experienced as daily routines require them to interact with the street ministers of education, dispute settlement, and health services. Collectively, street-level bureaucrats absorb a high share of public resources and become the focus of society's hopes for a healthy balance between provision of public services and a reasonable burden of public expenditures. As individuals, street-level bureaucrats represent the hopes of citizens for fair and effective treatment by government even as they are positioned to see clearly the limitations on effective intervention and the constraints on responsiveness engendered by mass processing.

NOTES

1. These definitions are analytical. They focus not on nominal occupational roles but on the characteristics of the particular work situations. Thus not every street-level bureaucrat works for a street-level bureaucracy [for example, a relocation specialist (a type of street-level bureaucrat) may work for an urban renewal agency whose employees are mostly planners, builders, and other technicians]. Conversely, not all employees of street-level bureaucracies are street-level bureaucrats (for example, file clerks in a welfare department or police officers on routine clerical assignments).

The conception of street-level bureaucracy was originally proposed in a paper prepared for the Annual Meeting of the American Political Science Association in 1969. "Toward a Theory of Street-Level Bureaucracy." It was later revised and published in Willis Hawley and Michael Lipsky, eds., *Theoretical Perspectives on Urban Politics* (Englewood Cliffs, N.J.: Prentice-Hall, 1977), pp. 196–213.

2. U.S. Bureau of the Census, Public Employment in 1973, Series GE 73 No. 1 (Washington, D.C.: Government Printing Office, 1974), p. 9. Presented in Alan Baker

and Barbara Grouby, "Employment and Payrolls of State and Local Governments, by Function: October 1973," *Municipal Year Book, 1975* (Washington, D.C.: International City Managers Association, 1975), pp. 109–112, table 4/3. Also, Marianne Stein Kah, "City Employment and Payrolls: 1975," *Municipal Year Book, 1977* (Washington, D.C.: International City Managers Association, 1977), pp. 173–179. These figures have been adjusted to represent full-time equivalents. For purposes of assessing public commitments to providing services, full-time equivalents are more appropriate statistics than total employment figures, which count many part-time employees.

3. Jeffry H. Galper, *The Politics of Social Services* (Englewood Cliffs, N.J.: Prentice-Hall, 1975), p. 56.

4. Lois Forer, *Death of the Law* (New York: McKay, 1975), p. 191.

5. *New York Times*, April 4, 1976, p. 22.

6. Baker and Grouby, "Employment and Payrolls of State and Local Governments."

7. *New York Times*, July 10, 1977, p. F13.

8. Of four cities with populations over one million responding to a *Municipal Year Book* survey, the proportion of personnel expenditures to total expenditures in police departments averaged 94 percent and did not go beyond 86 percent. Cities with smaller populations showed similar tendencies. These observations are derived from David Lewin, "Expenditure, Compensation, and Employment Data in Police, Fire and Refuse Collection and Disposal Departments," *Municipal Year Book, 1975*, pp. 39–98, table 1/21. However, the variation was much greater in the less populous cities because of smaller base figures and the fact that when cities with smaller bases make capital investments, the ratio of personnel to total expenditures changes more precipitously.

That public expenditures for street-level bureaucracies go to individuals primarily as salaries may also be demonstrated in the case of education. For example, more than 73 percent of all noncapital education expenditures inside Standard Metropolitan Statistical Areas goes toward personal services (i.e., salaries). See Government Finances, Number 1, Finances of School Districts, 1972 U.S. Census of Government (Bureau of the Census, Social and Economic Statistics Administration, U.S. Department of Commerce), table 4.

9. Many analysts have discussed the increasing role of services in the economy. See Daniel Bell, *The Coming of the Post-Industrial Society: A Venture in Social Forecasting* (New York: Basic Books, 1973); Alan Gartner and Frank Reissman, *The Service Society and the Consumer Vanguard* (New York: Harper & Row, 1974); Victor Fuchs, *The Service Economy* (New York: Columbia University Press, 1968). On transformations in public welfare, see Gilbert Steiner, *Social Insecurity* (Chicago: Rand McNally, 1966), chap. 1; on public safety, see Allan Silver, "The Demand for Order in Civil Society," in David Bordua, ed., *The Police: Six Sociological Essays* (New York: John Wiley, 1967), pp. 1–24.

10. Charles Reich, "The New Property," *Yale Law Journal*, vol. 72 (April, 1964): pp. 733–787.

11. Carl Hosticka, "Legal Services Lawyers Encounter Clients: A Study in Street-Level Bureaucracy" (Ph.D. diss., Massachusetts Institute of Technology, 1976), pp. 11–13.

12. See Frances Piven's convincing essay in which she argues that social service workers were the major beneficiaries of federal programs concerned with cities and poor people in the 1960s. Piven, "The Urban Crisis: Who Got What and Why," in

Richard Cloward and Frances Piven, *The Politics of Turmoil* (New York: Vintage Books, 1972), pp. 314–351.

13. J. Joseph Loewenberg and Michael H. Moskow, eds., *Collective Bargaining in Government* (Englewood Cliffs, N.J.: Prentice-Hall, 1972). A. Laurence Chickering, ed., *Public Employee Unions* (Lexington, Mass.: Lexington Books, 1976); and Margaret Levi, *Bureaucratic Insurgency* (Lexington, Mass.: Lexington Books, 1977).

14. The decline is a function of the lower birthrate and periodicity in the size of the school-age population originally resulting from the birth explosion following World War II. See Baker and Grouby, *Municipal Year Book, 1975*, pp. 109ff., on serviceability ratios.

15. This perspective remains applicable in the current period. However, in reaction to this tendency, programs that would eliminate service mediators and service providers, such as negative income taxation and housing allowances, have gained support. Fiscal scarcity has brought to public attention questions concerning the marginal utility of some of these service areas.

16. Consider the New York City policemen who, in October 1976, agreed to work overtime without pay so that a crop of rookie patrolmen would not be eliminated. *New York Times*, October 24, 1976, p. 24.

17. There can be no better illustration of the strength of the organized service workers and their support by relevant interests than the New York State Assembly's overriding of Gov. Hugh Carey's veto of the so-called Stavisky bill. This legislation, written in a period of massive concern for cutting the New York City budget, required the city to spend no less on education in the three years following the fiscal collapse than in the three years before the crisis, thus tying the hands of the city's financial managers even more. *New York Times*, April 4, 1976, p. E6; April 18, 1976, p. E6.

18. The seminal work here is Robert Rosenthal and Lenore Jacobson, *Pygmalion in the Classroom* (New York: Holt, Rinehart and Winston, 1968).

19. Martin Rein, "Welfare and Housing," Joint Center Working Paper Series, no. 4 (Cambridge, Mass.: Joint Center for Urban Studies, Spring, 1971, rev. Feb. 1972).

20. On the alleged importance of bureaucratic detachment in processing clients see Peter Blau, *Exchange and Power in Social Life* (New York: John Wiley, 1964), p. 66.

21. See National Advisory Commission on Civil Disorders, *Report* (New York: Bantam, 1968); Peter Rossi et al., *Roots of Urban Discontent* (New York: John Wiley, 1974).

22. Frances Fox Piven and Richard Cloward, *Poor People's Movements* (New York: Pantheon, 1977), pp. 20–21.

23. Michael Lipsky and Margaret Levi, "Community Organization as a Political Resource," in Harlan Hahn, ed., *People and Places in Urban Society* (Urban Affairs Annual Review, vol. 6) (Newbury Park, Calif.: Sage Publications, 1972), pp. 175–199.

24. See James O'Connor's discussion of "legitimation" and his general thesis concerning the role of the state service sector, in O'Connor, *The Fiscal Crisis of the State* (New York: St. Martin's, 1973). On social control functions in particular policy sectors see Samuel Bowles and Herbert Gintis, *Schooling in Capitalist America* (New York: Basic Books, 1976); Frances Fox Piven and Richard Cloward, *Regulating the Poor* (New York: Pantheon, 1971); Galper, *The Politics of Social Services*; Richard Quinney, *Criminology* (Boston: Little, Brown, 1975); Ira Katznelson, "Urban Counterrevolution," in Robert P. Wolff, ed., *1984 Revisited* (New York: Alfred Knopf, 1973), pp. 139–164.

7

Policy Paradox: The Art of Political Decision Making (1997)

Deborah Stone

Paradoxes are nothing but trouble. They violate the most elementary principle of logic: Something cannot be two different things at once. Two contradictory interpretations cannot both be true. A paradox is just such an impossible situation, and political life is full of them. Consider some examples.

Losing Is Winning

When the Republicans gained control of the House of Representatives after the 1994 midterm elections, passing a balanced-budget amendment to the U.S. Constitution was tops on their legislative agenda. Republicans had long criticized Democrats for profligate government spending and high deficits. Getting a constitutional amendment to require a balanced budget would be a powerful legal weapon they could use to cut government programs drastically. Early in 1995, it looked like both houses of Congress would pass the budget amendment easily. As time got closer to a Senate vote in March, however, the Republicans didn't seem to have the 67 votes necessary to pass a constitutional amendment. Senator Bob Dole, the Republican majority leader, kept postponing the vote, hoping to pick up more support, but eventually he brought the bill to a vote without having 67 votes lined up. Why would he bring the matter to a vote, knowing that the Republicans would fail to pass it? On the eve of the vote, he explained: "We really win if we win, but we may also win if we lose."[1]

    After the vote, the headlines were unanimous: "Senate Rejects Amendment on Balancing the Budget; Close Vote Is Blow to GOP," went the *New York Times'* verdict. "GOP is Loser on Budget Amendment," echoed the *Boston Globe.*[2] What did Dole mean by claiming that a loss could be a victory?

Source: Deborah Stone, *Policy Paradox: The Art of Political Decision Making,* 1997. Copyright © 1998, by Deborah Stone. Used by permission of W. W. Norton & Company, Inc.

Politicians always have at least two goals. First is a policy goal—whatever program or proposal they would like to see accomplished or defeated, whatever problem they would like to see solved. Perhaps even more important, though, is a political goal. Politicians always want to preserve their power, or gain enough power, to be able to accomplish their policy goals. Even though a defeat of the balanced-budget amendment was a loss for Republicans' policy goal, Dole thought it might be a gain for Republicans' political strength. (So, apparently, did the New York Times, whose sub-headline read "Risk to Democrats.") Republican leaders acknowledged that they had lost a constitutional device that would have helped them immensely in redeeming their campaign pledge to enact the "Contract with America." But they also saw some important political gains. Senator Orrin Hatch, the chief sponsor of the amendment, called the vote "a clear delineation between the parties." A Republican pollster explained how the vote might help Republican candidates in the next Congressional election: "It lays out the differences as sharply as we could want them: We want to cut spending, and they don't."[3] Dole, already campaigning for the presidency, used the occasion to lambaste President Clinton for "abdicating his responsibility" to control federal deficits, while Republicans in both houses talked about making Democrats pay at the polls in the next election. "As far as I'm concerned," Newt Gingrich crowed, "it's like a fork in chess. They can give us a victory today; they can give us a victory in November '96."[4]

Parades: Recreation or Speech?

An Irish gay and lesbian group wanted to march in Boston's annual Saint Patrick's day parade. The organizers of the parade wanted to stop them. The gay and lesbian group said a parade is a public recreational event, and therefore, civil rights law protected them against discrimination in public accommodations. The parade organizers claimed a parade is an expression of beliefs, really an act of speech. Their right to say what they wanted—by excluding from the parade those with a different message—should be protected by the First Amendment. Is a parade a public recreational event or an act of self-expression? Might it be both? What would you do if you were a justice on the Supreme Court and had to decide one way or the other?[5]

For or Against Welfare?

When asked about public spending on welfare, 48 percent of Americans say it should be cut. But when asked about spending on programs for poor children, 47 percent say it should be increased, and only 9 percent want cuts.[6]

Do Americans want to enlarge or curtail welfare spending? It all depends on how the question is framed. . . .

Which Came First—The Problem or the Solution?

In the 1950s, a federal program for mass transit was proposed as a solution to urban congestion. Subways and buses were presented as a more efficient means of transportation than private cars. In the late 1960s, environmental protection was the word of the day, and mass transit advocates peddled subways and buses as a way to reduce automobile pollution. Then with the OPEC oil embargo of 1972, Washington's attention was riveted by the energy crisis, and mass transit was sold as an energy-saving alternative to private automobiles. Was this a case of three problems for which mass transit just happened to be a solution, or a constant solution adapting to a changing problem?[7]

Babies: Product or Service?

New reproductive technologies have fundamentally changed the way people can have babies and create families. "Baby M" was born in 1986 as the result of a contract between William Stern and Marybeth Whitehead, both married, though not to each other. The contract provided for Mrs. Whitehead to be artificially inseminated with Mr. Stern's sperm, to bring the baby to term in her womb, and then to give the baby to Mr. and Mrs. Stern to raise as their child. In return, Mr. Stern would pay Mrs. Whitehead $10,000, plus expenses.

After the birth, Mrs. Whitehead decided she wanted to keep the baby, who was, after all, her biological daughter. The case went to court. Although the immediate issue was who would win the right to raise "Baby M," the policy question on everybody's mind was whether the courts should recognize and enforce surrogate motherhood contracts. Most states prohibit the sale of babies in their adoption laws. So the question of paramount importance was whether a surrogate motherhood contract is a contract for the sale of a baby or for a socially useful service.

On the one hand, Mrs. Whitehead could be seen as renting her womb. Like any professional service provider, she agreed to observe high standards of practice—in this case, prenatal care. According to the contract, she would not drink, smoke, or take drugs, and she would follow medical advice. Like any physical laborer, she was selling the use of her body for a productive purpose. By her own and the Sterns' account, she was altruistically helping to create a child for a couple who could not have their own.

On the other hand, Mrs. Whitehead could be seen as producing and selling a baby. She underwent artificial insemination in anticipation of a fee—no fee, no baby. She agreed to have amniocentesis and to have an abortion if the test showed any defects not acceptable to Mr. Stern. She agreed to accept a lower fee if the baby were born with any mental or physical handicaps—low-value baby, low price.

Is a surrogate motherhood contract for a service or for a baby?

How can we make sense of a world where such paradoxes occur? In an age of science, of human mastery over the innermost and outermost realms, how are we to deal with situations that will not observe the elementary rules of scientific decorum? Can we make public policy behave?

The fields of political science, public administration, law, and policy analysis have shared a common mission of rescuing public policy from the irrationalities and indignities of politics, hoping to make policy instead with rational, analytical, and scientific methods. This endeavor is what I call "the rationality project," and it has been a core part of American political culture almost since the beginning. The project began with James Madison's effort to "cure the mischiefs of faction" with proper constitutional design, thereby assuring that government policy would be protected from the self-interested motives of tyrannous majorities.[8] In the 1870s, Christopher Columbus Langdell, dean of the Harvard Law School, undertook to take the politics out of law by reforming legal training. Law was a science, he proclaimed, to be studied by examining appellate court decisions as specimens and distilling their common essence into a system of principles. There was no need for either students or professors to gain practical experience.

At the turn of the twentieth century, the rationality project was taken up in spades by the Progressive reformers, who removed policy-making authority from elected bodies and gave it to expert regulatory commissions and professional city managers, in an effort to render policy making more scientific and less political. The quest for an apolitical science of government continues in the twentieth century with Herbert Simon's search for a "science of administration," Harold Lasswell's dream of a "science of policy forming and execution," and the current effort of universities, foundations, and government to foster a profession of policy scientists.

This book has two aims. First, I argue that the rationality project misses the point of politics. Moreover, it is an impossible dream. From inside the rationality project, politics looks messy, foolish, erratic, and inexplicable. Events, actions, and ideas in the political world seem to leap outside the categories that logic and rationality offer. In the rationality project, the categories of analysis are somehow above politics or outside it. Rationality purports to offer a correct vantage point, from which we can judge the goodness of the real world.

I argue, instead, that the very categories of thought underlying rational analysis are themselves a kind of paradox, defined in political struggle. They do not exist before or without politics, and because they are necessarily abstract (they are categories of *thought*, after all), they can have multiple meanings. Thus, analysis is itself a creature of politics; it is strategically crafted argument, designed to create ambiguities and paradoxes and to resolve them in a particular direction. (This much is certainly awfully abstract for now, but each of the subsequent chapters is designed to show very concretely how one analytic category of politics and policy is a constantly evolving political creation.)

Beyond demonstrating this central misconception of the rationality project, my second aim is to derive a kind of political analysis that makes sense of policy paradoxes such as the ones depicted above. I seek to create a framework in which such phenomena, the ordinary situations of politics, do not have to be explained away as extraordinary, written off as irrational, dismissed as folly, or disparaged as "pure politics." Unfortunately, much of the literature about public policy proceeds from the idea that policy making in practice deviates from some hypothetical standards of good policy making, and that there is thus something fundamentally wrong with politics. In creating an alternative mode of political analysis, I start from the belief that politics is a creative and valuable feature of social existence.

The project of making public policy rational rests on three pillars: a model of reasoning, a model of society, and a model of policy making. The *model of reasoning* is rational decision making. In this model, decisions are or should be made in a series of well-defined steps:

1. Identify objectives.
2. Identify alternative courses of action for achieving objectives.
3. Predict the possible consequences of each alternative.
4. Evaluate the possible consequences of each alternative.
5. Select the alternative that maximizes the attainment of objectives.

This model of rational behavior is so pervasive it is a staple of check-out-counter magazines and self-help books. For all of its intuitive appeal, however, the rational decision-making model utterly fails to explain Bob Dole's thinking or behavior at the time of the balanced-budget amendment vote. Did he attain his objective or didn't he? Did he win or lose? Worse, the model could not help formulate political advice for Dole beforehand, for if we accept his reasoning that he wins either way, then it doesn't matter which way the vote goes and he should just sit back and enjoy the play. Of course, Dole was not only reasoning when he claimed that losing was winning. He was also trying to manipulate how the outcome of the vote would be perceived and how it would influence future political contests between the Republicans and the Democrats. In fact, all the Republican credit-claiming and victory speeches upon losing the vote suggest that politicians have a great deal of control over interpretations of events, and that the political analyst who wants to choose a wise course of action should focus less on assessing the objective consequences of actions and more on how the interpretations will go. If politicians can attain their objectives by portraying themselves as having attained them, then they should be studying portraiture, not cost-benefit analysis.

A model of political reason ought to account for the possibilities of changing one's objectives, of pursuing contradictory objectives simultaneously, of winning by appearing to lose and turning loss into an appearance of victory, and most unusual, of attaining objectives by portraying oneself as having attained them. Throughout this book, I develop a model of political reasoning quite different from the model of rational decision making. Political reasoning is reasoning by metaphor and analogy. It is trying to get others to see a situation as one thing rather than another. For example, parades can be seen as public recreational events, or as collective marches to express an idea. Each vision constructs a different political contest, and invokes a different set of rules for resolving the conflict. Babies created under surrogate motherhood contracts are a phenomenon quite unlike anything we already know. The situation is not exactly like professional service, not exactly like wage labor, not exactly like a contract for pork bellies, not exactly like a custody dispute between divorced parents, and not exactly like an adoption contract. Legislatures and courts deal with the issue by asking, "Of the things that surrogate motherhood isn't, which is it most like?"

Political reasoning is metaphor-making and category-making, but not just for beauty's sake or for insight's sake. It is strategic portrayal for persuasion's sake, and ultimately for policy's sake. This concept of political reason is developed and illustrated throughout the book, and I take up the idea directly again in the last chapter.

The *model of society* underlying the contemporary rationality project is the market. Society is viewed as a collection of autonomous, rational decision makers who have no community life. Their interactions consist entirely of trading with one another to maximize their individual well-being. They each have objectives or preferences, they each compare alternative ways of attaining their objectives, and they each choose the way that yields the most satisfaction. They maximize their self-interest through rational calculation. The market model and the rational decision-making model are thus very closely related.

The market model is not restricted to things we usually consider markets, that is, to systems where goods and services are bought and sold. Electoral voting, the behavior of legislators, political leadership, the size of the welfare rolls, and even marriage have all been explained in terms of the maximization of self-interest through rational calculation. The market model posits that individuals have relatively fixed, independent preferences for goods, services, and policies. In real societies, where people are psychologically and materially dependent, where they are connected through emotional bonds, traditions, and social groups, their preferences are based on loyalties and comparisons of images. How people define their preferences depends to a large extent on how choices are presented to them and by whom. They want greater welfare spending when it is called helping poor children, but not when it is called welfare. Sometimes, as in the case of "Baby M," they are not quite sure what they are buying and selling, or whether they have engaged in a sale at all.

In place of the model of society as a market, I construct a model of society as a political community. . . . [I set] forth the fundamental elements of human behavior and social life that I take to be axiomatic, and [contrast] them with the axioms of the market model. I start with a model of political community, or "polis," because I began my own intellectual odyssey in this territory with a simple reflection: Both policy and thinking about policy are produced in political communities.

The observation may be trite, but it has radical consequences for a field of inquiry that has been dominated by a conception of society as a market. To take just one example, the market model of society envisions societal welfare as the aggregate of individuals' situations. All behavior is explained as people striving to maximize their own self-interest. The market model therefore gives us no way to talk about how people fight over visions of the public interest or the nature of the community—the truly significant political questions underlying policy choices.

The *model of policy making* in the rationality project is a production model, where policy is created in a fairly orderly sequence of stages, almost as if on an assembly line. Many political scientists, in fact, speak of "assembling the elements" of policy. An issue is "placed on the agenda," and a problem gets defined. It moves through the legislative and executive branches of government, where alternative solutions are proposed, analyzed, legitimized, selected, and refined. A solution is implemented by the executive agencies and constantly challenged and revised by interested actors, perhaps using the judicial branch. And finally, if the policy-making process is managerially sophisticated, it provides a means of evaluating and revising implemented solutions.

So conceived, the policy-making process parallels the cognitive steps of the rational model of decision making. Government becomes a rational decision maker writ large—albeit not a very proficient one. Much of the political science literature in this genre is devoted to understanding where and how good policy gets derailed in the process of production. This model of policy making as rational problem solving cannot explain why sometimes policy solutions go looking for problems. It cannot tell us why solutions . . . turn into problems. It only tells us things are working "backward" or poorly.

The production model fails to capture what I see as the essence of policy making in political communities: the struggle over ideas. Ideas are a medium of exchange and a mode of influence even more powerful than money and votes and guns. Shared meanings motivate people to action and meld individual striving into collective action. Ideas are at the center of all political conflict. Policy making, in turn, is a constant struggle over the criteria for classification, the boundaries of categories, and the definition of ideals that guide the way people behave.

. . . Each idea is an argument, or more accurately, a collection of arguments in favor of different ways of seeing the world. Every chapter is devoted to showing how there are multiple understandings of what appears to be a single concept, how these understandings are created, and how they are manipulated as part of political strategy. Revealing the hidden arguments embedded in each concept illuminates, and may help resolve, the surface conflicts. . . .

As I demonstrate throughout the book, the political careers of most policy issues are not nearly so simple as this three-part formula would suggest. For example, people do not always perceive a goal first and then look for disparities between the goal and the status quo. Often, they see a problem first, which triggers a search for solutions and statement of goals. Or, they see a solution first, then formulate a problem that requires their solution (and their services). Nevertheless, I use this framework because it expresses a logic of problem solving that is widespread in the policy analysis literature and because it parallels the models of rational decision making and the policy-making process.

[I then present a discussion] about goals—not the specific goals of particular policy issues, such as expanding health insurance coverage or lowering health care costs, but the enduring values of community life that give rise to controversy over particular policies: equity, efficiency, security, and liberty. These values are "motherhood issues": everyone is for them when they are stated abstractly, but the fight begins as soon as we ask what people mean by them. These values not only express goals, but also serve as the standards we use to evaluate existing situations and policy proposals.

One tenet of the rationality project is that there are objective and neutral standards of evaluation that can be applied to politics, but that come from a vantage point outside politics, untainted by the interests of political players. . . . Behind every policy issue lurks a contest over conflicting, though equally plausible, conceptions of the same abstract goal or value. The abstractions are aspirations for a community, into which people read contradictory interpretations. It may not be possible to get everyone to agree on the same interpretation, but the first task of the political analyst is to reveal and clarify the underlying value disputes so that people can see where they differ and move toward some reconciliation.

There might well have been other ideas in the section on goals. Justice, privacy, social obligation, and democracy come to mind. Equity, efficiency, security, and liberty begged more insistently for political analysis only because, sadly, they are invoked more often as criteria in policy analysis. Once having read this book, the reader will have no trouble seeing some of the paradoxes in other criteria.

. . . There are many modes of defining problems in policy discourse, and each mode is like a language within which people offer and defend conflicting interpretations. "Symbols" and "Numbers" are about verbal and numerical languages, respectively, and both examine devices of symbolic representation within those languages. We also define problems in terms of what causes them ("Causes"), who is lined up on each side ("Interests"), or what kind of choice they pose ("Decisions"). Here, too, I might have chosen other categories; for example, one could examine problem formulation according to different disciplines, such as economics, law, political science, or ethics. I did not choose that framework because it would only perpetuate the somewhat artificial divisions of academia, and the categories I did choose seem to me a better representation of modes of discourse in political life.

. . . [I] start from the assumption that all policies involve deliberate attempts to change people's behavior, and each chapter in this section deals with a mechanism for bringing about such change—creating incentives and penalties ("Inducements"), mandating rules ("Rules"), informing and persuading ("Facts"), stipulating rights and duties ("Rights"), and reorganizing authority ("Powers").

The common theme of this part is that policy instruments are not just tools, each with its own function and its own appropriateness for certain kinds of jobs. In the standard political science model of the policy-making process, policy solutions are decided upon and then implemented, though things usually go awry at the implementation stage. The task of the analyst is to figure out which is the right or best tool to use, and then to fix mistakes when things don't go as planned. I argue, instead, that each type of policy instrument is a kind of political arena, with its peculiar ground rules, within which political conflicts are continued. Each mode of social regulation draws lines around what people may and may not do and how they may or may not treat each other. But these boundaries are constantly contested, either because they are ambiguous and do not settle conflicts, or because they allocate benefits and burdens to the people on either side, or both. Boundaries become real and acquire their meaning in political struggles. The job of the analyst, in this view, is to understand the rules of the game well enough to know the standard moves and have a repertoire of effective countermoves.

If deep down inside, you are a rationalist, you might want to know whether the topics covered by the chapters are "exhaustive" and "mutually exclusive." They are most assuredly not. Our categories of thought and modes of argument are intertwined and not easily delineated. That is one reason, I shall argue, why we have and always will have politics. Then, too, I remind you that I am trying to demonstrate precisely that essential political concepts are paradoxes. They have contradictory meanings that by formal logic ought to be mutually exclusive but by political logic are not. I do hope, however, that my categories at least provide a useful way to divide up an intellectual territory for exploration, and at best provide a new way of seeing it.

As for whether my categories are exhaustive, I can only plead the quintessential political defense: I had to draw the line somewhere.

NOTES

1. Quoted in Jill Zuckman, "No Voting, More Anger on Budget," *Boston Globe*, March 2, 1995, p. 1.

2. Both headlines on front page. *New York Times*, March 3, 1995; *Boston Globe*, March 5, 1995.

3. Quotations in "GOP Is Loser on Budget Amendment," *Boston Globe*, March 5, 1995, p. 1.

4. Quotation from "Senate Rejects Amendment on Balanced Budget," *New York Times*, March 3, 1995. p. A1.

5. Linda Greenhouse, "High Court Lets Parade in Boston Bar Homosexuals," *New York Times*, June 20, 1995, p. A1.

6. Jason DeParle, "Despising Welfare, Pitying Its Young," *New York Times*, December 18, 1994, p. E5.

7. John Kingdon, *Agendas, Alternatives and Public Policies* (Boston: Little Brown, 1984), p. 181.

8. This was the argument of his *Federalist Paper No. 10.*

Review Questions

1. Why is incrementalism the essence of Charles Lindblom's "Science of 'Muddling Through'"? How is incrementalism used to explain the politics behind all budgetary processes in government?

2. Why is the "mixed scanning" advocated by Amitai Etzioni considered a hybrid approach to decision making? Is "mixed scanning" a useful technique when reading a newspaper?

3. How does Michael Lipsky explain how bureaucrats at the lowest levels of their organizations get to make policy? Can you give examples of your personal interactions with "street-level bureaucrats"?

4. What does "the polis" refer to in Deborah Stone's *Policy Paradox and Political Reason?* How does her "polis model" differ from other models of political decision making?

Chapter 3

Interest Groups
and Public Policy

The importance of pluralism and the significance of groups in the democratic political process has been recognized for over two thousand years. For example, Aristotle in ancient Greece noted that political associations were both significant and commonplace because of the "general advantages" that members obtained. One of the first specific references to groups in the American political process was James Madison's famous discussion of factions in *The Federalist* No. 10. The *Federalist Papers*, published in 1787–1788, are considered by many political scientists to be the most important work of political theory written in the United States—the one product of the American mind counted among the classics of political philosophy.

The papers were originally newspaper articles written by Alexander Hamilton (1755–1804), the first Secretary of the Treasury, James Madison (1751–1839), the fourth President of the United States, and John Jay (1745–1829), the first Chief Justice of the United States, to encourage the state of New York to ratify the new Constitution. The papers reflect the genius of the balance achieved in the American system between the views of Madison, an exponent of limited government, and Hamilton, an admirer of an energetic national government. It has been suggested that the papers reflected the thinking of the minority of Americans, who sought a more nationalist government than most of the postrevolutionary generation wanted. They succeeded in getting it.

In *The Federalist* No. 10, reprinted here, Madison discusses the problem of factions (political groups) and the danger they pose to a political system. Madison feared that the interests of parties and pressure groups could destabilize a government; but he believed that an overarching representative government, with a functional as well as territorial separation of powers, could prevent this. Madison's brief essay, a defense of a pluralistic society, is the best known of the *Federalist Papers*. In the federal union he advocated, Madison envisioned "a republican remedy [a large republic] for the diseases most incident to republican government." The essay is one of the first attempts by an American to explain the political nature of humankind. Madison found the causes of political differences and the creation of factions to be "sown in the nature of man." Madison would famously lament this nature in *The Federalist* No. 51:

> Ambition must be made to counteract ambition. The interest of the man must be connected with the constitutional rights of the place. It may be a reflection on human nature that such devices should be necessary to control the abuses of government. But what is government itself but the greatest of all reflections on human nature? If men were angels, no government would be necessary. If angels were to govern men, neither external nor internal controls on government would be necessary. In framing a government which is to be administered by men over men, the great difficulty lies in this: you must first enable the government to control the governed; and in the next place oblige it to control itself.

In Madison's view, the group was inherent in the nature of people, and its causes were unremovable. The only choice then was to control the effects of group pressure and power.

The Federalist No. 10 has grown to be the classic explanation of why it is not easy to achieve change in the American political system. The constitutional structure is purposely designed to protect minorities from the possible tyranny of 50 percent plus one. The essay was more or less rediscovered by historian Charles A. Beard and other political analysts early in the twentieth century, when they sought to build an historical justification for modern interest group theory.

A more elaborate discussion of group theory can be traced to John C. Calhoun's (1782–1850) treatise on governance, *A Disquisition on Government* (1853). While essentially an argument for the protection of minority interests, the treatise suggested that ideal governance must deal with all interest groups, since they represent the legitimate interests of the citizens. If all groups participated on some level of parity within the policy-making process, then all individual interests would be recognized by the policymakers.

While the work of Calhoun represents the development of early group theory, modern political science group theory has taken greater impetus from the work of Arthur F. Bentley (1870–1957). Bentley was one of the pioneering voices in the behavioral analysis of politics and the intellectual creator of modern interest group theory. In *The Process of Government* (1908), Bentley argued that political analysis has had to shift its focus from forms of government to actions of individuals in the context of groups, because groups are the critical action mechanisms that enable numbers of individuals to achieve their political, economic, and social desires. Bentley's work was effectively "lost" until it was rediscovered and publicized by David B. Truman (1913–2003).

In Truman's *The Governmental Process* (1951), portions of which are reprinted here, group interactions are viewed as the real determinant of public policy and as the proper focal point of study. Truman defines the interest group as "a shared attitude group that makes certain claims upon other groups in the society. If and when it makes its claims through or upon any of the institutions of government, it becomes a public interest group." Group pressure is assured through the establishment of lines of access and influence. Truman notes that the administrative process provides a multitude of points of access comparable to the legislature. What Truman provides for group theory is a complete description and analysis of how groups interact, function, and influence in the overall political system. Two types of groups are identified by Truman: existing groups and potential groups. The potential group is constituted by people who have common values and attitudes but do not yet see their interests being threatened. Once they do, Truman argues, they form a group to protect their interests.

The concept of potential groups keeps the bureaucratic policy-making process honest (or perhaps balanced), given the possibility that new groups might surface or some issues may influence decision making. The potential groups concept also serves as a counterargument to the claim that group theory is undemocratic. Once the concept of potential groups is married to the active role of organized groups, the claim can be made, in Truman's words, that "all interests of society by definition are taken into account in one form or another by the institutions of government."

American political processes being inherently pluralistic emphasize the role of competitive groups in society. Pluralism assumes that power will shift from group to group as elements in the mass public transfer their allegiance in response to their perceptions of their individual interests. However, according to power-elite theory, if democracy is defined as popular participation in public affairs, then pluralist theory is inadequate as an explanation of modern U.S. government. Pluralism, according to this view, offers little direct participation, since the elite structure is closed, pyramidal, consensual, and unresponsive. Society is thus divided into two classes: the few who govern and the many who are governed; that is, pluralism is covert elitism, instead of a practical solution to preserve democracy in a mass society.

Power-elite theory asserts that the United States is basically ruled by a political, military, and business elite whose decisional powers essentially preempt the democratic process. Sociologist C. Wright Mills (1916–1962) wrote in *The Power Elite* (1956) that "the leading men in each of the three domains of power—the warlords, the corporation chieftains, the political directorate—tend to come together to form the power elite of America." Most contemporary analyses of elitism in American governance have their intellectual foundations in Mills's work, even if Mills himself is not acknowledged. The first chapter of Mills's seminal book is reprinted here.

American government is composed of multiple or pluralistic elements. First, its constitutional arrangement requires a separation of powers, the allocation of powers among the three branches of government so that they are a check upon each other. This separation, in theory, makes a tyrannical concentration of power impossible but also creates oft complained about inefficiencies. Justice Louis D. Brandeis offered as part of the opinion of the U.S. Supreme Court in the 1926 case of *Myers v. United States* this justification for inefficiency: "The doctrine of the separation of powers was adopted by the Convention of 1787, not to promote efficiency but to preclude the exercise of arbitrary power. The purpose was not to avoid friction, but, by means of the inevitable friction incident to the distribution of the governmental powers among three departments, to save the people from autocracy." And there exists parallel structural arrangements at the state and local level. In *Who Governs? Democracy and Power in an American City* (1961) political scientist Robert A. Dahl (1915–) produced what has become a classic analysis of how these inefficiencies meld into today's pluralistic governance, in which (in this case) local political power was seen as dispersed only to coalesce about different issues. Dahl found that political decisions were influenced more by coalitions and group rivalries than by power elites. Reprinted here is his first chapter on "The Nature of the Problem." This has grown to be the traditional, the standard, way in which the analysis of public policymaking is undertaken at all levels of American government.

The leading critic of the interest group pluralism espoused by Dahl is Theodore J. Lowi (1931–). His book, *The End of Liberalism: Ideology, Policy, and the Crisis of Public Authority* (1969) provided a provocative critique of the modern democratic government and a condemnation of the paralyzing effects of interest group pluralism. Lowi asserted that in Dahl's pluralistic world public authority is parceled out to private interest groups, resulting in a weak, decentralized government incapable of long-range planning. These powerful interest groups operate to promote private goals; they do not compete to promote the public interest. Government then becomes not an institution capable of making hard choices among conflicting values but a holding company for the special interests. The various interests are promoted by alliances of interest groups, relevant government agencies, and the appropriate legislative committees. Lowi's analysis is a scathing indictment of a governing process in which agencies charged with regulation are seen as basically protectors of those being regulated.

In the *End of Liberalism* Lowi offers a solution to the problem of interest group liberalism—juridical democracy. This calls for the federal courts to take a stronger role in achieving democratic ideals by forcing the Congress into a greater "rule of law" posture. Such force would come about by increasingly declaring statutes unconstitutional if they continue to be so vague that significant policy powers are delegated to government agencies who use this discretion to play the interest group game. Lowi views the competition of interest groups for influence over program implementation as inherently undemocratic, because these decisions should be made in great detail in the legislation itself. And only the courts can force the Congress to do this. Lowi is still waiting for the Congress to take his advice.

Lowi holds that different models should be constructed for different types of public policies. His now classic article, "American Business, Public Policy, Case Studies and Political Theory" (*World Politics*, July 1964), reprinted here, argued that policy contents should be an independent variable and that there are three major categories of public policies: distribution, regulation, and redistribution. "Each arena tends to develop its own characteristic political structure, political process, elites, and group relations." As one might expect, distribution policies involve actions that provide services and products to individuals and groups; regulatory policies involve transfers or transactions that take from one party and provide to another. Redistribution essentially means taking from the rich and giving to the poor; domestic policies and programs whose goal is to shift wealth or benefits from one segment of the population to another. The welfare state is founded on the notion of redistribution. The basic mechanism for redistribution is taxation. However, the laws themselves can sometimes redistribute benefits. For example, tax loopholes benefit one group of taxpayers at the expense of others; and the Civil Rights Act, through equal employment opportunity mandates, gave economic benefits to one segment of the population at the theoretical expense of another.

Redistribution is more popular with some classes of society than with others. French historian Alexis de Tocqueville (1805–1859) observed in *Democracy in America* (1835): "Countries . . . when lawmaking falls exclusively to the lot of the poor cannot hope for much economy in public expenditure; expenses will always be considerable, either because taxes cannot touch those who vote for them or because they are assessed in a way to prevent that." As the playwright George Bernard Shaw (1856–1950) said in *Everybody's Political What's What?* (1944): "A government which robs Peter to pay Paul can always depend on the support of Paul."

8

The Federalist No. 10 (1787)

James Madison

Among the numerous advantages promised by a well-constructed Union, none deserves to be more accurately developed than its tendency to break and control the violence of faction. The friend of popular governments never finds himself so much alarmed for their character and fate as when he contemplates their propensity to this dangerous vice. He will not fail, therefore, to set a due value on any plan, which, without violating the principles to which he is attached, provides a proper cure for it. The instability, injustice, and confusion introduced into the public councils have, in truth, been the mortal diseases under which popular governments have everywhere perished, as they continue to be the favorite and fruitful topics from which the adversaries to liberty derive their most specious declamations. The valuable improvements made by the American constitutions on the popular models, both ancient and modern, cannot certainly be too much admired; but it would be an unwarrantable partiality to contend that they have as effectually obviated the danger on this side, as was wished and expected. Complaints are everywhere heard from our most considerate and virtuous citizens, equally the friends of public and private faith and of public and personal liberty, that our governments are too unstable, that the public good is disregarded in the conflicts of rival parties, and that measures are too often decided, not according to the rules of justice and the rights of the minor party, but by the superior force of an interested and overbearing majority. However anxiously we may wish that these complaints had no foundation, the evidence of known facts will not permit us to deny that they are in some degree true. It will be found, indeed, on a candid review of our situation, that some of the distresses under which we labor have been erroneously charged on the operation of our governments; but it will be found, at the same time, that other causes will not alone account for many of our heaviest misfortunes; and, particularly, for that prevailing and increasing distrust of public engagements and alarm for private rights which are echoed from one

Source: James Madison, *The Federalist,* No. 10, 1787.

end of the continent to the other. These must be chiefly, if not wholly, effects of the unsteadiness and injustice with which a factious spirit has tainted our public administration.

By a faction I understand a number of citizens, whether amounting to a majority or minority of the whole, who are united and actuated by some common impulse of passion, or of interest, adverse to the rights of other citizens, or to the permanent and aggregate interests of the community.

There are two methods of curing the mischiefs of faction: the one, by removing its causes; the other, by controlling its effects.

There are again two methods of removing the causes of faction: the one, by destroying the liberty which is essential to its existence; the other, by giving to every citizen the same opinions, the same passions, and the same interests.

It could never be more truly said than of the first remedy that it was worse than the disease. Liberty is to faction what air is to fire, an aliment without which it instantly expires. But it could not be a less folly to abolish liberty, which is essential to political life, because it nourishes faction than it would be to wish the annihilation of air, which is essential to animal life, because it imparts to fire its destructive tendency.

The second expedient is as impracticable as the first would be unwise. As long as the reason of man continues fallible, and he is at liberty to exercise it, different opinions will be formed. As long as the connection subsists between his reason and his self-love, his opinions and his passions will have a reciprocal influence on each other; and the former will be objects to which the latter will attach themselves. The diversity in the faculties of men, from which the rights of property originate, is not less an insuperable obstacle to a uniformity of interests. The protection of these faculties is the first object of government. From the protection of different and unequal faculties of acquiring property, the possession of different degrees and kinds of property immediately results; and from the influence of these on the sentiments and views of the respective proprietors ensues a division of the society into different interests and parties.

The latent causes of faction are thus sown in the nature of man; and we see them everywhere brought into different degrees of activity, according to the different circumstances of civil society. A zeal for different opinions concerning religion, concerning government, and many other points, as well of speculation as of practice; an attachment to different leaders ambitiously contending for pre-eminence and power: or to persons of other descriptions whose fortunes have been interesting to the human passions, have, in turn, divided mankind into parties, inflamed them with mutual animosity, and rendered them much more disposed to vex and oppress each other than to cooperate for their common good. So strong is this propensity of mankind to fall into mutual animosities that where no substantial occasion presents itself the most frivolous and fanciful distinctions have been sufficient to kindle their unfriendly passions and excite their most violent conflicts. But the most common and durable source of factions has been the various and unequal distribution of property. Those who hold and those who are without property have ever formed distinct interests in society. Those who are creditors, and those who are debtors, fall under a like discrimination. A landed interest, a manufacturing interest, a mercantile interest, a moneyed interest, with many lesser interests, grow up of necessity in civilized nations, and divide them into different classes, actuated by different sentiments and views. The regulation of these various and interfering interests forms the principal task of modern legislation and involves the spirit of party and faction in the necessary and ordinary operations of government.

No man is allowed to be a judge in his own cause because his interest would certainly bias his judgment, and, not improbably, corrupt his integrity. With equal, nay with greater reason, a body of men are unfit to be both judges and parties at the same time; yet what are many of the most important acts of legislation but so many judicial determinations, not indeed concerning the rights of single persons, but concerning the rights of large bodies of citizens? And what are the different classes of legislators but advocates and parties to the causes which they determine? Is a law proposed concerning private debts? It is a question to which the creditors are parties on one side and the debtors on the other. Justice ought to hold the balance between them. Yet the parties are, and must be, themselves the judges; and the most numerous party, or in other words, the most powerful faction must be expected to prevail. Shall domestic manufacturers be encouraged, and in what degree, by restrictions on foreign manufacturers? are questions which would be differently decided by the landed and the manufacturing classes, and probably by neither with a sole regard to justice and the public good. The apportionment of taxes on the various descriptions of property is an act which seems to require the most exact impartiality; yet there is, perhaps, no legislative act in which greater opportunity and temptation are given to a predominant party to trample on the rules of justice. Every shilling with which they overburden the inferior number is a shilling saved to their own pockets.

It is in vain to say that enlightened statesmen will be able to adjust these clashing interests and render them all subservient to the public good. Enlightened statesmen will not always be at the helm. Nor, in many cases, can such an adjustment be made at all without taking into view indirect and remote considerations, which will rarely prevail over the immediate interest which one party may find in disregarding the rights of another or the good of the whole.

The inference to which we are brought is that the *causes* of faction cannot be removed and that relief is only to be sought in the means of controlling its *effects*.

If a faction consists of less than a majority, relief is supplied by the republican principle, which enables the majority to defeat its sinister views by regular vote. It may clog the administration, it may convulse the society; but it will be unable to execute and mask its violence under the forms of the Constitution. When a majority is included in a faction, the form of popular government, on the other hand, enables it to sacrifice to its ruling passion or interest both the public good and the rights of other citizens. To secure the public good and private rights against the danger of such a faction, and at the same time to preserve the spirit and the form of popular government, is then the great object to which our inquiries are directed. Let me add that it is the great desideratum by which alone this form of government can be rescued from the opprobrium under which it has so long labored and be recommended to the esteem and adoption of mankind.

By what means is this object attainable? Evidently by one of two only. Either the existence of the same passion or interest in a majority at the same time must be prevented, or the majority, having such coexistent passion or interest, must be rendered, by their number and local situation, unable to concert and carry into effect schemes of oppression. If the impulse and the opportunity be suffered to coincide, we well know that neither moral nor religious motives can be relied on as an adequate control. They are not found to be such on the injustice and violence of individuals, and lose their efficacy in proportion to the number combined together, that is, in proportion as their efficacy becomes needful.

From this view of the subject it may be concluded that a pure democracy, by which I mean a society consisting of a small number of citizens, who assemble and administer the government in person, can admit of no cure for the mischiefs of faction. A common passion or interest will, in almost every case, be felt by a majority of the whole; a communication and concert results from the form of government itself; and there is nothing to check the inducements to sacrifice the weaker party or an obnoxious individual. Hence it is that such democracies have ever been spectacles of turbulence and contention; have ever been found incompatible with personal security or the rights of property; and have in general been as short in their lives as they have been violent in their deaths. Theoretic politicians, who have patronized this species of government, have erroneously supposed that by reducing mankind to a perfect equality in their political rights, they would at the same time be perfectly equalized and assimilated in their possessions, their opinions, and their passions.

A republic, by which I mean a government in which the scheme of representation takes place, opens a different prospect and promises the cure for which we are seeking. Let us examine the points in which it varies from pure democracy, and we shall comprehend both the nature of the cure and the efficacy which it must derive from the Union.

The two great points of difference between a democracy and a republic are: first, the delegation of the government, in the latter, to a small number of citizens elected by the rest: secondly, the greater number of citizens and greater sphere of country over which the latter may be extended.

The effect of the first difference is, on the one hand, to refine and enlarge the public views by passing them through the medium of a chosen body of citizens, whose wisdom may best discern the true interest of their country and whose patriotism and love of justice will be least likely to sacrifice it to temporary or partial considerations. Under such a regulation it may well happen that the public voice, pronounced by the representatives of the people, will be more consonant to the public good than if pronounced by the people themselves, convened for the purpose. On the other hand, the effect may be inverted. Men of factious tempers, of local prejudices, or of sinister designs, may, by intrigue, by corruption, or by other means, first obtain the suffrages, and then betray the interests of the people. The question resulting is, whether small or extensive republics are most favorable to the election of proper guardians of the public weal; and it is clearly decided in favor of the latter by two obvious considerations.

In the first place it is to be remarked that however small the republic may be the representatives must be raised to a certain number in order to guard against the cabals of a few; and that however large it may be they must be limited to a certain number in order to guard against the confusion of a multitude. Hence, the number of representatives in the two cases not being in proportion to that of the constituents, and being proportionally greatest in the small republic, it follows that if the proportion of fit characters be not less in the large than in the small republic, the former will present a greater opinion, and consequently a greater probability of a fit choice.

In the next place, as each representative will be chosen by a greater number of citizens in the large than in the small republic, it will be more difficult for unworthy candidates to practise with success the vicious arts by which elections are too often carried; and the suffrages of people being more free, will be more likely to center on men who possess the most attractive merit and the most diffusive and established characters.

It must be confessed that in this, as in most other cases, there is a mean, on both sides of which inconveniencies will be found to lie. By enlarging too much the number of electors, you render the representative too little acquainted with all their local circumstances and lesser interests; as by reducing it too much, you render him unduly attached to these, and too little fit to comprehend and pursue great and national objects. The federal Constitution forms a happy combination in this respect; the great and aggregate interests being referred to the national, the local and particular to the State legislatures.

The other point of difference is the greater number of citizens and extent of territory which may be brought within the compass of republican than of democratic government; and it is this circumstance principally which renders factious combinations less to be dreaded in the former than in the latter. The smaller the society, the fewer probably will be the distinct parties and interests composing it; the fewer the distinct parties and interests, the more frequently will a majority be found of the same party; and the smaller the number of individuals composing a majority, and the smaller the compass within which they are placed, the more easily will they concert and execute their plans of oppression. Extend the sphere and you take in a greater variety of parties and interests; you make it less probable that a majority of the whole will have a common motive to invade the rights of other citizens; or if such a common motive exists, it will be more difficult for all who feel it to discover their own strength and to act in unison with each other. Besides other impediments, it may be remarked that, where there is a consciousness of unjust or dishonorable purposes, communication is always checked by distrust in proportion to the number whose concurrence is necessary.

Hence, it clearly appears that the same advantage which a republic has over a democracy in controlling the effects of faction is enjoyed by a large over a small republic—is enjoyed by the Union over the States composing it. Does this advantage consist in the substitution of representatives whose enlightened views and virtuous sentiments render them superior to local prejudices and to schemes of injustice? It will not be denied that the representation of the Union will be most likely to possess these requisite endowments. Does it consist in the greater security afforded by a greater variety of parties, against the event of any one party being able to outnumber and oppress the rest? In an equal degree does the increased variety of parties comprised within the Union increase this security? Does it, in fine, consist in the greater obstacles opposed to the concert accomplishment of the secret wishes of an unjust and interested majority? Here again the extent of the Union gives it the most palpable advantage.

The influence of factious leaders may kindle a flame within their particular States but will be unable to spread a general conflagration through the other States. A religious sect may degenerate into a political faction in a part of the Confederacy; but the variety of sects dispersed over the entire face of it must secure the national councils against any danger from that source. A rage for paper money, for an abolition of debts, for an equal division of property, or for any other improper or wicked project, will be less apt to pervade the whole body of the Union than a particular member of it, in the same proportion as such a malady is more likely to taint a particular county or district than an entire State.

In the extent and proper structure of the Union, therefore, we behold a republican remedy for the diseases most incident to republican government. And according to the degree of pleasure and pride we feel in being republicans ought to be our zeal in cherishing the spirit and supporting the character of federalists.

9

The Governmental Process (1951)

David Truman

Men, wherever they are observed, are creatures participating in those established patterns of interaction that we call groups. Excepting perhaps the most casual and transitory, these continuing interactions, like all such interpersonal relationships, involve power. This power is exhibited in two closely interdependent ways. In the first place, the group exerts power over its members; an individual's group affiliations largely determine his attitudes, values, and the frames of reference in terms of which he interprets his experiences. For a measure of conformity to the norms of the group is the price of acceptance within it. Such power is exerted not only by an individual's present group relationships; it also may derive from past affiliations such as the childhood family as well as from groups to which the individual aspires to belong and whose characteristic shared attitudes he also holds. In the second place, the group, if it is or becomes an interest group, which any group in a society may be, exerts power over other groups in the society when it successfully imposes claims upon them.

Many interest groups, probably an increasing proportion in the United States, are politicized. That is, either from the outset or from time to time in the course of their development they make their claims through or upon the institutions of government. Both the forms and functions of government in turn are a reflection of the activities and claims of such groups. The constitution-writing proclivities of Americans clearly reveal the influence of demands from such sources, and the statutory creation of new functions reflects their continuing operation. Many of these forms and functions have received such widespread acceptance from the start or in the course of time that they appear to be independent of the overt activities of organized interest groups. The judiciary is such a form. The building of city streets and the control of vehicular traffic are examples of such a function. However, if the judiciary or a segment of it

Source: David B. Truman, from *The Governmental Process*. New York: Knopf, 1951. Reprinted by permission of Elinor G. Truman.

operates in a fashion sharply contrary to the expectations of an appreciable portion of the community or if its role is strongly attacked, the group basis of its structure and powers is likely to become apparent. Similarly, if street construction greatly increases tax rates or if the control of traffic unnecessarily inconveniences either pedestrians or motorists, the exposure of these functions to the demands of competing interests will not be obscure. Interests that are widely held in the society may be reflected in government without their being organized in groups. They are what we have called potential groups. If the claims implied by the interests of these potential groups are quickly and adequately represented, interaction among those people who share the underlying interests or attitudes is unnecessary. But the interest base of accepted governmental forms and functions and their potential involvement in overt group activities are ever present even when not patently operative.

The institutions of government are centers of interest-based power; their connections with interest groups may be latent or overt and their activities range in political character from the routinized and widely accepted to the unstable and highly controversial. In order to make claims, political interest groups will seek access to the key points of decision within these institutions. Such points are scattered throughout the structure, including not only the formally established branches of government but also the political parties in their various forms and the relationships between governmental units and other interest groups.

The extent to which a group achieves effective access to the institutions of government is the resultant of a complex of interdependent factors. For the sake of simplicity these may be classified in three somewhat overlapping categories: (1) factors relating to a group's strategic position in the society; (2) factors associated with the internal characteristics of the group; and (3) factors peculiar to the governmental institutions themselves. In the first category are: the group's status or prestige in the society, affecting the ease with which it commands deference from those outside its bounds; the standing it and its activities have when measured against the widely held but largely unorganized interests or "rules of the game;" the extent to which government officials are formally or informally "members" of the group; and the usefulness of the group as a source of technical and political knowledge. The second category includes: the degree and appropriateness of the group's organization; the degree of cohesion it can achieve in a given situation, especially in the light of competing group demands upon its membership; the skills of the leadership; and the group's resources in numbers and money. In the third category, are: the operating structure of the government institutions, since such established features involve relatively fixed advantages and handicaps; and the effects of the group life of particular units or branches of the government. . . .

There are two elements in this conception of the political process in the United States that are of crucial significance and that require special emphasis. These are, first, the notion of multiple or overlapping membership and, second, the function of unorganized interests, or potential interest groups.

The idea of overlapping membership stems from the conception of a group as a standardized pattern of interactions rather than as a collection of human units. Although the former may appear to be a rather misty abstraction, it is actually far closer to complex reality than the latter notion. The view of a group as an aggregation of individuals abstracts from the observable fact that in any society, and especially a complex one, no single group affiliation accounts for all of the attitudes or interests of any individual except a fanatic or a compulsive neurotic. No tolerably normal person is totally absorbed in any group in which he participates. The diversity of an individual's activities and his attendant interests involve him in a variety of actual and potential groups. Moreover, the fact that the genetic experiences of no two individuals are identical and the consequent fact that the spectra of their attitudes are in varying degrees dissimilar means that the members of a single group will perceive the group's claims in terms of a diversity of frames of reference. Such heterogeneity may be of little significance until such time as these multiple memberships conflict. Then the cohesion and influence of the affected group depend upon the incorporation or accommodation of the conflicting loyalties of any significant segment of the group, an accommodation that may result in altering the original claims. Thus the leaders of a Parent-Teacher Association must take some account of the fact that their proposals must be acceptable to members who also belong to the local taxpayers' league, to the local chamber of commerce, and to the Catholic Church.

The notion of overlapping membership bears directly upon the problems allegedly created by the appearance of a multiplicity of interest groups. Yet the fact of such overlapping is frequently overlooked or neglected in discussions of the political role of groups. James Madison, whose brilliant analysis in the tenth essay in *The Federalist* we have frequently quoted, relied primarily upon diversity of groups and difficulty of communication to protect the new government from the tyranny of a factious majority. He barely touched on the notion of multiple membership when he observed, almost parenthetically: "Besides other impediments, it may be remarked that, where there is a consciousness of unjust or dishonorable purposes, communication is always checked by distrust in proportion to the number whose concurrence is necessary." John C. Calhoun's idea of the concurrent majority, developed in his posthumously published work, *A Disquisition on Government* (1851), assumed the unified, monolithic character of the groups whose liberties he was so anxious to protect. When his present-day followers unearth his doctrines, moreover, they usually make the same assumption, although implicitly.[1] Others, seeking a satisfactory means of accounting for the continued existence of the political system, sometimes assume that it is the nonparticipant citizens, aroused to unwonted activity, who act as a kind of counterbalance to the solid masses that constitute organized interest groups.[2] Although this phenomenon may occur in times of crisis, reliance upon it reckons insufficiently with the established observation that citizens who are nonparticipant in one aspect of the governmental process, such as voting, rarely show much concern for any phase of political activity. Multiple membership is more important as a restraint upon the activities of organized groups than the rarely aroused protests of chronic nonparticipants. . . .

Any mutual interest, however, any shared attitude, is a potential group. A disturbance in established relationships and expectations anywhere in the society may produce new patterns of interaction aimed at restricting or eliminating the disturbance. Sometimes it may be this possibility of organization that alone gives the potential group a minimum of influence in the political process. Thus Key notes that the Delta planters in Mississippi "must speak for their Negroes in such programs as health and education," although the latter are virtually unorganized and are denied the means of active political participation.[3] It is in this sense that Bentley speaks of a difference in degree between the politics of despotism and that of other "forms" of government. He notes that there is "a process of representation in despotisms which is inevitable in all democracies, and which may be distinguished by quantities and by elaboration of technique, but not in any deeper 'qualitative' way." He speaks of the despot as "representative of his own class, and to a smaller, but none the less real, extent of the ruled class as well."[4] Obstacles to the development of organized groups from potential ones may be presented by inertia or by the activities of opposed groups, but the possibility that severe disturbances will be created if these submerged, potential interests should organize necessitates some recognition of the existence of these interests and gives them at least a minimum of influence.

More important for present purposes than the potential groups representing separate minority elements are those interests or expectations that are so widely held in the society and are so reflected in the behavior of almost all citizens that they are, so to speak, taken for granted. Such "majority" interests are significant not only because they may become the basis for organized interest groups but also because the "membership" of such potential groups overlaps extensively the memberships of the various organized interest groups.[5] The resolution of conflicts between the claims of such organized interests and those of organized interest groups must grant recognition to the former not only because affected individuals may feel strongly attached to them but even more certainly because these interests are widely shared and are a part of many established patterns of behavior the disturbance of which would be difficult and painful. They are likely to be highly valued.

These widely held but unrecognized interests are what we have previously called the "rules of the game." Others have described these attitudes in such terms as "systems of belief," as a "general ideological consensus," and as "a broad body of attitudes and understandings regarding the nature and limits of authority."[6] Each of these interests (attitudes) may be wide or narrow, general or detailed. For the mass of the population they may be loose and ambiguous, though more precise and articulated at the leadership level. In any case the "rules of the game" are interests the serious disturbance of which will result in organized interaction and the assertion of fairly explicit claims for conformity. In the American system the "rules" would include the value generally attached to the dignity of the individual human being, loosely expressed in terms of "fair dealing" or more explicitly verbalized in formulations such as the Bill of Rights. They would embrace what we called "the democratic mold," that is, the approval of forms for broad mass participation in the designation of leaders and in the selection of policies in all social groups and institutions. They would also comprehend certain semi-egalitarian notions of material welfare. This is an illustrative, not an exclusive, list of such interests.

NOTES

1. Cf. John Fischer: "Unwritten Rules of American Politics," *Harper's Magazine* (November, 1948), pp. 27–36.

2. Cf. Herring: *The Politics of Democracy,* p. 32.

3. Key: *Southern Politics,* pp. 235 and *passim.*

4. Bentley: *The Process of Government,* pp. 314–5. Copyright 1908 by and used with the permission of Arthur F. Bentley.

5. See the suggestive discussion of this general subject in Robert Bierstedt: "The Sociology of Majorities," *American Sociological Review,* Vol. 13, no. 6 (December, 1948), pp. 700–10.

6. Kluckhohn: *Mirror for Man,* pp. 248 and *passim:* Sebastian de Grazia: *The Political Community: A Study of Anomie* (Chicago: University of Chicago Press, 1948), pp. ix, 80, and *passim;* Almond: *The American People and Foreign Policy,* p. 158; Charles E. Merriam: *Systematic Politics* (Chicago: University of Chicago Press, 1945), p. 213.

10

The Power Elite (1957)

C. Wright Mills

The powers of ordinary men are circumscribed by the everyday worlds in which they live, yet even in these rounds of job, family, and neighborhood they often seem driven by forces they can neither understand nor govern. 'Great changes' are beyond their control, but affect their conduct and outlook none the less. The very framework of modern society confines them to projects not their own, but from every side, such changes now press upon the men and women of the mass society, who accordingly feel that they are without purpose in an epoch in which they are without power.

But not all men are in this sense ordinary. As the means of information and of power are centralized, some men come to occupy positions in American society from which they can look down upon, so to speak, and by their decisions mightily affect, the everyday worlds of ordinary men and women. They are not made by their jobs; they set up and break down jobs for thousands of others; they are not confined by simple family responsibilities; they can escape. They may live in many hotels and houses, but they are bound by no one community. They need not merely meet the demands of the day and hour'; in some part, they create these demands, and cause others to meet them. Whether or not they profess their power, their technical and political experience of it far transcends that of the underlying population. What Jacob Burckhardt said of 'great men,' most Americans might well say of their elite: 'They are all that we are not.'[1]

The power elite is composed of men whose positions enable them to transcend the ordinary environments of ordinary men and women; they are in positions to make decisions having major consequences. Whether they do or do not make such decisions is less important than the fact that they do occupy such pivotal positions; their failure to act, their failure to make decisions, is itself an act that is often of greater consequence than the decisions they do make. For they are in command of the major hierarchies and organizations of modern society. They rule the big corporations. They run the machinery of the state and claim its prerogatives. They direct the military establishment. They occupy the strategic command posts of the social structure, in which are now centered the effective means of the power and the wealth and the celebrity which they enjoy.

The power elite are not solitary rulers. Advisers and consultants, spokesmen and opinion-makers are often the captains of their higher thought and decision. Immediately below the elite are the professional politicians of the middle levels of power, in the Congress and in the pressure groups, as well as among the new and old upper classes of town and city and region. Mingling with them, in curious ways which we shall explore, are those professional celebrities who live by being continually displayed but are never, so long as they remain celebrities, displayed enough. If such celebrities are not at the head of any dominating hierarchy, they do often have the power to distract the attention of the public or afford sensations to the masses, or, more directly, to gain the ear of those who do occupy positions of direct power. More or less unattached, as critics of morality and technicians of power, as spokesmen of God and creators of mass sensibility, such celebrities and consultants are part of the immediate scene in which the drama of the elite is enacted. But that drama itself is centered in the command posts of the major institutional hierarchies.

I

The truth about the nature and the power of the elite is not some secret which men of affairs know but will not tell. Such men hold quite various theories about their own roles in the sequence of event and decision. Often they are uncertain about their roles, and even more often they allow their fears and their hopes to affect their assessment of their own power. No matter how great their actual power, they tend to be less acutely aware of it than of the resistances of others to its use. Moreover, most American men of affairs have learned well the rhetoric of public relations, in some cases even to the point of using it when they are alone, and thus coming to believe it. The personal awareness of the actors is only one of the several sources one must examine in order to understand the higher circles. Yet many who believe that there is no elite, or at any rate none of any consequence, rest their argument upon what men of affairs believe about themselves, or at least assert in public.

There is, however, another view: those who feel, even if vaguely, that a compact and powerful elite of great importance does now prevail in America often base that feeling upon the historical trend of our time. They have felt, for example, the domination of the military event, and from this they infer that generals and admirals, as well as other men of decision influenced by them, must be enormously powerful. They hear that the Congress has again abdicated to a handful of men decisions clearly related to the issue of war or peace. They know that the bomb was dropped over Japan in the name of the United States of America, although they were at no time consulted about the matter. They feel that they live in a time of big decisions; they know that they are not making any. Accordingly, as they consider the present as history, they infer that at its center, making decisions or failing to make them, there must be an elite of power.

On the one hand, those who share this feeling about big historical events assume that there is an elite and that its power is great. On the other hand, those who listen carefully to the reports of men apparently involved in the great decisions often do not believe that there is an elite whose powers are of decisive consequence.

Both views must be taken into account, but neither is adequate. The way to understand the power of the American elite lies neither solely in recognizing the historic scale of events nor in accepting the personal awareness reported by men of apparent decision. Behind such men and behind the events of history, linking the two, are the major institutions of modern society. These hierarchies of state and corporation and army constitute the means of power; as such they are now of a consequence not before equaled in human history—and at their summits, there are now those command posts of modern society which offer us the sociological key to an understanding of the role of the higher circles in America.

Within American society, major national power now resides in the economic, the political, and the military domains. Other institutions seem off to the side of modern history, and, on occasion duly subordinated to these. No family is as directly powerful in national affairs as any major corporation; no church is as directly powerful in the external biographies of young men in America today as the military establishment; no college is as powerful in the shaping of momentous events as the National Security Council. Religious, educational, and family institutions are not autonomous centers of national power; on the contrary, these decentralized areas are increasingly shaped by the big three, in which developments of decisive and immediate consequence now occur.

Families and churches and schools adapt to modern life; governments and armies and corporations shape it; and, as they do so, they turn these lesser institutions into means for their ends. Religious institutions provide chaplains to the armed forces where they are used as a means of increasing the effectiveness of its morale to kill. Schools select and train men for their jobs in corporations and their specialized tasks in the armed forces. The extended family has of course, long been broken up by the industrial revolution, and now the son and the father are removed from the family, by compulsion if need be, whenever the army of the state sends out the call. And the symbols of all these lesser institutions are used to legitimate the power and the decisions of the big three.

The life-fate of the modern individual depends not only upon the family into which he was born or which he enters by marriage but increasingly upon the corporation in which he spends the most alert hours of his best years; not only upon the school where he is educated as a child and adolescent, but also upon the state which touches him throughout his life; not only upon the church in which on occasion he hears the word of God, but also upon the army in which he is disciplined.

If the centralized state could not rely upon the inculcation of nationalist loyalties in public and private schools, its leaders would promptly seek to modify the decentralized educational system. If the bankruptcy rate among the top five hundred corporations were as high as the general divorce rate among the thirty-seven million married couples, there would be economic catastrophe on an international scale. If members of armies gave to them no more of their lives than do believers to the churches to which they belong, there would be a military crisis.

Within each of the big three, the typical institutional unit has become enlarged, has become administrative, and, in the power of its decisions, has become centralized. Behind these developments there is a fabulous technology, for as institutions, they have incorporated this technology and guide it, even as it shapes and paces their developments.

The economy—once a great scatter of small productive units in autonomous balance—has become dominated by two or three hundred giant corporations, administratively and politically interrelated which together hold the keys to economic decisions.

The political order, once a decentralized set of several dozen states with a weak spinal cord, has become a centralized, executive establishment which has taken up into itself many powers previously scattered, and now enters into each and every cranny of the social structure.

The military order, once a slim establishment in a context of distrust fed by state militia, has become the largest and most expensive feature of government, and, although well versed in smiling public relations, now has all the grim and clumsy efficiency of a sprawling bureaucratic domain.

In each of these institutional areas, the means of power at the disposal of decision makers have increased enormously; their central executive powers have been enhanced; within each of them modern administrative routines have been elaborated and tightened up.

As each of these domains becomes enlarged and centralized, the consequences of its activities become greater, and its traffic with the others increases. The decisions of a handful of corporations bear upon military and political as well as upon economic developments around the world. The decisions of the military establishment rest upon and grievously affect political life as well as the very level of economic activity. The decisions made within the political domain determine economic activities and military programs. There is no longer, on the one hand, an economy, and, on the other hand, a political order containing a military establishment unimportant to politics and to money-making. There is a political economy linked, in a thousand ways, with military institutions and decisions. On each side of the world-split running through central Europe and around the Asiatic rimlands, there is an ever-increasing interlocking of economic, military, and political structures.[2] If there is government intervention in the corporate economy, so is there corporate intervention in the governmental process. In the structural sense, this triangle of power is the source of the interlocking directorate that is most important for the historical structure of the present.

The fact of the interlocking is clearly revealed at each of the points of crisis of modern capitalist society—slump, war, and boom. In each, men of decision are led to an awareness of the interdependence of the major institutional orders. In the nineteenth century, when the scale of all institutions was smaller, their liberal integration was achieved in the automatic economy, by an autonomous play of market forces, and in the automatic political domain, by the bargain and the vote. It was then assumed that out of the imbalance and friction that followed the limited decisions then possible a new equilibrium would in due course emerge. That can no longer be assumed, and it is not assumed by the men at the top of each of the three dominant hierarchies.

For given the scope of their consequences, decisions—and indecisions—in any one of these ramify into the others, and hence top decisions tend either to become co-ordinated or to lead to a commanding indecision. It has not always been like this. When numerous small entrepreneurs made up the economy, for example, many of them could fail and the consequences still remain local; political and military authorities did not intervene. But now, given political expectations and military commitments, can they afford to allow key units of the private corporate economy to break down in slump? Increasingly, they do intervene in economic affairs, and as they do so, the controlling decisions in each order are inspected by agents of the other two, and economic, military, and political structures are interlocked.

At the pinnacle of each of the three enlarged and centralized domains, there have arisen those higher circles which make up the economic, the political, and the military elites. At the top of the economy, among the corporate rich, there are the chief executives, at the top of the political order, the members of the political directorate; at the top of the military establishment, the elite of soldier-statesmen clustered in and around the Joint Chiefs of Staff and the upper echelon. As each of these domains has coincided with the others, as decisions tend to become total in their consequence, the leading men in each of the three domains of power—the warlords, the corporation chieftains, the political directorate—tend to come together, to form the power elite of America.

2

The higher circles in and around these command posts are often thought of in terms of what their members possess: they have a greater share than other people of the things and experiences that are most highly valued. From this point of view, the elite are simply those who have the most of what there is to have, which is generally held to include money, power, and prestige—as well as all the ways of life to which these lead.[3] But the elite are not simply those who have the most, for they could not 'have the most' were it not for their positions in the great institutions. For such institutions are the necessary bases of power, of wealth, and of prestige, and at the same time, the chief means of exercising power, of acquiring and retaining wealth, and of cashing in the higher claims for prestige.

By the powerful we mean, of course, those who are able to realize their will, even if others resist it. No one, accordingly, can be truly powerful unless he has access to the command of major institutions, for it is over these institutional means of power that the truly powerful are, in the first instance, powerful. Higher politicians and key officials of government command such institutional power; so do admirals and generals, and so do the major owners and executives of the larger corporations. Not all power, it is true, is anchored in and exercised by means of such institutions, but only within and through them can power be more or less continuous and important.

Wealth also is acquired and held in and through institutions. The pyramid of wealth cannot be understood merely in terms of the very rich; for the great inheriting families, as we shall see, are now supplemented by the corporate institutions of modern society; every one of the very rich families has been and is closely connected—always legally and frequently managerially as well—with one of the multi-million dollar corporations.

The modern corporation is the prime source of wealth, but, in latter-day capitalism, the political apparatus also opens and closes many avenues to wealth. The amount as well as the source of income, the power over consumer's goods as well as productive capital, are determined by position within the political economy. If our interest in the very rich goes beyond their lavish or their miserly consumption, we must examine their relations to modern forms of corporate property as well as to the state; for such relations now determine the chances of men to secure big property and to receive high income.

Great prestige increasingly follows the major institutional units of the social structure. It is obvious that prestige depends, often quite decisively, upon access to the publicity machines that are now a central and normal feature of all the big institutions of modern America. Moreover, one feature of these hierarchies of corporation, state, and military establishment is that their top positions are increasingly interchangeable. One result of this is the accumulative nature of prestige. Claims for prestige, for example may be initially based on military roles, then expressed in and augmented by an educational institution run by corporate executives, and cashed in, finally, in the political order, where, for General Eisenhower and those he represents, power and prestige finally meet at the very peak. Like wealth and power, prestige tends to be cumulative: the more of it you have, the more you can get. These values also tend to be translatable into one another: the wealthy find it easier than the poor to gain power; those with status find it easier than those without it to control opportunities for wealth.

If we took the one hundred most powerful men in America, the one hundred wealthiest, and the one hundred most celebrated away from the institutional positions they now occupy, away from their resources of men and women and money, away from the media of mass communication that are now focused upon them—then they would be powerless and poor and uncelebrated. For power is not of a man. Wealth does not center in the person of the wealthy. Celebrity is not inherent in any personality. To be celebrated, to be wealthy, to have power requires access to major institutions, for the institutional positions men occupy determine in large part their chances to have and to hold these valued experiences.

3

The people of the higher circles may also be conceived as members of a top social stratum, as a set of groups whose members know one another, see one another socially and at business, and so, in making decisions, take one another into account. The elite, according to this conception, feel themselves to be, and are felt by others to be, the inner circle of 'the upper social classes.'[4] They form a more or less compact social and psychological entity; they have become self-conscious members of a social class. People are either accepted into this class or they are not, and there is a qualitative split, rather than merely a numerical scale, separating them from those who are not elite. They are more or less aware of themselves as a social class and they behave toward one another differently from the way they do toward members of other classes. They accept one another, understand one another, marry one another, tend to work and to think if not together at least alike.

Now, we do not want by our definition to prejudge whether the elite of the command posts are conscious members of such a socially recognized class, or whether considerable proportions of the elite derive from such a clear and distinct class. These are matters to be investigated. Yet in order to be able to recognize what we intend to investigate, we must note something that all biographies and memoirs of the wealthy and the powerful and the eminent make clear: no matter what else they may be, the people of these higher circles are involved in a set of overlapping 'crowds' and intricately connected 'cliques.' There is a kind of mutual attraction among those who 'sit on the same terrace'—although this often becomes clear to them, as well as to others, only at the point at which they feel the need to draw the line; only when, in their common defense, they come to understand what they have in common, and so close their ranks against outsiders.

The idea of such ruling stratum implies that most of its members have similar social origins, that throughout their lives they maintain a network of informal connections, and that to some degree there is an interchangeability of position between the various hierarchies of money and power and celebrity. We must, of course, note at once that if such an elite stratum does exist, its social visibility and its form, for very solid historical reasons, are quite different from those of the noble cousinhoods that once ruled various European nations.

That American society has never passed through a feudal epoch is of decisive importance to the nature of the American elite, as well as to American society as a historic whole. For it means that no nobility or aristocracy, established before the capitalist era, has stood in tense opposition to the higher bourgeoisie. It means that this bourgeoisie has monopolized not only wealth but prestige and power as well. It means that no set of noble families has commanded the top positions and monopolized the values that are generally held in high esteem; and certainly that no set has done so explicitly by inherited right. It means that no high church dignitaries or court nobilities, no entrenched landlords with honorific accouterments, no monopolists of high army posts have opposed the enriched bourgeoisie and in the name of birth and prerogative successfully resisted its self-making.

But this does *not* mean that there are no upper strata in the United States. That they emerged from a 'middle class' that had no recognized aristocratic superiors does not mean they remained middle class when enormous increases in wealth made their own superiority possible. Their origins and their newness may have made the upper strata less visible in America than elsewhere. But in America today there are in fact tiers and ranges of wealth and power of which people in the middle and lower ranks know very little and may not even dream. There are families who, in their well-being, are quite insulated from the economic jolts and lurches felt by the merely prosperous and those farther down the scale. There are also men of power who in quite small groups make decisions of enormous consequence for the underlying population.

The American elite entered modern history as a virtually unopposed bourgeoisie. No national bourgeoisie, before or since, has had such opportunities and advantages. Having no military neighbors, they easily occupied an isolated continent stocked with natural resources and immensely inviting to a willing labor force. A framework of power and an ideology for its justification were already at hand. Against mercantilist restriction, they inherited the principle of *laissez-faire;* against Southern planters, they imposed the principle of industrialism. The Revolutionary War put an end to colonial pretensions to nobility, as loyalists fled the country and many estates were broken up. The Jacksonian upheaval with its status revolution put an end to pretensions to monopoly of descent by the old New England families. The Civil War broke the power, and so in due course the prestige, of the ante-bellum South's claimants for the higher esteem. The tempo of the whole capitalist development made it impossible for an inherited nobility to develop and endure in America.

No fixed ruling class, anchored in agrarian life and coming to flower in military glory, could contain in America the historic thrust of commerce and industry, or subordinate to itself the capitalist elite—as capitalists were subordinated, for example, in Germany and Japan. Nor could such a ruling class anywhere in the world contain that of the United States when industrialized violence came to decide history. Witness the fate of Germany and Japan in the two world wars of the twentieth century; and indeed the fate of Britain herself and her model ruling class, as New York became the inevitable economic, and Washington the inevitable political capital of the western capitalist world.

4

The elite who occupy the command posts may be seen as the possessors of power and wealth and celebrity; they may be seen as members of the upper stratum of a capitalistic society. They may also be defined in terms of psychological and moral criteria, as certain kinds of selected individuals. So defined, the elite, quite simply, are people of superior character and energy.

The humanist, for example, may conceive of the 'elite' not as a social level or category, but as a scatter of those individuals who attempt to transcend themselves, and accordingly, are more noble, more efficient, made out of better stuff. It does not matter whether they are poor or rich, whether they hold high position or low, whether they are acclaimed or despised; they are elite because of the kind of individuals they are. The rest of the population is mass, which, according to this conception, sluggishly relaxes into uncomfortable mediocrity.[5]

This is the sort of socially unlocated conception which some American writers with conservative yearnings have recently sought to develop. But most moral and psychological conceptions of the elite are much less sophisticated, concerning themselves not with individuals but with the stratum as a whole. Such ideas, in fact, always arise in a society in which some people possess more than do others of what there is to possess. People with advantages are loath to believe that they just happen to be people with advantages. They come readily to define themselves as inherently worthy of what they possess; they come to believe themselves 'naturally' elite; and, in fact, to imagine their possessions and their privileges as natural extensions of their own elite selves. In this sense, the idea of the elite as composed of men and women having a finer moral character is an ideology of the elite as a privileged ruling stratum, and this is true whether the ideology is elite-made or made up for it by others.

In eras of equalitarian rhetoric, the more intelligent or the more articulate among the lower and middle classes, as well as guilty members of the upper, may come to entertain ideas of a counter-elite. In western society, as a matter of fact, there is a long tradition and varied images of the poor, the exploited, and the oppressed as the truly virtuous, the wise, and the blessed. Stemming from Christian tradition, this moral idea of a counter-elite, composed of essentially higher types condemned to a lowly station, may be and has been used by the underlying population to justify harsh criticism of ruling elites and to celebrate utopian images of a new elite to come.

The moral conception of the elite, however, is not always merely an ideology of the overprivileged or a counter-ideology of the underprivileged. It is often a fact: having controlled experiences and select privileges, many individuals of the upper stratum do come in due course to approximate the types of character they claim to embody. Even when we give up—as we must—the idea that the elite man or woman is born with an elite character, we need not dismiss the idea that their experiences and trainings develop in them characters of a specific type.

Nowadays we must qualify the idea of elite as composed of higher types of individuals, for the men who are selected for and shaped by the top positions have many spokesmen and advisers and ghosts and make-up men who modify their self-conceptions and create their public images, as well as shape many of their decisions. There is, of course, considerable variation among the elite in this respect, but as a general rule in America today, it would be naïve to interpret any major elite group merely in terms of its ostensible personnel. The American elite often seems less a collection of persons than of corporate entities, which are in great part created and spoken for as standard types of 'personality.' Even the most apparently free-lance celebrity is usually a sort of synthetic production turned out each week by a disciplined staff which systematically ponders the effect of the easy ad-libbed gags the celebrity 'spontaneously' echoes.

Yet, in so far as the elite flourishes as a social class or as a set of men at the command posts, it will select and form certain types of personality, and reject others. The kind of moral and psychological beings men become is in large part determined by the values they experience and the institutional roles they are allowed and expected to play. From the biographer's point of view, a man of the upper classes is formed by his relations with others like himself in a series of small intimate groupings through which he passes and to which throughout his lifetime he may return. So conceived, the elite is a set of higher circles whose members are selected, trained and certified and permitted intimate access to those who command the impersonal institutional hierarchies of modern society. If there is any one key to the *psychological* idea of the elite, it is that they combine in their persons an awareness of impersonal decision-making with intimate sensibilities shared with one another. To understand the elite as a social class we must examine a whole series of smaller face-to-face milieux, the most obvious of which, historically, has been the upper class family, but the most important of which today are the proper secondary school and the metropolitan club.[6]

NOTES

1. Jacob Burckhardt, *Force and Freedom* (New York: Pantheon Books, 1943), pp. 303 ff.

2. Cf. Hans Gerth and C. Wright Mills, *Character and Social Structure* (New York: Harcourt, Brace, 1953), pp. 457 ff.

3. The statistical idea of choosing some value and calling those who have the most of it an elite derives, in modern times, from the Italian economist, Pareto, who puts the central point in this way: 'Let us assume that in every branch of human activity each individual is given an index which stands as a sign of his capacity, very much the way grades are given in the various subjects in examinations in school. The highest type of lawyer, for instance, will be given 10. The man who does not get a client will be given 1—reserving zero for the man who is an out-and-out idiot. To the man who has made

his millions—honestly or dishonestly as the case may be—we will give 10. To the man who has earned his thousands we will give 6; to such as just manage to keep out of the poor-house, 1, keeping zero for those who get in . . . So let us make a class of people who have the highest indices in their branch of activity, and to that class give the name of *elite*.' Vilfredo Pareto, *The Mind and Society* (New York: Harcourt, Brace, 1935), par. 2027 and 2031. Those who follow this approach end up not with one elite, but with a number corresponding to the number of values they select. Like many rather abstract ways of reasoning, this one is useful because it forces us to think in a clear-cut way. For a skillful use of this approach, see the work of Harold D. Lasswell, in particular, *Politics: Who Gets What, When, How* (New York: McGraw-Hill, 1936); and for a more systematic use, H. D. Lasswell and Abraham Kaplan, *Power and Society* (New Haven: Yale University Press, 1950).

4. The conception of the elite as members of a top social stratum, is, of course, in line with the prevailing common-sense view of stratification. Technically, it is closer to 'status group' than to 'class,' and has been very well stated by Joseph A. Schumpeter, 'Social Classes in an Ethically Homogeneous Environment,' *Imperialism and Social Classes* (New York: Augustus M. Kelley, Inc., 1951), pp. 133 ff, especially pp. 137-47. Cf. also his *Capitalism, Socialism and Democracy,* 3rd ed. (New York: Harper, 1950), Part II. For the distinction between class and status groups, see *From Max Weber: Essays in Sociology* (trans. and ed. by Gerth and Mills; New York: Oxford University Press, 1946). For analysis of Pareto's conception of the elite compared with Marx's conception of classes, as well as data on France, see Raymond Aron, "Social Structure and Ruling Class,' *British Journal of Sociology*, vol. 1, nos. 1 and 2 (1950).

5. The most popular essay in recent years which defines the elite and the mass in terms of a morally evaluated character-type is probably José Ortega y Gasset's, *The Revolt of the Masses,* 1932 (New York: New American Library, Mentor Edition, 1950), esp. pp. 91 ff.

6. 'The American elite' is a confused and confusing set of images, and yet when we hear or when we use such words as Upper Class, Big Shot, Top Brass, The Millionaire Club, The High and The Mighty, we feel at least vaguely that we know what they mean, and often do. What we do not often do, however, is connect each of these images with the others; we make little effort to form a coherent picture in our minds of the elite as a whole. Even when, very occasionally, we do try to do this, we usually come to believe that it is indeed no 'whole'; that, like our images of it, there is no one elite, but many, and that they are not really connected with one another. What we must realize is that until we do try to see it as a whole, perhaps our impression that it may not be is a result merely of our lack of analytic rigor and sociological imagination.

The first conception defines the elite in terms of the sociology of institutional position and the social structure these institutions form; the second, in terms of the statistics of selected values; the third, in terms of membership in a clique-like set of people; and the fourth, in terms of the morality of certain personality types. Or, put into inelegant shorthand: what they head up, what they have, what they belong to, who they really are.

In this chapter, as in this book as a whole, I have taken as generic the first view—of the elite defined in terms of institutional position—and have located the other views within it. This straight-forward conception of the elite has one practical and two theoretical advantages. The practical advantage is that it seems the easiest and the most concrete 'way into' the whole problem—if only because a good deal of information is more or less readily available for sociological reflection about such circles and institutions.

But the theoretical advantages are much more important. The institutional or structural definition, first of all, does not force us to prejudge by definition that we ought properly to leave open for investigation. The elite conceived morally, for example, as people having a certain type of character is not an ultimate definition, for apart from being rather morally arbitrary, it leads us immediately to ask *why* these people have this or that sort of character. Accordingly, we should leave open the type of characters which the members of the elite in fact turn out to have, rather than by definition select them in terms of one type or another. In a similar way, we do not want, by mere definition, to prejudge whether or not the elite are conscious members of a social class. The second theoretical advantage of defining the elite in terms of major institutions, which I hope this book as a whole makes clear, is the fact that it allows us to fit the other three conceptions of the elite into place in a systematic way: (1) The institutional positions men occupy throughout their lifetime determine their chances to get and to hold selected values. (2) The kind of psychological beings they become is in large part determined by the values they thus experience and the institutional roles they play. (3) Finally, whether or not they come to feel that they belong to a select social class, and whether or not they act according to what they hold to be its interests—these are also matters in large part determined by their institutional position, and in turn, the select values they possess and the characters they acquire.

11

Who Governs? (1961)

Robert A. Dahl

In a political system where nearly every adult may vote but where knowledge, wealth, social position, access to officials, and other resources are unequally distributed, who actually governs?

The question has been asked, I imagine, wherever popular government has developed and intelligent citizens have reached the stage of critical self-consciousness concerning their society. It must have been put many times in Athens even before it was posed by Plato and Aristotle.

The question is peculiarly relevant to the United States and to Americans. In the first place, Americans espouse democratic beliefs with a fervency and a unanimity that have been a regular source of astonishment to foreign observers from Tocqueville and Bryce to Myrdal and Brogan. Not long ago, two American political scientists reported that 96 per cent or more of several hundred registered voters interviewed in two widely separated American cities agreed that: "Democracy is the best form of government" and "Every citizen should have an equal chance to influence government policy," and subscribed to other propositions equally basic to the democratic credo.[1] What, if anything, do these beliefs actually mean in the face of extensive inequalities in the resources different citizens can use to influence one another?

These beliefs in democracy and equality first gained wide acceptance as a part of what Myrdal later called the "American Creed" during a period when the problem of inequality was (if we can disregard for the moment the question of slavery) much less important than it is today. Indeed, the problem uppermost in the minds of the men at the Constitutional Convention in Philadelphia in 1787 could probably have been stated quite the other way around. To men concerned with what was then a unique task of adapting

---

Source: Robert A. Dahl, from *Who Governs?* Copyright © 1961 by Yale University Press. Reprinted by permission of the publisher.

[1] James W. Prothro and Charles M. Grigg, "Fundamental Principles of Democracy: Bases of Agreement and Disagreement," *Journal of Politics*, 22 (1960), 276–94.

republican institutions to a whole nation, the very *equality* in resources of power that American society and geography tended to generate seemed to endanger political stability and liberty. In a society of equals, what checks would there be against an impetuous, unenlightened, or unscrupulous majority? A half century later, this was also the way an amazing and gifted observer, Alexis de Tocqueville, posed the question in probably the most profound analysis of American democracy ever written. For Tocqueville, the United States was the most advanced representative of a new species of society emerging from centuries of development: "In running over the pages of [European] history, we shall scarcely find a single great event of the last seven hundred years that has not promoted equality of condition." So he wrote in the introduction to the first volume of his *Democracy in America*.

> Whither, then, are we tending? [he went on to ask] No one can say, for terms of comparison already fail us. There is greater equality of condition in Christian countries at the present day than there has been at any previous time, in any part of the world, so that the magnitude of what already has been done prevents us from foreseeing what is yet to be accomplished.

In the United States he had looked upon the future, on

> one country in the world where the great social revolution that I am speaking of seems to have nearly reached its natural limits . . . Men are there seen on a greater equality in point of fortune and intellect, or, in other words, more equal in their strength, than in any other country of the world, or in any age of which history has preserved the remembrance.[2]

The America that Tocqueville saw, however, was the America of Andrew Jackson. It was an agrarian democracy, remarkably close to the ideal often articulated by Jefferson.

Commerce, finance, and industry erupted into this agrarian society in a gigantic explosion. By the time the century approached its last decade, and another distinguished foreign observer looked upon the United States, the America of Tocqueville had already passed away. In how many senses of the word, James Bryce asked in 1899, does equality exist in the United States?

> Clearly not as regards material conditions. Sixty years ago there were no great fortunes in America, few large fortunes, no poverty. Now there is some poverty (though only in a few places can it be called pauperism), many large fortunes, and a greater number of gigantic fortunes than in any other country of the world.

He found also an intellectual elite, among whose members the "level of exceptional attainment . . . rises faster than does the general level of the multitude, so that in this regard also it appears that equality has diminished and will diminish further."

---

[2]Alexis de Tocqueville, *Democracy in America* (New York, Vintage Books, 1955), 1, 5, 6, 14, 55.

It was true that in America there were no formal marks of rank in the European sense. However, this did not

> prevent the existence of grades and distinctions in society which, though they may find no tangible expression, are sometimes as sharply drawn as in Europe . . . The nature of a man's occupation, his education, his manners and breeding, his income, his connections, all come into view in determining whether he is in this narrow sense of the word "a gentleman."

Yet, remarkably, the universal belief in equality that Tocqueville had found sixty years earlier still persisted. "It is in this," Bryce wrote, "that the real sense of equality comes out. In America men hold others to be at bottom exactly like themselves." A man may be enormously rich, or a great orator, or a great soldier or writer, "but it is not a reason for bowing down to him, or addressing him in deferential terms, or treating him as if he was porcelain and yourself only earthenware."[3]

Now it has always been held that if equality of power among citizens is possible at all—a point on which many political philosophers have had grave doubts—then surely considerable equality of social conditions is a necessary prerequisite. But if, even in America, with its universal creed of democracy and equality, there are great inequalities in the conditions of different citizens, must there not also be great inequalities in the capacities of different citizens to influence the decisions of their various governments? And if, because they are unequal in other conditions, citizens of a democracy are unequal in power to control their government, then who in fact does govern? How does a "democratic" system work amid inequality of resources? These are the questions I want to explore by examining one urban American community, New Haven, Connecticut.

I have said "explore" because it is obvious that one cannot do more by concentrating on one community. However, New Haven embodies most of the equalities and inequalities that lend this enterprise its significance. In the course of the book, I shall examine various aspects of these that may be related to differences in the extent to which citizens can and do influence local government. But it will not hurt to start putting a little paint on the canvas now.

One might argue whether the political system of New Haven is "democratic" or "truly democratic," but only because these terms are always debatable. In everyday language, New Haven is a democratic political community. Most of its adult residents are legally entitled to vote. A relatively high proportion do vote. Their votes are, by and large, honestly counted—though absentee votes, a small fraction of the total, are occasionally manipulated. Elections are free from violence and, for all practical purposes, free from fraud. Two political parties contest elections, offer rival slates of candidates, and thus present the voters with at least some outward show of choice.

---

[3]James Bryce, *The American Commonwealth* (London, Macmillan, 1889), *2*, 602–03, 606–07.

Running counter to this legal equality of citizens in the voting booth, however, is an unequal distribution of the resources that can be used for influencing the choices of voters and, between elections, of officials. Take property, for example. In 1957, the fifty largest property owners, in number less than one-sixteenth of one per cent of the taxpayers, held nearly one-third of the total assessed value of all real property in the city. Most of the fifty largest property owners were, of course, corporations: public utilities like the United Illuminating Company, which had the largest assessment ($22 million) and the Southern New England Telephone Company ($12 million); big industries like Olin Mathieson ($21 million) which had bought up the Winchester Repeating Arms Company, the famous old New Haven firearms firm; family-held firms like Sargent and A. C. Gilbert; or department stores like the century-old firm of Malley's. Of the fifty largest property owners, sixteen were manufacturing firms, nine were retail and wholesale businesses, six were privately-owned public utilities, and five were banks. Yale University was one of the biggest property owners, though it ranked only tenth in assessed value ($3.6 million) because much of its property was tax-free. A few individuals stood out boldly on the list, like John Day Jackson, the owner and publisher of New Haven's two newspapers.

Or consider family income. In 1949, the average (median) family income in New Haven was about $2,700 a year. One family out of forty had an income of $10,000 or more; over one family out of five had an income of less than $1,000. In the Thirtieth Ward, which had the highest average family income, one family out of four had an income of $7,000 or more; in the Fifth, the poorest, over half the families had incomes of less than $2,000 a year. (Technically, the First Ward was even poorer than the Fifth for half the families there had incomes of less than $700 a year, but three-quarters of the residents of the First were students at Yale.)

The average adult in New Haven had completed the ninth grade, but in the Tenth Ward half the adults had never gone beyond elementary school. About one out of six adults in the city had gone to college. The extremes were represented by the Thirty-first Ward, where nearly half had attended college, and the Twenty-seventh, where the proportion was only one out of thirty.[4]

Thus one is forced back once more to the initial question. Given the existence of inequalities like these, who actually governs in a democracy?

Since the question is not new, one may wonder whether we do not, after all, pretty well know the answer by now. Do we not at least know what answer must be given for the present-day political system of the United States? Unfortunately no. Students of politics have provided a number of conflicting explanations for the way in which democracies can be expected to operate in the

---

[4]Assessments are from the city records. The average ratio of assessed value to actual prices on property sold in 1957 was 49.2, according to the New Haven Taxpayers Research Council, "Assessment of Real Estate," Council Comment, No. 36 (Mar. 9, 1959). Data on incomes and education are from a special tabulation by wards of the data in U.S. Census, Characteristics of the Population, 1950. Income data are estimates by the Census Bureau from a 20% sample.

midst of inequalities in political resources. Some answers are a good deal more optimistic than others. For example, it is sometimes said that political parties provide competition for public office and thereby guarantee a relatively high degree of popular control. By appealing to the voters, parties organize the unorganized, give power to the powerless, present voters with alternative candidates and programs, and insure that during campaigns they have an opportunity to learn about the merits of these alternatives. Furthermore, after the election is over, the victorious party, which now represents the preferences of a majority of voters, takes over the task of governing. The voter, therefore, does not need to participate actively in government; it is enough for him to participate in elections by the simple act of voting. By his vote he registers a preference for the general direction in which government policy should move; he cannot and does not need to choose particular policies. One answer to the question, "Who governs?" is then that competing political parties govern, but they do so with the consent of voters secured by competitive elections.

However, no sooner had observers begun to discover the extraordinary importance of political parties in the operation of democratic political systems than others promptly reduced the political party to little more than a collection of "interest groups," or sets of individuals with some values, purposes, and demands in common. If the parties were the political molecules, the interest groups were the atoms. And everything could be explained simply by studying the atoms. Neither people nor parties but interest groups, it was said, are the true units of the political system. An individual, it was argued, is politically rather helpless, but a group unites the resources of individuals into an effective force. Thus some theorists would answer our question by replying that interest groups govern; most of the actions of government can be explained, they would say, simply as the result of struggles among groups of individuals with differing interests and varying resources of influence.

The first explanation was developed by English and American writers, the second almost entirely by Americans. A third theory, much more pessimistic than the other two, was almost exclusively European in origin, though it subsequently achieved a considerable vogue in the United States. This explanation, which has both a "Left" and a "Right" interpretation, asserts that beneath the façade of democratic politics a social and economic elite will usually be found actually running things. Robert and Helen Lynd used this explanation in their famous two books on "Middletown" (Muncie, Indiana), and many studies since then have also adopted it, most notably Floyd Hunter in his analysis of the "power structure" of Atlanta.[5] Because it fits nicely with the very factors that give rise to our question, the view that a social and economic elite controls government is highly persuasive. Concentration of power in the hands of

---

[5]Robert S. Lynd and Helen M. Lynd, *Middletown* (New York, Harcourt Brace, 1929) and *Middletown in Transition* (New York, Harcourt Brace, 1937). Floyd Hunter *Community Power Structure* (Chapel Hill, University of North Carolina Press, 1953) and *Top Leadership, U.S.A.* (Chapel Hill, University of North Carolina Press, 1959).

an elite is a necessary consequence, in this view, of the enormous inequalities in the distribution of resources of influence—property, income, social status, knowledge, publicity, local position, and all the rest.

One difficulty with all of these explanations was that they left very little room for the politician. He was usually regarded merely as an agent—of majority will, the political parties, interest groups, or the elite. He had no independent influence. But an older view that could be traced back to Machiavelli's famous work, *The Prince,* stressed the enormous political potential of the cunning, resourceful, masterful leader. In this view, majorities, parties, interest groups, elites, even political systems are all to some extent pliable; a leader who knows how to use his resources to the maximum is not so much the agent of others as others are his agents. Although a gifted political entrepreneur might not exist in every political system, wherever he appeared he would make himself felt.

Still another view commingled elements of all the rest. This explanation was set out by Tocqueville as a possible course of degeneration in all democratic orders, restated by the Spanish philosopher, Ortega y Gassett, in his highly influential book, *The Revolt of the Masses* (1930), and proposed by a number of European intellectuals, after the destruction of the German Republic by Nazism, as an explanation for the origins of modern dictatorships. Although it is a theory proposed mainly by Europeans about European conditions, it is so plausible an alternative that we cannot afford to ignore it. Essentially, this theory (which has many variants) argues that under certain conditions of development (chiefly industrialization and urbanization) older, stratified, class-based social structures are weakened or destroyed; and in their place arises a mass of individuals with no secure place in the social system, rootless, aimless, lacking strong social ties, ready and indeed eager to attach themselves to any political entrepreneur who will cater to their tastes and desires. Led by unscrupulous and exploitative leaders, these rootless masses have the capacity to destroy whatever stands in their way without the ability to replace it with a stable alternative. Consequently the greater their influence on politics, the more helpless they become; the more they destroy, the more they depend upon strong leaders to create some kind of social, economic, and political organization to replace the old. If we ask, "Who governs?" the answer is not the mass nor its leaders but both together; the leaders cater to mass tastes and in return use the strength provided by the loyalty and obedience of the masses to weaken and perhaps even to annihilate all opposition to their rule.

A superficial familiarity with New Haven (or for that matter with almost any modern American city) would permit one to argue persuasively that each of these theories really explains the inner workings of the city's political life. However, a careful consideration of the points at which the theories diverge suggests that the broad question, "Who governs?" might be profitably subdivided into a number of more specific questions. These questions, listed below, have guided the study of New Haven recorded in this book:

Are inequalities in resources of influence "cumulative" or "noncumulative?" That is, are people who are better off in one resource also better off in others? In other words, does the way in which political resources are distributed encourage oligarchy or pluralism?

How are important political decisions actually made?

What kinds of people have the greatest influence on decisions? Are different kinds of decisions all made by the same people? From what strata of the community are the most influential people, the leaders, drawn?

Do leaders tend to cohere in their policies and form a sort of ruling group, or do they tend to divide, conflict, and bargain? Is the pattern of leadership, in short, oligarchical or pluralistic?

What is the relative importance of the most widely distributed political resource—the right to vote? Do leaders respond generally to the interests of the few citizens with the greatest wealth and highest status—or do they respond to the many with the largest number of votes? To what extent do various citizens use their political resources? Are there important differences that in turn result in differences in influence?

Are the patterns of influence durable or changing? For example, was democracy stronger in New Haven when Tocqueville contemplated the American scene? And in more recent years, as New Haven has grappled with a gigantic program of urban reconstruction, what has happened to popular control and to patterns of leadership? In general, what are the sources of change and stability in the political system?

Finally, how important is the nearly universal adherence to the "American Creed" of democracy and equality? Is the operation of the political system affected in any way by what ordinary citizens believe or profess to believe about democracy? If so, how?

12

American Business, Public Policy, Case-Studies, and Political Theory (1963–1964)

Theodore J. Lowi

Raymond A. Bauer, Ithiel de Sola Pool, and Lewis A. Dexter, *American Business and Public Policy: The Politics of Foreign Trade*, New York, Atherton Press, 1963, 499 pp. $8.95.

Case-Studies of the policy-making process constitute one of the more important methods of political science analysis. Beginning with Schattschneider, Herring, and others in the 1930's, case-studies have been conducted on a great variety of decisions. They have varied in subject-matter and format, in scope and rigor, but they form a distinguishable body of literature which continues to grow year by year. The most recent addition, a book-length study by Raymond Bauer and his associates, stands with Robert A. Dahl's prize-winning *Who Governs?* (New Haven 1961) as the best yet to appear. With its publication a new level of sophistication has been reached. The standards of research its authors have set will indeed be difficult to uphold in the future. *American Business and Public Policy* is an analysis of political relationships within the context of a single, well-defined issue—foreign trade. It is an analysis of business attitudes, strategies, communications and, through these, business relationships in politics. The analysis makes use of the best behavioral research techniques without losing sight of the rich context of policies, traditions, and institutions. Thus, it does not, in Dahl's words, exchange relevance for rigor; rather it is standing proof that the two—relevance and rigor—are not mutually exclusive goals.

Source: Theodore J. Lowi, from "American Business, Public Policy, Case-Studies, and Political Theory," *World Politics* 16:4 (1964), 677–681; 689–693; 695; 697; 699; 701; 703; 705; 707; 709; 711; 713; 715. Copyright © The John Hopkins University Press. Reprinted with permission of The John Hopkins University Press.

But what do all the case-studies, including *American Business and Public Policy*, add up to? As a result of these case materials, how much farther along the road of political theory are we? What questions have the authors of these studies raised, and what non-obvious hypotheses and generalizations about "who rules and why" would we have lacked without them?[1] Because of what it does, what it implies and what it does not do, *American Business and Public Policy* provides a proper occasion for asking these questions and for attempting once again to formulate theories that will convert the discrete facts of the case-studies into elements that can be assessed, weighed, and cumulated. But, first, what theories have we now, and how does this significant new study relate to them?

I. Existing Notions:
The Non-Theories of Power in America

It was inevitable that some general notions about power and public policy would develop out of the case-study literature. Together, these notions form what is variously called the group theory, the pressure-group, or the pluralist model of the democratic political system (a model recently also applied to non-democratic systems). No theory or approach has ever come closer to defining and unifying the field of political science than pluralism, perhaps because it fitted so nicely both the outlook of revered Federalist #10 and the observables of the New Deal. Group theory provided a rationale for the weakness of parties and the electoral process. It provided an appropriate defense for the particular programs pursued by the New Deal and successive Administrations. And, more importantly, it seemed to provide an instant explanation, in more or less generalizable terms, of the politics of each decision. Analysis requires simply an inventory of the group participants and their strategies, usually in chronological form—for, after all, politics is a process. Each group participant is a *datum*, and power is attributed in terms of inferred patterns of advantage and indulgence in the final decision. The extremists have treated government ("formal institutions") as a *tabula rasa*, with policy as the residue of the "interplay of forces" measurable as a "parallelogram." More sophisticated analysts avoided the government-as-blank-key approach by treating officials as simply other units in the group process, where Congressman and bureaucrat were brokers but with their own interests and resources.

In group theory, all resources are treated as equivalent and interchangeable. And all the varieties of interaction among groups and between groups and officials are also treated as equivalent, to such an extent that only one term is employed for all forms of political interaction: the *coalition*. Coalitions, so the argument goes, form around "shared attitudes" and are extended by expansion of the stakes of the controversy. Two types of strategies comprise the

---

[1] For similar question's and a critique, see Herbert Kaufman, "The Next Step in Case Studies," *Public Administration Review*, XVIII (Winter 1958), 52–59.

dynamics of the process: internal and external. The first refers to the problem of cohesion in the midst of overlapping memberships; cohesion is a determinant of full use of group resources. The second refers to expansion of the coalition and the strategy of its use. Large coalitions beat small coalitions. System equilibrium (of unquestionably high-priority value to pluralists) is maintained by the requirement of majority-size coalitions, which are extremely difficult to create but which must be created virtually from scratch for each issue. Thus, power is highly decentralized, fluid, and situational. There is no single elite, but a "multicentered" system in which the centers exist in a conflict-and-bargaining relation to each other.

As an argument that the group must be the major unit of analysis, pluralism excites little controversy. But controversy is unavoidable insofar as the pluralist model implies a theory of power or power distribution. Most importantly, the pluralist model has, until recently, failed to take into account the general economic *and* political structure within which the group process takes place.[2] On this basis, the leading type of critique of the pluralist model is a set of explicit propositions about power structure and elites. The typical answer to pluralism is a straightforward Marxian assumption that there is a one-for-one relation between socio-economic status and power over public decisions. Perhaps the more sophisticated version is a combination Marx-Weber approach which specifies the particular status bases most closely related to power—i.e., the major "orders" of society (*ständen*) in our day are the military, the industrial, and the political hierarchies.

This is no place to enter into an elaborate critique of either of these approaches or of the pluralist approach itself. Suffice it to say that while the pluralist model has failed to take the abiding, institutional factors sufficiently into account, the "social stratification" and "power elite" schools wrongly assume a simple relation between status and power. Both these latter schools mistake the resources of power for power itself, and escape analytic and empirical problems by the route of definition.[3] There is no denying, however, that the social-stratification or power-elite approaches can explain *certain* important outcomes in a more intuitively satisfactory manner than the pluralist model precisely because each emphasizes that, while coalition-forming may be universal, not all coalitions are equivalent. For certain types of issues (without accepting Mills's argument that these are all the "key" issues), it seems clear that decisions are made by high public and private "officials" in virtually a public

---

[2]David Truman's rather weak and diffuse "potential interest group" is a doff of the hat in this direction, but this concept is so non-directive and non-observable as to be disregarded even by its creator.

[3]The best critiques and analyses of all the various currents of thought are found in Nelson W. Polsby, *Community Power and Political Theory* (New Haven 1963); Daniel Bell, "The Power Elite—Revisited," *American Journal of Sociology*, LXIV (November 1958), 238–50; Robert A. Dahl, "Critique of the Ruling Elite Model," *American Political Science Review*, LII (June 1958), 463–69; and Raymond Wolfinger, "Reputation and Reality in the Study of Community Power," *American Sociological Review*, XXV (October 1960), 636–44.

opinion and interest-group opinion vacuum. One does not have to go all the way with Mills and insist that behind all apparent conflict there is an elite whose members all agree on specific major policy goals as well as long-range aims. But the pluralist is equally unwise who refuses to recognize that "command post" positions in all orders of society are highly legitimate, and that the recruitment and grooming of these institutional leaders make possible a reduction in the number of basic conflicts among them, and equally possible (1) many stable and abiding agreements on policy, (2) accommodation to conflict by more formal, hierarchical means ("through channels") than coalition politics, and (3) settlement of conflict by more informal means (i.e., among gentlemen, without debates and votes) that maintain the leaders' legitimacy and stability.

There is still a third approach to power and policy-making, no less important than the others, which has not been self-consciously employed since its creation in 1935 because it was mistakenly taken as a case of pluralism. I refer to E. E. Schattschneider's conclusions in *Politics, Pressures and the Tariff* (New York 1935). Schattschneider observed a multiplicity of groups in a decentralized and bargaining arena, but the nature of relations among participants was not in the strictest sense pluralistic. The pluralist model stresses conflict and conflict resolution through bargaining among groups and coalitions organized around shared interests. The elitists stress conflict *reduction* among formal officeholders in a much more restricted, centralized, and stable arena. What Schattschneider saw was neither, but contained elements of both. His political arena was decentralized and multicentered, but relationships among participants were based upon "mutual non-interference" among uncommon interests. The "power structure" was stabilized toward the "command posts" (in this case, the House Ways and Means Committee), not because the officials were above pressure groups, but because the pattern of access led to supportive relations between pressure groups and officials. What may appear to one observer as evidence of a power elite appears to another as decentralized pluralism (to such an extent, indeed, that Schattschneider is often credited with an important share in the founding of pluralist political analysis). Schattschneider's masterful case-study actually reveals neither. At one point he concludes: "A policy that is so hospitable and catholic as the protective tariff disorganizes the opposition."[4] In many important cases completely unrelated to the tariff and much more recent than 1930, we can find plenty of evidence to support this third or fourth[5] approach to a "theory" of power and policy-making. But as

---

[4] *Politics, Pressures and the Tariff*, 88. The fact that Schattschneider holds his generalizations to the particular policy in question should be noted here as a point central to my later arguments.

[5] There are four approaches here if the "social stratification" school is kept separate from the "power elite" school. While both make the same kinds of errors, each leads to different kinds of propositions. In some hands they are, of course, indistinguishable and, for good reason, Polsby in *Community Power and Political Theory* treats the two as one. Since the distinction, once made, is not important here, I will more or less follow Polsby's lead.

a general theory Schattschneider's conclusions would be no more satisfactory than any one approach identified earlier.

The main trouble with all these approaches is that they do not generate related propositions that can be tested by research and experience. Moreover, the findings of studies based upon any one of them are not cumulative. Finally, in the absence of logical relations between the "theory" and the propositions, the "theory" becomes self-directing and self-supportive. This is why I have employed the term "theory" only with grave reservations and quotation marks.

The pluralist approach has generated case-study after case-study that "proves" the model with findings directed by the approach itself. Issues are chosen for research because conflict made them public; group influence is found because in public conflict groups participate whether they are influential or not. Group influence can be attributed because groups so often share in the *definition* of the issue and have taken positions that are more or less directly congruent with the outcomes. An indulged group was influential, and a deprived group was uninfluential; but that leaves no room for group irrelevancy. . . .

Obviously, the major analytic problem is that of identifying types of outputs or policies. The approach I have taken is to define policies in terms of their impact or expected impact on the society. When policies are defined this way, there are only a limited number of types; when all is said and done, there are only a limited number of functions that governments can perform. This approach cashiers the "politics of agriculture" and the "politics of education" or, even more narrowly but typically, "the politics of the ARA bill" or "the politics of the 1956 Aid to Education bill," in which the composition and strategy of the participants are fairly well-known before the study is begun. But it maintains the pluralist's resistance to the assumption that there is only one power structure for every political system. My approach replaces the descriptive, subject-matter categories of the pluralists with functional categories. There is no need to argue that the classification scheme exhausts all the possibilities even among domestic policies; it is sufficient if most policies and the agencies that implement them can be categorized with little, if any, damage to the nuances.

There are three major categories of public policies in the scheme: distribution, regulation, and redistribution. These types are historically as well as functionally distinct, distribution being almost the exclusive type of national domestic policy from 1789 until virtually 1890. Agitation for regulatory and redistributive policies began at about the same time, but regulation had become an established fact before any headway at all was made in redistribution.[6]

---

[6]Foreign policy, for which no appropriate "-tion" word has been found, is obviously a fourth category. It is not dealt with here for two reasons. First, it overly extends the analysis. Second, and of greater importance, it is in many ways not part of the same universe, because in foreign policy-making America is only a subsystem. Winston Churchill, among other foreigners, has consistently participated in our foreign policy decisions. Of course, those aspects of foreign and military policy that have direct domestic implications are included in my scheme.

These categories are not mere contrivances for purposes of simplification. They are meant to correspond to real phenomena—so much so that the major hypotheses of the scheme follow directly from the categories and their definitions. Thus, *these areas of policy or government activity constitute real arenas of power.* Each arena tends to develop its own characteristic political structure, political process, elites, and group relations. What remains is to identify these arenas, to formulate hypotheses about the attributes of each, and to test the scheme by how many empirical relationships it can anticipate and explain.

Areas of Policy Defined

(1) In the long run, all governmental policies may be considered redistributive, because in the long run some people pay in taxes more than they receive in services. Or, all may be thought regulatory because, in the long run, a governmental decision on the use of resources can only displace a private decision about the same resource or at least reduce private alternatives about the resource. But politics works in the short run, and in the short run certain kinds of government decisions can be made without regard to limited resources. Policies of this kind are called "distributive," a term first coined for nineteenth century land policies, but easily extended to include most contemporary public land and resource policies; rivers and harbors ("pork barrel") programs; defense procurement and R & D; labor, business, and agricultural "clientele" services; and the traditional tariff. Distributive policies are characterized by the ease with which they can be disaggregated and dispensed unit by small unit, each unit more or less in isolation from other units and from any general rule. "Patronage" in the fullest meaning of the word can be taken as a synonym for "distributive." These are policies that are virtually not policies at all but are highly individualized decisions that only by accumulation can be called a policy. They are policies in which the indulged and the deprived, the loser and the recipient, need never come into direct confrontation. Indeed, in many instances of distributive policy, the deprived cannot as a class be identified, because the most influential among them can be accommodated by further disaggregation of the stakes.

(2) Regulatory policies are also specific and individual in their impact, but they are not capable of the almost infinite amount of disaggregation typical of distributive policies. Although the laws are stated in general terms ("Arrange the transportation system artistically." "Thou shalt not show favoritism in pricing."), the impact of regulatory decisions is clearly one of directly raising costs and/or reducing or expanding the alternatives of private individuals ("Get off the grass!" "Produce kosher if you advertise kosher!"). Regulatory policies are distinguishable from distributive in that in the short run the regulatory decision involves a direct choice as to who will be indulged and who deprived. Not all applicants for a single television channel or an overseas air route can be propitiated. Enforcement of an unfair labor practice on the part of management weakens management in its dealings with labor. So, while implementation is

firm-by-firm and case-by-case, policies cannot be disaggregated to the level of the individual or the single firm (as in distribution), because individual decisions must be made by application of a general rule and therefore become interrelated within the broader standards of law. Decisions cumulate among all individuals affected by the law in roughly the same way. Since the most stable lines of perceived common impact are the basic sectors of the economy, regulatory decisions are cumulative largely along sectoral lines; regulatory policies are usually disaggregable only down to the sector level.[7]

(3) Redistributive policies are like regulatory policies in the sense that relations among broad categories of private individuals are involved and, hence, individual decisions must be interrelated. But on all other counts there are great differences in the nature of impact. The categories of impact are much broader, approaching social classes. They are, crudely speaking, haves and have-nots, bigness and smallness, bourgeoisie and proletariat. The aim involved is not use of property but property itself, not equal treatment but equal possession, not behavior but being. The fact that our income tax is in reality only mildly redistributive does not alter the fact of the aims and the stakes involved in income tax policies. The same goes for our various "welfare state" programs, which are redistributive only for those who entered retirement or unemployment rolls without having contributed at all. The nature of a redistributive issue is not determined by the outcome of a battle over how redistributive a policy is going to be. Expectations about what it *can* be, what it threatens to be, are determinative.

Arenas of Power

Once one posits the general tendency of these areas of policy or governmental activity to develop characteristic political structures, a number of hypotheses become compelling. And when the various hypotheses are accumulated, the general contours of each of the three arenas begin quickly to resemble, respectively, the three "general" theories of political process identified earlier. The arena that develops around distributive policies is best characterized in the terms of Schattschneider's findings. The regulatory arena corresponds to the pluralist school, and the school's general notions are found to be limited

---

[7]A "sector" refers to any set of common or substitutable commodities or services or any other form of established economic interaction. Sectors therefore vary in size because of natural economic forces and because of the different ways they are identified by economists or businessmen. They vary in size also because they are sometimes defined *a priori* by the observer's assessment of what constitutes a common product and at other times are defined *a posteriori* by the trade associations that represent the identification of a sector by economic actors themselves.

pretty much to this one arena. The redistributive arena most closely approximates, with some adaptation, an elitist view of the political process.

(1) The distributive arena can be identified in considerable detail from Schattschneider's case-study alone. What he and his pluralist successors did not see was that the traditional structure of tariff politics is also in largest part the structure of politics of all those diverse policies identified earlier as distributive. The arena is "pluralistic" only in the sense that a large number of small, intensely organized interests are operating. In fact, there is even greater multiplicity of participants here than the pressure-group model can account for, because essentially it is a politics of every man for himself. The single person and the single firm are the major activists. Bauer, Pool, and Dexter, for instance, are led to question seriously the "pressure-group model" because of the ineffectiveness of virtually all the groups that should have been most active and effective.

Although a generation removed, Schattschneider's conclusions about the politics of the Smoot-Hawley Tariff are almost one-for-one applicable to rivers and harbors and land development policies, tax exemptions, defense procurement, area redevelopment, and government "services." Since there is no real basis for discriminating between those who should and those who should not be protected [indulged], says Schattschneider, Congress seeks political support by "giving a limited protection [indulgence] to all interests strong enough to furnish formidable resistance." Decision-makers become "responsive to considerations of equality, consistency, impartiality, uniformity, precedent, and moderation, however formal and insubstantial these may be."[8] Furthermore, a "policy that is so hospitable and catholic . . . disorganizes the opposition."[9]

When a billion-dollar issue can be disaggregated into many millions of nickel-dime items and each item can be dealt with without regard to the others, multiplication of interests and of access is inevitable, and so is reduction of conflict. All of this has the greatest of bearing on the relations among participants and, therefore, the "power structure." Indeed, coalitions must be built to pass legislation and "make policy," but what of the nature and basis of the coalitions? In the distributive arena, political relationships approximate what Schattschneider called "mutual non-interference"—"a mutuality under which it is proper for each to seek duties [indulgences] for himself but improper and unfair to oppose duties [indulgences] sought by others."[10] In the area of rivers and harbors, references are made to "pork barrel" and "log-rolling," but these colloquialisms have not been taken sufficiently seriously. A log-rolling coalition is not one forged of conflict, compromise, and tangential interest but, on the contrary, one composed of members who have absolutely nothing in common; and this is possible because the "pork barrel" is a container for unrelated items. This is the typical form of relationship in the distributive arena.

---

[8] *Politics, Pressures,* 85.
[9] *Ibid.,* 88.
[10] *Ibid.,* 135–36.

The structure of these log-rolling relationships leads typically, though not always, to Congress; and the structure is relatively stable because all who have access of any sort usually support whoever are the leaders. And there tend to be "elites" of a peculiar sort in the Congressional committees whose jurisdictions include the subject-matter in question. Until recently, for instance, on tariff matters the House Ways and Means Committee was virtually the government. Much the same can be said for Public Works on rivers and harbors.[11] It is a broker leadership, but "policy" is best understood as cooptation rather than conflict and compromise. . . .

Distributive issues individualize conflict and provide the basis for highly stable coalitions that are virtually irrelevant to the larger policy outcomes; thousands of obscure decisions are merely accumulated into a "policy" of protection or of natural-resources development or of defense subcontracting. And Congress did not "give up" the tariff; as the tariff became a matter of regulation (see below), committee elites lost their power to contain the participants because obscure decisions became interrelated, therefore less obscure, and more controversy became built in and unavoidable.[12]

(2) The regulatory arena could hardly be better identified than in the thousands of pages written for the whole polity by the pluralists. But, unfortunately, some translation is necessary to accommodate pluralism to its more limited universe. The regulatory arena appears to be composed of a multiplicity of groups organized around tangential relations or David Truman's "shared attitudes." Within this narrower context of regulatory decisions, one can even go so far as to accept the most extreme pluralist statement that policy tends to be a residue of the interplay of group conflict. This statement can be severely criticized only by use of examples drawn from non-regulatory decisions.

As I argued before, there is no way for regulatory policies to be disaggregated into very large numbers of unrelated items. Because individual regulatory decisions involve direct confrontations of indulged and deprived, the typical political coalition is born of conflict and compromise among tangential interests that usually involve a total sector of the economy. Thus, while the typical basis for coalition in distributive politics is uncommon interests

---

[11]The stable, intimate interlocking of Congressional committeemen and their support groups in the Rivers and Harbors Congress and the Corps of Engineers has been made famous by Arthur Maass; see *Muddy Waters: The Army Engineers and the Nation's Rivers* (Cambridge, Mass., 1951), and especially "Congress and Water Resources," *American Political Science Review*, XLIV (September 1950), 576–92, reprinted in my reader, *Legislative Politics USA* (Boston 1962). Cited widely as an example of interest-group strategy and access, this case has not until now, as far as I know, been given its proper significance. That significance comes clear within my scheme. The pattern approaches that of the tariff but not of regulatory situations.

[12]Schattschneider, in his more recent book *The Semi-sovereign People* (New York 1960), offers some fascinating propositions about the "scope of conflict" which can easily be subsumed within the scheme offered here.

(log-rolling), an entirely different basis is typical in regulatory politics. The pluralist went wrong only in assuming the regulatory type of coalition is *the* coalition . . . .[13]

Owing to the unrelatedness of issues in distributive politics, the activities of single participants need not be related but rather can be specialized as the situation warrants it. But the relatedness of regulatory issues, at least up to the sector level of the trade association, leads to the containment of all these within the association and, therefore, to the dynamic situation ascribed erroneously by Truman to all intergroup relations in all issues. When all the stakes are contained in one organization, constituents have no alternative but to fight against each other to shape the policies of that organization or actually to abandon it.

What this suggests is that the typical power structure in regulatory politics is far less stable than that in the distributive arena. Since coalitions form around shared interests, the coalitions will shift as the interests change or as conflicts of interest emerge. With such group-based and shifting patterns of conflict built into every regulatory issue, it is in most cases impossible for a Congressional committee, an administrative agency, a peak association governing board, or a social elite to contain all the participants long enough to establish a stable power elite. Policy outcomes seem inevitably to be the residue remaining after all the reductions of demands by all participants have been made in order to extend support to majority size. But a majority-sized coalition of shared interests on one issue could not possibly be entirely appropriate for some other issue. In regulatory decision-making, relationships among group leadership elements and between them on any one or more points of governmental access are too unstable to form a single policy-making elite. As a consequence, decision-making tends to pass from administrative agencies and Congressional committees to Congress, the place where uncertainties in the policy process have always been settled. Congress as an institution is the last resort for breakdowns in bargaining over policy, just as in the case of parties the primary is a last resort for breakdowns in bargaining over nominations. No one leadership group can contain the conflict by an almost infinite subdivision and distribution of the stakes. In the regulatory political

---

[13]I was surprised and pleased on rereading Truman's *The Governmental Process* (New York 1951), after completing the first draft of this article, to find that he identified two types of "mutual assistance," alliances and log-rolling (pp. 362–68). In my scheme, as will soon be clear, there are two types of "alliance," tangential interest and ideology. But what is of interest here is that Truman supports his distinction with examples perfectly congruent with my theory. His case of the alliance is the aggregation of interests around the 1946 Employment Act (redistribution, even if a peculiar "law"). The typical log-rolling situation he identifies with rivers and harbors appropriations (distribution). The difference between us is that my scheme considers these patterns of coalition as revealing fundamental political relations that are limited to certain types of issues, while Truman implies that they are two strategies in an inventory of strategies more or less appropriate to any issue.

process, Congress and the "balance of power" seem to play the classic role attributed to them by the pluralists. . . .

Beginning with reciprocity in the 1930's, the tariff began to lose its capacity for infinite disaggregation because it slowly underwent redefinition, moving away from its purely domestic significance towards that of an instrument of international politics. In brief, the tariff, especially following World War II and our assumption of peacetime international leadership, became a means of regulating the domestic economy for international purposes. The significant feature here is not the international but the regulatory part of the redefinition. As the process of redefinition took place, a number of significant shifts in power relations took place as well, because it was no longer possible to deal with each dutiable item in isolation. . . . The political problem of the South was the concentration of textile industry there. Coal, oil, and rails came closer and closer to coalition. The final shift came with the 1962 Trade Expansion Act, which enabled the President for the first time to deal with broad categories (to the sector) rather than individual commodities.

Certain elements of distributive politics remain, for two obvious reasons. First, there are always efforts on the part of political leaders to disaggregate policies because this is the best way to spread the patronage and to avoid conflict. (Political actors, like economic actors, probably view open competition as a necessary evil or a last resort to be avoided at almost any cost.) Second, until 1962, the basic tariff law and schedules were still contained in the Smoot-Hawley Act. This act was amended by Reciprocal Trade but only to the extent of allowing negotiated reductions rather than reductions based on comparative costs. Until 1962, tariff politics continued to be based on commodity-by-commodity transactions, and thus until then tariff coalitions could be based upon individual firms (or even branches of large and diversified firms) and log-rolling, unrelated interests. The escape clause and peril point were maintained in the 1950's so that transactions could be made on individual items even within reciprocity. And the coalitions of strange bedfellows continued: "Offered the proper coalition, they both [New England textiles and Eastern railroads] might well have been persuaded that their interest was in the opposite direction" (p. 398).

But despite the persistence of certain distributive features, the true nature of tariff in the 1960's emerges as regulatory policy with a developing regulatory arena. Already we can see some changes in Congress even more clearly than the few already observed in the group structure. Out of a committee (House Ways and Means) elite, we can see the emergence of Congress in a pluralist setting. Even as early as 1954–1955, the compromises eventually ratified by Congress were worked out, not in committee through direct cooptation of interests, but in the Randall Commission, a collection of the major interests in conflict (p. 47). Those issues that could not be thrashed out through the "group process" also could not be thrashed out in committee but had to pass on to Congress and the floor. After 1954 the battle centered on major categories of goods (even to the extent of a textile management-union entente) and the battle took place more or less openly on the floor (e.g., pp. 60, 62, and 67).

The weakening of the Ways and Means Committee as the tariff elite is seen in the fact that in 1955 Chairman Cooper was unable to push a closed rule through. The Rules Committee, "in line with tradition," granted a closed rule but the House voted it down 207–178 (p. 63).[14] Bauer, Pool, and Dexter saw this as a victory for protectionism, but it is also evidence of the emerging regulatory arena—arising from the difficulty of containing conflict and policy within the governing committee. The last effort to keep the tariff as a traditional instrument of distributive politics—a motion by Reed to recommit, with instructions to write in a provision that Tariff Commission rulings under the escape clause be final except where the President finds the national security to be involved—was voted down 206–199 (pp. 64–65). After that, right up to 1962, it was clear that tariff decisions would not be made piecemeal. Tariff became a regulatory policy in 1962; all that remains of distributive politics now are quotas and subsidies for producers of specific commodities injured by general tariff reductions.

(3) If Bauer, Pool, and Dexter had chosen a line of cases from the redistributive arena for their intensive analysis, most assuredly they would have found themselves in an altogether different universe, proposing different generalizations, expressing different doubts. The same would have been true of Schattschneider and of the pluralist students of regulatory cases. Compared particularly with the regulatory area, very few case-studies of redistributive decisions have ever been published. This in itself is a significant datum— which Mills attributes to the middle-level character of the issues that have gotten attention. But, whatever the reasons, it reduces the opportunities for elaborating upon and testing the scheme. Most of the propositions to follow are illustrated by a single case, the "welfare state" battle of the 1930's. But this case is a complex of many decisions that became one of the most important acts of policy ever achieved in the United States. A brief review of the facts of the case will be helpful.[15] Other cases will be referred to in less detail from time to time.

As the 1934 mid-term elections approached, pressures for a federal social security system began to mount. The Townsend Plan and the Lundeen Bill had become nationally prominent and were gathering widespread support. Both schemes were severely redistributive, giving all citizens access to government-

---

[14]Sam Rayburn made one of his rare trips from rostrum to floor to support the closed rule and the integrity of Ways and Means: "Only once in the history of the House, in forty-two years in my memory, has a bill *of this kind and character* been considered except under a closed rule . . ." (p. 64, emphasis added). It was on the following morning that Rayburn expressed his now-famous warning to the frosh: "If you want to get along, go along" (p. 64).

[15]The facts and events are taken from Paul H. Douglas, *Social Security in the United States* (New York 1936); Edwin E. Witte, *The Development of the Social Security Act* (Madison, Wis., 1962); Committee on Economic Security, *Report to the President* (Washington, GPO, 1935); and Frances Perkins, *The Roosevelt I Knew* (New York 1946).

based insurance as a matter of right. In response, the President created in June of 1934 a Committee on Economic Security (CES) composed of top cabinet members with Secretary of Labor Perkins as chairman. In turn, they set up an Advisory Council and a Technical Board, which held hearings, conducted massive studies, and emerged on January 17, 1935, with a bill. The insiders around the CES were representatives of large industries, business associations, unions, and the most interested government bureaucracies. And the detailed legislative histories reveal that virtually all of the debate was contained within the CES and its committees until a mature bill emerged. Since not all of the major issues had been settled in the CES's bill, its members turned to Congress with far from a common front. But the role of Congress was still not what would have been expected. Except for a short fight over committee jurisdiction (won by the more conservative Finance and Ways and Means committees) the legislative process was extraordinarily quiet, despite the import of the issues. Hearings in both Houses brought forth very few witnesses, and these were primarily CES members supporting the bill, and Treasury Department officials, led by Morgenthau, opposing it with "constructive criticism."

The Congressional battle was quiet because the real struggle was taking place elsewhere, essentially between the Hopkins-Perkins bureaucracies and the Treasury. The changes made in the CES bill had all been proposed by Morgenthau (the most important one being the principle of contribution, which took away the redistributive sting). And the final victory for Treasury and mild redistribution came with the removal of administrative responsibility from both Labor and Hopkins's FERA. Throughout all of this some public expressions of opinion were to be heard from the peak associations, but their efforts were mainly expended in the quieter proceedings in the bureaucracies. The Congress's role seems largely to have been one of ratifying agreements that arose out of the bureaucracies and the class agents represented there. Revisions attributable to Congress concerned such matters as exceptions in coverage, which are part of the distributive game that Congress plays at every opportunity. The *principle* of the Act was set in an interplay involving (quietly) top executives and business and labor leaders.

With only slight changes in the left-right positions of the participants, the same pattern has been observed in income tax decisions.[16] Professor Surrey notes: "The question, 'Who speaks for tax equity and tax fairness?,' is answered today largely in terms of only the Treasury Department" (p. 1164). "Thus, in tax bouts . . . it is the Treasury versus percentage legislation, the Treasury versus capital gains, the Treasury versus this constituent, the Treasury versus that private group. . . . As a consequence, the congressman . . . [sees] a dispute . . . only as a contest between a private group and a government department" (pp. 1165–66). Congress, says Surrey, "occupies the role of mediator between the tax views of the executive and the demands of the pressure

[16]Stanley S. Surrey, "The Congress and the Tax Lobbyist: How Special Tax Provisions Get Enacted," *Harvard Law Review*, LXX (May 1957), 1145–82.

groups" (p. 1154). And when the tax issues "are at a major political level, as are tax rates or personal exemptions, then pressure groups, labor organizations, the Chamber of Commerce, the National Association of Manufacturers, and the others, become concerned" (p. 1166). The "average congressman does not basically believe in the present income tax in the upper brackets" (p. 1150), but rather than touch the principle he deals in "special hardship" and "penalizing" and waits for decisions on principle to come from abroad. Amidst the 1954–1955 tax controversies, for example, Ways and Means members decided to allow each member one bill to be favorably reported if the bill met with unanimous agreement (p. 1157).

Issues that involve[17] redistribution cut closer than any others along class lines and activate interests in what are roughly class terms. If there is ever any cohesion within the peak associations, it occurs on redistributive issues, and their rhetoric suggests that they occupy themselves most of the time with these.[18] In a ten-year period just before and after, but not including, the war years, the Manufacturers' Association of Connecticut, for example, expressed itself overwhelmingly more often on redistributive than on any other types of issues.[19] Table 1 summarizes the pattern, showing that expressions on generalized issues involving basic relations between bourgeoisie and proletariat outnumbered expressions on regulation of business practices by 870 to 418, despite the larger number of issues in the latter category.[20] This pattern goes contrary to the one observed by Bauer, Pool, and Dexter in tariff politics, where they discovered, much to their surprise, that self-interest did not activate both "sides" equally. Rather, they found, the concreteness and specificity of protectionist interests activated them much more often and intensely than did the general, ideological position of the liberal-traders (pp. 192–93). This was

---

[17]"Involve" may appear to be a weasel word, but it is used advisedly. As I argued earlier when defining redistribution, it is not the actual outcomes but the expectations as to what the outcomes *can be* that shape the issues and determine their politics. One of the important strategies in any controversial issue is to attempt to define it in redistributive terms in order to broaden the base of opposition or support.

[18]In personal conversations, Andrew Biemiller of AFL-CIO has observed that this is true even of his group. He estimates that perhaps from 80 to 90 per cent of their formal policy expressions deal with welfare and general rights of collective bargaining and that only occasionally does the central board touch specific regulatory issues.

[19]Robert E. Lane, *The Regulation of Businessmen* (New Haven 1953), 38ff.

[20]Note also in the table the fairly drastic contrast in the proportion of references that expressed approval. Similarly drastic differences are revealed in Lane's figures on the reasons given for expressing disapproval. On those issues I call redistributive, the overwhelmingly most important reason is "coerciveness." In contrast, this reason was given for about 10 per cent of general trade regulation and anti-trust references, 3 per cent of the basing-point negative references, and not once when Miller-Tydings and Robinson-Patman were denounced. For regulatory issues, the reason for disapproval given most frequently was that the policy was confused and that it failed to achieve its purposes. And there were equally high percentages of residual or "other" responses, suggesting a widespread lack of agreement as to the very meaning of the policy.

Table I Published Expressions of Manufacturers' Association of Connecticut on Selected Issues

		Number of References in Ten-year Period (1934–40, 1946–48)	Per Cent of Favorable References
1.	Unspecified regulation	378	7.7%
2.	Labor relations, general	297	0.0
3.	Wages and hours	195	0.5
	Total expressions, redistribution	870	
4.	Trade practices	119	13.8
5.	Robinson-Patman	103	18.4
6.	Anti-trust	72	26.4
7.	Basing points	55	20.0
8.	Fair-trade (Miller-Tydings)	69	45.5
	Total expressions, regulation	418	

Source: Lane, *Regulation of Businessmen*, 38ff. The figures are his; their arrangement is mine.

true in tariff, as they say, because there the "structure of the communications system favored the propagation of particular demands" (p. 191). But there is also a structure of communications favoring generalized and ideological demands; this structure consists of the peak associations (which were seen as ineffective in tariffs—pp. 334, 335–36, 337–38, and 340); and it is highly effective when the issues are generalizable. This is the case consistently for redistributive issues, almost never for distributive issues, and only seldom for regulatory issues.

As the pluralists would argue, there will be a vast array of organized interests for any item on the policy agenda. But the relations among the interests and between them and government vary, and the nature of and conditions for this variation are what our political analyses should be concerned with. Let us say, in brief, that on Monday night the big associations meet in agreement and considerable cohesion on "the problem of government," the income tax, the Welfare State. On Tuesday, facing regulatory issues, the big associations break up into their constituent trade and other specialized groups, each prepared to deal with special problems in its own special ways, usually along subject-matter lines. On Wednesday night still another fission takes place as the pork barrel and the other forms of subsidy and policy patronage come under consideration. The parent groups and "catalytic groups" still exist, but by Wednesday night they have little identity. As Bauer, Pool, and Dexter would say, they have preserved their unanimity through overlapping memberships. They gain identity to the extent that they can define the issues in redistributive terms. And when interests in issues are more salient in sectoral or geographic or individual terms, the common or generalized factor will be lost in abstractness and diffuseness. This is what happened to the liberal trade groups in the tariff battles of the 1950's, when "the protectionist position was more firmly grounded in direct business considerations and . . . the liberal-trade position fitted better with the ideology of the times . . ." (p. 150).

Where the peak associations, led by elements of Mr. Mills's power elite, have reality, their resources and access are bound to affect power relations. Owing to their stability and the impasse (or equilibrium) in relations among broad classes of the entire society, the political structure of the redistributive arena seems to be highly stabilized, virtually institutionalized. Its stability, unlike that of the distributive arena, derives from shared interests. But in contrast to the regulatory arena, these shared interests are sufficiently stable and clear and consistent to provide the foundation for ideologies. Table 2 summarizes the hypothesized differences in political relationships drawn above.

Many of the other distinctive characteristics of this arena are related to, perhaps follow from, the special role of the peak associations. The cohesion of peak associations means that the special differences among related but competing groups are likely to be settled long before the policies reach the governmental agenda. In many respects the upper-class directors perform the functions in the redistributive arena that are performed by Congressional committees in the distributive arena and by committees and Congress in the regulatory arena. But the differences are crucial. In distributive policies there are as many "sides" as there are tariff items, bridges and dams to be built, parcels of public land to be given away or leased, and so on. And there are probably as many elites as there are Congressional committees and subcommittees which have jurisdiction over distributive policies. In redistribution, there will never be more than two sides and the sides are clear, stable, and consistent. Negotiation is possible, but only for the purpose of strengthening or softening the impact of redistribution. And there is probably one elite for each side. The elites do not correspond directly to bourgeoisie and proletariat; they are better understood under Wallace Sayre's designation of "money-providing" and "service-demanding" groups. Nonetheless, the basis for coalition is broad, and it centers around those individuals most respected and best known for worth and wealth. If the top leaders did not know each other and develop common perspectives as a result of common schooling, as Mills would argue, these commonalities could easily develop later in life because the kinds of stakes involved in redistributive issues are always the same. So institutionalized does the conflict become that governmental bureaucracies themselves begin to reflect them, as do national party leaders and Administrations. Finally, just as the nature of redistributive policies influences politics towards the centralization and stabilization of conflict, so does it further influence the removal of decision-making from Congress. A decentralized and bargaining Congress can cumulate but it cannot balance, and redistributive policies require complex balancing on a very large scale. What Riker has said of budget-making applies here: ". . . legislative governments cannot endure a budget. Its finances must be totted up by party leaders in the legislature itself. In a complex fiscal system, however, haphazard legislative judgments cannot bring revenue into even rough alignment with supply. So budgeting is introduced—which transfers financial control to the budget maker. . . ."[21] Congress can provide exceptions

---

[21]William H. Riker, *Democracy in the United States* (New York 1953), 216.

Table 2 Arenas and Political Relationships: A Diagramatic Summary

Arena	Primary Political Unit	Relation Among Units	Power Structure	Stability of Structure	Primary Decisional Locus	Implementation
Distribution	Individual, firm, corporation	Log-rolling, mutual non-interference, uncommon interests	Non-conflictual elite with support groups	Stable	Congressional committee and/or agency**	Agency centralized to primary functional unit ("bureau")
Regulation*	Group	"The coalition," shared subject-matter interest, bargaining	Pluralistic, multi-centered, "theory of balance"	Unstable	Congress, in classic role	Agency decentralized from center by "delegation," mixed control
Redistribution	Association	The "peak association," class, ideology	Conflictual elite, i.e. elite and counterelite	Stable	Executive and peak associations	Agency centralized toward top (above "bureau"), elaborate standards

*Given the multiplicity of organized interests in the regulatory arena, there are obviously many cases of successful log-rolling coalitions that resemble the coalitions prevailing in distributive politics. In this respect, the difference between the regulatory and the distributive arenas is thus one of degree. The predominant form of coalition in regulatory politics is deemed to be that of common or tangential interest. Although the difference is only one of degree, it is significant because this prevailing type of coalition makes the regulatory arena so much more unstable, unpredictable, and non-elitist ("balance of power"). When we turn to the redistributive arena, however, we find differences of principle in every sense of the word.

**Distributive politics tends to stabilize around an institutional unit. In most cases, it is the Congressional committee (or subcommittee). But in others, particularly in the Department of Agriculture, the focus is the agency or the agency and the committee. In the cities, this is the arena where machine domination continues, if machines were in control in the first place.

to principles and it can implement those principles with elaborate standards of implementation as a condition for the concessions that money-providers will make. But the makers of principles of redistribution seem to be the holders of the "command posts."

None of this suggests a power elite such as Mills would have had us believe existed, but it does suggest a type of stable and continual conflict that can only be understood in class terms. The foundation upon which the social-stratification and power-elite school rested, especially when dealing with national power, was so conceptually weak and empirically unsupported that its critics were led to err in the opposite direction by denying the direct relevance of social and institutional positions and the probability of stable decision-making elites. But the relevance of that approach becomes stronger as the scope of its application is reduced and as the standards for identifying the scope are clarified. But this is equally true of the pluralist school and of those approaches based on a "politics of this-or-that policy."

Review Questions

1. What advantages did James Madison in *The Federalist* No. 10 see in the United States being a large republic? How did Madison believe the American political system would function to control the problem of "factions"

2. How does David Truman's defense of a pluralistic political system square with the continual denunciation of "special interests" that now seems to be a permanent part of American politics? How does Truman's concept of potential groups temper the political process

3. Who made up the core elements of C. Wright Mills's "power elite"? Do we have a power elite in present day American society?

4. Why did Robert Dahl assert that political decisions at the local level were influenced more by coalitions and group rivalries than by power elites? Does Dahl's finding apply to American national government as well?

5. What are the basic features of Theodore Lowi's three major categories of public policies: distribution, regulation and redistribution? Why is redistribution always more popular with some classes of society than with others?

Chapter 4

Agenda Setting

Agenda setting is the process by which ideas or issues bubble up through the various political channels to come up for consideration by a political institution such as a legislature or court. The two greatest sources of new agenda items are elective executives and legislators. Each of their constituencies expects that they will seek the enactment into law of the policies that they advocated in their campaigns for elective office. Additionally, the administrative agencies of a government often generate legislative proposals. Sometimes these are incorporated into the executive's legislative recommendations.

Admittedly, the agenda-setting process often makes extensive use of the mass media to take a relatively unknown or unsupported issue and, through publicity, expand the numbers of people who care about the issue so that an institution, whether it be city hall or the Congress, is forced to take some action. A famous example started in 1955, when Rosa Parks (1913–), an African American woman, was arrested for refusing to take a seat in the back of a bus in Montgomery, Alabama. This confrontation sparked the modern civil rights movement. Dr. Martin Luther King Jr. (1929–1968) would later use the tactics of nonviolent confrontation with southern segregational policies to arouse sufficient sympathy and support in the rest of the nation, which would lead to the passage of landmark civil rights legislation in Congress. When these nonviolent demonstrations turned violent, it was all the better—because it made better television and thus ensured a bigger audience for the message of the cause.

Agenda setting, which is usually confined to professional politicians, is a game that anybody can play. A federal judge could rule that a state prison is unconstitutionally overcrowded and thus force the state's legislature to deal with the issue by appropriating funds for new prisons. A citizens' group could grow so excited about an issue that they organize themselves to gather enough signatures of registered voters to put the issue as a proposition on the ballot of the next election. A public interest law firm could challenge the legality of an agency's action and force the courts to ascertain its constitutionality. Or an interest group could get thousands of its members to write (or e-mail) letters to their legislative representatives demanding action on a controversy. While there are only a few places—such as a legislature, court, or regulatory commission—where agendas can be formally enacted, there are infinite numbers of sources from which agenda items spring. And like hope, they spring eternally.

While agenda setting as a concept is as old as the ancient desire to gain an audience before a king, the first full scale modern analysis was by Roger W. Cobb and Charles D. Elder in *Participation in American Politics: The Dynamics of Agenda-Building* (1972). Reprinted here is their chapter on "Issue Creation and Agenda Context."

Anthony Downs (1930–) is the economist and policy analyst who is generally credited with establishing the intellectual framework for public choice economics in his *An Economic Theory of Democracy* (1957). His classic book on bureaucracy, *Inside Bureaucracy* (1967), sought to justify bureaucratic government on economic grounds and to develop laws and propositions that would aid in predicting the behavior of bureaus and bureaucrats. The issue-attention cycle, a model developed by Downs, in his 1972 *Public Interest* article, "Up and Down With Ecology—The Issue-Attention Cycle," is reprinted here. It attempts to explain how many policy problems evolve on the political agenda. The cycle is premised on the notion that the public's atten-

Figure 4.1

The Agenda Setting Process

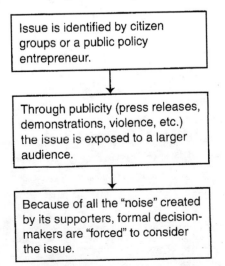

tion rarely remains focused on any one issue, regardless of the objective nature of the problem. The cycle consists of five steps:

1. The pre-problem stage (an undesirable social condition exists, but has not captured public attention);

2. Alarmed discovery and euphoric enthusiasm (a dramatic event catalyzes the public attention, accompanied by an enthusiasm to solve the problem);

3. Recognition of the cost of change (the public gradually realizes the difficulty of implementing meaningful change);

4. Decline of public interest (people become discouraged or bored or a new issue claims attention); and

5. The postproblem stage (although the issue has not been solved, it has been dropped from the nation's agenda).

According to John Kingdon in his award winning *Agendas, Alternatives, and Public Policies* (1995), portions of which are reprinted here: "If Anthony Downs is right, problems often fade from public view because a short period of awareness and optimism gives way to a realization of the financial and social costs of action. As people become impressed with the sacrifices, dislocations, and costs to be borne, they lose their enthusiasm for addressing the problem." For example, during the first Clinton administration there was initially great enthusiasm and support for a major reform in the nation's systems of medical insurance.

Kingdon, expanding upon the work of Cobb and Elder posits three sources, three explanations, for how issues arrive on governmental agendas: problems, politics, and visible participants. Kingdon uses these three elements to explore how ideas find their way onto policy agendas and how agendas change over time. He conceives of these elements as "three process streams flowing through the system" that, when they come together at critical junctures—when windows of opportunity open up—are able to make policy.

13

The Dynamics of
Agenda-Building (1972)

Roger W. Cobb and Charles D. Elder

An issue is a conflict between two or more identifiable groups over proce-dural or substantive matters relating to the distribution of positions or resources. Generally, there are four means by which issues are created. The most common method is the manufacturing of an issue by one or more of the contending parties who perceive an unfavorable bias in the distribution of positions or resources. For example, in 1950 truckers in Pennsylvania thought the railroads had an inherent advantage in carrying freight over long distances and sought to create an issue to redress this imbalance.[1] Such initiators are labeled "readjustors."

Another form of issue creation can be traced to a person or group who manufacture an issue for their own gain; for example, individuals who want to run for public office and are looking for an issue to advance their cause. Such individuals may be labeled "exploiters." As Herbert Blumer has written:

> The gaining of sympathizers or members rarely occurs through a mere combi-nation of a pre-established appeal and a pre-established individual psycholog-ical bent on which it is brought to bear. Instead the prospective sympathizer has to be aroused, nurtured and directed.[2]

Hans Toch echoes a similar sentiment when he writes:

> People are brought into social movements through the skills of leaders and agitators rather than because of pre-existing problems. . . . Appeals seem to

Source: Roger W. Cobb and Charles D. Elder, *Participation in American Politics; The Dynamics of Agenda-Building.* Copyright © 1972, 1983. Reprinted by permission of the authors.

[1] For a case study of this conflict, see Andrew Hacker, "Pressure Politics in Penn-sylvania: The Truckers vs. The Railroads," in Alan Westin (ed.), *The Uses of Power: 7 Cases in American Politics* (New York: Harcourt, 1962), pp. 323–76.

[2] Herbert Blumer, "Collective Behavior," in J. B. Gittler (ed.), *Review of Sociology* (New York: Wiley, 1957), 148.

originate with people who are primarily interested in other ends than the solution of the problems of potential members.[3]

Another means of issue initiation is through an unanticipated event. Such events could be called "circumstantial reactors." Examples include the development of an oil slick off the California coast near Santa Barbara in early 1969 that led to a reconsideration of the whole question of offshore drilling regulations. Other examples are the assassination of President Kennedy, which led to the gun control issue, and Eisenhower's heart attack in the mid-1950's, which raised the question of presidential disability.

Issues can be generated by persons or groups who have no positions or resources to gain for themselves. Often, they merely acquire a psychological sense of well-being for doing what they believe is in the public interest. These initiators might be called "do-gooders." The efforts to support Biafran relief programs fall in this category.

The above categories are not mutually exclusive, as an individual or group may have more than one motive for a particular action. For example, some people supported civil rights legislation because they felt it was humanitarian, while others supported it because they sought personal or collective gains.

Triggering Devices

At least two classes of triggering mechanisms, or unforeseen events, help shape issues that will be defined by the initiators. These can be subdivided into internal and external events that correspond to the domestic and foreign spheres.

Within the internal subdivision, there are five types of triggering devices. The first is a natural catastrophe, such as a mine cave-in, air inversion, flooding, and fire. The second is an unanticipated human event, such as a spontaneous riot, assassination of public officials, air hijackings, and murder of private individuals. The third is a technological change in the environment that creates heretofore undiscussed questions. It might involve mass transportation, air and water pollution, or air travel congestion. The fourth category is an actual imbalance, or bias, in the distribution of resources leading to such things as civil rights protest and union strikes.[4] A fifth type is ecological change, such as population explosion and black migration to Northern cities.

There are four types of external trigger mechanisms. The first is an act of war or military violence involving the United States as a direct combatant. Examples include the Vietnam war, the Pueblo seizure, and the dropping of atomic bombs on Hiroshima. The second category includes innovations in weapons technology involving such things as arms control, the Hotline

---

[3]Hans Toch, *The Psychology of Social Movements* (Indianapolis: Bobbs-Merrill, 1965), 87.

[4]Here the focus is on *actual* maldistribution of resources. A *perceived* maldistribution is covered by the "readjustor" type of issue initiator.

between the Kremlin and the White House, and the deployment of an anti-ballistic system. The third type is an international conflict in which the United States is not a direct combatant, such as the conflicts in the Middle East and the Congo. The final category involves changing world alignment patterns that may affect American membership in the United Nations, troop commitments in the North Atlantic Treaty Organization, and the American role in the Organization of American States.

Issue Initiation and Trigger Mechanisms

The formation of an issue is dependent on the dynamic interplay between the initiator and the trigger device. This can be seen in the following diagram:

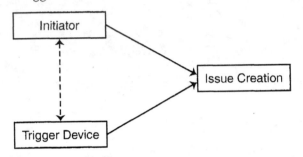

For example, a mine disaster itself does not create an issue. Many times in the past such an event has occurred with no ameliorative action. A link must be made between a grievance (or a triggering event) and an initiator who converts the problem into an issue for a private or a public reason.

In a system perspective, the inputs consist of the initiator and the event, or triggering mechanism, that transform the problem into an issue. The output is the agenda, which will be the focus of the next section. Transforming an issue into an agenda item will be the focus of succeeding chapters.

Agendas: What Are They?

In general terms, we have identified two basic types of political agendas. The first of these is the systemic agenda for political controversy. *The systemic agenda consists of all issues that are commonly perceived by members of the political community as meriting public attention and as involving matters within the legitimate jurisdiction of existing governmental authority.* Every local, state, and national political community will have a systemic agenda. The systemic agenda of the larger community may subsume items from the systemic agendas of subsidiary communities, but the two agendas will not necessarily correspond. For example, the systemic agenda of Boston may include items on the national agenda of controversy, such as pollution and crime in the streets, but will also include such items as the need for a new sports arena.

There are three prerequisites for an issue to obtain access to the systemic agenda: (1) widespread attention or at least awareness; (2) shared concern of a sizeable portion of the public that some type of action is required; and (3) a shared perception that the matter is an appropriate concern of some governmental unit and falls within the bounds of its authority. The terms "shared concern" and "shared perception" refer to the prevailing climate of opinion, which will be conditioned by the dominant norms, values, and ideology of a community. An issue requires the recognition of only a major portion of the polity, not the entire citizenry.

For an item or an issue to acquire public recognition, its supporters must have either access to the mass media or the resources necessary to reach people. They may require more than money and manpower; often the use of action rhetoric is essential. For example, use of terms such as *communist-inspired* or *anti-American* is a useful verbal ploy in attracting a larger audience than the original adherents of a cause.

In addition to gaining popular recognition, the issue must be perceived by a large number of people as both being subject to remedial action and requiring such action. In other words, action must be considered not only possible, but also necessary for the resolution of the issue. To foster such popular conviction, the mobilization of a significant number of groups or persons will normally be required.

Often, the fate of an issue in gaining systemic agenda status will hinge on whether or not it can be defined as being within the purview of legitimate governmental action. Perhaps one of the most devastating tactics that may be used to prevent an issue from reaching the systemic agenda is to deny that it falls within the bounds of governmental authority. For example, equal access to public accommodations was kept off the systemic agenda for some time because opponents successfully argued that the grievance fell outside the proper bounds of governmental authority.

The second type of agenda is the institutional, governmental, or formal agenda, which may be defined as *that set of items explicitly up for the active and serious consideration of authoritative decision-makers.* Therefore, any set of items up before any governmental body at the local, state, or national level will constitute an institutional agenda.

Two clarifications are in order regarding key terms in the above definition of a formal agenda. "Explicitly" refers to an issue involving action or policy alternatives or involving simply the identification of a problem requiring some action. An example of the former would be a proposal to raise the minimum wage to a specific level per hour. An illustration of the latter would be a reconsideration of certain restrictive loan practices of savings and loan institutions in the ghetto.

"Active and serious" are used to distinguish formal agenda items from what might be called "pseudo-agenda items." By pseudo-agenda, we mean any form of registering or acknowledging a demand without explicitly considering its merit. Decision-makers will often use such an agenda to assuage frustrations of constituency groups and to avoid political ramifications of a failure to acknowledge the demand. This typically occurs in a legislature where bills are placed in the hopper to placate some groups of activists with no real chance of action being taken.

Policy-makers will participate in the building of both systemic and institutional agendas. However, the natures of the two agendas are substantially different. The systemic agenda will be composed of fairly abstract and general items that do little more than identify a problem area. It will not necessarily suggest either the alternatives available or the means of coping with the problem. For example, it might include a vague item like "ending discrimination."

An institutional agenda will tend to be more specific, concrete, and limited in the number of items. It will identify, at least implicitly, those facets of a problem that are to be seriously considered by a decision-making body. An example would be a city council's consideration of alternative forms of local taxation for the support of public schools. It is possible for an item to get onto the formal agenda without having been a part of the systemic agenda. Each year, Congress considers many private bills of little social import or concern. However, it is unlikely that any issue involving substantial social consequences will gain standing on a governmental agenda unless it has first attained systemic agenda status.

Content of Formal Agendas

Formal agenda items can be divided into two major categories: *old items* and *new items*. *Old items* are those that have action alternatives delineated. They are predefined in most instances, except in specific cases (for example, the issue may not be whether workers will receive a 5 percent or a 10 percent raise, but whether they will get a raise at all).

There are two agenda components under the general heading of *old items*. Habitual items include those that come up for regular review. Examples would be budget items such as personnel pay and fights between existing agencies for a larger slice of the federal budget.

Recurrent items are those that occur with some periodicity, but need not appear at regular intervals. Examples would include governmental reorganization and regulation arising from a concern for efficiency or economy or both, rules changes in the legislature (for example, the filibuster in the Senate), Congressional reform, tariff items, tax reform, and social security increases or extensions.

The second general heading, *new items*, refers to those components that have no predetermined definitions, but are flexible in their interpretation or development. The first subdivision would include automatic or spontaneous issues appearing as an action or reaction of a key decision-maker in a specific situation. Examples include public employee or major industry strikes with a substantial impact on the economy or our military strength, the steel crisis under President Truman during the Korean War, foreign policy crises (e.g., Korea, Cuba, and the Dominican Republic), and innovations in foreign policy (e.g., American entrance into the United Nations, the test ban treaty, and the nuclear proliferation treaty).

A second component of *new items* is channeled items, those issues channeled to the agenda by the mobilization of mass support or by the activation of significant public groups (e.g., unions). Examples of issues with mass support include the civil rights issues of the 1960's and the gun control issue. Illustrations of issues backed by significant public groups include the Taft-Hartley repeal effort and the farm parity program.

An issue need not be static or confined to one category throughout its existence. At any point in time, it may be redefined. An example of a dynamic issue is the Vietnam policy. Initially, it became a spontaneous issue when President Eisenhower committed several hundred advisers in the late 1950's. The issue of expanded commitment became recurrent under Presidents Kennedy and Johnson. By 1963, the dispute appeared on the docket with great regularity. It continued in this form until opposition to the war—a channelized item begun by peace groups—raised the question of the legitimacy of American involvement. The peace groups expanded concern with American involvement until it became the policy stance of a major presidential candidate in 1968.

The Form of an Institutional Agenda

The explicit form of the formal agenda may be found in the calendar of authoritative decision-making bodies such as legislatures, high courts, or regulatory agencies.[5] Unless an item appears on some docket, it will not be considered to be an agenda item. Agenda composition will vary over time. However, recurrent or habitual items will be the most numerous. They tend to receive priority from the decision-makers, who constantly find that their time is limited and that their agenda is overloaded. Spontaneous, or automatic, items take precedence over channeled items, so it is very difficult to get new issues on the agenda. Decision-makers presume that older problems warrant more attention because of their longevity and the greater familiarity officials have with them.

Differential Access to Institutional Gatekeepers

The content of a formal agenda will tend to reflect structural and institutional biases found within the system. These biases arise from differential resources among individuals and groups and concomitant differences in access. For an issue to attain agenda status, it must command the support of at least some key decision-makers, for they are the ultimate guardians of the formal agenda.

---

[5]Calendars normally provide predefined agendas for both the legislature and the court. However, most legislatures have some procedure to allow items to be entered on the agenda at the request of one decision-maker without going through the normal procedures of agenda specification. For example, in the Congress, this procedure involves the private calendar. That calendar will be excluded from our analysis, which focuses on the public and union calendars, where most issues of public import will be found.

Political leaders are active participants in the agenda-building process, not simply impartial arbiters of issue disputes. As Bauer, Pool, and Dexter note:

> Congress is not a passive body, registering already-existent public views forced on its attention by public pressures. Congress, second only to the president, is, rather the major institution for initiating and creating political issues and projecting them into a national civic debate.[6]

The strategic location of these leaders assures them of media visibility when they want to promote an issue and places them in an excellent position to bargain with other decision-makers over formal agenda content. Because they have fairly direct control over what will appear on the formal agenda and considerable freedom to choose among the plethora of issues competing for attention, they can insist that an issue of concern to them be considered in return for agreement to consider an issue that is salient to another decision-maker or set of decision-makers.

It is easy then to understand why access to one or more key officials is so important to political groups. As one commentator noted,

> The development and improvement of such access is a common denominator of the tactics of all of them, frequently leading to efforts to exclude competing groups from equivalent access or to set up new decision points access to which can be monopolized by a particular group.[7]

Some groups have a greater ease of access than others, and are thus more likely to get their demands placed on an agenda.

This differential responsiveness arises from a variety of factors. First, the decision-maker may be indebted to a particular group or identify himself as a member of that group. Second, some groups have more resources than others or are better able to mobilize their resources. Third, some groups are located so strategically in the social or economic structure of society that their interests cannot be ignored (for example, big business and agriculture). Fourth, some groups (such as doctors, lawyers and church leaders) are held in greater esteem by the public than others and thus can command greater access to decision-makers. As a consequence, certain groups are more likely than others to receive attention from decision-makers when they come up with new demands. Farmers have an inherent advantage over many other groups in obtaining action on their needs because there are many decision-makers who identify themselves with farm groups and because agriculture occupies a pivotal position in the American economy.

A group may encounter different types of responses from different levels or branches of the government. When the National Association for the Advancement of Colored People first started to press its demands, it focused on the Congress and the presidency, but received no support. However, the group

---

[6]Raymond Bauer, Ithiel Pool and Lewis Dexter, *American Business and Public Policy* (New York: Atherton Press, 1963), p. 478.

[7]David Truman, *The Governmental Process* (New York: Knopf, 1964), p. 264.

was much more effective when it focused on a judicial strategy of making gains in civil rights through a series of court cases. Thus, differential responsiveness may result from the type of governmental unit petitioned as well as from differences among groups themselves.

Political parties also play an important part in translating issues into agenda items.[8] To assure support, they will often seek out and identify themselves with issues that are salient to large portions of the populace. Typically, these issues are identified in the party platform in general terms and with considerable ambiguity. However, as Truman notes:

> The significance of preparing a platform lies primarily in the evidence that the negotiations provide concerning what groups will have access to the developing national party organization. . . . Interest group leaders are aware that the real settlement of the issues they are concerned with . . . will take place later; in the platform, they seek tentative assurance of a voice in that settlement. To maximize this assurance, political interest groups normally seek recognition in the platforms of both major parties.[9]

Certainly recognition on a party platform is at least indicative of an issue attaining standing on the systemic agenda of political controversy.[10]

The media can also play a very important role in elevating issues to the systemic agenda and increasing their chances of receiving formal agenda consideration. Certain personages in the media can act as opinion leaders in bringing publicity to a particular issue. Examples of individuals who have gained a larger audience for a dispute include Walter Lippmann, Jack Anderson, and Drew Pearson. Individuals who have acquired an audience simply by constantly appearing in the news can also publicize an issue. Ralph Nader has a readymade constituency stemming from his many attacks on various inefficient and unscrupulous business practices.

Differential Legitimacy

While most observers grant that there are inequalities in access to decision-makers, they argue that the existence of multiple points of access owing to different levels and branches of government has the net effect of insuring widespread contacts. Further, the existence of dispersed inequalities (that is,

---

[8]See, for example, Everett C. Ladd, Jr., *American Political Parties* (New York: W. W. Norton and Company, 1970).

[9]Truman, *op. cit.,* p. 285.

[10]Significant differences in the platforms of the two major parties may portend a major alteration in the national systemic agenda. This change may be realized through what Key called "a critical election." Certainly a critical, or realigning, election may be taken as an indicator of a major shift in the systemic agenda. See V. O. Key, *Politics, Parties and Pressure Groups,* 5th ed. (New York: Thomas Crowell Company, 1964), pp. 520–36.

the fact that groups having great resources in one area may not have comparable resources in other areas) supposedly assures that no group will be without political influence in some areas. However, this argument fails to consider the relatively stable pattern of differential legitimacy accorded various social groupings. Differences in accessibility to decision-makers are a function of the relative legitimacy of various groups. For example, a proposal advanced by a group of businessmen to improve traffic flows into the downtown business area is more likely to receive the attention of decision-makers than a counter-proposal by ghetto residents to develop more extensive and effective mass transit systems.

The problem confronted by any newly formed group is often how to legitimize the group and the interest represented rather than how to legitimize a particular issue position. The legitimacy of the group will be greatly enhanced by the status and community standing of its members. In other words, people without resources (for example, lower-income groups) will have greater difficulty attaining legitimacy than their higher-income counterparts. For example, the antiwar movement initially promoted by student groups who traditionally have little political standing received little public support until more socially prominent persons and groups entered the fray on their behalf (for example, business groups, military leaders, clergymen, and senators).

Systemic Constraints on Agenda Entrance

Even if an issue is promoted by a group that is perceived to be legitimate, its appearance on a formal agenda may be problematic owing to cultural constraints on the range of issues that are considered legitimate topics for governmental action. Any institutional agenda will be restricted by the prevailing popular sentiment as to what constitutes appropriate matters for governmental attention. For example, federal aid to education was long considered by many to be an inappropriate area for federal governmental action, a fact that precluded active and serious consideration of the merits of the issue for decades. Legitimizing issues that are considered outside of the governmental realm is difficult and normally takes a long time. The net effect of this is that new demands of particularly disadvantaged or deprived groups are the least likely to receive attention on either the systemic agenda of controversy or the institutional agenda.

14

Up and Down with Ecology: The Issue-Attention Cycle (1972)

Anthony Downs

American public attention rarely remains sharply focused upon any one domestic issue for very long—even if it involves a continuing problem of crucial importance to society. Instead, a systematic "issue-attention cycle" seems strongly to influence public attitudes and behavior concerning most key domestic problems. Each of these problems suddenly leaps into prominence, remains there for a short time, and then—though still largely unresolved—gradually fades from the center of public attention. A study of the way this cycle operates provides insights into whether public attention is likely to remain sufficiently focused upon any given issue to generate enough political pressure to cause effective change.

The shaping of American attitudes toward improving the quality of our environment provides both an example and a potential test of this "issue-attention cycle." In the past few years, there has been a remarkably widespread upsurge of interest in the quality of our environment. This change in public attitudes has been much faster than any changes in the environment itself. What has caused this shift in public attention? Why did this issue suddenly assume so high a priority among our domestic concerns? And how long will the American public sustain high-intensity interest in ecological matters? I believe that answers to these questions can be derived from analyzing the "issue-attention cycle."

The Dynamics of the "Issue-Attention Cycle"

Public perception of most "crises" in American domestic life does not reflect changes in real conditions as much as it reflects the operation of a systematic

Source: Anthony Downs, "Up and Down with Ecology: The 'Issue Attention Cycle.'" Reprinted with permission of the author from *The Public Interest*, No. 28 (Summer 1972) pp. 38–50. Copyright © 1972 by National Affairs, Inc.

cycle of heightening public interest and then increasing boredom with major issues. This "issue-attention cycle" is rooted both in the nature of certain domestic problems and in the way major communications media interact with the public. The cycle itself has five stages, which may vary in duration depending upon the particular issue involved, but which almost always occur in the following sequence:

1. **The pre-problem stage.** This prevails when some highly undesirable social condition exists but has not yet captured much public attention, even though some experts or interest groups may already be alarmed by it. Usually, objective conditions regarding the problem are far worse during the pre-problem stage than they are by the time the public becomes interested in it. For example, this was true of racism, poverty, and malnutrition in the United States.

2. **Alarmed discovery and euphoric enthusiasm.** As a result of some dramatic series of events (like the ghetto riots in 1965 to 1967) or for other reasons, the public suddenly becomes both aware of and alarmed about the evils of a particular problem. This alarmed discovery is invariably accompanied by euphoric enthusiasm about society's ability to "solve this problem" or "do something effective" within a relatively short time. The combination of alarm and confidence results in part from the strong public pressure in America for political leaders to claim that every problem can be "solved." This outlook is rooted in the great American tradition of optimistically viewing most obstacles to social progress as external to the structure of society itself. The implication is that every obstacle can be eliminated and every problem solved without any fundamental reordering of society itself, if only we devote sufficient effort to it. In older and perhaps wiser cultures, there is an underlying sense of irony or even pessimism which springs from a widespread and often confirmed belief that many problems cannot be "solved" at all in any complete sense. Only recently has this more pessimistic view begun to develop in our culture.

3. **Realizing the cost of significant progress.** The third stage consists of a gradually spreading realization that the cost of "solving" the problem is very high indeed. Really doing so would not only take a great deal of money but would also require major sacrifices by large groups in the population. The public thus begins to realize that part of the problem results from arrangements that are providing significant benefits to someone—often to millions. For example, traffic congestion and a great deal of smog are caused by increasing automobile usage. Yet this also enhances the mobility of millions of Americans who continue to purchase more vehicles to obtain these advantages.

   In certain cases, technological progress can eliminate some of the undesirable results of a problem without causing any major restructuring of society or any loss of present benefits by others (except for higher money costs). In the optimistic American tradition, such a technological solution is initially assumed to be possible in the case of nearly every problem. Our most pressing social problems, however, usually involve either deliberate or unconscious exploitation of one group in society by another, or the prevention of one group from enjoying something that others want to keep for themselves. For example, most upper-middle-class whites value geographic separation from poor people and blacks. Hence any equality of access to the advantages of suburban living for the poor and for blacks cannot be achieved without some sacrifice by middle-class whites of the "benefits" of separation. The increasing recognition that there is this type of relationship between the problem and its "solution" constitutes a key part of the third stage.

4. **Gradual decline of intense public interest.** The previous stage becomes almost imperceptibly transformed into the fourth stage: a gradual decline in the intensity of public interest in the problem. As more and more people realize how difficult, and how costly to themselves, a solution to the problem would be, three reactions set in. Some people just get discouraged. Others feel positively threatened by thinking about the problem; so they suppress such thoughts. Still others become bored by the issue. Most people experience some combination of these feelings. Consequently, public desire to keep attention focused on the issue wanes. And by this time, some other issue is usually entering Stage Two; so it exerts a more novel and thus more powerful claim upon public attention.

5. **The post-problem stage.** In the final stage, an issue that has been replaced at the center of public concern moves into a prolonged limbo—a twilight realm of lesser attention or spasmodic recurrences of interest. However, the issue now has a different relation to public attention than that which prevailed in the "pre-problem" stage. For one thing, during the time that interest was sharply focused on this problem, new institutions, programs, and policies may have been created to help solve it. These entities almost always persist and often have some impact even after public attention has shifted elsewhere. For example, during the early stages of the "War on Poverty," the Office of Economic Opportunity (OEO) was established, and it initiated many new programs. Although poverty has now faded somewhat as a central public issue, many of these programs have experienced significant success, even though funded at a far lower level than would be necessary to reduce poverty decisively.

Any major problem that once was elevated to national prominence may sporadically recapture public interest; or important aspects of it may become attached to some other problem that subsequently dominates center stage. Therefore, problems that have gone through the cycle almost always receive a higher average level of attention, public effort, and general concern than those still in the pre-discovery stage.

Which Problems Are Likely to Go
through the Cycle?

Not all major social problems go through this "issue-attention cycle." Those which do generally possess to some degree three specific characteristics. First, the majority of persons in society are not suffering from the problem nearly as much as some minority (a numerical minority, not necessarily an ethnic one). This is true of many pressing social problems in America today—poverty, racism, poor public transportation, low-quality education, crime, drug addiction, and unemployment, among others. The number of persons suffering from each of these ills is very large absolutely—in the millions. But the numbers are small relatively—usually less than 15 percent of the entire population. Therefore, most people do not suffer directly enough from such problems to keep their attention riveted on them.

Second, the sufferings caused by the problem are generated by social arrangements that provide significant benefits to a majority or a powerful minority of the population. For example, Americans who own cars—plus the powerful automobile and highway lobbies—receive short-run benefits from the prohibition of using motor-fuel tax revenues for financing public transportation systems, even though such systems are desperately needed by the urban poor.

Third, the problem has no intrinsically exciting qualities—or no longer has them. When big-city racial riots were being shown nightly on the nation's television screens, public attention naturally focused upon their causes and consequences. But when they ceased (or at least the media stopped reporting them so intensively), public interest in the problems related to them declined sharply. Similarly, as long as the National Aeronautics and Space Administration (NASA) was able to stage a series of ever more thrilling space shots, culminating in the worldwide television spectacular of Americans walking on the moon, it generated sufficient public support to sustain high-level congressional appropriations. But NASA had nothing half so dramatic for an encore, and repetition of the same feat proved less and less exciting (though a near disaster on the third try did revive audience interest). So NASA's congressional appropriations plummeted.

A problem must be dramatic and exciting to maintain public interest because news is "consumed" by much of the American public (and by publics everywhere) largely as a form of entertainment. As such, it competes with other types of entertainment for a share of each person's time. Every day, there is a fierce struggle for space in the highly limited universe of newsprint and television viewing time. Each issue vies not only with all other social problems and public events, but also with a multitude of "non-news" items that are often far more pleasant to contemplate. These include sporting news, weather reports, crossword puzzles, fashion accounts, comics, and daily horoscopes. In fact, the amount of television time and newspaper space devoted to sports coverage, as compared to international events, is a striking commentary on the relative value that the public places on knowing about these two subjects.

When all three of the above conditions exist concerning a given problem that has somehow captured public attention, the odds are great that it will soon move through the entire "issue-attention cycle"—and therefore will gradually fade from the center of the stage. The first condition means that most people will not be continually reminded of the problem by their own suffering from it. The second condition means that solving the problem requires sustained attention and effort, plus fundamental changes in social institutions or behavior. This in turn means that significant attempts to solve it are threatening to important groups in society. The third condition means that the media's sustained focus on this problem soon bores a majority of the public. As soon as the media realize that their emphasis on this problem is threatening many people and boring even more, they will shift their focus to some "new" problem. This is particularly likely in America because nearly all the media are run for profit, and they make the most money by appealing to the largest possible audiences. Thus, as Marshall McLuhan has pointed out, it is largely the audience itself—the American public—that "manages the news" by maintaining or losing interest in a given subject. As long as this pattern persists, we will continue to be confronted by a stream of "crises" involving particular social problems. Each will rise into public view, capture center stage for a while, and then gradually fade away as it is replaced by more fashionable issues moving into their "crisis" phases.

The Rise of Environmental Concern

Public interest in the quality of the environment now (1972) appears to be about midway through the "issue-attention cycle." Gradually, more and more people are beginning to realize the immensity of the social and financial costs of cleaning up our air and water and of preserving and restoring open spaces. Hence much of the enthusiasm about prompt, dramatic improvement in the environment is fading. There is still a great deal of public interest, however, so it cannot be said that the "post-problem stage" has been reached. In fact, as will be discussed later, the environmental issue may well retain more attention than social problems that affect smaller proportions of the population. Before evaluating the prospects of long-term interest in the environment, though, it is helpful to analyze how environmental concern passed through the earlier stages in the "issue-attention cycle."

The most obvious reason for the initial rise in concern about the environment is the recent deterioration of certain easily perceived environmental conditions. A whole catalogue of symptoms can be arrayed, including ubiquitous urban smog, greater proliferation of solid waste, oceanic oil spills, greater pollution of water supplies by DDT and other poisons, the threatened disappearance of many wildlife species, and the overcrowding of a variety of facilities from commuter expressways to national parks. Millions of citizens observing these worsening conditions became convinced that someone ought to "do something" about them. But "doing something" to reduce environmental deterioration is not easy. For many of our environmental problems have been caused by developments which are highly valued by most Americans.

The very abundance of our production and consumption of material goods is responsible for an immense amount of environmental pollution. For example, electric power generation, if based on fossil fuels, creates smoke and air pollution or, if based on nuclear fuels, causes rising water temperatures. Yet a key foundation for rising living standards in the United States during this century has been the doubling of electric power consumption every 10 years. So more pollution is the price we have paid for the tremendous advantages of being able to use more and more electricity. Similarly, much of the litter blighting even our remotest landscapes stems from the convenience of using "throwaway packages." Thus, to regard environmental pollution as a purely external negative factor would be to ignore its direct linkage with material advantages most citizens enjoy.

Another otherwise favorable development that has led to rising environmental pollution is what I would call the democratization of privilege. Many more Americans are now able to participate in certain activities that were formerly available only to a small, wealthy minority. Some members of that minority are incensed by the consequences of having their formerly esoteric advantages spread to "the common man." The most frequent irritant caused by the democratization of privilege is congestion. Rising highway congestion, for example, is denounced almost everywhere. Yet its main cause is the rapid spread of automobile ownership and usage. In 1950, about 59 percent of all families had at least one automobile, and 7 percent owned two or more. By 1968, the proportion of families owning at least one automobile had climbed to 79 percent, and 26 percent had two or more cars. In the 10 years from 1960 to 1970, the total number of registered automotive vehicles rose by 35 million (or 47 percent), as compared to a rise in human population of 23 million (or only 13 percent). Moreover, it has been estimated that motor vehicles cause approximately 60 percent of all air pollution. So the tremendous increase in smog does not result primarily from larger population, but rather from the democratization of automobile ownership.

The democratization of privilege also causes crowding in national parks, rising suburban housing density, the expansion of new subdivisions into formerly picturesque farms and orchards, and the transformation of once tranquil resort areas like Waikiki Beach into forests of high-rise buildings. It is now difficult for the wealthy to flee from busy urban areas to places of quiet seclusion, because so many more people can afford to go with them. *The elite's environmental deterioration is often the common man's improved standard of living.*

Our Soaring Aspirations

A somewhat different factor which has contributed to greater concern with environmental quality is a marked increase in our aspirations and standards concerning what our environment ought to be like. In my opinion, rising dissatisfaction with the "system" in the United States does not result primarily from poorer performance by that system. Rather, it stems mainly from a rapid escalation of our aspirations as to what the system's performance ought to be. Nowhere is this phenomenon more striking than in regard to the quality of the environment. One hundred years ago, white Americans were eliminating whole Indian tribes without a qualm. Today, many serious-minded citizens seek to make important issues out of the potential disappearance of the whooping crane, the timber wolf, and other exotic creatures. Meanwhile, thousands of Indians in Brazil are still being murdered each year—but American conservationists are not focusing on that human massacre. Similarly, some aesthetes decry "galloping sprawl" in metropolitan fringe areas, while they ignore acres of rat-infested housing a few miles away. Hence the escalation of our environmental aspirations is more selective than might at first appear.

Yet regarding many forms of pollution, we are now rightly upset over practices and conditions that have largely been ignored for decades. An example is our alarm about the dumping of industrial wastes and sewage into rivers and lakes. This increase in our environmental aspirations is part of a general cultural phenomenon stimulated both by our success in raising living standards and by the recent emphases of the communications media. Another cause of the rapid rise in interest in environmental pollution is the "explosion" of alarmist rhetoric on this subject. According to some well-publicized experts, all life on earth is threatened by an "environmental crisis." Some claim human life will end within three decades or less if we do not do something drastic about current behavior patterns.

Are things really that bad? Frankly, I am not enough of an ecological expert to know. But I am skeptical concerning all highly alarmist views because so many previous prophets of doom and disaster have been so wrong concerning many other so-called "crises" in our society. There are two reasonable definitions of "crisis." One kind of crisis consists of a rapidly deteriorating situation moving toward a single disastrous event at some future moment. The second kind consists of a more gradually deteriorating situation that will eventually pass some subtle "point of no return." At present, I do not believe either of these definitions applies to most American domestic problems. Although many social critics hate to admit it, the American "system" actually serves the majority of citizens rather well in terms of most indicators of well-being. Concerning such things as real income, personal mobility, variety and choice of consumption patterns, longevity, health, leisure time, and quality of housing, most Americans are better off today than they have ever been and extraordinarily better off than most of mankind. What is not improving is the gap between society's performance and what most people—or at least highly vocal minorities—believe society ought to be doing to solve these problems. Our aspirations and standards have risen far faster than the beneficial outputs of our social system. Therefore, although most Americans, including most of the poor, are receiving more now, they are enjoying it less.

This conclusion should not be confused with the complacency of some super-patriots. It would be unrealistic to deny certain important negative trends in American life. Some conditions are indeed getting worse for nearly everyone. Examples are air quality and freedom from thievery. Moreover, congestion and environmental deterioration might forever destroy certain valuable national amenities if they are not checked. Finally, there has probably been a general rise in personal and social anxiety in recent years. I believe this is due to increased tensions caused by our rapid rate of technical and social change, plus the increase in worldwide communication through the media. These developments rightly cause serious and genuine concern among millions of Americans.

The Future of the Environmental Issue

Concern about the environment has passed through the first two stages of the "issue-attention cycle" and is by now well into the third. In fact, we have already begun to move toward the fourth stage, in which the intensity of public interest in environmental improvement must inexorably decline. And this raises an interesting question: Will the issue of environmental quality then move on into the "post-problem" stage of the cycle?

My answer to this question is: Yes, but not soon, because certain characteristics of this issue will protect it from the rapid decline in public interest typical of many other recent issues. First of all, many kinds of environmental pollution are much more visible and more clearly threatening than most other social problems. This is particularly true of air pollution. The greater the apparent threat from visible forms of pollution and the more vividly this can be dramatized, the more public support environmental improvement will receive and the longer it will sustain public interest. Ironically, the cause of ecologists would therefore benefit from an environmental disaster like a "killer smog" that would choke thousands to death in a few days. Actually, this is nothing new; every cause from early Christianity to the Black Panthers has benefitted from martyrs. Yet even the most powerful symbols lose their impact if they are constantly repeated. The piteous sight of an oil-soaked seagull or a dead soldier pales after it has been viewed even a dozen times. Moreover, some of the worst environmental threats come from forms of pollution that are invisible. Thus, our propensity to focus attention on what is most visible may cause us to clean up the pollution we can easily perceive while ignoring even more dangerous but hidden threats.

Pollution is also likely to be kept in the public eye because it is an issue that threatens almost everyone, not just a small percentage of the population. Since it is not politically divisive, politicians can safely pursue it without fearing adverse repercussions. Attacking environmental pollution is therefore much safer than attacking racism or poverty. For an attack upon the latter antagonizes important blocs of voters who benefit from the sufferings of others or at least are not threatened enough by such suffering to favor spending substantial amounts of their money to reduce it.

A third strength of the environmental issue is that much of the "blame" for pollution can be attributed to a small group of "villains" whose wealth and power make them excellent scapegoats. Environmental defenders can therefore "courageously" attack these scapegoats without antagonizing most citizens. Moreover, at least in regard to air pollution, that small group actually has enough power to greatly reduce pollution if it really tries. If leaders of the nation's top auto-producing, power-generating, and fuel-supplying firms would change their behavior significantly, a drastic decline in air pollution could be achieved very quickly. This has been demonstrated at many locations already.

Gathering support for attacking any problem is always easier if its ills can be blamed on a small number of "public enemies," as is shown by the success of Ralph Nader. This tactic is especially effective if the "enemies" exhibit extreme wealth and power, eccentric dress and manners, obscene language, or some other uncommon traits. Then society can aim its outrage at a small, alien group without having to face up to the need to alter its own behavior. It is easier to find such scapegoats for almost all forms of pollution than for other major problems like poverty, poor housing, or racism. Solutions to those problems would require millions of Americans to change their own behavior patterns, to accept higher taxes, or both.

The possibility that technological solutions can be devised for most pollution problems may also lengthen the public prominence of this issue. To the extent that pollution can be reduced through technological change, most people's basic attitudes, expectations, and behavior patterns will not have to be altered. The traumatic difficulties of achieving major institutional change could thus be escaped through the "magic" of purely technical improvements in automobile engines, water purification devices, fuel composition, and sewage treatment facilities.

Financing the Fight Against Pollution

Another aspect of anti-pollution efforts that will strengthen their political support is that most of the costs can be passed on to the public through higher product prices rather than higher taxes. Therefore, politicians can demand enforcement of costly environmental quality standards without paying the high political price of raising the required funds through taxes. True, water pollution is caused mainly by the actions of public bodies, especially municipal sewer systems, and effective remedies for this form of pollution require higher taxes or at least higher prices for public services. But the major costs of reducing most kinds of pollution can be added to product prices and thereby quietly shifted to the ultimate consumers of the outputs concerned. This is a politically painless way to pay for attacking a major social problem. In contrast, effectively combatting most social problems requires large-scale income redistribution attainable only through both higher taxes and higher transfer payments or subsidies. Examples of such politically costly problems are poverty, slum housing, low-quality health care for the poor, and inadequate public transportation.

Many ecologists oppose paying for a cleaner environment through higher product prices. They would rather force the polluting firms to bear the required cost through lower profits. In a few oligopolistic industries, like petroleum and automobile production, this might work. But in the long run, not much of the total cost could be paid this way without driving capital out of the industries concerned and thereby eventually forcing product prices upwards. Furthermore, it is just that those who use any given product should pay the full cost of making it—including the cost of avoiding excessive pollution in its production. Such payment is best made through higher product prices. In my opinion, it would be unwise in most cases to try to pay these costs by means of government subsidies in order to avoid shifting the load onto consumers. We need to conserve our politically limited taxing capabilities to attack those problems that cannot be dealt with in any other way.

Still another reason why the cleaner-environment issue may last a long time is that it could generate a large private industry with strong vested interests in continued spending against pollution. Already dozens of firms with "eco" or "environ" in their names have sprung up to exploit supposedly burgeoning anti-pollution markets. In time, we might even generate an "environmental-industrial complex" about which some future president could vainly warn us in his retirement speech! Any issue gains longevity if its sources of political support and the programs related to it can be institutionalized in large bureaucracies. Such organizations have a powerful desire to keep public attention focused on the problems that support them. However, it is doubtful that the anti-pollution industry will ever come close to the defense industry in size and power. Effective anti-pollution activities cannot be carried out separately from society as a whole because they require changes in behavior by millions of people. In contrast, weapons are produced by an industry that imposes no behavioral changes (other than higher taxes) on the average citizen.

Finally, environmental issues may remain at center stage longer than most domestic issues because of their very ambiguity. "Improving the environment" is a tremendously broad and all-encompassing objective. Almost everyone can plausibly claim that his or her particular cause is another way to upgrade the quality of our life. This ambiguity will make it easier to form a majority-sized coalition favoring a variety of social changes associated with improving the environment. The inability to form such a coalition regarding problems that adversely affect only minority-sized groups usually hastens the exit of such problems from the center of public attention.

All the factors set forth above indicate that circumstances are unusually favorable for launching and sustaining major efforts to improve the quality of our environment. Yet we should not underestimate the American public's capacity to become bored—especially with something that does not immediately threaten them, or promise huge benefits for a majority, or strongly appeal to their sense of injustice. In the present mood of the nation, I believe most citizens do not want to confront the need for major social changes on any issues except those that seem directly to threaten them—such as crime and other urban violence. And even in regard to crime, the public does not yet wish to support really effective changes in our basic system of justice. The present administration has apparently concluded that a relatively "low-profile" government—one that does not try to lead the public into accepting truly significant institutional changes—will most please the majority of Americans at this point. Regardless of the accuracy of this view, if it remains dominant within the federal government, then no major environmental programs are likely to receive long-sustained public attention or support.

Some proponents of improving the environment are relying on the support of students and other young people to keep this issue at the center of public attention. Such support, however, is not adequate as a long-term foundation. Young people form a highly unstable base for the support of any policy because they have such short-lived "staying power." For one thing, they do not long enjoy the large amount of free time they possess while in college. Also, as new individuals enter the category of "young people" and older ones leave it, different issues are stressed and accumulated skills in marshaling opinion are dissipated. Moreover, the radicalism of the young has been immensely exaggerated by the media's tendency to focus attention upon those with extremist views. In their attitudes toward political issues, most young people are not very different from their parents.

There is good reason, then, to believe that the bundle of issues called "improving the environment" will also suffer the gradual loss of public attention characteristic of the later stages of the "issue-attention cycle." However, it will be eclipsed at a much slower rate than other recent domestic issues. So it may be possible to accomplish some significant improvements in environmental quality—if those seeking them work fast.

15

Agendas, Alternatives and Public Policies (1995)

John W. Kingdon

Agenda Setting

How are governmental agendas set? Our answer has concentrated on three explanations: problems, politics, and visible participants.

Problems

Why do some problems come to occupy the attention of governmental officials more than other problems? The answer lies both in the means by which those officials learn about conditions and in the ways in which conditions become defined as problems. As to means, we have discussed indicators, focusing events, and feedback. Sometimes, a more or less systematic indicator simply shows that there is a condition out there. Indicators are used to assess the magnitude of the condition (e.g., the incidence of a disease or the cost of a program), and to discern changes in a condition. Both large magnitude and change catch officials' attention. Second, a focusing event—a disaster, crisis, personal experience, or powerful symbol—draws attention to some conditions more than to others. But such an event has only transient effects unless accompanied by a firmer indication of a problem, by a preexisting perception, or by a combination with other similar events. Third, officials learn about conditions through feedback about the operation of existing programs, either formal (e.g., routine monitoring of costs or program evaluation studies) or informal (e.g., streams of complaints flowing into congressional offices).

There is a difference between a condition and a problem. We put up with all kinds of conditions every day, and conditions do not rise to prominent places on policy agendas. Conditions come to be defined as problems, and have a better chance of rising on the agenda, when we come to believe that we should do something to change them. People in and around government define conditions as problems in several ways. First, conditions that violate important values are transformed into problems. Second, conditions become problems by comparison with other countries or other relevant units. Third, classifying a condition into one category rather than another may define it as one kind of problem or another. The lack of public transportation for handicapped people, for instance, can be classified as a transportation problem or as a civil rights problem, and the treatment of the subject is dramatically affected by the category.

Problems not only rise on governmental agendas, but they also fade from view. Why do they fade? First, government may address the problem, or fail to address it. In both cases, attention turns to something else, either because something has been done or because people are frustrated by failure and refuse to invest more of their time in a losing cause. Second, conditions that highlighted a problem may change—indicators drop instead of rise, or crises go away. Third, people may become accustomed to a condition or relabel a problem. Fourth, other items emerge and push the highly placed items aside. Finally, there may simply be inevitable cycles in attention; high growth rates level off, and fads come and go.

Problem recognition is critical to agenda setting. The chances of a given proposal or subject rising on an agenda are markedly enhanced if it is connected to an important problem. Some problems are seen as so pressing that they set agendas all by themselves. Once a particular problem is defined as pressing, whole classes of approaches are favored over others, and some alternatives are highlighted while others fall from view. So policy entrepreneurs invest considerable resources bringing their conception of problems to officials' attention, and trying to convince them to see problems their way. The recognition and definition of problems affect outcomes significantly.

Politics

The second family of explanations for high or low agenda prominence is in the political stream. Independently of problem recognition or the development of policy proposals, political events flow along according to their own dynamics and their own rules. Participants perceive swings in national mood, elections bring new administrations to power and new partisan or ideological distributions to Congress, and interest groups of various descriptions press (or fail to press) their demands on government.

Developments in this political sphere are powerful agenda setters. A new administration, for instance, changes agendas all over town as it highlights its conceptions of problems and its proposals, and makes attention to subjects that are not among its high priorities much less likely. A national mood that is perceived to be profoundly conservative dampens attention to costly new initiatives, while a more tolerant national mood would allow for greater spending. The opposition of a powerful phalanx of interest groups makes it difficult—not impossible, but difficult—to contemplate some initiatives.

Consensus is built in the political stream by bargaining more than by persuasion. When participants recognize problems or settle on certain proposals in the policy stream, they do so largely by persuasion. They marshal indicators and argue that certain conditions ought to be defined as problems, or they argue that their proposals meet such logical tests as technical feasibility or value acceptability. But in the political stream, participants build consensus by bargaining—trading provisions for support, adding elected officials to coalitions by giving them concessions that they demand, or compromising from ideal positions that will gain wider acceptance.

The combination of national mood and elections is a more potent agenda setter than organized interests. Interest groups are often able to block consideration of proposals they do not prefer, or to adapt to an item already high on a governmental agenda by adding elements a bit more to their liking. They less often initiate considerations or set agendas on their own. And when organized interests come into conflict with the combination of national mood and elected politicians, the latter combination is likely to prevail, at least as far as setting an agenda is concerned.

Visible Participants

Third, we made a distinction between visible and hidden participants. The visible cluster of actors, those who receive considerable press and public attention, include the president and his high-level appointees, prominent members of Congress, the media, and such elections-related actors as political parties and campaigners. The relatively hidden cluster includes academic specialists, career bureaucrats, and congressional staffers. We have discovered that the visible cluster affects the agenda and the hidden cluster affects the alternatives. So the chances of a subject rising on a governmental agenda are enhanced if that subject is pushed by participants in the visible cluster, and dampened if it is neglected by those participants. The administration—the president and his appointees—is a particularly powerful agenda setter, as are such prominent members of Congress as the party leaders and key committee chairs.

At least as far as agenda setting is concerned, elected officials and their appointees turn out to be more important than career civil servants or participants outside of government. To those who look for evidences of democracy at work, this is an encouraging result. These elected officials do not necessarily get their way in specifying alternatives or implementing decisions, but they do affect agendas rather substantially. To describe the roles of various participants in agenda setting, a fairly straightforward top-down model, with elected officials at the top, comes surprisingly close to the truth.

Alternative Specification

How is the list of potential alternatives for public policy choices narrowed to the ones that actually receive serious consideration? There are two families of answers: (1) Alternatives are generated and narrowed in the policy stream; and

(2) Relatively hidden participants, specialists in the particular policy area, are involved.

Hidden Participants: Specialists

Alternatives, proposals, and solutions are generated in communities of special-ists. This relatively hidden cluster of participants includes academics, researchers, consultants, career bureaucrats, congressional staffers, and ana-lysts who work for interest groups. Their work is done, for instance, in planning and evaluation or budget shops in the bureaucracy or in the staff agencies on the Hill.

These relatively hidden participants form loosely knit communities of spe-cialists. There is such a community for health, for instance, which includes analogous subcommunities for more specialized areas like the direct delivery of medical services and the regulation of food and drugs. Some of these com-munities, such as the one for transportation, are highly fragmented, while oth-ers are more tightly knit. Each community is composed of people located throughout the system and potentially of very diverse orientations and inter-ests, but they all share one thing: their specialization and acquaintance with the issues in that particular policy area.

Ideas bubble around in these communities. People try out proposals in a variety of ways: through speeches, bill introductions, congressional hearings, leaks to the press, circulation of papers, conversations, and lunches. They float their ideas, criticize one another's work, hone and revise their ideas, and float new versions. Some of these ideas are respectable, while others are out of the question. But many, many ideas are possible and are considered in some fash-ion somewhere along the line.

The Policy Stream

The generation of policy alternatives is best seen as a selection process, analo-gous to biological natural selection. In what we have called the policy primeval soup, many ideas float around, bumping into one another, encoun-tering new ideas, and forming combinations and recombinations. The origins of policy may seem a bit obscure, hard to predict and hard to understand or to structure.

While the origins are somewhat haphazard, the selection is not. Through the imposition of criteria by which some ideas are selected out for survival while others are discarded, order is developed from chaos, pattern from ran-domness. These criteria include technical feasibility, congruence with the val-ues of community members, and the anticipation of future constraints, including a budget constraint, public acceptability, and politicians' receptivity. Proposals that are judged infeasible—that do not square with policy commu-nity values, that would cost more than the budget will allow, that run afoul of opposition in either the mass or specialized publics, or that would not find a receptive audience among elected politicians—are less likely to survive than proposals that meet these standards. In the process of consideration in the policy community, ideas themselves are important. Pressure models do not completely describe the process. Proposals are evaluated partly in terms of their political support and opposition, to be sure, but partly against logical or analytical criteria as well.

There is a long process of softening up the system. Policy entrepreneurs do not leave consideration of their pet proposals to accident. Instead, they push for consideration in many ways and in many forums. In the process of policy development, recombination (the coupling of already-familiar elements) is more important than mutation (the appearance of wholly new forms). Thus entrepreneurs, who broker people and ideas, are more important than inventors. Because recombination is more important than invention, there may be "no new thing under the sun" at the same time that there may be dramatic change and innovation. There is change, but it involves the recombination of already-familiar elements.

The long softening-up process is critical to policy change. Opportunities for serious hearings, the policy windows we explored in Chapter 8, pass quickly and are missed if the proposals have not already gone through the long gestation process before the window opens. The work of floating and refining proposals is not wasted if it does not bear fruit in the short run. Indeed, it is critically important if the proposal is to be heard at the right time.

Coupling and Windows

The separate streams of problems, policies, and politics each have lives of their own. Problems are recognized and defined according to processes that are different from the ways policies are developed or political events unfold. Policy proposals are developed according to their own incentives and selection criteria, whether or not they are solutions to problems or responsive to political considerations. Political events flow along on their own schedule and according to their own rules, whether or not they are related to problems or proposals.

But there come times when the three streams are joined. A pressing problem demands attention, for instance, and a policy proposal is coupled to the problem as its solution. Or an event in the political stream, such as a change of administration, calls for different directions. At that point, proposals that fit with that political event, such as initiatives that fit with a new administration's philosophy, come to the fore and are coupled with the ripe political climate. Similarly, problems that fit are highlighted, and others are neglected.

Decision Agendas

A complete linkage combines all three streams—problems, policies, and politics—into a single package. Advocates of a new policy initiative not only take advantage of politically propitious moments but also claim that their proposal is a solution to a pressing problem. Likewise, entrepreneurs concerned about a particular problem search for solutions in the policy stream to couple to their problem, then try to take advantage of political receptivity at certain points in time to push the package of problem and solution. At points along the way, there are partial couplings: solutions to problems, but without a receptive political climate: politics to proposals, but without a sense that a compelling problem is being solved: politics and problems both calling for action, but without an available alternative to advocate. But the complete joining of all three streams dramatically enhances the odds that a subject will become firmly fixed on a decision agenda.

Governmental agendas, lists of subjects to which governmental officials are paying serious attention, can be set solely in either problems or political streams, and solely by visible actors. Officials can pay attention to an important problem, for instance, without having a solution to it. Or politics may highlight a subject, even in the absence of either problem or solution. A decision agenda, a list of subjects that is moving into position for an authoritative decision, such as legislative enactment or presidential choice, is set somewhat differently. The probability of an item rising on a decision agenda is dramatically increased if all three elements—problem, policy proposal, and political receptivity—are linked in a single package. Conversely, partial couplings are less likely to rise on decision agendas. Problems that come to decisions without solutions attached, for instance, are not as likely to move into position for an authoritative choice as if they did have solutions attached. And proposals that lack political backing are less likely to move into position for a decision than ones that do have that backing.

A return to our case studies in Chapter 1 illustrates these points. With aviation deregulation, awareness of problems, development of proposals, and swings of national mood all proceeded separately in their own streams. Increasingly through the late 1960s and early 1970s, people became convinced that the economy contained substantial inefficiencies to which the burdens of government regulation contributed. Proposals for deregulation were formed among academics and other specialists, through a softening-up process that included journal articles, testimony, conferences, and other forums. In the 1970s, politicians sensed a change in national mood toward increasing hostility to government size and intrusiveness. All three of the components, therefore, came together at about the same time. The key to movement was the coupling of the policy stream's literature on deregulation with the political incentive to rein in government growth, and those two elements with the sense that there was a real, important, and increasing problem with economic inefficiency.

The waterway user charge case illustrates a similar coupling. A proposal, some form of user charge, had been debated among transportation specialists for years. The political stream produced an administration receptive to imposing a user charge. This combination of policy and politics was coupled with a problem—the necessity, in a time of budget stringency, to repair or replace aging facilities like Lock and Dam 26. Thus did the joining of problem, policy, and politics push the waterway user charge into position on a decision agenda.

By contrast, national health insurance during the Carter years did not have all three components joined. Proponents could argue that there were real problems of medical access, though opponents countered that many of the most severe problems were being addressed through Medicare, Medicaid, and private insurance. The political stream did produce a heavily Democratic Congress and an administration that favored some sort of health insurance initiative. It seemed for a time that serious movement was under way. But the policy stream had not settled on a single, worked-up, viable alternative from among the many proposals floating around. The budget constraint, itself a severe problem, and politicians' reading of the national mood, which seemed to be against costly new initiatives, also proved to be too much to overcome. The coupling was incomplete, and the rise of national health insurance on the agenda proved fleeting. Then the election of Ronald Reagan sealed its fate, at least for the time being.

Success in one area contributes to success in adjacent areas. Once aviation deregulation passed, for instance, government turned with a vengeance to other deregulation proposals, and passed several in short order. These spillovers, as we have called them, occur because politicians sense the payoff in repeating a successful formula in a similar area, because the winning coalition can be transferred, and because advocates can argue from successful precedent. These spillovers are extremely powerful agenda setters, seemingly bowling over even formidable opposition that stands in the way.

Policy Windows

An open policy window is an opportunity for advocates to push their pet solutions or to push attention to their special problems. Indeed, advocates in and around government keep their proposals and their problems at hand, waiting for these opportunities to occur. They have pet solutions, for instance, and wait for problems to float by to which they can attach their solutions, or for developments in the political stream that they can use to their advantage. Or they wait for similar opportunities to bring their special problems to the fore, such as the appearance of a new administration that would be concerned with these problems. That administration opens a window for them to bring greater attention to the problems about which they are concerned.

Windows are opened by events in either the problems or political streams. Thus there are problems windows and political windows. A new problem appears, for instance, creating an opportunity to attach a solution to it. Or such events in the political stream as turnover of elected officials, swings of national mood, or vigorous lobbying might create opportunities to push some problems and proposals to the fore and dampen the chances to highlight other problems and proposals.

Sometimes, windows open quite predictably. Legislation comes up for renewal on a schedule, for instance, creating opportunities to change, expand, or abolish certain programs. At other times, windows open quite unpredictably, as when an airliner crashes or a fluky election produces an unexpected turnover in key decision makers. Predictable or unpredictable, open windows are small and scarce. Opportunities come, but they also pass. Windows do not stay open long. If a chance is missed, another must be awaited.

The scarcity and the short duration of the opening of a policy window create a powerful magnet for problems and proposals. When a window opens, problems and proposals flock to it. People concerned with particular problems see the open window as their opportunity to address or even solve these problems. Advocates of particular proposals see the open window as the opportunity to enact them. As a result, the system comes to be loaded down with problems and proposals. If participants are willing to invest sufficient resources, some of the problems can be resolved and some of the proposals enacted. Other problems and proposals drift away because insufficient resources are mobilized.

Open windows present opportunities for the complete linkage of problems, proposals, and politics, and hence opportunities to move packages of the three joined elements up on decision agendas. One particularly crucial coupling is the link of a solution to something else. Advocates of pet proposals watch for developments in the political stream that they can take advantage of, or try to couple their solution to whatever problems are floating by at the moment. Once they have made the partial coupling of proposal to either problem or politics, they attempt to join all three elements, knowing that the chances for enactment are considerably enhanced if they can complete the circle. Thus they try to hook packages of problems and solutions to political forces, packages of proposals and political incentives to perceived problems, or packages of problems and politics to some proposal taken from the policy stream.

Entrepreneurs

Policy entrepreneurs are people willing to invest their resources in return for future policies they favor. They are motivated by combinations of several things: their straightforward concern about certain problems, their pursuit of such self-serving benefits as protecting or expanding their bureaucracy's budget or claiming credit for accomplishment, their promotion of their policy values, and their simple pleasure in participating. We have encountered them at three junctures: pushing their concerns about certain problems higher on the agenda, pushing their pet proposals during a process of softening up the system, and making the couplings we just discussed. These entrepreneurs are found at many locations; they might be elected officials, career civil servants, lobbyists, academics, or journalists. No one type of participant dominates the pool of entrepreneurs.

As to problems, entrepreneurs try to highlight the indicators that so importantly dramatize their problems. They push for one kind of problem definition rather than another. Because they know that focusing events can move subjects higher on the agenda, entrepreneurs push to create such things as personal viewings of problems by policy makers and the diffusion of a symbol that captures their problem in a nutshell. They also may prompt the kinds of feedback about current governmental performance that affect agendas: letters, complaints, and visits to officials.

As to proposals, entrepreneurs are central to the softening-up process. They write papers, give testimony, hold hearings, try to get press coverage, and meet endlessly with important and not-so-important people. They float their ideas as trial balloons, get reactions, revise their proposals in the light of reactions, and float them again. They aim to soften up the mass public, specialized publics, and the policy community itself. The process takes years of effort.

As to coupling, entrepreneurs once again appear when windows open. They have their pet proposals or their concerns about problems ready, and push them at the propitious moments. In the pursuit of their own goals, they perform the function for the system of coupling solutions to problems, problems to political forces, and political forces to proposals. The joining of the separate streams described earlier depends heavily on the appearance of the right entrepreneur at the right time. In our case study of Health Maintenance Organizations in Chapter 1, Paul Ellwood appeared on the scene to link his pet proposal (HMOs) to the problem of medical care costs and to the political receptivity created by the Nixon administration casting about for health initiatives. The problems and political streams had opened a window, and Ellwood cleverly took advantage of that opportunity to push his HMO proposal, joining all three streams in the process.

The appearance of entrepreneurs when windows are open, as well as their more enduring activities of trying to push their problems and proposals into prominence, are central to our story. They bring several key resources into the fray: their claims to a hearing, their political connections and negotiating skills, and their sheer persistence. An item's chances for moving up on an agenda are enhanced considerably by the presence of a skillful entrepreneur, and dampened considerably if no entrepreneur takes on the cause, pushes it, and makes the critical couplings when policy windows open.

Conclusion

The ideas we have explored in the pages of this book have a few important properties which it is appropriate to highlight as we draw to a close. These properties fall into two general categories: the differences between our model of these processes and other notions, and the places of randomness and pattern.

Other Notions

The ideas developed in this book are quite unlike many other theories that could have captured our attention. For example, events do not proceed nearly in stages, steps, or phases. Instead, independent streams that flow through the system all at once, each with a life of its own and equal with one another, become coupled when a window opens. Thus participants do not first identify problems and then seek solutions for them; indeed, advocacy of solutions often precedes the highlighting of problems to which they become attached. Agendas are not first set and then alternatives generated; instead, alternatives must be advocated for a long period before a short-run opportunity presents itself on an agenda. Events do not necessarily proceed in similar order in several different case studies: instead, many things happen separately in each case, and become coupled at critical points.

Other notions have elements of truth, and do describe parts of the processes, but they are incomplete. A pressure model, for instance, does describe parts of the political stream, but ideas are as important as pressure in other parts of the processes. Agenda items do not necessarily start in a larger systemic or public arena and transfer to a formal or governmental agenda; indeed, the flow is just as often in the reverse direction. As we argued in Chapter 4, a concentration on origins does not take us very far because ideas come from many locations, nobody has a monopoly on leadership or prescience, and tracing origins involves an infinite regress. We were drawn to the importance of combinations rather than single origins, and to a climate of receptivity that allows ideas to take off. Also in Chapter 4, we portrayed comprehensive-rational and incremental models as incomplete. Participants sometimes do approach their decisions quite comprehensively and decide quite rationally, but the larger process is less tidy. Incrementalism does describe the slow process of generating alternatives, and often does describe small legislative and bureaucratic changes stretching over many years, but does not describe agenda change well. Thus, In addition to arguing for one way of looking at the policy formation world, we have argued what the world does *not* look like.

On Randomness and Pattern

We still encounter considerable doses of messiness, accident, fortuitous coupling, and dumb luck. Subjects sometimes rise on agendas without our understanding completely why. We are sometimes surprised by the couplings that take place. The fortuitous appearance or absence of key participants affect outcomes. There remains some degree of unpredictability.

Yet it would be a grave mistake to conclude that the processes explored in this book are essentially random. Some degree of pattern is evident in three fundamental sources: processes within each stream, processes that structure couplings, and general constraints on the system.

First, processes operating within each stream limit randomness. Within the problems stream, not every problem has an equal chance of surfacing. Those conditions that are not highlighted by indicators, focusing events, or feedback are less likely to be brought to the attention of governmental officials than conditions that do have those advantages. Furthermore, not all conditions are defined as problems. Conditions that do not conflict with important values or that are placed in an inappropriate category are less likely to be translated into problems than conditions that are evaluated or categorized appropriately. In the policy stream, not every proposal surfaces. Selection criteria make patterns out of initial noise. Proposals that meet such standards as technical feasibility, value acceptability, public acquiescence, politicians' receptivity, and budgetary stringency are more likely to survive than those that fail to meet such standards. In the political stream, not every environment or event is equally likely. Some groups lack the resources that others have, some swings of national mood (e.g., to socialism) are unlikely, and some types of turnover of elected officials are more likely than others.

Second, some couplings are more likely than others. Everything cannot interact with everything else. For one thing, the timing of an item's arrival in its stream affects its ability to be joined to items in other streams. A window may open, for instance, but a solution may not be available at that time in the policy stream, so the window closes without a coupling of solution to problem or politics. Or a proposal may be ready in the policy stream, but the political conditions are not right for it to be pushed, again limiting the coupling possibilities. In addition to timing, germaneness limits the coupling possibilities. Not all solutions have an equal possibility of being discussed with all problems. Instead, participants have some sense of what would constitute an appropriate solution to a problem. There is some room for different solutions being hooked to a given problem or different problems being hooked to a given solution, but participants also set some limits on the appropriate couplings. Finally, the appearance of a skillful entrepreneur enhances the probability of a coupling. Potential couplings without entrepreneurs are less likely because they fail for lack of someone willing to invest resources in them.

Third, there are various constraints on the system, limits that provide a basic structure within which the participants play the games we have described.[1] The political stream provides many of these constraints. Participants sense some boundaries that are set on their actions by the mood of the mass public, and narrower boundaries set by the preferences of specialized publics and elected politicians. As I have argued elsewhere, governmental officials sense these limits and believe they must operate within them.[2] The budget imposes constraints as well. Costly proposals are not likely to be addressed in times of economic contraction or budget stringency, but might be more likely to receive attention in more robust times. Various rules of procedure, including the constitution, statutes, prescribed jurisdictions, precedents, customary decision-making modes, and other legal requirements, all impose structures on the participants. Finally, the scarcity of open windows constrains participants. They compete for limited space on agendas, and queue up for their turn. Even the selection criteria used by specialists in the policy stream anticipate these constraints.

---

[1] For a good discussion of constraints, see Roger W. Cobb and Charles D. Elder, "Communications and Public Policy," in Dan Nimmo and Keith Sanders, eds., *Handbook of Political Communications* (Beverly Hills: Sage, 1981), pp. 402–408.

[2] John W. Kingdon, *Congressmen's Voting Decisions*, 3rd ed. (Ann Arbor: University of Michigan Press, 1989), Chapter 12.

These various types of pattern—dynamics internal to each stream, limits on coupling possibilities, and more general constraints—help us understand why some items never rise on policy agendas. Chapter 1 set forth several such items in health and transportation in the late 1970s. Some of them, such as long-term care and mental health, remained low, not because participants would not recognize real problems there but because they had little sense for alternatives that might be available as solutions. Some agenda items, such as buses, did not have powerful constituencies behind them in the political stream and failed to receive attention for lack of such advocates. Items such as rail nationalization failed because of powerful opposition. Others were not prominent on health and transportation agendas because systems of special-ization and jurisdiction limited their movement. Items like direct delivery of medical care and food and drug regulation were indeed high on certain spe-cialized agendas, but not on the larger health agenda. Finally, some items like environmental impact and transportation safety had been prominent earlier, but were played out by the time of these interviews, according to dynamics we explored when examining why problems fade. Thus this study helps to under-stand not only the appearance of some items on agendas, but also the failure of other items to appear.

Finally, it should be noted that all of our ideas are probabilistic. I have tried to adhere to such formulations as "the chances are improved or lessened" and "these events are more likely than others." In describing these processes, hard-and-fast rules and the specification of conditions that *must* be met seem less fruitful than a quotation of odds. Constraints, for instance, are not absolutes. Instead, they are conditions that make some events highly unlikely and other events more likely to occur. They do impose structure on the system, but it is structure that still allows room for some gray areas and some unpre-dictability. A budget constraint, for instance, is subject to some interpretation in the light of knowledge gaps and participants' values, but its operation still does make attention to some proposals at some points in time highly unlikely.

Thus we have made some progress in understanding the vague and imprecise phenomena we wanted to understand at the beginning of our jour-ney. To the extent that our vision is still obscured, the world itself may be somewhat opaque.

Review Questions

1. According to Roger Cobb and Charles Elder how does the agenda-setting process work in the American political system? Can you provide an example of how an issue has been nurtured by its supporters so that it eventually ended up on a governmental agenda for resolution?

2. What are the five phases in the issue-attention cycle put forth by Anthony Downs? Can you state any recent policy issue and trace its progress through the Downs's cycle?

3. How does John Kingdon explain the agenda-setting process using the "three process streams" of problems, policies, and politics? Why are windows of opportunity so critical for allowing issues to come onto a policy-making agenda for resolution?

Chapter 5

The Political
Economy of
Public Policy

Economics is the study of how people or states use their limited resources to satisfy their unlimited wants; how scarce resources are allocated among competing needs. Political economy is the conjunction of politics and economics, the field that studied the intersections between the economy and the state before either political science or economics became distinct disciplines. According to the "father" of modern economics, Adam Smith (1723–1790) in his *Wealth of Nations* (1776), political economy is that "branch of the science of a statesman or legislator" that provides "a plentiful revenue or subsistence for the people . . . and [provides] the state or commonwealth with a revenue sufficient for the public service. It proposes to enrich both the people and the sovereign."

A contemporary that Smith never met, Alexander Hamilton (1755–1804) took this science very seriously. While President George Washington's Secretary of the Treasury, Hamilton wrote his *Report on Manufactures* (1791) that explained why government intervention in the economy was desirable. The *Report*, which calls for a tariff system to protect American industry and for federal public works for roads and canals, was to influence American economic policy for generations. Hamilton felt that the general welfare required that government encourage infant industries to avoid overdependence on other countries for essential supplies. Ever since, American politicians have been intervening in an effort to achieve Smith's goal of enriching "both the people and the sovereign."

Political economy is a paramount public policy concern because of the primacy of economic prosperity to U.S. governments. Not only does the government account for one-third of the gross national product, it also regulates the basic economic conditions of society. For example, it can specify production of a product, regulate the wages of the production workers, prescribe working conditions, and establish standards for and inspect the quality of the finished product. The recurring policy questions have to do with whether interest rates should be higher or lower, whether government spending on public works should be increased or decreased, and whether inflation should be modestly encouraged or severely discouraged. The perpetual policy problem here is that there is seldom consensus on how to achieve any of these goals even if the goals themselves could be agreed upon.

American government has been concerned with economic issues even before its beginning. Remember that the 1776 Declaration of Independence contained a long list of the reasons for claiming independence, many of which had economic implications—such as taxation. So it is hardly surprising that economic issues were prominent when the founders met at the Constitutional Convention of 1787. While it is incontestable that the Constitution addressed economic concerns such as a common currency and the regulation of commerce, it is an open question whether the U.S. Constitution was primarily written to further the economic interests of its authors.

This is the contention of historian Charles A. Beard (1874–1948) in *An Economic Interpretation of the Constitution of the United States* (1913), portions reprinted here. He contended that the founders wrote the Constitution in large measure to protect their personal economic interests and that it is "an economic document drawn with superb skill by men whose property interests were immediately at stake." While best known for this explanation of how the founders developed a political system to protect their fortunes and prospects, Beard was one of the most influential of all twentieth-century American historians in part because of the sheer number of his books (more than fifty), often written with his wife Mary (1876–1958), and which in their totality sold many millions. In addition to being both a major scholar and popular historian, Beard was also an important figure in the early evolution of public administration.

In one of the most influential of all economics books, *The General Theory of Employment, Interest, and Money* (1936), John Maynard Keynes (1883–1946) wrote: "The ideas of economists and political philosophers, both when they are right and when they are wrong, are more powerful than is commonly understood. Indeed the world is ruled by little else. Practical men, who believe themselves to be quite exempt from any intellectual influences, are usually the slaves of some defunct economist."

"Defunct" is too strong a word for our next classic author. While the economist in question is certainly defunct meaning "dead" (though only recently so), he is far from defunct meaning "finished." Indeed, with the elevation of George W. Bush to the American presidency, the Austrian-born Friedrich A. Hayek (1899–1992) has never been more influential.

After being educated at the University of Vienna, Hayek produced pioneering work on business cycles. He became so acclaimed that in 1931 at age 32 he effectively reached the top of his profession when he was appointed the Tooke Professor of Economic Science and Statistics at the University of London. He thrived in England, produced a series of papers on how capitalism's price system functions as an information processing machine, and became a British subject in 1938. But when World War II broke out and his academic peers, such as his close friend Keynes, were offered significant positions in the civil service, he was blacklisted from such work because of his Austrian background. (Austria had been incorporated into Germany; and no German—even a forsworn one—could be trusted with war work.) This had the unintentional but beneficial effect of giving him the time to write what became his most enduring and influential book, *The Road to Serfdom* (1944).

Hayek's *Road*, written for a popular audience, argued that "the unforeseen but inevitable consequences of socialist planning create a state of affairs in which, if the policy is to be pursued, totalitarian forces will get the upper hand." To Hayek state intervention in the economy in Great Britain and the United States differed only in degree, not in kind, from the fascism of Hitler and the communism of Stalin. The evil to be resisted was collectivism whether it wore a swastika or not. By asserting that allied economic policies were headed in the direction of Nazi policies, Hayek was being deliberately provocative and controversial. According to Hayek, "there is scarcely a leaf out of Hitler's [economic] book which somebody or other in England or America has not recommended us to take and use for our own purposes." Thus the "road" to serfdom was a collectivism that would ultimately lead to a Hitler-like totalitarianism. Consequently, open market capitalism, a political system with minimal state planning and regulation, offered the only logical means to maintain prosperous and free societies.

Hayek's book, which can be condensed into five words—government planning leads to dictatorship—was an immediate sensation on both sides of the Atlantic. But it made Hayek decidedly unpopular in a postwar Britain that was implementing the socialist agenda of the Labour Party. So after a messy divorce that alienated him from even more friends and colleagues, Hayek moved across the pond to the University of Chicago.

In a world moving increasingly toward centralized planning, Hayek seemed more like a crank than a prophet during the next two decades. Nevertheless, in 1974 he was awarded the Nobel Prize in Economics and his work became the foundation of the modern conservative movement. The ascent to power of British Prime Minister Margaret Thatcher in 1979 and U.S. President Ronald Reagan in 1981 created an informal trans-Atlantic coalition to advance Hayek's principles of less government and market rule. The movement toward privatization and deregulation then had as its champions the two most influential political voices in the English speaking world. Reprinted here is Chapter 2, "Planning and Democracy," from Hayek's attack on socialism. He considered socialism to be, quite literally, "the road to serfdom."

John Kenneth Galbraith (1908–) is the Harvard professor who knew John F. Kennedy as an undergraduate and then became President Kennedy's ambassador to India. The author of many best-sellers on economic history, Galbraith is a noted Democratic Party activist who has long called for the public ownership of those private corporations doing most of their business with the government. Galbraith finds public administration to be a major impediment to his socialistic vision: "No argument against public ownership is so much used or so effective as the allegation that it is incompetent," *The New Republic* (August 16, 1975). Galbraith concludes that the "extension of the area of public ownership is only possible politically or economically as the reputation for efficient public management is affirmed." So it is the reputation of American public administration that protects the republic from the socialism Galbraith prefers and Hayek abhors.

In 1958, Galbraith published his most famous book, *The Affluent Society.* Here he described American society as one in which scarcity of resources was not a major problem, but where "private affluence and public squalor" existed continuously side by side. Today, this trend is becoming even more pronounced. Journalists such as Michael Lind in *Harpers* (June 1995) are observing a "new feudalism" which "reverses the trend of the past thousand years toward the government's provision of basic public goods like policing, public roads, and transport networks, and public schools." Lind echoes Galbraith when he concludes that "in the United States—to a degree unmatched in any other industrialized democracy—these public goods are once again becoming private luxuries."

When public services deteriorate—especially in urban areas—those with enough money increasingly buy their way out of the problem. They send their children to private schools and hire private police. And in the best feudal tradition, they retire each night behind walled cities where guards at a gate check the identity of all who seek to enter. We are not just talking about an apartment building with a doorkeeper. We are talking about millions of citizens living in suburban "gated communities" with their own private police, private streets, and private parks. Present trends have made Galbraith's *Affluent Society* more current than ever. A portion of Galbraith's prophetic analysis is reprinted here. Note that this book introduced the term "conventional wisdom" meaning that which is generally believed to be true. However, any writer who uses the phrase is setting something up to be knocked down; so conventional wisdom really means that which most people believe to be true, but really isn't. Galbraith observed: "Only posterity is unkind to the man of conventional wisdom, and all posterity does is bury him in a blanket of neglect."

Milton Friedman, (1912–) is the conservative economist generally considered the leading proponent of a return to laissez-faire economics. A 1976 Nobel Prize winner, he has been a major influence on thinking about monetary policy, consumption, and government regulation. His most important work, *A Monetary History of the United States, 1867–1960* (1963), with Anna Schwartz, is a major reconstruction of the history of money and banking. In it, he argues that the Great Depression was caused not by a failure of free markets but by a sharp and continuous decline in the money supply for which the government was responsible. Consequently, Friedman is the leading advocate for a monetary policy that calls for a constant and predictable money growth.

Contemporary analysis of the utility of school vouchers begins with the work of Milton Friedman. As early as 1955 he argued that all parents should be provided with unrestricted vouchers that would allow them to send their students to either public or private schools. Friedman's advocacy of school vouchers follows in the tradition of Hayek's aversion to state planning. As with Hayek's notions, Friedman's ideas on education were met with heavy skepticism. He was proposing nothing less than the abolition of the public schools as we knew them. However, as many public schools faced with the related problems of busing and white flight deteriorated, his ideas became newly appealing.

On May 9, 2002, on his 90th birthday, Friedman was once again honored at a White House reception. (He was awarded the Presidential Medal of Freedom in 1988). In his speech to President George W. Bush and his guests, Friedman used this four part typology to explain his philosophy of public policy:

> When a man spends his own money to buy something for himself, he is very careful how much he spends and how he spends it.
>
> When a man spends his own money to buy something for someone else, he is still very careful about how much he spends, but somewhat less what he spends it on.
>
> When a man spends someone else's money to buy something for himself, he is very careful about what he buys, but doesn't care at all how much he spends.
>
> And when a man spends someone else's money on someone else, he doesn't care how much he spends or what he spends it on.
>
> And that's government for you.

Friedman is generally considered to be the intellectual godfather to the movement toward government deregulation, the lifting of restrictions on business, industry, and other professional activities for which government rules were established and bureaucracies created to administer. The modern movement toward deregulation, which really began in the late 1970s during the Jimmy Carter administration, was supported by both parties, but for different reasons. Republicans tended to support it because they were inclined to be philosophically hostile toward government interference with business in the first place. Democrats tended to support it because they felt that greater market competition would bring down prices for the consumer. Reprinted here is the introduction from Friedman's 1962 *Capitalism and Freedom*, his highly influential rationale for deregulation in which he also explains the evolution of the word "liberal" as it reversed its meaning from the nineteenth to the twentieth centuries.

Sometimes the best way to figure out what to do is to play games—literally. Game theory is a quantitative approach to the analysis of policy decisions related to problems of conflict and collaboration between rational actors in an uncertain world. Game theory is often illustrated by the "Prisoners' Dilemma." This supposes that two men have been arrested on a suspicion of committing a crime together and are being held in separate cells. There is not enough evidence to prosecute unless one confesses and implicates the other. Both of them know this, but cannot talk to each other. The dilemma is that the best outcome, not being convicted, is only available if they trust each other. So if X decides to trust Y, but Y fears X may not be trustworthy, Y may confess to get a lesser sentence; X then gets a worse one. This dilemma calls for both to cooperate, to minimize the worst that can happen, rather than trying for the outcome that is maximum. This is called the "Minimax" strategy; game theorists consider it to be the most probable outcome.

"Prisoner's Dilemma" and other game structures are often used to describe or explain relations among states. Particularly noteworthy is Robert Axelrod's *Evolution of Cooperation* (1984), which demonstrates very clearly that when games are iterative and tit-for-tat strategies are followed as in the Prisoner's Dilemma, the long-term benefits of cooperative strategies become very clear. This can be illustrated in relation to the arms race or to highlight the dangers of escalation as a strategy. When both states strive to achieve superiority in armaments, especially at the nuclear level, the most likely outcome is that they will simply achieve stalemate at a higher level of arms and at great cost. If they have a degree of trust and neither tries to maximize gains at the expense of the adversary, then they can find solutions that are less costly. Similarly, escalatory strategies can simply lead both sides in a crisis to become much worse off than if they cooperated to keep things under control.

A zero-sum game is a perspective that views potential gains for one side as a loss for the other; for one player to win, another must lose. This brings the overall outcome to zero. Once used only in game theory, the idea of zero-sum conflict has gradually gained wider usage. One example of a zero-sum conflict is the fight for the control of disputed territories. If one side has the land, then the other side is basically dispossessed. Zero-sum conflicts of this kind are especially difficult conflicts to resolve as there is so little common ground between the parties.

Lester Thurow (1938–), the Harvard University trained economist who has spent his academic career at the nearby Massachusetts Institute of Technology, seems to have inherited John Kenneth Galbraith's mantle as the best selling left of center economist. In his best known book, *The Zero-Sum Society* (1980), portions reprinted here, he takes the zero-sum idea from game theory and applies it to the "game" of the national economy. Here he discussed the human cost of economic stagnation. All workers were involved in a zero-sum game in which some lose and some win. In these domestic economic wars the winners get lower taxes and economic policies favorable to their interests; the losers often get higher relative taxes and the joys of unemployment. Consequently, he contends that there is no way elected officials can avoid hurting some segments of society in the process of making economic policy. That is why he considers economic policymaking to be a zero-sum game.

16

An Economic Interpretation of the Constitution (1913)

Charles A. Beard

The requirements for an economic interpretation of the formation and adoption of the Constitution may be stated in a hypothetical proposition which, although it cannot be verified absolutely from ascertainable data, will at once illustrate the problem and furnish a guide to research and generalization.

It will be admitted without controversy that the Constitution was the creation of a certain number of men, and it was opposed by a certain number of men. Now, if it were possible to have an economic biography of all those connected with its framing and adoption,—perhaps about 160,000 men altogether,—the materials for scientific analysis and classification would be available. Such an economic biography would include a list of the real and personal property owned by all of these men and their families: lands and houses, with incumbrances, money at interest, slaves, capital invested in shipping and manufacturing, and in state and continental securities.

Suppose it could be shown from the classification of the men who supported and opposed the Constitution that there was no line of property division at all; that is, that men owning substantially the same amounts of the same kinds of property were equally divided on the matter of adoption or rejection— it would then become apparent that the Constitution had no ascertainable relation to economic groups or classes, but was the product of some abstract causes remote from the chief business of life—gaining a livelihood.

Suppose, on the other hand, that substantially all of the merchants, money lenders, security holders, manufacturers, shippers, capitalists, and financiers and their professional associates are to be found on one side in support of the Constitution and that substantially all or the major portion of the opposition came from the non-slaveholding farmers and the debtors—would it not be pretty conclusively demonstrated that our fundamental law was not the

Source: Charles A. Beard, *An Economic Interpretation of the Constitution,* 1913.

product of an abstraction known as "the whole people," but of a group of economic interests which must have expected beneficial results from its adoption. Obviously all the facts here desired cannot be discovered, but the data presented in the following chapters bear out the latter hypothesis, and thus a reasonable presumption in favor of the theory is created.

Of course, it may be shown (and perhaps can be shown) that the farmer and debtors who opposed the Constitution were, in fact, benefited by the general improvement which resulted from its adoption. It may likewise be shown to take an extreme case, that the English nation derived immense advantage from the Norman Conquest and the orderly administrative processes which were introduced, as it undoubtedly did; nevertheless, it does not follow that the vague thing known as "the advancement of general welfare" or some abstraction known as "justice" was the immediate, guiding purpose of the leaders in either of these great historic changes. The point is, that the direct impelling motive in both cases was the economic advantages which the beneficiaries expected would accrue to themselves first, from their action. Further than this, economic interpretation cannot go. It may be that some large world-process is working through each series of historical events; but ultimate causes lie beyond our horizon. . . .

A survey of the economic interests of the members of the Convention presents certain conclusions:

A majority of the members were lawyers by profession.

Most of the members came from towns, on or near the coast, that is, from the regions in which personalty was largely concentrated.

Not one member represented in his immediate personal economic interests the small farming or mechanic classes.

The overwhelming majority of members, at least five-sixths, were immediately, directly, and personally interested in the outcome of their labors at Philadelphia, and were to a greater or less extent economic beneficiaries from the adoption of the Constitution. . . .

It cannot be said, therefore, that the members of the Convention were "disinterested." On the contrary, we are forced to accept the profoundly significant conclusion that they knew through their personal experiences in economic affairs the precise results which the new government that they were setting up was designed to attain. As a group of doctrinaries, like the Frankfort assembly of 1848, they would have failed miserably; but as practical men they were able to build the new government upon the only foundations which could be stable: fundamental economic interests. . . .

Conclusions

At the close of this long and arid survey—partaking of the nature of catalogue—it seems worth while to bring together the important conclusions for political science which the data presented appear to warrant.

The movement for the Constitution of the United States was originated and carried through principally by four groups of personalty interests which had been adversely affected under the Articles of Confederation: money, public securities, manufactures, and trade and shipping.

The first firm steps toward the formation of the Constitution were taken by a small and active group of men immediately interested through their personal possessions in the outcome of their labors.

No popular vote was taken directly or indirectly on the proposition to call the Convention which drafted the Constitution.

A large propertyless mass was, under the prevailing suffrage qualifications, excluded at the outset from participation (through representatives) in the work of framing the Constitution.

The members of the Philadelphia Convention which drafted the Constitution were, with a few exceptions, immediately, directly, and personally interested in, and derived economic advantages from, the establishment of the new system.

The Constitution was essentially an economic document based upon the concept that the fundamental private rights of property are anterior to government and morally beyond the reach of popular majorities.

The major portion of the members of the Convention are on record as recognizing the claim of property to a special and defensive position in the Constitution.

In the ratification of the Constitution, about three-fourths of the adult males failed to vote on the question, having abstained from the elections at which delegates to the state conventions were chosen, either on account of their indifference or their disenfranchisement by property qualifications.

The Constitution was ratified by a vote of probably not more than one-sixth of the adult males.

It is questionable whether a majority of the voters participating in the elections for the state conventions in New York, Massachusetts, New Hampshire, Virginia, and South Carolina, actually approved the ratification of the Constitution.

The leaders who supported the Constitution in the ratifying conventions represented the same economic groups as the members of the Philadelphia Convention; and in a large number of instances they were also directly and personally interested in the outcome of their efforts.

In the ratification, it became manifest that the line of cleavage for and against the Constitution was between substantial personalty interests on the one hand and the small farming and debtor interests on the other.

The Constitution was not created by "the whole people" as the jurists have said; neither was it created by "the states" as Southern nullifiers long contended; but it was the work of a consolidated group whose interests knew no state boundaries and were truly national in their scope.

17

The Road to Serfdom (1944)

Friedrich A. Hayek

The statesman who should attempt to direct private people in what manner they ought to employ their capitals, would not only load himself with a most unnecessary attention, but assume an authority which could safely be trusted to no council and senate whatever, and which would nowhere be so dangerous as in the hands of a man who had folly and presumption enough to fancy himself fit to exercise it.

—ADAM SMITH

The common features of all collectivist systems may be described, in a phrase ever dear to socialists of all schools, as the deliberate organization of the labors of society for a definite social goal. That our present society lacks such "conscious" direction toward a single aim, that its activities are guided by the whims and fancies of irresponsible individuals, has always been one of the main complaints of its socialist critics.

In many ways this puts the basic issue very clearly. And it directs us at once to the point where the conflict arises between individual freedom and collectivism. The various kinds of collectivism, communism, fascism, etc., differ among themselves in the nature of the goal toward which they want to direct the efforts of society. But they all differ from liberalism and individualism in wanting to organize the whole of society and all its resources for this unitary end and in refusing to recognize autonomous spheres in which the ends of the individuals are supreme. In short, they are totalitarian in the true sense of this new word which we have adopted to describe the unexpected but nevertheless inseparable manifestations of what in theory we call collectivism.

The "social goal," or "common purpose," for which society is to be organized is usually vaguely described as the "common good," the "general welfare," or the "general interest." It does not need much reflection to see that these terms have no sufficiently definite meaning to determine a particular course of action. The welfare and the happiness of millions cannot be measured on a single scale of less and more. The welfare of a people, like the happiness of a man, depends on a great many things that can be provided in an infinite variety of combinations. It cannot be adequately expressed as a single end, but only as a hierarchy of ends, a comprehensive scale of values in which every need of every person is given its place. To direct all our activities according to a single plan presupposes that every one of our needs is given its rank in an order of values which must be complete enough to make it possible to decide among all the different courses which the planner has to choose. It presupposes, in short, the existence of a complete ethical code in which all the different human values are allotted their due place.

The conception of a complete ethical code is unfamiliar, and it requires some effort of imagination to see what it involves. We are not in the habit of thinking of moral codes as more or less complete. The fact that we are constantly choosing between different values without a social code prescribing how we ought to choose does not surprise us and does not suggest to us that our moral code is incomplete. In our society there is neither occasion nor reason why people should develop common views about what should be done in such situations. But where all the means to be used are the property of society and are to be used in the name of society according to a unitary plan, a "social" view about what ought to be done must guide all decisions. In such a world we should soon find that our moral code is full of gaps.

We are not concerned here with the question whether it would be desirable to have such a complete ethical code. It may merely be pointed out that up to the present the growth of civilization has been accompanied by a steady diminution of the sphere in which individual actions are bound by fixed rules. The rules of which our common moral code consists have progressively become fewer and more general in character. From the primitive man, who was bound by an elaborate ritual in almost every one of his daily activities, who was limited by innumerable taboos, and who could scarcely conceive of doing things in a way different from his fellows, morals have more and more tended to become merely limits circumscribing the sphere within which the individual could behave as he liked. The adoption of a common ethical code comprehensive enough to determine a unitary economic plan would mean a complete reversal of this tendency.

The essential point for us is that no such complete ethical code exists. The attempt to direct all economic activity according to a single plan would raise innumerable questions to which the answer could be provided only by a moral rule, but to which existing morals have no answer and where there exists no agreed view on what ought to be done. People will have either no definite views or conflicting views on such questions, because in the free society in which we have lived there has been no occasion to think about them and still less to form common opinions about them.

Not only do we not possess such an all-inclusive scale of values: it would be impossible for any mind to comprehend the infinite variety of different needs of different people which compete for the available resources and to attach a definite weight to each. For our problem it is of minor importance whether the ends for which any person cares comprehend only his own individual needs, or whether they include the needs of his closer or even those of his more distant fellows—that is, whether he is egoistic or altruistic in the ordinary senses of these words. The point which is so important is the basic fact that it is impossible for any man to survey more than a limited field, to be aware of the urgency of more than a limited number of needs. Whether his interests center round his own physical needs, or whether he takes a warm interest in the welfare of every human being he knows, the ends about which he can be concerned will always be only an infinitesimal fraction of the needs of all men.

This is the fundamental fact on which the whole philosophy of individualism is based. It does not assume, as is often asserted, that man is egoistic or selfish or ought to be. It merely starts from the indisputable fact that the limits of our powers of imagination make it impossible to include in our scale of values more than a sector of the needs of the whole society, and that, since, strictly speaking, scales of value can exist only in individual minds, nothing but partial scales of values exist—scales which are inevitably different and often inconsistent with each other. From this the individualist concludes that the individuals should be allowed, within defined limits, to follow their own values and preferences rather than somebody else's; that within these spheres the individual's system of ends should be supreme and not subject to any dictation by others. It is this recognition of the individual as the ultimate judge of his ends, the belief that as far as possible his own views ought to govern his actions, that forms the essence of the individualist position.

This view does not, of course, exclude the recognition of social ends, or rather of a coincidence of individual ends which makes it advisable for men to combine for their pursuit. But it limits such common action to the instances where individual views coincide; what are called "social ends" are for it merely identical ends of many individuals—or ends to the achievement of which individuals are willing to contribute in return for the assistance they receive in the satisfaction of their own desires. Common action is thus limited to the fields where people agree on common ends. Very frequently these common ends will not be ultimate ends to the individuals but means which different persons can use for different purposes. In fact, people are most likely to agree on common action where the common end is not an ultimate end to them but a means capable of serving a great variety of purposes.

When individuals combine in a joint effort to realize ends they have in common, the organizations, like the state, that they form for this purpose are given their own system of ends and their own means. But any organization thus formed remains one "person" among others, in the case of the state much more powerful than any of the others, it is true, yet still with its separate and limited sphere in which alone its ends are supreme. The limits of this sphere are determined by the extent to which the individuals agree on particular ends; and the probability that they will agree on a particular course of action necessarily decreases as the scope of such action extends. There are certain functions of the state on the exercise of which there will be practical unanimity among its citizens; there will be others on which there will be agreement of a substantial majority; and so on, until we come to fields where, although each individual might wish the state to act in some way, there will be almost as many views about what the government should do as there are different people.

We can rely on voluntary agreement to guide the action of the state only so long as it is confined to spheres where agreement exists. But not only when the state undertakes direct control in fields where there is no such agreement is it bound to suppress individual freedom. We can unfortunately not indefinitely extend the sphere of common action and still leave the individual free in his own sphere. Once the communal sector, in which the state controls all the means, exceeds a certain proportion of the whole, the effects of its actions dominate the whole system. Although the state controls directly the use of only a large part of the available resources, the effects of its decisions on the remaining part of the economic system become so great that indirectly it controls almost everything. Where, as was, for example, true in Germany as early as 1928, the central and local authorities directly control the use of more than half the national income (according to an official German estimate then, 53 percent), they control indirectly almost the whole economic life of the nation. There is, then, scarcely an individual end which is not dependent for its achievement on the action of the state, and the "social scale of values" which guides the state's action must embrace practically all individual ends.

It is not difficult to see what must be the consequences when democracy embarks upon a course of planning which in its execution requires more agreement than in fact exists. The people may have agreed on adopting a system of directed economy because they have been convinced that it will produce great prosperity. In the discussions leading to the decision, the goal of planning will have been described by some such term as "common welfare," which only conceals the absence of real agreement on the ends of planning. Agreement will in fact exist only on the mechanism to be used. But it is a mechanism which can be used only for a common end; and the question of the precise goal toward which all activity is to be directed will arise as soon as the executive power has to translate the demand for a single plan into a particular plan. Then it will appear that the agreement on the desirability of planning is not supported by agreement on the ends the plan is to serve. The effect of the people's agreeing that there must be central planning, without agreeing on the ends, will be rather as if a group of people were to commit themselves to take a journey together without agreeing where they want to go: with the result that they may all have to make a journey which most of them do not want at all. That planning creates a situation in which it is necessary for us to agree on a much larger number of topics than we have been used to, and that in a planned system we cannot confine collective action to the tasks on which we can agree but are forced to produce agreement on everything in order that any action can be taken at all, is one of the features which contributes more than most to determining the character of a planned system.

It may be the unanimously expressed will of the people that its parliament should prepare a comprehensive economic plan, yet neither the people nor its representatives need therefore be able to agree on any particular plan. The inability of democratic assemblies to carry out what seems to be a clear mandate of the people will inevitably cause dissatisfaction with democratic institutions. Parliaments come to be regarded as ineffective "talking shops," unable or incompetent to carry out the tasks for which they have been chosen. The conviction grows that if efficient planning is to be done, the direction must be "taken out of politics" and placed in the hands of experts—permanent officials or independent autonomous bodies.

The difficulty is well known to socialists. It will soon be half a century since the Webbs began to complain of "the increased incapacity of the House of Commons to cope with its work."[1] More recently, Professor Laski has elaborated the argument:

"It is common ground that the present parliamentary machine is quite unsuited to pass rapidly a great body of complicated legislation. The National Government, indeed, has in substance admitted this by implementing its economy and tariff measures not by detailed debate in the House of Commons but by a wholesale system of delegated legislation. A Labour Government would, I presume, build upon the amplitude of this precedent. It would confine the House of Commons to the two functions it can properly perform: the ventilation of grievances and the discussion of general principles of its measures. Its Bills would take the form of general formulae conferring wide powers on the appropriate government departments; and those powers would be exercised by Order in Council which could, if desired, be attacked in the House by means of a vote of no confidence. The necessity and value of delegated legislation has recently been strongly reaffirmed by the Donoughmore Committee; and its extension is inevitable if the process of socialisation is not to be wrecked by the normal methods of obstruction which existing parliamentary procedure sanctions."

And to make it quite clear that a socialist government must not allow itself to be too much fettered by democratic procedure, Professor Laski at the end of the same article raised the question "whether in a period of transition to Socialism, a Labour Government can risk the overthrow of its measures as a result of the next general election"—and left it significantly unanswered.[2]

---

[1] Sidney and Beatrice Webb, *Industrial Democracy* (1897), p. 800 n.

[2] H. J. Laski, "Labour and the Constitution," *New Statesman and Nation,* No. 81 (new ser.), September 10, 1932, p. 277. In a book (*Democracy in Crisis* [1933], particularly p. 87) in which Professor Laski later elaborated these ideas, his determination that parliamentary democracy must not be allowed to form an obstacle to the realization of socialism is even more plainly expressed: not only would a socialist government "take vast powers and legislate under them by ordinance and decree" and "suspend the classic formulae of normal opposition" but the "continuance of parliamentary government would depend on its [i.e., the Labour government's] possession of guarantees from the Conservative Party that its work of transformation would not be disrupted by repeal in the event of its defeat at the polls"!

As Professor Laski invokes the authority of the Donoughmore Committee, it may be worth recalling that Professor Laski was a member of that committee and presumably one of the authors of its report.

It is important clearly to see the causes of this admitted ineffectiveness of parliaments when it comes to a detailed administration of the economic affairs of a nation. The fault is neither with the individual representatives nor with parliamentary institutions as such but with the contradictions inherent in the task with which they are charged. They are not asked to act where they can agree, but to produce agreement on everything—the whole direction of the resources of the nation. For such a task the system of majority decision is, however, not suited. Majorities will be found where it is a choice between limited alternatives; but it is a superstition to believe that there must be a majority view on everything. There is no reason why there should be a majority in favor of any one of the different possible courses of positive action if their number is legion. Every member of the legislative assembly might prefer some particular plan for the direction of economic activity to no plan, yet no one plan may appear preferable to a majority to no plan at all.

Nor can a coherent plan be achieved by breaking it up into parts and voting on particular issues. A democratic assembly voting and amending a comprehensive economic plan clause by clause, as it deliberates on an ordinary bill, makes nonsense. An economic plan, to deserve the name, must have a unitary conception. Even if a parliament could, proceeding step by step, agree on some scheme, it would certainly in the end satisfy nobody. A complex whole in which all the parts must be most carefully adjusted to each other cannot be achieved through a compromise between conflicting views. To draw up an economic plan in this fashion is even less possible than, for example, successfully to plan a military campaign by democratic procedure. As in strategy it would become inevitable to delegate the task to the experts.

Yet the difference is that, while the general who is put in charge of a campaign is given a single end to which, for the duration of the campaign, all the means under his control have to be exclusively devoted, there can be no such single goal given to the economic planner, and no similar limitation of the means imposed upon him. The general has not got to balance different independent aims against each other; there is for him only one supreme goal. But the ends of an economic plan, or of any part of it, cannot be defined apart from the particular plan. It is the essence of the economic problem that the making of an economic plan involves the choice between conflicting or competing ends—different needs of different people. But which ends do so conflict, which will have to be sacrificed if we want to achieve certain others, in short, which are the alternatives between which we must choose, can only be known to those who know all the facts; and only they, the experts, are in a position to decide which of the different ends are to be given preference. It is inevitable that they should impose their scale of preferences on the community for which they plan.

This is not always clearly recognized, and delegation is usually justified by the technical character of the task. But this does not mean that only the technical detail is delegated, or even that the inability of parliaments to understand the technical detail is the root of the difficulty.[3] Alterations in the structure of civil law are no less technical and no more difficult to appreciate in all their implications; yet nobody has yet seriously suggested that legislation there should be delegated to a body of experts. The fact is that in these fields legislation does not go beyond general rules on which true majority agreement can be achieved, while in the direction of economic activity the interests to be reconciled are so divergent that no true agreement is likely to be reached in a democratic assembly.

It should be recognized, however, that it is not the delegation of law-making power as such which is so objectionable. To oppose delegation as such is to oppose a symptom instead of the cause and, as it may be a necessary result of other causes, to weaken the case. So long as the power that is delegated is merely the power to make general rules, there may be very good reasons why such rules should be laid down by local rather than by the central authority. The objectionable feature is that delegation is so often resorted to because the matter in hand cannot be regulated by general rules but only by the exercise of discretion in the decision of particular cases. In these instances delegation means that some authority is given power to make with the force of law what to all intents and purposes are arbitrary decisions (usually described as "judging the case on its merits").

The delegation of particular technical tasks to separate bodies, while a regular feature, is yet only the first step in the process whereby a democracy which embarks on planning progressively relinquishes its powers. The expedient of

---

[3]It is instructive in this connection briefly to refer to the government document in which in recent years these problems have been discussed. As long as thirteen years ago, that is before England finally abandoned economic liberalism, the process of delegating legislative powers had already been carried to a point where it was felt necessary to appoint a committee to investigate "what safeguards are desirable or necessary to secure the sovereignty of Law." In its report the Donoughmore Committee (*Report of the [Lord Chancellor's] Committee in Ministers' Powers*, Cmd. 4060 [1932]) showed that even at that date Parliament had resorted "to the practice of wholesale and indiscriminate delegation" but regarded this (it was before we had really glanced into the totalitarian abyss!) as an inevitable and relatively innocuous development. And it is probably true that delegation as such need not be a danger to freedom. The interesting point is why delegation had become necessary on such a scale. First place among the causes enumerated in the report is given to the fact that "Parliament nowadays passes so many laws every year" and that "much of the detail is so technical as to be unsuitable for Parliamentary discussion." But if this were all there would be no reason why the detail should not be worked out *before* rather than after Parliament passes a law. What is probably in many cases a much more important reason why, "if Parliament were not willing to delegate law-making power, Parliament would be unable to pass the kind and quantity of legislation which public opinion requires" is innocently revealed in the little sentence that "many of the laws affect people's lives so closely that elasticity is essential"! What does this mean if not conferment of arbitrary power—power limited by no fixed principles and which in the opinion of Parliament cannot be limited by definite and unambiguous rules?

delegation cannot really remove the causes which make all the advocates of comprehensive planning so impatient with the impotence of democracy. The delegation of particular powers to separate agencies creates a new obstacle to the achievement of a single co-ordinated plan. Even if, by this expedient, a democracy should succeed in planning every sector of economic activity, it would still have to face the problem of integrating these separate plans into a unitary whole. Many separate plans do not make a planned whole—in fact, as the planners ought to be the first to admit, they may be worse than no plan. But the democratic legislature will long hesitate to relinquish the decisions on really vital issues, and so long as it does so it makes it impossible for anyone else to provide the comprehensive plan. Yet agreement that planning is necessary, together with the inability of democratic assemblies to produce a plan, will evoke stronger and stronger demands that the government or some single individual should be given powers to act on their own responsibility. The belief is becoming more and more widespread that, if things are to get done, the responsible authorities must be freed from the fetters of democratic procedure.

The cry for an economic dictator is a characteristic stage in the movement toward planning. It is now several years since one of the most acute of foreign students of England, the late Élie Halévy, suggested that, "if you take a composite photograph of Lord Eustace Percy, Sir Oswald Mosley, and Sir Stafford Cripps, I think you would find this common feature—you would find them all agreeing to say: 'We are living in economic chaos and we cannot get out of it except under some kind of dictatorial leadership.'"[4] The number of influential public men whose inclusion would not materially alter the features of the "composite photograph" has since grown considerably.

In Germany, even before Hitler came into power, the movement had already progressed much further. It is important to remember that, for some time before 1933, Germany had reached a stage in which it had, in effect, had to be governed dictatorially. Nobody could then doubt that for the time being democracy had broken down and that sincere democrats like Brüning were no more able to govern democratically than Schleicher or von Papen. Hitler did not have to destroy democracy; he merely took advantage of the decay of democracy and at the critical moment obtained the support of many to whom, though they detested Hitler, he yet seemed the only man strong enough to get things done.

The argument by which the planners usually try to reconcile us with this development is that, so long as democracy retains ultimate control, the essentials of democracy are not affected. Thus Karl Mannheim writes:

"The only [sic] way in which a planned society differs from that of the nineteenth century is that more and more spheres of social life, and ultimately each and all of them, are subjected to state control. But if a few controls can be held in check by parliamentary sovereignty, so can many. . . . In a

---

[4]"Socialism and the Problems of Democratic Parliamentarism," *International Affairs*, XIII, 501.

democratic state sovereignty can be boundlessly strengthened by plenary powers without renouncing democratic control."[5]

This belief overlooks a vital distinction. Parliament can, of course, control the execution of tasks where it can give definite directions, where it has first agreed on the aim and merely delegates the working-out of the detail. The situation is entirely different when the reason for the delegation is that there is no real agreement on the ends, when the body charged with the planning has to choose between ends of whose conflict parliament is not even aware, and when the most that can be done is to present to it a plan which has to be accepted or rejected as a whole. There may and probably will be criticism; but as no majority can agree on an alternative plan, and the parts objected to can almost always be represented as essential parts of the whole, it will remain quite ineffective. Parliamentary discussion may be retained as a useful safety valve and even more as a convenient medium through which the official answers to complaints are disseminated. It may even prevent some flagrant abuses and successfully insist on particular shortcomings being remedied. But it cannot direct. It will at best be reduced to choosing the persons who are to have practically absolute power. The whole system will tend toward that plebiscitarian dictatorship in which the head of the government is from time to time confirmed in his position by popular vote, but where he has all the powers at his command to make certain that the vote will go in the direction he desires.

It is the price of democracy that the possibilities of conscious control are restricted to the fields where true agreement exists and that in some fields things must be left to chance. But in a society which for its functioning depends on central planning this control cannot be made dependent on a majority's being able to agree; it will often be necessary that the will of a small minority be imposed upon the people, because this minority will be the largest group able to agree among themselves on the question at issue. Democratic government has worked successfully where, and so long as, the functions of government were, by a widely accepted creed, restricted to fields where agreement among a majority could be achieved by free discussion; and it is the great merit of the liberal creed that it reduced the range of subjects on which agreement was necessary to one on which it was likely to exist in a society of free men. It is now often said that democracy will not tolerate "capitalism." If "capitalism" means here a competitive system based on free disposal over private property, it is far more important to realize that only within this system is democracy possible. When it becomes dominated by a collectivist creed, democracy will inevitably destroy itself.

We have no intention, however, of making a fetish of democracy. It may well be true that our generation talks and thinks too much of democracy and too little of the values which it serves. It cannot be said of democracy, as Lord Acton truly said of liberty, that it "is not a means to a higher political end.

---

[5] *Man and Society in an Age of Reconstruction* (1940), p. 340.

It is itself the highest political end. It is not for the sake of a good public administration that it is required, but for the security in the pursuit of the highest objects of civil society, and of private life." Democracy is essentially a means, a utilitarian device for safeguarding internal peace and individual freedom. As such it is by no means infallible or certain. Nor must we forget that there has often been much more cultural and spiritual freedom under an autocratic rule than under some democracies—and it is at least conceivable that under the government of a very homogeneous and doctrinaire majority democratic government might be as oppressive as the worst dictatorship. Our point, however, is not that dictatorship must inevitably extirpate freedom but rather that planning leads to dictatorship because dictatorship is the most effective instrument of coercion and the enforcement of ideals and, as such, essential if central planning on a large scale is to be possible. The clash between planning and democracy arises simply from the fact that the latter is an obstacle to the suppression of freedom which the direction of economic activity requires. But in so far as democracy ceases to be a guaranty of individual freedom, it may well persist in some form under a totalitarian regime. A true "dictatorship of the proletariat," even if democratic in form, if it undertook centrally to direct the economic system, would probably destroy personal freedom as completely as any autocracy has ever done.

The fashionable concentration on democracy as the main value threatened is not without danger. It is largely responsible for the misleading and unfounded belief that, so long as the ultimate source of power is the will of the majority, the power cannot be arbitrary. The false assurance which many people derive from this belief is an important cause of the general unawareness of the dangers which we face. There is no justification for the belief that, so long as power is conferred by democratic procedure, it cannot be arbitrary; the contrast suggested by this statement is altogether false: it is not the source but the limitation of power which prevents it from being arbitrary. Democratic control *may* prevent power from becoming arbitrary, but it does not do so by its mere existence. If democracy resolves on a task which necessarily involves the use of power which cannot be guided by fixed rules, it must become arbitrary power.

18

The Affluent Society (1958)

John Kenneth Galbraith

I

The first requirement for an understanding of contemporary economic and social life is a clear view of the relation between events and the ideas which interpret them. For each of these has a life of its own, and much as it may seem a contradiction in terms each is capable for a considerable period of pursuing an independent course.

The reason is not difficult to discover. Economic, like other social life, does not conform to a simple and coherent pattern. On the contrary, it often seems incoherent, inchoate, and intellectually frustrating. But one must have an explanation or interpretation of economic behavior. Neither man's curiosity nor his inherent ego allows him to remain contentedly oblivious to anything that is so close to his life.

Because economic and social phenomena are so forbidding, or at least so seem, and because they yield few hard tests of what exists and what does not, they afford to the individual a luxury not given by physical phenomena. Within a considerable range he is permitted to believe what he pleases. He may hold whatever view of this world he finds most agreeable or otherwise to his taste.

As a consequence in the interpretation of all social life, there is a persistent and never-ending competition between what is relevant and what is merely acceptable. In this competition, while a strategic advantage lies with what exists, all tactical advantage is with the acceptable. Audiences of all kinds most applaud what they like best. And in social comment the test of audience approval, far more than the test of truth, comes to influence comment. The speaker or writer who addresses his audience with the proclaimed intent of telling the hard, shocking facts invariably goes on to expound what the audience most wants to hear.

Just as truth ultimately serves to create a consensus, so in the short run does acceptability. Ideas come to be organized around what the community as a whole or particular audiences find acceptable. And as the laboratory worker devotes himself to discovering scientific verities, so the ghost writer and the public relations man concern themselves with identifying the acceptable. If their clients are rewarded with applause, these artisans are qualified in their craft. If not they have failed. However, by sampling audience reaction in advance, or by pretesting speeches, articles, and other communications, the risk of failure can now be greatly minimized.

Numerous factors contribute to the acceptability of ideas. To a very large extent, of course, we associate truth with convenience—with what most closely accords with self-interest and individual well-being or promises best to avoid awkward effort or unwelcome dislocation of life. We also find highly acceptable what contributes most to self-esteem. Speakers before the United States Chamber of Commerce rarely denigrate the businessman as an economic force. Those who appear before the AFL-CIO are prone to identify social progress with a strong trade union movement. But perhaps most important of all, people approve most of what they best understand. As just noted, economic and social behavior are complex and mentally tiring. Therefore we adhere, as though to a raft, to those ideas which represent our understanding. This is a prime manifestation of vested interest. For a vested interest in understanding is more preciously guarded than any other treasure. It is why men react, not infrequently with something akin to religious passion, to the defense of what they have so laboriously learned. Familiarity may breed contempt in some areas of human behavior, but in the field of social ideas it is the touchstone of acceptability.

Because familiarity is such an important test of acceptability, the acceptable ideas have great stability. They are highly predictable. It will be convenient to have a name for the ideas which are esteemed at any time for their acceptability, and it should be a term that emphasizes this predictability. I shall refer to these ideas henceforth as the conventional wisdom.

II

The conventional wisdom is not the property of any political group. On a great many modern social issues, as we shall see in the course of this essay, the consensus is exceedingly broad. Nothing much divides those who are liberals by common political designation from those who are conservatives. The test of what is acceptable is much the same for both. On some questions, however, ideas must be accommodated to the political preferences of the particular audience. The tendency to make this adjustment, either deliberately or more often unconsciously, is not greatly different for different political groups. The conservative is led by disposition, not unmixed with pecuniary self-interest, to adhere to the familiar and the established. These underly his test of acceptability. But the liberal brings moral fervor and passion, even a sense of righteousness, to the ideas with which he is most familiar. While the ideas he cherishes are different from those of the conservative, he is not likely to be much less emphatic in making familiarity a test of acceptability. Deviation in the form of originality is condemned as faithlessness or backsliding. A "good" liberal or a "tried and true" liberal or a "true blue" liberal is one who is adequately predictable. This means that he forswears any serious striving toward original-ity. In both the United States and Britain, in recent times, liberals and their British counterparts of the left have proclaimed themselves in search of new ideas. To proclaim the need for new ideas has served, in some measure, as a substitute for them.

Thus we may, as necessary, speak of the conventional wisdom of conserv-atives or the conventional wisdom of liberals.

The conventional wisdom is also articulated on all levels of sophistication. At the highest levels of social science scholarship some novelty of formulation or statement is not resisted. On the contrary, considerable store is set by the device of putting an old truth in a new form, and minor heresies are much cherished. And the very vigor of minor debate makes it possible to exclude as irrelevant, and without seeming to be unscientific or parochial, any challenge to the framework itself. Moreover, with time and aided by the debate, the accepted ideas become increasingly elaborate. They have a large literature, even a mystique. The defenders are able to say that the challengers of the con-ventional wisdom have not mastered their intricacies. Indeed these ideas can be appreciated only by a stable, orthodox, and patient man—in brief, by someone who closely resembles the man of conventional wisdom. The con-ventional wisdom having been made more or less identical with sound schol-arship, its position is virtually impregnable. The skeptic is disqualified by his very tendency to go brashly from the old to the new. Were he a sound scholar he would remain with the conventional wisdom.

At the same time in the higher levels of the conventional wisdom origi-nality remains highly acceptable in the abstract. Here again the conventional wisdom often makes vigorous advocacy of originality a substitute for original-ity itself.

III

As noted, the hallmark of the conventional wisdom is acceptability. It has the approval of those to whom it is addressed. There are many reasons why people like to hear articulated that which they approve. It serves the ego: the individ-ual has the satisfaction of knowing that other and more famous people share his conclusions. To hear what he believes is also a source of reassurance. The individual knows that he is supported in his thoughts—that he has not been left behind and alone. Further, to hear what one approves serves the evangeliz-ing instinct. It means that others are also hearing and are thereby in process of being persuaded.

In some measure the articulation of the conventional wisdom is a religious rite. It is an act of affirmation like reading aloud from the Scriptures or going to church. The business executive listening to a luncheon address on the virtues of free enterprise and the evils of Washington is already persuaded, and so are his fellow listeners, and all are secure in their convictions. Indeed, although a display of rapt attention is required, the executive may not feel it necessary to listen. But he does placate the gods by participating in the ritual. Having been present, maintained attention, and having applauded, he can depart feeling that the economic system is a little more secure. Scholars gather in scholarly assemblages to hear in elegant statement what all have heard before. Yet it is not a negligible rite, for its purpose is not to convey knowledge but to beatify learning and the learned.

With so extensive a demand, it follows that a very large part of our social comment—and nearly all that is well regarded—is devoted at any time to articulating the conventional wisdom. To some extent this has been professionalized. Individuals, most notably the great television and radio commentators, make a profession of knowing and saying with elegance and unction what their audience will find most acceptable. But in general the articulation of the conventional wisdom is a prerogative of academic, public, or business position. Thus any individual, on being elected president of a college or university, automatically wins the right to enunciate the conventional wisdom should he choose to do so. It is one of the rewards of high academic rank, although such rank is also a reward for expounding the conventional wisdom at a properly sophisticated level.

The high public official is expected, and indeed is to some extent required, to expound the conventional wisdom. His, in many respects, is the purest case. Before assuming office he ordinarily commands little attention. But on taking up his position he is immediately assumed to be gifted with deep insights. He does not, except in the rarest instances, write his own speeches or articles; and these are planned, drafted, and scrupulously examined to insure their acceptability. The application of any other test, e.g., their effectiveness as a simple description of the economic or political reality, would be regarded as eccentric in the extreme. . . .

As surely as an increase in the output of automobiles puts new demands on the steel industry so, also, it places new demands on public services. Similarly, every increase in the consumption of private goods will normally mean some facilitating or protective step by the state. In all cases if these services are not forthcoming, the consequences will be in some degree ill. It will be convenient to have a term which suggests a satisfactory relationship between the supply of privately produced goods and services and those of the state, and we may call it social balance.

The problem of social balance is ubiquitous, and frequently it is obtrusive. As noted, an increase in the consumption of automobiles requires a facilitating supply of streets, highways, traffic control, and parking space. The protective services of the police and the highway patrols must also be available, as must those of the hospitals. Although the need for balance here is extraordinarily clear, our use of privately produced vehicles has, on occasion, got far out of line with the supply of the related public services. The result has been hideous road congestion, an annual massacre of impressive proportions, and chronic colitis in the cities. As on the ground, so also in the air. Planes collide with disquieting consequences for those within when the public provision for air traffic control fails to keep pace with private use of the airways.

But the auto and the airplane, versus the space to use them, are merely an exceptionally visible example of a requirement that is pervasive. The more goods people procure, the more packages they discard and the more trash that must be carried away. If the appropriate sanitation services are not provided, the counterpart of increasing opulence will be deepening filth. The greater the wealth the thicker will be the dirt. This indubitably describes a tendency of our time. As more goods are produced and owned, the greater are the opportunities for fraud and the more property that must be protected. If the provision of public law enforcement services do not keep pace, the counterpart of increased well-being will, we may be certain, be increased crime.

The city of Los Angeles, in modern times, is a near-classic study in the problem of social balance. Magnificently efficient factories and oil refineries, a lavish supply of automobiles, a vast consumption of handsomely packaged products, coupled with the absence of a municipal trash collection service which forced the use of home incinerators, made the air nearly unbreathable for an appreciable part of each year. Air pollution could be controlled only by a complex and highly developed set of public services—by better knowledge stemming from more research, better policing, a municipal trash collection service, and possibly the assertion of the priority of clean air over the production of goods. These were long in coming. The agony of a city without usable air was the result.

The issue of social balance can be identified in many other current problems. Thus an aspect of increasing private production is the appearance of an extraordinary number of things which lay claim to the interest of the young. Motion pictures, television, automobiles, and the vast opportunities which go with the mobility, together with such less enchanting merchandise as narcotics, comic books, and pornographia, are all included in an advancing gross national product. The child of a less opulent as well as a technologically more primitive age had far fewer such diversions. The red schoolhouse is remembered mainly because it had a paramount position in the lives of those who attended it that no modern school can hope to attain.

In a well-run and well-regulated community, with a sound school system, good recreational opportunities, and a good police force—in short a community where public services have kept pace with private production—the diversionary forces operating on the modern juvenile may do no great damage. Television and the violent mores of Hollywood and Madison Avenue must contend with the intellectual discipline of the school. The social, athletic, dramatic, and like attractions of the school also claim the attention of the child. These, together with the other recreational opportunities of the community, minimize the tendency to delinquency. Experiments with violence and immorality are checked by an effective law enforcement system before they become epidemic.

In a community where public services have failed to keep abreast of private consumption things are very different. Here, in an atmosphere of private opulence and public squalor, the private goods have full sway. Schools do not compete with television and the movies. The dubious heroes of the latter, not Miss Jones, become the idols of the young. The hot rod and the wild ride take the place of more sedentary sports for which there are inadequate facilities or provision. Comic books, alcohol, narcotics, and switchblade knives are, as noted, part of the increased flow of goods, and there is nothing to dispute their enjoyment. There is an ample supply of private wealth to be appropriated and not much to be feared from the police. An austere community is free from temptation. It can be austere in its public services. Not so a rich one.

Moreover, in a society which sets large store by production and which has highly effective machinery for synthesizing private wants, there are strong pressures to have as many wage earners in the family as possible. As always all social behavior is part of a piece. If both parents are engaged in private production, the burden on the public services is further increased. Children, in effect, become the charge of the community for an appreciable part of the time. If the services of the community do not keep pace, this will be another source of disorder.

19

Capitalism and Freedom (1962)

Milton Friedman

In a much quoted passage in his inaugural address, President Kennedy said, "Ask not what your country can do for you—ask what you can do for your country." It is a striking sign of the temper of our times that the controversy about this passage centered on its origin and not on its content. Neither half of the statement expresses a relation between the citizen and his government that is worthy of the ideals of free men in a free society. The paternalistic "what your country can do for you" implies that government is the patron, the citizen the ward, a view that is at odds with the free man's belief in his own responsibility for his own destiny. The organismic, "what you can do for your country" implies that government is the master or the deity, the citizen, the servant or the votary. To the free man, the country is the collection of individuals who compose it, not something over and above them. He is proud of a common heritage and loyal to common traditions. But he regards government as a means, an instrumentality, neither a grantor of favors and gifts, nor a master or god to be blindly worshipped and served. He recognizes no national goal except as it is the consensus of the goals that the citizens severally serve. He recognizes no national purpose except as it is the consensus of the purposes for which the citizens severally strive.

The free man will ask neither what his country can do for him nor what he can do for his country. He will ask rather "What can I and my compatriots do through government" to help us discharge our individual responsibilities, to achieve our several goals and purposes, and above all, to protect our freedom? And he will accompany this question with another: How can we keep the government we create from becoming a Frankenstein that will destroy the very freedom we establish it to protect? Freedom is a rare and delicate plant. Our minds tell us, and history confirms, that the great threat to freedom is the concentration of power. Government is necessary to preserve our freedom, it is an instrument through which we can exercise our freedom; yet by concentrating power in political hands, it is also a threat to freedom. Even though the men who wield this power initially be of good will and even though they be not corrupted by the power they exercise, the power will both attract and form men of a different stamp.

How can we benefit from the promise of government while avoiding the threat to freedom? Two broad principles embodied in our Constitution give an answer that has preserved our freedom so far, though they have been violated repeatedly in practice while proclaimed as precept.

First, the scope of government must be limited. Its major function must be to protect our freedom both from the enemies outside our gates and from our fellow-citizens: to preserve law and order, to enforce private contracts, to foster competitive markets. Beyond this major function, government may enable us at times to accomplish jointly what we would find it more difficult or expensive to accomplish severally. However, any such use of government is fraught with danger. We should not and cannot avoid using government in this way. But there should be a clear and large balance of advantages before we do. By relying primarily on voluntary co-operation and private enterprise, in both economic and other activities, we can insure that the private sector is a check on the powers of the governmental sector and an effective protection of freedom of speech, of religion, and of thought.

The second broad principle is that government power must be dispersed. If government is to exercise power, better in the county than in the state, better in the state than in Washington. If I do not like what my local community does, be it in sewage disposal, or zoning, or schools, I can move to another local community, and though few may take this step, the mere possibility acts as a check. If I do not like what my state does, I can move to another. If I do not like what Washington imposes, I have few alternatives in this world of jealous nations.

The very difficulty of avoiding the enactments of the federal government is of course the great attraction of centralization to many of its proponents. It will enable them more effectively, they believe, to legislate programs that—as they see it—are in the interest of the public, whether it be the transfer of income from the rich to the poor or from private to governmental purposes. They are in a sense right. But this coin has two sides. The power to do good is also the power to do harm; those who control the power today may not tomorrow; and, more important, what one man regards as good, another may regard as harm. The great tragedy of the drive to centralization, as of the drive to extend the scope of government in general, is that it is mostly led by men of good will who will be the first to rue its consequences.

The preservation of freedom is the protective reason for limiting and decentralizing governmental power. But there is also a constructive reason. The great advances of civilization, whether in architecture or painting, in science or literature, in industry or agriculture, have never come from centralized government. Columbus did not set out to seek a new route to China in response to a majority directive of a parliament, though he was partly financed by an absolute monarch. Newton and Leibnitz; Einstein and Bohr; Shakespeare, Milton, and Pasternak; Whitney, McCormick, Edison, and Ford; Jane Addams, Florence Nightingale, and Albert Schweitzer; no one of these opened new frontiers in human knowledge and understanding, in literature, in technical possibilities, or in the relief of human misery in response to governmental directives. Their achievements were the product of individual genius, of strongly held minority views, of a social climate permitting variety and diversity.

Government can never duplicate the variety and diversity of individual action. At any moment in time, by imposing uniform standards in housing, or nutrition, or clothing, government could undoubtedly improve the level of living of many individuals; by imposing uniform standards in schooling, road construction, or sanitation, central government could undoubtedly improve the level of performance in many local areas and perhaps even on the average of all communities. But in the process, government would replace progress by stagnation, it would substitute uniform mediocrity for the variety essential for that experimentation which can bring tomorrow's laggards above today's mean.

This book discusses some of these great issues. Its major theme is the role of competitive capitalism—the organization of the bulk of economic activity through private enterprise operating in a free market—as a system of economic freedom and a necessary condition for political freedom. Its minor theme is the role that government should play in a society dedicated to freedom and relying primarily on the market to organize economic activity.

The first two chapters deal with these issues on an abstract level, in terms of principles rather than concrete application. The later chapters apply these principles to a variety of particular problems.

An abstract statement can conceivably be complete and exhaustive, though this ideal is certainly far from realized in the two chapters that follow. The application of the principles cannot even conceivably be exhaustive. Each day brings new problems and new circumstances. That is why the role of the state can never be spelled out once and for all in terms of specific functions. It is also why we need from time to time to re-examine the bearing of what we hope are unchanged principles on the problems of the day. A by-product is inevitably a retesting of the principles and a sharpening of our understanding of them.

It is extremely convenient to have a label for the political and economic viewpoint elaborated in this book. The rightful and proper label is liberalism. Unfortunately, "As a supreme, if unintended compliment, the enemies of the system of private enterprise have thought it wise to appropriate its label",[1] so that liberalism has, in the United States, come to have a very different meaning than it did in the nineteenth century or does today over much of the Continent of Europe.

As it developed in the late eighteenth and early nineteenth centuries, the intellectual movement that went under the name of liberalism emphasized freedom as the ultimate goal and the individual as the ultimate entity in the society. It supported laissez faire at home as a means of reducing the role of the state in economic affairs and thereby enlarging the role of the individual; it supported free trade abroad as a means of linking the nations of the world together peacefully and democratically. In political matters, it supported the development of representative government and of parliamentary institutions, reduction in the arbitrary power of the state, and protection of the civil freedoms of individuals.

Beginning in the late nineteenth century, and especially after 1930 in the United States, the term liberalism came to be associated with a very different emphasis, particularly in economic policy. It came to be associated with a readiness to rely primarily on the state rather than on private voluntary arrangements to achieve objectives regarded as desirable. The catchwords became welfare and equality rather than freedom. The nineteenth-century liberal regarded an extension of freedom as the most effective way to promote welfare and equality; the twentieth-century liberal regards welfare and equality as either prerequisites of or alternatives to freedom. In the name of welfare and equality, the twentieth-century liberal has come to favor a revival of the very policies of state intervention and paternalism against which classical liberalism fought. In the very act of turning the clock back to seventeenth-century mercantilism, he is fond of castigating true liberals as reactionary!

The change in the meaning attached to the term liberalism is more striking in economic matters than in political. The twentieth-century liberal, like the nineteenth-century liberal, favors parliamentary institutions, representative government, civil rights, and so on. Yet even in political matters, there is a notable difference. Jealous of liberty, and hence fearful of centralized power, whether in governmental or private hands, the nineteenth-century liberal favored political decentralization. Committed to action and confident of the beneficence of power so long as it is in the hands of a government ostensibly controlled by the electorate, the twentieth-century liberal favors centralized government. He will resolve any doubt about where power should be located in favor of the state instead of the city, of the federal government instead of the state, and of a world organization instead of a national government.

---

[1]Joseph Schumpeter, *History of Economic Analysis* (New York: Oxford University Press, 1954) p. 394.

Because of the corruption of the term liberalism, the views that formerly went under that name are now often labeled conservatism. But this is not a satisfactory alternative. The nineteenth-century liberal was a radical, both in the etymological sense of going to the root of the matter, and in the political sense of favoring major changes in social institutions. So too must be his modern heir. We do not wish to conserve the state interventions that have interfered so greatly with our freedom, though, of course, we do wish to conserve those that have promoted it. Moreover, in practice, the term conservatism has come to cover so wide a range of views, and views so incompatible with one another, that we shall no doubt see the growth of hyphenated designations, such as libertarian-conservative and aristocratic-conservative.

Partly because of my reluctance to surrender the term to proponents of measures that would destroy liberty, partly because I cannot find a better alternative, I shall resolve these difficulties by using the word liberalism in its original sense—as the doctrines pertaining to a free man.

20

The Zero-Sum Society (1980)

Lester Thurow

A Zero-Sum Game

This is the heart of our fundamental problem. Our economic problems are solvable. For most of our problems there are several solutions. But all these solutions have the characteristic that someone must suffer large economic losses. No one wants to volunteer for this role, and we have a political process that is incapable of forcing anyone to shoulder this burden. Everyone wants someone else to suffer the necessary economic losses, and as a consequence none of the possible solutions can be adopted.

Basically we have created the world described in Robert Ardrey's *The Territorial Imperative*. To beat an animal of the same species on his home turf, the invader must be twice as strong as the defender. But no majority is twice as strong as the minority opposing it. Therefore we each veto the other's initiatives, but none of us has the ability to create successful initiatives ourselves.

Our political and economic structure simply isn't able to cope with an economy that has a substantial zero-sum element. A zero-sum game is any game where the losses exactly equal the winnings. All sporting events are zero-sum games. For every winner there is a loser, and winners can only exist if losers exist. What the winning gambler wins, the losing gambler must lose.

When there are large losses to be allocated, any economic decision has a large zero-sum element. The economic gains may exceed the economic losses, but the losses are so large as to negate a very substantial fraction of the gains. What is more important, the gains and losses are not allocated to the same individuals or groups. On average, society may be better off, but this average hides a large number of people who are much better off and large numbers of people who are much worse off. If you are among those who are worse off, the fact that someone else's income has risen by more than your income has fallen is of little comfort.

To protect our own income, we will fight to stop economic change from occurring or fight to prevent society from imposing the public policies that hurt us. From our perspective they are not good public policies even if they do result in a larger GNP. We want a solution to the problem, say the problem of energy, that does not reduce our income, but all solutions reduce someone's income. If the government chooses some policy option that does not lower our income, it will have made a supporter out of us, but it will have made an opponent out of someone else, since someone else will now have to shoulder the burden of large income reductions.

The problem with zero-sum games is that the essence of problem solving is loss allocation. But this is precisely what our political process is least capable of doing. When there are economic gains to be allocated, our political process can allocate them. When there are large economic losses to be allocated, our political process is paralyzed. And with political paralysis comes economic paralysis.

The importance of economic losers has also been magnified by a change in the political structure. In the past, political and economic power was distributed in such a way that substantial economic losses could be imposed on parts of the population if the establishment decided that it was in the general interest. Economic losses were allocated to particular powerless groups rather than spread across the population. These groups are no longer willing to accept losses and are able to raise substantially the costs for those who wish to impose losses upon them.

There are a number of reasons for this change. Vietnam and the subsequent political scandals clearly lessened the population's willingness to accept their nominal leader's judgments that some project was in their general interest. With the civil rights, poverty, black power, and women's liberation move-ments, many of the groups that have in the past absorbed economic losses have become militant. They are no longer willing to accept losses without a political fight. The success of their militancy and civil disobedience sets an example that spreads to other groups representing the environment, neighbor-hoods, and regions.

All minority groups have gone through a learning process. They have dis-covered that it is relatively easy with our legal system and a little militancy to delay anything for a very long period of time. To be able to delay a program is often to be able to kill it. Legal and administrative costs rise, but the delays and uncertainties are even more important. When the costs of delays and uncer-tainties are added into their calculations, both government and private indus-try often find that it pays to cancel projects that would otherwise be profitable. Costs are simply higher than benefits.

In one major environmental group, delays are such a major part of their strategy that they have a name for it—analysis paralysis. Laws are to be passed so that every project must meet a host of complicated time-consuming require-ments. The idea is not to learn more about the costs and benefits of projects, but to kill them. If such requirements were to be useful in deciding whether a project should be undertaken, environmental-impact statements, for example, would have to be inexpensive, simple, and quick to complete. Then a firm might undertake the studies to help determine whether they should or should not start a project.

Instead, the studies are to be expensive and complex to serve as a finan-cial deterrent to undertaking any project, to substantially lengthen the time necessary to complete any project, and to ensure that they can be challenged in court (another lengthy process). As a consequence, the developer will start the process only if he has already decided on other grounds to go ahead with the project. The result is an adversary situation where the developer cannot get his project underway—and where the environmentalists also cannot get exist-ing plants (such as Reserve Mining) to clean up their current pollution. Where it helps them, both sides have learned the fine art of delay.

Consider the interstate highway system. Whatever one believes about the merits of completing the remaining intracity portion of the system, it is clear that it gives the country an intercity transportation network that would be sorely missed had it not been built. Even those who argue against it do so on the grounds that if it had not been built, some better (nonauto) system would have been devised. Yet most observers would agree that the interstate highway system could not have been built if it had been proposed in the mid-1970s rather than in the mid-1950s.

Exactly the same factors that would prevent the initiation of an interstate highway system would also prevent the initiation of any alternative transporta-tion system. A few years ago, when a high-speed rail system was being consid-ered for the Boston-Washington corridor, a former governor of Connecticut announced that he would veto any relocation of the Boston-to-New York line on the grounds that it would be of prime benefit to those at either end of the line, but would tear up Connecticut homes. The groups opposing an intercity rail network would be slightly different from the groups opposing an intercity highway network, but they would be no less effective in stopping the project. Any transportation system demands that land be taken and homes be torn down. At one time, this was possible; at the moment, it is impossible.

The Balkanization of nations is a worldwide phenomenon that the United States has not escaped. Regions and localities are less and less willing to incur costs that will primarily help people in other parts of the same country. Consider the development of the coalfields of Wyoming and Montana. There is no question that most of the benefits will accrue to those living in urban areas in the rest of the country while most of the costs will be imposed on those living in that region. As a result, the local population objects. More coal mining might be good for the United States, but it will be bad for local constituents. Therefore they will impose as many delays and uncertainties as possible.

The same problem is visible in the location of nuclear power plants. Whatever one believes about the benefits of nuclear power, it is clear that lengthy delays in approving sites serve no purpose other than as a strategy for killing the projects. If the projects are undertaken anyway, the consumer will have to suffer the same risks and pay the higher costs associated with these delays. What is wanted is a quick yes or no answer; but this is just what we find impossible to do. The question of nuclear power sites also raises the Balkanization issue. Whatever the probabilities of accidents, the consequences of such failures are much less if the plants are located in remote areas. But those who live in remote areas do not want the plants, since they suffer all the potential hazards and do not need the project. Everyone wants power, but no one wants a power plant next to his own home.

Domestic problems also tend to have a much longer time horizon. In modern times, even long wars are won or lost in relatively short periods of time. In contrast, a project such as energy independence would take decades to achieve. The patience and foresight necessary for long-range plans is generally not an American virtue. Consequently, representatives seeking reelection every two, four, or six years want to support programs that will bring them votes. They do not want to stick their necks out for a good cause that may conflict with their careers. Even more fundamentally, domestic problems often involve long periods where costs accrue, with the benefits following much later. Think about energy independence. For a long time, sacrifices must be made to construct the necessary mines and plants. Benefits emerge only near the end of the process. The politician who must incur the costs (raise the necessary revenue and incur the anger of those who are hurt as the projects are constructed) is unlikely to be around to collect the credits when energy independence has been achieved.

The Retreat to Government

Given the problem of loss allocation, it is not surprising that government stands in the middle of an adversary relationship. Each group wants government to use its power to protect it and to force others to do what is in the general interest. Energy producers want prices to go up and the real income of energy consumers to go down. Energy consumers want prices to go down and a reduction in the income of producers. Each understands that the government could stop them from having to suffer such losses. Each of us demands what collectively is impossible. But as the demands for protection grow, the basic assumptions of the democratic process are undermined.

To be workable, a democracy assumes that public decisions are made in a framework where there is a substantial majority of concerned but disinterested citizens who will prevent policies from being shaped by those with direct economic self-interests. Decisions in the interests of the general welfare are supposed to be produced by those concerned but disinterested citizens. They are to arbitrate and judge the disputes of the interested parties. As government grows, however, the number of such citizens shrinks. Almost everyone now has a direct economic stake in what government does in an area such as energy.

The Watergate and associated corporate bribery scandals revealed the illegal side of this problem, but the real problem is not so much illegal acts as it is the incentive to use legal ones. With everyone's economic self-interest at stake, we all form perfectly proper lobbying groups to bend decisions in our favor. But with the disinterested citizen in a minority, how are decisions to reflect the general welfare? Who is to arbitrate? Our natural inclination is to rely on the adversary process, where different self-interested groups present their case. But somewhere there has to be a disinterested judge with the power to decide or tip a political decision in the right way. The general welfare is not always on the side of those who can mobilize the most economic and political power in their own behalf. If we really were to enforce the rule that no one could vote on an issue if his or her income would go up or down as a result of the action, we would end up with few or no voters on most issues. The problem is to establish a modicum of speedy, disinterested decision-making capacity in a political process where everyone has a direct self-interest.

The Need for Distribution Judgments

We have a governmental process that goes to great lengths to avoid having to overtly lower someone's income. Such decisions are always being made of course, but they are made implicitly, under the guise of accomplishing other objectives. Conservatives are now arguing for a restructuring of taxes and expenditures that would make the distribution of income more unequal, but they do not defend this goal overtly. Inequality is simply a regrettable necessity on the way to higher growth.

Fortunately or unfortunately we have reached a point where it is no longer possible to solve our economic problems and still make such implicit distributional decisions. The problems are stark enough and the options clear enough that everyone both knows and cares about the distributional consequences that will follow. Deregulating the price of energy might be the efficient thing to do, but we have great trouble doing so. Everyone whose income will go down knows it, objects, and stands ready to fight the proposal.

Since government must alter the distribution of income if it is to solve our economic problems, we have to have a government that is capable of making equity decisions. Whose income ought to go up and whose income ought to go down? To do this, however, we need to know what is equitable. What is a fair or just distribution of economic resources? What is a fair or just procedure for distributing income? Unless we can specify what is equitable, we cannot say whose income ought to go down. Unless we can say whose income ought to go down, we cannot solve our economic problems.

The difficulties of specifying economic equity neither obviate the need for equity decisions nor stop such decisions from being made. Every time a tax is levied or repealed, every time public expenditures are expanded or contracted, every time regulations are extended or abolished, an equity decision has to be made. Since economic gains are relatively easy to allocate, the basic problem comes down to one of allocating economic losses. Whose income "ought" to go down?

Historically we have used economic growth to avoid having to make this judgment. If we just have more growth, we can have more good jobs for everyone, and we won't have to worry about taking jobs away from whites and giving them to blacks. If we just have more economic growth, we won't have to worry about government collecting taxes in the Northeast and spending them in the Southwest. More is obviously better than less, and economic growth has been seen as the social lubricant that can keep different groups working together.

American liberals and conservatives both used to regard economic growth as unambiguously good. Through the magic of economic growth and individual self-interest, everyone would have more. If everyone had a higher income, then society would not have to address the divisive issue of equity or what constitutes a just distribution of economic resources. Individuals would be happy with their new, higher incomes regardless of their relative status.

We now know that almost all the implicit assumptions in this social consensus are false. When we are talking about incomes above the range of psychological necessities, individual perceptions of the adequacy of their economic performance depend almost solely on relative as opposed to absolute position. The poor in the United States might be rich in India, but they actually live in the United States and feel poor. The middle class may have fresh fruits and vegetables that the richest kings could not afford in the Middle Ages, but they feel deprived relative to the upper-middle class, who can afford things they cannot afford.

The proportion of any population that report themselves satisfied with their economic performance rises not at all as that population's average income rises. Those happiest with their economic circumstances have above-average incomes. There is no minimum absolute standard of living that will make people content. Individual wants are not satiated as incomes rise, and individuals do not become more willing to transfer some of their resources to the poor as they grow richer. If their income rises less rapidly than someone else's, or less rapidly than they expect, they may even feel poorer as their incomes rise.

This immediately forces a democracy into a no-win situation where, whatever it decides about the just distribution of resources, there will be a large number (perhaps even a majority) of unhappy voters. Distributional issues are highly contentious and precisely the kind of issues that democracies find it most difficult to solve. It is not *we* versus *them*, but *us* versus *us* in a zero-sum game.

Review Questions

1. Was historian Charles Beard correct when he asserted that the framers of the U.S. Constitution were primarily motivated by personal economic concerns? If you believe Beard's contention, does this in any way diminish, in your eyes, the value and values of the constitutional government they created?

2. What kind of government does Friedrich Hayek consider to be the "road to serfdom"? Why did Hayek consider extensive government planning for a national economy to be ultimately inefficient?

3. What did John Kenneth Galbraith mean by his phrase "the conventional wisdom"? Does the America that Galbraith saw in 1958, one of "private wealth" amid "public squalor" still exist? If so, why?

4. Why is Milton Friedman considered to be the father of the modern movement toward government deregulation? What did Friedman mean when he asserted that he was a classical liberal?

5. Who does Lester Thurow consider to be the winners and losers in the zero-sum society? How does Thurow differ from Hayek and Friedman in his idea of how governments should manage their economies?

Chapter 6

Policymaking by Legislatures

A legislature is the lawmaking branch of a representative government. It is not necessary for a legislature to have the word "legislature" in its formal title. It could be an assembly or a city council. The U.S. Congress is the lawmaking branch of the government of the United States. Article I, Section 1, of the U.S. Constitution states that all legislative power shall be vested in the Congress. This means that the president is specifically denied the power to make laws. All his authority must be based either on expressed or implicit powers granted by the Constitution or on statutes enacted by the Congress.

While there are three "coequal" branches of government, the legislature is nevertheless supreme. After all it has the greatest number of enumerated powers and the executive and judicial branches must enforce its laws. As James Madison wrote in *The Federalist*, No. 51: "In republican government, the legislative authority necessarily predominates." President Franklin D. Roosevelt in a press conference on July 23, 1937 put it another way: "It is the duty of the President to propose and it is the privilege of the Congress to dispose." Thus presidents make policy proposals to a congress that is the final authority on their merit.

This chapter offers classic answers to three seemingly eternal questions about legislatures. In making policy should the individual legislators primarily represent the interests of the constituency that elected them or the interests of the nation as a whole? How does the policy-making process work within the legislative institution? Why is it that the same people who express disdain for their legislatures overwhelmingly reelect the representatives from their own districts?

Edmund Burke (1729–1797) was the British political philosopher and Member of Parliament who is often referred to as the "father" of modern conservative thought. In his 1770 pamphlet "Thoughts on the Cause of the Present Discontents," he provided the first modern definition of a political party as a group united on public principle that could act as a link between the executive branch (the king) and the legislative branch (Parliament), providing consistency and strength while in power and principled criticism when out of power. In a 1774 election speech he presented his now famous analysis of the role of a member of a legislature regarding policymaking. In his "Speech to the Electors of Bristol," reprinted here, Burke asserted that the role of an elected member of a legislature should be that of a representative or trustee (free to exercise his own best judgment) rather than that of a delegate (bound by prior instructions from a constituency). Even though the speech was made in the context of the British parliamentary system, the doctrine Burke advocated for himself as a legislator is valid for all legislators.

Woodrow Wilson (1856–1924) is best known as the president of the United States from 1913 to 1921. But he also was president of Princeton University (1902–1910), governor of New Jersey (1911–1913), and a president of the American Political Science Association. While a college professor, he published the classic account of congressional policymaking, *Congressional Government: A Study in American Politics* (1885), portions reprinted here. He found Congress to be "predominant over its so-called coordinate branches" with congressional power parceled out to the various congressional committees.

A standing committee is a regular committee of a legislature that deals with bills within a specified subject area. In the U.S. Congress, each of the two principal parties has a committee on committees, which recommends committee assignments subject to caucus or conference approval. At the beginning of each Congress, members can express assignment preferences to their respective committee on committees. This committee then prepares and approves an assignment slate of members for each committee and submits it to the caucus or conference for approval. Normally, the recommendations are approved without challenge, but procedures exist by which other members can be nominated for vacant committee posts. The House, generally by strict party vote, adopts the slates presented by the two parties. The proportion of Republicans to Democrats is fixed by the majority party of the House. A similar method is used in the Senate.

The influence of the standing committees of the Congress cannot be overstated. As Woodrow Wilson declared more than a century ago: "I know not how better to describe our form of government in a single phrase than by calling it a government by the Chairman of the Standing Committees of Congress." But because of the various subcommittees, select committees and conference committees overall authority "is perplexingly subdivided and distributed, and responsibility has to be hunted down in out-of-the-way corners." This is why Wilson, in perhaps the most famous statement from *Congressional Government*, wrote that: "Congress in session is Congress on public exhibition, whilst Congress in its committee-rooms is Congress at work."

Depending on one's attitude toward a bill, the best legislation may be no legislation. Woodrow Wilson poetically wrote in *Congressional Government* that "once begin the dance of legislation, and you must struggle through its mazes as best you can to its breathless end,—if any end there be." The legislative policy-making process is inherently messy. It is so full of compromise, hypocrisy, and self-interest that its end product, legislation, is sometimes compared to sausage, in that a wise person will avoid watching either of them being made.

Disdain for the Congress as a whole is longstanding. Mark Twain (1835–1910) wrote: "Suppose you were an idiot. And suppose you were a number of Congress. But I repeat myself." The chaplain of the Senate, Edward Everett Hale (1822–1909) was asked if he prayed for the senators. He replied: "No, I look at the senators and pray for the country." But you don't have to go back into history for disdainful remarks about the Congress. Just turn on the radio or television. More so than baseball, America's national pastime is making fun of the Congress. Yet, in a seeming contradiction, its individual members are overwhelmingly reelected.

An explanation of this, of why the Congress as a whole is respected so much less than its individual members is offered by Glenn R. Parker and Roger H. Davidson. Their article, "Why Do Americans Love Their Congressmen So Much More Than Their Congress?" in *Legislative Studies Quarterly* (February 1979) is reprinted here.

Their research found that Americans paradoxically do indeed seem to love their own member of Congress while thinking little of the Congress itself. Based on national survey data, Parker and Davidson conclude that Americans use one set of standards for evaluating Congress and another for evaluating individual members of Congress. The slowness of Congress along with dissatisfaction with the policy results of Congressional action lead to negative evaluations of the institution as a whole. On the other hand, individual members are rarely held accountable for policy decisions of the Congress, but are evaluated according to their personal qualities and level of service to constituents.

Casework is the term used for the services performed by legislators and their staffs at the request of and on behalf of constituents. For example, a U.S. representative may be asked to discover why a social security check has been delayed or why a veteran's claim for benefits has been denied. Casework is an important means by which legislators maintain oversight of the bureaucracy and solidify their political base with constituents.

Casework offers many advantages for legislators. First, its cheap and noncontroversial. For the price of some minor staff time, they can make a voter happy. After dealing with thousands of cases over several years, this can pay back big on election day. Of course, there is always the danger that the legislator will not be able to solve the constituent's problem. But if the situation is handled with promptness and tactfulness, the case can still be a net gain from a public relations viewpoint. Even if the "customer" did not get what was wanted from the bureaucracy, a perception of fair treatment will still go a long way—especially on election day.

21

Speech to the Electors of Bristol (1774)

Edmund Burke

Certainly, gentlemen, it ought to be the happiness and glory of a representative to live in the strictest union, the closest correspondence, and the most unreserved communication with his constituents. Their wishes ought to have great weight with him; their opinion, high respect; their business, unremitted attention. It is his duty to sacrifice his repose, his pleasures, his satisfactions, to theirs; and above all, ever, and in all cases, to prefer their interest to his own. But his unbiased opinion, his mature judgment, his enlightened conscience, he ought not to sacrifice to you, to any man, or to any set of men living. These he does not derive from your pleasure; no, nor from the law and the constitution. They are a trust from Providence, for the abuse of which he is deeply answerable. Your representative owes you, not his industry only, but his judgment; and he betrays, instead of serving you, if he sacrifices it to your opinion.

My worthy colleague says, his will ought to be subservient to yours. If that be all, the thing is innocent. If government were a matter of will upon any side, yours, without question, ought to be superior. But government and legislation are matters of reason and judgment, and not of inclination; and what sort of reason is that, in which the determination precedes the discussion; in which one set of men deliberate, and another decide; and where those who form the conclusion are perhaps three hundred miles distant from those who hear the arguments?

To deliver an opinion, is the right of all men; that of constituents is a weighty and respectable opinion, which a representative ought always to rejoice to hear; and which he ought always most seriously to consider. But *authoritative* instructions; *mandates* issued, which the member is bound blindly and implicitly to obey, to vote, and to argue for, though contrary to the clearest conviction of his judgment and conscience,—these are things utterly unknown to the laws of this land, and which arise from a fundamental mistake of the whole order and tenor of our constitution.

Source: Edmund Burke, "Speech to the Electors of Bristol," November 3, 1774.

Parliament is not a *congress* of ambassadors from different and hostile interests; which interests each must maintain, as an agent and advocate, against other agents and advocates; but parliament is a *deliberative* assembly of *one* nation, with *one* interest, that of the whole; where, not local purposes, not local prejudices, ought to guide, but the general good, resulting from the general reason of the whole. You choose a member indeed; but when you have chosen him, he is not member of Bristol, but he is a member of *parliament.* If the local constituent should have an interest, or should form an hasty opinion, evidently opposite to the real good of the rest of the community, the member for that place ought to be as far, as any other, from any endeavor to give it effect. I beg pardon for saying so much on this subject. I have been unwillingly drawn into it; but I shall ever use a respectful frankness of communication with you. Your faithful friend, your devoted servant, I shall be to the end of my life: a flatterer you do not wish for. On this point of instruction, however, I think it scarcely possible we ever can have any sort of difference. Perhaps I may give you too much, rather than too little, trouble.

From the first hour I was encouraged to court your favor, to this happy day of obtaining it, I have never promised you anything but humble and persevering endeavors to do my duty. The weight of that duty, I confess, makes me tremble; and whoever well considers what it is, of all things in the world, will fly from what has the least likeness to a positive and precipitate engagement. To be a good member of parliament is, let me tell you, no easy task; especially at this time, when there is so strong a disposition to run into the perilous extreme of servile compliance or wild popularity. To unite circumspection with vigor, is absolutely necessary; but it is extremely difficult. We are now members for a rich commercial *city*; this city, however, is but a part of a rich commercial *nation,* the interests of which are various, multiform, and intricate. We are members for that great nation, which however is itself but part of a great *empire,* extended by our virtue and our fortune to the farthest limits of the east and of the west. All these wide-spread interests must be considered; must be compared; must be reconciled, if possible. We are members for a *free* country; and surely we all know, that the machine of a free constitution is no simple thing; but as intricate and as delicate as it is valuable. We are members in a great and ancient *monarchy;* and we must preserve religiously the true legal rights of the sovereign, which form the key-stone that binds together the noble and well-constructed arch of our empire and our constitution. A constitution made up of balanced powers must ever be a critical thing. As such I mean to touch that part of it which comes within my reach. I know my inability, and I wish for support from every quarter. In particular I shall aim at the friendship, and shall cultivate the best correspondence, of the worthy colleague you have given me.

I trouble you no further than once more to thank you all; you, gentlemen, for your favors; the candidates, for their temperate and polite behavior; and the sheriffs, for a conduct which may give a model for all who are in public stations.

22

Congressional Government (1885)

Woodrow Wilson

Like a vast picture thronged with figures of equal prominence and crowded with elaborate and obtrusive details, Congress is hard to see satisfactorily and appreciatively at a single view and from a single stand-point. Its complicated forms and diversified structure confuse the vision, and conceal the system which underlies its composition. It is too complex to be understood without an effort, without a careful and systematic process of analysis. Consequently, very few people do understand it, and its doors are practically shut against the comprehension of the public at large. If Congress had a few authoritative leaders whose figures were very distinct and very conspicuous to the eye of the world, and who could represent and stand for the national legislature in the thoughts of that very numerous, and withal very respectable, class of persons who must think specifically and in concrete forms when they think at all, those persons who can make something out of men but very little out of intangible generalizations, it would be quite within the region of possibilities for the majority of the nation to follow the course of legislation without any very serious confusion of thought. I suppose that almost everybody who just now gives any heed to the policy of Great Britain, with regard even to the reform of the franchise and other like strictly legislative questions, thinks of Mr. Gladstone and his colleagues rather than of the House of Commons, whose servants they are. The question is not, What will Parliament do? but, What will Mr. Gladstone do? And there is even less doubt that it is easier and more natural to look upon the legislative designs of Germany as locked up behind Bismarck's heavy brows than to think of them as dependent upon the determinations of the Reichstag, although as a matter of fact its consent is indispensable even to the plans of the imperious and domineering Chancellor.

But there is no great minister or ministry to represent the will and being of Congress in the common thought. The Speaker of the House of Representatives

Source: Woodrow Wilson, *Congressional Government,* 1885.

stands as near to leadership as any one; but his will does not run as a formative and imperative power in legislation much beyond the appointment of the committees who are to lead the House and do its work for it, and it is, therefore, not entirely satisfactory to the public mind to trace all legislation to him. He may have a controlling hand in starting it; but he sits too still in his chair, and is too evidently not on the floor of the body over which he presides, to make it seem probable to the ordinary judgment that he has much immediate concern in legislation after it is once set afoot. Everybody knows that he is a staunch and avowed partisan, and that he likes to make smooth, whenever he can, the legislative paths of his party; but it does not seem likely that all important measures originate with him, or that he is the author of every distinct policy. And in fact he is not. He is a great party chief, but the hedging circumstances of his official position as presiding officer prevent his performing the part of active leadership. He appoints the leaders of the House, but he is not himself its leader.

The leaders of the House are the chairmen of the principal Standing Committees. Indeed, to be exactly accurate, the House has as many leaders as there are subjects of legislation; for there are as many Standing Committees as there are leading classes of legislation, and in the consideration of every topic of business the House is guided by a special leader in the person of the chairman of the Standing Committee, charged with the superintendence of measures of the particular class to which that topic belongs. It is this multiplicity of leaders, this many-headed leadership, which makes the organization of the House too complex to afford uninformed people and unskilled observers any easy clue to its methods of rule. For the chairmen of the Standing Committees do not constitute a coöperative body like a ministry. They do not consult and concur in the adoption of homogeneous and mutually helpful measures; there is no thought of acting in concert. Each Committee goes its own way at its own pace. It is impossible to discover any unity or method in the disconnected and therefore unsystematic, confused, and desultory action of the House, or any common purpose in the measures which its Committees from time to time recommend.

And it is not only to the unanalytic thought of the common observer who looks at the House from the outside that its doings seem helter-skelter, and without comprehensible rule; it is not at once easy to understand them when they are scrutinized in their daily headway through open session by one who is inside the House. The newly-elected member, entering its doors for the first time, and with no more knowledge of its rules and customs than the more intelligent of his constituents possess, always experiences great difficulty in adjusting his preconceived ideas of congressional life to the strange and unlooked-for conditions by which he finds himself surrounded after he has been sworn in and has become a part of the great legislative machine. Indeed there are generally many things connected with his career in Washington to disgust and dispirit, if not to aggrieve, the new member. In the first place, his local reputation does not follow him to the federal capital. Possibly the members from his own State know him, and receive him into full fellowship; but no one else knows him, except as an adherent of this or that party, or as a new-comer from this or that State. He finds his station insignificant, and his identity indistinct. But this social humiliation which he experiences in circles in which to be a congressman does not of itself confer distinction, because it is only to be one among many, is probably not to be compared with the chagrin and disappointment which come in company with the inevitable discovery that he is equally without weight or title to consideration in the House itself. No man, when chosen to the membership of a body possessing great powers and exalted prerogatives, likes to find his activity repressed, and himself suppressed, by imperative rules and precedents which seem to have been framed for the deliberate purpose of making usefulness unattainable by individual members. Yet such the new member finds the rules and precedents of the House to be. It matters not to him, because it is not apparent on the face of things, that those rules and precedents have grown, not out of set purpose to curtail the privileges of new members as such, but out of the plain necessities of business; it remains the fact that he suffers under their curb, and it is not until "custom hat made it in him a property of easiness" that he submits to them with anything like good grace.

Not all new members suffer alike, of course, under this trying discipline; because it is not every new member that comes to his seat with serious purposes of honest, earnest, and duteous work. There are numerous tricks and subterfuges, soon learned and easily used, by means of which the most idle and self-indulgent members may readily make such show of exemplary diligence as will quite satisfy, if it does not positively delight, constituents in Buncombe. But the number of congressmen who deliberately court uselessness and counterfeit well-doing is probably small. The great majority doubtless have a keen enough sense of their duty, and a sufficiently unhesitating desire to do it; and it may safely be taken for granted that the zeal of new members is generally hot and insistent. If it be not hot to begin with, it is like to become so by reason of friction with the rules, because such men must inevitably be chafed by the bonds of restraint drawn about them by the inexorable observances of the House.

Often the new member goes to Washington as the representative of a particular line of policy, having been elected, it may be, as an advocate of free trade, or as a champion of protection; and it is naturally his first care upon entering on his duties to seek immediate opportunity for the expression of his views and immediate means of giving them definite shape and thrusting them upon the attention of Congress. His disappointment is, therefore, very keen when he finds both opportunity and means denied him. He can introduce his bill; but that is all he can do, and he must do that at a particular time and in a particular manner. This he is likely to learn through rude experience, if he be not cautious to inquire beforehand the details of practice. He is likely to make a rash start, upon the supposition that Congress observes the ordinary rules of parliamentary practice to which he has become accustomed in the debating clubs familiar to his youth, and in the mass-meetings known to his later experience. His bill is doubtless ready for presentation early in the session, and some day, taking advantage of a pause in the proceedings, when there seems to be no business before the House, he rises to read it and move its adoption. But he finds getting the floor an arduous and precarious undertaking. There are certain to be others who want it as well as he; and his indignation is stirred by the fact that the Speaker does not so much as turn towards him, though he must have heard his call, but recognizes some one else readily and as a matter of course. If he be obstreperous and persistent in his cries of "Mr. Speaker," he may get that great functionary's attention for a moment,—only to be told, however, that he is out of order, and that his bill can be introduced at that stage only by unanimous consent: immediately there are mechanically-uttered but emphatic exclamations of objection, and he is forced to sit down confused and disgusted. He has, without knowing it, obtruded himself in the way of the "regular order of business," and been run over in consequence, without being quite clear as to how the accident occurred.

Moved by the pain and discomfiture of this first experience to respect, if not to fear, the rules, the new member casts about, by study or inquiry, to find out, if possible, the nature and occasion of his privileges. He learns that his only safe day is Monday. On that day the roll of the States is called, and members may introduce bills as their States are reached in the call. So on Monday he essays another bout with the rules, confident this time of being on their safe side,—but mayhap indiscreetly and unluckily over-confident. For if he supposes, as he naturally will, that after his bill has been sent up to be read by the clerk he may say a few words in its behalf, and in that belief sets out upon his long-considered remarks, he will be knocked down by the rules as surely as he was on the first occasion when he gained the floor for a brief moment. The rap of Mr. Speaker's gavel is sharp, immediate, and peremptory. He is curtly informed that no debate is in order; the bill can only be referred to the appropriate Committee.

This is, indeed, disheartening; it is his first lesson in committee government, and the master's rod smarts; but the sooner he learns the prerogatives and powers of the Standing Committees the sooner will he penetrate the mysteries of the rules and avoid the pain of further contact with their thorny side. The privileges of the Standing Committees are the beginning and the end of the rules. Both the House of Representatives and the Senate conduct their business by what may figuratively, but not inaccurately, be called an odd device of *disintegration*. The House virtually both deliberates and legislates in small sections. Time would fail it to discuss all the bills brought in, for they every session number thousands; and it is to be doubted whether, even if time allowed, the ordinary processes of debate and amendment would suffice to sift the chaff from the wheat in the bushels of bills every week piled upon the clerk's desk. Accordingly, no futile attempt is made to do anything of the kind. The work is parceled out, most of it to the forty-seven Standing Committees which constitute the regular organization of the House, some of it to select committees appointed for special and temporary purposes. Each of the almost numberless bills that come pouring in on Mondays is "read a first and second time,"—simply perfunctorily read, that is, by its title, by the clerk, and passed by silent assent through its first formal courses, for the purpose of bringing it to the proper stage for commitment,—and referred without debate to the appropriate Standing Committee. Practically, no bill escapes commitment—save, of course, bills introduced by committees, and a few which may now and then be crowded through under a suspension of the rules, granted by a two-thirds vote—though the exact disposition to be made of a bill is not always determined easily and as a matter of course. Besides the great Committee of Ways and Means and the equally great Committee on Appropriations, there are Standing Committees on Banking and Currency, on Claims, on Commerce, on the Public Lands, on Post-Offices and Post-Roads, on the Judiciary, on Public Expenditures, on Manufactures, on Agriculture, on Military Affairs, on Naval Affairs, on Mines and Mining, on Education and Labor, on Patents, and on a score of other branches of legislative concern; but careful and differential as is the topical division of the subjects of legislation which is represented in the titles of these Committees, it is not always evident to which Committee each particular bill should go. Many bills affect subjects which may be regarded as lying as properly within the jurisdiction of one as of another of the Committees; for no hard and fast lines separate the various classes of business which the Committees are commissioned to take in charge. Their jurisdictions overlap at many points, and it must frequently happen that bills are read which cover just this common ground. Over the commitment of such bills sharp and interesting skirmishes often take place. There is active competition for them, the ordinary, quiet routine of matter-of-course reference being interrupted by rival motions seeking to give very different directions to the disposition to be made of them. To which Committee should a bill "to fix and establish the maximum rates of fares of the Union Pacific and Central Pacific Railroads" be sent,—to the Committee on Commerce or to the Committee on the Pacific Railroads? Should a bill which prohibits the mailing of certain classes of letters and circulars go to the Committee on Post-Offices and Post-Roads, because it relates to the mails, or to the Committee on the Judiciary, because it proposes to make any transgression of its prohibition a crime? What is the proper disposition of any bill which thus seems to lie within two distinct committee jurisdictions?

The fate of bills committed is generally not uncertain. As a rule, a bill committed is a bill doomed. When it goes from the clerk's desk to a committee-room it crosses a parliamentary bridge of sighs to dim dungeons of silence whence it will never return. The means and time of its death are unknown, but its friends never see it again. Of course no Standing Committee is privileged to take upon itself the full powers of the House it represents, and formally and decisively reject a bill referred to it; its disapproval, if it disapproves, must be reported to the House in the form of a recommendation that the bill "do not pass." But it is easy, and therefore common, to let the session pass without making any report at all upon bills deemed objectionable or unimportant, and to substitute for reports upon them a few bills of the Committee's own drafting; so that thousands of bills expire with the expiration of each Congress, not having been rejected, but having been simply neglected. There was not time to report upon them.

Of course it goes without saying that the practical effect of this Committee organization of the House is to consign to each of the Standing Committees the entire direction of legislation upon those subjects which properly come to its consideration. As to those subjects it is entitled to the initiative, and all legislative action with regard to them is under its overruling guidance. It gives shape and course to the determinations of the House. In one respect, however, its initiative is limited. Even a Standing Committee cannot report a bill whose subject-matter has not been referred to it by the House, "by the rules or otherwise"; it cannot volunteer advice on questions upon which its advice has not been asked. But this is not a serious, not even an operative, limitation upon its functions of suggestion and leadership; for it is a very simple matter to get referred to it any subject it wishes to introduce to the attention of the House. Its chairman, or one of its leading members, frames a bill covering the point upon which the Committee wishes to suggest legislation; brings it in, in his capacity as a private member, on Monday, when the call of States is made; has it referred to his Committee; and thus secures an opportunity for the making of the desired report.

It is by this imperious authority of the Standing Committees that the new member is stayed and thwarted whenever he seeks to take an active part in the business of the House. Turn which way he may, some privilege of the Committees stands in his path. The rules are so framed as to put all business under their management; and one of the discoveries which the new member is sure to make, albeit after many trying experiences and sobering adventures and as his first session draws towards its close, is, that under their sway freedom of debate finds no place of allowance, and that his long-delayed speech must remain unspoken. For even a long congressional session is too short to afford time for a full consideration of all the reports of the forty-seven Committees, and debate upon them must be rigidly cut short, if not altogether excluded, if any considerable part of the necessary business is to be gotten through with before adjournment. There are some subjects to which the House must always give prompt attention; therefore reports from the Committees on Printing and on Elections are always in order; and there are some subjects to which careful consideration must always be accorded; therefore the Committee of Ways and Means and the Committee on Appropriations are clothed with extraordinary privileges; and revenue and supply bills may be reported, and will ordinarily be considered, at any time. But these four are the only specially licensed Committees. The rest must take their turns in fixed order as they are called on by the Speaker, contenting themselves with such crumbs of time as fall from the tables of the four Committees of highest prerogative. . . .

These are some of the plainer points of the rules. They are full of complexity, and of confusion to the uninitiated, and the confusions of practice are greater than the confusions of the rules. For the regular order of business is constantly being interrupted by the introduction of resolutions offered "by unanimous consent," and of bills let in under a "suspension of the rules." Still, it is evident that there is one principle which runs through every stage of procedure, and which is never disallowed or abrogated,—the principle that the Committees shall rule without let or hindrance. And this is a principle of extraordinary formative power. It is the mould of all legislation. In the first place, the speeding of business under the direction of the Committees determines the character and the amount of the discussion to which legislation shall be subjected. The House is conscious that time presses. It knows that, hurry as it may, it will hardly get through with one eighth of the business laid out for the session, and that to pause for lengthy debate is to allow the arrears to accumulate. Besides, most of the members are individually anxious to expedite action on every pending measure, because each member of the House is a member of one or more of the Standing Committees, and is quite naturally desirous that the bills prepared by his Committees, and in which he is, of course, specially interested by reason of the particular attention which he has been compelled to give them, should reach a hearing and a vote as soon as possible. It must, therefore, invariably happen that the Committee holding the floor at any particular time is the Committee whose proposals the majority wish to dispose of as summarily as circumstances will allow, in order that the rest of the forty-two unprivileged Committees to which the majority belong may gain the earlier and the fairer chance of a hearing. A reporting Committee, besides, is generally as glad to be pushed as the majority are to push it. It probably has several bills matured, and wishes to see them disposed of before its brief hours of opportunity are passed and gone.

Consequently, it is the established custom of the House to accord the floor for one hour to the member of the reporting Committee who has charge of the business under consideration; and that hour is made the chief hour of debate. The reporting committee-man seldom, if ever, uses the whole of the hour himself for his opening remarks; he uses part of it, and retains control of the rest of it; for by undisputed privilege it is his to dispose of, whether he himself be upon the floor or not. No amendment is in order during that hour, unless he consent to its presentation; and he does not, of course, yield his time indiscriminately to any one who wishes to speak. He gives way, indeed, as in fairness he should, to opponents as well as to friends of the measure under his charge; but generally no one is accorded a share of his time who has not obtained his previous promise of the floor; and those who do speak must not run beyond the number of minutes he has agreed to allow them. He keeps the course both of debate and of amendment thus carefully under his own supervision, as a good tactician, and before he finally yields the floor, at the expiration of his hour, he is sure to move the previous question. To neglect to do so would be to lose all control of the business in hand; for unless the previous question is ordered the debate may run on at will, and his Committee's chance for getting its measures through slip quite away; and that would be nothing less than his disgrace. He would be all the more blameworthy because he had but to ask for the previous question to get it. As I have said, the House is as eager to hurry business as he can be, and will consent to almost any limitation of discussion that he may demand; though, probably, if he were to throw the reins upon its neck, it would run at large from very wantonness, in scorn of such a driver. The previous question once ordered, all amendments are precluded, and one hour remains for the summing-up of this same privileged committee-man before the final vote is taken and the bill disposed of.

These are the customs which baffle and perplex and astound the new member. In these precedents and usages, when at length he comes to understand them, the novice spies out the explanation of the fact, once so confounding and seemingly inexplicable, that when he leaped to his feet to claim the floor other members who rose after him were coolly and unfeelingly preferred before him by the Speaker. Of course it is plain enough now that Mr. Speaker knew beforehand to whom the representative of the reporting Committee had agreed to yield the floor; and it was no use for any one else to cry out for recognition. Whoever wished to speak should, if possible, have made some arrangement with the Committee before the business came to a hearing, and should have taken care to notify Mr. Speaker that he was to be granted the floor for a few moments.

Unquestionably this, besides being a very interesting, is a very novel and significant method of restricting debate and expediting legislative action,—a method of very serious import, and obviously fraught with far-reaching constitutional effects. The practices of debate which prevail in its legislative assembly are manifestly of the utmost importance to a self-governing people; for that legislation which is not thoroughly discussed by the legislating body is practically done in a corner. It is impossible for Congress itself to do wisely what it does so hurriedly; and the constituencies cannot understand what Congress does not itself stop to consider. The prerogatives of the Committees represent something more than a mere convenient division of labor. There is only one part of its business to which Congress, as a whole, attends,—that part, namely, which is embraced under the privileged subjects of revenue and supply. The House never accepts the proposals of the Committee of Ways and Means, or of the Committee on Appropriations, without due deliberation; but it allows almost all of its other Standing Committees virtually to legislate for it. In form, the Committees only digest the various matter introduced by individual members, and prepare it, with care, and after thorough investigation, for the final consideration and action of the House; but, in reality, they dictate the course to be taken, prescribing the decisions of the House not only, but measuring out, according to their own wills, its opportunities for debate and deliberation as well. The House sits, not for serious discussion, but to sanction the conclusions of its Committees as rapidly as possible. It legislates in its committee-rooms; not by the determinations of majorities, but by the resolutions of specially-commissioned minorities; so that it is not far from the truth to say that Congress in session is Congress on public exhibition, whilst Congress in its committee-rooms is Congress at work.

23

Popular Congressmen and Unpopular Congress (1979)

Glenn R. Parker and Roger H. Davidson

The past decade has witnessed the spread of public cynicism concerning established political institutions. The available evidence suggests that alienation from the polity is a fairly widespread phenomenon, penetrating all countries, and bringing to the surface fundamental questions about the legitimacy of political institutions and authorities.

A recurring theme in critiques of the American political system is the citizen's dismay at the inability of the government to perform, an impediment that Seymour Lipset (1963, pp. 64–70) singles out as detrimental to political stability. Felix Frankfurter (1930, p. 3) characterized distrust of Depression-era government as an indication that people felt that government was unable to satisfy the needs of a modern society. In a later and presumably more benign era, Morris Rosenberg (1951, p. 14) contended that politics meant "very little to people because it literally does little for them," and that governmental action was considered by many as "irrelevant to their lives" (1954, p. 364). Such a posture toward government probably affects the public's image of political officials. In fact, William C. Mitchell (1959, p. 693) has suggested that such officials are not viewed as performing vital services because political functions themselves are not considered as providing a societal contribution.

Public assessments of governmental performance can be described in terms of three components: confidence, impact, and evaluation. *Confidence* reflects the degree to which individuals have faith in the actions of their officials and/or institutions. The extent to which governmental activity is perceived as affecting an individual's life is a measure of the *impact* of governmental

Source: Glenn R. Parker and Roger H. Davidson, from "Why Do Americans Love Their Congressmen So Much More Than Their Congress?" *Legislative Studies Quarterly*, IV, 1, February 1979. Reprinted by permission of Comparative Legislative Research Center and the authors.

performance. *Evaluations* are explicit judgments of the value the individual assigns to that impact. In this research note we focus on the last-mentioned component—the content of public evaluations of one political institution, the United States Congress.

Citizens' evaluations are certainly important in and of themselves. But in reporting these assessments, we too often overlook the bases of their judgments—that is, the criteria individuals use in forming their evaluations. Thus, the objective of this analysis is to describe the standards used in appraising Congress and its membership and to examine response categories in an effort to gauge the likelihood that certain standards generate favorable evaluations.

The findings are based on opinion surveys administered to national population samples (Harris, 1968; U.S. House of Representatives, 1977). Of particular interest are the responses elicited from two open-ended survey items concerning evaluations of Congress and the respondent's representative. In both surveys, individuals were first asked how they would evaluate the performance of Congress—excellent, pretty good, only fair, or poor. Respondents were then queried about the criteria upon which they based their evaluation. Later in the interview sessions, the same questioning was used to ascertain respondent's judgment of their representative's performance in the U.S. House of Representatives. The multiple-response nature of the open-ended questionnaire items allowed individuals the opportunity to provide as many different criteria as they desired. The responses to the above items were then coded and categorized on the basis of the criteria volunteered and, if discernible, the favorable or unfavorable nature of the responses.[1]

Analysis

Domestic policy is the most frequently mentioned criteria for evaluating Congress (Table 1). Although the centrality of domestic policy appears to have declined somewhat since late 1968, it still is the most frequently cited basis for evaluating Congress. The valence associated with domestic policy has also changed in the last several years. While in 1968 domestic policy seemed to divide the electorate equally into those satisfied and dissatisfied with congressional actions, such policy actions had a distinctly negative effect in 1977; 93 percent of those citing domestic policy as a basis for their evaluations of Congress were negative in their assessments of congressional performance.

In late 1968, the Vietnam War's salience took its toll on the popularity of Congress: of those who cited foreign policy as a basis for evaluation, nearly two-thirds had negative evaluations. Several years later, in the absence of major American involvement in a foreign war, few people mentioned foreign policy considerations in evaluating Congress. As the Vietnam War and other foreign ventures began to fade from media attention and public consciousness, domestic policy conflicts gained greater saliency with the public.

Table I Bases of Evaluations of Congress (in percentages)

Bases of Evaluation	1968[a]			1977[b]		
	Percent of all Responses (n = 1370)	Favorable	Unfavorable	Percent of all Responses (n = 1813)	Favorable	Unfavorable
Policy	51.8			30.8		
Domestic	46.3	54	46	30.1	7	93
Foreign-Defense	5.5	35	65	0.7	100	—
Legislative-Executive Relations	6.5			19.6		
Presidential Support	3.1	72	28	—	—	—
Presidential Opposition	3.4	56	44	19.6	25	75
Congressional Environment	16.0			37.1		
Congressional Style and Pace	10.2	38	62	23.1	30	70
Congressional Ethics	2.4	—	100	4.9	—	100
Congressional Self-Seeking	3.4	—	100	9.1	—	100
Group Treatment	4.2	66	34	1.4	50	50
Other	6.4	27	73	8.4	33	67
Repeat of Closed-Ended Question	12.0					
Don't Know/Not Ascertained	3.0			2.8		
Total	99.9			100.1		

[a] *Question:* "How would you rate the job Congress did this past year in 1968—excellent, pretty good, only fair, or poor? Why do you feel this way? Any other reasons?"

[b] *Question:* "Overall, how would you rate the job Congress as a whole—that is the House of Representatives—has done during the past 2 or 3 years—would you say Congress has done an excellent job, a pretty good job, only a fair job, or a poor job? Why do you feel this way? Any other reasons?"

The ideological and partisan differences between those controlling the White House and Congress served to exacerbate the natural conflicts that the "sharing of power" produces. The resulting policy statements generated negative evaluations of congressional performance: in 1977, three of every four mentions of legislative-executive relations as a basis for evaluating Congress were negative.

Another frequently mentioned basis for assessing Congress is the style and pace of the legislative process. In fact, there appears to be an increase in the saliency of the congressional environment as a basis for congressional evaluations: In 1977, one of every three responses made reference to the congressional environment, and these references were distinctly negative. It seems clear that the congressional environment, like legislative-executive relations, tends to foster negative evaluations of Congress.

In light of the saliency of the various criteria, it is not too surprising that evaluations of Congress are often negative. The range and volume of policies and problems for which Congress is held accountable—by the media and the public—create numerous opportunities for dissatisfaction with congressional performance. The cumbersome legislative process, which often gives the appearance of delay and inaction, may be a necessary evil for the constitutional system, but it is not an attribute that appeals to the public. Further, both domestic policy and the legislative environment are frequently mentioned as bases for evaluating Congress. In short, the most salient concerns of the public appear to be those that frequently generate negative impressions of congressional performance.

The criteria for evaluating Congress and those applied in evaluating individual representatives show few parallels. Evaluations of representatives tend to be based upon constituency service provided the district and the personal attributes of incumbents (Table 2). In addition, these criteria tend to place incumbent House members in a favorable light: most of what people hear (or retain) about incumbents is favorable. In fact, the reputation of House members was the most frequently mentioned criterion for evaluating the performance of incumbents: more than 70 percent of the responses refer to some aspect of the incumbents' constituency service or personal attributes.

Policy actions, in contrast, are infrequently cited as criteria for evaluating the representative. This may be a blessing to House members, inasmuch as references to public policy tend to be negative in content. The infrequent use of policy criteria and the emphasis on personal characteristics and district service promote positive evaluations of the incumbent. Rarely are the latter elements viewed in a negative light. In sum, evaluations of Congress and of individual members are apt to differ in valence because of the disparate criteria that are applied to each. Congress is held responsible for policy and for management of the legislative environment, while individual representatives are evaluated in terms of their personal characteristics or constituency service.

Table 2 Bases of Evaluations of Members of Congress (in percentages)

Bases of Evaluation	1968[a]			1977[b]		
	Percent of all Responses (n = 1258)	Favorable	Unfavorable	Percent of all Responses (n = 1232)	Favorable	Unfavorable
Policy	11.2			3.0		
Vague Reference	7.9	69	31	1.5	—	100
Specific Reference	3.3	46	54	1.5	—	100
Constituency Service	49.8			37.7		
District Service	28.1	74	26	13.3	100	—
Constituent Assistance	2.1	100	—	12.6	100	—
Direct Conditions	2.7	91	9	3.7	100	—
Informs Constituents	16.9	18	82	8.1	82	18
Personal Attributes	26.9			35.6		
Personal Characteristics	16.5	84	16	6.7	100	—
Reputation	9.4	95	5	28.9	67	33
Personal Acquaintance	1.0	—	—	—	—	—
Group Treatment	6.4	58	42	3.7	100	—
Other	0.3	50	50	10.4	57	43
Repeat of Closed-Ended Question	2.7					
Don't Know/Not Ascertained	2.7			9.7		
Total	100.0			100.1		

[a] Question: "How would you rate the service your representative gives in looking after this district in Washington—excellent, pretty good, only fair, or poor? Why do you feel this way? Any other reasons?"

[b] Question: "Overall, how would you rate the job congressman who has been representing this area during the past 2 or 3 years has done—would you say your congressman has done an excellent job, a pretty good job, a fair job, or a poor job? Why do you feel this way? Any other reasons?"

Conclusions

Clearly, quite disparate criteria are used in evaluating Congress and individual representatives. Furthermore, one's evaluative criteria influence the nature of one's appraisal: *certain criteria are associated with positive evaluations, while other criteria are identified with negative appraisals.* That is, the features of congressional activity that attract the concern and attention of individuals affect how congressional performance is evaluated. It also seems clear that evaluations of representatives rest more on service to the district than on policy concerns; moreover, such service generally is perceived in a favorable light by constituents. It is no wonder, then, that members of Congress pay so much attention to constituency service—it generates a positive image. Congress, on the other hand, is assessed more in terms of its policy actions, which tend to produce mixed (or negative) evaluations of the institution.

These findings cast new light on a paradox posed by Richard F. Fenno, Jr.: How can we account for the contrast in the popularity of Congress on the one hand, and individual representatives on the other? "If our congressmen are so good," he asks (1975, p. 278), "how can our Congress be so bad? If it is the individuals that make up the institution, why should there be such a disparity in our judgments?"

One possible explanation for this disparity is that people simply apply divergent standards of judgment to Congress as an institution and to individual legislators. Fenno speculates (1975, pp. 278–280) that individual legislators are judged on the basis of personal style and policy views. Stylistically, we expect our legislators to display a solicitous attitude toward constituents—to appear frequently in the district, to maintain contact through the media, and to work on local projects and individual cases. As for policy views, we ask merely that our legislators not stray too far from the norm as expressed by a majority of constituents.

Our data support Fenno's speculations, and they further indicate how much precedence stylistic considerations take over policy concerns. No more than 15 percent of our respondents, by the most generous reckoning, cited policies in explaining how they rated their representative. Unless they were specific, these policy references tended to tilt in the incumbents' favor. Fortunately for incumbents, few voters voice specific policy concerns—indeed, few voice policy concerns of any kind—in evaluating members' performance.

For Congress as an institution, in contrast, citizens enunciate the task of resolving national problems. This is a far more hazardous assignment than citizens set for individual representatives. Many problems are virtually insoluble on a national scale; even if they were solved, would we be able to ascertain that fact? As we have seen, in assessing Congress, respondents mention policy factors more frequently than any other considerations. In the late 1960s, domestic policy concerns tended to produce favorable assessments, while foreign policy concerns yielded critical assessments by almost a two-to-one margin. A decade later, the valences were reversed. Legislative-executive relations also produce mixed reviews: some people expect Congress to fall into line behind the president; others want it to resist White House initiatives and act as a watchdog. Finally, what citizens read and hear of Capitol Hill style carries an overwhelmingly negative message. Scandal and venality are highly visible features of legislative institutions; expertise or courage are less well publicized.

The present data, in short, give eloquent testimony to the reasons why we "love our congressmen so much" yet denigrate the institution of Congress. Individual legislators are evaluated in terms of personal style and district service—attributes upon which few voters are able to make comparisons with other legislators. But Congress-as-institution is evaluated largely on the basis of policies—which tend to be intractable and divisive.

In view of the divergence we have found in the public's premises in assessing congressmen and Congress, incumbents are entirely rational in emphasizing constituency service and equipping themselves with the necessary staff and perquisites to do the job. Members of the U.S. House have historically had a firm grassroots base, cultivated by constituency service as well as by localism legislative roles. There is nothing novel about this: indeed, the House was designed to operate in this fashion (*Wesberry v. Sanders,* 1964). Yet, students of Congress agree that recently legislative roles have shifted perceptibly in the direction of constituency service. As Florin (1977, p. 61) puts it:

> Congressmen are going home more, pressing the flesh, getting around. They are building a personal base of support, one dependent on personal contacts and favors.

The present emphasis upon constituency errand-running, which appears to date from the mid-1960s, contrasts with at least some of the dominant House norms of the previous generation or two.

If the push toward errand-running is conceded, there remains a critical issue of cause and effect. Put bluntly, the question is: In erecting the machinery for constituency communication and service, did legislators mainly contrive to ensure their own re-election, or did they simply respond to what they assumed the public demanded?

Perhaps this question will never be answered with certainty. At the very least, we need to review carefully the sequence of events that produced the present congressional establishment, with special attention to the decade of the 1960s. Survey data should be re-analyzed to determine legislators' and citizens' states of mind during this period of time, even though such data are bound to yield a fragmentary and inconclusive picture.

The present findings nonetheless leave little room for doubt concerning the public's expectations for legislators' performance. The data indicate that, whereas citizens' expectations for Congress are vague and anchored to generalized policy and stylistic concerns, their expectations for their own representatives are unmistakable. Legislators are judged very largely on the way they serve their districts and communicate with them. Successful performance of this aspect of the representative's job typically pays off handsomely, as indicated by incumbents' high rates of re-election. Yet such judgments on the part of voters imply sanctions as well: legislators who lose touch or who seem preoccupied with national issues may be disciplined by declining support or even defeat. A few "lessons" of this type will suffice to persuade other legislators, who after all are politicians, to shift their job priorities.

Is it possible then that public expectation, rather than legislative connivance, is the cause of the bureaucratic establishment that supports constituency-oriented policy making? If so, we may wish to modify the currently popular notion (Florin, 1977, p. 3) that congressmen are to blame for this state of affairs. The public may well be the key to the Washington establishment. If the public did not create this establishment, they have inspired and sustained it, and are apt to continue to do so.

NOTES

1. The data for the open-ended congressional evaluation questions in the 1977 survey were obtained from: U.S. House of Representatives (1977). We have recoded these data into the categories utilized in coding the 1968 data in order to facilitate comparisons and sharpen patterns of congressional evaluations. A description of the recoding scheme is available from the authors.

REFERENCES

Fenno, Richard F., Jr., 1975. "If, as Ralph Nader Says, Congress Is 'The Broken Branch,' How Come We Love Our Congressmen So Much?" in Norman J. Ornstein, ed., *Congress in Change: Evolution and Reform.* New York: Praeger, pp. 277–287.

Fiorina, Morris P. 1977. *Congress: Keystone of the Washington Establishment.* New Haven: Yale University Press.

Frankfurter, Felix. 1930. *The Public and Its Government.* New Haven: Yale University Press.

Harris, Louis & Associates. 1968. Study No. 1900, contracted by Roger H. Davidson, under a grant from the Committee on Governmental and Legal Services, Social Science Research Council.

Lipset, Seymour M. 1963. *Political Man.* New York: Anchor Books.

Mitchell, William C. 1959. "The Ambivalent Social Status of the American Politician," *Western Political Quarterly* 12 (September, 1959): 683–698.

Rosenberg, Morris. 1951. "The Meaning of Politics in Mass Society," *Public Opinion Quarterly* 15 (Spring, 1951): 5–15.

———. 1954. "Some Determinants of Political Apathy," *Public Opinion Quarterly* 18 (Winter, 1954): 349–366.

U.S. House of Representatives, Commission on Administrative Review. 1977. *Final Report: Survey Materials.* H. Doc. 95–272 (95th Congress, 1st session): Vol. 2, pp. 817–819.

Review Questions

1. Why does Edmund Burke assert that elected legislators should represent their constituents by relying on their own best judgment rather than reflecting the views of those who elected them? Do you prefer your elected representatives to follow Burke's advice?

2. Is the U.S. Congress still run by the committee system described by Woodrow Wilson in 1885? Would this selection still be worth reading if it hadn't been written by a future president?

3. How do Parker and Davidson explain the apparent contradictions between the views held by the public about their members of Congress and the Congress as a whole? Do you like your member of Congress better than the Congress as a whole?

Chapter 7

Policy Implementation by the Executive

Implementation is the process of putting a government program into effect; it is the total process of translating a legal mandate, whether an executive order or an enacted statute, into appropriate program directives and structures that provide services or create goods. Implementation, the doing part of public administration, is an inherently political process. Architects often say that "God is in the details." So is implementation. Its essence is in the details. A law is passed but the process of putting it into effect requires countless small decisions that necessarily alter it. According to President Carter's National Security Adviser Zbigniew Brzezinski, "policy-makers are overwhelmed by events and information . . . a great deal of decision-making is done through implementation by the bureaucracy, which often distorts it." "Distort" is a harsh word. It implies intentional change. But most administrative implementators act in good faith. There is seldom intentional distortion. However, there is substantial friction. This means that no matter how well planned a large operation is, the reality of delays, misunderstandings, etc., will make its inevitable execution less than ideal. While military in origin, friction has become a generally recognized phenomenon in all aspects of the administration of public and international affairs.

While implementation is obviously at the heart of public policy and its administration, it has only recently been self-consciously studied. The first major analysis of implementation as a new focus for public administration was Jeffrey Pressman and Aaron Wildavsky's 1973 study of federal programs in the city of Oakland, California. The unabridged title of their work tells part of the story in itself: *Implementation: How Great Expectations in Washington Are Dashed in Oakland; Or, Why It's Amazing that Federal*

Programs Work at All; This being a Saga of the Economic Development Administration as Told by Two Sympathetic Observers Who Seek to Build Morals on a Foundation of Ruined Hopes. What Pressman and Wildavsky related in their landmark book seems almost simplistic—that policy planning and analysis were not taking into account the difficulties of execution or "implementation." The goal of their book was to consider how a closer nexus between policy and implementation could be achieved. A direct result of this book was a spate of works explaining how policy analysis can accomplish this objective—an objective, it is fair to say, that has yet to be comprehensively implemented.

Pressman and Wildavsky formally define implementation as "a process of interaction between the setting of goals and actions geared to achieving them" as well as "an ability to forge subsequent links in the causal chain so as to obtain the desired results." This definition usefully calls attention to the interaction between setting goals and carrying them out. This helps clarify that implementation is political in a very fundamental sense in that the activities that go on under its banner shape who gets what, when, and how from government. Like lawmakers, administrators and those with whom they interact during the implementation process exert power over program objectives and influence program inputs and outcomes. Implementation involves administrators, interest groups, and other actors with diverse values, mobilizing power resources, forming coalitions, consciously plotting strategies, and generally engaging in strategic behavior designed to ensure that their point of view prevails. The terrain may be different from that found in Congress or other legislatures, but the basic staples of the political process are very much present.

The executive branch of any government is the element responsible for the implementation of programs. But political executives, whether mayors, governors or presidents, cannot manage alone. They need staff. The job of the staff, whether a single individual or a bureaucratic behemoth, is to assist line managers in carrying out their duties. Generally, staff officers or units do not have the power of decision, command or control of operations. Rather they are usually restricted to making recommendations to executives and line managers. To the extent that staff recommendations carry the weight of demonstrated (via academic degrees or previous accomplishment) expertise, those recommendations are more likely to be adopted. Staff has its origins with the young assistants of old generals. They are called "staff" in the first place because these young aides de camp carried the general's tent posts (or staffs) and ropes. Even today staff officers in the military are known by the vestigial ropes over their shoulders.

While presidents have always had aides as secretaries and personal staff as household servants, the presidency as an institution did not get significant professional staff assistance until just before World War II. The impetus for this was the President's Committee on Administrative Management (1936–1937), popularly known as the Brownlow Committee, after its chairman Louis Brownlow (1879–1963), a major figure in the development of city management as a profession. The two other members of the committee were Charles E. Merriam (1874–1953), the University of Chicago political scientist, and Luther Gulick (1892–1993), founder of the Institute of Public Administration in New York.

Government grew rapidly during the New Deal period and there was little time or inclination for planning. It was largely believed that there existed many poorly conceived and poorly implemented organizational designs that were neither economical nor effective. These poor designs were often a reflection of the considerable political conflict between the executive and legislative branches. Both the president's office and the Congress had deliberately contributed to this problem by establishing programs in new organizations or agencies only with regard to political objectives—without taking managerial considerations into account. This persistent struggle over organizational control would be addressed by the Brownlow Committee—which provided the first formal assessment of government organization from a managerial perspective.

The Brownlow Committee submitted its report to President Roosevelt in January 1937. The core proposals of the committee were simple enough. Essentially the report indicated that "the president needs help"; that he needs professional staff members around him who possessed a "passion for anonymity." This particular passion seems to have faded in recent years along with the public's belief that a modern president writes his own speeches.

Overall the committee recommended a major reorganization of the executive branch. The president agreed and appropriate legislation was submitted to Congress in 1938. But Congress, in the wake of the president's 1937 court packing plan to enlarge and thus control the Supreme Court and fearful of too much power in the presidency, killed the bill. The president resubmitted a considerably modified reorganization bill the following year and the Congress passed the Reorganization Act of 1939. This law created the present Executive Office of the President, brought into it the Bureau of the Budget (later to be the Office of Management and Budget) from the Department of the Treasury, and authorized the president to prepare future reorganization plans subject to an after-the-fact congressional veto.

The Brownlow report, the Executive Office of the President, and many of the other recommendations of the Brownlow Committee which would eventually become law have been sanctified by time. Yet the Brownlow Committee's major proposals initially aroused considerable controversy. The Congress in the context of the times was naturally cautious about allowing the executive branch too much power even in the good cause of more rational implementation. In the late 1930s Europe was full of dictators (in Germany, Italy, Spain, Russia, etc.) who offered awful examples of what could happen when there is too much power in the executive branch. So it was not unreasonable to be suspicious of the president. After all, didn't he just try to take over the Supreme Court? The argument over who should have more power over the machinery of government, the executive or the legislature, still resonates in the budgetary struggles between the president and the Congress over the size and scope of the governmental machine. Most of the Brownlow Report's introduction and a portion of its section on the White House staff are reprinted here.

Because of constitutionally mandated checks and balances many political executives—whether mayors, governors or presidents—occupy inherently weak offices. Harvard political scientist Richard Neustadt (1919–2003) wrote the classic book on the fragility and elusiveness of executive power with regard to implementation of programs, plans and policy initiatives. Neustadt's *Presidential Power*, published in 1960 on the eve of John F. Kennedy taking office, was greeted as a pioneering addition to our understanding of presidential power as if a modern day Machiavelli had written a new version of *The Prince* (1532) just for the American presidency. The exercise of power, Neustadt argued, is more than office holding, role enactment, or hat wearing; it is the "power to persuade." A president as mere office holder is so weak that he or she must persuade significant numbers of other political actors, especially members of Congress, that what the White House wants of them matches their appraisal of what their own responsibilities require them to do in their own interest and on their own authority.

Neustadt concludes that a president's capacity to persuade will rest mightily on his bargaining skills, on his professional reputation, and on his popular prestige. The higher a president's ratings are in the public opinion polls, the greater his reputation and concomitant ability to influence others. And visa versa. As a president's ratings sink, so too, his bargaining strength. This is why the last two years of the presidencies of Presidents Richard Nixon and Bill Clinton were effectively crippled. In each case a scandal-racked president, deprived of the traditionally high prestige of the office by their own misdeeds, was unable to fully function as the persuader in chief.

But no matter how low a president goes in public esteem, he can still issue orders and directives. True. However, it is often the case that a presidential order indicates a failure to persuade, a failure to adroitly exercise the primary presidential power. Neustadt offered three major examples of this: (1) when President Harry S. Truman had to fire General Douglas MacArthur for publicly contradicting the president on military policy during the Korean War, (2) when Truman had the government take over the steel mills to forestall a strike that would have interfered with Korean War armaments production, and (3) when President Dwight D. Eisenhower had to send federal troops to Little Rock, Arkansas, to racially integrate Central High School. In each case the president failed: (1) to get MacArthur to shut up, (2) to have labor and management reach agreement, and (3) to get the governor of Arkansas to use local police to have integration proceed as a federal court had ordered. Their subsequent formal orders only highlighted their initial failure to persuade. Reprinted here is Neustadt's chapter exploring the "Power to Persuade."

The Constitution, the precedents, the Supreme Court decisions, and legislative enactments all have led the president to assume a dominant role in foreign policy matters. This led Aaron Wildavsky (1930–1993), the author of *The Politics of the Budgetary Process* (1964) which reveals the tactics public managers use to get their budgets passed, to conclude that there are two presidencies: a foreign policy presidency and a domestic policy presidency. And since World War II, presidents have been more successful in foreign than in domestic policy.

The logic behind Wildavsky's hypothesis was his assumption that a number of events and conditions emanating from the development of the modern presidency, which rested in considerable part on the rise of internationalism over isolationism since 1941, paved the way for increasing presidential leadership in foreign policy.

To test his hypothesis Wildavsky examined congressional action on presidential proposals from 1948 to 1964. For this period Congress approved 58.5 percent of foreign policy bills, including 73.3 percent of defense policy bills, and 70.8 percent of the treaties, general foreign relations, State Department, and foreign aid bills. During this same period Congress approved only 40.2 percent of the president's domestic policy proposals. Thus, the two presidencies thesis, reprinted here, was confirmed.

Wildavsky's work has spawned a bevy of research articles, none of which has materially diminished his original thesis. Some of this research does not reflect Wildavsky's neatly differentiated two presidencies because of an insurgent Congress's challenges to the president for control of foreign policy in the aftermath of the Vietnam War and the Watergate scandal. Nevertheless, the president remains preeminent in foreign policy matters—and this is no where more so than with war powers.

A model is a simplification of reality, a reduction in time and space that allows for a better understanding of reality. The representation may be expressed in words, numbers, or diagrams. For example, a book may describe how something works. That is a model. Then it may have diagrams representing how the thing works. That, too, is a model. Models are simplified representations of more complex phenomena intended to facilitate understanding.

We all use models all the time. It's how we think of the world. When you think of the government, what do you see? If you see a diagram of the three equal branches (executive, legislative and judicial), that's a model. If you think of driving to Washington, D.C., and imagine all the links on the interstate highway system you will take to get there, that's a model. The question is not "to model or not to model" but what models are most useful?

A leading example of a conceptual model of public policymaking is provided by Graham T. Allison (1940–), a former dean of Harvard University's Kennedy School of Government. His study of government decision making showed the inadequacies of the view that policies are made by a "single calculating decisionmaker" such as a president who has complete control over the organizational units and individual officials within his or her government. Instead, Allison—using the John F. Kennedy administration's Cuban Missile Crisis of 1962—demonstrated that differing bureaucratic viewpoints (such as those of the Defense Department, State Department, and National Security Council) fight over policy—and over how policy is implemented.

Although Allison's ideas were not new, he helped to crystallize thinking about foreign policymaking by dealing with the different approaches in terms of three models. He argued that the traditionally dominant model, that of the "single calculating decisionmaker," obscured more than it illuminated. He described this as the Rational Actor Model or Model One. He wrote that this needed to be replaced by two other models. Allison's Model Two, the Organizational Processes Model, basically argued that government action could be understood as the output of large organizations which operated according to standard operational procedures. Model Three, Allison described as a Governmental Politics Model, the essence of which was that decisions were the outcome of a bargaining process between different groups and individuals with different bureaucratic perspectives and different political interests. Consequently, foreign policy decisions are not the product of a rational calculation about what is good for the state; rather they are a compromise—and often compromised—product of the internal bargaining process.

Allison's models became some of the best-known models of foreign policymaking—indeed, all public policymaking—because they are useful ways of thinking about how policy is made and implemented. That's the test of the utility of a model. Allison first presented his models as an article in the *American Political Science Review*. An abridged version of this is reprinted here. These are the same models that he later expanded upon in a book, *Essence of Decision: Explaining the Cuban Missile Crisis* (1971).

24

Report of the President's Committee on Administrative Management (1937)

Louis Brownlow, Charles E. Merriam, and Luther Gulick

The American Executive

The need for action in realizing democracy was as great in 1789 as it is today. It was thus not by accident but by deliberate design that the founding fathers set the American Executive in the Constitution on a solid foundation. Sad experience under the Articles of Confederation, with an almost headless Government and committee management, had brought the American

Source: Louis Brownlow, Charles E. Merriam, and Luther Gulick, "Report of the President's Committee on Administrative Management," *Administrative Management in the Government of the United States*, 1937.

Republic to the edge of ruin. Our forefathers had broken away from hereditary government and pinned their faith on democratic rule, but they had not found a way to equip the new democracy for action. Consequently, there was grim purpose in resolutely providing for a Presidency which was to be a national office. The President is indeed the one and only national officer representative of the entire Nation. There was hesitation on the part of some timid souls in providing the President with an election independent of the Congress; with a longer term than most governors of that day; with the duty of informing the Congress as to the state of the Union and of recommending to its consideration "such Measures as he shall judge necessary and expedient"; with a two-thirds veto; with a wide power of appointment; and with military and diplomatic authority. But this reluctance was overcome in the face of need and a democratic executive established.

Equipped with these broad constitutional powers, reenforced by statute, by custom, by general consent, the American Executive must be regarded as one of the very greatest contributions made by our Nation to the development of modern democracy—a unique institution the value of which is as evident in times of stress and strain as in periods of quiet.

As an instrument for carrying out the judgment and will of the people of a nation, the American Executive occupies an enviable position among the executives of the states of the world, combining as it does the elements of popular control and the means for vigorous action and leadership—uniting stability and flexibility. The American Executive as an institution stands across the path of those who mistakenly assert that democracy must fail because it can neither decide promptly not act vigorously.

Our Presidency unites at least three important functions. From one point of view the President is a political leader—leader of a party, leader of the Congress, leader of a people. From another point of view he is head of the Nation in the ceremonial sense of the term, the symbol of our American national solidarity. From still another point of view the President is the Chief Executive and administrator within the Federal system and service. In many types of government these duties are divided or only in part combined, but in the United States they have always been united in one and the same person whose duty it is to perform all of these tasks.

Your Committee on Administrative Management has been asked to investigate and report particularly upon the last function; namely, that of administrative management—the organization for the performance of the duties imposed upon the President in exercising the executive power vested in him by the Constitution of the United States.

Improving the Machinery of Government

Throughout our history we have paused now and then to see how well the spirit and purpose of our Nation is working out in the machinery of everyday government with a view to making such modifications and improvements as prudence and the spirit of progress might suggest. Our Government was the first to set up in its formal Constitution a method of amendment, and the spirit of America has been from the beginning of our history the spirit of progressive changes to meet conditions shifting perhaps more rapidly here than elsewhere in the world.

Since the Civil War, as the tasks and responsibilities of our Government have grown with the growth of the Nation in sweep and power, some notable attempts have been made to keep our administrative system abreast of the new times. The assassination of President Garfield by a disappointed office seeker aroused the Nation against the spoils system and led to the enactment of the civil-service law of 1883. We have struggled to make the principle of this law effective for half a century. The confusion in fiscal management led to the establishment of the Bureau of the Budget and the budgetary system in 1921. We still strive to realize the goal set for the Nation at that time. And, indeed, many other important forward steps have been taken.

Now we face again the problem of governmental readjustment, in part as the result of the activities of the Nation during the desperate years of the industrial depression, in part because of the very growth of the Nation, and in part because of the vexing social problems of our times. There is room for vast increase in our national productivity and there is much bitter wrong to set right in neglected ways of human life. There is need for improvement of our governmental machinery to meet new conditions and to make us ready for the problems just ahead.

Facing one of the most troubled periods in all the troubled history of mankind, we wish to set our affairs in the very best possible order to make the best use of all of our national resources and to make good our democratic claims. If America fails, the hopes and dreams of democracy over all the world go down. We shall not fail in our task and our responsibility, but we cannot live upon our laurels alone.

We seek modern types of management in National Government best fitted for the stern situations we are bound to meet, both at home and elsewhere. As to ways and means of improvement, there are naturally sincere differences of judgment and opinion, but only a treasonable design could oppose careful attention to the best and soundest practices of government available for the American Nation in the conduct of its heavy responsibilities.

The Foundations of Governmental Efficiency

The efficiency of government rests upon two factors: the consent of the governed and good management. In a democracy consent may be achieved readily, though not without some effort, as it is the cornerstone of the Constitution. Efficient management in a democracy is a factor of peculiar significance.

Administrative efficiency is not merely a matter of paper clips, time clocks, and standardized economies of motion. These are but minor gadgets. Real efficiency goes much deeper down. It must be built into the structure of a government just as it is built into a piece of machinery.

Fortunately the foundations of effective management in public affairs, no less than in private, are well known. They have emerged universally wherever men have worked together for some common purpose, whether through the state, the church, the private association, or the commercial enterprise. They have been written into constitutions, charters, and articles of incorporation, and exist as habits of work in the daily life of all organized peoples. Stated in simple terms these canons of efficiency require the establishment of a responsible and effective chief executive as the center of energy, direction, and administrative management; the systematic organization of all activities in the hands of qualified personnel under the direction of the chief executive; and to aid him in this, the establishment of appropriate managerial and staff agencies. There must also be provision for planning, a complete fiscal system, and means for holding the Executive accountable for his program.

Taken together, these principles, drawn from the experience of mankind in carrying on large-scale enterprises, may be considered as the first requirement of good management. They comprehend the subject matter of administrative management as it is dealt with in this report. Administrative management concerns itself in a democracy with the executive and his duties, with managerial and staff aides, with organization, with personnel, and with the fiscal system because these are the indispensable means of making good the popular will in a people's government.

Modernizing Our Governmental Management

In the light of these canons of efficiency, what must be said of the Government of the United States today? Speaking in the broadest terms at this point, and in detail later on, we find in the American Government at the present time that the effectiveness of the Chief Executive is limited and restricted, in spite of the clear intent of the Constitution to the contrary; that the work of the Executive Branch is badly organized; that the managerial agencies are weak and out of date; that the public service does not include its share of men and women of outstanding capacity and character; and that the fiscal and auditing systems are inadequate. These weaknesses are found at the center of our Government and involve the office of the Chief Executive itself.

While in general principle our organization of the Presidency challenges the admiration of the world, yet in equipment for administrative management our Executive Office is not fully abreast of the trend of our American times, either in business or in government. Where, for example, can there be found an executive in any way comparable upon whom so much petty work is thrown? Or who is forced to see so many persons on unrelated matters and to make so many decisions on the basis of what may be, because of the very press of work, incomplete information? How is it humanly possible to know fully the affairs and problems of over 100 separate major agencies, to say nothing of being responsible for their general direction and coordination?

These facts have been known for many years and are so well appreciated that it is not necessary for us to prove again that the President's administrative equipment is far less developed than his responsibilities, and that a major task before the American Government is to remedy this dangerous situation. What we need is not a new principle, but a modernizing of our managerial equipment.

This is not a difficult problem in itself. In fact, we have already dealt with it successfully in State governments, in city governments, and in large-scale private industry. Gov. Frank O. Lowden in Illinois, Gov. Alfred E. Smith in New York, Gov. Harry F. Byrd in Virginia, and Gov. William Tudor Gardiner in Maine, among others, have all shown how similar problems can be dealt with in large governmental units. The Federal Government is more extensive and more complicated, but the principles of reorganization are the same. On the basis of this experience and our examination of the Executive Branch we conclude that the following steps should now be taken:

1. To deal with the greatly increased duties of executive management falling upon the President the White House staff should be expanded.
2. The managerial agencies of the Government, particularly those dealing with the budget, efficiency research, personnel, and planning, should be greatly strengthened and developed as arms of the Chief Executive.
3. The merit system should be extended upward, outward, and downward to cover all non-policy-determining posts, and the civil service system should be reorganized and opportunities established for a career system attractive to the best talent of the Nation.
4. The whole Executive Branch of the Government should be overhauled and the present 100 agencies reorganized under a few large departments in which every executive activity would find its place.
5. The fiscal system should be extensively revised in the light of the best governmental and private practice, particularly with reference to financial records, audit, and accountability of the Executive to the Congress.

These recommendations are explained and discussed in the following sections of this report.

The Purpose of Reorganization

In proceeding to the reorganization of the Government it is important to keep prominently before us the ends of reorganization. Too close a view of machinery must not cut off from sight the true purpose of efficient management. Economy is not the only objective, though reorganization is the first step to savings; the elimination of duplication and contradictory policies is not the only objective, though this will follow; a simple and symmetrical organization is not the only objective, though the new organization will be simple and symmetrical; higher salaries and better jobs are not the only objectives, though these are necessary; better business methods and fiscal controls are not the only objectives, though these too are demanded. There is but one grand purpose, namely, to make democracy work today in our National Government; that is, to make our Government an up-to-date, efficient, and effective instrument for carrying out the will of the Nation. It is for this purpose that the Government needs thoroughly modern tools of management.

As a people we congratulate ourselves justly on our skill as managers—in the home, on the farm, in business big and little—and we properly expect that management in government shall be of the best American model. We do not always get these results, and we must modestly say "we count not ourselves to have attained," but there is a steady purpose in America to press forward until the practices of our governmental administration are as high as the purpose and standards of our people. We know that bad management may spoil good purposes, and that without good management democracy itself cannot achieve its highest goals.

The White House Staff

In this broad program of administrative reorganization the White House itself is involved. The President needs help. His immediate staff assistance is entirely inadequate. He should be given a small number of executive assistants who would be his direct aides in dealing with the managerial agencies and administrative departments of the Government. These assistants, probably not exceeding six in number, would be in addition to his present secretaries, who deal with the public, with the Congress, and with the press and the radio. These aides would have no power to make decisions or issue instructions in their own right. They would not be interposed between the President and the heads of his departments. They would not be assistant presidents in any sense. Their function would be, when any matter was presented to the President for action affecting any part of the administrative work of the Government, to assist him in obtaining quickly and without delay all pertinent information possessed by any of the executive departments so as to guide him in making his responsible decisions; and then when decisions have been made, to assist him in seeing to it that every administrative department and agency affected is promptly informed. Their effectiveness in assisting the President will, we think, be directly proportional to their ability to discharge their functions with restraint. They would remain in the background, issue no orders, make no decisions, emit no public statements. Men for these positions should be carefully chosen by the President from within and without the Government. They should be men in whom the President has personal confidence and whose character and attitude is such that they would not attempt to exercise power on their own account. They should be possessed of high competence, great physical vigor, and a passion for anonymity. They should be installed in the White House itself, directly accessible to the President. In the selection of these aides the President should be free to call on departments from time to time for the assignment of persons who, after a tour of duty as his aides, might be restored to their old positions.

This recommendation arises from the growing complexity and magnitude of the work of the President's office. Special assistance is needed to insure that all matters coming to the attention of the President have been examined from the over-all managerial point of view, as well as from all standpoints that would bear on policy and operation. It also would facilitate the flow upward to the President of information upon which he is to base his decisions and the flow downward from the President of the decisions once taken for execution by the department or departments affected. Thus such a staff would not only aid the President but would also be of great assistance to the several executive departments and to the managerial agencies in simplifying executive contacts, clearance, and guidance.

The President should also have at his command a contingent fund to enable him to bring in from time to time particular persons possessed of particular competency for a particular purpose and whose services he might usefully employ for short periods of time.

The President in his regular office staff should be given a greater number of positions so that he will not be compelled, as he has been compelled in the past, to use for his own necessary work persons carried on the payrolls of other departments.

If the President be thus equipped he will have but the ordinary assistance that any executive of a large establishment is afforded as a matter of course.

In addition to this assistance in his own office the President must be given direct control over and be charged with immediate responsibility for the great managerial functions of the Government which affect all of the administrative departments, as is outlined in the following sections of this report. These functions are personnel management, fiscal and organizational management, and planning management. Within these three groups may be comprehended all of the essential elements of business management.

The development of administrative management in the Federal Government requires the improvement of the administration of these managerial activities, not only by the central agencies in charge, but also by the departments and bureaus. The central agencies need to be strengthened and developed as managerial arms of the Chief Executive, better equipped to perform their central responsibilities and to provide the necessary leadership in bringing about improved practices throughout the Government.

The three managerial agencies, the Civil Service Administration, the Bureau of the Budget, and the National Resources Board should be a part and parcel of the Executive Office. Thus the President would have reporting to him directly the three managerial institutions whose work and activities would affect all of the administrative departments.

The budgets for the managerial agencies should be submitted to the Congress by the President as a part of the budget for the Executive Office. This would distinguish these agencies from the operating administrative departments of the Government, which should report to the President through the heads of departments who collectively compose his Cabinet. Such an arrangement would materially aid the President in his work of supervising the administrative agencies and would enable the Congress and the people to hold him to strict accountability for their conduct.

25

Presidential Power: The Power to Persuade (1959)

Richard E. Neustadt

The limits on command suggest the structure of our government. The Constitutional Convention of 1787 is supposed to have created a government of "separated powers." It did nothing of the sort. Rather, it created a government of separated institutions *sharing* powers.[1] "I am part of the legislative process," Eisenhower often said in 1959 as a reminder of his veto.[2] Congress, the dispenser of authority and funds, is no less part of the administrative process. Federalism adds another set of separated institutions. The Bill of Rights adds others. Many public purposes can only be achieved by voluntary acts of private institutions; the press, for one, in Douglass Cater's phrase, is a "fourth branch of government."[3] And with the coming of alliances abroad, the separate institutions of a London, or a Bonn, share in the making of American public policy.*

What the Constitution separates our political parties do not combine. The parties are themselves composed of separated organizations sharing public authority. The authority consists of nominating powers. Our national parties are confederations of state and local party institutions, with a headquarters that represents the White House, more or less, if the party has a President in office. These confederacies manage presidential nominations. All other public offices depend upon electorates confined within the states.[4] All other nominations are controlled within the states. The President and congressmen who bear one party's label are divided by dependence upon different sets of voters. The differences are sharpest at the stage of nomination. The White House has too

Source: Richard E. Neustadt, from "The Power to Persuade." Reprinted with the permission of The Free Press, a Division of Simon & Schuster Adult Publishing Group, from *Presidential Power and the Modern Presidents: The Politics of Leadership from Roosevelt to Reagan* by Richard E. Neustadt. Copyright © 1990 by Richard E. Neustadt. All rights reserved.
    *For distinctions drawn throughout between powers and power see note 1.

small a share in nominating congressmen, and Congress has too little weight in nominating presidents for party to erase their constitutional separation. Party links are stronger than is frequently supposed, but nominating processes assure the separation.[5]

The separateness of institutions and the sharing of authority prescribe the terms on which a President persuades. When one man shares authority with another, but does not gain or lose his job upon the other's whim, his willingness to act upon the urging of the other turns on whether he conceives the action right for him. The essence of a President's persuasive task is to convince such men that what the White House wants of them is what they ought to do for their sake and on their authority. (Sex matters not at all; for *man* read *woman.*)

Persuasive power, thus defined, amounts to more than charm or reasoned argument. These have their uses for a President, but these are not the whole of his resources. For the individuals he would induce to do what he wants done on their own responsibility will need or fear some acts by him on his responsibility. If they share his authority, he has some share in theirs. Presidential "powers" may be inconclusive when a President commands, but always remain relevant as he persuades. The status and authority inherent in his office reinforce his logic and his charm.

Status adds something to persuasiveness; authority adds still more. When Truman urged wage changes on his secretary of commerce while the latter was administering the steel mills, he and Secretary Sawyer were not just two men reasoning with one another. Had they been so, Sawyer probably would never have agreed to act. Truman's status gave him special claims to Sawyer's loyalty or at least attention. In Walter Bagehot's charming phrase "no man can argue on his knees." Although there is no kneeling in this country, few men—and exceedingly few cabinet officers—are immune to the impulse to say "yes" to the President of the United States. It grows harder to say "no" when they are seated in his Oval Office at the White House, or in his study on the second floor, where almost tangibly he partakes of the aura of his physical surroundings. In Sawyer's case, moreover, the President possessed formal authority to intervene in many matters of concern to the secretary of commerce. These matters ranged from jurisdictional disputes among the defense agencies to legislation pending before Congress and, ultimately, to the tenure of the secretary, himself. There is nothing in the record to suggest that Truman voiced specific threats when they negotiated over wage increases. But given his formal powers and their relevance to Sawyer's other interests, it is safe to assume that Truman's very advocacy of wage action conveyed an implicit threat.

A President's authority and status give him great advantages in dealing with the men he would persuade. Each "power" is a vantage point for him in the degree that other men have use for his authority. From the veto to appointments, from publicity to budgeting, and so down a long list, the White House now controls the most encompassing array of vantage points in the American political system. With hardly an exception, those who share in governing this country are aware that at some time, in some degree, the doing of *their* jobs, the furthering of *their* ambitions, may depend upon the President of the United

States. Their need for presidential action, or their fear of it, is bound to be recurrent if not actually continuous. Their need or fear is his advantage.

A President's advantages are greater than mere listing of his "powers" might suggest. Those with whom he deals must deal with him until the last day of his term. Because they have continuing relationships with him, his future, while it lasts, supports his present influence. Even though there is no need or fear of him today, what he could do tomorrow may supply today's advantage. Continuing relationships may convert any "power," any aspect of his status, into vantage points in almost any case. When he induces other people to do what he wants done, a President can trade on their dependence now and later.

The President's advantages are checked by the advantages of others. Continuing relationships will pull in both directions. These are relationships of mutual dependence. A President depends upon the persons whom he would persuade; he has to reckon with his need or fear of them. They too will possess status, or authority, or both, else they would be of little use to him. Their vantage points confront his own; their power tempers his.

Persuasion is a two-way street. Sawyer, it will be recalled, did not respond at once to Truman's plan for wage increases at the steel mills. On the contrary, the secretary hesitated and delayed and only acquiesced when he was satisfied that publicly he would not bear the onus of decision. Sawyer had some points of vantage all his own from which to resist presidential pressure. If he had to reckon with coercive implications in the President's "situations of strength," so had Truman to be mindful of the implications underlying Sawyer's place as a department head, as steel administrator, and as a cabinet spokesman for business. Loyalty is reciprocal. Having taken on a dirty job in the steel crisis, Sawyer had strong claims to loyal support. Besides, he had authority to do some things that the White House could ill afford. Emulating Wilson, he might have resigned in a huff (the removal power also works two ways). Or, emulating Ellis Arnall, he might have declined to sign necessary orders. Or he might have let it be known publicly that he deplored what he was told to do and protested its doing. By following any of these courses Sawyer almost surely would have strengthened the position of management, weakened the position of the White House, and embittered the union. But the whole purpose of a wage increase was to enhance White House persuasiveness in urging settlement upon union and companies alike. Although Sawyer's status and authority did not give him the power to prevent an increase outright, they gave him capability to undermine its purpose. If his authority over wage rates had been vested by a statute, not by revocable presidential order, his power of prevention might have been complete. So Harold Ickes demonstrated in the famous case of helium sales to Germany before the Second World War.[6]

The power to persuade is the power to bargain. Status and authority yield bargaining advantages. But in a government of "separated institutions sharing powers," they yield them to all sides. With the array of vantage points at his disposal, a President may be far more persuasive than his logic or his charm could make him. But outcomes are not guaranteed by his advantages. There remain the counter pressures those whom he would influence can bring to bear on him from vantage points at their disposal. Command has limited utility; persuasion becomes give-and-take. It is well that the White House holds the vantage points it does. In such a business any President may need them all—and more.

NOTES

1. The reader will want to keep in mind the distinction between two senses in which the word *power* is employed. When I have used the word (or its plural) to refer to formal constitutional, statutory, or customary authority, it is either qualified by the adjective "formal" or placed in quotation marks as "power(s)." Where I have used it in the sense of effective influence on the conduct of others, it appears without quotation marks (and always in the singular). Where clarity and convenience permit, *authority* is substituted for "power" in the first sense and *influence* for power in the second.

2. See, for example, his press conference of July 22, 1959, as reported in the *New York Times,* July 23, 1959.

3. See Douglass Cater, *The Fourth Branch of Government* (Boston: Houghton Mifflin, 1959).

4. With the exception of the vice presidency, of course.

5. See David B. Truman's illuminating study of party relationships in the Eighty-first Congress, *The Congressional Party* (New York: Wiley, 1959), especially chaps. 4, 6, 8.

6. As secretary of the interior in 1939, Harold Ickes refused to approve the sale of helium to Germany despite the insistence of the State Department and the urging of President Roosevelt. Without the Secretary's approval, such sales were forbidden by statute. See *The Secret Diaries of Harold L. Ickes* (New York: Simon & Schuster, 1954), vol. 2, especially pp. 391–93, 396–99. See also Michael J. Reagan, "The Helium Controversy," in the forthcoming casebook on civil-military relations prepared for the Twentieth Century Fund under the editorial direction of Harold Stein.

In this instance the statutory authority ran to the secretary as a matter of his discretion. A President is unlikely to fire cabinet officers for the conscientious exercise of such authority. If the President did so, their successors might well be embarrassed both publicly and at the Capitol were they to reverse decisions previously taken. As for a President's authority to set aside discretionary determinations of this sort, it rests, if it exists at all, on shaky legal ground not likely to be trod save in the gravest of situations.

26

The Two Presidencies (1966)

Aaron Wildavsky

The United States has one President, but it has two presidencies; one presidency is for domestic affairs, and the other is concerned with defense and foreign policy. Since World War II, Presidents have had much greater success in controlling the nation's defense and foreign policies than in dominating its domestic policies. Even Lyndon Johnson has seen his early record of victories in domestic legislation diminish as his concern with foreign affairs grows.

What powers does the President have to control defense and foreign policies and so completely overwhelm those who might wish to thwart him?

The President's normal problem with domestic policy is to get congressional support for the programs he prefers. In foreign affairs, in contrast, he can almost always get support for policies that he believes will protect the nation—but his problem is to find a viable policy.

Whoever they are, whether they begin by caring about foreign policy like Eisenhower and Kennedy or about domestic policies like Truman and Johnson, Presidents soon discover they have more policy preferences in domestic matters than in foreign policy. The Republican and Democratic parties possess a traditional roster of policies, which can easily be adopted by a new President—for example, he can be either for or against Medicare and aid to education. Since existing domestic policy usually changes in only small steps, Presidents find it relatively simple to make minor adjustments. However, although any President knows he supports foreign aid and NATO, the world outside changes much more rapidly than the nation inside—Presidents and their parties have no prior policies on Argentina and the Congo. The world has

Source: Aaron Wildavsky, "The Two Presidencies," from *Transaction*, Vol. 4, Issue 2, December 1966. Copyright © 1966 by Transaction Publishers. Reprinted by permission of the publisher.

become a highly intractable place with a whirl of forces we cannot or do not know how to alter.

The Record of Presidential Control

It takes great crises, such as Roosevelt's hundred days in the midst of the depression, or the extraordinary majorities that Barry Goldwater's candidacy willed to Lyndon Johnson, for Presidents to succeed in controlling domestic policy. From the end of the 1930s to the present (what may roughly be called the modern era), Presidents have often been frustrated in their domestic programs. From 1938, when conservatives regrouped their forces, to the time of his death, Franklin Roosevelt did not get a single piece of significant domestic legislation passed. Truman lost out on most of his intense domestic preferences, except perhaps for housing. Since Eisenhower did not ask for much domestic legislation, he did not meet consistent defeat, yet he failed in his general policy of curtailing governmental commitments. Kennedy, of course, faced great difficulties with domestic legislation.

In the realm of foreign policy there has not been a single major issue on which Presidents, when they were serious and determined, have failed. The list of their victories is impressive: entry into the United Nations, the Marshall Plan, NATO, the Truman Doctrine, the decisions to stay out of Indochina in 1954 and to intervene in Vietnam in the 1960s, aid to Poland and Yugoslavia, the test-ban treaty, and many more. Serious setbacks to the President in controlling foreign policy are extraordinary and unusual.

Table 1, compiled from the Congressional Quarterly Service tabulation of presidential initiative and congressional response from 1948 through 1964, shows that Presidents have significantly better records in foreign and defense matters than in domestic policies. When refugees and immigration—which Congress considers primarily a domestic concern—are removed from the general

Table I Congressional Action on Presidential Proposals from 1948 to 1964

Policy Area	Congressional Action		
	% Pass	% Fail	Number of Proposals
Domestic policy (natural resources, labor, agriculture, taxes, etc.)	40.2	59.8	2,499
Defense policy (defense, disarmament, manpower, misc.)	73.3	26.7	90
Foreign policy	58.5	41.5	655
Immigration, refugees	13.2	86.0	129
Treaties, general foreign relations, State Department, foreign aid	70.8	29.2	445

Source: Congressional Quarterly Service, Congress and the Nation, 1945–1964 (Washington, 1965).

foreign policy area, it is clear that Presidents prevail about 70 percent of the time in defense and foreign policy, compared with 40 percent in the domestic sphere.

World Events and Presidential Resources

Power in politics is control over governmental decisions. How does the President manage his control of foreign and defense policy? The answer does not reside in the greater constitutional power in foreign affairs that Presidents have possessed since the founding of the Republic. The answer lies in the changes that have taken place since 1945.

The number of nations with which the United States has diplomatic relations has increased from 53 in 1939 to 113 in 1966. But sheer numbers do not tell enough; the world has also become a much more dangerous place. However remote it may seem at times, our government must always be aware of the possibility of nuclear war.

Yet the mere existence of great powers with effective thermonuclear weapons would not, in and of itself, vastly increase our rate of interaction with most other nations. We see events in Assam or Burundi as important because they are also part of a larger worldwide contest, called the cold war, in which great powers are rivals for the control or support of other nations. Moreover, the reaction against the blatant isolationism of the 1930s has led to a concern with foreign policy that is worldwide in scope. We are interested in what happens everywhere because we see these events as connected with larger interests involving, at the worst, the possibility of ultimate destruction.

Given the overriding fact that the world is dangerous and that small causes are perceived to have potentially great effects in an unstable world, it follows that Presidents must be interested in relatively "small" matters. So they give Azerbaijan or Lebanon or Vietnam huge amounts of their time. Arthur Schlesinger, Jr., wrote of Kennedy that "in the first two months of his administration he probably spent more time on Laos than on anything else." Few failures in domestic policy, Presidents soon realize, could have as disastrous consequences as any one of dozens of mistakes in the international arena.

The result is that foreign policy concerns tend to drive out domestic policy. Except for occasional questions of domestic prosperity and for civil rights, foreign affairs have consistently higher priority for Presidents. Once, when trying to talk to President Kennedy about natural resources, Secretary of the Interior Stewart Udall remarked, "He's imprisoned by Berlin."

The importance of foreign affairs to Presidents is intensified by the increasing speed of events in the international arena. The event and its consequences follow closely on top of one another. The blunder at the Bay of Pigs is swiftly followed by the near catastrophe of the Cuban missile crisis. Presidents can no longer count on passing along their most difficult problems to their successors. They must expect to face the consequences of their actions—or failure to act—while still in office.

Domestic policy-making is usually based on experimental adjustments to an existing situation. Only a few decisions, such as those involving large dams, irretrievably commit future generations. Decisions in foreign affairs, however, are often perceived to be irreversible. This is expressed, for example, in the fear of escalation or the various "spiral" or "domino" theories of international conflict.

If decisions are perceived to be both important and irreversible, there is every reason for Presidents to devote a great deal of resources to them. Presidents have to be oriented toward the future in the use of their resources. They serve a fixed term in office, and they cannot automatically count on support from the populace, Congress, or the administrative apparatus. They have to be careful, therefore, to husband their resources for pressing future needs. But because the consequences of events in foreign affairs are potentially more grave, faster to manifest themselves, and less easily reversible than in domestic affairs, Presidents are more willing to use up their resources.

The Power to Act

Their formal powers to commit resources in foreign affairs and defense are vast. Particularly important is their power as Commander-in-Chief to move troops. Faced with situations like the invasion of South Korea or the emplacement of missiles in Cuba, fast action is required. Presidents possess both the formal power to act and the knowledge that elites and the general public expect them to act. Once they have committed American forces, it is difficult for Congress or anyone else to alter the course of events. The Dominican venture is a recent case in point.

Presidential discretion in foreign affairs also makes it difficult (though not impossible) for Congress to restrict their actions. Presidents can use executive agreements instead of treaties, enter into tacit agreements instead of written ones, and otherwise help create de facto situations not easily reversed. Presidents also have far greater ability than anyone else to obtain information on developments abroad through the Departments of State and Defense. The need for secrecy in some aspects of foreign and defense policy further restricts the ability of others to compete with Presidents. These things are well known. What is not so generally appreciated is the growing presidential ability to use information to achieve goals.

In the past Presidents were amateurs in military strategy. They could not even get much useful advice outside of the military. As late as the 1930s the number of people outside the military establishment who were professionally engaged in the study of defense policy could be numbered on the fingers. Today there are hundreds of such men. The rise of the defense intellectuals has given the President of the United States enhanced ability to control defense policy. He is no longer dependent on the military for advice. He can choose among defense intellectuals from the research corporations and the academies for alternative sources of advice. He can install these men in his own office. He can play them off against each other or use them to extend spheres of coordination.

Even with these advisers, however, Presidents and Secretaries of Defense might still be too bewildered by the complexity of nuclear situations to take action—unless they had an understanding of the doctrine and concepts of deterrence. But knowledge of the doctrine about deterrence has been widely diffused; it can be picked up by any intelligent person who will read books or listen to enough hours of conversation. Whether or not the doctrine is good is a separate question; the point is that civilians can feel they understand what is going on in defense policy. Perhaps the most extraordinary feature of presidential action during the Cuban missile crisis was the degree to which the Commander-in-Chief of the Armed Forces insisted on controlling even the smallest moves. From the positioning of ships to the methods of boarding, to the precise words and actions to be taken by individual soldiers and sailors, the President and his civilian advisers were in control.

Although Presidents have rivals for power in foreign affairs, the rivals do not usually succeed. Presidents prevail not only because they may have superior resources but because their potential opponents are weak, divided, or believe that they should not control foreign policy. Let us consider the potential rivals—the general citizenry, special interest groups, the Congress, the military, the so-called military-industrial complex, and the State Department.

COMPETITORS FOR CONTROL OF POLICY

The Public

The general public is much more dependent on Presidents in foreign affairs than in domestic matters. While many people know about the impact of social security and Medicare, few know about the politics in Malawi. So it is not surprising that people expect the President to act in foreign affairs and reward him with their confidence. Gallup Polls consistently show that presidential popularity rises after he takes action in a crisis—whether the action is disastrous as in the Bay of Pigs or successful as in the Cuban missile crisis. Decisive action, such as the bombing of oil fields near Haiphong, resulted in a sharp (though temporary) increase in Johnson's popularity.

The Vietnam situation illustrates another problem of public opinion in foreign affairs: it is extremely difficult to get operational policy directions from the general public. It took a long time before any sizable public interest in the subject developed. Nothing short of the large scale involvement of American troops under fire probably could have brought about the current high level of concern. Yet this relatively well developed popular opinion is difficult to interpret. While a majority appear to support President Johnson's policy, it appears that they could easily be persuaded to withdraw from Vietnam if the administration changed its line. Although a sizable majority would support various initiatives to end the war, they would seemingly be appalled if this action led to Communist encroachments elsewhere in Southeast Asia. (See

"The President, the Polls, and Vietnam" by Seymour Martin Lipset, *Transaction*, Sept/Oct 1966.)

Although Presidents lead opinion in foreign affairs, they know they will be held accountable for the consequences of their actions. President Johnson has maintained a large commitment in Vietnam. His popularity shoots up now and again in the midst of some imposing action. But the fact that a body of citizens do not like the war comes back to damage his overall popularity. We will support your initiatives, the people seem to say, but we will reserve the right to punish you (or your party) if we do not like the results.

Special Interest Groups

Opinions are easier to gauge in domestic affairs because, for one thing, there is a stable structure of interest groups that covers virtually all matters of concern. The farm, labor, business, conservation, veteran, civil rights, and other interest groups provide cues when a proposed policy affects them. Thus people who identify with these groups may adopt their views. But in foreign policy matters the interest group structure is weak, unstable, and thin rather than dense. In many matters affecting Africa and Asia, for example, it is hard to think of well-known interest groups. While ephemeral groups arise from time to time to support or protest particular policies, they usually disappear when the immediate problem is resolved. In contrast, longer-lasting elite groups like the Foreign Policy Association and Council on Foreign Relations are composed of people of diverse views; refusal to take strong positions on controversial matters is a condition of their continued viability.

The strongest interest groups are probably the ethnic associations whose members have strong ties with a homeland, as in Poland or Cuba, so they are rarely activated simultaneously on any specific issue. They are most effective when most narrowly and intensely focused—as in the fierce pressure from Jews to recognize the state of Israel. But their relatively small numbers limits their significance to Presidents in the vastly more important general foreign policy picture—as continued aid to the Arab countries shows. Moreover, some ethnic groups may conflict on significant issues such as American acceptance of the Oder-Neisse line separating Poland from what is now East Germany.

The Congress

Congressmen also exercise power in foreign affairs. Yet they are ordinarily not serious competitors with the President because they follow a self-denying ordinance. They do not think it is their job to determine the nation's defense policies. Lewis A. Dexter's extensive interviews with members of the Senate Armed Services Committee, who might be expected to want a voice in defense policy, reveal that they do not desire for men like themselves to run the nation's defense establishment. Aside from a few specific conflicts among the armed services which allow both the possibility and desirability of direct intervention, the Armed Services Committee constitutes a sort of real estate committee dealing with the regional economic consequences of the location of military facilities.

The congressional appropriations power is potentially a significant resource, but circumstances since the end of World War II have tended to reduce its effectiveness. The appropriations committees and Congress itself might make their will felt by refusing to allot funds unless basic policies were altered. But this has not happened. While Congress makes its traditional small cuts in the military budget, Presidents have mostly found themselves warding off congressional attempts to increase specific items still further.

Most of the time, the administration's refusal to spend has not been seriously challenged. However, there have been occasions when individual legislators or committees have been influential. Senator Henry Jackson in his campaign (with the aid of colleagues on the Joint Committee on Atomic Energy) was able to gain acceptance for the Polaris weapons system and Senator Arthur H. Vandenberg played a part in determining the shape of the Marshall Plan and so on. The few congressmen who are expert in defense policy act, as Samuel P. Huntington says, largely as lobbyists with the executive branch. It is apparently more fruitful for these congressional experts to use their resources in order to get a hearing from the executive than to work on other congressmen.

When an issue involves the actual use or threat of violence, it takes a great deal to convince congressmen not to follow the President's lead. James Robinson's tabulation of foreign and defense policy issues from the late 1930s to 1961 (Table 2) shows dominant influence by Congress in only one case out of seven—the 1954 decision not to intervene with armed force in Indochina. In that instance President Eisenhower deliberately sounded out congressional opinion and, finding it negative, decided not to intervene—against the advice of Admiral Radford, chairman of the Joint Chiefs of Staff. This attempt to abandon responsibility did not succeed, as the years of American involvement demonstrate.

The Military

The outstanding feature of the military's participation in making defense policy is their amazing weakness. Whether the policy decisions involve the size of the armed forces, the choice of weapons systems, the total defense budget, or its division into components, the military have not prevailed. Let us take budgetary decisions as representative of the key choices to be made in defense policy. Since the end of World War II the military has not been able to achieve significant (billion dollar) increases in appropriations by their own efforts. Under Truman and Eisenhower defense budgets were determined by what Huntington calls the remainder method: the two Presidents estimated revenues, decided what they could spend on domestic matters, and the remainder was assigned to defense. The usual controversy was between some military and congressional groups supporting much larger expenditures while the

Table 2 Congressional Involvement in Foreign and Defense Policy Decisions

Issue	Congressional Involvement (High, Low, None)	Initiator (Congress or Executive)	Predominant Influence (Congress or Executive)	Legislation or Resolution (Yes or No)	Violence at Stake (Yes or No)	Decision Time (Long or Short)
Neutrality legislation, the 1930s	High	Exec	Cong	Yes	No	Long
Lend-lease, 1941	High	Exec	Exec	Yes	Yes	Long
Aid to Russia, 1941	Low	Exec	Exec	No	No	Long
Repeal of Chinese exclusion, 1943	High	Cong	Cong	Yes	No	Long
Fulbright Resolution, 1943	High	Cong	Cong	Yes	No	Long
Building the atomic bomb, 1944	Low	Exec	Exec	Yes	Yes	Long
Foreign Services Act of 1946	High	Exec	Exec	Yes	No	Long
Truman Doctrine, 1947	High	Exec	Exec	Yes	No	Long
The Marshall Plan, 1947–48	High	Exec	Exec	Yes	No	Long
Berlin airlift, 1948	None	Exec	Exec	No	Yes	Long
Vandenberg Resolution, 1948	High	Exec	Cong	Yes	No	Long
North Atlantic Treaty, 1947–49	High	Exec	Exec	Yes	No	Long
Korean decision, 1950	None	Exec	Exec	No	Yes	Short
Japanese peace treaty, 1952	High	Exec	Exec	Yes	No	Long
Bohlen nomination, 1953	High	Exec	Exec	Yes	No	Long
Indo-China, 1954	High	Exec	Cong	No	Yes	Short
Formosan Resolution, 1955	High	Exec	Exec	Yes	Yes	Long
International Finance Corporation, 1956	Low	Exec	Exec	Yes	No	Long
Foreign aid, 1957	High	Exec	Exec	Yes	No	Long
Reciprocal trade agreements, 1958	High	Exec	Exec	Yes	No	Long
Monroney Resolution, 1958	High	Cong	Cong	Yes	No	Long
Cuban decision, 1961	Low	Exec	Exec	No	Yes	Long

Source: James A. Robinson, Congress and Foreign Policy-Making (Homewood, Ill.: Dorsey Press, 1962).

President and his executive allies refused. A typical case, involving the desire of the Air Force to increase the number of groups of planes is described by Huntington in *The Common Defense:*

> The FY [fiscal year] 1949 budget provided 48 groups. After the Czech coup, the Administration yielded and backed an Air Force of 55 groups in its spring rearmament program. Congress added additional funds to aid Air Force expansion to 70 groups. The Administration refused to utilize them, however, and in the gathering economy wave of the summer and fall of 1948, the Air Force goal was cut back again to 48 groups. In 1949 the House of Representatives picked up the challenge and appropriated funds for 58 groups. The President impounded the money. In June, 1950, the Air Force had 48 groups.

The great increases in the defense budget were due far more to Stalin and modern technology than to the military. The Korean War resulted in an increase from 12 to 44 billions and much of the rest followed Sputnik and the huge costs of missile programs. Thus modern technology and international conflict put an end to the one major effort to subordinate foreign affairs to domestic policies through the budget.

It could be argued that the President merely ratifies the decisions made by the military and their allies. If the military and/or Congress were united and insistent on defense policy, it would certainly be difficult for Presidents to resist these forces. But it is precisely the disunity of the military that has characterized the entire postwar period. Indeed, the military have not been united on any major matter of defense policy. The apparent unity of the Joint Chiefs of Staff turns out to be illusory. The vast majority of their recommendations appear to be unanimous and are accepted by the Secretary of Defense and the President. But this facade of unity can only be achieved by methods that vitiate the impact of the recommendations. Genuine disagreements are hidden by vague language that commits no one to anything. Mutually contradictory plans are strung together so everyone appears to get something, but nothing is decided. Since it is impossible to agree on really important matters, all sorts of trivia are brought in to make a record of agreement. While it may be true, as Admiral Denfield, a former Chief of Naval Operations, said, that "On nine-tenths of the matters that come before them the joint Chiefs of Staff reach agreement themselves," the vastly more important truth is that "normally the *only* disputes are on strategic concepts, the size and composition of forces, and budget matters."

Military-Industrial

But what about the fabled military-industrial complex? If the military alone is divided and weak, perhaps the giant industrial firms that are so dependent on defense contracts play a large part in making policy.

First, there is an important distinction between the questions "Who will get a given contract?" and "What will our defense policy be?" It is apparent that different answers may be given to these quite different questions. There are literally tens of thousands of defense contractors. They may compete vigorously for business. In the course of this competition, they may wine and dine military officers, use retired generals, seek intervention by their congressmen, place ads in trade journals, and even contribute to political campaigns. The famous TFX controversy—should General Dynamics or Boeing get the expensive contract?—is a larger than life example of the pressure brought to bear in search of lucrative contracts.

But neither the TFX case nor the usual vigorous competition for contracts is involved with the making of substantive defense policy. Vital questions like the size of the defense budget, the choice of strategic programs, massive retaliation vs. a counter-city strategy, and the like were far beyond the policy aims of any company. Industrial firms, then, do not control such decisions, nor is there much evidence that they actually try. No doubt a precipitous and drastic rush to disarmament would meet with opposition from industrial firms among other interests. However, there has never been a time when any significant element in the government considered a disarmament policy to be feasible.

It may appear that industrial firms had no special reason to concern themselves with the government's stance on defense because they agree with the national consensus on resisting communism, maintaining a large defense establishment, and rejecting isolationism. However, this hypothesis about the climate of opinion explains everything and nothing. For every policy that is adopted or rejected can be explained away on the grounds that the cold war climate of opinion dictated what happened. Did the United States fail to intervene with armed force in Vietnam in 1954? That must be because the climate of opinion was against it. Did the United States send troops to Vietnam in the 1960s? That must be because the cold war climate demanded it. If the United States builds more missiles, negotiates a test-ban treaty, intervenes in the Dominican Republic, fails to intervene in a dozen other situations, all these actions fit the hypothesis by definition. The argument is reminiscent of those who defined the Soviet Union as permanently hostile and therefore interpreted increases of Soviet troops as menacing and decreases of troop strength as equally sinister.

If the growth of the military establishment is not directly equated with increasing military control of defense policy, the extraordinary weakness of the professional soldier still requires explanation. Huntington has written about how major military leaders were seduced in the Truman and Eisenhower years into believing that they should bow to the judgment of civilians that the economy could not stand much larger military expenditures. Once the size of the military pie was accepted as a fixed constraint, the military services were compelled to put their major energies into quarreling with one another over who should get the larger share. Given the natural rivalries of the military and their traditional acceptance of civilian rule, the President and his advisers—who could claim responsibility for the broader picture of reconciling defense and domestic policies—had the upper hand. There are, however, additional explanations to be considered.

The dominant role of the congressional appropriations committee is to be guardian of the treasury. This is manifested in the pride of its members in cutting the President's budget. Thus it was difficult to get this crucial committee to recommend even a few hundred million increase in defense; it was practically impossible to get them to consider the several billion jump that might really have made a difference. A related budgetary matter concerned the planning, programming, and budgetary system introduced by Secretary of Defense McNamara. For if the defense budget contained major categories that crisscrossed the services, only the Secretary of Defense could put it together. Whatever the other debatable consequences of program budgeting, its major consequence was to grant power to the secretary and his civilian advisers.

The subordination of the military through program budgeting is just one symptom of a more general weakness of the military. In the past decade the military has suffered a lack of intellectual skills appropriate to the nuclear age. For no one has (and no one wants) direct experience with nuclear war. So the usual military talk about being the only people to have combat experience is not very impressive. Instead, the imaginative creation of possible future wars—in order to avoid them—requires people with a high capacity for abstract thought combined with the ability to manipulate symbols using quantitative methods. West Point has not produced many such men.

The State Department

Modern Presidents expect the State Department to carry out their policies. John F. Kennedy felt that State was "in some particular sense 'his' department." If a Secretary of State forgets this, as was apparently the case with James Byrnes under Truman, a President may find another man. But the State Department, especially the Foreign Service, is also a highly professional organization with a life and momentum of its own. If a President does not push hard, he may find his preferences somehow dissipated in time. Arthur Schlesinger fills his book on Kennedy with laments about the bureaucratic inertia and recalcitrance of the State Department.

Yet Schlesinger's own account suggests that State could not ordinarily resist the President. At one point, he writes of "the President, himself, increasingly the day-to-day director of American foreign policy." On the next page, we learn that "Kennedy dealt personally with almost every aspect of policy around the globe. He knew more about certain areas than the senior officials at State and probably called as many issues to their attention as they did to his." The President insisted on his way in Laos. He pushed through his policy on the Congo against strong opposition with the State Department. Had Kennedy wanted to get a great deal more initiative out of the State Department, as Schlesinger insists, he could have replaced the Secretary of State, a man who did not command special support in the Democratic party or in Congress. It may be that Kennedy wanted too strongly to run his own foreign policy. Dean Rusk may have known far better than Schlesinger that the one thing Kennedy did not want was a man who might rival him in the field of foreign affairs.

Schlesinger comes closest to the truth when he writes that "the White House could always win any battle it chose over the [Foreign] Service; but the prestige and proficiency of the Service limited the number of battles any White

House would find it profitable to fight." When the President knew what he wanted, he got it. When he was doubtful and perplexed, he sought good advice and frequently did not get that. But there is no evidence that the people on his staff came up with better ideas. The real problem may have been a lack of good ideas anywhere. Kennedy undoubtedly encouraged his staff to prod the State Department. But the President was sufficiently cautious not to push so hard that he got his way when he was not certain what that way should be. In this context Kennedy appears to have played his staff off against elements in the State Department.

The growth of a special White House staff to help Presidents in foreign affairs expresses their need for assistance, their refusal to rely completely on the regular executive agencies, and their ability to find competent men. The deployment of this staff must remain a presidential prerogative, however, if its members are to serve Presidents and not their opponents. Whenever critics do not like existing foreign and defense policies, they are likely to complain that the White House staff is screening out divergent views from the President's attention. Naturally, the critics recommend introducing many more different viewpoints. If the critics could maneuver the President into counting hands all day ("on the one hand and on the other"), they would make it impossible for him to act. Such a viewpoint is also congenial to those who believe that action rather than inaction is the greatest present danger in foreign policy. But Presidents resolutely refuse to become prisoners of their advisers by using them as other people would like. Presidents remain in control of their staff as well as of major foreign policy decisions.

How Complete Is the Control?

Some analysts say that the success of Presidents in controlling foreign policy decisions is largely illusory. It is achieved, they say, by anticipating the reactions of others, and eliminating proposals that would run into severe opposition. There is some truth in this objection. In politics, where transactions are based on a high degree of mutual interdependence, what others may do has to be taken into account. But basing presidential success in foreign and defense policy on anticipated reactions suggests a static situation which does not exist. For if Presidents propose only those policies that would get support in Congress, and Congress opposes them only when it knows that it can muster overwhelming strength, there would never be any conflict. Indeed, there might never be any action.

How can "anticipated reaction" explain the conflict over policies like the Marshall Plan and the test-ban treaty in which severe opposition was overcome only by strenuous efforts? Furthermore, why doesn't "anticipated reaction" work in domestic affairs? One would have to argue that for some reason presidential perception of what would be successful is consistently confused on domestic issues and most always accurate on major foreign policy issues. But the role of "anticipated reactions" should be greater in the more familiar domestic situations, which provide a backlog of experience for forecasting, than in foreign policy with many novel situations such as the Suez crisis or the Rhodesian affair.

Are there significant historical examples which might refute the thesis of presidential control of foreign policy? Foreign aid may be a case in point. For many years, Presidents have struggled to get foreign aid appropriations because of hostility from public and congressional opinion. Yet several billion dollars a year are appropriated regularly despite the evident unpopularity of the program. In the aid programs to Communist countries like Poland and Yugoslavia, the Congress attaches all sorts of restrictions to the aid, but Presidents find ways of getting around them.

What about the example of recognition of Communist China? The sentiment of the country always has been against recognizing Red China or admitting it to the United Nations. But have Presidents wanted to recognize Red China and been hamstrung by opposition? The answer, I suggest, is a qualified "no." By the time recognition of Red China might have become a serious issue for the Truman administration, the war in Korea effectively precluded its consideration. There is no evidence that President Eisenhower or Secretary Dulles ever thought it wise to recognize Red China or help admit her to the United Nations. The Kennedy administration viewed the matter as not of major importance and, considering the opposition, moved cautiously in suggesting change. Then came the war in Vietnam. If the advantages for foreign policy had been perceived to be much higher, then Kennedy or Johnson might have proposed changing American policy toward recognition of Red China.

One possible exception, in the case of Red China, however, does not seem sufficient to invalidate the general thesis that Presidents do considerably better in getting their way in foreign and defense policy than in domestic policies.

The World Influence

The forces impelling Presidents to be concerned with the widest range of foreign and defense policies also affect the ways in which they calculate their power stakes. As Kennedy used to say, "Domestic policy . . . can only defeat us; foreign policy can kill us."

It no longer makes sense for Presidents to "play politics" with foreign and defense policies. In the past, Presidents might have thought that they could gain by prolonged delay or by not acting at all. The problem might disappear or be passed on to their successors. Presidents must now expect to pay the high costs themselves if the world situation deteriorates. The advantages of pursuing a policy that is viable in the world, that will not blow up on Presidents or their fellow citizens, far outweigh any temporary political disadvantages accrued in supporting an initially unpopular policy. Compared with domestic affairs, Presidents engaged in world politics are immensely more concerned with meeting problems on their own terms. Who supports and opposes a policy, though a matter of considerable interest, does not assume the crucial importance that it does in domestic affairs. The best policy Presidents can find is also the best politics.

The fact that there are numerous foreign and defense policy situations competing for a President's attention means that it is worthwhile to organize political activity in order to effect his agenda. For if a President pays more attention to certain problems he may develop different preferences; he may seek and receive different advice; his new calculations may lead him to devote greater resources to seeking a solution. Interested congressmen may exert influence not by directly determining a presidential decision, but indirectly by making it costly for a President to avoid reconsidering the basis for his action. For example, citizen groups, such as those concerned with a change in China policy, may have an impact simply by keeping their proposals on the public agenda. A President may be compelled to reconsider a problem even though he could not overtly be forced to alter the prevailing policy.

In foreign affairs we may be approaching the stage where knowledge is power. There is a tremendous receptivity to good ideas in Washington. Most anyone who can present a convincing rationale for dealing with a hard world finds a ready audience. The best way to convince Presidents to follow a desired policy is to show that it might work. A man like McNamara thrives because he performs; he comes up with answers he can defend. It is, to be sure, extremely difficult to devise good policies or to predict their consequences accurately. Nor is it easy to convince others that a given policy is superior to other alternatives. But it is the way to influence with Presidents. For if they are convinced that the current policy is best, the likelihood of gaining sufficient force to compel a change is quite small. The man who can build better foreign policies will find Presidents beating a path to his door.

27

Conceptual Models and the Cuban Missile Crisis (1969)

Graham T. Allison

The Cuban missile crisis is a seminal event. For thirteen days of October 1962, there was a higher probability that more human lives would end suddenly than ever before in history. Had the worst occurred, the death of 100 million Americans, over 100 million Russians, and millions of Europeans as well would make previous natural calamities and inhumanities appear insignificant. Given the probability of disaster—which President Kennedy estimated as "between 1 out of 3 and even"—our escape seems awesome.[1] This event symbolizes a central, if only partially thinkable, fact about our existence. That such consequences could follow from the choices and actions of national governments obliges students of government as well as participants in governance to think hard about these problems.

Improved understanding of this crisis depends in part on more information and more probing analyses of available evidence. To contribute to these efforts is part of the purpose of this study. But here the missile crisis serves primarily as grist for a more general investigation. This study proceeds from the premise that marked improvement in our understanding of such events depends critically on more self-consciousness about what observers bring to the analysis. What each analyst sees and judges to be important is a function not only of the evidence about what happened but also of the "conceptual lenses" through which he looks at the evidence. The principal purpose of this essay is to explore some of the fundamental assumptions and categories employed by analysts in thinking about problems of governmental behavior, especially in foreign and military affairs.

Source: Graham T. Allison, from "Conceptual Models and the Cuban Missile Crisis," *American Political Science Review,* LXIII (3) (September 1969). Copyright © 1969 American Political Science Association, published by Cambridge University Press. Reproduced with permission.

The general argument can be summarized in three propositions:

1. Analysts think about problems of foreign and military policy in terms of largely implicit conceptual models that have significant consequences for the content of their thought.[2]

Though the present product of foreign policy analysis is neither systematic nor powerful, if one carefully examines explanations produced by analysts, a number of fundamental similarities emerge. Explanations produced by particular analysts display quite regular, predictable features. This predictability suggests a substructure. These regularities reflect an analyst's assumptions about the character of puzzles, the categories in which problems should be considered, the types of evidence that are relevant, and the determinants of occurrences. The first proposition is that clusters of such related assumptions constitute basic frames of reference or conceptual models in terms of which analysts both ask and answer the questions: What happened? Why did the event happen? What will happen?[3] Such assumptions are central to the activities of explanation and prediction, for in attempting to explain a particular event, the analyst cannot simply describe the full state of the world leading up to that event. The logic of explanation requires that he single out the occurrence.[4] Moreover, as the logic of prediction underscores, the analyst must summarize the various determinants as they bear on the event in question. Conceptual models both fix the mesh of the nets that the analyst drags through the material in order to explain a particular action or decision and direct casting that net in select ponds, at certain depths, in order to catch the desired fish.

2. Most analysts explain (and predict) the behavior of national governments in terms of various forms of one basic conceptual model, here entitled the Rational Policy Model.[5]

In terms of this conceptual model, analysts attempt to understand happenings as the more or less purposive acts of unified national governments. For these analysts, the point of an explanation is to show how the nation or government could have chosen the action in question, given the strategic problem that it faced. For example, in confronting the problem posed by the Soviet installation of missiles in Cuba, rational policy model analysts attempt to show how this was a reasonable act from the point of view of the Soviet Union, given Soviet strategic objectives.

3. Two "alternative" conceptual models, here labeled an Organizational Process model (model II) and a Bureaucratic Politics model (model III) provide a base for improved explanation and prediction. . . .

Model I: Rational Policy

Rational Policy Model Illustrated

Where is the pinch of the puzzle raised by the New York Times over Soviet deployment of an antiballistic missile system?[6] The question, as the Times states it, concerns the Soviet Union's objective in allocating such large sums of money for this weapon system while at the same time seeming to pursue a policy of increasing détente. In former President Johnson's words, "the paradox is that this [Soviet deployment of an antiballistic missile system] should be happening at a time when there is abundant evidence that our mutual antagonism is beginning to ease."[7] This question troubles people primarily because Soviet antiballistic missile deployment, and evidence of Soviet actions towards détente, when juxtaposed in our implicit model, produce a question. With reference to what objective could the Soviet government have rationally chosen the simultaneous pursuit of these two courses of action? This question arises only when the analyst attempts to structure events as purposive choices of consistent actors.

How do analysts attempt to explain the Soviet emplacement of missiles in Cuba? The most widely cited explanation of this occurrence has been produced by two RAND Sovietologists, Arnold Horelick and Myron Rush.[8] They conclude that "the introduction of strategic missiles into Cuba was motivated chiefly by the Soviet leaders' desire to overcome . . . the existing large margin of US strategic superiority."[9] How do they reach this conclusion? In Sherlock Holmes style, they seize several salient characteristics of this action and use these features as criteria against which to test alternative hypotheses about Soviet objectives. For example, the size of the Soviet deployment, and the simultaneous emplacement of more expensive, more visible intermediate-range missiles as well as medium-range missiles, it is argued, exclude an explanation of the action in terms of Cuban defense—since the objective could have been secured with a much smaller number of medium-range missiles alone. Their explanation presents an argument for one objective that permits interpretation of the details of Soviet behavior as a value-maximizing choice.

How do analysts account for the coming of the First World War? According to Hans Morgenthau, "the first World War had its origin exclusively in the fear of a disturbance of the European balance of power."[10] In the period preceding World War I, the Triple Alliance precariously balanced the Triple Entente. If either power combination could gain a decisive advantage in the Balkans, it would achieve a decisive advantage in the balance of power. "It was this fear," Morgenthau asserts, "that motivated Austria in July 1914 to settle its accounts with Serbia once and for all, and that induced Germany to support Austria unconditionally. It was the same fear that brought Russia to the support of Serbia, and France to the support of Russia."[11] How is Morgenthau able to resolve this problem so confidently? By imposing on the data a "rational outline."[12] The value of this method, according to Morgenthau, is that "it provides for rational discipline in action and creates astounding continuity in foreign policy which makes American, British, or Russian foreign policy appear as an intelligent, rational continuum . . . regardless of the different motives, preferences, and intellectual and moral qualities of successive statesmen."[13] . . .

Most contemporary analysts (as well as laymen) proceed predominantly—albeit most often implicitly—in terms of this model when attempting to explain happenings in foreign affairs. Indeed, that occurrences in foreign affairs are the *acts of nations* seems so fundamental to thinking about such problems that this underlying model has rarely been recognized: to explain an occurrence in foreign policy simply means to show how the government could have rationally chosen that action.[14] These brief examples illustrate five uses of the model. To prove that most analysts think largely in terms of the rational policy model is not possible. In this limited space it is not even possible to illustrate the range of employment of the framework. Rather, my purpose is to convey to the reader a grasp of the model and a challenge: let the readers examine the literature with which they are most familiar and make a judgment.

The general characterization can be sharpened by articulating the rational policy model as an "analytic paradigm" in the technical sense developed by Robert K. Merton for sociological analyses.[15] Systematic statement of basic assumptions, concepts, and propositions employed by model I analysts highlights the distinctive thrust of this style of analysis. To articulate a largely implicit framework is of necessity to caricature. But caricature can be instructive.

Rational Policy Paradigm

Basic Unit of Analysis: Policy as National Choice

Happenings in foreign affairs are conceived as actions chosen by the nation or national government.[16] Governments select the action that will maximize strategic goals and objectives. These "solutions" to strategic problems are the fundamental categories in terms of which the analyst perceives what is to be explained.

Organizing Concepts

NATIONAL ACTOR

The nation or government, conceived as a rational, unitary decision-maker, is the agent. This actor has one set of specified goals (the equivalent of a consistent utility function), one set of perceived options, and a single estimate of the consequences that follow from each alternative.

THE PROBLEM

Action is chosen in response to the strategic problem which the nation faces. Threats and opportunities arising in the "international strategic market place" move the nation to act.

STATIC SELECTION

The sum of activity of representatives of the government relevant to a problem constitutes what the nation has chosen as its "solution." Thus the action is conceived as a steady-state choice among alternative outcomes (rather than, for example, a large number of partial choices in a dynamic stream).

ACTION AS RATIONAL CHOICE

The components include:

1. *Goals and Objectives.* National security and national interests are the principal categories in which strategic goals are conceived. Nations seek security and a range of further objectives. (Analysts rarely translate strategic goals and objectives into an explicit utility function; nevertheless, analysts do focus on major goals and objectives and trade off side effects in an intuitive fashion.)
2. *Options.* Various courses of action relevant to a strategic problem provide the spectrum of options.
3. *Consequences.* Enactment of each alternative course of action will produce a series of consequences. The relevant consequences constitute benefits and costs in terms of strategic goals and objectives.
4. *Choice.* Rational choice is value-maximizing. The rational agent selects the alternative whose consequences rank highest in terms of his goals and objectives.

Dominant Inference Pattern

This paradigm leads analysts to rely on the following pattern of inference: if a nation performed a particular action, that nation must have had ends towards which the action constituted an optimal means. The rational policy model's explanatory power stems from this inference pattern. Puzzlement is relieved by revealing the purposive pattern within which the occurrence can be located as a value-maximizing means.

General Propositions

The disgrace of political science is the infrequency with which propositions of any generality are formulated and tested. "Paradigmatic analysis" argues for explicitness about the terms in which analysis proceeds, and seriousness about the logic of explanation. Simply to illustrate the kind of propositions on which analysts who employ this model rely, the formulation includes several.

The basic assumption of value-maximizing behavior produces propositions central to most explanations. The general principle can be formulated as follows: the likelihood of any particular action results from a combination of the nation's (1) relevant values and objectives, (2) perceived alternative courses of action, (3) estimates of various sets of consequences (which will follow from each alternative), and (4) net valuation of each set of consequences. This yields two propositions.

1. An increase in the cost of an alternative, i.e., a reduction in the value of the set of consequences which will follow from that action, or a reduction in the probability of attaining fixed consequences, reduces the likelihood of that alternative being chosen.

2. A decrease in the costs of an alternative, i.e., an increase in the value of the set of consequences which will follow from that alternative, or an increase in the probability of attaining fixed consequences, increases the likelihood of that action being chosen.[17]

Specific Propositions

DETERRENCE

The likelihood of any particular attack results from the factors specified in the general proposition. Combined with factual assertions, this general proposition yields the propositions of the subtheory of deterrence.

1. A stable nuclear balance reduces the likelihood of nuclear attack. This proposition is derived from the general proposition plus the asserted fact that a second-strike capability affects the potential attacker's calculations by increasing the likelihood and the costs of one particular set of consequences which might follow from attack—namely, retaliation.

2. A stable nuclear balance increases the probability of limited war. This proposition is derived from the general proposition plus the asserted fact that though increasing the costs of a nuclear exchange, a stable nuclear balance nevertheless produces a more significant reduction in the probability that such consequences would be chosen in response to a limited war. Thus this set of consequences weighs less heavily in the calculus.

SOVIET FORCE POSTURE

The Soviet Union chooses its force posture (i.e., its weapons and their deployment) as a value-maximizing means of implementing Soviet strategic objectives and military doctrine. A proposition of this sort underlies Secretary of Defense Laird's inference from the fact of 200 SS-9s (large intercontinental missiles) to the assertion that, "the Soviets are going for a first-strike capability, and there's no question about it."[18]

Variants of the Rational Policy Model

This paradigm exhibits the characteristics of the most refined version of the rational model. The modern literature of strategy employs a model of this sort. Problems and pressures in the "international strategic marketplace" yield probabilities of occurrence. The international actor, which could be any national actor, is simply a value-maximizing mechanism for getting from the strategic problem to the logical solution. But the explanations and predictions produced by most analysts of foreign affairs depend primarily on variants of this "pure" model. The point of each is the same: to place the action within a value-maximizing framework, given certain constraints. Nevertheless, it may be helpful to identify several variants, each of which might be exhibited similarly as a paradigm. The first focuses upon the national actor and his choice in a particular situation, leading analysts to further constrain the goals, aalternatives, and consequences considered. Thus, (1) national propensities or personality traits reflected in an "operational code," (2) concern with certain objectives, or (3) special principles of action, narrow the "goals" or "alternatives" or "consequences" of the paradigm. For example, the Soviet deployment of ABMs is sometimes explained by reference to the Soviets' "defense-mindedness." Or a particular Soviet action is explained as an instance of a special rule of action in the Bolshevik operational code.[19] A second, related, cluster of variants focuses on the individual leader or leadership group as the actor whose preference function is maximized and whose personal (or group) characteristics are allowed to modify the alternatives, consequences and rules of choice. Explanations of the US involvement in Vietnam as a natural consequence of the Kennedy-Johnson administration's axioms of foreign policy rely on this variant. A third, more complex variant of the basic model recognizes the existence of several actors within a government, for example, hawks and doves or military and civilians, but attempts to explain (or predict) an occurrence by reference to the objectives of the victorious actor. Thus, for example, some revisionist histories of the cold war recognize the forces of light and the forces of darkness within the US government, but explain American actions as a result of goals and perceptions of the victorious forces of darkness.

Each of these forms of the basic paradigm constitutes a formalization of what analysts typically rely upon implicitly. In the transition from implicit conceptual model to explicit paradigm much of the richness of the best employment of this model has been lost. But the purpose in raising loose, implicit conceptual models to an explicit level is to reveal the basic logic of analysts' activity. Perhaps some of the remaining artificiality that surrounds the statement of the paradigm can be erased by noting a number of the standard additions and modifications employed by analysts who proceed *predominantly* within the rational policy model. First, in the course of a document, analysts shift from one variant of the basic model to another, occasionally appropriating in an ad hoc fashion aspects of a situation which are logically incompatible with the basic model. Second, in the course of explaining a number of occurrences, analysts sometimes pause over a particular event about which they have a great deal of information and unfold it in such detail that an impression of randomness is created. Third, having employed other assumptions and categories in deriving an explanation or prediction, analysts will present their product in a neat, convincing rational policy model package. (This accommodation is a favorite of members of the intelligence community whose association with the details of a process is considerable, but who feel that by putting an occurrence in a larger rational framework, it will be more comprehensible to their audience.) Fourth, in attempting to offer an explanation—particularly in cases where a prediction derived from the basic model has failed—the notion of a "mistake" is invoked. Thus, the failure in the prediction of a "missile gap" is written off as a Soviet mistake in not taking advantage of their opportunity. Both these and other modifications permit model I analysts considerably more variety than the paradigm might suggest. But such accommodations are essentially appendages to the basic logic of these analyses. . . .

Model II: Organizational Process

For some purposes, governmental behavior can be usefully summarized as action chosen by a unitary, rational decision-maker: centrally controlled, completely informed, and value maximizing. But this simplification must not be allowed to conceal the fact that a "government" consists of a conglomerate of semifeudal, loosely allied organizations, each with a substantial life of its own. Government leaders do sit formally, and to some extent in fact, on top of this conglomerate. But governments perceive problems through organizational sensors. Governments define alternatives and estimate consequences as organizations process information. Governments act as these organizations enact routines. Government behavior can therefore be understood according to a second conceptual model, less as deliberate choices of leaders and more as *outputs* of large organizations functioning according to standard patterns of behavior.

To be responsive to a broad spectrum of problems, governments consist of large organizations among which primary responsibility for particular areas is divided. Each organization attends to a special set of problems and acts in quasi-independence on these problems. But few important problems fall exclusively within the domain of a single organization. Thus government behavior relevant to any important problem reflects the independent output of several organizations, partially coordinated by government leaders. Government leaders can substantially disturb, but not substantially control, the behavior of these organizations.

To perform complex routines, the behavior of large numbers of individuals must be coordinated. Coordination requires standard operating procedures: rules according to which things are done. Assured capability for reliable performance of action that depends upon the behavior of hundreds of persons requires established "programs." Indeed, if the eleven members of a football team are to perform adequately on any particular down, each player must not "do what he thinks needs to be done" or "do what the quarterback tells him to do." Rather, each player must perform the maneuvers specified by a previously established play which the quarterback has simply called in this situation.

At any given time, a government consists of *existing* organizations, each with a *fixed* set of standard operating procedures and programs. The behavior of these organizations—and consequently of the government—relevant to an issue in any particular instance is, therefore, determined primarily by routines established in these organizations prior to that instance. But organizations do change. Learning occurs gradually, over time. Dramatic organizational change occurs in response to major crises. Both learning and change are influenced by existing organizational capabilities.

Borrowed from studies of organizations, these loosely formulated propositions amount simply to *tendencies*. Each must be hedged by modifiers like "other things being equal" and "under certain conditions." In particular instances, tendencies hold—more or less. In specific situations, the relevant question is: more or less? But this is as it should be. For, on the one hand, "organizations" are no more homogeneous a class than "solids." When scientists tried to generalize about "solids," they achieved similar results. Solids tend to expand when heated, but some do and some don't. More adequate categorization of the various elements now lumped under the rubric "organizations" is thus required. On the other hand, the behavior of particular organizations seems considerably more complex than the behavior of solids. Additional information about a particular organization is required for further specification of the tendency statements. In spite of these two caveats, the characterization of government action as organizational output differs distinctly from model I. Attempts to understand problems of foreign affairs in terms of this frame of reference should produce quite different explanations.[20]

Organizational Process Paradigm[21]

Basic Unit of Analysis: Policy as Organizational Output

The happenings of international politics are, in three critical senses, outputs of organizational processes. First, the actual occurrences are organizational outputs. For example, Chinese entry into the Korean War—that is, the fact that Chinese soldiers were firing at UN soldiers south of the Yalu in 1950—is an organizational action: the action of men who are soldiers in platoons which are in companies, which in turn are in armies, responding as privates to lieutenants who are responsible to captains and so on to the commander, moving into Korea, advancing against enemy troops, and firing according to fixed routines of the Chinese Army. Government leaders' decisions trigger organizational routines. Government leaders can trim the edges of this output and exercise some choice in combining outputs. But the mass of behavior is determined by previously established procedures. Second, existing organizational routines for employing present physical capabilities constitute the effective options open to government leaders confronted with any problem. Only the existence of men, equipped and trained as armies and capable of being transported to North Korea, made entry into the Korean War a live option for the Chinese leaders. The fact that fixed programs (equipment, men, and routines which exist at the particular time) exhaust the range of buttons that leaders can push is not always perceived by these leaders. But in every case it is critical for an understanding of what is actually done. Third, organizational outputs structure the situation within the narrow constraints of which leaders must contribute their "decision" concerning an issue. Outputs raise the problem, provide the information, and make the initial moves that color the face of the issue that is turned to the leaders. As Theodore Sorensen has observed: "Presidents rarely, if ever, make decisions—particularly in foreign affairs—in the sense of writing their conclusions on a clean slate . . . The basic decisions, which confine their choices, have all too often been previously made."[22] If one understands the structure of the situation and the face of the issue—which are determined by the organizational outputs—the formal choice of the leaders is frequently anticlimactic.

Organizing Concepts

ORGANIZATIONAL ACTORS

The actor is not a monolithic "nation" or "government" but rather a constellation of loosely allied organizations on top of which government leaders sit. This constellation acts only as component organizations perform routines.[23]

FACTORED PROBLEMS AND FRACTIONATED POWER

Surveillance of the multiple facets of foreign affairs requires that problems be cut up and parceled out to various organizations. To avoid paralysis, primary power must accompany primary responsibility. But if organizations are permitted to do anything, a large part of what they do will be determined within the organization. Thus each organization perceives problems, processes information, and performs a range of actions in quasi-independence (within broad guidelines of national policy). Factored problems and fractionated power are two edges of the same sword. Factoring permits more specialized attention to particular facets of problems than would be possible if government leaders tried to cope with these problems by themselves. But this additional attention must be paid for in the coin of discretion for *what* an organization attends to, and *how* organizational responses are programmed.

PAROCHIAL PRIORITIES, PERCEPTIONS, AND ISSUES

Primary responsibility for a narrow set of problems encourages organizational parochialism. These tendencies are enhanced by a number of additional factors: (1) selective information available to the organization, (2) recruitment of personnel into the organization, (3) tenure of individuals in the organization, (4) small group pressures within the organization, and (5) distribution of rewards by the organization. Clients (e.g., interest groups), government allies (e.g., Congressional committees), and extranational counterparts (e.g., the British Ministry of Defense for the Department of Defense, ISA, or the British Foreign Office for the Department of State, EUR) galvanize this parochialism. Thus organizations develop relatively stable propensities concerning operational priorities, perceptions, and issues.

ACTION AS ORGANIZATIONAL OUTPUT

The preeminent feature of organizational activity is its programmed character: the extent to which behavior in any particular case is an enactment of preestablished routines. In producing outputs, the activity of each organization is characterized by:

1. *Goals. Constraints Defining Acceptable Performance.* The operational goals of an organization are seldom revealed by formal mandates. Rather, each organization's operational goals emerge as a set of constraints defining acceptable performance. Central among these constraints is organizational health, defined usually in terms of bodies assigned and dollars appropriated. The set of constraints emerges from a mix of expectations and demands of other organizations in the government, statutory authority, demands from citizens and special

interest groups, and bargaining within the organization. These constraints represent a quasi-resolution of conflict—the constraints are relatively stable, so there is some resolution. But conflict among alternative goals is always latent; hence, it is a quasi-resolution. Typically, the constraints are formulated as imperatives to avoid roughly specified discomforts and disasters.[24]

2. *Sequential Attention to Goals.* The existence of conflict among operational constraints is resolved by the device of sequential attention. As a problem arises, the subunits of the organization most concerned with that problem deal with it in terms of the constraints they take to be most important. When the next problem arises, another cluster of subunits deals with it, focusing on a different set of constraints.

3. *Standard Operating Procedures.* Organizations perform their "higher" functions, such as attending to problem areas, monitoring information, and preparing relevant responses for likely contingencies, by doing "lower" tasks, for example, preparing budgets, producing reports, and developing hardware. Reliable performance of these tasks requires standard operating procedures (hereafter SOPs). Since procedures are "standard" they do not change quickly or easily. Without these standard procedures, it would not be possible to perform certain concerted tasks. But because of standard procedures, organizational behavior in particular instances often appears unduly formalized, sluggish, or inappropriate.

4. *Programs and Repertoires.* Organizations must be capable of performing actions in which the behavior of large numbers of individuals is carefully coordinated. Assured performance requires clusters of rehearsed SOPs for producing specific actions, e.g., fighting enemy units or answering an embassy's cable. Each cluster comprises a "program" (in the terms both of drama and computers) which the organization has available for dealing with a situation. The list of programs relevant to a type of activity, e.g., fighting, constitutes an organizational repertoire. The number of programs in a repertoire is always quite limited. When properly triggered, organizations execute programs; programs cannot be substantially changed in a particular situation. The more complex the action and the greater the number of individuals involved, the more important are programs and repertoires as determinants of organizational behavior.

5. *Uncertainty Avoidance.* Organizations do not attempt to estimate the probability distribution of future occurrences. Rather, organizations avoid uncertainty. By arranging a *negotiated environment,* organizations regularize the reactions of other actors with whom they have to deal. The primary environment, relations with other organizations that comprise the government, is stabilized by such arrangements as agreed budgetary splits, accepted areas of responsibility, and established conventional practices. The secondary environment, relations with the international world, is stabilized between allies by the establishment of contracts (alliances) and "club relations" (US State and UK Foreign Office and US Treasury and UK Treasury). Between enemies, contracts and accepted conventional practices perform a similar function, for example, the rules of the "precarious status quo" which President Kennedy referred to in

the missile crisis. Where the international environment cannot be negotiated, organizations deal with remaining uncertainties by establishing a set of *standard scenarios* that constitute the contingencies for which they prepare. For example, the standard scenario for Tactical Air Command of the US Air Force involves combat with enemy aircraft. Planes are designed and pilots trained to meet this problem. That these preparations are less relevant to more probable contingencies, e.g., provision of close-in ground support in limited wars like Vietnam, has had little impact on the scenario.

6. *Problem-directed Search.* Where situations cannot be construed as standard, organizations engage in search. The style of search and the solution are largely determined by existing routines. Organizational search for alternative courses of action is problem-oriented: it focuses on the atypical discomfort that must be avoided. It is simple-minded: the neighborhood of the symptom is searched first; then, the neighborhood of the current alternative. Patterns of search reveal biases which in turn reflect such factors as specialized training or experience and patterns of communication.

7. *Organizational Learning and Change.* The parameters of organizational behavior mostly persist. In response to nonstandard problems, organizations search and routines evolve, assimilating new situations. Thus learning and change follow in large part from existing procedures. But marked changes in organizations do sometimes occur. Conditions in which dramatic changes are more likely include: (1) Periods of budgetary feast. Typically, organizations devour budgetary feasts by purchasing additional items on the existing shopping list. Nevertheless, if committed to change, leaders who control the budget can use extra funds to effect changes. (2) Periods of prolonged budgetary famine. Though a single year's famine typically results in few changes in organizational structure but a loss of effectiveness in performing some programs, prolonged famine forces major retrenchment. (3) Dramatic performance failures. Dramatic change occurs (mostly) in response to major disasters. Confronted with an undeniable failure of procedures and repertoires, authorities outside the organization demand change, existing personnel are less resistant to change, and critical members of the organization are replaced by individuals committed to change.

CENTRAL COORDINATION AND CONTROL

Action requires decentralization of responsibility and power. But problems lap over the jurisdictions of several organizations. Thus the necessity for decentralization runs headlong into the requirement for coordination. (Advocates of one horn or the other of this dilemma—responsive action entails decentralized power versus coordinated action requires central control—account for a considerable part of the persistent demand for government reorganization.) Both the necessity for coordination and the centrality of foreign policy to national welfare guarantee the involvement of government leaders in the procedures of the organizations among which problems are divided and power shared. Each organization's propensities and routines can be disturbed by government leaders' intervention. Central direction and persistent control of organizational activity, however, are not possible. The relation among organizations, and between organizations and the government leaders depends critically on a number of structural variables including: (1) the nature of the job, (2) the measures and information available to government leaders, (3) the system of rewards and punishments for organizational members, and (4) the procedures by which human and material resources get committed. For example, to the extent that rewards and punishments for the members of an organization are distributed by higher authorities, these authorities can exercise some control by specifying criteria in terms of which organizational output is to be evaluated. These criteria become constraints within which organizational activity proceeds. But constraint is a crude instrument of control.

Intervention by government leaders does sometimes change the activity of an organization in an intended direction. But instances are fewer than might be expected. As Franklin Roosevelt, the master manipulator of government organizations, remarked:

> The Treasury is so large and far-flung and ingrained in its practices that I find it is almost impossible to get the action and results I want . . . But the Treasury is not to be compared with the State Department. You should go through the experience of trying to get any changes in the thinking, policy, and action of the career diplomats and then you'd know what a real problem was. But the Treasury and the State Department put together are nothing compared with the Na-a-vy . . . To change anything in the Na-a-vy is like punching a feather bed. You punch it with your right and you punch it with your left until you are finally exhausted, and then you find the damn bed just as it was before you started punching.[25]

John Kennedy's experience seems to have been similar: "The State Department," he asserted, "is a bowl full of jelly."[26] And lest the McNamara revolution in the Defense Department seem too striking a counterexample, the Navy's recent rejection of McNamara's major intervention in Naval weapons procurement, the F-111B, should be studied as an antidote.

DECISIONS OF GOVERNMENT LEADERS

Organizational persistence does not exclude shifts in governmental behavior. For government leaders sit atop the conglomerate of organizations. Many important issues of governmental action require that these leaders decide what organizations will play out which programs where. Thus stability in the parochialisms and SOPs of individual organizations is consistent with some important shifts in the behavior of governments. The range of these shifts is defined by existing organizational programs.

Dominant Inference Pattern

If a nation performs an action of this type today, its organizational components must yesterday have been performing (or have had established routines for performing) an action only marginally different from this action. At any specific point in time, a government consists of an established conglomerate of organizations, each with existing goals, programs, and repertoires. The characteristics of a government's action in any instance follow from those established routines, and from the choice of government leaders—on the basis of information and estimates provided by existing routines—among existing programs. The best explanation of an organization's behavior at t is $t - 1$; the prediction of $t + 1$ is t. Model II's explanatory power is achieved by uncovering the organizational routines and repertoires that produced the outputs that comprise the puzzling occurrence.

General Propositions

A number of general propositions have been stated above. In order to illustrate clearly the type of proposition employed by model II analysts, this section formulates several more precisely.

ORGANIZATIONAL ACTION

Activity according to SOPs and programs does not constitute farsighted, flexible adaptation to "the issue" (as it is conceived by the analyst). Detail and nuance of actions by organizations are determined predominantly by organizational routines, not government leaders' directions.

SOPs constitute routines for dealing with *standard* situations. Routines allow large numbers of ordinary individuals to deal with numerous instances, day after day, without considerable thought, by responding to basic stimuli. But this regularized capability for adequate performance is purchased at the price of standardization. If the SOPs are appropriate, average performance, I.e., performance averaged over the range of cases, is better than it would be if each instance were approached individually (given fixed talent, timing, and resource constraints). But specific instances, particularly critical instances that typically do not have "standard" characteristics, are often handled sluggishly or inappropriately.

A program, i.e., a complex action chosen from a short list of programs in a repertoire, is rarely tailored to the specific situation in which it is executed. Rather, the program is (at best) the most appropriate of the programs in a previously developed repertoire.

Since repertoires are developed by parochial organizations for standard scenarios defined by that organization, programs available for dealing with a particular situation are often ill-suited.

LIMITED FLEXIBILITY AND INCREMENTAL CHANGE

Major lines of organizational action are straight, i.e., behavior at one time is marginally different from that behavior at $t - 1$. Simpleminded predictions work best: Behavior at $t + 1$ will be marginally different from behavior at the present time.

Organizational budgets change incrementally—both with respect to totals and with respect to intraorganizational splits. Though organizations could divide the money available each year by carving up the pie anew (in the light of changes in objectives or environment), in practice, organizations take last year's budget as a base and adjust incrementally. Predictions that require large budgetary shifts in a single year between organizations or between units within an organization should be hedged.

Once undertaken, an organizational investment is not dropped at the point where "objective" costs outweigh benefits. Organizational stakes in adopted projects carry them quite beyond the loss point.

ADMINISTRATIVE FEASIBILITY

Adequate explanation, analysis, and prediction must include administrative feasibility as a major dimension. A considerable gap separates what leaders choose (or might rationally have chosen) and what organizations implement.

Organizations are blunt instruments. Projects that require several organizations to act with high degrees of precision and coordination are not likely to succeed.

Projects that demand that existing organizational units depart from their accustomed functions and perform previously unprogrammed tasks are rarely accomplished in their designed form.

Government leaders can expect that each organization will do its "part" in terms of what the organization knows how to do.

Government leaders can expect incomplete and distorted information from each organization concerning its part of the problem.

Where an assigned piece of a problem is contrary to the existing goals of an organization, resistance to implementation of that piece will be encountered.

Specific Propositions

DETERRENCE

The probability of nuclear attack is less sensitive to balance and imbalance, or stability and instability (as these concepts are employed by model I strategists) than it is to a number of organizational factors. Except for the special case in which the Soviet Union acquires a credible capability to destroy the US with a disarming blow, US superiority or inferiority affects the probability of a nuclear attack less than do a number of organizational factors.

First, if a nuclear attack occurs, it will result from organizational activity: the firing of rockets by members of a missile group. The enemy's *control system*, i.e., physical mechanisms and standard procedures which determine who can launch rockets when, is critical. Second, the enemy's programs for bringing his strategic forces to *alert status* determine probabilities of accidental firing and momentum. At the outbreak of World War I, if the Russian tsar had understood the organizational processes which his order of full mobilization triggered, he would have realized that he had chosen war. Third, organizational repertoires fix the range of effective choice open to enemy leaders. The menu available to Tsar Nicholas in 1914 has two entrees: full mobilization and no mobilization. Partial mobilization was not an organizational option. Fourth, since organizational routines set the chessboard, the training and deployment of troops and nuclear weapons is crucial. Given that the outbreak of hostilities in Berlin is more probable than most scenarios for nuclear war, facts about deployment, training, and tactical nuclear equipment of Soviet troops stationed in East Germany—which will influence the face of the issue seen by Soviet leaders at the outbreak of hostilities and the manner in which choice is implemented—are as critical as the question of "balance."

SOVIET FORCE POSTURE

Soviet Force posture, i.e., the fact that certain weapons rather than others are procured and deployed, is determined by organizational factors such as the goals and procedures of existing military services and the goals and processes of research and design labs, within budgetary constraints that emerge from the government leader's choices. The frailty of the Soviet Air Force within the Soviet military establishment seems to have been a crucial element in the Soviet failure to acquire a large bomber force in the 1950s (thereby faulting American intelligence predictions of a "bomber gap"). The fact that missiles were controlled until 1960 in the Soviet Union by the Soviet Ground Forces, whose goals and procedures reflected no interest in an intercontinental mission, was not irrelevant to the slow Soviet buildup of ICBMs (thereby faulting US intelligence predictions of a "missile gap"). These organizational factors (Soviet Ground Forces' control of missiles and that service's fixation with European scenarios) make the Soviet deployment of so many MRBMs that European targets could be destroyed three times over, more understandable. Recent weapon developments, e.g., the testing of a Fractional Orbital Bombardment System (FOBS) and multiple warheads for the SS-9, very likely reflect the activity and interests of a cluster of Soviet research and development organizations, rather than a decision by Soviet leaders to acquire a first-strike weapon system. Careful attention to the organizational components of the Soviet military establishment (Strategic Rocket Forces, Navy, Air Force, Ground Forces, and National Air Defense), the missions and weapons systems to which each component is wedded (an independent weapon system assists survival as an independent service), and existing budgetary splits (which probably are relatively stable in the Soviet Union as they tend to be everywhere) offer potential improvements in medium- and longer-term predictions. . . .

Model III: Bureaucratic Politics

The leaders who sit on top of organizations are not a monolithic group. Rather, each is, in his own right, a player in a central, competitive game. The name of the game is bureaucratic politics: bargaining along regularized channels among players positioned hierarchically within the government. Government behavior can thus be understood according to a third conceptual model not as organizational outputs, but as outcomes of bargaining games. In contrast with model I, the bureaucratic politics model sees no unitary actor but rather many actors as players, who focus not on a single strategic issue but on many diverse intranational problems as well, in terms of no consistent set of strategic objectives but rather according to various conceptions of national, organizational, and personal goals, making government decisions not by rational choice but by the pulling and hauling that is politics.

The apparatus of each national government constitutes a complex arena for the intranational game. Political leaders at the top of this apparatus plus the men who occupy positions on top of the critical organizations form the circle of central players. Ascendancy to this circle assures some independent standing. The necessary decentralization of decisions required for action on the broad range of foreign policy problems guarantees that each player has considerable discretion. Thus power is shared.

The nature of problems of foreign policy permits fundamental disagreement among reasonable men concerning what ought to be done. Analyses yield conflicting recommendations. Separate responsibilities laid on the shoulders of individual personalities encourage differences in perceptions and priorities. But the issues are of first-order importance. What the nation does really matters. A wrong choice could mean irreparable damage. Thus responsible men are obliged to fight for what they are convinced is right.

Men share power. Men differ concerning what must be done. The differences matter. This milieu necessitates that policy be resolved by politics. What the nation does is sometimes the result of the triumph of one group over others. More often, however, different groups pulling in different directions yield a result distinct from what anyone intended. What moves the chess pieces is not simply the reasons which support a course of action, nor the routines of organizations which enact an alternative, but the power and skill of proponents and opponents of the action in question.

This characterization captures the thrust of the bureaucratic politics orientation. If problems of foreign policy arose as discrete issues, and decisions were determined one game at a time, this account would suffice. But most "issues," e.g., Vietnam or the proliferation of nuclear weapons, emerge piecemeal, over time, one lump in one context, a second in another. Hundreds of issues compete for players' attention every day. Each player is forced to fix upon his issues for that day, fight them on their own terms, and rush on to the next. Thus the character of emerging issues and the pace at which the game is played converge to yield government "decisions" and "actions" as collages. Choices by one player, outcomes of minor games, outcomes of central games, and "foulups"—these pieces, when stuck to the same canvas, constitute government behavior relevant to an issue.

The concept of national security policy as political outcome contradicts both public imagery and academic orthodoxy. Issues vital to national security, it is said, are too important to be settled by political games. They must be "above" politics. To accuse someone of "playing politics with national security" is a most serious charge. What public conviction demands, the academic penchant for intellectual elegance reinforces. Internal politics is messy; moreover, according to prevailing doctrine, politicking lacks intellectual content. As such, it constitutes gossip for journalists rather than a subject for serious investigation. Occasional memoirs, anecdotes in historical accounts, and several detailed case studies to the contrary, most of the literature of foreign policy avoids bureaucratic politics. The gap between academic literature and the experience of participants in government is nowhere wider than at this point.

Bureaucratic Politics Paradigm[27]

Basic Unit of Analysis: Policy as Political Outcome

The decisions and actions of governments are essentially intranational political outcomes: outcomes in the sense that what happens is not chosen as a solution to a problem but rather results from compromise, coalition, competition, and confusion among government officials who see different faces of an issue; political in the sense that the activity from which the outcomes emerge is best characterized as bargaining. Following Wittgenstein's use of the concept of a "game," national behavior in international affairs can be conceived as outcomes of intricate and subtle, simultaneous, overlapping games among players located in positions, the hierarchical arrangement of which constitutes the government.[28] These games proceed neither at random nor at leisure. Regular channels structure the game. Deadlines force issues to the attention of busy players. The moves in the chess game are thus to be explained in terms of the bargaining among players with separate and unequal power over particular pieces and with separable objectives in distinguishable subgames.

Organizing Concepts

PLAYERS IN POSITIONS

The actor is neither a unitary nation, nor a conglomerate of organizations, but rather a number of individual players. Groups of these players constitute the agent for particular government decisions and actions. Players are men in jobs.

Individuals become players in the national security policy game by occupying a critical position in an administration. For example, in the US government the players include "Chiefs": the president, secretaries of state, defense, and treasury, director of the CIA, Joint Chiefs of Staff, and, since 1961, the special assistant for national security affairs,[29] "Staffer": the immediate staff of each Chief, "Indians": the political appointees and permanent government officials within each of the departments and agencies; and "Ad Hoc Players": actors in the wider government game (especially "Congressional Influentials"), members of the press, spokesmen for important interest groups (especially the "bipartisan foreign policy establishment" in and out of Congress), and surrogates for each of these groups. Other members of the Congress, press, interest groups, and public form concentric circles around the central arena—circles which demarcate the permissive limits within which the game is played.

Positions define what players both may and must do. The advantages and handicaps with which each player can enter and play in various games stems from his position. So does a cluster of obligations for the performance of certain tasks. The two sides of this coin are illustrated by the position of the modern secretary of state. First, in form and usually in fact, he is the primary repository of political judgment on the political-military issues that are the stuff of contemporary foreign policy; consequently, he is a senior personal adviser to the president. Second, he is the colleague of the president's other senior advisers on the problems of foreign policy, the secretaries of defense and treasury, and the special assistant for national security affairs. Third, he is the ranking US diplomat for serious negotiation. Fourth, he serves as an administration voice to Congress, the country, and the world. Finally, he is "Mr. State Department" or "Mr. Foreign Office," "leader of officials, spokesman for their causes, guardian of their interests, judge of their disputes, superintendent of their work, master of their careers."[30] But he is not first one, and then the other. All of these obligations are his simultaneously. His performance in one affects his credit and power in the others. The perspective stemming from the daily work which he must oversee—the cable traffic by which his department maintains relations with other foreign offices—conflicts with the president's requirement that he serve as a generalist and coordinator of contrasting perspectives. The necessity that he be close to the president restricts the extent to which, and the force with which, he can front for his department. When he defers to the secretary of defense rather than fighting for his department's position—as he often must—he strains the loyalty of his officialdom. The secretary's resolution of these conflicts depends not only upon the position, but also upon the player who occupies the position.

For players are also people. Men's metabolisms differ. The core of the bureaucratic politics mix is personality. How each man manages to stand the heat in his kitchen, each player's basic operating style, and the complementarity or contradiction among personalities and styles in the inner circles are irreducible pieces of the policy blend. Moreover, each person comes to his position with baggage in tow, including sensitivities to certain issues, commitments to various programs, and personal standing and debts with groups in society.

PAROCHIAL PRIORITIES, PERCEPTIONS AND ISSUES

Answers to the questions: "What is the issue?" and "What must be done?" are colored by the position from which the questions are considered. For the factors which encourage organizational parochialism also influence the players who occupy positions on top of (or within) these organizations. To motivate members of his organization, a player must be sensitive to the organization's orientation. The games into which the player can enter and the advantages with which he plays enhance these pressures. Thus propensities of perception stemming from position permit reliable prediction about a player's stances in many cases. But these propensities are filtered through the baggage which players bring to positions. Sensitivity to both the pressures and the baggage is thus required for many predictions.

INTERESTS, STAKES, AND POWER

Games are played to determine outcomes. But outcomes advance and impede each player's conceptions of the national interest, specific programs to which he is committed, the welfare of his friends, and his personal interests. These overlapping interests constitute the stakes for which games are played. Each player's ability to play successfully depends upon his power. Power, i.e., effective influence on policy outcomes, is an elusive blend of at least three elements: bargaining advantages (drawn from formal authority and obligations, institutional backing, constituents, expertise, and status), skill and will in using bargaining advantages, and other players' perceptions of the first two ingredients. Power wisely invested yields an enhanced reputation for effectiveness. Unsuccessful investment depletes both the stock of capital and the reputation. Thus each player must pick the issues on which he can play with a reasonable probability of success. But no player's power is sufficient to guarantee satisfactory outcomes. Each player's needs and fears run to many other players. What ensues is the most intricate and subtle of games known to man.

THE PROBLEM AND THE PROBLEMS

"Solutions" to strategic problems are not derived by detached analysts focusing coolly on *the* problem. Instead, deadlines and events raise issues in games, and demand decisions of busy players in contexts that influence the face the issue wears. The problems for the players are both narrower and broader than *the* strategic problem. For each player focuses not on the total strategic problem but rather on the decision that must be made now. But each decision has critical consequences not only for the strategic problem but for each player's organizational, reputational, and personal stakes. Thus the gap between the problems the player was solving and the problem upon which the analyst focuses is often very wide.

ACTION-CHANNELS

Bargaining games do not proceed randomly. Action-channels, i.e., regularized ways of producing action concerning types of issues, structure the game by preselecting the major players, determining their points of entrance into the game, and distributing particular advantages and disadvantages for each game. Most critically, channels determine "who's got the action," that is, which department's Indians actually do whatever is chosen. Weapon procurement decisions are made within the annual budgeting process; embassies' demands for action cables are answered according to routines of consultation and clearance from State to Defense and White House; requests for instructions from military groups (concerning assistance all the time, concerning operations during war) are composed by the military in consultation with the Office of the Secretary of Defense, State, and White House; crisis responses are debated among White House, State, Defense, CIA, and Ad Hoc players; major political speeches, especially by the President but also by other Chiefs, are cleared through established channels.

ACTION AS POLITICS

Government decisions are made, and government actions emerge neither as the calculated choice of a unified group, nor as a formal summary of leaders' preferences. Rather the context of shared power but separate judgments concerning important choices, determines that politics is the mechanism of choice. Note the *environment* in which the game is played: inordinate uncertainty about what must be done, the necessity that something be done, and crucial consequences of whatever is done. These features force responsible men to become active players. The *pace of the game*—hundreds of issues, numerous games, and multiple channels—compels players to fight to "get others' attention," to make them "see the facts," to assure that they "take the time to think seriously about the broader issue." The *structure of the game*—power shared by individuals with separate responsibilities—validates each player's feeling that "others don't see my problem," and "others must be persuaded to look at the issue from a less parochial perspective." The *rules of the game*—he who hesitates loses his chance to play at that point, and he who is uncertain about his recommendation is overpowered by others who are sure—pressures players to come down on one side of a 51–49 issue and play. The *rewards of the game*—effectiveness, i.e., impact on outcomes, as the immediate measure of performance—encourages hard play. Thus, most players come to fight to "make the government do what is right." The strategies and tactics employed are quite similar to those formalized by theorists of international relations.

STREAMS OF OUTCOMES

Important government decisions or actions emerge as collages composed of individual acts, outcomes of minor and major games, and foul-ups. Outcomes which could never have been chosen by an actor and would never have emerged from bargaining in a single game over the issue are fabricated piece by piece. Understanding of the outcome requires that it be disaggregated.

Dominant Inference Pattern

If a nation performed an action, that action was the *outcome* of bargaining among individuals and groups within the government. That outcome included *results* achieved by groups committed to a decision or action, *resultants* which emerged from bargaining among groups with quite different positions and *foul-ups*. Model III's explanatory power is achieved by revealing the pulling and hauling of various players, with different perceptions and priorities, focusing on separate problems, which yielded the outcomes that constitute the action in question.

General Propositions

ACTION AND INTENTION

Action does not presuppose intention. The sum of behavior of representatives of a government relevant to an issue was rarely intended by any individual or group. Rather separate individuals with different intentions contributed pieces which compose an outcome distinct from what anyone would have chosen.

WHERE YOU STAND DEPENDS ON WHERE YOU SIT[31]

Horizontally, the diverse demands upon each player shape his priorities, perceptions, and issues. For large classes of issues, e.g., budgets and procurement decisions, the stance of a particular player can be predicted with high reliability from information concerning his seat. In the notorious B-36 controversy, no one was surprised by Admiral Radford's testimony that "the B-36 under any theory of war, is a bad gamble with national security," as opposed to Air Force Secretary Symington's claim that "a B-36 with an A-bomb can destroy distant objectives which might require ground armies years to take."[32]

CHIEFS AND INDIANS

The aphorism "where you stand depends on where you sit" has vertical as well as horizontal application. Vertically, the demands upon the president, Chiefs, Staffers, and Indians are quite distinct.

The foreign policy issues with which the president can deal are limited primarily by his crowded schedule: the necessity of dealing first with what comes next. His problem is to probe the special face worn by issues that come to his attention, to preserve his leeway until time has clarified the uncertainties, and to assess the relevant risks.

Foreign policy Chiefs deal most often with the hottest issue *de jour*, though they can get the attention of the president and other members of the government for other issues which they judge important. What they cannot guarantee is that "the President will pay the price" or that "the others will get on board." They must build a coalition of the relevant powers that be. They must "give the President confidence" in the right course of action.

Most problems are framed, alternatives specified, and proposals pushed, however, by Indians. Indians fight with Indians of other departments; for example, struggles between International Security Affairs of the Department of Defense and Political-Military of the State Department are a microcosm of the action at higher levels. But the Indian's major problem is how to get the *attention* of Chiefs, how to get an issue decided, how to get the government "to do what is right."

In policymaking then, the issue looking *down* is options: how to preserve my leeway until time clarifies uncertainties. The issue looking *sideways* is commitment: how to get others committed to my coalition. The issue looking *upwards* is confidence: how to give the boss confidence in doing what must be done. To paraphrase one of Neustadt's assertions which can be applied down the length of the ladder, the essence of a responsible official's task is to induce others to see that what needs to be done is what their own appraisal of their own responsibilities requires them to do in their own interests.

Specific Propositions

DETERRENCE

The probability of nuclear attack depends primarily on the probability of attack emerging as an outcome of the bureaucratic politics of the attacking government. First, which players can decide to launch an attack? Whether the effective power over action is controlled by an individual, a minor game, or the central game is critical. Second, though model I's confidence in nuclear deterrence stems from an assertion that, in the end, governments will not commit suicide, model III recalls historical precedents. Admiral Yamamoto, who designed the Japanese attack on Pearl Harbor, estimated accurately: "In the first six months to a year of war against the US and England I will run wild, and I will show you an uninterrupted succession of victories; I must also tell you that, should the war be prolonged for two or three years, I have no confidence in our ultimate victory."[33] But Japan attacked. Thus, three questions might be considered. One: could any member of the government solve his problem by attack? What patterns of bargaining could yield attack as an outcome? The major difference between a stable balance of terror and a questionable balance may simply be that in the first case most members of the government appreciate fully the consequences of attack and are thus on guard against the emergence of this outcome. Two: what stream of outcomes might lead to an attack? At what point in that stream is the potential attacker's politics? If members of the US government had been sensitive to the stream of decisions from which the Japanese attack on Pearl Harbor emerged, they would have been aware of a considerable probability of that attack. Three: how might miscalculation and confusion generate foul-ups that yield attack as an outcome? For example, in a crisis or after the beginning of conventional war, what happens to the information available to, and the effective power of, members of the central game. . . .

Conclusion

This essay has obviously bitten off more than it has chewed. For further developments and synthesis of these arguments the reader is referred to the larger study.[34] In spite of the limits of space, however, it would be inappropriate to stop without spelling out several implications of the argument and addressing the question of relations among the models and extensions of them to activity beyond explanation.

At a minimum, the intended implications of the argument presented here are four. First, formulation of alternative frames of reference and demonstration that different analysts, relying predominantly on different models, produce quite different explanations should encourage the analyst's self-consciousness about the nets he employs. The effect of these "spectacles" in sensitizing him to particular aspects of what is going on—framing the puzzle in one way rather than another, encouraging him to examine the problem in terms of certain categories rather than others, directing him to particular kinds of evidence, and relieving puzzlement by one procedure rather than another—must be recognized and explored.

Second, the argument implies a position on the problem of "the state of the art." While accepting the commonplace characterization of the present condition of foreign policy analysis—personalistic, noncumulative, and sometimes insightful—this essay rejects both the counsel of despair's justification of this condition as a consequence of the character of the enterprise, and the "new frontiersmen's" demand for a priori theorizing on the frontiers and ad hoc appropriation of "new techniques."[35] What is required as a first step is noncasual examination of the present product: inspection of existing explanations, articulation of the conceptual models employed in producing them, formulation of the propositions relied upon, specification of the logic of the various intellectual enterprises, and reflection on the questions being asked. Though it is difficult to overemphasize the need for more systematic processing of more data, these preliminary matters of formulating questions with clarity and sensitivity to categories and assumptions so that fruitful acquisition of large quantities of data is possible are still a major hurdle in considering most important problems.

Third, the preliminary, partial paradigms presented here provide a basis for serious reexamination of many problems of foreign and military policy. Model II and model III cuts at problems typically treated in model I terms can permit significant improvements in explanation and prediction.[36] Full model II and III analyses require large amounts of information. But even in cases where the information base is severely limited, improvements are possible. Consider the problem of predicting Soviet strategic forces. In the mid-1950s, model I style calculations led to predictions that the Soviets would rapidly deploy large numbers of long-range bombers. From a model II perspective, both the frailty of the Air Force within the Soviet military establishment and the budgetary implications of such a buildup, would have led analysts to hedge this prediction. Moreover, model II would have pointed to a sure, visible indicator of such a buildup: noisy struggles among the Services over major budgetary shifts. In the late 1950s and early 1960s, model I calculations led to the prediction of immediate, massive Soviet deployment of ICBMs. Again, a model II cut would have reduced this number because, in the earlier period, strategic rockets were controlled by the Soviet Ground Forces rather than an independent service, and in the later period, this would have necessitated massive shifts in budgetary splits. Today, model I considerations lead many analysts both to recommend that an agreement not to deploy ABMs be a major American objective in upcoming strategic negotiations with the USSR, and to predict success. From a model II vantage point, the existence of an on-going Soviet ABM program, the strength of the organization (National Air Defense) that controls ABMs, and the fact that an agreement to stop ABM deployment would force the virtual dismantling of this organization, make a viable agreement of this sort much less likely. A model III cut suggests that (a) there must be significant differences among perceptions and priorities of Soviet leaders over strategic negotiations, (b) any agreement will affect some players' power bases, and (c) agreements that do not require extensive cuts in the sources of some major players' power will prove easier to negotiate and more viable.

Fourth, the present formulation of paradigms is simply an initial step. As such it leaves a long list of critical questions unanswered. Given any action, an imaginative analyst should always be able to construct some rationale for the government's choice. By imposing, and relaxing, constraints on the parameters of rational choice (as in variants of model I) analysts can construct a large number of accounts of any act as a rational choice. But does a statement of reasons why a rational actor would choose an action constitute an explanation of the *occurrence* of that action? How can model I analysis be forced to make more systematic contributions to the question of the determinants of occurrences? Model II's explanation of t in terms of $t - 1$ is explanation. The world is contiguous. But governments sometimes make sharp departures. Can an organizational process model be modified to suggest where change is likely? Attention to organizational change should afford greater understanding of why particular programs and SOPs are maintained by identifiable types of organizations and also how a manager can improve organizational performance. Model III tells a fascinating "story." But its complexity is enormous, the information requirements are often overwhelming, and many of the details of the bargaining may be superfluous. How can such a model be made parsimonious? The three models are obviously not exclusive alternatives. Indeed, the paradigms highlight the partial emphasis of the framework—what each emphasizes and what it leaves out. Each concentrates on one class of variables, in effect, relegating other important factors to a *ceteris paribus* clause. Model I concentrates on "market factors": pressures and incentives created by the "international strategic marketplace." Models II and III focus on the internal mechanism of the government that chooses in this environment. But can these relations be more fully specified? Adequate synthesis would require a typology of decisions and actions, some of which are more amenable to treatment in terms of one model and some to another. Government behavior is but one cluster of factors relevant to occurrences in foreign affairs. Most students of foreign policy adopt this focus (at least when explaining and predicting). Nevertheless, the dimensions of the chess board, the character of the pieces, and the rules of the game—factors considered by international systems theorists—constitute the context in which the pieces are moved. Can the major variables in the full function of determinants of foreign policy outcomes be identified?

Both the outline of a partial, ad hoc working synthesis of the models, and a sketch of their uses in activities other than explanation can be suggested by generating predictions in terms of each. Strategic surrender is an important problem of international relations and diplomatic history. War termination is a new, developing area of the strategic literature. Both of these interests lead scholars to address a central question: *Why* do nations surrender *when?* Whether implicit in explanations or more explicit in analysis, diplomatic historians and strategists rely upon propositions which can be turned forward to produce predictions. Thus at the risk of being timely—and in error—the present situation (August, 1968) offers an interesting test case: Why will North Vietnam surrender when?[37]

In a nutshell, analysis according to model I asserts: nations quit when costs outweigh the benefits. North Vietnam will surrender when it realizes "that continued fighting can only generate additional costs without hope of compensating gains, this expectation being largely the consequence of the previous application of force by the dominant side."[38] US actions can increase or decrease Hanoi's strategic costs. Bombing North Vietnam increases the pain and thus increases the probability of surrender. This proposition and prediction are not without meaning. That—"other things being equal"—nations are more likely to surrender when the strategic cost-benefit balance is negative, is true. Nations rarely surrender when they are winning. The proposition specifies a range within which nations surrender. But over this broad range, the relevant question is: why do nations surrender?

Models II and III focus upon the government machine through which this fact about the international strategic marketplace must be filtered to produce a surrender. These analysts are considerably less sanguine about the possibility of surrender *at the point* that the cost-benefit calculus turns negative. Never in history (i.e., in none of the five cases I have examined) have nations surrendered at that point. Surrender occurs sometime thereafter. *When* depends on process of organizations and politics of players within these governments—as they are affected by the opposing government. Moreover, the effects of the victorious power's action upon the surrendering nation cannot be adequately summarized as increasing or decreasing strategic costs. Imposing additional costs by bombing a nation may increase the probability of surrender. But it also may reduce it. An appreciation of the impact of the acts of one nation upon another thus requires some understanding of the machine which is being influenced. For more precise prediction, models II and III require considerably more information about the organizations and politics of North Vietnam than is publicly available. On the basis of the limited public information, however, these models can be suggestive.

Model II examines two subproblems. First, to have lost is not sufficient. The government must know that the strategic cost-benefit calculus is negative. But neither the categories, nor the indicators, of strategic costs and benefits are clear. And the sources of information about both are organizations whose parochial priorities and perceptions do not facilitate accurate information of estimation. Military evaluation of military performance, military estimates of factors like "enemy morale," and military predictions concerning when "the tide will turn" or "the corner will have been turned" are typically distorted. In cases of highly decentralized guerrilla operations, like Vietnam, these problems are exacerbated. Thus strategic costs will be underestimated. Only highly *visible* costs can have direct impact on leaders without being filtered through organizational channels. Second, since organizations define the details of options and execute actions, surrender (and negotiation) is likely to entail considerable bungling in the early stages. No organization can define options or prepare programs for this treasonous act. Thus, early overtures will be uncoordinated with the acts of other organizations, e.g., the fighting forces, creating contradictory "signals" to the victor.

Model III suggests that surrender will not come at the point that strategic costs outweigh benefits, but that it will not wait until the leadership group concludes that the war is lost. Rather the problem is better understood in terms of four additional propositions. First, strong advocates of the war effort, whose careers are closely identified with the war, rarely come to the conclusion that costs outweigh benefits. Second, quite often from the outset of a war, a number of members of the government (particularly those whose responsibilities sensitize them to problems other than war, e.g., economic planners or intelligence experts) are convinced that the war effort is futile. Third, surrender is likely to come as the result of a political shift that enhances the effective power of the latter group (and adds swing members to it). Fourth, the course of the war, particularly actions of the victor, can influence the advantages and disadvantages of players in the loser's government. Thus, North Vietnam will surrender not when its leaders have a change of heart, but when Hanoi has a change of leaders (or a change of effective power within the central circle). How US bombing (or pause), threats, promises, or action in the South affect the game in Hanoi is subtle but nonetheless crucial.

That these three models could be applied to the surrender of governments other than North Vietnam should be obvious. But that exercise is left for the reader.

NOTES

1. Theodore Sorensen, *Kennedy* (New York: Harper and Row, 1965), p. 705.

2. In attempting to understand problems of foreign affairs, analysts engage in a number of related, but logically separable enterprises: (a) description, (b) explanation, (c) prediction, (d) evaluation, and (e) recommendation. This essay focuses primarily on explanation (and by implication, prediction).

3. In arguing that explanations proceed in terms of implicit conceptual models, this essay makes no claim that foreign policy analysts have developed any satisfactory, empirically tested theory. In this essay, the use of the term "model" without qualifiers should be read "conceptual scheme."

4. For the purpose of this argument we shall accept Carl G. Hempel's characterization of the logic of explanation: an explanation "answers the question,' *Why* did the explanadum-phenomenon occur?' by showing that the phenomenon resulted from particular circumstances, specified in $C_1, C_2, \ldots C_x$, in accordance with laws $L_1, L_2, \ldots L_r$. By pointing this out, the argument shows that, given the particular circumstances and the laws in question, the occurrence of the phenomenon was to be *expected;* and it is in this sense that the explanation enables us to understand why the phenomenon occurred." *Aspects of Scientific Explanation* (New York: Harcourt, Brace and World, 1961), p. 337. While various patterns of explanation can be distinguished, viz., Ernest Nagel, T*he Structure of Science: Problems in the Logic of Scientific Explanation* (New York: Harcourt, Brace and World, 1961), satisfactory scientific explanations exhibit this basic logic. Consequently prediction is the converse of explanation.

5. Earlier drafts of this argument have aroused heated arguments concerning proper names for these models. To choose names from ordinary language is to court confusion, as well as familiarity. Perhaps it is best to think of these models as I, II, and III.

6. *New York Times*, 18 Feb., 1967.

7. Ibid.

8. Arnold Horelick and Myron Rush, *Strategic Power and Soviet Foreign Policy* (Chicago: University of Chicago Press, 1965). Based on A. Horelick, "The Cuban Missile Crisis: An Analysis of Soviet Calculations and Behavior," *World Politics* 16 (Apr. 1964).

9. Horelick and Rush, *Strategic Power,* p. 154.

10. Hans Morgenthau, *Politics among Nations* 3d ed. (New York: Knopf, 1960), p. 191.

11. Ibid., p. 192.

12. Ibid., p. 5.

13. Ibid., pp. 5–6.

14. The larger study examines several exceptions to this generalization. Sidney Verba's excellent essay "Assumptions of Rationality and Non-Rationality in Models of the International System" is less an exception than it is an approach to a somewhat different problem. Verba focuses upon models of rationality and irrationality of *individual* statesmen: in Knorr and Verba, *International System.*

15. Robert K. Merton, *Social Theory and Social Structures,* rev. and enl. ed. (New York: Free Press, 1957), pp. 12–16. Considerably weaker than a satisfactory theoretical model, paradigms nevertheless represent a short step in that direction from looser, implicit conceptual models. Neither the concepts nor the relations among the variables are sufficiently specified to yield propositions deductively. "Paradigmatic Analysis" nevertheless has considerable promise for clarifying and codifying styles of analysis in political science. Each of the paradigms stated here can be represented rigorously in mathematical terms. For example, model I lends itself to mathematical formulation along the lines of Herbert Simon's "Behavioral Theory of Rationality," *Models of Man* (New York: Wiley, 1957). But this does not solve the most difficult problem of "measurement and estimation."

16. Though a variant of this model could easily be stochastic, this paradigm is stated in nonprobabilistic terms. In contemporary strategy, a stochastic version of this model is sometimes used for predictions; but it is almost impossible to find an explanation of an occurrence in foreign affairs that is consistently probabilistic.

Analogies between model I and the concept of explanation developed by R. G. Collingwood, William Dray, and other "revisionists" among philosophers concerned with the critical philosophy of history are not accidental. For a summary of the "revisionist position" see Maurice Mandelbaum, "Historical Explanation: The Problem of Covering Laws," *History and Theory* 1 (1960).

17. This model is an analogue of the theory of the rational entrepreneur which has been developed extensively in economic theories of the firm and the consumer. These two propositions specify the "substitution effect." Refinement of this model and specification of additional general propositions by translating from the economical theory is straightforward.

18. *New York Times,* 22 Mar., 1969.

19. See Nathan Leites, *A Study of Bolshevism* (Glencoe, Ill.: Free Press, 1953).

20. The influence of organizational studies upon the present literature of foreign affairs is minimal. Specialists in international politics are not students of organization theory. Organization theory has only recently begun to study organizations as decision-makers and has not yet produced behavioral studies of national security organizations from a decision-making perspective. It seems unlikely, however, that these gaps will remain unfilled much longer. Considerable progress has been made in the study of the business firm as an organization. Scholars have begun applying these insights to government organizations, and interest in an organizational perspective is spreading

among institutions and individuals concerned with actual government operations. The "decision-making" approach represented by Richard Snyder, R. Bruck, and B. Sapin, *Foreign Policy Decision-Making* (Glencoe, Ill.: Free Press, 1962), incorporates a number of insights from organization theory.

21. The formulation of this paradigm is indebted both to the orientation and insights of Herbert Simon and to the behavioral model of the firm stated by Richard Cyert and James March, *A Behavioral Theory of the Firm* (Englewood Cliffs, N.J.: Prentice-Hall, 1963). Here, however, one is forced to grapple with the less routine, less quantified functions of the less differentiated elements in government organizations.

22. Theodore Sorensen, "You Get to Walk to Work," *New York Times Magazine,* 19 Mar., 1967.

23. Organizations are not monolithic. The proper level of disaggregation depends upon the objectives of a piece of analysis. This paradigm is formulated with reference to the major organizations that constitute the US government. Generalization to the major components of each department and agency should be relatively straight forward.

24. The stability of these constraints is dependent on such factors as rules for promotion and reward, budgeting and accounting procedures, and mundane operating procedures.

25. Marriner Eccles, *Beckoning Frontiers* (New York: A. A. Knopf, 1951), p. 336.

26. Arthur Schlesinger, *A Thousand Days* (Boston: Houghton-Mifflin, 1965), p. 406.

27. This paradigm relies upon the small group of analysts who have begun to fill the gap. My primary source is the model implicit in the work of Richard E. Neustadt, though his concentration on presidential action has been generalized to a concern with policy as the outcome of political bargaining among a number of independent players, the president amounting to no more than a "superpower" among many lesser but considerable powers. As Warner Schilling argues, the substantive problems are of such inordinate difficulty that uncertainties and differences with regard to goals, alternatives, and consequences are inevitable. This necessitates what Roger Hilsman describes as the process of conflict and consensus building. The techniques employed in this process often resemble those used in legislative assemblies, though Samuel Huntington's characterization of the process as "legislative" overemphasizes the equality of participants as opposed to the hierarchy which structures the game. Moreover, whereas for Huntington, foreign policy (in contrast to military policy) is set by the executive, this paradigm maintains that the activities which he describes as legislative are characteristic of the process by which foreign policy is made.

28. The theatrical metaphor of stage, roles, and actors is more common than this metaphor of games, positions, and players. Nevertheless, the rigidity connotated by the concept of "role" both in the theatrical sense of actors reciting fixed lines and in the sociological sense of fixed responses to specified social situations makes the concept of names, positions, and players more useful for this analysis of active participants in the determination of national policy. Objections to the terminology on the grounds that "game" connotes nonserious play overlook the concept's application to most serious problems both in Wittgenstein's philosophy and in contemporary game theory. Game theory typically treats more precisely structured games, but Wittgenstein's examination of the "language game" wherein men use words to communicate is quite analogous to this analysis of the less specified game of bureaucratic politics. See Ludwig Wittgenstein, *Philosophical Investigations,* 3d. ed. (New York: Macmillan, 1968), and Thomas

Schelling, "What Is Game Theory?" in James Charlesworth, *Contemporary Political Analysis* (New York: Free Press 1967).

29. Inclusion of the president's special assistant for national security affairs in the tier of "Chiefs" rather than among the "Staffers" involves a debatable choice. In fact he is both super-staffer and near-chief. His position has no statutory authority. He is especially dependent upon good relations with the president and the secretaries of defense and state. Nevertheless, he stands astride a genuine action-channel. The decision to include this position among the Chiefs reflects my judgment that the Bundy function is becoming institutionalized.

30. Richard E. Neustadt, Testimony, United States Senate, Committee on Government Operations, Subcommittee on National Security Staffing, *Administration of National Security,* 26 Mar. 1963, pp. 82–83.

31. This aphorism was stated first, I think, by Don K. Price.

32. Paul Y. Hammond, "Super Carriers and B-36 Bombers," in Harold Stein, ed., *American Civil-Military Decisions* (Birmingham: University of Alabama Press, 1963).

33. Roberta Wohlstetter, *Pearl Harbor* (Stanford: Stanford University Press, 1962), p. 350.

34. Graham T. Allison, *Essence of Decision* (Boston: Little, Brown, 1971).

35. Thus my position is quite distinct from both poles in the recent "great debate" about international relations. While many "traditionalists" of the sort Kaplan attacks adopt the first posture and many "scientists" of the sort attacked by Bull adopt the second, this third posture is relatively neutral with respect to whatever is in substantive dispute. See Hedley Bull, "International Theory: The Case for a Classical Approach," *World Politics* 18 (Apr. 1966); and Morton Kaplan, "The New Great Debate: Traditionalism vs. Science in International Relations," *World Politics* 19 (Oct. 1966).

36. A number of problems are now being examined in these terms both in the Bureaucracy Study Group on Bureaucracy and Policy of the Institute of Politics at Harvard University and at the RAND Corporation.

37. In response to several readers' recommendations, what follows is reproduced verbatim from the paper delivered at the Sept. 1968 Association meetings (RAND P-3919). The discussion is heavily indebted to Ernest R. May.

38. Richard Snyder, *Deterrence and Defense* (Princeton: Princeton University Press, 1961), p. 11. For a more general presentation of this position see Paul Kecskemeti, *Strategic Surrender* (New York: Stanford University Press, 1964).

Review Questions

1. How did the Brownlow *Report* contribute to the growth of the modern institutionalized presidency? Why did the *Report* recommend that the president have working for him staff members with "a passion for anonymity?

2. Are a president's powers more related to his "power to persuade" than to his formal authority? Can Richard Neustadt's "power to persuade" thesis be applied to any executive or is it limited to the president?

3. What is meant by Aaron Wildavsky's theory of the "two presidencies"? Is this theory still valid today?

4. What are the three conceptual models used by Graham Allison to explain American actions during the Cuban missile crisis of 1962? Can these models by applied to domestic as well as foreign policy issues?

Chapter 8

Policy Reviewing by the Judiciary

Judicial activism is the making of new public policies through the decisions of judges. This may take the form of a reversal or modification of a prior court decision, the nullification of a law passed by a legislature, or the overturning of some action of the executive branch. The concept of judicial activism is most associated with the U.S. Supreme Court, which from time to time has found new laws when none were there before. However, judges at any level can be said to engage in judicial activism when their judicial positions are used to promote what they consider to be desirable social goals. The main argument against judicial activism is that it tends to usurp the power of the legislature or negate the words of a constitution. The counterargument holds that, because laws—being products of compromise—tend to be vague on "hot" issues, the courts are in effect forced by the nature of the cases they receive to sort things out in a manner that seems "activist" to critics.

Those who oppose judicial activism and believe that constitutions should be interpreted narrowly and literally, are known as strict constructionists. They favor judicial self-restraint, a self-imposed limitation on judicial decision making; the tendency on the part of judges to favor a narrow interpretation of the laws and to defer to the policy judgments of the legislative and executive branches.

A loose constructionist, in contrast, believes that the Constitution should be interpreted liberally in order to reflect changing times. Chief Justice John Marshall (1755–1835) first made the case for loose construction in *McCulloch v. Maryland* (1819), when he asserted: "Let the end be legitimate, let it be within the scope of the Constitution, and all means which are appropriate, which are plainly adapted to that end, which are not prohibited, but consist with the letter and spirit of the Constitution, are constitutional."

Note that the strict versus loose construction construct is highly subjective and has no meaning or consistent application in practice. After all, even a strict constructionist could be an activist in reversing loose construction.

The role that the Supreme Court would play in American government was left vague by its new constitution. But Alexander Hamilton was not the least bit shy in delineating the functions of what he famously called "the least dangerous branch" in *The Federalist* No. 78 (reprinted here). What followed from Hamilton's logic was the most powerful court the world has ever seen, one strong enough to, in effect, force a president to resign as in *United States v. Nixon* (1974) and radically change the premises of American society. This chapter continues with five of the most influential Supreme Court cases in American history: the first established the Court's power, the second made racial segregation illegal, the third established the right to bedroom privacy, the fourth forced the police to respect the constitutional rights of criminal defendants no matter how poor or "obviously guilty" they were, and the fifth dealt with abortion.

1. *Marbury v. Madison* (1803), reprinted here, became the preeminent U.S. Supreme Court case because of its famous declaration of the Court's power of judicial review—the power to declare federal legislation or executive actions unconstitutional and consequently unenforceable through the courts. It was in this case that Chief Justice John Marshall held that it was the duty of the judiciary to say what the law is, including expounding and interpreting that law. The law contained in the Constitution, he said, was paramount, and laws repugnant to its provisions must fall. He concluded that it was the province of the courts to decide when other law was in violation of the basic law of the Constitution and, where this was found to occur, to declare that law null and void. This is the doctrine known as judicial review, which has become the basis for the Court's application of constitutional guarantees.

Judicial review was used rarely by the Court in the nineteenth century but it became commonplace in the twentieth century. While many books have been written about the implementation of this or that government program, there is ultimately only one thing that government is in essence capable of implementing—that is the law. Of course the law is often in turmoil. The legislative basis of programs, or specific agency rules and regulations, are constantly being challenged in court by those who oppose as well as those who support the program involved. The opposition wants the enabling legislation declared unconstitutional and the program destroyed while supporters often want the program administered even more generously. Ever since the New Deal of the 1930s, a pattern has emerged with controversial legislation. After its passage, opponents challenge its legality in court, hoping that the judicial branch will overturn it. In effect, there is a new final phase to the legislative policymaking process, a judicial review to see if the new law is constitutional.

2. The essence of the *Brown v. Board of Education of Topeka, Kansas* (1954) decision was whether black and white children should attend the same schools. Prior to *Brown*

the prevailing doctrine on civil rights was "separate but equal." This meant that blacks did not suffer an infringement of their constitutional rights as citizens if they were not allowed to use the same facilities as whites—so long as "separate but equal" facilities were also provided. While this sounded fair on the surface, there were two insurmountable arguments against this doctrine. First, there was the simple reality that what was provided separately was hardly ever equal. Second, there was the inherent stigma of being treated differently.

What made this doctrine particularly insidious was the fact that it derived not just from custom and the Jim Crow (racial segregation) laws of the South; it was famously promulgated by the U.S. Supreme Court. In *Plessy v. Ferguson* (1896) the Court held that segregated railroad facilities for African Americans, facilities that were considered equal in quality to those provided for whites, were legal.

Plessy put the stamp of inferiority on every American of African descent. One justice saw this clearly. In his lone dissenting opinion Justice John Marshall Harlan (1833–1911), ironically a former slave owner from Kentucky, wrote: "We boast of the freedom enjoyed by our people. . . . But it is difficult to reconcile that boast with a state of the law which, practically, puts the brand of servitude and degradation upon a large class of our fellow citizens, our equals before the law. The thin disguise of 'equal' accommodations for passengers in the railroad coaches will not mislead anyone, or atone for the wrong this day done."

More than half a century later, future Supreme Court Justice Thurgood Marshall (1908–1993) of the National Association for the Advancement of Colored People led the legal team that urged the Court to overturn the "wrong this day done" in the *Plessy* decision and nullify this doctrine when it asserted that separate was "inherently unequal."

Linda Brown was a seven year old girl in Topeka, Kansas, when her famous case started winding its way to the high court. She lived just a few blocks from a local elementary school. But since that was for whites only, she had to attend a "colored" school on the other side of town. This required that she cross railroad tracks to then take a long bus ride. Her father, Oliver, joined a group of African Americans who sought for three years to get Topeka to improve the "colored" schools. Finally they filed a lawsuit and Brown found his name as the first of the plaintiffs.

In *Brown* the Court decided that the separation of children by race and according to law in public schools "generates a feeling of inferiority as to their [the minority group's] status in the community that may affect their hearts and minds in a way unlikely ever to be undone." Consequently, it held that "separate educational facilities are inherently unequal" and therefore violate the equal protection clause of the Fourteenth Amendment. Chief Justice Earl Warren (1891–1974), in delivering the unanimous opinion of the Court, stated that public education "is the very foundation of good citizenship." It was so important to the nation that considerations of the original intent of the Fourteenth Amendment were less important than remedying the present situation. So the Court effectively brushed aside the question of whether the

Fourteenth Amendment was ever intended to cover public education. Warren stated: "In approaching this problem we cannot turn the clock back to 1868 when the Amendment was adopted, or even to 1896 when *Plessy v. Ferguson* was written. We must consider public education in the light of its full development and present place in American life."

Then Warren proceeded to dismantle the doctrine of separate but equal. "We come then to the question presented: does segregation of children in public schools solely on the basis of race, even though the physical facilities and other 'tangible' factors may be equal, deprive the children of the minority group of equal educational opportunities? We believe that it does."

Warren acknowledged that the Court accepted the validity of various psychologists that segregated schools damaged minority students by creating "a feeling of inferiority." Finally he concluded that "in the field of public education the doctrine of 'separate but equal' has no place."

3. In the 1965 case of *Griswold v. Connecticut* (reprinted here) the Supreme Court first asserted that there was a constitutional right to bedroom privacy even when the word privacy does not appear in the constitution. *Griswold* ruled that state regulation of birth control devices was an impermissible invasion of privacy. This helped to establish privacy as a constitutionally protected right under the Ninth and Fourteenth amendments. Justice William O. Douglas wrote, in the majority opinion: "The First Amendment has a penumbra where privacy is protected from governmental intrusion." He asked: "Would we allow the police to search the sacred precincts of marital bedrooms for telltale signs of the use of contraceptives? The very idea is repulsive to the notions of privacy surrounding the marriage relationship." The logic behind *Griswold* would be reasserted in two other landmark cases: *Roe v. Wade* (discussed below) and *Lawrence v. Texas* (2003).

The core problem of dealing with the civil rights of gays and lesbians is the activity that defines them (consensual sodomy) has been considered a crime in many states. But no longer. In 2003 the Supreme Court in *Lawrence v. Texas* declared unconstitutional the Texas ban on consensual sodomy and in effect asserted a broad constitutional right to sexual privacy. Justice Anthony M. Kennedy in the majority opinion wrote that the case concerned "two adults who, with full and mutual consent from each other, engaged in sexual practices common to a homosexual lifestyle. The petitioners are entitled to respect for their private lives. The State cannot demean their existence or control their destiny by making their private sexual conduct a crime."

In an extremely strong dissenting opinion Justice Antonin Scalia said that the ruling "effectively decrees the end of all morals legislation," and could possibly pave the way for "judicial imposition of homosexual marriage, as has recently occurred in Canada." This case overruled a 1986 decision in which the court upheld Georgia's sodomy law (*Bowers v. Hardwick*). The 2003 decision effectively nullified sodomy laws in the 13 other states besides Texas that still had such laws.

4. Before you have read your first college textbook, you have seen the ritual played out hundreds of times in movies and on television—if not in real life. The

police first arrest someone; then immediately read them their rights. These rights are "read" instead of "told" because it is important that the wording reflect the demands established by the U.S. Supreme Court in the 1966 case of *Miranda v. Arizona.*

The *Miranda* rights, consists of all those rights that a person accused or suspected of having committed a crime has during interrogation and of which he or she must be informed prior to questioning. The act of informing a person of these rights is often called admonition of rights, or admonishment of rights. The information given is called the Miranda warning. Once rights have been read, the arrestee is said to have been "Mirandized."

In *Miranda* the Supreme Court held that an arrested person must be warned of the right to be silent and the right to have a lawyer, who will be provided if the arrested person cannot afford one, as soon as the arrest is made. The Court stated that "the prosecution may not use statements . . . stemming from custodial interrogation of the defendant unless it demonstrates the use of procedural safeguards effective to secure the privilege against self-incrimination." When the police arrest individuals and "read them their rights," it is the rights embedded in the *Miranda* decision they refer to. The Court made a major exception to *Miranda* when in *New York v. Quarles* (1984) it held that suspects could be questioned before advising them of their rights if there were "overriding considerations of public safety."

And what happened to Ernesto Miranda, the ex-con whose confession to kidnapping and rape was the basis for this famous case? His confession was disallowed. When retried in 1967, he was again convicted. Later paroled, he was killed in a barroom knife fight in 1976. Thereupon, the person arrested for his murder was read his Miranda rights.

The basic reason for the *Miranda* decision is that it was too often customary for police to arrest someone and then use psychological or physical methods to force a confession. And even assuming no coercion, ordinary people are at a severe disadvantage dealing with the police without legal advice. In this sense *Miranda* expanded upon the 1963 decision of *Gideon v. Wainwright* in which the Supreme Court held that the due process clause of the Fourteenth Amendment required that persons brought to trial in state courts on felony charges are entitled to have a court-appointed lawyer if they cannot afford to pay for one of their own. Previously, state courts were required to provide legal counsel to indigent defendants only in cases where the death penalty was at issue (*Powell v. Alabama* [1932]) or when the defendant was young or mentally incompetent (*Betts v. Brady* [1942]). *Gideon* extended the right to legal assistance to all felony defendants in all state criminal trials. Justice Hugo Black wrote that "reason and reflection require us to recognize that, in our adversary system of criminal justice, any person hauled into court, who is too poor to hire a lawyer, cannot be assured a fair trial unless counsel is provided for him. This seems to be an obvious truth."

The Sixth Amendment provides a right to be represented by counsel. For many years, this was interpreted to mean only that the defendant had a right to be represented by a lawyer if the defendant could obtain one. But the Supreme Court has since held in a series of cases that the amendment imposes an affirmative obligation on the part of federal and state governments to provide legal counsel at public expense for those who cannot afford it.

Unfortunately our right to a lawyer when we become embroiled in the criminal justice system is similar to our access to medical care when we are sick. Without medical insurance all but the very rich are one major illness away from bankruptcy. This is why anyone with even modest assets to protect will strive to maintain medical insurance coverage. But there does not exist a similar tradition with legal insurance. The rich don't need it. The poor, as *Miranda* states, will have public defenders or court appointed attorneys. All fine attorneys to be sure. But with houses, cars, and lawyers, you tend to get what you pay for. And if all you can afford is a "free" or low priced lawyer, you may not get the best possible defense. Nevertheless, thanks to *Miranda* you have a right to be defended.

5. *Roe v. Wade* (reprinted here) is the 1973 Supreme Court case that (by a vote of seven to two) made abortions legal in the United States by ruling that governments lacked the power to prohibit them. Associate Justice Harry Blackmun wrote regarding this case that "freedom of personal choice in matters of marriage and family life is one of the liberties protected by the due process clause of the Fourteenth Amendment. . . . That right necessarily includes the right of a woman to decide whether or not to terminate her pregnancy." This has been one of the most controversial Supreme Court decisions, heralded by some groups as a landmark for women's rights and denounced by others, especially the new Right, as the legalization of murder.

Ever since, as the Court has grown more conservative, this right to abortion has been increasingly curtailed. In *Webster v. Reproductive Health Services* (1989), the Court stopped just short of reversing *Roe v. Wade* when it held that states could regulate or abolish a woman's right to have an abortion. Justice Harry Blackmun, who wrote the Court's opinion in *Roe v. Wade*, wrote a stinging dissent in the *Webster* case. He said the Court "casts into darkness the hopes and visions of every woman in this country who had come to believe that the Constitution guaranteed her the right to exercise some control over her unique ability to bear children."

The *Webster* decision suddenly made abortion *the* issue of state politics. Now many candidates for a governorship or state legislature must take a stand. This is vexing for politicians of both parties because abortion is not clearly an issue of the left or right.

Roe v. Wade remains the most contentious Supreme Court case in American politics. The Republican Party wants it reversed while the Democratic Party wants to see it sustained. Thus this case has become part of every recent presidential contest. The continuing issue is whether future presidential appointments to the Court will oppose or support *Roe v. Wade*.

28

The Federalist No. 78 (1778)

Alexander Hamilton

To the People of the State of New York:

We proceed now to an examination of the judiciary department of the proposed government.

In unfolding the defects of the existing Confederation, the utility and necessity of a federal judicature have been clearly pointed out. It is the less necessary to recapitulate the considerations there urged, as the propriety of the institution in the abstract is not disputed; the only questions which have been raised being relative to the manner of constituting it, and to its extent. To these points, therefore, our observations shall be confined.

The manner of constituting it seems to embrace these several objects: 1st. The mode of appointing the judges, 2d. The tenure by which they are to hold their places. 3d. The partition of the judiciary authority between different courts, and their relations to each other.

First. As to the mode of appointing the judges; this is the same with that of appointing the officers of the Union in general, and has been so fully discussed in the two last numbers, that nothing can be said here which would not be useless repetition.

Second. As to the tenure by which the judges are to hold their places: this chiefly concerns their duration in office; the provisions for their support; the precautions for their responsibility.

According to the plan of the convention, all judges who may be appointed by the United States are to hold their offices *during good behavior;* which is conformable to the most approved of the State constitutions, and among the rest, to that of this State. Its propriety having been drawn into question by the adversaries of that plan, is no light symptom of the rage for objection, which disorders their imaginations and judgments. The standard of good behavior for the continuance in office of the judicial magistracy, is certainly one of the most

Source: Alexander Hamilton, *The Federalist,* No. 78, 1778.

valuable of the modern improvements in the practice of government. In a monarchy it is an excellent barrier to the despotism of the prince; in a republic it is a no less excellent barrier to the encroachments and oppressions of the representative body. And it is the best expedient which can be devised in any government, to secure a steady, upright, and impartial administration of the laws.

Whoever attentively considers the different departments of power must perceive, that, in a government in which they are separated from each other, the judiciary, from the nature of its functions, will always be the least dangerous to the political rights of the Constitution; because it will be least in a capacity to annoy or injure them. The Executive not only dispenses the honors, but holds the sword of the community. The legislature not only commands the purse, but prescribes the rules by which the duties and rights of every citizen are to be regulated. The judiciary, on the contrary, has no influence over either the sword or the purse; no direction either of the strength or of the wealth of the society; and can take no active resolution whatever. It may truly be said to have neither force nor will, but merely judgment; and must ultimately depend upon the aid of the executive arm even for the efficacy of its judgments.

This simple view of the matter suggests several important consequences. It proves incontestably, that the judiciary is beyond comparison the weakest of the three departments of power; that it can never attack with success either of the other two; and that all possible care is requisite to enable it to defend itself against their attacks. It equally proves, that though individual oppression may now and then proceed from the courts of justice, the general liberty of the people can never be endangered from that quarter; I mean so long as the judiciary remains truly distinct from both the legislature and the Executive. For I agree, that "there is no liberty, if the power of judging be not separated from the legislative and executive powers." And it proves, in the last place, that as liberty can have nothing to fear from the judiciary alone, but would have every thing to fear from its union with either of the other departments; that as all the effects of such a union must ensue from a dependence of the former on the latter, notwithstanding a nominal and apparent separation; that as, from the natural feebleness of the judiciary, it is in continual jeopardy of being overpowered, awed, or influenced by its coördinate branches; and that as nothing can contribute so much to its firmness and independence as permanency in office, this quality may therefore be justly regarded as an indispensable ingredient in its constitution, and, in a great measure, as the citadel of the public justice and the public security.

The complete independence of the courts of justice is peculiarly essential in a limited Constitution. By a limited Constitution, I understand one which contains certain specified exceptions to the legislative authority; such, for instance, as that it shall pass no bills at attainder, no *ex-post-facto* laws, and the like. Limitations of this kind can be preserved in practice no other way than through the medium of courts of justice, whose duty it must be to declare all acts contrary to the manifest tenor of the Constitution void. Without this, all the reservations of particular rights and privileges would amount to nothing.

Some perplexity respecting the rights of the courts to pronounce legislative acts void, because contrary to the constitution, has arisen from an imagination that the doctrine would imply a superiority of the judiciary to the legislative power. It is urged that the authority which can declare the acts of another void, must necessarily be superior to the one whose acts may be declared void. As this doctrine is of great importance in all the American constitutions, a brief discussion of the ground on which it rests cannot be unacceptable.

There is no position which depends on clearer principles, than that every act of a delegated authority, contrary to the tenor of the commission under which it is exercised, is void. No legislative act, therefore, contrary to the Constitution, can be valid. To deny this, would be to affirm, that the deputy is greater than his principal; that the servant is above his master; that the representatives of the people are superior to the people themselves; that men acting by virtue of powers, may do not only what their powers do not authorize, but what they forbid.

If it be said that the legislative body are themselves the constitutional judges of their own powers, and that the construction they put upon them is conclusive upon the other departments, it may be answered, that this cannot be the natural presumption, where it is not to be collected from any particular provisions in the Constitution. It is not otherwise to be supposed, that the Constitution could intend to enable the representatives of the people to substitute their *will* to that of their constituents. It is far more rational to suppose, that the courts were designed to be an intermediate body between the people and the legislature, in order, among other things, to keep the latter within the limits assigned to their authority. The interpretation of the laws is the proper and peculiar province of the courts. A constitution is, in fact, and must be regarded by the judges, as a fundamental law. It therefore belongs to them to ascertain its meaning, as well as the meaning of any particular act proceeding from the legislative body. If there should happen to be an irreconcilable variance between the two, that which has the superior obligation and validity ought, of course, to be preferred; or, in other words, the Constitution ought to be preferred to the statute, the intention of the people to the intention of their agents.

Nor does this conclusion by any means suppose a superiority of the judicial to the legislative power. It only supposes that the power of the people is superior to both; and that where the will of the legislature, declared in its statutes, stands in opposition to that of the people, declared in the Constitution, the judges ought to be governed by the latter rather than the former. They ought to regulate their decisions by the fundamental laws, rather than by those which are not fundamental.

This exercise of judicial discretion, in determining between two contradictory laws, is exemplified in a familiar instance. It not uncommonly happens, that there are two statutes existing at one time, clashing in whole or in part with each other, and neither of them containing any repealing clause or expression. In such a case, it is the province of the courts to liquidate and fix their meaning and operation. So far as they can, by any fair construction, be reconciled to each other, reason and law conspire to dictate that this should be done; where this is impracticable, it becomes a matter of necessity to give effect to one, in exclusion of the other. The rule which has obtained in the courts for determining their relative validity is, that the last in order of time shall be preferred to the first. But there is a mere rule of construction, not derived from any positive law, but from the nature and reason of the thing. It is a rule not enjoined upon the courts by legislative provision, but adopted by themselves, as consonant to truth and propriety, for the direction of their conduct as interpreters of the law. They thought it reasonable, that between the interfering acts of an *equal authority*, that which was the last indication of its will should have the preference.

But in regard to the interfering acts of a superior and subordinate authority, of an original and derivative power, the nature and reason of the thing indicate the converse of that rule as proper to be followed. They teach us that the prior act of a superior ought to be preferred to the subsequent act of an inferior and subordinate authority; and that accordingly, whenever a particular statute contravenes the Constitution, it will be the duty of the judicial tribunals to adhere to the latter and disregard the former.

It can be of no weight to say that the courts, on the pretence of a repugnancy, may substitute their own pleasure to the constitutional intentions of the legislature. This might as well happen in the case of two contradictory statutes; or it might as well happen in every adjudication upon any single statute. The courts must declare the sense of the law; and if they should be disposed to exercise will instead of judgment, the consequence would equally be the substitution of their pleasure to that of the legislative body. The observation, if it prove any thing, would prove that there ought to be no judges distinct from that body.

If, then, the courts of justice are to be considered as the bulwarks of a limited Constitution against legislative encroachments, this consideration will afford a strong argument for the permanent tenure of judicial offices, since nothing will contribute so much as this to that independent spirit in the judges which must be essential to the faithful performance of so arduous a duty.

This independence of the judges is equally requisite to guard the Constitution and the rights of individuals from the effects of those ill humors, which the arts of designing men, or the influence of particular conjectures, sometimes disseminate among the people themselves, and which, though they speedily give place to better information, and more deliberate reflection, have a tendency, in the meantime, to occasion dangerous innovations in the government, and serious oppressions of the minor party in the community. Though I trust the friends of the proposed Constitution will never concur with its enemies, in questioning that fundamental principle of republican government, which admits the right of the people to alter or abolish the established Constitution, whenever they find it inconsistent with their happiness, yet it is not to be inferred from this principle, that the representatives of the people, whenever a momentary inclination happens to lay hold of a majority of their constituents, incompatible with the provisions in the existing Constitution, would, on that account, be justifiable in a violation of those provisions; or that the courts would be under a greater obligation to connive at infractions in this shape, than when they had proceeded wholly from the cabals of the representative body. Until the people have, by some solemn and authoritative act, annulled or changed the established form, it is binding upon themselves collectively, as well as individually; and no presumption, or even knowledge, of their sentiments, can warrant their representatives in a departure from it, prior to such an act. But it is easy to see, that it would require an uncommon portion of fortitude in the judges to do their duty as faithful guardians of the Constitution, where legislative invasions of it had been instigated by the major voice of the community.

But it is not with a view to infractions of the Constitution only, that the independence of the judges may be an essential safeguard against the effects of occasional ill humors in the society. These sometimes extend no farther than to the injury of the private rights of particular classes of citizens, by unjust and partial laws. Here also the firmness of the judicial magistracy is of vast importance in mitigating the severity and confining the operation of such laws. It not only serves to moderate immediate mischiefs of those which may have been passed, but it operates as a check upon the legislative body in passing them; who, perceiving that obstacles to the success of iniquitous intention are to be expected from the scruples of the courts, are in a manner compelled, by the very motives of the injustice they mediate, to qualify their attempts. This is a circumstance calculated to have more influence upon the character of our governments, than but few may be aware of. The benefits of the integrity and moderation of the judiciary have already been felt in more States than one; and though they may have displeased those whose sinister expectations they may have disappointed, they must have commanded the esteem and applause of all the virtuous and disinterested. Considerate men, of every description, ought to prize whatever will tend to beget or fortify that temper in the courts; as no man can be sure that he may not be to-morrow the victim of a spirit of injustice, by which he may be a gainer today. And every man must now feel, that the inevitable tendency of such a spirit is to sap the foundations of public and private confidence, and to introduce in its stead universal distrust and distress.

That inflexible and uniform adherence to the rights of the Constitution, and of individuals, which we perceive to be indispensable in the courts of justice, can certainly not be expected from judges who hold their offices by a temporary commission. Periodical appointments, however regulated, or by whomsoever made, would, in some way or other, be fatal to their necessary independence. If the power of making them was committed either to the Executive or legislature, there would be danger of an improper complaisance to the branch which possessed it; if to both, there would be an unwillingness to hazard the displeasure of either; if to the people, or to persons chosen by them for the special purpose, there would be too great a disposition to consult popularity, to justify a reliance that nothing would be consulted but the Constitution and the laws.

There is yet a further and a weightier reason for the permanency of the judicial offices, which is deducible from the nature of the qualifications they require. It has been frequently remarked, with great propriety, that a voluminous code of laws is one of the inconveniences necessarily connected with the advantages of a free government. To avoid an arbitrary discretion in the courts, it is indispensable that they should be bound down by strict rules and precedents, which serve to define and point out their duty in every particular case that comes before them; and it will readily be conceived from the variety of controversies which grow out of the folly and wickedness of mankind, that the records of those precedents must unavoidably swell to a very considerable bulk, and must demand long and laborious study to acquire a competent knowledge of them. Hence it is, that there can be but few men in the society who will have sufficient skill in the laws to qualify them for the stations of judges. And making the proper deductions for the ordinary depravity of human nature, the number must be still smaller of those who unite the requisite integrity with the requisite knowledge. These considerations apprise us, that the government can have no great option between fit character; and that a temporary duration in office, which would naturally discourage such characters from quitting a lucrative line of practice to accept a seat on the bench, would have a tendency to throw the administration of justice into hands less able, and less well qualified, to conduct it with utility and dignity. In the present circumstances of this country, and in those in which it is likely to be for a long time to come, the disadvantages on this score would be greater than they may at first sight appear; but it must be confessed, that they are far inferior to those which present themselves under the other aspects of the subject.

Upon the whole, there can be no room to doubt that the convention acted wisely in copying from the models of those constitutions which have established *good behavior* as the tenure of their judicial offices, in point of duration; and that so far from being blamable on this account, their plan would have been inexcusably defective, if it had wanted this important feature of good government. The experience of Great Britain affords an illustrious comment on the excellence of the institution.

29

Marbury v. Madison (1803)

Chief Justice MARSHALL delivers the opinion of the Court.

At the last term on the affidavits then read and filed with the clerk, a rule was granted in this case, requiring the secretary of state to show cause why a mandamus should not issue, directing him to deliver to William Marbury his commission as a justice of the peace for the county of Washington, in the District of Columbia.

No cause has been shown, and the present motion is for a *mandamus*. The peculiar delicacy of this case, the novelty of some of its circumstances, and the real difficulty attending the points which occur in it, require a complete exposition of the principles on which the opinion to be given by the court is founded.

These principles have been, on the side of the applicant very ably argued at the bar. In rendering the opinion of the court, there will be some departure in form, though not in substance, from the points stated in that argument.

In the order in which the court has viewed this subject, the following questions have been considered and decided.

1st. Has the applicant a right to the commission he demands?

2d. If he has a right, and that right has been violated, do the laws of his country afford him a remedy?

3d. If they do afford him a remedy, is it a *mandamus* issuing from this court? The first object of inquiry is,

1st. Has the applicant a right to the commission he demands?

His right originates in an act of congress passed in February, 1801, concerning the District of Columbia.

After dividing the district into two counties, the 11th section of this law enacts, "that there shall be appointed in and for each of the said counties, such number of discreet persons to be justices of the peace as the president of the United States shall, from time to time, think expedient, to continue in office for five years."

It appears, from the affidavits, that in compliance with this law, a commission for William Marbury, as a justice of the peace for the county of Washington,

---

Source: U.S. Supreme Court, *Marbury v. Madison*, 1803.

was signed by John Adams, then President of the United States; after which the seal of the United States was affixed to it; but the commission has never reached the person for whom it was made out. . . .

Mr. Marbury, then, since his commission was signed by the president, and sealed by the secretary of state, was appointed; and as the law creating the office, gave the officer a right to hold for five years, independent of the executive, the appointment was not revocable, but vested in the officer legal rights, which are protected by the laws of his country.

To withhold his commission, therefore, is an act deemed by the court not warranted by law, but violative of a vested legal right.

This brings us to the second inquiry; which is,

2d. If he has a right, and that right has been violated, do the laws of this country afford him a remedy?

The very essence of civil liberty certainly consists in the right of every individual to claim the protection of the laws, whenever he receives an injury. One of the first duties of government is to afford that protection. In Great Britain the king himself is sued in the respectful form of a petition, and he never fails to comply with the judgment of his court. . . .

By the constitution of the United States, the president is invested with certain important political powers, in the exercise of which he is to use his own discretion, and is accountable only to his country in his political character and to his own conscience. To aid him in the performance of these duties, he is authorized to appoint certain officers, who act by his authority, and in conformity with his orders.

In such cases, their acts are his acts; and whatever opinion may be entertained of the manner in which executive discretion may be used, still there exists, and can exist, no power to control that discretion. The subjects are political. They respect the nation, not individual rights, and being intrusted to the executive, the decision of the executive is conclusive. . . .

But when the legislature proceeds to impose on that officer other duties; when he is directed peremptorily to perform certain acts; when the rights of individuals are dependent on the performance of those acts; he is so far the officer of the law; is amenable to the laws for his conduct; and cannot at his discretion sport away the vested rights of others.

The conclusion from this reasoning is, that where the heads of departments are the political or confidential agents of the executive, merely to execute the will of the president, or rather to act in cases in which the executive possesses a constitutional or legal discretion, nothing can be more perfectly clear than that their acts are only politically examinable. But where a specific duty is assigned by law, and individual rights depend upon the performance of that duty, it seems equally clear that the individual who considers himself injured, has a right to resort to the laws of his country for a remedy. . . .

It is, then, the opinion of the Court,

1st. That by signing the commission of Mr. Marbury, the President of the United States appointed him a justice of peace for the county of Washington, in the District of Columbia; and that the seal of the United States, affixed thereto by the secretary of state, is conclusive testimony of the verity of the signature, and of the completion of the appointment; and that the appointment conferred on him a legal right to the office for the space of five years.

2d. That, having this legal title to the office, he has a consequent right to the commission; a refusal to deliver which is a plain violation of that right, for which the laws of his country afford him a remedy.

It remains to be inquired whether,

3d. He is entitled to the remedy for which he applies. This depends on,

1st. The nature of the writ applied for; and

2d. The power of this court.

1st. The nature of the writ. . . .

[T]o render the *mandamus* a proper remedy, the officer to whom it is to be directed, must be one to whom, on legal principles, such writ may be directed; and the person applying for it must be without any other specific and legal remedy. . . .

The act to establish the judicial courts of the United States authorizes the Supreme Court "to issue writs of *mandamus* in cases warranted by the principles and usages of law, to any courts appointed, or persons holding office, under the authority of the United States."

The secretary of state, being a person holding an office under the authority of the United States, is precisely within the letter of the description, and if this court is not authorized to issue a writ of mandamus to such an officer, it must be because the law is unconstitutional, and therefore absolutely incapable of conferring the authority, and assigning the duties which its words purport to confer and assign.

The constitution vests the whole judicial power of the United States in one supreme court, and such inferior courts as congress shall, from time to time, ordain and establish. This power is expressly extended to all cases arising under the laws of the United States; and, consequently, in some form, may be exercised over the present case; because the right claimed is given by a law of the United States.

In the distribution of this power it is declared that "the supreme court shall have original jurisdiction in all cases affecting ambassadors, other public ministers and consuls, and those in which a state shall be a party. In all other cases, the supreme court shall have appellate jurisdiction."

It has been insisted, at the bar, that as the original grant of jurisdiction, to the supreme and inferior courts, is general, and the clause, assigning original jurisdiction to the supreme court, contains no negative or restrictive words, the power remains to the legislature, to assign original jurisdiction to that court in other cases than those specified in the article which has been recited; provided those cases belong to the judicial power of the United States.

If it had been intended to leave it in the discretion of the legislature to apportion the judicial power between the supreme and inferior courts according to the will of that body, it would certainly have been useless to have proceeded further than to have defined the judicial power, and the tribunals in which it should be vested. The subsequent part of the section is mere surplusage, is entirely without meaning, if such is to be the construction. If congress remains at liberty to give this court appellate jurisdiction, where the constitution has declared their jurisdiction shall be original; and original jurisdiction where the constitution has declared it shall be appellate; the distribution of jurisdiction, made in the constitution, is form without substance. . . .

To enable this court, then, to issue a *mandamus,* it must be shown to be an exercise of appellate jurisdiction, or to be necessary to enable them to exercise appellate jurisdiction.

It has been stated at the bar that the appellate jurisdiction may be exercised in a variety of forms, and that if it be the will of the legislature that a *mandamus* should be used for that purpose, that will must be obeyed. This is true, yet the jurisdiction must be appellate, not original.

It is the essential criterion of appellate jurisdiction, that it revises and corrects the proceedings in a cause already instituted, and does not create that cause. Although, therefore, a mandamus may be directed to courts, yet to issue such a writ to an officer for the delivery of a paper, is in effect the same as to sustain an original action for that paper, and, therefore, seems not to belong to appellate, but to original jurisdiction. Neither is it necessary in such a case as this, to enable the court to exercise its appellate jurisdiction.

The authority, therefore, given to the supreme court, by the act establishing the judicial courts of the United States, to issue writs of *mandamus* to public officers, appears not to be warranted by the constitution; and it becomes necessary to inquire whether a jurisdiction so conferred can be exercised. . . .

The distinction between a government with limited and unlimited powers is abolished, if those limits do not confine the persons on whom they are imposed, and if acts prohibited and acts allowed, are of equal obligation. It is a proposition too plain to be contested, and the constitution controls any legislative act repugnant to it; or, that the legislature may alter the constitution by an ordinary act.

Between these alternatives there is no middle ground. The constitution is either a superior paramount law, unchangeable by ordinary means, or it is on a level with ordinary legislative acts, and, like other acts, is alterable when the legislature shall please to alter it.

If the former part of the alternative be true, then a legislative act contrary to the constitution is not law: if the latter part be true, then written constitutions are absurd attempts, on the part of the people, to limit a power in its own nature illimitable.

Certainly all those who have framed written constitutions contemplate them as forming the fundamental and paramount law of the nation, and consequently, the theory of every such government must be, that an act of the legislature, repugnant to the constitution, is void.

This theory is essentially attached to a written constitution, and, is consequently, to be considered, by this court, as one of the fundamental principles of our society. It is not therefore to be lost sight of in the further consideration of this subject.

If an act of the legislature, repugnant to the constitution, is void, does it, notwithstanding its invalidity, bind the courts, and oblige them to give it effect?

Or, in other words, though it be not law, does it constitute a rule as operative as if it was a law? This would be to overthrow in fact what was established in theory; and would seem, at first view, an absurdity too gross to be insisted on. It shall, however, receive a more attentive consideration.

It is emphatically the province and duty of the judicial department to say what the law is. Those who apply the rule to particular cases, must of necessity expound and interpret that rule. If two laws conflict with each other, the courts must decide on the operation of each.

So if a law be in opposition to the constitution; if both the law and the constitution apply to a particular case, so that the court must either decide that case conformably to the law, disregarding the constitution; or conformably to the constitution, disregarding the law; the court must determine which of these conflicting rules governs the case. This is of the very essence of judicial duty.

If, then, the courts are to regard the constitution, and the constitution is superior to any ordinary act of the legislature, the constitution, and not such ordinary act, must govern the case to which they both apply.

Those, then, who controvert the principle that the constitution is to be considered, in court, as a paramount law, are reduced to the necessity of maintaining that courts must close their eyes on the constitution, and see only the law.

This doctrine would subvert the very foundation of all written constitutions. It would declare that an act which, according to the principles and theory of our government, is entirely void, is yet, in practice, completely obligatory. It would declare that if the legislature shall do what is expressly forbidden, such act, notwithstanding the express prohibition, is in reality effectual. It would be given to the legislature a practical and real omnipotence, with the same breath which professes to restrict their powers within narrow limits. It is prescribing limits, and declaring that those limits may be passed at pleasure.

That it thus reduces to nothing what we have deemed the greatest improvement on political institutions, a written constitution, would of itself be sufficient, in America, where written constitutions have been viewed with so much reverence, for rejecting the construction. But the peculiar expressions of the constitution of the United States furnish additional arguments in favour of its rejection.

The judicial power of the United States is extended to all cases arising under the constitution.

Could it be the intention of those who gave this power, to say that in using it the constitution should not be looked into? That a case arising under the constitution should be decided without examining the instrument under which it arises?

This is too extravagant to be maintained.

In some cases, then, the constitution must be looked into by the judges. And if they can open it at all, what part of it are they forbidden to read or to obey?

There are many other parts of the constitution which serve to illustrate this subject.

It is declared that "no tax or duty shall be laid on articles exported from any state." Suppose a duty on the export of cotton, of tobacco, or of flour; and a suit instituted to recover it. Ought judgment to be rendered in such a case? Ought the judges to close their eyes on the constitution, and only see the law?

The constitution declares "that no bill of attainder or *ex post facto* law shall be passed."

If, however, such a bill should be passed, and a person should be prosecuted under it; must the court condemn to death those victims whom the constitution endeavors to preserve?

"No person," says the constitution, "shall be convicted of treason unless on the testimony of two witnesses to the same overt act, or on confession in open court."

Here the language of the constitution is addressed especially to the courts. It prescribes, directly for them, a rule of evidence not to be departed from. If the legislature should change that rule, and declare one witness, or a confession out of court, sufficient for conviction, must the constitutional principle yield to the legislative act?

From these, and many other selections which might be made, it is apparent, that the framers of the constitution contemplated that instrument as a rule for the government of courts, as well as of the legislature.

Why otherwise does it direct the judges to take an oath to support it? This oath certainly applies in an especial manner, to their conduct in their official character. How immoral to impose it on them, if they were to be used as the instruments, and the knowing instruments, for violating what they swear to support!

The oath of office, too, imposed by the legislature, is completely demonstrative of the legislative opinion on this subject. It is in these words: "I do solemnly swear that I will administer justice without respect to persons, and do equal right to the poor and to the rich; and that I will faithfully and impartially discharge all the duties incumbent on me as ———, according to the best of my abilities and understanding agreeably to the constitution and laws of the United States."

Why does a judge swear to discharge his duties agreeably to the constitution of the United States, if that constitution forms no rule for his government? if it is closed upon him, and cannot be inspected by him?

If such be the real state of things, this is worse than solemn mockery. To prescribe, or to take this oath, becomes equally a crime.

It is also not entirely unworthy of observation, that in declaring what shall be the *supreme law* of the land, *the constitution* itself is first mentioned; and not the laws of the United States generally, but those only which shall be made in *pursuance* of the constitution, have that rank.

Thus, the particular phraseology of the constitution of the United States confirms and strengthens the principle, supposed to be essential to all written constitutions, that a law repugnant to the constitution is void; and that *courts,* as well as other departments, are bound by that instrument.

The rule must be discharged.

30

Brown v. Board of Education (1954)

Mr. Chief Justice Warren, delivering the opinion of the Court in the Brown case, said in part:

These cases come to us from the States of Kansas, South Carolina, Virginia, and Delaware. They are premised on different facts and different local conditions, but a common legal question justifies their consideration together in this consolidated opinion.

In each of the cases, minors of the Negro race, through their legal representatives, seek the aid of the courts in obtaining admission to the public schools of their community on a nonsegregated basis. In each instance, they had been denied admission to schools attended by white children under laws requiring or permitting segregation according to race. This segregation was alleged to deprive plaintiffs of the equal protection of the laws under the Fourteenth Amendment. . . .

The plaintiffs contend that segregated public schools are not "equal" and cannot be made "equal," and that hence they are deprived of the equal protection of the laws. Because of the obvious importance of the question presented, the Court took jurisdiction. Argument was heard in the 1952 Term, and reargument was heard this Term on certain questions propounded by the Court.

Reargument was largely devoted to the circumstances surrounding the adoption of the Fourteenth Amendment in 1868. It covered exhaustively consideration of the Amendment in Congress, ratification by the states, then existing practices in racial segregation, and the views of proponents and opponents of the Amendment. This discussion and our own investigation convince us that, although these sources cast some light, it is not enough to resolve the problem with which we are faced. At best, they are inconclusive. The most avid proponents of the post-War Amendments undoubtedly intended them to remove all legal distinctions among "all persons born or naturalized in the United States." Their opponents, just as certainly, were antagonistic to both the letter and the spirit of the Amendments and wished them to have the most limited effect. What others in Congress and the state legislatures had in mind cannot be determined with any degree of certainty.

Source: U.S. Supreme Court, *Brown v. Board of Education of Topeka,* 1954.

An additional reason for the inconclusive nature of the Amendment's history, with respect to segregated schools, is the status of public education at that time. In the South, the movement toward free common schools, supported by general taxation, had not yet taken hold. Education of white children was largely in the hands of private groups. Education of Negroes was almost nonexistent, and practically all of the race were illiterate. In fact, any education of Negroes was forbidden by law in some states. Today, in contrast, many Negroes have achieved outstanding success in the arts and sciences as well as in the business and professional world. It is true that public school education at the time of the Amendment had advanced further in the North, but the effect of the Amendment on Northern States was generally ignored in the congressional debates. Even in the North, the conditions of public education did not approximate those existing today. The curriculum was usually rudimentary; ungraded schools were common in rural areas; the school term was but three months a year in many states; and compulsory school attendance was virtually unknown. As a consequence, it is not surprising that there should be so little in the history of the Fourteenth Amendment relating to its intended effect on public education.

In the first cases in this Court construing the Fourteenth Amendment, decided shortly after its adoption the Court interpreted it as proscribing all state-imposed discriminations against the Negro race. The doctrine of "separate but equal" did not make its appearance in this Court until 1896 in the case of *Plessy v. Ferguson,* involving not education but transportation. American courts have since labored with the doctrine for over half a century. In this Court, there have been six cases involving the "separate but equal" doctrine in the field of public education. In *Cumming v. Board of Education of Richmond County* [1899] and *Gong Lum v. Rice* [1927] the validity of the doctrine itself was not challenged. In more recent cases, all on the graduate school level, inequality was found in that specific benefits enjoyed by white students were denied to Negro students of the same educational qualifications. *State of Missouri ex rel. Gaines v. Canada* [1938], *Sipuel v. Board of Regents of University of Oklahoma* [1948], *Sweatt v. Painter* [1950], *McLaurin v. Oklahoma State Regents* [1950]. In none of these cases was it necessary to reexamine the doctrine to grant relief to the Negro plaintiff. And in *Sweatt v. Painter* the Court expressly reserved decision on the question whether *Plessy v. Ferguson* should be held inapplicable to public education.

In the instant cases, that question is directly presented. Here, unlike *Sweatt v. Painter,* there are findings below that the Negro and white schools involved have been equalized, or are being equalized, with respect to buildings, curricula, qualifications and salaries of teachers, and other "tangible" factors. Our decision, therefore, cannot turn on merely a comparison of these tangible factors in the Negro and white schools involved in each of the cases. We must look instead to the effect of segregation itself on public education.

In approaching this problem, we cannot turn the clock back to 1868 when the Amendment was adopted, or even to 1896 when *Plessy v. Ferguson* was written. We must consider public education in the light of its full development and its present place in American life throughout the Nation. Only in this way can it be determined if segregation in public schools deprives these plaintiffs of the equal protection of the laws.

Today, education is perhaps the most important function of state and local governments. Compulsory school attendance laws and the great expenditures for education both demonstrate our recognition of the importance of education to our democratic society. It is required in the performance of our most basic public responsibilities, even service in the armed forces. It is the very foundation of good citizenship. Today it is a principal instrument in awakening the child to cultural values, in preparing him to adjust normally to his environment. In these days, it is doubtful that any child may reasonably be expected to succeed in life if he is denied the opportunity of an education. Such an opportunity, where the state has undertaken to provide it, is a right which must be made available to all on equal terms.

We come then to the question presented: Does segregation of children in public schools, solely on the basis of race, even though the facilities and other "tangible" factors may be equal, deprive the children of the minority group of equal educational opportunities? We believe that it does.

In *Sweatt v. Painter,* in finding that a segregated law school for Negroes could not provide them equal educational opportunities, this Court relied in large part on "those qualities which are incapable of objective measurement but which make for greatness in a law school." In *McLaurin v. Oklahoma State Regents,* the Court, in requiring that a Negro admitted to a white graduate school be treated like all other students, again resorted to intangible considerations: ". . . his ability to study, to engage in discussions and exchange views with other students, and, in general, to learn his profession." Such considerations apply with added force to children in grade and high schools. To separate them from others of similar age and qualifications solely because of their race generates a feeling of inferiority as to their status in the community that may effect their hearts and minds in a way unlikely ever to be undone. The effect of this separation on their educational opportunities was well stated by a finding in the Kansas case by a court which nevertheless felt compelled to rule against the Negro plaintiffs:

"Segregation of white and colored children in public schools has a detrimental effect upon the colored children. The impact is greater when it has the sanction of the law; for the policy of separating the races is usually interpreted as denoting the inferiority of the Negro group. A sense of inferiority affects the motivation of a child to learn. Segregation with the sanction of law, therefore, has a tendency to [retard] the educational and mental development of Negro children and to deprive them of some of the benefits they would receive in a racial[ly] integrated school system." Whatever may have been the extent of psychological knowledge at the time of *Plessy v. Ferguson,* this finding is amply supported by modern authority. Any language in *Plessy v. Ferguson* contrary to this finding is rejected.

We conclude that in the field of public education the doctrine of "separate but equal" has no place. Separate educational facilities are inherently unequal. Therefore, we hold that the plaintiffs and others similarly situated for whom the actions have been brought are, by reason of the segregation complained of, deprived of the equal protection of the laws guaranteed by the Fourteenth Amendment. This disposition makes unnecessary any discussion whether such segregation also violates the Due Process Clause of the Fourteenth Amendment.

Because these are class actions, because of the wide applicability of this decision, and because of the great variety of local conditions, the formulation of decrees in these cases presents problems of considerable complexity. On reargument, the consideration of appropriate relief was necessarily subordinated to the primary question—the constitutionality of segregation in public education. We have now announced that such segregation is a denial of the equal protection of the laws. In order that we may have the full assistance of the parties in formulating decrees, the cases will be restored to the docket, and the parties are requested to present further argument on Questions 4 and 5 previously propounded by the Court for the reargument this Term. The Attorney General of the United States is again invited to participate. The Attorneys General of the states requiring or permitting segregation in public education will also be permitted to appear as amici curiae upon request to do so by September 15, 1954, and submission of briefs by October 1, 1954.

It is so ordered.

31

Griswold v. Connecticut (1965)

Justice Douglas delivered the opinion of the Court.

[A Connecticut statute makes it a crime to use contraceptives. Another statute makes it illegal to provide or assist another in using contraceptives. A married couple, their doctor, and the director of Planned Parenthood of Connecticut challenge their convictions under these statutes.]

Source: U.S. Supreme Court, *Griswold v. Connecticut,* 1965.

. . . [W]e are met with a wide range of questions that implicate the Due Process Clause of the Fourteenth Amendment. Overtones of some arguments suggest that *Lochner v. New York* should be our guide. But we decline that invitation. We do not sit as a super-legislature to determine the wisdom, need, and propriety of laws that touch economic problems, business affairs, or social conditions. This law, however, operates directly on an intimate relation of husband and wife and their physician's role in one aspect of that relation.

The association of people is not mentioned in the Constitution nor in the Bill of Rights. The right to educate a child in a school of the parents' choice—whether public or private or parochial—is also not mentioned. Nor is the right to study any particular subject or any foreign language. Yet the First Amendment has been construed to include certain of those rights.

By *Pierce v. Society of Sisters,* the right to educate one's children as one chooses is made applicable to the States by the force of the First and Fourteenth Amendments. By *Myer v. Nebraska,* the same dignity is given the right to study the German language in a private school. In other words, the State may not, consistently with the spirit of the First Amendment, contract the spectrum of available knowledge. The right of freedom of speech and press includes not only the right to utter or to print, but the right to distribute, the right to receive, the right to read and freedom of inquiry, freedom of thought, and freedom to teach, indeed the freedom of the entire university community. Without those peripheral rights the specific rights would be less secure. And so we reaffirm the principle of the *Pierce* and the *Meyer* cases.

In *NAACP v. Alabama,* we protected the "freedom to associate and privacy in one's associations," noting that freedom of association was a peripheral First Amendment right. . . .

The foregoing cases suggest that specific guarantees in the Bill of Rights have penumbras, formed by emanations from those guarantees that help give them life and substance. Various guarantees create zones of privacy. The right of association contained in the penumbra of the First Amendment is one, as we have seen. The Third Amendment in its prohibition against the quartering of soldiers "in any house" in time of peace without the consent of the owner is another facet of that privacy. The Fourth Amendment explicitly affirms the "right of the people to be secure in their persons, houses, papers, and effects, against unreasonable searches and seizures." The Fifth Amendment in its Self-Incrimination Clause enables the citizen to create a zone of privacy which government may not force him to surrender to his detriment. The Ninth Amendment provides: "The enumeration in the Constitution, of certain rights, shall not be construed to deny or disparage others retained by the people."

The present case concerns a relationship lying within the zone of privacy created by several fundamental constitutional guarantees. And it concerns a law which, in forbidding the use of contraceptives rather than regulating their manufacture or sale, seeks to achieve its goals by means having a maximum destructive impact upon that relationship. Would we allow the police to search the sacred precincts of marital bedrooms for telltale signs of the use of contraceptives? The very idea is repulsive to the notions of privacy surrounding the marriage relationship. . . .

We deal with a right of privacy older than the Bill of Rights—older than our political parties, older than our school system. Marriage is a coming together for better or for worse, hopefully enduring, and intimate to the degree of being sacred. It is an association that promotes a way of life, not causes; a harmony in living, not political faiths; a bilateral loyalty, not commercial or social projects. Yet it is an association for as noble a purpose as any involved in our prior decisions.

Reversed.

32

Miranda v. Arizona (1966)

MR. CHIEF JUSTICE WARREN delivered the opinion of the Court.

The cases before us raise questions which go to the roots of our concepts of American criminal jurisprudence: the restraints society must observe consistent with the Federal Constitution in prosecuting individuals for crime. More specifically, we deal with the admissibility of statements obtained from an individual who is subjected to custodial police interrogation and the necessity for procedures which assure that the individual is accorded his privilege under the Fifth Amendment to the Constitution not to be compelled to incriminate himself.

We dealt with certain phases of this problem recently in *Escobedo v. Illinois,* 378 U.S. 478 (1964). There, as in the four cases before us, law enforcement officials took the defendant into custody and interrogated him in a police station for the purpose of obtaining a confession. The police did not effectively advise him of his right to remain silent or of his right to consult with his

Source: U.S. Supreme Court, *Miranda v. Arizona,* 1966.

attorney. Rather, they confronted him with an alleged accomplice who accused him of having perpetrated a murder. When the defendant denied the accusation and said "I didn't shoot Manuel, you did it," they handcuffed him and took him to an interrogation room. There, while handcuffed and standing, he was questioned for four hours until he confessed. During the interrogation, the police denied his request to speak to his attorney, and they prevented his retained attorney, who had come to the police station, from consulting with him. At his trial, the State, over his objection, introduced the confession against him. We held that the statements thus made were constitutionally inadmissible.

This case has been the subject of judicial interpretation and spirited legal debate since it was decided two years ago. Both state and federal courts, in assessing its implications, have arrived at varying conclusions. A wealth of scholarly material has been written tracing its ramifications and underpinnings. Police and prosecutor have speculated on its range and desirability. We granted certiorari in these cases, 382 U.S. 924, 925, 937, in order further to explore some facets of the problems, thus exposed, of applying the privilege against self-incrimination to in-custody interrogation, and to give concrete constitutional guidelines for law enforcement agencies and courts to follow.

We start here, as we did in *Escobedo,* with the premise that our holding is not an innovation in our jurisprudence, but is an application of principles long recognized and applied in other settings. We have undertaken a thorough re-examination of the *Escobedo* decision and the principles it announced, and we reaffirm it. That case was but an explication of basic rights that are enshrined in our Constitution—that "No person . . . shall be compelled in any criminal case to be a witness against himself," and that "the accused shall . . . have the Assistance of Counsel"—rights which were put in jeopardy in that case through official overbearing. These precious rights were fixed in our Constitution only after centuries of persecution and struggle. And in the words of Chief Justice Marshall, they were secured "for ages to come, and . . . designed to approach immortality as nearly as human institutions can approach it," *Cohens v. Virginia,* 6 Wheat. 264, 387 (1821).

. . .

Our holding will be spelled out with some specificity in the pages which follow but briefly stated it is this: the prosecution may not use statements, whether exculpatory or inculpatory, stemming from custodial interrogation of the defendant unless it demonstrates the use of procedural safeguards effective to secure the privilege against self-incrimination. By custodial interrogation, we mean questioning initiated by law enforcement officers after a person has been taken into custody or otherwise deprived of his freedom of action in any significant way. As for the procedural safeguards to be employed, unless other fully effective means are devised to inform accused persons of their right of silence and to assure a continuous opportunity to exercise it, the following measures are required. Prior to any questioning, the person must be warned that he has a right to remain silent, that any statement he does make may be used as evidence against him, and that he has a right to the presence of an attorney, either retained or appointed. The defendant may waive effectuation of these rights, provided the waiver is made voluntarily, knowingly and intelligently. If, however, he indicates in any manner and at any stage of the process that he wishes to consult with an attorney before speaking there can be no questioning. Likewise, if the individual is alone and indicates in any manner that he does not wish to be interrogated, the police may not question him. The mere fact that he may have answered some questions or volunteered some statements on his own does not deprive him of the right to refrain from answering any further inquiries until he has consulted with an attorney and thereafter consents to be questioned.

I

The constitutional issue we decide in each of these cases is the admissibility of statements obtained from a defendant questioned while in custody or otherwise deprived of his freedom of action in any significant way. In each, the defendant was questioned by police officers, detectives, or a prosecuting attorney in a room in which he was cut off from the outside world. In none of these cases was the defendant given a full and effective warning of his rights at the outset of the interrogation process. In all the cases, the questioning elicited oral admissions, and in three of them, signed statements as well which were admitted at their trials. They all thus share salient features—incommunicado interrogation of individuals in a police-dominated atmosphere, resulting in self-incriminating statements without full warnings of constitutional rights.

An understanding of the nature and setting of this in-custody interrogation is essential to our decisions today. The difficulty in depicting what transpires at such interrogations stems from the fact that in this country they have largely taken place incommunicado. From extensive factual studies undertaken in the early 1930's, including the famous Wickersham Report to Congress by a Presidential Commission, it is clear that police violence and the "third degree" flourished at that time. In a series of cases decided by this Court long after these studies, the police resorted to physical brutality—beating, hanging, whipping—and to sustained and protracted questioning incommunicado in order to extort confessions. The Commission on Civil Rights in 1961 found much evidence to indicate that "some policeman still resort to physical force to obtain confessions," 1961 Comm'n on Civil Rights Rep., Justice, pt. 5, 17. The use of physical brutality and violence is not, unfortunately, relegated to the past or to any part of the country. Only recently in Kings County, New York, the police brutally beat, kicked and placed lighted cigarette butts on the back of a potential witness under interrogation for the purpose of securing a statement incriminating a third party. . . .

To highlight the isolation and unfamiliar surroundings, the manuals instruct the police to display an air of confidence in the suspect's guilt and from outward appearance to maintain only an interest in confirming certain details. The guilt of the subject is to be posited as a fact. The interrogator should direct his comments toward the reasons why the subject committed the act, rather than court failure by asking the subject whether he did it. Like other men, perhaps the subject has had a bad family life, had an unhappy childhood, had too much to drink, had an unrequited desire for women. The officers are instructed to minimize the moral seriousness of the offense, to cast blame on the victim or on society. These tactics are designed to put the subject in a psychological state where his story is but an elaboration of what the police purport to know already—that he is guilty. Explanations to the contrary are dismissed and discouraged. . . .

From these representative samples of interrogation techniques, the setting prescribed by the manuals and observed in practice becomes clear. In essence, it is this: To be alone with the subject is essential to prevent distraction and to deprive him of any outside support. The aura of confidence in his guilt undermines his will to resist. He merely confirms the preconceived story the police seek to have him describe. Patience and persistence, at times relentless questioning, are employed. To obtain a confession, the interrogator must "patiently maneuver himself or his quarry into a position from which the desired objective may be obtained." When normal procedures fail to produce the needed result, the police may resort to deceptive stratagems such as giving false legal advice. It is important to keep the subject off balance, for example, by trading on his insecurity about himself or his surroundings. The police then persuade, trick, or cajole him out of exercising his constitutional rights.

Even without employing brutality, the "third degree" or the specific stratagems described above, the very fact of custodial interrogation exacts a heavy toll on individual liberty and trades on the weakness of individuals. This fact may be illustrated simply by referring to three confession cases decided by this Court in the Term immediately preceding our *Escobedo* decision. In *Townsend v. Sain,* 372 U.S. 293 (1963), the defendant was a 19-year-old heroin addict, described as a "near mental defective," id., at 307–310. The defendant in *Lynumn v. Illinois,* 372 U.S. 528 (1963), was a woman who confessed to the arresting officer after being importuned to "cooperate" in order to prevent her children from being taken by relief authorities. This Court as in those cases reversed the conviction of a defendant in *Haynes v. Washington,* 373 U.S. 503 (1963), whose persistent request during his interrogation was to phone his wife or attorney. In other settings, these individuals might have exercised their constitutional rights. In the incommunicado police-dominated atmosphere, they succumbed.

In the cases before us today, given this background, we concern ourselves primarily with this interrogation atmosphere and the evils it can bring. In No. 759, *Miranda v. Arizona,* the police arrested the defendant and took him to a special interrogation room where they secured a confession. In No. 760, *Vignera v. New York,* the defendant made oral admissions to the police after interrogation in the afternoon, and then signed an inculpatory statement upon being questioned by an assistant district attorney later the same evening. In No. 761, *Westover v. United States,* the defendant was handed over to the Federal Bureau of Investigation by local authorities after they had detained and interrogated him for a lengthy period, both at night and the following morning. After some two hours of questioning, the federal officers had obtained signed statements from the defendant. Lastly, in No. 584, *California v. Stewart,* the local police held the defendant five days in the station and interrogated him on nine separate occasions before they secured his inculpatory statement.

In these cases, we might not find the defendants' statements to have been involuntary in traditional terms. Our concern for adequate safeguards to protect precious Fifth Amendment rights is, of course, not lessened in the slightest. In each of the cases, the defendant was thrust into an unfamiliar atmosphere and run through menacing police interrogation procedures. The potentiality for compulsion is forcefully apparent, for example, in *Miranda,* where the indigent Mexican defendant was a seriously disturbed individual with pronounced sexual fantasies, and in *Stewart,* in which the defendant was an indigent Los Angeles Negro who had dropped out of school in the sixth grade. To be sure, the records do not evince overt physical coercion or patent psychological ploys. The fact remains that in none of these cases did the officers undertake to afford appropriate safeguards at the outset of the interrogation to insure that the statements were truly the product of free choice.

It is obvious that such an interrogation environment is created for no purpose other than to subjugate the individual to the will of his examiner. This atmosphere carries its own badge of intimidation. To be sure, this is not physical intimidation, but it is equally destructive of human dignity. The current practice of incommunicado interrogation is at odds with one of our Nation's most cherished principles—that the individual may not be compelled to incriminate himself. Unless adequate protective devices are employed to dispel the compulsion inherent in custodial surroundings, no statement obtained from the defendant can truly be the product of his free choice. . . .

Accordingly we hold that an individual held for interrogation must be clearly informed that he has the right to consult with a lawyer and to have the lawyer with him during interrogation under the system for protecting the privilege we delineate today. As with the warnings of the right to remain silent and that anything stated can be used in evidence against him, this warning is an absolute prerequisite to interrogation. No amount of circumstantial evidence that the person may have been aware of this right will suffice to stand in its stead. Only through such a warning is there ascertainable assurance that the accused was aware of this right.

If an individual indicates that he wishes the assistance of counsel before any interrogation occurs, the authorities cannot rationally ignore or deny his request on the basis that the individual does not have or cannot afford a retained attorney. The financial ability of the individual has no relationship to the scope of the rights involved here. The privilege against self-incrimination secured by the Constitution applies to all individuals. The need for counsel in order to protect the privilege exists for the indigent as well as the affluent. In fact, were we to limit these constitutional rights to those who can retain an attorney, our decisions today would be of little significance. The cases before us as well as the vast majority of confession cases with which we have dealt in the past involve those unable to retain counsel. While authorities are not required to relieve the accused of his poverty, they have the obligation not to take advantage of indigence in the administration of justice. Denial of counsel to the indigent at the time of interrogation while allowing an attorney to those who can afford one would be no more supportable by reason or logic than the similar situation at trial and on appeal struck down in *Gideon v. Wainwright,* 372 U.S. 335 (1963), and *Douglas v. California,* 372 U.S. 353 (1963).

In order fully to apprise a person interrogated of the extent of his rights under this system then, it is necessary to warn him not only that he has the right to consult with an attorney, but also that if he is indigent a lawyer will be appointed to represent him. Without this additional warning, the admonition of the right to consult with counsel would often be understood as meaning only that he can consult with a lawyer if he has one or has the funds to obtain one. The warning of a right to counsel would be hollow if not couched in terms that would convey to the indigent—the person most often subjected to interrogation—the knowledge that he too has a right to have counsel present. As with the warnings of the right to remain silent and of the general right to counsel, only by effective and express explanation to the indigent of this right can there be assurance that he was truly in a position to exercise it.

Once warnings have been given, the subsequent procedure is clear. If the individual indicates in any manner, at any time prior to or during questioning, that he wishes to remain silent, the interrogation must cease. At this point he has shown that he intends to exercise his Fifth Amendment privilege; any statement taken after the person invokes his privilege cannot be other than the product of compulsion, subtle or otherwise. Without the right to cut off questioning, the setting of in-custody interrogation operates on the individual to overcome free choice in producing a statement after the privilege has been once invoked. If the individual states that he wants an attorney, the interrogation must cease until an attorney is present. At that time, the individual must have an opportunity to confer with the attorney and to have him present during any subsequent questioning. If the individual cannot obtain an attorney and he indicates that he wants one before speaking to police, they must respect his decision to remain silent.

This does not mean, as some have suggested, that each police station must have a "station house lawyer" present at all times to advise prisoners. It does mean, however, that if police propose to interrogate a person they must make known to him that he is entitled to a lawyer and that if he cannot afford one, a lawyer will be provided for him prior to any interrogation. If authorities conclude that they will not provide counsel during a reasonable period of time in which investigation in the field is carried out, they may refrain from doing so without violating the person's Fifth Amendment privilege so long as they do not question him during that time.

If the interrogation continues without the presence of an attorney and a statement is taken, a heavy burden rests on the government to demonstrate that the defendant knowingly and intelligently waived his privilege against self-incrimination and his right to retained or appointed counsel. *Escobedo v. Illinois,* 378 U.S. 478, 490, n. 14. This Court has always set high standards of proof for the waiver of constitutional rights, *Johnson v. Zerbst,* 304 U.S. 458 (1938), and we re-assert these standards as applied to in-custody interrogation. Since the State is responsible for establishing the isolated circumstances under which the interrogation takes place and has the only means of making available corroborated evidence of warnings given during incommunicado interrogation, the burden is rightly on its shoulders. . . .

The principles announced today deal with the protection which must be given to the privilege against self-incrimination when the individual is first subjected to police interrogation while in custody at the station or otherwise deprived of his freedom of action in any significant way. It is at this point that our adversary system of criminal proceedings commences, distinguishing itself at the outset from the inquisitorial system recognized in some countries. Under the system of warnings we delineate today or under any other system which may be devised and found effective, the safeguards to be erected about the privilege must come into play at this point.

Our decision is not intended to hamper the traditional function of police officers investigating crime. See *Escobedo v. Illinois,* 378 U.S. 478, 492. When an individual is in custody on probable cause, the police may, of course, seek out evidence in the field to be used at trial against him. Such investigation may include inquiry of persons not under restraint. General on-the-scene questioning as to facts surrounding a crime or other general questioning of citizens in the fact-finding process is not affected by our holding. It is an act of responsible citizenship for individuals to give whatever information they may have to aid in law enforcement. In such situations the compelling atmosphere inherent in the process of in-custody interrogation is not necessarily present.

In dealing with statements obtained through interrogation, we do not purport to find all confessions inadmissible. Confessions remain a proper element in law enforcement. Any statement given freely and voluntarily without any compelling influences is, of course, admissible in evidence. The fundamental import of the privilege while an individual is in custody is not whether he is allowed to talk to the police without the benefit of warnings and counsel, but whether he can be interrogated. There is no requirement that police stop a person who enters a police station and states that he wishes to confess to a crime, or a person who calls the police to offer a confession or any other statement he desires to make. Volunteered statements of any kind are not barred by the Fifth Amendment and their admissibility is not affected by our holding today.

To summarize, we hold that when an individual is taken into custody or otherwise deprived of his freedom by the authorities in any significant way and is subjected to questioning, the privilege against self-incrimination is jeopardized. Procedural safeguards must be employed to protect the privilege, and unless other fully effective means are adopted to notify the person of his right of silence and to assure that the exercise of the right will be scrupulously honored, the following measures are required. He must be warned prior to any questioning that he has the right to remain silent, that anything he says can be used against him in a court of law, that he has the right to the presence of an attorney, and that if he cannot afford an attorney one will be appointed for him prior to any questioning if he so desires. Opportunity to exercise these rights must be afforded to him throughout the interrogation. After such warnings have been given, and such opportunity afforded him, the individual may knowingly and intelligently waive these rights and agree to answer questions or make a statement. But unless and until such warnings and waiver are demonstrated by the prosecution at trial, no evidence obtained as a result of interrogation can be used against him.

IV

A recurrent argument made in these cases is that society's need for interrogation outweighs the privilege. This argument is not unfamiliar to this Court. See, e.g., *Chambers v. Florida*, 309 U.S. 227, 240–241 (1940). The whole thrust of our foregoing discussion demonstrates that the Constitution has prescribed the rights of the individual when confronted with the power of government when it provided in the Fifth Amendment that an individual cannot be compelled to be a witness against himself. That right cannot be abridged. . . .

If the individual desires to exercise his privilege, he has the right to do so. This is not for the authorities to decide. An attorney may advise his client not to talk to police until he has had an opportunity to investigate the case, or he may wish to be present with his client during any police questioning. In doing so an attorney is merely exercising the good professional judgment he has been taught. This is not cause for considering the attorney a menace to law enforcement. He is merely carrying out what he is sworn to do under his oath—to protect to the extent of his ability the rights of his client. In fulfilling this responsibility the attorney plays a vital role in the administration of criminal justice under our Constitution.

In announcing these principles, we are not unmindful of the burdens which law enforcement officials must bear, often under trying circumstances. We also fully recognize the obligation of all citizens to aid in enforcing the criminal laws. This Court, while protecting individual rights, has always given ample latitude to law enforcement agencies in the legitimate exercise of their duties. The limits we have placed on the interrogation process should not constitute an undue interference with a proper system of law enforcement. As we have noted, our decision does not in any way preclude police from carrying out their traditional investigatory functions. Although confessions may play an important role in some convictions, the cases before us present graphic examples of the overstatement of the "need" for confessions. In each case authorities conducted interrogations ranging up to five days in duration despite the presence, through standard investigating practices, of considerable evidence against each defendant. Further examples are chronicled in our prior cases.

33

Roe v. Wade (1973)

Justice Blackmun delivered the opinion of the Court.

The Texas statutes that concern us here make it a crime to "procure an abortion," or to attempt one, except with respect to "an abortion procured or attempted by medical advice for the purpose of saving the life of the mother." Similar statutes are in existence in a majority of the States. . . .

The principle thrust of appellant's attack on the Texas statutes is that they improperly invade a right, said to be possessed by the pregnant woman, to choose to terminate her pregnancy. Appellant would discover this right in the concept of personal "liberty" embodied in the Fourteenth Amendment's Due Process Clause; or in personal, marital, familial, and sexual privacy said to be protected by the Bill of Rights or its penumbras; or among those rights reserved to the people by the Ninth Amendment. . . .

The Constitution does not explicitly mention any right of privacy. In a line of decisions, however, the Court has recognized that a right of personal privacy, or a guarantee of certain areas or zones of privacy, does exist under the Constitution. In varying contexts, the Court or individual Justices have, indeed, found at least the roots of that right in the First Amendment, *Stanley v. Georgia,* 394 U.S. 557 (1969); in the Fourth and Fifth Amendments, *Terry v. Ohio,* 392 U.S. 1 (1968); in the penumbras of the Bill of Rights, *Griswold v. Connecticut;* in the Ninth Amendment, id., at 486 (Goldberg, J., concurring); or in the concept of liberty guaranteed by the first section of the Fourteenth Amendment. These decisions make it clear that only personal rights that can be deemed "fundamental" or "implicit in the concept of ordered liberty," *Palko v. Connecticut,* 302 U.S. 319 (1937), are included in this guarantee of personal privacy. They also make it clear that the right has some extension to activities relating to marriage, procreation, contraception, family relationships, child rearing and education.

This right of privacy, whether it be founded in the Fourteenth Amendment's concept of personal liberty and restrictions upon state action, as we feel it is, or, as the District Court determined, in the Ninth Amendment's reservation of rights to the people, is broad enough to encompass a woman's decision whether or not to terminate her pregnancy. The detriment that the State would

---

Source: U.S. Supreme Court, *Roe v. Wade,* 1973.

impose upon the pregnant woman by denying this choice altogether is apparent. Specific and direct harm medically diagnosable even in early pregnancy may be involved. Maternity, or additional offspring, may force upon the woman a distressful life and future. Psychological harm may be imminent. Mental and physical health may be taxed by child care. There is also the distress, for all concerned, associated with the unwanted child, and there is the problem of bringing a child into a family already unable, psychologically and otherwise, to care for it. In other cases, as in this one, the additional difficulties and continuing stigma of unwed motherhood may be involved. All these are factors the woman and her responsible physician necessarily will consider in consultation.

On the basis of elements such as these, appellant and some amici argue that the woman's right is absolute and that she is entitled to terminate her pregnancy at whatever time, in whatever way, and for whatever reason she alone chooses. With this we do not agree. Appellant's arguments that Texas either has no valid interest at all in regulating the abortion decision, or no interest strong enough to support any limitation upon the woman's sole determination, is unpersuasive. The Court's decisions recognizing a right of privacy also acknowledge that some state regulation in areas protected by that right is appropriate. . . . A state may properly assert important interests in safeguarding health, in maintaining medical standards, and in protecting potential life. At some point in pregnancy, these respective interests become sufficiently compelling to sustain regulation of the factors that govern the abortion decision. The privacy right involved, therefore, cannot be said to be absolute. In fact, it is not clear to us that the claim asserted by some amici that one has an unlimited right to do with one's body as one pleases bears a close relationship to the right of privacy previously articulated in the Court's decisions. The Court has refused to recognize an unlimited right of this kind in the past.

We, therefore, conclude that the right of personal privacy includes the abortion decision, but that this right is not unqualified and must be considered against important state interests in regulation. . . .

Where certain "fundamental rights" are involved, the Court has held that regulation limiting these rights may be justified only by a "compelling state interest," and that legislative enactments must be narrowly drawn to express only the legitimate state interests at stake. . . .

Texas urges that . . . life begins at conception and is present throughout pregnancy, and that, therefore, the State has a compelling interest in protecting that life from and after conception. We need not resolve the difficult question of when life begins. When those trained in the respective disciplines of medicine, philosophy, and theology are unable to arrive at any consensus, the judiciary, at this point in the development of man's knowledge, is not in a position to speculate as to the answer.

[The Court concludes that the point where the state's interest in the life of the unborn fetus may supersede the woman's right to privacy is at viability— the point where the fetus is potentially able to live outside the mother's womb, albeit with aid. This occurs at approximately 7 months, but can occur as early as 24 weeks.]

. . . . [W]e do not agree that, by adopting one theory of life, Texas may override the rights of the pregnant woman that are at stake. We repeat, however, that the State does have an important and legitimate interest in preserving and protecting the health of the pregnant woman, whether she be a resident of the State or a non-resident who seeks medical consultation and treatment there, and that it has still another important and legitimate interest in protecting the potentiality of human life. These interests are separate and distinct. Each grows in substantiality as the woman approaches term and, at a point during pregnancy, each becomes "compelling."

With respect to the State's important and legitimate interest in the health of the mother, the "compelling" point, in the light of present medical knowledge, is at approximately the end of the first trimester. This is so because of the now-established medical fact, that until the end of the first trimester mortality in abortion may be less than mortality in normal childbirth. It follows that, from and after this point, a State may regulate the abortion procedure to the extent that the regulation reasonably relates to the preservation and protection of maternal health. Examples of permissible state regulation in this area are requirements as to the qualifications of the person who is to perform the abortion; as to the licensure of that person; as to the facility in which the procedure is to be performed, that is, whether it must be a hospital or may be a clinic or some other place of less-than-hospital status; as to the licensing of the facility; and the like.

This means, on the other hand, that, for the period of pregnancy prior to this "compelling" point, the attending physician, in consultation with his patient, is free to determine, without regulation by the State, that, in his medical judgment, the patient's pregnancy should be terminated. If that decision is reached, the judgment may be effectuated by an abortion free of interference by the State.

With respect to the State's important and legitimate interest in potential life, the "compelling" point is at viability. This is so because the fetus then presumably has the capability of meaningful life outside the mother's womb. State regulation protective of fetal life after viability thus has both logical and biological justifications. If the State is interested in protecting fetal life after viability, it may go so far as to proscribe abortion during that period, except when it is necessary to preserve the life or health of the mother.

Review Questions

1. Why is it that the U.S. Supreme Court has evolved to be even stronger than the court envisioned by Alexander Hamilton in *Federalist* No. 78? How does a powerful court mesh with democratic ideals of accountability when it can overturn the acts of elected executives and legislators?

2. How did Chief Justice John Marshall use the *Marbury v. Madison* case to establish judicial review? How has judicial review evolved to make the U.S. Supreme Court so powerful?

3. Why did the *Brown v. Board of Education* decision reverse the "separate but equal" doctrine of the *Plessy v. Ferguson* case? Since the *Brown* decision outlawed racial segregation in the public schools in 1954, why are so many public schools still effectively segregated?

4. How did the logic behind the *Griswold* decision lead to future decisions regarding matters of sexual privacy? How can the Supreme Court in *Griswold* assert that there is a "right to privacy" when the word "privacy" does not even appear in the Constitution?

5. How does the fact that *Miranda* rights exist protect citizens from possible abuses by agents of the state—such as police? Does a suspect's right to have a lawyer present when being questioned necessarily hinder the police in obtaining the truth of a situation?

6. Was *Roe V. Wade* a pro-choice or pro-life decision? How logical is the *Roe* decision as medical technology increasingly makes it possible for younger and younger fetuses to survive?

Chapter 9

Foreign Policy

Foreign policy is the totality of a state's relations with and policies toward other states. According to George F. Kennan, *Realities of American Foreign Policy* (1954): "A political society does not live to conduct foreign policy; it would be more correct to say that it conducts foreign policy in order to live." A nation's foreign policy, even though it may be largely the prerogative of an executive branch, is always grounded in its domestic policy and must be defined in terms of national interest.

As an academic discipline international relations focuses upon the relations among states and other actors in the international system. It examines the political, military, and economic interactions among nations; the analysis of who gets what, when, and how on the world's political stage. International relations did not really develop as an academic discipline until the twentieth century—partly because traditional political philosophy focused on the principles and practices of governance within political units rather than on the relations between them.

Two intellectual traditions underpin the contemporary study of international relations and the practice of foreign policy: (I) the Grotian tradition, after Hugo Grotius (1583–1645), the Dutch jurist considered the "founder of international law," emphasizes that there is a society of states bound by common rules, customs and shared norms, and (2) Hobbesian realism, after Thomas Hobbes (1588–1679), the English political philosopher and social contract theorist, which focuses on the anarchical nature of the international system and sees international relations as dominated by the political struggle for power.

During the period between the First and Second World Wars, the Grotian tradition with its emphasis on the norms of international society was not only dominant but became closely bound up with an idealism which was based upon the desire fundamentally to transform international relations in ways which would ensure that the horror of the First World War would never be repeated. Consequently, the studies of international relations done during this period were predominantly prescriptive (what should be) in tone and aim. Idealists believed that flawed political arrangements, especially international anarchy and secret diplomacy, led to war—and had done so in 1914. The concomitant was that once the problems were correctly identified they could then be eradicated—so long as governments listened to the prescriptions.

The problem with the idealist approach according to Edward H. Carr (1892–1982), the British diplomat and scholar who was one of the first modern proponents of political realism, was that "wishing prevailed over thinking." Although the development of realism grew out of the reaction against idealism, its roots can be traced back to antiquity. Realism's main theorist in the post World War II period was Hans J. Morgenthau (1904–1980) who assumed that international politics, like all politics, was a struggle for power and that states defined their national interest in terms of power.

Even today foreign policy issues are frequently examined by placing them on a continuum that starts with the purest idealism and extends to an almost criminal realism. The United Nations was founded on idealist sentiments in 1945 after a world war was fought and won to repulse the criminal realism of Germany and Japan. Foreign policy analysts constantly measure the degree of idealism and realism in considering actions. Too much idealism and you may be taken advantage of— Uncle Sam as "Uncle Sucker." Too much realism and you may be seen as a bully and engender unnecessary enmity. How much of each? That's the essential question of foreign policymaking.

A decision to go to war is arguably the most important public policy decision made by a state. Not surprisingly then, the four selections in this chapter all deal with the issues of war and peace—and how idealism and realism influence all such considerations. All intellectual discussions of war and peace begin with Thucydides (455–400 B.C.E.), the Athenian historian and political analyst whose *History of the Peloponnesian War* remains the most influential study of war and politics ever written.

His *History* includes the famous observation on what causes war. "What made war inevitable was the growth of Athenian power and the fear which this caused in Sparta." This has subsequently been termed the security dilemma, a situation in which one state takes action to enhance its security only to have this action seen as threatening by other states. The result is that the other states engage in counter-measures, which intensify the first state's insecurity. The dilemma arises from the fact that because of this process, actions taken to enhance security can actually end up diminishing it. There is also a dilemma for the second state in that if it regards the action as defensive and takes no counters it leaves itself vulnerable, whereas if it responds vigorously, it will exacerbate the first state's insecurity.

The Melian debate (reprinted here) refers to Thucydides' account in his *History* of the discussions between the Athenians and the Melians about whether the island of Melos should surrender to the obviously superior Athenian forces. Melos was a colony of Sparta and, because of this, had refused to join the Athenian empire. Before attacking Melos, the Athenians decided to offer the Melians the choice between war and surrender. Their arguments and the rejoinders are full of ideas about the interactions of great and small powers, about the balance of power and the role of power in political relations.

The Athenians made no pretense that their arguments were couched in terms of justice, contending instead that "when these matters are discussed by practical people, the standard of justice depends on the equality of power to compel and in fact the strong do what they have the power to do and the weak accept what they have to accept." The reason the Athenians put forward for the conquest of Melos was one of self-interest and credibility. The argument was that if Athens was seen to be on friendly terms with Melos and failed to attack, this would be viewed by the other subject peoples of Athens as a sign of weakness—a perception that would threaten the security of Athens.

Against this line of reasoning the Melians contended that military action against them would be counterproductive for Athens as an attack on Melos would frighten other neutral states that would fear for their own safety in the future and would consequently ally against what they would see as a potential threat to themselves. In this argument, it is possible to discern a sophisticated and subtle kind of balance of power thinking: although Melos had little power, its inferiority would be offset by its alliance with Sparta. Against Athenian arguments that this alliance meant very little, and that the Melians were "most completely deluded" in counting on the Spartans, the Melians claimed that it was not in Sparta's self interest to betray them. This would only result in Sparta losing the confidence of its friends and thus be of benefit to its enemies.

The Athenians were not convinced, however, and faced the Melians with a choice. "You will see that there is nothing disgraceful in giving way to the greatest city in Hellas [Greece] when she is offering you such reasonable terms—alliance on a tribute-paying basis and liberty to enjoy your own property. And, when you are allowed to choose between war and safety, you will not be so insensitively arrogant as to make the wrong choice." The Athenian delegation essentially argued that the safe rule was to "stand up to one's equals, to behave with deference towards one's superiors and to treat one's inferiors with moderation." Although this can be understood as an attempt to use coercion rather than resort to brute military force, it failed.

The final outcome was that the Melians decided to fight. When reinforcements came from Athens, however, the Melians were forced to surrender unconditionally. The Athenians then killed all the men and sold the women and children into slavery. So much for depending on one's Spartan allies! A military policy dependent upon allies to create a balance of power has ever since been considered only as strong as the credibility of those allies. A balance with allies that won't fight with you is no balance at all.

While Thucydides' *History* contains the origins of balance of power theory, it is also the seminal work of political realism or realpolitik—the school of thought which examines political relations on the basis of might rather than right. Thucydides' concepts are often applied to politics—whether of the organizational or societal variety—premised on material or practical factors rather than on theoretical or ethical considerations. This is the politics of realism; an injunction not to allow wishful thinking or sentimentality to cloud one's judgment.

Carl Maria von Clausewitz (1780–1831), was the Prussian general who wrote *On War* (1832), the most famous book on Western military strategy and tactics. All students of public policy should be familiar with at least these three of his concepts:

1. That "war is the continuation of policy by other means" meaning that, if diplomacy or other efforts fail to get you what you want, war is "simply" your next policy option. This is realism in action.

2. That "war is the province of uncertainty; three-fourths of the things on which action in war is based lie hidden in the fog." The fog of war is the descriptive phrase for the confusion inherent in combat. It is as if a literal fog descends upon the battlefield and blinds the combatants to what the enemy and even other elements of their own forces are doing. Today, wherever far-flung or large-scale operations have to be coordinated, whether military or managerial, fog or uncertainty is always a possibility. The field of management information systems has grown up in recent decades to reduce the inevitable fog to manageable proportions. But the reduction mechanisms themselves—computer data and memorandums in a seemingly endless stream—often create more problems than the fog they were designed to dispel.

3. That no matter how well designed an operation may be, "friction"—the reality of delays and misunderstandings—inevitably makes its execution less than ideal. This is why Clausewitz said: "Arrange maneuvers in peacetime to include . . . causes of friction, in order that the judgment . . . of the separate leaders may be exercised. . . . It is of immense importance that the soldier . . . whatever be his rank, should not see for the first time in war those phenomena of war which, when seen for the first time, astonish and perplex him."

Reprinted here is the best known portion of *On War,* "War as an Instrument of Policy."

Containment, to contain the expansion of communist influence, was the underlying basis of U.S. foreign and military policy during the Cold War which lasted from the end of World War II to the demise of the Soviet Union in 1991. George F. Kennan, (1904–) was the United States career foreign service officer and Ambassador to Yugoslavia (1961–1963) and the Soviet Union (1952) who was literally the author of the United States policy of containment in the post World War II period. Kennan's famous 8,000 word "long telegram" from Moscow to the State Department in 1946 outlined what he regarded as Soviet objectives as well as the need for a United States response. The ideas in the telegram subsequently provided the basis for the Truman Doctrine and Kennan's article "The Sources of Soviet Conduct" which appeared under the X pseudonym in *Foreign Affairs* (1947). (The official author of this article was X because Kennan wrote it while serving as a Foreign Service officer; but it was never a secret who the actual author was.) This provided the public rationale for the United States policy of containment.

Although Kennan used military analogies in this article, reprinted here, he saw containment as essentially political in character and believed that it was crucial that the United States rebuild Western Europe economically so that it provided indigenous countervailing power to that of the Soviet Union. Kennan believed that Soviet expansionist probes were not the result of feelings about recent injustices from the West, but of long term Russian expanionist tendencies which had to be opposed. President George H. W. Bush said in a speech at Texas A & M University on May 12, 1989: "Wise men . . . crafted the strategy of containment. They believed that the Soviet Union, denied the easy course of expansion, would turn inward and address the contradictions of its inefficient, repressive and inhumane system. And they were right. . . . Containment worked."

The domestic implications of the Truman Doctrine of containment were equally important. For example, the communist threat justified the Federal Aid Highway Act of 1956 (which built the U.S. interstate road network—the National Defense Highway System), the National Defense Education Act of 1958 (which provides loans and fellowships for students and grants to schools and colleges), and the National Aeronautics and Space Administration Act of 1958 (for the peaceful exploration of space).

Of course, Truman never envisioned his doctrine supporting local public works or graduate student education. But the Cold War goal of defeating communism meant that anything that could be presented as part of this international struggle would get a more sympathetic legislative reception. Thus graduate student fellowships and academic research in almost every field were justified as aiding the national defense effort. As more and more people got with the plan, it turned out that there was hardly any worthwhile government project that could not be designed, however farfetched, to defeat communism. It turned out that every single member of Congress was willing, indeed eager, to fight the worldwide Communist menace by bringing pork barrel projects home to his or her district.

This combination of limited wars on the perimeter, interstate highways, and fellowships for graduate students was more than the Soviet Union could bear. When the great Communist experiment finally failed, credit was given to the containment policies of the Truman administration and its successors and more recently to the Reagan administration's massive arms buildup that the Soviets could not match.

Samuel P. Huntington (1927–), author of a classic analysis of civil-military relations, *The Professional Soldier* (1957), has long been a highly respected Harvard University political scientist. But the events of September 11, 2001, seem to have made him a prophet of almost biblical proportions because a few years prior he argued that the wars of the future are likely to be of civilizations rather than states. Huntington's analysis, which initially appeared as "The Clash of Civilizations" in *Foreign Affairs* (1993), has generated intense debate and controversy. Although Huntington subsequently developed the argument into a book entitled *The Clash of Civilizations and the Making of World Order* (1996), we have reprinted the initial article.

According to Huntington, world politics is entering a new phase in which the fundamental sources of conflict will not be primarily ideological or economic, but cultural. Although Huntington conceds that nation-states will remain the most powerful actors in world affairs, he contends that the principal conflicts of global politics will occur between nations and groups of different civilizations. As he puts it, "the fault lines between civilizations will be the battle lines of the future." He suggests that the differences among the world's seven or eight major civilizations—Western, Confucian, Japanese, Islamic, Hindu, Slavic-Orthodox, Latin American and possibly African—are fundamental in character. Because the world is becoming a smaller place, interactions among these civilizations are becoming more intense.

Additionally, this clash appears to exist at two distinct but related levels, "At the micro-level, adjacent groups along the fault lines between civilizations struggle, often violently, over the control of territory and each other. At the macro-level, states from different civilizations compete for relative military and economic power, struggle over the control of international institutions and third parties, and competitively promote their particular political and religious values."

Almost a decade before the War on Terror Huntington predicted that the clash between the West and Islam was likely to become more rather than less intense. Part of the reason for this is that the West is now at an extraordinary peak of power in relation to other civilizations. Not surprisingly, there has been a hostile reaction to Western dominance.

Huntington's thesis is not without its critics. For example, he seems to be attributing civilization-related motives to Chinese arms sales which might have more to do with economic opportunity than with an affinity or tacit alliance with Islamic states. Huntington also downplays the potential for clashes among states that are part of the same civilization. Nevertheless, Huntington's prophetic analysis has given an alternative name to the War on Terror (The Clash of Civilizations) and has indirectly helped to justify President George W. Bush's policy of preemption.

34

History of the Peloponnesian War: The Melian Debate (5th century B.C.E.)

Thucydides

Next summer Alcibiades sailed to Argos with twenty ships and seized 300 Argive citizens who were still suspected of being pro-Spartan. These were put by the Athenians into the nearby islands under Athenian control.

The Athenians also made an expedition against the island of Melos. They had thirty of their own ships, six from Chios, and two from Lesbos; 1,200 hoplites, 300 archers, and twenty mounted archers, all from Athens; and about 1,500 hoplites from the allies and the islanders.

The Melians are a colony from Sparta. They had refused to join the Athenian empire like the other islanders, and at first had remained neutral without helping either side; but afterwards, when the Athenians had brought force to bear on them by laying waste their land, they had become open enemies of Athens.

Now the generals Cleomedes, the son of Lycomedes, and Tisias, the son of Tisimachus, encamped with the above force in Melian territory and, before doing any harm to the land, first of all sent representatives to negotiate. The Melians did not invite these representatives to speak before the people, but asked them to make the statement for which they had come in front of the governing body and the few. The Athenian representatives then spoke as follows:

Athenians: So we are not to speak before the people, no doubt in case the mass of the people should hear once and for all and without interruption an argument from us which is both persuasive and incontrovertible, and should so be led astray. This, we realize, is your motive in bringing us here to speak before the few. Now suppose that you who sit here should make assurance doubly sure. Suppose that you, too, should refrain from dealing with every point in detail in a set speech, and should instead interrupt us whenever we say something controversial and deal with that before going on to the next point? Tell us first whether you approve of this suggestion of ours.

The Council of the Melians replied as follows:

Melians: No one can object to each of us putting forward our own views in a calm atmosphere. That is perfectly reasonable. What is scarcely consistent with such a proposal is the present threat, indeed the certainly, of your making war on us. We see that you have come prepared to judge the argument your-selves, and that the likely end of it all will be either war, if we prove that we are in the right, and so refuse to surrender, or else slavery.

Athenians: If you are going to spend the time in enumerating your suspi-cions about the future, or if you have met here for any other reason except to look the facts in the face and on the basis of these facts to consider how you can save your city from destruction, there is no point in our going on with this discussion. If, however, you will do as we suggest, then we will speak on.

Melians: It is natural and understandable that people who are placed as we are should have recourse to all kinds of arguments and different points of view. However, you are right in saying that we are met together here to discuss the safety of our country and, if you will have it so, the discussion shall pro-ceed on the lines that you have laid down.

Athenians: Then we on our side will use no fine phrases saying, for exam-ple, that we have a right to our empire because we defeated the Persians, or that we have come against you now because of the injuries you have done us—a great mass of words that nobody would believe. And we ask you on your side not to imagine that you will influence us by saying that you, though a colony of Sparta, have not joined Sparta in the war, or that you have never done us any harm. Instead we recommend that you should try to get what it is possible for you to get, taking into consideration what we both really do think; since you know as well as we do that, when these matters are discussed by practical people, the standard of justice depends on the equality of power to compel and that in fact the strong do what they have the power to do and the weak accept what they have to accept.

Melians: Then in our view (since you force us to leave justice out of account and to confine ourselves to self-interest)—in our view it is at any rate useful that you should not destroy a principle that is to the general good of all men—namely, that in the case of all who fall into danger there should be such a thing as fair play and just dealing, and that such people should be allowed to use and to profit by arguments that fall short of a mathematical accuracy. And this is a principle which affects you as much as anybody, since your own fall would be visited by the most terrible vengeance and would be an example to the world.

Athenians: As for us, even assuming that our empire does come to an end, we are not despondent about what would happen next. One is not so much frightened by being conquered by a power which rules over others, as Sparta does (not that we are concerned with Sparta now), as of what would happen if a ruling power is attacked and defeated by its own subjects. So far as this point is concerned, you can leave it to us to face the risks involved. What we shall do now is to show you that it is for the good of our own empire that we are here and that it is for the preservation of your city that we shall say what we are going to say. We do not want any trouble in bringing you into our empire, and we want you to be spared for the good both of yourselves and of ourselves.

Melians: And how could it be just as good for us to be the slaves as for you to be the masters?

Athenians: You, by giving in, would save yourselves from disaster; we, by not destroying you, would be able to profit from you.

Melians: So you would not agree to our being neutral, friends instead of enemies, but allies of neither side?

Athenians: No, because it is not so much your hostility that injures us; it is rather the case that, if we were on friendly terms with you, our subjects would regard that as a sign of weakness in us, whereas your hatred is evidence of our power.

Melians: Is that your subjects' idea of fair play—that no distinction should be made between people who are quite unconnected with you and people who are mostly your own colonists or else rebels whom you have conquered?

Athenians: So far as right and wrong are concerned they think that there is no difference between the two, that those who still preserve their independence do so because they are strong, and that if we fail to attack them it is because we are afraid. So that by conquering you we shall increase not only the size but the security of our empire. We rule the sea and you are islanders, and weaker islanders too than the others; it is therefore particularly important that you should not escape.

Melians: But do you think there is no security for you in what we suggest? For here again, since you will not let us mention justice, but tell us to give in to your interests, we, too, must tell you what our interests are and, if yours and ours happen to coincide, we must try to persuade you of the fact. Is it not certain that you will make enemies of all states who are at present neutral, when they see what is happening here and naturally conclude that in course of time you will attack them too? Does not this mean that you are strengthening the enemies you have already and are forcing others to become your enemies even against their intentions and their inclinations?

Athenians: As a matter of fact we are not so much frightened of states on the continent. They have their liberty, and this means that it will be a long time before they begin to take precautions against us. We are more concerned about islanders like yourselves, who are still unsubdued, or subjects who have already become embittered by the constraint which our empire imposes on them. These are the people who are most likely to act in a reckless manner and to bring themselves and us, too, into the most obvious danger.

Melians: Then surely, if such hazards are taken by you to keep your empire and by your subjects to escape from it, we who are still free would show ourselves great cowards and weaklings if we failed to face everything that comes rather than submit to slavery.

Athenians: No, not if you are sensible. This is no fair fight, with honour on one side and shame on the other. It is rather a question of saving your lives and not resisting those who are far too strong for you.

Melians: Yet we know that in war fortune sometimes makes the odds more level than could be expected from the difference in numbers of the two sides. And if we surrender, then all our hope is lost at once, whereas, so long as we remain in action, there is still a hope that we may yet stand upright.

Athenians: Hope, that comforter in danger! If one already has solid advantages to fall back upon, one can indulge in hope. It may do harm, but will not destroy one. But hope is by nature an expensive commodity, and those who are risking their all on one cast find out what it means only when they are already ruined; it never fails them in the period when such a knowledge would enable them to take precautions. Do not let this happen to you, you who are weak and whose fate depends on a single movement of the scale. And do not be like those people who, as so commonly happens, miss the chance of saving themselves in a human and practical way, and, when every clear and distinct hope has left them in their adversity, turn to what is blind and vague, to prophecies and oracles and such things which by encouraging hope lead men to ruin.

Melians: It is difficult, and you may be sure that we know it, for us to oppose your power and fortune, unless the terms be equal. Nevertheless we trust that the gods will give us fortune as good as yours, because we are standing for what is right against what is wrong; and as for what we lack in power, we trust that it will be made up for by our alliance with the Spartans, who are bound, if for no other reason, then for honour's sake, and because we are their kinsmen, to come to our help. Our confidence, therefore, is not so entirely irrational as you think.

Athenians: So far as the favour of the gods is concerned, we think we have as much right to that as you have. Our aims and our actions are perfectly consistent with the beliefs men hold about the gods and with the principles which govern their own conduct. Our opinion of the gods and our knowledge of men lead us to conclude that it is a general and necessary law of nature to rule wherever one can. This is not a law that we made ourselves, nor were we the first to act upon it when it was made. We found it already in existence, and we shall leave it to exist for every among those who come after us. We are merely acting in accordance with it, and we know that you or anybody else with the same power as ours would be acting in precisely the same way. And therefore, so far as the gods are concerned, we see no good reason why we should fear to be at a disadvantage. But with regard to your views about Sparta and your confidence that she, out of a sense of honour, will come to your aid, we must say that we congratulate you on your simplicity but do not envy you your folly. In matters that concern themselves or their own constitution the Spartans are quite remarkably good; as for their relations with others, that is a long story, but it can be expressed shortly and clearly by saying that of all people we know the Spartans are most conspicuous for believing that what they like doing is honourable and what suits their interests is just. And this kind of attitude is not going to be of much help to you in your absurd quest for safety at the moment.

Melians: But this is the very point when we can feel most sure. Their own self-interest will make them refuse to betray their own colonists, the Melians, for that would mean losing the confidence of their friends among the Hellenes and doing good to their enemies.

Athenians: You seem to forget that if one follows one's self-interest one wants to be safe, whereas the path of justice and honour involves one in danger. And, where danger is concerned, the Spartans are not, as a rule very venturesome.

Melians: But we think that they would even endanger themselves for our sake and count the risk more worth taking than in the case of others, because we are so close to the Peloponnese that they could operate more easily, and because they can depend on us more than on others, since we are of the same race and share the same feelings.

Athenians: Goodwill shown by the part that is asking for help does not mean security for the prospective ally. What is looked for is a positive preponderance of power in action. And the Spartans pay attention to this point even more than others do. Certainly they distrust their own native resources so much that when they attack a neighbour they bring a great army of allies with them. It is hardly likely therefore that, while we are in control of the sea, they will cross over to an island.

Melians: But they still might send others. The Cretan sea is a wide one, and it is harder for those who control it to intercept others than for those who want to slip through to do so safely. And even if they were to fail in this, they would turn against your own land and against those of your allies left unvisited by Brasidas. So, instead of troubling about a country which has nothing to do with you, you will find trouble nearer home, among your allies, and in your own country.

Athenians: It is a possibility, something that has in fact happened before. It may happen in your case, but you are well aware that the Athenians have never yet relinquished a single siege operation through fear of others. But we are somewhat shocked to find that, though you announced your intention of discussing how you could preserve yourselves, in all this talk you have said absolutely nothing which could justify a man in thinking that he could be preserved. Your chief points are concerned with what you hope may happen in the future, while your actual resources are too scanty to give you a chance of survival against the forces that are opposed to you at this moment. You will therefore be showing an extraordinary lack of common sense if, after you have asked us to retire from this meeting, you still fail to reach a conclusion wiser than anything you have mentioned so far. Do not be led astray by a false sense of honour—a thing which often brings men to ruin when they are faced with an obvious danger that somehow affects their pride. For in many cases men have still been able to see the dangers ahead of them, but this thing called dishonour, this word, by its own force of seduction, has drawn them into a state where they have surrendered to an idea, while in fact they have fallen voluntarily into irrevocable disaster, in dishonour that is all the more dishonourable because it has come to them from their own folly rather than their misfortune. You, if you take the right view, will be careful to avoid this. You will see that there is nothing disgraceful in giving way to the greatest city in Hellas when she is offering you such reasonable terms—alliance on a tribute-paying basis and liberty to enjoy your own property. And, when you are allowed to choose between war and safety, you will not be so insensitively arrogant as to make the wrong choice. This is the safe rule—to stand up to one's equals, to behave with deference towards one's superiors, and to treat one's inferiors with moderation. Think it over again, then, when we have withdrawn from the meeting, and let this be a point that constantly recurs to your minds—that you are discussing the fate of your country, that you have only one country, and that its future for good or ill depends on this one single decision which you are going to make.

The Athenians then withdrew from the discussion. The Melians, left to themselves, reached a conclusion which was much the same as they had indicated in their previous replies. Their answer was as follows:

Melians: Our decision, Athenians, is just the same as it was at first. We are not prepared to give up in a short moment the liberty which our city has enjoyed from its foundation for 700 years. We put our trust in the fortune that the gods will send and which has saved us up to now, and in the help of men—that is, of the Spartans; and so we shall try to save ourselves. But we invite you to allow us to be friends of yours and enemies to neither side, to make a treaty which shall be agreeable to both you and us, and so to leave our country.

The Melians made this reply, and the Athenians, just as they were breaking off the discussion, said:

Athenians: Well, at any rate, judging from this decision of yours, you seem to us quite unique in your ability to consider the future as something more certain than what is before your eyes, and to see uncertainties as realities, simply because you would like them to be so. As you have staked most on and trusted most in Spartans, luck, and hopes, so in all these you will find yourselves most completely deluded.

The Athenian representatives then went back to the army, and the Athenian generals, finding that the Melians would not submit, immediately commenced hostilities and built a wall completely around the city of Melos, dividing the work out among the various states. Later they left behind a garrison of some of their own and some allied troops to blockade the place by land and sea, and with the greater part of their army returned home. The force left behind stayed on and continued with the siege.

About the same time the Argives invaded Phliasia and were ambushed by the Phliasians and the exiles from Argos, losing about eighty men.

Then, too, the Athenians at Pylos captured a great quantity of plunder from Spartan territory. Not even after this did the Spartans renounce the treaty and make war, but they issued a proclamation saying that any of their people who wished to do so were free to make raids on the Athenians. The Corinthians also made some attacks on the Athenians because of private quarrels of their own, but the rest of the Peloponnesians stayed quiet.

Meanwhile the Melians made a night attack and captured the part of the Athenian lines opposite the market-place. They killed some of the troops, and then, after bringing in corn and everything else useful that they could lay their hands on, retired again and made no further move, while the Athenians took measures to make their blockade more efficient in future. So the summer came to an end.

In the following winter the Spartans planned to invade the territory of Argos, but when the sacrifices for crossing the frontier turned out unfavourably, they gave up the expedition. The fact that they had intended to invade made the Argives suspect certain people in their city, some of whom they arrested, though others succeeded in escaping.

About this same time the Melians again captured another part of the Athenian lines where there were only a few of the garrison on guard. As a result of this, another force came out afterwards from Athens under the command of Philocrates, the son of Demeas. Siege operations were now carried on vigorously and, as there was also some treachery from inside, the Melians surrendered unconditionally to the Athenians, who put to death all the men of military age whom they took, and sold the women and children as slaves. Melos itself they took over for themselves, sending out later a colony of 500 men.

35

On War: War as an Instrument of Policy (1832)

Carl von Clausewitz

Influence of the Political Object on the Military Object

We never find that a State joining in the cause of another State takes it up with the same earnestness as its own. An auxiliary Army of moderate strength is sent; if it is not successful, then the Ally looks upon the affair as in a manner ended, and tries to get out of it on the cheapest terms possible.

In European politics it has been usual for States to pledge themselves to mutual assistance by an alliance offensive and defensive, not so far that the one takes part in the interests and quarrels of the other, but only so far as to promise one another beforehand the assistance of a fixed, generally very moderate, contingent of troops, without regard to the object of the War or the scale on which it is about to be carried on by the principals. In a treaty of alliance of this kind the Ally does not look upon himself as engaged with the enemy in a War properly speaking, which should necessarily begin with a declaration of War and end with a treaty of peace. Still, this idea also is nowhere fixed with any distinctness, and usage varies one way and another.

The thing would have a kind of consistency, and it would be less embarrassing to the theory of War if this promised contingent of ten, twenty, or thirty thousand men was handed over entirely to the State engaged in War, so that it could be used as required; it might then be regarded as a subsidised force. But the usual practice is widely different. Generally the auxiliary force has its own Commander, who depends only on his own Government, and to whom it prescribes an object such as best suits the shilly-shally measures it has in view.

But even if two States go to War with a third, they do not always both look in like measure upon this common enemy as one that they must destroy or be destroyed by themselves. The business is often settled like a commercial

---

Source: Carl von Clausewitz, *On War*. J.J. Graham, trans., 1911.

transaction; each, according to the amount of the risk he incurs or the advantage to be expected, takes shares in the concern to the extent of 30,000 or 40,000 men, and acts as if he could not lose more than the amount of his investment.

Not only is this the point of view taken when a State comes to the assistance of another in a cause in which it has, in a manner, little concern, but even when both have a common and very considerable interest at stake nothing can be done except under diplomatic reservation, and the contracting parties usually only agree to furnish a small stipulated contingent, in order to employ the rest of the forces according to the special ends to which policy may happen to lead them.

This way of regarding Wars entered into by reason of alliances was quite general, and was only obliged to give place to the natural way in quite modern times, when the extremity of danger drove men's minds into the natural direction (as in the Wars *against* Buonaparte), and when the most boundless power compelled them to it (as *under* Buonaparte). It was an abnormal thing, an anomaly, for War and Peace are ideas which in their foundation can have no gradations; nevertheless it was no mere diplomatic offspring which the reason could look down upon, but deeply rooted in the natural limitedness and weakness of human nature.

Lastly, even in Wars carried on without Allies, the political cause of a War has a great influence on the method in which it is conducted.

If we only require from the enemy a small sacrifice, then we content ourselves with aiming at a small equivalent by the War, and we expect to attain that by moderate efforts. The enemy reasons in very much the same way. Now, if one or the other finds that he has erred in his reckoning—that in place of being slightly superior to the enemy, as he supposed, he is, if anything, rather weaker, still, at that moment, money and all other means, as well as sufficient moral impulse for greater exertions, are very often deficient: in such a case he just does what is called "the best he can"; hopes better things in the future, although he has not the slightest foundation for such hope, and the War in the meantime drags itself feebly along, like a body worn out with sickness.

Thus it comes to pass that the reciprocal action, the rivalry, the violence and impetuosity of War lose themselves in the stagnation of weak motives, and that both parties move with a certain kind of security in very circumscribed spheres.

If this influence of the political object is once permitted, as it then must be, there is no longer any limit, and we must be pleased to come down to such warfare as consists in a *mere threatening of the enemy* and in *negotiating*.

That the theory of War, if it is to be and to continue a philosophical study, finds itself here in a difficulty is clear. All that is essentially inherent in the conception of War seems to fly from it, and it is in danger of being left without any point of support. But the natural outlet soon shows itself. According as a modifying principle gains influence over the act of War, or rather, the weaker the motives to action become, the more the action will glide into a passive resistance, the less eventful it will become, and the less it will require guiding principles. All military art then changes itself into mere prudence, the principal object of which will be to prevent the trembling balance from suddenly turning to our disadvantage, and the half War from changing into a complete one.

War as an Instrument of Policy

Having made the requisite examination on both sides of that state of antagonism in which the nature of War stands with relation to other interests of men individually and of the bond of society, in order not to neglect any of the opposing elements—an antagonism which is founded in our own nature, and which, therefore, no philosophy can unravel—we shall now look for that unity into which, in practical life, these antagonistic elements combine themselves by partly neutralising each other. We should have brought forward this unity at the very commencement if it had not been necessary to bring out this contradiction very plainly, and also to look at the different elements separately. Now, this unity is *the conception that War is only a part of political intercourse, therefore by no means an independent thing in itself.*

We know, certainly, that War is only called forth through the political intercourse of Governments and Nations; but in general it is supposed that such intercourse is broken off by War, and that a totally different state of things ensues, subject to no laws but its own.

We maintain, on the contrary, that War is nothing but a continuation of political intercourse, with a mixture of other means. We say mixed with other means in order thereby to maintain at the same time that this political intercourse does not cease by the War itself, is not changed into something quite different, but that, in its essence, it continues to exist, whatever may be the form of the means which it uses, and that the chief lines on which the events of the War progress, and to which they are attached, are only the general features of policy which run all through the War until peace takes place. And how can we conceive it to be otherwise? Does the formation of diplomatic notes stop the political relations between different Nations and Governments? Is not War merely another kind of writing and language for political thoughts? It has certainly a grammar of its own, but its logic is not peculiar to itself.

Accordingly, War can never be separated from political intercourse, and if, in the consideration of the matter, this is done in any way, all the threads of the different relations are, to a certain extent, broken, and we have before us a senseless thing without an object.

This kind of idea would be indispensable even if War was perfect War, the perfectly unbridled element of hostility, for all the circumstances on which it rests, and which determine its leading features, viz., our own power, the enemy's power, Allies on both sides, the characteristics of the people and their Governments respectively, &c., as enumerated in the first chapter of the first book—are they not of a political nature, and are they not so intimately connected with the whole political intercourse that it is impossible to separate them? But this view is doubly indispensable if we reflect that real War is no such consistent effort tending to an extreme, as it should be according to the abstract idea, but a half-and-half thing, a contradiction in itself; that, as such, it cannot follow its own laws, but must be looked upon as a part of another whole—and this whole is policy.

Policy in making use of War avoids all those rigorous conclusions which proceed from its nature; it troubles itself little about final possibilities, confining its attention to immediate probabilities. If such uncertainty in the whole action ensues therefrom, if it thereby becomes a sort of game, the policy of each Cabinet places its confidence in the belief that in this game it will surpass its neighbor in skill and sharpsightedness.

Thus policy makes out of the all-overpowering element of War a mere instrument, changes the tremendous battlesword, which should be lifted with both hands and the whole power of the body to strike once for all, into a light handy weapon, which is even sometimes nothing more than a rapier to exchange thrusts and feints and parries.

Thus the contradictions in which man, naturally timid, becomes involved by War may be solved, if we choose to accept this as a solution.

If War belongs to policy, it will naturally take its character from thence. If policy is grand and powerful, so also will be the War, and this may be carried to the point at which War attains to *its absolute form.*

In this way of viewing the subject, therefore, we need not shut out of sight the absolute form of War, we rather keep it continually in view in the background.

Only through this kind of view War recovers unity; only by it can we see all Wars as things of *one* kind; and it is only through it that the judgment can obtain the true and perfect basis and point of view from which great plans may be traced out and determined upon.

It is true the political element does not sink deep into the details of War. Vedettes are not planted, patrols do not make their rounds from political considerations; but small as is its influence in this respect, it is great in the formation of a plan for a whole War, or a campaign, and often even for a battle.

For this reason we were in no hurry to establish this view at the commencement. While engaged with particulars, it would have given us little help, and, on the other hand, would have distracted our attention to a certain extent; in the plan of a War or campaign it is indispensable.

There is, upon the whole, nothing more important in life than to find out the right point of view from which things should be looked at and judged of, and then to keep to that point; for we can only apprehend the mass of events in their unity from *one* standpoint; and it is only the keeping to one point of view that guards us from inconsistency.

If, therefore, in drawing up a plan of a War, it is not allowable to have a two-fold or three-fold point of view, from which things may be looked at, now with the eye of a soldier, then with that of an administrator, and then again with that of a politician, &c., then the next question is, whether *policy* is necessarily paramount and everything else subordinate to it.

That policy unites in itself, and reconciles all the interests of internal administrations, even those of humanity, and whatever else are rational subjects of consideration is presupposed, for it is nothing in itself, except a mere representative and exponent of all these interests towards other States. That policy may take a false direction, and may promote unfairly the ambitious ends, the private interests, the vanity of rulers, does not concern us here; for, under no circumstances can the Art of War be regarded as its preceptor, and we can only look at policy here as the representative of the interests generally of the whole community.

The only question, therefore, is whether in framing plans for a War the political point of view should give way to the purely military (if such a point is conceivable), that is to say, should disappear altogether, or subordinate itself to it, or whether the political is to remain the ruling point of view and the military to be considered subordinate to it.

That the political point of view should end completely when War begins is only conceivable in contests which are Wars of life and death, from pure hatred: as Wars are in reality, they are, as we before said, only the expressions or manifestations of policy itself. The subordination of the political point of view to the military would be contrary to common sense, for policy has declared the War; it is the intelligent faculty, War only the instrument, and not the reverse. The subordination of the military point of view to the political is, therefore, the only thing which is possible.

If we reflect on the nature of real War, and call to mind . . . *that every War should be viewed above all things according to the probability of its character, and its leading features as they are to be deduced from the political forces and proportions,* and that often—indeed we may safely affirm, in our days, *almost always*—War is to be regarded as an organic whole, from which the single branches are not to be separated, in which therefore every individual activity flows into the whole, and also has its origin in the idea of this whole, then it becomes certain and palpable to us that the superior standpoint for the conduct of the War, from which its leading lines must proceed, can be no other than that of policy.

From this point of view the plans come, as it were, out of a cast; the apprehension of them and the judgment upon them become easier and more natural, our convictions respecting them gain in force, motives are more satisfying, and history more intelligible.

At all events from this point of view there is no longer in the nature of things a necessary conflict between the political and military interests, and where it appears it is therefore to be regarded as imperfect knowledge only. That policy makes demands on the War which it cannot respond to, would be contrary to the supposition that it knows the instrument which it is going to use, therefore, contrary to a natural and indispensable supposition. But if policy judges correctly of the march of military events, it is entirely its affair to determine what are the events and what the direction of events most favourable to the ultimate and great end of the War.

In one word, the Art of War in its highest point of view is policy, but, no doubt, a policy which fights battles instead of writing notes.

According to this view, to leave a great military enterprise, or the plan for one, to *a purely military judgment and decision* is a distinction which cannot be allowed, and is even prejudicial; indeed, it is an irrational proceeding to consult professional soldiers on the plan of a War, that they may give a *purely military opinion* upon what the Cabinet ought to do; but still more absurd is the demand of Theorists that a statement of the available means of War should be laid before the General, that he may draw out a purely military plan for the War or for a campaign in accordance with those means. Experience in general also teaches us that notwithstanding the multifarious branches and scientific character of military art in the present day, still the leading outlines of a War are always determined by the Cabinet, that is, if we would use technical language, by a political not a military organ.

This is perfectly natural. None of the principal plans which are required for a War can be made without an insight into the political relations; and, in reality, when people speak, as they often do, of the prejudicial influence of policy on the conduct of a War, they say in reality something very different to what they intend. It is not this influence but the policy itself which should be found fault with. If policy is right, that is, if it succeeds in hitting the object, then it can only act with advantage on the War. If this influence of policy causes a divergence from the object, the cause is only to be looked for in a mistaken policy.

It is only when policy promises itself a wrong effect from certain military means and measures, an effect opposed to their nature, that it can exercise a prejudicial effect on War by the course it prescribes. Just as a person in a language with which he is not conversant sometimes says what he does not intend, so policy, when intending right, may often order things which do not tally with its own views.

This happened times without end, and it shows that a certain knowledge of the nature of War is essential to the management of political intercourse.

But before going further, we must guard ourselves against a false interpretation of which this is very susceptible. We are far from holding the opinion that a War Minister smothered in official papers, a scientific engineer, or even a soldier who has been well tried in the field, would, any of them, necessarily make the best Minister of State where the Sovereign does not act for himself; or, in other words, we do not mean to say that this acquaintance with the nature of War is the principal qualification for a War Minister; elevation, superiority of mind, strength of character, these are the principal qualifications which he must possess; a knowledge of War may be supplied in one way or the other. France was never worse advised in its military and political affairs than by the two brothers Belleisle and the Duke of Choiseul, although all three were good soldiers.

If War is to harmonise entirely with the political views and policy, to accommodate itself to the means available for War, there is only one alternative to be recommended when the statesman and soldier are not combined in one person, which is, to make the Commander-in-Chief a member of the Cabinet, that he may take part in its councils and decisions on important occasions. But then, again, this is only possible when the Cabinet, that is, the

Government itself, is near the theatre of War, so that things can be settled without a serious waste of time.

This is what the Emperor of Austria did in 1809, and the allied Sovereigns in 1813, 1814, 1815, and the arrangement proved completely satisfactory.

The influence of any military man except the General-in-Chief in the Cabinet is extremely dangerous; it very seldom leads to able vigorous action. The example of France in 1793, 1794, 1795, when Carnot, while residing in Paris, managed the conduct of the War, is to be avoided, as a system of terror is not at the command of any but a revolutionary government.

We shall now conclude with some reflections derived from history.

In the last decade of the past century, when that remarkable change in the Art of War in Europe took place by which the best Armies found that a part of their method of War had become utterly unserviceable, and events were brought about of a magnitude far beyond what any one had any previous conception of, it certainly appeared that a false calculation of everything was to be laid to the charge of the Art of War. It was plain that while confined by habit within a narrow circle of conceptions, she had been surprised by the force of a new state of relations, lying, no doubt, outside that circle, but still not outside the nature of things.

Those observers who took the most comprehensive view ascribed the circumstance to the general influence which policy had exercised for centuries on the Art of War, and undoubtedly to its very great disadvantage, and by which it had sunk into a half-measure, often into mere sham-fighting. They were right as to fact, but they were wrong in attributing it to something accidental, or which might have been avoided.

Others thought that everything was to be explained by the momentary influence of the particular policy of Austria, Prussia, England, &c., with regard to their own interests respectively.

But is it true that the real surprise by which men's minds were seized was confined to the conduct of War, and did not rather relate to policy itself? That is: Did the ill success proceed from the influence of policy on the War, or from a wrong policy itself?

The prodigious effects of the French Revolution abroad were evidently brought about much less through new methods and views introduced by the French in the conduct of War than through the changes which it wrought in state-craft and civil administration, in the character of Governments, in the condition of the people, &c. That other Governments took a mistaken view of all these things; that they endeavored, with their ordinary means, to hold their own against forces of a novel kind and overwhelming in strength—all that was a blunder in policy.

Would it have been possible to perceive and mend this error by a scheme for the War from a purely military point of view? Impossible. For if there had been a philosophical strategist, who merely from the nature of the hostile elements had foreseen all the consequences, and prophesied remote possibilities, still it would have been practically impossible to have turned such wisdom to account.

If policy had risen to a just appreciation of the forces which had sprung up in France, and of the new relations in the political state of Europe, it might have foreseen the consequences which must follow in respect to the great features of War, and it was only in this way that it could arrive at a correct view of the extent of the means required as well as of the best use to make of those means. We may therefore say, that the twenty years' victories after the Revolution are chiefly to be ascribed to the erroneous policy of the Governments by which it was opposed.

It is true these errors first displayed themselves in the War, and the events of the War completely disappointed the expectations which policy entertained. But this did not take place because policy neglected to consult its military advisers. That Art of War in which the politician of the day could believe, namely, that derived from the reality of War at that time, that which belonged to the policy of the day, that familiar instrument which policy had hitherto used—*that* Art of War, I say, was naturally involved in the error of policy, and therefore could not teach it anything better. It is true that War itself underwent important alterations both in its nature and forms, which brought it nearer to its absolute form; but these changes were not brought about because the French Government had, to a certain extent, delivered itself from the leading-strings of policy; they arose from an altered policy, produced by the French Revolution, not only in France, but over the rest of Europe as well. This policy had called forth other means and other powers, by which it became possible to conduct War with a degree of energy which could not have been thought of otherwise.

Therefore, the actual changes in the Art of War are a consequence of alterations in policy; and, so far from being an argument for the possible separation of the two, they are, on the contrary, very strong evidence of the intimacy of their connection.

Therefore, once more: War is an instrument of policy: it must necessarily bear its character, it must measure with its scale: the conduct of War, in its great features, is therefore policy itself, which takes up the sword in place of the pen, but does not on that account cease to think according to its own laws.

36

The Sources of Soviet Conduct (1947)

X (George F. Kennan)

The political personality of Soviet power as we know it today is the product of ideology and circumstances: ideology inherited by the present Soviet leaders from the movement in which they had their political origin, and circumstances of the power which they now have exercised for nearly three decades in Russia. There can be few tasks of psychological analysis more difficult than to try to trace the interaction of these two forces and the relative role of each in the determination of official Soviet conduct. Yet the attempt must be made if that conduct is to be understood and effectively countered.

It is difficult to summarize the set of ideological concepts with which the Soviet leaders came into power. Marxian ideology, in its Russian-Communist projection, has always been in process of subtle evolution. The materials on which it bases itself are extensive and complex. But the outstanding features of Communist thought as it existed in 1916 may perhaps be summarized as follows: (a) that the central factor in the life of man, the factor which determines the character of public life and the "physiognomy of society," is the system by which material goods are produced and exchanged; (b) that the capitalist system of production is a nefarious one which inevitably leads to the exploitation of the working class by the capital-owning class and is incapable of developing adequately the economic resources of society or of distributing fairly the material goods produced by human labor; (c) that capitalism contains the seeds of its own destruction and must, in view of the inability of the capital-owning class to adjust itself to economic change, result eventually and inescapably in a revolutionary transfer of power to the working class; and (d) that imperialism, the final phase of capitalism, leads directly to war and revolution. . . .

Source: X (George F. Kennan), "The Sources of Soviet Conduct." Reprinted by permission of *Foreign Affairs*, Vol. 25, No. 4 (July 1947). Copyright © 1947 by the Council on Foreign Relations.

Now it must be noted that through all the years of preparation for revolution, the attention of these men, as indeed of Marx himself, had been centered less on the future form which Socialism[1] would take than on the necessary overthrow of rival power which, in their view, had to precede the introduction of Socialism. Their views, therefore, on the positive program to be put into effect, once power was attained, were for the most part nebulous, visionary and impractical. Beyond the nationalization of industry and the expropriation of large private capital holdings there was no agreed program. The treatment of the peasantry, which according to the Marxist formulation was not of the proletariat, had always been a vague spot in the pattern of Communist thought; and it remained an object of controversy and vacillation for the first ten years of Communist power.

The circumstances of the immediate post-revolution period—the existence in Russia of civil war and foreign intervention, together with the obvious fact that the Communists represented only a tiny minority of the Russian people—made the establishment of dictatorial power a necessity. The experiment with "war Communism" and the abrupt attempt to eliminate private production and trade had unfortunate economic consequences and caused further bitterness against the new revolutionary régime. While the temporary relaxation of the effort to communize Russia, represented by the New Economic Policy, alleviated some of this economic distress and thereby served its purpose, it also made it evident that the "capitalistic sector of society" was still prepared to profit at once from any relaxation of governmental pressure, and would, if permitted to continue to exist, always constitute a powerful opposing element to the Soviet régime and a serious rival for influence in the country. Somewhat the same situation prevailed with respect to the individual peasant who, in his own small way, was also a private producer.

Lenin, had he lived, might have proved a great enough man to reconcile these conflicting forces to the ultimate benefit of Russian society, though this is questionable. But be that as it may, Stalin, and those whom he led in the struggle for succession to Lenin's position of leadership, were not the men to tolerate rival political forces in the sphere of power which they coveted. Their sense of insecurity was too great. Their particular brand of fanaticism, unmodified by any of the Anglo-Saxon traditions of compromise, was too fierce and too jealous to envisage any permanent sharing of power. From the Russian-Asiatic world out of which they had emerged they carried with them a skepticism as to the possibilities of permanent and peaceful coexistence of rival forces. Easily persuaded of their own doctrinaire "rightness," they insisted on the submission or destruction of all competing power. Outside of the Communist Party, Russian society was to have no rigidity. There were to be no forms of collective human activity or association which would not be dominated by the Party. No other force in Russian society was to be permitted to achieve vitality or integrity. Only the Party was to have structure. All else was to be an amorphous mass.

And within the Party the same principle was to apply. The mass of Party members might go through the motions of election, deliberation, decision and action; but in these motions they were to be animated not by their own individual wills but by the awesome breath of the Party leadership and the over-brooding presence of "the word."

Let it be stressed again that subjectively these men probably did not seek absolutism for its own sake. They doubtless believed—and found it easy to believe—that they alone knew what was good for society and that they would accomplish that good once their power was secure and unchallengeable. But in seeking that security of their own rule they were prepared to recognize no restrictions, either of God or man, on the character of their methods. And until such time as that security might be achieved, they placed far down on their scale of operational priorities the comforts and happiness of the peoples entrusted to their care.

Now the outstanding circumstance concerning the Soviet régime is that down to the present day this process of political consolidation has never been completed and the men in the Kremlin have continued to be predominantly absorbed with the struggle to secure and make absolute the power which they seized in November 1917. They have endeavored to secure it primarily against forces at home, within Soviet society itself. But they have also endeavored to secure it against the outside world. For ideology, as we have seen, taught them that the outside world was hostile and that it was their duty eventually to over-throw the political forces beyond their borders. The powerful hands of Russian history and tradition reached up to sustain them in this feeling. Finally, their own aggressive intransigence with respect to the outside world began to find its own reaction; and they were soon forced, to use another Gibbonesque phrase, "to chastise the contumacy" which they themselves had provoked. It is an undeniable privilege of every man to prove himself right in the thesis that the world is his enemy; for if he reiterates it frequently enough and makes it the background of his conduct he is bound eventually to be right.

Now it lies in the nature of the mental world of the Soviet leaders, as well as in the character of their ideology, that no opposition to them can be offi-cially recognized as having any merit or justification whatsoever. Such opposi-tion can flow, in theory, only from the hostile and incorrigible forces of dying capitalism. As long as remnants of capitalism were officially recognized as existing in Russia, it was possible to place on them, as an internal element, part of the blame for the maintenance of a dictatorial form of society. But as these remnants were liquidated, little by little, this justification fell away; and when it was indicated officially that they had been finally destroyed, it disap-peared altogether. And this fact created one of the most basic of the compul-sions which came to act upon the Soviet régime: since capitalism no longer existed in Russia and since it could not be admitted that there could be serious or widespread opposition to the Kremlin springing spontaneously from the lib-erated masses under its authority, it became necessary to justify the retention of the dictatorship by stressing the menace of capitalism abroad. . . .

Now the maintenance of this pattern of Soviet power, namely, the pursuit of unlimited authority domestically, accompanied by the cultivation of the semi-myth of implacable foreign hostility, has gone far to shape the actual machinery of Soviet power as we know it today. Internal organs of administration which did not serve this purpose withered on the vine. Organs which did serve this purpose became vastly swollen. The security of Soviet power came to rest on the iron discipline of the Party, on the severity and ubiquity of the secret police, and on the uncompromising economic monopolism of the state. The "organs of suppression," in which the Soviet leaders had sought security from rival forces, became in large measure the masters of those whom they were designed to serve. Today the major part of the structure of Soviet power is committed to the perfection of the dictatorship and to the maintenance of the concept of Russia as in a state of siege, with the enemy lowering beyond the walls. And the millions of human beings who form that part of the structure of power must defend at all costs this concept of Russia's position, for without it they are themselves superfluous.

As things stand today, the rulers can no longer dream of parting with these organs of suppression. The quest for absolute power, pursued now for nearly three decades with a ruthlessness unparalleled (in scope at least) in modern times, has again produced internally, as it did externally, its own reaction. The excesses of the police apparatus have fanned the potential opposition to the régime into something far greater and more dangerous that it could have been before those excesses began.

But least of all can the rulers dispense with the fiction by which the maintenance of dictatorial power has been defended. For this fiction has been canonized in Soviet philosophy by the excesses already committed in its name; and it is now anchored in the Soviet structure of thought by bonds far greater than those of mere ideology. . . .

So much for the historical background. What does it spell in terms of the political personality of Soviet power as we know it today?

Of the original ideology, nothing has been officially junked. Belief is maintained in the basic badness of capitalism, in the inevitability of its destruction, in the obligation of the proletariat to assist in that destruction and to take power into its own hands. But stress has come to be laid primarily on those concepts which relate most specifically to the Soviet régime itself: to its position as the sole truly Socialist régime in a dark and misguided world, and to the relationship of power within it.

The first of these concepts is that of the innate antagonism between capitalism and Socialism. We have seen how deeply that concept has become imbedded in foundations of Soviet power. It has profound implications for Russia's conduct as a member of international society. It means that there can never be on Moscow's side any sincere assumption of a community of aims between the Soviet Union and powers which are regarded as capitalist. It must invariably be assumed in Moscow that the aims of the capitalist world are antagonistic to the Soviet régime, and therefore to the interests of the people it controls. If the Soviet Government occasionally sets its signature to documents which would indicate the contrary, this is to be regarded as a tactical manœuvre permissible in dealing with the enemy (who is without honor) and should be taken in the spirit of *caveat emptor.* Basically, the antagonism remains. It is postulated. And from it flow many of the phenomena which we find disturbing in the Kremlin's conduct of foreign policy: the secretiveness, the lack of frankness, the duplicity, the wary suspiciousness, and the basic unfriendliness of purpose. These phenomena are there to stay, for the foreseeable future. There can be variations of degree and of emphasis. When there is something the Russians want from us, one or the other of these features of their policy may be thrust temporarily into the background; and when that happens there will always be Americans who will leap forward with gleeful announcements that "the Russians have changed," and some who will even try to take credit for having brought about such "changes." But we should not be misled by tactical manœuvres. These characteristics of Soviet policy, like the postulate from which they flow, are basic to the internal nature of Soviet power, and will be with us, whether in the foreground or the background, until the internal nature of Soviet power is changed.

This means that we are going to continue for a long time to find the Russians difficult to deal with it. It does not mean that they should be considered as embarked upon a do-or-die program to overthrow our society by a given date. The theory of the inevitability of the eventual fall of capitalism has the fortunate connotation that there is no hurry about it. . . .

The Kremlin is under no ideological compulsion to accomplish its purposes in a hurry. Like the Church, it is dealing in ideological concepts which are of long-term validity, and it can afford to be patient. It has no right to risk the existing achievements of the revolution for the sake of vain baubles of the future. The very teachings of Lenin himself require great caution and flexibility in the pursuit of Communist purposes. Again, these precepts are fortified by the lessons of Russian history: of centuries of obscure battles between nomadic forces over the stretches of a vast unfortified plain. Here caution, circumspection, flexibility and deception are the valuable qualities; and their value finds natural appreciation in the Russian or the Asian mind. Thus the Kremlin has no compunction about retreating in the face of superior force. And being under the compulsion of no timetable, it does not get panicky under the necessity for such retreat. Its political action is a fluid stream which moves constantly, wherever it is permitted to move, toward a given goal. Its main concern is to make sure that it has filled every nook and cranny available to it in the basin of the world power. But if it finds unassailable barriers in its path, it accepts these philosophically and accommodates itself to them. The main thing is that there should always be pressure, unceasing constant pressure, toward the desired goal. There is no trace of any feeling in Soviet psychology that that goal must be reached at any given time.

These considerations make Soviet diplomacy at once easier and more difficult to deal with than the diplomacy of individual aggressive leaders like Napoleon and Hitler. On the one hand it is more sensitive to contrary force, more ready to yield on individual sectors of the diplomatic front when that force is felt to be too strong, and thus more rational in the logic and rhetoric of power. On the other hand it cannot be easily defeated or discouraged by a single victory on the part of its opponents. And the patient persistence by which it is animated means that it can be effectively countered not by sporadic acts which represent the momentary whims of democratic opinion but only by intelligent long-range policies on the part of Russia's adversaries—policies no less steady in their purpose, and no less variegated and resourceful in their application, than those of the Soviet Union itself.

In these circumstances it is clear that the main element of any United States policy toward the Soviet Union must be that of a long-term, patient but firm and vigilant containment of Russian expansive tendencies. It is important to note, however, that such a policy has nothing to do with outward histrionics: with threats or blustering or superfluous gestures of outward "toughness." While the Kremlin is basically flexible in its reaction to political realities, it is by no means unamenable to considerations of prestige. Like almost any other government, it can be placed by tactless and threatening gestures in a position where it cannot afford to yield even though this might be dictated by its sense of realism. The Russian leaders are keen judges of human psychology, and as such they are highly conscious that loss of temper and of self-control is never a source of strength in political affairs. They are quick to exploit such evidences of weakness. For these reasons, it is a *sine qua non* of successful dealing with Russia that the foreign government in question should remain at all times cool and collected and that its demands on Russian policy should be put forward in such a manner as to leave the way open for a compliance not too detrimental to Russian prestige.

In the light of the above, it will be clearly seen that the Soviet pressure against the free institutions of the western world is something that can be contained by the adroit and vigilant application of counter-force at a series of constantly shifting geographical and political points, corresponding to the shifts and manœuvres of Soviet policy, but which cannot be charmed or talked out of existence. . . . Russia, as opposed to the western world in general, is still by far the weaker party, . . . Soviet policy is highly flexible, and . . . Soviet society may well contain deficiencies which will eventually weaken its own total potential. This would of itself warrant the United States entering with reasonable confidence upon a policy of firm containment, designed to confront the Russians with unalterable counter-force at every point where they show signs of encroaching upon the interests of a peaceful and stable world.

But in actuality the possibilities for American policy are by no means limited to holding the line and hoping for the best. It is entirely possible for the United States to influence by its actions the internal developments, both within Russia and throughout the international Communist movement, by which Russian policy is largely determined. This is not only a question of the modest measure of informational activity which this government can conduct in the Soviet Union and elsewhere, although that, too, is important. It is rather a question of the degree to which the United States can create among the peoples of the world generally the impression of a country which knows what it wants, which is coping successfully with the problems of its internal life and with the responsibilities of a World Power, and which has a spiritual vitality capable of holding its own among the major ideological currents of the time. To the extent that such an impression can be created and maintained, the aims of Russian Communism must appear sterile and quixotic, the hopes and enthusiasm of Moscow's supporters must wane, and added strain must be imposed on the Kremlin's foreign policies. For the palsied decrepitude of the capitalist world is the keystone of Communist philosophy. Even the failure of the United States to experience the early economic depression which the ravens of the Red Square have been predicting with such complacent confidence since hostilities ceased would have deep and important repercussions throughout the Communist world.

By the same token, exhibitions of indecision, disunity and internal disintegration within this country have an exhilarating effect on the whole Communist movement. . . .

The United States has it in its power to increase enormously the strains under which Soviet policy must operate, to force upon the Kremlin a far greater degree of moderation and circumspection than it has had to observe in recent years, and in this way to promote tendencies which must eventually find their outlet in either the break-up or the gradual mellowing of Soviet power. For no mystical, Messianic movement—and particularly not that of the Kremlin—can face frustration indefinitely without eventually adjusting itself in one way or another to the logic of that state of affairs.

NOTES

1. Here and elsewhere in this [article] "Socialism" refers to Marxist or Leninist Communism, not to liberal Socialism of the Second International variety.

37

The Clash of Civilizations? (1993)

Samuel P. Huntington

The Next Pattern of Conflict

World politics is entering a new phase, and intellectuals have not hesitated to proliferate visions of what it will be—the end of history, the return of traditional rivalries between nation states, and the decline of the nation state from the conflicting pulls of tribalism and globalism, among others. Each of these visions catches aspects of the emerging reality. Yet they all miss a crucial, indeed a central, aspect of what global politics is likely to be in the coming years.

It is my hypothesis that the fundamental source of conflict in this new world will not be primarily ideological or primarily economic. The great divisions among humankind and the dominating source of conflict will be cultural. Nation states will remain the most powerful actors in world affairs, but the principal conflicts of global politics will occur between nations and groups of different civilizations. The clash of civilizations will dominate global politics. The fault lines between civilizations will be the battle lines of the future.

Conflict between civilizations will be the latest phase in the evolution of conflict in the modern world. For a century and a half after the emergence of the modern international system with the Peace of Westphalia, the conflicts of the Western world were largely among princes—emperors, absolute monarchs and constitutional monarchs attempting to expand their bureaucracies, their armies, their mercantilist economic strength and, most important, the territory they ruled. In the process they created nation states, and beginning with the French Revolution the principal lines of conflict were between nations rather than princes. In 1793, as R. R. Palmer put it, "The wars of kings were over; the wars of peoples had begun." This nineteenth-century pattern lasted until the end of World War I. Then, as a result of the Russian Revolution and the reaction against it, the conflict of nations yielded to the conflict of ideologies, first among communism, fascism-Nazism and liberal democracy, and

Source: Samuel P. Huntington, "The Clash of Civilizations?" Reprinted by permission of *Foreign Affairs,* Vol. 72, No. 3 (Summer 1993). Copyright © 1993 by the Council on Foreign Relations.

then between communism and liberal democracy. During the Cold War, this latter conflict became embodied in the struggle between the two superpowers, neither of which was a nation state in the classical European sense and each of which defined its identity in terms of its ideology.

These conflicts between princes, nation states and ideologies were primarily conflicts within Western civilization, "Western civil wars," as William Lind has labeled them. This was as true of the Cold War as it was of the world wars and the earlier wars of the seventeenth, eighteenth and nineteenth centuries. With the end of the Cold War, international politics moves out of its Western phase, and its centerpiece becomes the interaction between the West and non-Western civilizations and among non-Western civilizations. In the politics of civilizations, the peoples and governments of non-Western civilizations no longer remain the objects of history as targets of Western colonialism but join the West as movers and shapers of history.

The Nature of Civilizations

During the Cold War the world was divided into the First, Second and Third Worlds. Those divisions are no longer relevant. It is far more meaningful now to group countries not in terms of their political or economic systems or in terms of their level of economic development but rather in terms of their culture and civilization.

What do we mean when we talk of a civilization? A civilization is a cultural entity. Villages, regions, ethnic groups, nationalities, religious groups, all have distinct cultures at different levels of cultural heterogeneity. The culture of a village in southern Italy may be different from that of a village in northern Italy, but both will share in a common Italian culture that distinguishes them from German villages. European communities, in turn, will share cultural features that distinguish them from Arab or Chinese communities. Arabs, Chinese and Westerners, however, are not part of any broader cultural entity. They constitute civilizations. A civilization is thus the highest cultural grouping of people and the broadest level of cultural identity people have short of that which distinguishes humans from other species. It is defined both by common objective elements, such as language, history, religion, customs, institutions, and by the subjective self-identification of people. People have levels of identity: a resident of Rome may define himself with varying degrees of intensity as a Roman, an Italian, a Catholic, a Christian, a European, a Westerner. The civilization to which he belongs is the broadest level of identification with which he intensely identifies. People can and do redefine their identities and, as a result, the composition and boundaries of civilizations change.

Civilizations may involve a large number of people, as with China ("a civilization pretending to be a state," as Lucian Pye put it), or a very small number of people, such as the Anglophone Caribbean. A civilization may include several nation states, as is the case with Western, Latin American and Arab civilizations, or only one, as is the case with Japanese civilization. Civilizations obviously blend and overlap, and may include subcivilizations. Western civilization has two major variants, European and North American, and Islam has its Arab, Turkic and Malay subdivisions. Civilizations are nonetheless meaningful entities, and while the lines between them are seldom sharp, they are real. Civilizations are dynamic; they rise and fall; they divide and merge. And, as any student of history knows, civilizations disappear and are buried in the sands of time.

Westerners tend to think of nation states as the principal actors in global affairs. They have been that, however, for only a few centuries. The broader reaches of human history have been the history of civilizations. In *A Study of History,* Arnold Toynbee identified 21 major civilizations; only six of them exist in the contemporary world.

Why Civilizations Will Clash

Civilization identity will be increasingly important in the future, and the world will be shaped in large measure by the interactions among seven or eight major civilizations. These include Western, Confucian, Japanese, Islamic, Hindu, Slavic-Orthodox, Latin American and possibly African civilization. The most important conflicts of the future will occur along the cultural fault lines separating these civilizations from one another.

Why will this be the case?

First, differences among civilizations are not only real; they are basic. Civilizations are differentiated from each other by history, language, culture, tradition and, most important, religion. The people of different civilizations have different views on the relations between God and man, the individual and the group, the citizen and the state, parents and children, husband and wife, as well as differing views of the relative importance of rights and responsibilities, liberty and authority, equality and hierarchy. These differences are the product of centuries. They will not soon disappear. They are far more fundamental than differences among political ideologies and political regimes. Differences do not necessarily mean conflict, and conflict does not necessarily mean violence. Over the centuries, however, differences among civilizations have generated the most prolonged and the most violent conflicts.

Second, the world is becoming a smaller place. The interactions between peoples of different civilizations are increasing; these increasing interactions intensify civilization consciousness and awareness of differences between civilizations and commonalities within civilizations. North African immigration to France generates hostility among Frenchmen and at the same time increased receptivity to immigration by "good" European Catholic Poles. Americans react far more negatively to Japanese investment than to larger investments from Canada and European countries. Similarly, as Donald Horowitz has pointed out, "An Ibo may be . . . an Owerri Ibo or an Onitsha Ibo in what was the Eastern region of Nigeria. In Lagos, he is simply an Ibo. In London, he is a Nigerian. In New York, he is an African." The interactions among peoples of different civilizations enhance the civilization-consciousness of people that, in turn, invigorates differences and animosities stretching or thought to stretch back deep into history.

Third, the processes of economic modernization and social change throughout the world are separating people from longstanding local identities. They also weaken the nation state as a source of identity. In much of the world religion has moved in to fill this gap, often in the form of movements that are labeled "fundamentalist." Such movements are found in Western Christianity, Judaism, Buddhism and Hinduism, as well as in Islam. In most countries and most religions the people active in fundamentalist movements are young, college-educated, middle-class technicians, professionals and business persons. The "unsecularization of the world," George Weigel has remarked, "is one of the dominant social facts of life in the late twentieth century." The revival of religion, "la revanche de Dieu," as Gilles Kepel labeled it, provides a basis for identity and commitment that transcends national boundaries and unites civilizations.

Fourth, the growth of civilization-consciousness is enhanced by the dual role of the West. On the one hand, the West is at a peak of power. At the same time, however, and perhaps as a result, a return to the roots phenomenon is occurring among non-Western civilizations. Increasingly one hears references to trends toward a turning inward and "Asianization" in Japan, the end of the Nehru legacy and the "Hinduization" of India, the failure of Western ideas of socialism and nationalism and hence "re-Islamization" of the Middle East, and now a debate over Westernization versus Russianization in Boris Yeltsin's country. A West at the peak of its power confronts non-Wests that increasingly have the desire, the will and the resources to shape the world in non-Western ways.

In the past, the elites of non-Western societies were usually the people who were most involved with the West, had been educated at Oxford, the Sorbonne or Sandhurst, and had absorbed Western attitudes and values. At the same time, the populace in non-Western countries often remained deeply imbued with the indigenous culture. Now, however, these relationships are being reversed. A de-Westernization and indigenization of elites is occurring in many non-Western countries at the same time that Western, usually American, cultures, styles and habits become more popular among the mass of the people.

Fifth, cultural characteristics and differences are less mutable and hence less easily compromised and resolved than political and economic ones. In the former Soviet Union, communists can become democrats, the rich can become poor and the poor rich, but Russians cannot become Estonians and Azeris cannot become Armenians. In class and ideological conflicts, the key question was "Which side are you on?" and people could and did choose sides and change sides. In conflicts between civilizations, the question is "What are you?" That is a given that cannot be changed. And as we know, from Bosnia to the Caucasus to the Sudan, the wrong answer to that question can mean a bullet in the head. Even more than ethnicity, religion discriminates sharply and exclusively among people. A person can be half-French and half-Arab and simultaneously even a citizen of two countries. It is more difficult to be half-Catholic and half-Muslim.

Finally, economic regionalism is increasing. The proportions of total trade that were intraregional rose between 1980 and 1989 from 51 percent to 59 percent in Europe, 33 percent to 37 percent in East Asia, and 32 percent to 36 percent in North America. The importance of regional economic blocs is likely to continue to increase in the future. On the one hand, successful economic regionalism will reinforce civilization-consciousness. On the other hand, economic regionalism may succeed only when it is rooted in a common civilization. The European Community rests on the shared foundation of European culture and Western Christianity. The success of the North American Free Trade Area depends on the convergence now underway of Mexican, Canadian and American cultures. Japan, in contrast, faces difficulties in creating a comparable economic entity in East Asia because Japan is a society and civilization unique to itself. However strong the trade and investment links Japan may develop with the other East Asian countries, its cultural differences with those countries inhibit and perhaps preclude its promoting regional economic integration like that in Europe and North America.

Common culture, in contrast, is clearly facilitating the rapid expansion of the economic relations between the People's Republic of China and Hong Kong, Taiwan, Singapore and the overseas Chinese communities in other Asian countries. With the Cold War over, cultural commonalities increasingly overcome ideological differences, and mainland China and Taiwan move closer together. If cultural commonality is a prerequisite for economic integration, the principal East Asian economic bloc of the future is likely to be centered on China. This bloc is, in fact, already coming into existence. As Murray Weidenbaum has observed,

> Despite the current Japanese dominance of the region, the Chinese-based economy of Asia is rapidly emerging as a new epicenter for industry, commerce and finance. This strategic area contains substantial amounts of technology and manufacturing capability (Taiwan), outstanding entrepreneurial, marketing and services acumen (Hong Kong), a fine communications network (Singapore), a tremendous pool of financial capital (all three), and very large endowments of land, resources and labor (mainland China). . . . From Guangzhou to Singapore, from Kuala Lumpur to Manila, this influential network—often based on extensions of the traditional clans—has been described as the backbone of the East Asian economy.[1]

Culture and religion also form the basis of the Economic Cooperation Organization, which brings together ten non-Arab Muslim countries: Iran, Pakistan, Turkey, Azerbaijan, Kazakhstan, Kyrgyzstan, Turkmenistan, Tadjikistan, Uzbekistan and Afghanistan. One impetus to the revival and expansion of this organization, founded originally in the 1960s by Turkey, Pakistan and Iran, is the realization by the leaders of several of these countries that they had no chance of admission to the European Community. Similarly, Caricom, the Central American Common Market and Mercosur rest on common cultural foundations. Efforts to build a broader Caribbean-Central American economic entity bridging the Anglo-Latin divide, however, have to date failed.

As people define their identity in ethnic and religious terms, they are likely to see an "us" versus "them" relation existing between themselves and people of different ethnicity or religion. The end of ideologically defined states in Eastern Europe and the former Soviet Union permits traditional ethnic identities and animosities to come to the fore. Differences in culture and religion create differences over policy issues, ranging from human rights to immigration to trade and commerce to the environment. Geographical propinquity gives rise to conflicting territorial claims from Bosnia to Mindanao. Most important, the efforts of the West to promote its values of democracy and liberalism as universal values, to maintain its military predominance and to advance its economic interests engender countering responses from other civilizations. Decreasingly able to mobilize support and form coalitions on the basis of ideology, governments and groups will increasingly attempt to mobilize support by appealing to common religion and civilization identity.

The clash of civilizations thus occurs at two levels. At the micro-level, adjacent groups along the fault lines between civilizations struggle, often violently, over the control of territory and each other. At the macro-level, states from different civilizations compete for relative military and economic power, struggle over the control of international institutions and third parties, and competitively promote their particular political and religious values.

The Fault Lines between Civilizations

The fault lines between civilizations are replacing the political and ideological boundaries of the Cold War as the flash points for crisis and bloodshed. The Cold War began when the Iron Curtain divided Europe politically and ideologically. The Cold War ended with the end of the Iron Curtain. As the ideological division of Europe has disappeared, the cultural division of Europe between Western Christianity, on the one hand, and Orthodox Christianity and Islam, on the other, has reemerged. The most significant dividing line in Europe, as William Wallace has suggested, may well be the eastern boundary of Western Christianity in the year 1500. This line runs along what are now the boundaries between Finland and Russia and between the Baltic states and Russia, cuts through Belarus and Ukraine separating the more Catholic western Ukraine from Orthodox eastern Ukraine, swings westward separating Transylvania from the rest of Romania, and then goes through Yugoslavia almost exactly along the line now separating Croatia and Slovenia from the rest of Yugoslavia. In the Balkans this line, of course, coincides with the historic boundary between the Hapsburg and Ottoman empires. The peoples to the north and west of this line are Protestant or Catholic; they shared the common experiences of European history—feudalism, the Renaissance, the Reformation, the Enlightenment, the French Revolution, the Industrial Revolution; they are generally economically better off than the peoples to the east; and they may now look forward to increasing involvement in a common European economy and to the consolidation of democratic political systems. The peoples to the east and south of this line are Orthodox or Muslim; they historically belonged to the Ottoman or Tsarist empires and were only lightly touched by the shaping events in the rest of Europe; they are generally less advanced economically; they seem much less likely to develop stable democratic political systems. The Velvet Curtain of culture has replaced the Iron Curtain of ideology as the most significant dividing line in Europe. As the events in Yugoslavia show, it is not only a line of difference; it is also at times a line of bloody conflict.

Conflict along the fault line between Western and Islamic civilizations has been going on for 1,300 years. After the founding of Islam, the Arab and Moorish surge west and north only ended at Tours in 732. From the eleventh to the thirteenth century the Crusaders attempted with temporary success to bring Christianity and Christian rule to the Holy Land. From the fourteenth to the seventeenth century, the Ottoman Turks reversed the balance, extended their sway over the Middle East and the Balkans, captured Constantinople, and twice laid siege to Vienna. In the nineteenth and early twentieth centuries as Ottoman power declined Britain, France, and Italy established Western control over most of North Africa and the Middle East.

After World War II, the West, in turn, began to retreat; the colonial empires disappeared; first Arab nationalism and then Islamic fundamentalism manifested themselves; the West became heavily dependent on the Persian Gulf countries for its energy; the oil-rich Muslim countries became money-rich and, when they wished to, weapons-rich. Several wars occurred between Arabs and Israel (created by the West). France fought a bloody and ruthless war in Algeria for most of the 1950s; British and French forces invaded Egypt in 1956; American forces went into Lebanon in 1958; subsequently American forces returned to Lebanon, attacked Libya, and engaged in various military encounters with Iran; Arab and Islamic terrorists, supported by at least three Middle Eastern governments, employed the weapon of the weak and bombed Western planes and installations and seized Western hostages. This warfare between Arabs and the West culminated in 1990, when the United States sent a massive army to the Persian Gulf to defend some Arab countries against aggression by another. In its aftermath NATO planning is increasingly directed to potential threats and instability along its "southern tier."

This centuries-old military interaction between the West and Islam is unlikely to decline. It could become more virulent. The Gulf War left some Arabs feeling proud that Saddam Hussein had attacked Israel and stood up to the West. It also left many feeling humiliated and resentful of the West's military presence in the Persian Gulf, the West's overwhelming military dominance, and their apparent inability to shape their own destiny. Many Arab countries, in addition to the oil exporters, are reaching levels of economic and social development where autocratic forms of government become inappropriate and efforts to introduce democracy become stronger. Some openings in Arab political systems have already occurred. The principal beneficiaries of these openings have been Islamist movements. In the Arab world, in short, Western democracy strengthens anti-Western political forces. This may be a passing phenomenon, but it surely complicates relations between Islamic countries and the West.

Those relations are also complicated by demography. The spectacular population growth in Arab countries, particularly in North Africa, has led to increased migration to Western Europe. The movement within Western Europe toward minimizing internal boundaries has sharpened political sensitivities with respect to this development. In Italy, France and Germany, racism is increasingly open, and political reactions and violence against Arab and Turkish migrants have become more intense and more widespread since 1990.

On both sides the interaction between Islam and the West is seen as a clash of civilizations. The West's "next confrontation," observes M. J. Akbar, an Indian Muslim author, "is definitely going to come from the Muslim world. It is in the sweep of the Islamic nations from the Maghreb to Pakistan that the struggle for a new world order will begin." Bernard Lewis comes to a similar conclusion:

> We are facing a mood and a movement far transcending the level of issues and policies and the governments that pursue them. This is no less than a clash of civilizations—the perhaps irrational but surely historic reaction of an ancient rival against our Judeo-Christian heritage, our secular present, and the world-wide expansion of both.[2]

Historically, the other great antagonistic interaction of Arab Islamic civilization has been with the pagan, animist, and now increasingly Christian black peoples to the south. In the past, this antagonism was epitomized in the image of Arab slave dealers and black slaves. It has been reflected in the ongoing civil war in the Sudan between Arabs and blacks, the fighting in Chad between Libyan-supported insurgents and the government, the tensions between Orthodox Christians and Muslims in the Horn of Africa, and the political conflicts, recurring riots and communal violence between Muslims and Christians in Nigeria. The modernization of Africa and the spread of Christianity are likely to enhance the probability of violence along this fault line. Symptomatic of the intensification of this conflict was the Pope John Paul II's speech in Khartoum in February 1993 attacking the actions of the Sudan's Islamist government against the Christian minority there.

On the northern border of Islam, conflict has increasingly erupted between Orthodox and Muslim peoples, including the carnage of Bosnia and Sarajevo, the simmering violence between Serb and Albanian, the tenuous relations between Bulgarians and their Turkish minority, the violence between Ossetians and Ingush, the unremitting slaughter of each other by Armenians and Azeris, the tense relations between Russians and Muslims in Central Asia, and the deployment of Russian troops to protect Russian interests in the Caucasus and Central Asia. Religion reinforces the revival of ethnic identities and restimulates Russian fears about the security of their southern borders. This concern is well captured by Archie Roosevelt:

> Much of Russian history concerns the struggle between the Slavs and the Turkic peoples on their borders, which dates back to the foundation of the Russian state more than a thousand years ago. In the Slavs' millennium-long

confrontation with their eastern neighbors lies the key to an understanding not only of Russian history, but Russian character. To understand Russian realities today one has to have a concept of the great Turkic ethnic group that has pre-occupied Russians through the centuries.[3]

The conflict of civilizations is deeply rooted elsewhere in Asia. The historic clash between Muslim and Hindu in the subcontinent manifests itself now not only in the rivalry between Pakistan and India but also in intensifying religious strife within India between increasingly militant Hindu groups and India's substantial Muslim minority. The destruction of the Ayodhya mosque in December 1992 brought to the fore the issue of whether India will remain a secular democratic state or become a Hindu one. In East Asia, China has outstanding territorial disputes with most of its neighbors. It has pursued a ruthless policy toward the Buddhist people of Tibet, and it is pursuing an increasingly ruthless policy toward its Turkic-Muslim minority. With the Cold War over, the underlying differences between China and the United States have reasserted themselves in areas such as human rights, trade and weapons proliferation. These differences are unlikely to moderate. A "new cold war," Deng Xaioping reportedly asserted in 1991, is under way between China and America.

The same phrase has been applied to the increasingly difficult relations between Japan and the United States. Here cultural difference exacerbates economic conflict. People on each side allege racism on the other, but at least on the American side the antipathies are not racial but cultural. The basic values, attitudes, behavioral patterns of the two societies could hardly be more different. The economic issues between the United States and Europe are no less serious than those between the United States and Japan, but they do not have the same political salience and emotional intensity because the differences between American culture and European culture are so much less than those between American civilization and Japanese civilization.

The interactions between civilizations vary greatly in the extent to which they are likely to be characterized by violence. Economic competition clearly predominates between the American and European subcivilizations of the West and between both of them and Japan. On the Eurasian continent, however, the proliferation of ethnic conflict, epitomized at the extreme in "ethnic cleansing," has not been totally random. It has been most frequent and most violent between groups belonging to different civilizations. In Eurasia the great historic fault lines between civilizations are once more aflame. This is particularly true along the boundaries of the crescent-shaped Islamic bloc of nations from the bulge of Africa to central Asia. Violence also occurs between Muslims, on the one hand, and Orthodox Serbs in the Balkans, Jews in Israel, Hindus in India, Buddhists in Burma and Catholics in the Philippines. Islam has bloody borders.

Civilization Rallying: The Kin-Country Syndrome

Groups or states belonging to one civilization that become involved in war with people from a different civilization naturally try to rally support from other members of their own civilization. As the post-Cold War world evolves, civilization commonality, what H. D. S. Greenway has termed the "kin-country" syndrome, is replacing political ideology and traditional balance of power considerations as the principal basis for cooperation and coalitions. It can be seen gradually emerging in the post-Cold War conflicts in the Persian Gulf, the Caucasus and Bosnia. None of these was a full-scale war between civilizations, but each involved some elements of civilizational rallying, which seemed to become more important as the conflict continued and which may provide a foretaste of the future.

First, in the Gulf War one Arab state invaded another and then fought a coalition of Arab, Western and other states. While only a few Muslim governments overtly supported Saddam Hussein, many Arab elites privately cheered him on, and he was highly popular among large sections of the Arab publics. Islamic fundamentalist movements universally supported Iraq rather than the Western-backed governments of Kuwait and Saudi Arabia. Forswearing Arab nationalism, Saddam Hussein explicitly invoked an Islamic appeal. He and his supporters attempted to define the war as a war between civilizations. "It is not the world against Iraq," as Safar Al-Hawali, dean of Islamic Studies at the Umm Al-Qura University in Mecca, put it in a widely circulated tape. "It is the West against Islam." Ignoring the rivalry between Iran and Iraq, the chief Iranian religious leader, Ayatollah Ali Khamenei, called for a holy war against the West: "The struggle against American aggression, greed, plans and policies will be counted as a jihad, and anybody who is killed on that path is a martyr." "This is a war," King Hussein of Jordan argued, "against all Arabs and all Muslims and not against Iraq alone."

The rallying of substantial sections of Arab elites and publics behind Saddam Hussein caused those Arab governments in the anti-Iraq coalition to moderate their activities and temper their public statements. Arab governments opposed or distanced themselves from subsequent Western efforts to apply pressure on Iraq, including enforcement of a no-fly zone in the summer of 1992 and the bombing of Iraq in January 1993. The Western-Soviet-Turkish-Arab anti-Iraq coalition of 1990 had by 1993 become a coalition of almost only the West and Kuwait against Iraq.

Muslims contrasted Western actions against Iraq with the West's failure to protect Bosnians against Serbs and to impose sanctions on Israel for violating U.N. resolutions. The West, they alleged, was using a double standard. A world of clashing civilizations, however, is inevitably a world of double standards: people apply one standard to their kin-countries and a different standard to others.

Second, the kin-country syndrome also appeared in conflicts in the former Soviet Union. Armenian military successes in 1992 and 1993 stimulated Turkey to become increasingly supportive of its religious, ethnic and linguistic brethren in Azerbaijan. "We have a Turkish nation feeling the same sentiments as the Azerbaijanis," said one Turkish official in 1992. "We are under pressure. Our newspapers are full of the photos of atrocities and are asking us if we are still serious about pursuing our neutral policy. Maybe we should show Armenia that there's a big Turkey in the region." President Turgut Özal agreed, remarking that Turkey should at least "scare the Armenians a little bit." Turkey, Özal threatened again in 1993, would "show its fangs." Turkish Air Force jets flew reconnaissance flights along the Armenia border; Turkey suspended food shipments and air flights to Armenia; and Turkey and Iran announced they would not accept dismemberment of Azerbaijan. In the last years of its existence, the Soviet government supported Azerbaijan because its government was dominated by former communists. With the end of the Soviet Union, however, political considerations gave way to religious ones. Russian troops fought on the side of the Armenians, and Azerbaijan accused the "Russian government of turning 180 degrees" toward support for Christian Armenia.

Third, with respect to the fighting in the former Yugoslavia, Western publics manifested sympathy and support for the Bosnian Muslims and the horrors they suffered at the hands of the Serbs. Relatively little concern was expressed, however, over Croatian attacks on Muslims and participation in the dismemberment of Bosnia-Herzegovina. In the early stages of the Yugoslav breakup, Germany, in an unusual display of diplomatic initiative and muscle, induced the other 11 members of the European Community to follow its lead in recognizing Slovenia and Croatia. As a result of the pope's determination to provide strong backing to the two Catholic countries, the Vatican extended recognition even before the Community did. The United States followed the European lead. Thus the leading actors in Western civilization rallied behind their coreligionists. Subsequently Croatia was reported to be receiving substantial quantities of arms from Central European and other Western countries. Boris Yeltsin's government, on the other hand, attempted to pursue a middle course that would be sympathetic to the Orthodox Serbs but not alienate Russia from the West. Russian conservative and nationalist groups, however, including many legislators, attacked the government for not being more forthcoming in its support for the Serbs. By early 1993 several hundred Russians apparently were serving with the Serbian forces, and reports circulated of Russian arms being supplied to Serbia.

Islamic governments and groups, on the other hand, castigated the West for not coming to the defense of the Bosnians. Iranian leaders urged Muslims from all countries to provide help to Bosnia; in violation of the U.N. arms embargo, Iran supplied weapons and men for the Bosnians; Iranian-supported Lebanese groups sent guerrillas to train and organize the Bosnian forces. In 1993 up to 4,000 Muslims from over two dozen Islamic countries were reported to be fighting in Bosnia. The governments of Saudi Arabia and other countries felt under increasing pressure from fundamentalist groups in their own societies to provide more vigorous support for the Bosnians. By the end of 1992, Saudi Arabia had reportedly supplied substantial funding for weapons and supplies for the Bosnians, which significantly increased their military capabilities vis-à-vis the Serbs.

In the 1930s the Spanish Civil War provoked intervention from countries that politically were fascist, communist and democratic. In the 1990s the Yugoslav conflict is provoking intervention from countries that are Muslim, Orthodox and Western Christian. The parallel has not gone unnoticed.

"The war in Bosnia-Herzegovina has become the emotional equivalent of the fight against fascism in the Spanish Civil War," one Saudi editor observed. "Those who died there are regarded as martyrs who tried to save their fellow Muslims."

Conflicts and violence will also occur between states and groups within the same civilization. Such conflicts, however, are likely to be less intense and less likely to expand than conflicts between civilizations. Common membership in a civilization reduces the probability of violence in situations where it might otherwise occur. In 1991 and 1992 many people were alarmed by the possibility of violent conflict between Russia and Ukraine over territory, particularly Crimea, the Black Sea fleet, nuclear weapons and economic issues. If civilization is what counts, however, the likelihood of violence between Ukrainians and Russians should be low. They are two Slavic, primarily Orthodox peoples who have had close relationships with each other for centuries. As of early 1993, despite all the reasons for conflict, the leaders of the two countries were effectively negotiating and defusing the issues between the two countries. While there has been serious fighting between Muslims and Christians elsewhere in the former Soviet Union and much tension and some fighting between Western and Orthodox Christians in the Baltic states, there has been virtually no violence between Russians and Ukrainians.

Civilization rallying to date has been limited, but it has been growing, and it clearly has the potential to spread much further. As the conflicts in the Persian Gulf, the Caucasus and Bosnia continued, the positions of nations and the cleavages between them increasingly were along civilizational lines. Populist politicians, religious leaders and the media have found it a potent means of arousing mass support and of pressuring hesitant governments. In the coming years, the local conflicts most likely to escalate into major wars will be those, as in Bosnia and the Caucasus, along the fault lines between civilizations. The next world war, if there is one, will be a war between civilizations.

The West Versus The Rest

The West is now at an extraordinary peak of power in relation to other civilizations. Its superpower opponent has disappeared from the map. Military conflict among Western states is unthinkable, and Western military power is unrivaled. Apart from Japan, the West faces no economic challenge. It dominates international political and security institutions and with Japan international economic institutions. Global political and security issues are effectively settled by a directorate of the United States, Britain and France, world economic issues by a directorate of the United States, Germany and Japan, all of which maintain extraordinarily close relations with each other to the exclusion of lesser and largely non-Western countries. Decisions made at the U.N. Security Council or in the International Monetary Fund that reflect the interests of the West are presented to the world as reflecting the desires of the world community. The very phrase "the world community" has become the euphemistic collective noun (replacing "the Free World") to give global legitimacy to actions reflecting the interests of the United States and other Western powers.[4] Through the IMF and other international economic institutions, the West promotes its economic interests and imposes on other nations the economic policies it thinks appropriate. In any poll of non-Western peoples, the IMF undoubtedly would win the support of finance ministers and a few others, but get an overwhelmingly unfavorable rating from just about everyone else, who would agree with Georgy Arbatov's characterization of IMF officials as "neo-Bolsheviks who love expropriating other people's money, imposing undemocratic and alien rules of economic and political conduct and stifling economic freedom."

Western domination of the U.N. Security Council and its decisions, tempered only by occasional abstention by China, produced U.N. legitimation of the West's use of force to drive Iraq out of Kuwait and its elimination of Iraq's sophisticated weapons and capacity to produce such weapons. It also produced the quite unprecedented action by the United States, Britain and France in getting the Security Council to demand that Libya hand over the Pan Am 103 bombing suspects and then to impose sanctions when Libya refused. After defeating the largest Arab army, the West did not hesitate to throw its weight around in the Arab world. The West in effect is using international institutions, military power and economic resources to run the world in ways that will maintain Western predominance, protect Western interests and promote Western political and economic values.

That at least is the way in which non-Westerners see the new world, and there is a significant element of truth in their view. Differences in power and struggles for military, economic and institutional power are thus one source of conflict between the West and other civilizations. Differences in culture, that is basic values and beliefs, are a second source of conflict. V. S. Naipaul has argued that Western civilization is the "universal civilization" that "fits all men." At a superficial level much of Western culture has indeed permeated the rest of the world. At a more basic level, however, Western concepts differ fundamentally from those prevalent in other civilizations. Western ideas of individualism, liberalism, constitutionalism, human rights, equality, liberty, the rule of law, democracy, free markets, the separation of church and state, often have little resonance in Islamic, Confucian, Japanese, Hindu, Buddhist or Orthodox cultures. Western efforts to propagate such ideas produce instead a reaction against "human rights imperialism" and a reaffirmation of indigenous values, as can be seen in the support for religious fundamentalism by the younger generation in non-Western cultures. The very notion that there could be a "universal civilization" is a Western idea, directly at odds with the particularism of most Asian societies and their emphasis on what distinguishes one people from another. Indeed, the author of a review of 100 comparative studies of values in different societies concluded that "the values that are most important in the West are least important worldwide."[5] In the political realm, of course, these differences are most manifest in the efforts of the United States and other Western powers to induce other peoples to adopt Western ideas concerning democracy and human rights. Modern democratic government originated in the West. When it has developed in non-Western societies it has usually been the product of Western colonialism or imposition.

The central axis of world politics in the future is likely to be, in Kishore Mahbubani's phrase, the conflict between "the West and the Rest" and the responses of non-Western civilizations to Western power and values.[6] Those responses generally take one or a combination of three forms. At one extreme, non-Western states can, like Burma and North Korea, attempt to pursue a course of isolation, to insulate their societies from penetration or "corruption" by the West, and, in effect, to opt out of participation in the Western-dominated global community. The costs of this course, however, are high, and few states have pursued it exclusively. A second alternative, the equivalent of "bandwagoning" in international relations theory, is to attempt to join the West and accept its values and institutions. The third alternative is to attempt to "balance" the West by developing economic and military power and cooperating with other non-Western societies against the West, while preserving indigenous values and institutions; in short, to modernize but not to Westernize.

The Torn Countries

In the future, as people differentiate themselves by civilization, countries with large numbers of peoples of different civilizations, such as the Soviet Union and Yugoslavia, are candidates for dismemberment. Some other countries have a fair degree of cultural homogeneity but are divided over whether their society belongs to one civilization or another. These are torn countries. Their leaders typically wish to pursue a bandwagoning strategy and to make their countries members of the West, but the history, culture and traditions of their countries are non-Western. The most obvious and prototypical torn country is Turkey. The late twentieth-century leaders of Turkey have followed in the Attatürk tradition and defined Turkey as a modern, secular, Western nation state. They allied Turkey with the West in NATO and in the Gulf War; they applied for membership in the European Community. At the same time, however, elements in Turkish society have supported an Islamic revival and have argued that Turkey is basically a Middle Eastern Muslim society. In addition, while the elite of Turkey has defined Turkey as a Western society, the elite of the West refuses to accept Turkey as such. Turkey will not become a member of the European Community, and the real reason, as President Özal said, "is that we are Muslim and they are Christian and they don't say that." Having rejected Mecca, and then being rejected by Brussels, where does Turkey look? Tashkent may be the answer. The end of the Soviet Union gives Turkey the opportunity to become the leader of a revived Turkic civilization involving seven countries from the borders of Greece to those of China. Encouraged by the West, Turkey is making strenuous efforts to carve out this new identity for itself.

During the past decade Mexico has assumed a position somewhat similar to that of Turkey. Just as Turkey abandoned its historic opposition to Europe and attempted to join Europe, Mexico has stopped defining itself by its opposition to the United States and is instead attempting to imitate the United States and to join it in the North American Free Trade Area. Mexican leaders are engaged in the great task of redefining Mexican identity and have introduced fundamental economic reforms that eventually will lead to fundamental political change. In 1991 a top adviser to President Carlos Salinas de Gortari described at length to me all the changes the Salinas government was making. When he finished, I remarked: "That's most impressive. It seems to me that basically you want to change Mexico from a Latin American country into a North American country." He looked at me with surprise and exclaimed: "Exactly! That's precisely what we are trying to do, but of course we could never say so publicly." As his remark indicates, in Mexico as in Turkey, significant elements in society resist the redefinition of their country's identity. In Turkey, European-oriented leaders have to make gestures to Islam (Özal's pilgrimage to Mecca); so also Mexico's North American-oriented leaders have to make gestures to those who hold Mexico to be a Latin American country (Salinas' Ibero-American Guadalajara summit).

Historically Turkey has been the most profoundly torn country. For the United States, Mexico is the most immediate torn country. Globally the most important torn country is Russia. The question of whether Russia is part of the West or the leader of a distinct Slavic-Orthodox civilization has been a recurring one in Russian history. That issue was obscured by the communist victory in Russia, which imported a Western ideology, adapted it to Russian conditions and then challenged the West in the name of that ideology. The dominance of communism shut off the historic debate over Westernization versus Russification. With communism discredited Russians once again face that question.

President Yeltsin is adopting Western principles and goals and seeking to make Russia a "normal" country and a part of the West. Yet both the Russian elite and the Russian public are divided on this issue. Among the more moderate dissenters, Sergei Stankevich argues that Russia should reject the "Atlanticist" course, which would lead it "to become European, to become a part of the world economy in rapid and organized fashion, to become the eighth member of the Seven, and to put particular emphasis on Germany and the United States as the two dominant members of the Atlantic alliance." While also rejecting an exclusively Eurasian policy, Stankevich nonetheless argues that Russia should give priority to the protection of Russians in other countries, emphasize its Turkic and Muslim connections, and promote "an appreciable redistribution of our resources, our options, our ties, and our interests in favor of Asia, of the eastern direction." People of this persuasion criticize Yeltsin for subordinating Russia's interests to those of the West, for reducing Russian military strength, for failing to support traditional friends such as Serbia, and for pushing economic and political reform in ways injurious to the Russian people. Indicative of this trend is the new popularity of the ideas of Petr Savitsky, who in the 1920s argued that Russia was a unique Eurasian civilization.[7] More extreme dissidents voice much more blatantly nationalist, anti-Western and anti-Semitic views, and urge Russia to redevelop its military strength and to establish closer ties with China and Muslim countries. The people of Russia are as divided as the elite. An opinion survey in European Russia in the spring of 1992 revealed that 40 percent of the public had positive attitudes toward the West and 36 percent had negative attitudes. As it has been for much of its history, Russia in the early 1990s is truly a torn country.

To redefine its civilization identity, a torn country must meet three requirements. First, its political and economic elite has to be generally supportive of and enthusiastic about this move. Second, its public has to be willing to acquiesce in the redefinition. Third, the dominant groups in the recipient civilization have to be willing to embrace the convert. All three requirements in large part exist with respect to Mexico. The first two in large part exist with respect to Turkey. It is not clear that any of them exist with respect to Russia's joining the West. The conflict between liberal democracy and Marxism-Leninism was between ideologies which, despite their major differences, ostensibly shared ultimate goals of freedom, equality and prosperity. A traditional, authoritarian, nationalist Russia could have quite different goals. A Western democrat could carry on an intellectual debate with a Soviet Marxist. It would be virtually impossible for him to do that with a Russian traditionalist. If, as the Russians stop behaving like Marxists, they reject liberal democracy and begin behaving like Russians but not like Westerners, the relations between Russia and the West could again become distant and conflictual.[8]

The Confucian-Islamic Connection

The obstacles to non-Western countries joining the West vary considerably. They are least for Latin American and East European countries. They are greater for the Orthodox countries of the former Soviet Union. They are still greater for Muslim, Confucian, Hindu and Buddhist societies. Japan has established a unique position for itself as an associate member of the West: it is in the West in some respects but clearly not of the West in important dimensions. Those countries that for reason of culture and power do not wish to, or cannot, join the West compete with the West by developing their own economic, military and political power. They do this by promoting their internal development and by cooperating with other non-Western countries. The most prominent form of this cooperation is the Confucian-Islamic connection that has emerged to challenge Western interests, values and power.

Almost without exception, Western countries are reducing their military power; under Yeltsin's leadership so also is Russia. China, North Korea and several Middle Eastern states, however, are significantly expanding their military capabilities. They are doing this by the import of arms from Western and non-Western sources and by the development of indigenous arms industries. One result is the emergence of what Charles Krauthammer has called

"Weapon States," and the Weapon States are not Western states. Another result is the redefinition of arms control, which is a Western concept and a Western goal. During the Cold War the primary purpose of arms control was to establish a stable military balance between the United States and its allies and the Soviet Union and its allies. In the post-Cold War world the primary objective of arms control is to prevent the development by non-Western societies of military capabilities that could threaten Western interests. The West attempts to do this through international agreements, economic pressure and controls on the transfer of arms and weapons technologies.

The conflict between the West and the Confucian-Islamic states focuses largely, although not exclusively, on nuclear, chemical and biological weapons, ballistic missiles and other sophisticated means for delivering them, and the guidance, intelligence and other electronic capabilities for achieving that goal. The West promotes nonproliferation as a universal norm and nonproliferation treaties and inspections as means of realizing that norm. It also threatens a variety of sanctions against those who promote the spread of sophisticated weapons and proposes some benefits for those who do not. The attention of the West focuses, naturally, on nations that are actually or potentially hostile to the West.

The non-Western nations, on the other hand, assert their right to acquire and to deploy whatever weapons they think necessary for their security. They also have absorbed, to the full, the truth of the response of the Indian defense minister when asked what lesson he learned from the Gulf War: "Don't fight the United States unless you have nuclear weapons." Nuclear weapons, chemical weapons and missiles are viewed, probably erroneously, as the potential equalizer of superior Western conventional power. China, of course, already has nuclear weapons; Pakistan and India have the capability to deploy them. North Korea, Iran, Iraq, Libya and Algeria appear to be attempting to acquire them. A top Iranian official has declared that all Muslim states should acquire nuclear weapons, and in 1988 the president of Iran reportedly issued a directive calling for development of "offensive and defensive chemical, biological and radiological weapons."

Centrally important to the development of counter-West military capabilities is the sustained expansion of China's military power and its means to create military power. Buoyed by spectacular economic development, China is rapidly increasing its military spending and vigorously moving forward with the modernization of its armed forces. It is purchasing weapons from the former Soviet states; it is developing long-range missiles; in 1992 it tested a one-megaton nuclear device. It is developing power-projection capabilities, acquiring aerial refueling technology, and trying to purchase an aircraft carrier. Its military buildup and assertion of sovereignty over the South China Sea are provoking a multilateral regional arms race in East Asia. China is also a major exporter of arms and weapons technology. It has exported materials to Libya and Iraq that could be used to manufacture nuclear weapons and nerve gas. It has helped Algeria build a reactor suitable for nuclear weapons research and production. China has sold to Iran nuclear technology that American officials believe could only be used to create weapons and apparently has shipped components of 300-mile-range missiles to Pakistan. North Korea has had a nuclear weapons program under way for some while and has sold advanced missiles and missile technology to Syria and Iran. The flow of weapons and weapons technology is generally from East Asia to the Middle East. There is, however, some movement in the reverse direction; China has received Stinger missiles from Pakistan.

A Confucian-Islamic military connection has thus come into being, designed to promote acquisition by its members of the weapons and weapons technologies needed to counter the military power of the West. It may or may not last. At present, however, it is, as Dave McCurdy has said, "a renegades' mutual support pact, run by the proliferators and their backers." A new form of arms competition is thus occurring between Islamic-Confucian states and the West. In an old-fashioned arms race, each side developed its own arms to balance or to achieve superiority against the other side. In this new form of arms competition, one side is developing its arms and the other side is attempting not to balance but to limit and prevent that arms build-up while at the same time reducing its own military capabilities.

Implications for the West

This article does not argue that civilization identities will replace all other identities, that nation states will disappear, that each civilization will become a single coherent political entity, that groups within a civilization will not conflict with and even fight each other. This paper does set forth the hypotheses that differences between civilizations are real and important; civilization-consciousness is increasing; conflict between civilizations will supplant ideological and other forms of conflict as the dominant global form of conflict; international relations, historically a game played out within Western civilization, will increasingly be de-Westernized and become a game in which non-Western civilizations, are actors and not simply objects; successful political, security and economic international institutions are more likely to develop within civilizations than across civilizations; conflicts between groups in different civilizations will be more frequent, more sustained and more violent than conflicts between groups in the same civilization; violent conflicts between groups in different civilizations are the most likely and most dangerous source of escalation that could lead to global wars; the paramount axis of world politics will be the relations between "the West and the Rest"; the elites in some torn non-Western countries will try to make their countries part of the West, but in most cases face major obstacles to accomplishing this; a central focus of conflict for the immediate future will be between the West and several Islamic-Confucian states.

This is not to advocate the desirability of conflicts between civilizations. It is to set forth descriptive hypotheses as to what the future may be like. If these are plausible hypotheses, however, it is necessary to consider their implications for Western policy. These implications should be divided between short-term advantage and long-term accommodation. In the short term it is clearly in the interest of the West to promote greater cooperation and unity within its own civilization, particularly between its European and North American components; to incorporate into the West societies in Eastern Europe and Latin America whose cultures are close to those of the West; to promote and maintain cooperative relations with Russia and Japan; to prevent escalation of local inter-civilization conflicts into major inter-civilization wars; to limit the expansion of the military strength of Confucian and Islamic states; to moderate the reduction of Western military capabilities and maintain military superiority in East and Southwest Asia; to exploit differences and conflicts among Confucian and Islamic states; to support in other civilizations groups sympathetic to Western values and interests; to strengthen international institutions that reflect and legitimate Western interests and values and to promote the involvement of non-Western states in those institutions.

In the longer term other measures would be called for. Western civilization is both Western and modern. Non-Western civilizations have attempted to become modern without becoming Western. To date only Japan has fully succeeded in this quest. Non-Western civilizations will continue to attempt to acquire the wealth, technology, skills, machines and weapons that are part of being modern. They will also attempt to reconcile this modernity with their traditional culture and values. Their economic and military strength relative to the West will increase. Hence the West will increasingly have to accommodate these non-Western modern civilizations whose power approaches that of the West but whose values and interests differ significantly from those of the West. This will require the West to maintain the economic and military power necessary to protect its interests in relation to these civilizations. It will also, however, require the West to develop a more profound understanding of the basic religious and philosophical assumptions underlying other civilizations and the ways in which people in those civilizations see their interests. It will require an effort to identify elements of commonality between Western and other civilizations. For the relevant future, there will be no universal civilization, but instead a world of different civilizations, each of which will have to learn to coexist with the others.

NOTES

1. Murray Weidenbaum, *Great China: The Next Economic Superpower?*, St. Louis: Washington University Center for the Study of American Business, Contemporary Issues, Series 57, February 1993, pp. 2–3.

2. Bernard Lewis, "The Roots of Muslim Rage," *The Atlantic Monthly*, vol. 266, September 1990, p. 60; *Time*, June 15, 1992, pp. 24–28.

3. Archie Roosevelt, *For Lust of Knowing*, Boston: Little, Brown, 1988, pp. 332–333.

4. Almost invariably Western leaders claim they are acting on behalf of "the world community." One minor lapse occurred during the run-up to the Gulf War. In an interview on "Good Morning America," Dec. 21, 1990, British Prime Minister John Major referred to the actions "the West" was taking against Saddam Hussein. He quickly cor-

rected himself and subsequently referred to "the world community." He was, however, right when he erred.

5. Harry C. Triandis, *The New York Times*, Dec. 25, 1990, p. 41, and "Cross-Cultural Studies of Individualism and Collectivism," Nebraska Symposium on Motivation, vol. 37, 1989, pp. 41–133.

6. Kishore Mahbubani, "The West and the Rest," *The National Interest*, Summer 1992, pp. 3–13.

7. Sergei Stankevich, "Russia in Search of Itself," *The National Interest*, Summer 1992, pp. 47–51; Daniel Schneider, "A Russian Movement Rejects Western Tilt," *Christian Science Monitor*, Feb. 5, 1993, pp. 5–7.

8. Owen Harries has pointed out that Australia is trying (unwisely in his view) to become a torn country in reverse. Although it has been a full member not only of the West but also of the ABCA military and intelligence core of the West, its current leaders are in effect proposing that it defect from the West, redefine itself as an Asian country and cultivate close ties with its neighbors. Australia's future, they argue, is with the dynamic economies of East Asia. But, as I have suggested, close economic cooperation normally requires a common cultural base. In addition, none of the three conditions necessary for a torn country to join another civilization is likely to exist in Australia's case.

Review Questions

1. How does Thucydides's classical analysis of the balance of power concept resonate through the ages to the present day? Can you apply any of Thucydides's early concepts of international relations to modern issues of war and peace?
2. Do you agree with Clausewitz that war is essentially just another way of implementing policy? How are Clausewitz's concepts of friction and the fog of war still valid today?
3. Why did George Kennon believe that containment, as opposed to war, would be the best way to deal with the Soviet Union during the Cold War? Why did the policy of containment ultimately prove to be so successful?
4. What does Samuel Huntington mean by the "clash of civilizations"? Does Huntington deserve credit for predicting the War on Terrorism that began on September 11, 2001?

Chapter 10

Public Policy as Public Relations

All great leaders have been spinners—public opinion manipulators—to some extent. Is there any greater spin than the divine right of kings? The Vikings called a frozen island in the North Atlantic "Greenland" and their foothold in what is now eastern Canada, "Vineland." While there was not much green and fewer vines, some settlers were initially encouraged by the sharply spun names.

Propaganda at its core is the spinning of people's beliefs, values, and behavior by using symbols (such as flags, music, or oratory) and other psychological tools. In effect, it is the management of public opinion. Propaganda is the older term for what is now called public relations, a government's mass dissemination of true information about its policies and the policies of its adversaries; or alternatively, similar dissemination that is untruthful (sometimes called black propaganda).

Propaganda has a long history. Genghis Kahn (1162–1227), for example, used exaggerated rumors of the strength of his army to terrorize populations and leaders into surrender. The term itself stems from the Congregation of Propaganda set up by the Roman Catholic Church in 1622 to propagate its views and to refute those of Protestants and those considered heretics.

The growth of democracy and mass political awareness presented new possibilities for propaganda. So too has the development of the mass media which all governments use to influence their publics. The concept was introduced into American political science after World War I when British news reports of German atrocities (both real and imagined) were indicted as having influenced American attitudes toward entry into the war. This fostered Harold D. Lasswell's landmark analysis,

Propaganda Technique in World War I (1927). Ever since World War II, when the German Ministry of Propaganda under Joseph Goebbels (1897–1945) broadcast one lie after another, the term has taken on a sinister connotation. Goebbels musically advised to: "Think of the press as a great keyboard on which the government can play" (*Time*, March 27, 1933).

Playing counterpoint at the time was George Orwell (1903–1950). He spent the 1940s writing novels, articles and radio broadcasts refuting the fascist propaganda of Nazi Germany and the communist propaganda of the Soviet Union. Orwell first became famous with the publication of *Animal Farm*, his 1945 novella— the classic satire on Soviet communism and a warning that all revolutions may eventually betray their evolutionary ideals. His last novel, *1984* (1950) was published the year he died and he never knew how repellently influential his conception of "big brother"—a government so big and intrusive that it literally oversaw and regulated every aspect of life—would be.

Orwell knew that the fascists and communists were using language to hide some of the most despicable crimes of the twentieth century. His 1946 essay; "Politics and the English Language," sought not only to expose their diction but to demonstrate how "political language . . . is designed to make lies sound truthful and murder respectable. . . ." Inasmuch as Americans experience politics almost exclusively through the words of political leaders and the description of political events by reporters and commentators, the use of language continues to play a crucial role in determining who wins and loses elections and how Americans will define political events at home and abroad. Orwell's classic recognition that "The great enemy of clear language is insincerity" remains as significant today as when he wrote it. The public would be well advised to heed Orwell's message that political language always has as its goal persuasion rather than clarity, and that "political chaos is connected with the decay of language."

Propaganda today is no longer presented with the heavy hand of the mailed fist. It is subtle, delicate, almost subliminal. Modern propaganda is offered to a television addicted public as a media event, an activity undertaken as a means of generating publicity from the news media. The defining criterion for a media event is that it would not be done if cameras and reporters were not present. Examples include an orchestrated news leak, the releasing of trial balloons (deliberate leak of a potential policy to see what public response will be), protest demonstrations scheduled for the convenience of the early evening television news programs or a walk through a poor or ethnic neighborhood by a candidate for public office to demonstrate meaningful (meaning photogenic) concern. These pseudoevents, historian Daniel J. Boorstin's term for nonspontaneous, planted, or manufactured "news," are designed to gain publicity for the person or cause which arranged the "event." Once you read his analyses of the "synthetic novelty which has flooded our experience," reprinted here, you will never again look at a presidential appearance, a campaign speech or a political demonstration in the same old way. You will see it anew as less than it seems.

Cunning politicos throughout the ages have instinctively practiced effective public relations using symbols. Some techniques are timeless. When William Shakespeare's Richard III wanted to enhance his seeming worthiness to be king among the masses, he conspicuously went about carrying a Bible. President Bill Clinton did the same when the Monica Lewinsky scandal broke in 1998. The following Sunday he went hand in hand with his wife to church while conspicuously carrying his Bible. The Bible, in addition to its other uses, is a time honored public relations prop.

Since prehistory, people have been controlled by their leaders by means of taboos and rituals. The associated symbolism portends either terror or hope. Political leaders in the United States have evoked terror with dire predictions about the international communist conspiracy and hope with a call to arms to fight the war on poverty. Similarly, U.S. business leaders evoke terror by reminding us of the perils of bad breath, dull teeth, and unsprayed body areas. These fears fade when the various sprays, creams, gels, and pastes are purchased and used. The public is assured that they, too, can be "beautiful people" if they take the right vitamin supplements, drive the appropriate car, and drink the correct diet cola or wine cooler. We are all subliminally (if not consciously) aware of the symbolism in political rhetoric and business advertising. As Murray Edelman (1919–2001) has written in *The Symbolic Uses of Politics* (1967): "For most people most of the time politics is a series of pictures in the mind, placed there by television news, newspapers, magazines, and discussions. . . . Politics for most of us is a passing parade of symbols."

A political executive wishing to impose a sanction upon a congressional committee that is holding up the funding of his program might suggest that the committee is not acting in "the national interest." The notion of the national interest, while vague, is a powerful symbol because it represents a commonly accepted good. Because it is so widely revered, it has great legitimacy. By wrapping his program in a symbol of such weight and using that symbol punitively against legislators in opposition to his program, a political executive may succeed in influencing those legislators. The success or failure of such a gambit depends upon a variety of interrelated factors. How susceptible to this particular symbol are the legislators that he is trying to influence? Is the symbol of appropriate weight relative to the symbols of the opposition? While the political executive might wish to use a more powerful symbol, such a tactic might backfire. One does not fight the opposition's symbol of "economy and efficiency" by calling them "communist dupes."

Reprinted here is Edelman's chapter on "Symbols and Political Quiescence" which explains how symbols manipulate citizens' attitudes and beliefs so that they are acquiescent to policies that they might otherwise oppose. Note that Edelman's analysis is opposed to traditional rational choice theory which holds that citizens make rational choices after considering the options. To Edelman rational choice is in large measure taken away from the citizenry when their emotions are played upon by the symbols and propaganda of the state.

38

Politics and the English Language (1946)

George Orwell

In our time it is broadly true that political writing is bad writing. Where it is not true, it will generally be found that the writer is some kind of rebel, expressing his private opinions and not a "party line." Orthodoxy, of whatever color, seems to demand a lifeless, imitative style. The political dialects to be found in pamphlets, leading articles, manifestos, White Papers and the speeches of undersecretaries do, of course, vary from party to party, but they are all alike in that one almost never finds in them a fresh, vivid, home-made turn of speech. When one watches some tired hack on the platform mechanically repeating the familiar phrases—*bestial atrocities, iron heel, bloodstained tyranny, free peoples of the world, stand shoulder to shoulder*—one often has a curious feeling that one is not watching a live human being but some kind of dummy: a feeling which suddenly becomes stronger at moments when the light catches the speaker's spectacles and turns them into blank discs which seem to have no eyes behind them. And this in not altogether fanciful. A speaker who uses that kind of phraseology has gone some distance towards turning himself into a machine. The appropriate noises are coming out of his larynx, but his brain is not involved as it would be if he were choosing his words for himself. If the speech he is making is one that he is accustomed to make over and over again, he may be almost unconscious of what he is saying, as one is when one utters the responses in church. And this reduced state of consciousness, if not indispensable, is at any rate favorable to political conformity.

In our time, political speech and writing are largely the defence of the indefensible. Things like the continuance of British rule in India, the Russian purges and deportations, the dropping of the atom bombs on Japan, can indeed be defended, but only by arguments which are too brutal for most people to face, and which do not square with the professed aims of political parties. Thus political language has to consist largely of euphemism, question-begging and sheer cloudy vagueness. Defenceless villages are bombarded from the air, the inhabitants driven out into the countryside, the cattle machine-gunned, the huts set on fire with incendiary bullets: this is called *pacification*. Millions of peasants are robbed of their farms and sent trudging along the roads with no more than they can carry: this is called *transfer of population* or *rectification of frontiers*. People are imprisoned for years without trial, or shot in the back of the neck or sent to die of scurvy in Arctic lumber camps: this is called *elimination of unreliable elements*. Such phraseology is needed if one wants to name things without calling up mental pictures of them. Consider for instance some comfortable English professor defending Russian totalitarianism. He cannot say outright, "I believe in killing off your opponents when you can get good results by doing so." Probably, therefore, he will say something like this:

"While freely conceding that the Soviet régime exhibits certain features which the humanitarian may be inclined to deplore, we must, I think, agree that a certain curtailment of the right to political opposition is an unavoidable concomitant of transitional periods, and that the rigors which the Russian people have been called upon to undergo have been amply justified in the sphere of concrete achievement."

The inflated style is itself a kind of euphemism. A mass of Latin words falls upon the facts like soft snow, blurring the outlines and covering up all the details. The great enemy of clear language is insincerity. When there is a gap between one's real and one's declared aims, one turns as it were instinctively to long words and exhausted idioms, like a cuttlefish squirting out ink. In our age there is no such thing as "keeping out of politics." All issues are political issues, and politics itself is a mass of lies, evasions, folly, hatred and schizophrenia. When the general atmosphere is bad, language must suffer. I should expect to find—this is a guess which I have not sufficient knowledge to verify—that the German, Russian and Italian languages have all deteriorated in the last ten or fifteen years, as a result of dictatorship.

But if thought corrupts language, language can also corrupt thought. A bad usage can spread by tradition and imitation, even among people who should and do know better. The debased language that I have been discussing is in some ways very convenient. Phrases like *a not unjustifiable assumption, leaves much to be desired, would serve no good purpose, a consideration which we should do well to bear in mind,* are a continuous temptation, a packet of aspirins always at one's elbow. Look back through this essay, and for certain you will find that I have again and again committed the very faults I am protesting against. By this morning's post I have received a pamphlet dealing with conditions in Germany. The author tells me that he "felt impelled" to write it. I open it at random, and here is almost the first sentence that I see: "[The Allies] have an opportunity not only of achieving a radical transformation of Germany's social and political structure in such a way as to avoid a nationalistic reaction in Germany itself, but at the same time of laying the foundations of a co-operative and unified Europe." You see, he "feels impelled" to write—feels, presumably, that he has something new to say—and yet his words, like cavalry horses answering the bugle, group themselves automatically into the familiar dreary pattern. This invasion of one's mind by ready-made phrases (*lay the foundations, achieve a radical transformation*) can only be prevented if one is constantly on guard against them, and every such phrase anaesthetizes a portion of one's brain.

I said earlier that the decadence of our language is probably curable. Those who deny this would argue, if they produced an argument at all, that language merely reflects existing social conditions, and that we cannot influence its development by any direct tinkering with words and constructions. So far as the general tone or spirit of a language goes, this may be true, but it is not true in detail. Silly words and expressions have often disappeared, not through any evolutionary process but owing to the conscious action of a minority. Two recent examples were *explore every avenue* and *leave no stone unturned*, which were killed by the jeers of a few journalists. There is a long list of flyblown metaphors which could similarly be got rid of if enough people would interest themselves in the job; and it should also be possible to laugh the *not un-* formation out of existence, to reduce the amount of Latin and Greek in the average sentence, to drive out foreign phrases and strayed scientific words, and, in general, to make pretentiousness unfashionable. But all these are minor points. The defence of the English language implies more than this, and perhaps it is best to start by saying what it does *not* imply.

To begin with it has nothing to do with archaism, with the salvaging of obsolete words and turns of speech, or with the setting up of a "standard English" which must never be departed from. On the contrary, it is especially concerned with the scrapping of every word or idiom which has outworn its usefulness. It has nothing to do with correct grammar and syntax, which are of no importance so long as one makes one's meaning clear, or with the avoidance of Americanisms, or with having what is called a "good prose style." On the other hand it is not concerned with fake simplicity and the attempt to make written English colloquial. Nor does it even imply in every case preferring the Saxon word to the Latin one, though it does imply using the fewest and shortest words that will cover one's meaning. What is above all needed is to let the meaning choose the word, and not the other way about. In prose, the worst thing one can do with words is to surrender to them. When you think of a concrete object, you think wordlessly, and then, if you want to describe the thing you have been visualizing you probably hunt about till you find the exact words that seem to fit it. When you think of something abstract you are more inclined to use words from the start, and unless you make a conscious effort to prevent it, the existing dialect will come rushing in and do the the job for you, at the expense of blurring or even changing your meaning. Probably it is better to put off using words as long as possible and get one's meaning as clear as one can through pictures or sensations. Afterwards one can choose—not simply *accept*—the phrases that will best cover the meaning, and then switch round and decide what impression one's words are likely to make on another person. This last effort of the mind cuts out all stale or mixed images, all prefabricated phrases, needless repetitions, and humbug and vagueness generally. But one can often be in doubt about the effect of a word or a phrase, and one needs rules that one can rely on when instinct fails. I think the following rules will cover most cases:

(i)   Never use a metaphor, simile or other figure of speech which you are used to seeing in print.
(ii) Never use a long word where a short one will do.
(iii) If it is possible to cut a word out, always cut it out.
(iv) Never use the passive where you can use the active.
(v)   Never use a foreign phrase, a scientific word or a jargon word if you can think of an everyday English equivalent.
(vi) Break any of these rules sooner than say anything outright barbarous.

These rules sound elementary, and so they are, but they demand a deep change of attitude in anyone who has grown used to writing in the style now fashionable. One could keep all of them and still write bad English, but one could not write the kind of stuff that I quoted in those five specimens at the beginning of this article.

I have not here been considering the literary use of language, but merely language as an instrument for expressing and not for concealing or preventing thought. Stuart Chase and others have come near to claiming that all abstract words are meaningless, and have used this as a pretext for advocating a kind of political quietism. Since you don't know what Fascism is, how can you struggle against Fascism? One need not swallow such absurdities as this, but one ought to recognize that the present political chaos is connected with the decay of language, and that one can probably bring about some improvement by starting at the verbal end. If you simplify your English, you are freed from the worst follies of orthodoxy. You cannot speak any of the necessary dialects, and when you make a stupid remark its stupidity will be obvious, even to yourself. Political language—and with variations this is true of all political parties, from Conservatives to Anarchists—is designed to make lies sound truthful and murder respectable, and to give an appearance of solidity to pure wind. One cannot change this all in a moment, but one can at least change one's own habits, and from time to time one can even, if one jeers loudly enough, send some worn-out and useless phrase—some *jackboot, Achilles' heel, hotbed, melting pot, acid test, veritable inferno* or other lump of verbal refuse—into the dustbin where it belongs.

39

The Image: A Guide to Pseudo-Events in America (1961)

Daniel J. Boorstin

The new kind of synthetic novelty which has flooded our experience I will call "pseudo-events." The common prefix "pseudo" comes from the Greek word meaning false, or intended to deceive. Before I recall the historical forces which have made these pseudo-events possible, have increased the supply of them and the demand for them, I will give a commonplace example.

The owners of a hotel, in an illustration offered by Edward L. Bernays in his pioneer *Crystallizing Public Opinion* (1923), consult a public relations counsel. They ask how to increase their hotel's prestige and so improve their business. In less sophisticated times, the answer might have been to hire a new chef, to improve the plumbing, to paint the rooms, or to install a crystal chandelier in the lobby. The public relations counsel's technique is more indirect. He proposes that the management stage a celebration of the hotel's thirtieth anniversary. A committee is formed, including a prominent banker, a leading society matron, a well-known lawyer, an influential preacher, and an "event" is planned (say a banquet) to call attention to the distinguished service the hotel has been rendering the community. The celebration is held, photographs are taken, the occasion is widely reported, and the object is accomplished. Now this occasion is a pseudo-event, and will illustrate all the essential features of pseudo-events.

This celebration, we can see at the outset, is somewhat—but not entirely—misleading. Presumably the public relations counsel would not have been able to form his committee of prominent citizens if the hotel had not actually been rendering service to the community. On the other hand, if the hotel's services had been all that important, instigation by public relations counsel might not have been necessary. Once the celebration has been held, the celebration itself becomes evidence that the hotel really is a distinguished institution. The occasion actually gives the hotel the prestige to which it is pretending.

It is obvious, too, that the value of such a celebration to the owners depends on its being photographed and reported in newspapers, magazines, newsreels, on radio, and over television. It is the report that gives the event its force in the minds of potential customers. The power to make a reportable event is thus the power to make experience. One is reminded of Napoleon's apocryphal reply to his general, who objected that circumstances were unfavorable to a proposed campaign: "Bah, I make circumstances!" The modern public relations counsel—and he is, of course; only one of many twentieth-century creators of pseudo-events—has come close to fulfilling Napoleon's idle boast. "The counsel on public relations," Mr. Bernays explains, "not only knows what news value is, but knowing it, he is in a position to *make news happen*. He is a creator of events."

The intriguing feature of the modern situation, however, comes precisely from the fact that the modern news makers are not God. The news they make happen, the events they create, are somehow not quite real. There remains a tantalizing difference between man-made and God-made events.

A pseudo-event, then, is a happening that possesses the following characteristics:

1. It is not spontaneous, but comes about because someone has planned, planted, or incited it. Typically, it is not a train wreck or an earthquake, but an interview.
2. It is planted primarily (not always exclusively) for the immediate purpose of being reported or reproduced. Therefore, its occurrence is arranged for the convenience of the reporting or reproducing media. Its success is measured by how widely it is reported. Time relations in it are commonly fictitious or factitious: the announcement is given out in advance "for future release" and written as if the event had occurred in the past. The question, "Is it real?" is less important than, "Is it newsworthy?"
3. Its relation to the underlying reality of the situation is ambiguous. Its interest arises largely from this very ambiguity. Concerning a pseudo-event the question, "What does it mean?" has a new dimension. While the news interest in a train wreck is in *what* happened and in the real consequences, the interest in an interview is always, in a sense, in *whether* it really happened and in what might have been the motives. Did the statement really mean what it said? Without some of this ambiguity a pseudo-event cannot be very interesting.
4. Usually it is intended to be a self-fulfilling prophecy. The hotel's thirtieth-anniversary celebration, by saying that the hotel is a distinguished institutional, actually makes it one. . . .

In the age of pseudo-events it is less the artificial simplification than the artificial complication of experience that confuses us. Whenever in the public mind a pseudo-event competes for attention with a spontaneous event in the same field, the pseudo-event will tend to dominate. What happens on television will overshadow what happens off television. Of course I am concerned here not with our private worlds but with our world of public affairs.

Here are some characteristics of pseudo-events which make them overshadow spontaneous events:

1. Pseudo-events are more dramatic. A television debate between candidates can be planned to be more suspenseful (for example, by reserving questions which are then popped suddenly) than a casual encounter or consecutive formal speeches planned by each separately.

2. Pseudo-events, being planned for dissemination, are easier to disseminate and to make vivid. Participants are selected for their newsworthy and dramatic interest.

3. Pseudo-events can be reported at will, and thus their impression can be re-enforced.

4. Pseudo-events cost money to create; hence somebody has an interest in disseminating, magnifying, advertising, and extolling them as events worth watching or worth believing. They are therefore advertised in advance, and rerun in order to get money's worth.

5. Pseudo-events, being planned for intelligibility, are more intelligible and hence more reassuring. Even if we cannot discuss intelligently the qualifications of the candidates or the complicated issues, we can at least judge the effectiveness of a television performance. How comforting to have some political matter we can grasp!

6. Pseudo-events are more sociable, more conversable, and more convenient to witness. Their occurrence is planned for our convenience. The Sunday newspaper appears when we have a lazy morning for it. Television programs appear when we are ready with our glass of beer. In the office the next morning, Jack Paar's (or any other star performer's) regular late-night show at the usual hour will overshadow in conversation a casual event that suddenly came up and had to find its way into the news.

7. Knowledge of pseudo-events—of what has been reported, or what has been staged, and how—becomes the test of being "informed." News magazines provide us regularly with quiz questions concerning not what has happened but concerning "names in the news"—what has been reported in the news magazines. Pseudo-events begin to provide that "common discourse" which some of my old-fashioned friends have hoped to find in the Great Books.

8. Finally, pseudo-events spawn other pseudo-events in geometric progression. They dominate our consciousness simply because there are more of them, and ever more.

By this new Gresham's law of American public life, counterfeit happenings tend to drive spontaneous happenings out of circulation. The rise in the power and prestige of the Presidency is due not only to the broadening powers of the office and the need for quick decisions, but also to the rise of centralized news gathering and broadcasting, and the increase of the Washington press corps. The President has an ever more ready, more frequent, and more centralized access to the world of pseudo-events. A similar explanation helps account for the rising prominence in recent years of the Congressional investigating committees. In many cases these committees have virtually no legislative impulse, and sometimes no intelligible legislative assignment. But they do have an almost unprecedented power, possessed now by no one else in the Federal government except the President, to make news. Newsmen support the committees because the committees feed the newsmen: they live together in happy symbiosis. The battle for power among Washington agencies becomes a contest to dominate the citizen's information of the government. This can most easily be done by fabricating pseudo-events.

A perfect example of how pseudo-events can dominate is the recent popularity of the quiz show format. Its original appeal came less from the fact that such shows were tests of intelligence (or of dissimulation) than from the fact that the situations were elaborately contrived—with isolation booths, armed bank guards, and all the rest—and they purported to inform the public.

The application of the quiz show format to the so-called "Great Debates" between Presidential candidates in the election of 1960 is only another example. These four campaign programs, pompously and self-righteously advertised by the broadcasting networks, were remarkably successful in reducing great national issues to trivial dimensions. With appropriate vulgarity, they might have been called the $400,000 Question (Prize: a $100,000-a-year job for four years). They were a clinical example of the pseudo-event, of how it is made, why it appeals, and of its consequences for democracy in America.

In origin the Great Debates were confusedly collaborative between politicians and news makers. Public interest centered around the pseudo-event itself: the lighting, make-up, ground rules, whether notes would be allowed, etc. Far more interest was shown in the performance than in what was said. The pseudo-events spawned in turn by the Great Debates were numberless. People who had seen the shows read about them the more avidly, and listened eagerly for interpretations by news commentators. Representatives of both parties made "statements" on the probable effects of the debates. Numerous interviews and discussion programs were broadcast exploring their meaning. Opinion polls kept us informed on the nuances of our own and other people's reactions. Topics of speculation multiplied. Even the question whether there should be a fifth debate became for a while a lively "issue."

The drama of the situation was mostly specious, or at least had an extremely ambiguous relevance to the main (but forgotten) issue: which participant was better qualified for the Presidency. Of course, a man's ability, while standing under klieg lights, without notes, to answer in two and a half minutes a question kept secret until that moment, had only the most dubious relevance—if any at all—to his real qualifications to make deliberate Presidential decisions on long-standing public questions after being instructed by a corps of advisers. The great Presidents in our history (with the possible exception of F.D.R.) would have done miserably; but our most notorious demagogues would have shone. A number of exciting pseudo-events were created—for example, the Quemoy-Matsu issue. But that, too, was a good example of a pseudo-event: it was created to be reported, it concerned a then-quiescent problem, and it put into the most factitious and trivial terms the great and real issue of our relation to Communist China.

The television medium shapes this new kind of political quiz-show spectacular in many crucial ways. Theodore H. White has proven this with copious detail in his *The Making of the President: 1960* (1961). All the circumstances of this particular competition for votes were far more novel than the old word "debate" and the comparisons with the Lincoln-Douglas Debates suggested. Kennedy's great strength in the critical first debate, according to White, was that he was in fact not "debating" at all, but was seizing the opportunity to address the whole nation; while Nixon stuck close to the issues raised by his opponent, rebutting them one by one. Nixon, moreover, suffered a handicap that was serious only on television: he has a light, naturally transparent skin. On an ordinary camera that takes pictures by optical projection, this skin photographs well. But a television camera projects electronically, by an "image-orthicon tube" which has an x-ray effect. This camera penetrates Nixon's transparent skin and brings out (even just after a shave) the tiniest hair growing in the follicles beneath the surface. For the decisive first program Nixon wore a makeup called "Lazy Shave" which was ineffective under these conditions. He therefore looked haggard and heavy-bearded by contrast to Kennedy, who looked pert and clean-cut.

This greatest opportunity in American history to educate the voters by debating the large issues of the campaign failed. The main reason, as White points out, was the compulsions of the medium. "The nature of both TV and radio is that they abhor silence and 'dead time.' All TV and radio discussion programs are compelled to snap question and answer back and forth as if the contestants were adversaries in an intellectual tennis match. Although every experienced newspaperman and inquirer knows that the most thoughtful and responsive answers to any difficult question come after long pause, and that the longer the pause the more illuminating the thought that follows it, nonetheless the electronic media cannot bear to suffer a pause of more than five seconds; a pause of thirty seconds of dead time on air seems interminable. Thus, snapping their two-and-a-half-minute answers back and forth, both candidates could only react for the cameras and the people, they could not think." Whenever either candidate found himself touching a thought too large for two-minute exploration, he quickly retreated. Finally the television-watching voter was left to judge, not on issues explored by thoughtful men, but on the relative capacity of the two candidates to perform under television stress.

Pseudo-events thus lead to emphasis on pseudo-qualifications. Again the self-fulfilling prophecy. If we test Presidential candidates by their talents on TV quiz performances, we will, of course, choose presidents for precisely these qualifications. In a democracy, reality tends to conform to the pseudo-event. Nature imitates art.

We are frustrated by our very efforts publicly to unmask the pseudo-event. Whenever we describe the lighting, the make-up, the studio setting, the rehearsals, etc., we simply arouse more interest. One newsman's interpretation makes us more eager to hear another's. One commentator's speculation that the debates may have little significance makes us curious to hear whether another commentator disagrees.

Pseudo-events do, of course, increase our illusion of grasp on the world, what some have called the American illusion of omnipotence. Perhaps, we come to think, the world's problems can really be settled by "statements," by "Summit" meetings, by a competition of "prestige," by overshadowing images, and by political quiz shows.

Once we have tasted the charm of pseudo-events, we are tempted to believe they are the only important events. Our progress poisons the sources of our experience. And the poison tastes so sweet that it spoils our appetite for plain fact. Our seeming ability to satisfy our exaggerated expectations makes us forget that they are exaggerated.

40

Symbols and Political Quiescence (1964)

Murray Edelman

Few explanations of political phenomena are more common than the assertion that the success of some group was facilitated by the "apathy" of other groups with opposing interests. If apathy is not observable in a political context because it connotes an individual's mental state, quiescence is observable. This chapter specifies some conditions associated with political quiescence in the formation of business regulation policies. Although the same general conditions are apparently applicable to the formation of public policies in any area, the argument and the examples used here focus upon the field of government regulation of business in order to permit more intensive treatment.

Political quiescence toward a policy area can be assumed to be a function either of lack of interest or of the satisfaction of whatever interest the quiescent group may have in the policy in question. Our concern here is with the forms of satisfaction. In analyzing the various means by which it can come to pass, the following discussion distinguishes between interests in resources (whether goods or freedoms to act) and interests in symbols connoting the suppression of threats to the group in question.

Three related hypotheses will be considered:

1. The interests of organized groups in tangible resources or in substantive power are less easily satiable than are interests in symbolic reassurance.
2. Conditions associated with the occurrence of an interest in symbolic reassurance are:
   a. the existence of economic conditions threatening the security of a large group;

    b. 'the absence of organization for the purpose of furthering the common interest of that group.

3. The pattern of political activity represented by lack of organization, interests in symbolic reassurance, and quiescence is a key element in the ability of organized groups to use political agencies in order to make good their claims on tangible resources and power, thus continuing the threat to the unorganized.

Evidence bearing on these hypotheses is marshaled as follows. First, some widely accepted propositions regarding group claims, quiescence, and techniques for satisfying group interests in governmental regulation of business are summarized. Next, some pertinent experimental and empirical findings of other disciplines are considered. Finally, we explore the possibility of integrating the various findings and applying them to the propositions listed above.

I

If the regulatory process is examined in terms of a divergence between political and legal promises on the one hand and resource allocations and group reactions on the other hand, the largely symbolic character of the entire process becomes apparent. What do the studies of government regulation of business tell us of the role and functions of that amorphous group who are affected by these policies, but who are not organized to pursue their interests? The following generalizations would probably be accepted by most students, perhaps with occasional changes of emphasis:

    1. Tangible resources and benefits are frequently not distributed to unorganized political group interests as promised in regulatory statutes and the propaganda attending their enactment.

    This is true of the values held out to (or demanded by) groups which regard themselves as disadvantaged and which presumably anticipate benefits from a regulatory policy. There is virtually unanimous agreement among students of the antitrust laws, the Clayton and Federal Trade Commission acts, the Interstate Commerce acts, the public utility statutes and the right-to-work laws, for example, that through much of the history of their administration these statutes have been ineffective in the sense that many of the values they promised have not in fact been realized. The story has not been uniform, of course; but the general point hardly needs detailed documentation at this late date. Herring,[1] Leiserson,[2] Truman,[3] and Bernstein[4] all conclude that few regulatory policies have been pursued unless they proved acceptable to the regu-

---

    [1] E. Pendleton Herring, *Public Administration and the Public Interest* (New York, 1936), p. 213.

    [2] Avery Leiserson, *Administrative Regulation: A Study in Representation of Interests* (Chicago, 1942), p. 14.

    [3] David Truman, *The Governmental Process* (New York, 1951), Chap. 5.

    [4] Marver Bernstein, *Regulating Business by Independent Commission* (New York, 1955), Chap. 3.

lated groups or served the interests of these groups. Redford,[5] Bernstein,[6] and others have offered a "life cycle" theory of regulatory history, showing a more or less regular pattern of loss of vigor by regulatory agencies. For purposes of the present argument it need not be assumed that this always happens but only that it frequently happens in important cases.[7]

2. When it does happen, the deprived groups often display little tendency to protest or to assert their awareness of the deprivation.

The fervent display of public wrath, or enthusiasm, in the course of the initial legislative attack on forces seen as threatening "the little man" is a common American spectacle. It is about as predictable as the subsequent lapse of the same fervor. Again, it does not always occur, but it happens often enough to call for thorough explanation. The leading students of regulatory processes have all remarked upon it; but most of these scholars, who ordinarily display a close regard for rigor and full exploration, dismiss this highly significant political behavior rather casually. Thus, Redford declares that, "In the course of time the administrator finds that the initial public drive and congressional sentiment behind his directive has wilted and that political support for change from the existing pattern is lacking."[8]

Although the presumed beneficiaries of regulatory legislation often show little or no concern with its failure to protect them, they are nevertheless assumed to constitute a potential base of political support for the retention of these statutes in the law books. The professional politician is probably quite

---

[5]Emmette S. Redford, *Administration of National Economic Control* (New York, 1952), pp. 385–386.

[6]Bernstein, *op. cit.*

[7]In addition to the statements in these analytical treatments of the administrative process, evidence for the proposition that regulatory statutes often fail to have their promised consequences in terms of resource allocation are found in general studies of government regulation of business and in empirical research on particular statutes. As an example of the former see Clair Wilcox, *Public Policies Toward Business* (Chicago, 1955). As examples of the latter see Frederic Meyers, *"Right to Work" in Practice* (New York, 1959); Walton Hamilton and Irene Till, *Antitrust in Action,* TNEC Monograph 16 (Washington, D.C., GPO, 1940).

[8]Redford, *op. cit.,* p. 383. Similar explanations appear in Herring, *op. cit.,* p. 227, and Bernstein, *op. cit.,* pp. 82–83. Some writers have briefly suggested more rigorous explanations, consistent with the hypotheses discussed in this paper, though they do not consider the possible role of interests in symbolic reassurance. Thus Truman calls attention to organizational factors, emphasizing the ineffectiveness of interest groups "whose interactions on the basis of the interest are not sufficiently frequent or stabilized to produce an intervening organization and whose multiple memberships, on the same account, are a constant threat to the strength of the claim." Truman, *op. cit.,* p. 441. Multiple group memberships are, of course, characteristic of individuals in all organizations, stable and unstable; and "infrequent interactions" is a phenomenon that itself calls for explanation if a common interest is recognized. Bernstein, *loc. cit.,* refers to the "undramatic nature" of administration and to the assumption that the administrative agency will protect the public.

correct when he acts on the assumption that his advocacy of this regulatory legislation, in principle, is a widely popular move, even though actual resource allocations inconsistent with the promise of the statutes are met with quiescence. These responses (support of the statute together with apathy toward failure to allocate resources as the statute promises) define the meanings of the law so far as the presumed beneficiaries are concerned.[9] It is the frequent inconsistency between the two types of response that is puzzling.

3. The most intensive dissemination of symbols commonly attends the enactment of legislation which is most meaningless in its effects upon resource allocation. In the legislative history of particular regulatory statutes the provisions least significant for resource allocation are most widely publicized and the most significant provisions are least widely publicized.

The statutes listed under Proposition 1 as having promised something substantially different from what was delivered are also the ones which have been most intensively publicized as symbolizing protection of widely shared interests. Trust-busting, "Labor's Magna Carta" (the Clayton Act), protection against price discrimination and deceptive trade practices, protection against excessive public utility charges, tight control of union bureaucracies (or, by other groups, the "slave labor law"), federal income taxation according to "ability to pay," are the terms and symbols widely disseminated to the public as descriptive of much of the leading federal and state regulation of the last seven decades, and they are precisely the descriptions shown by careful students to be most misleading. Nor is it any less misleading if one quotes the exact language of the most widely publicized specific provisions of these laws: Section 1 of the Sherman Act, Sections 6 and 20 of the Clayton Act, or the closed shop, secondary boycott, or emergency strike provisions of Taft-Hartley, for example. In none of these instances would a reading of either the text of the statutory provision or the attendant claims and publicity enable an observer to predict even the direction of future regulatory policy, let alone its precise objectives.

Other features of these statutes also stand as the symbols of threats stalemated, if not checkmated, by the forces of right and justice. Typically, a preamble (which does not pretend to be more than symbolic, even in legal theory) includes strong assurances that the public or the public interest will be protected, and the most widely publicized regulatory provisions always include other nonoperational standards connoting fairness, balance, or equity.

If one asks, on the other hand, for examples of changes in resource allocations that have been influenced substantially and directly by public policy, it quickly appears that the outstanding examples have been publicized relatively little. One thinks of such legislation as the silver purchase provisions, the court

---

[9]Compare the discussion of meaning in George Herbert Mead, *Mind, Self and Society* (Chicago, 1934), pp. 78–79.

definitions of the word "lawful" in the Clayton Act's labor sections, the procedural provisions of Taft-Hartley and the Railway Labor Act, the severe postwar
cuts in grazing service appropriations, and changes in the parity formula
requiring that such items as interest, taxes, freight rates, and wages be included
as components of the index of prices paid by farmers.

Illuminating descriptions of the operational meaning of statutory mandates
are found in Truman's study and in Earl Latham's *The Group Basis of Politics*.[10]
Both emphasize the importance of contending groups and organizations in
day-to-day decision-making as the dynamic element in policy formation; and
both distinguish this element from statutory language as such.[11]

We are only beginning to get some serious studies of the familiarity of
voters with current public issues and of the intensity of their feelings about
issues; but successful political professionals have evidently long acted on the
assumption that there is in fact relatively little familiarity, that expressions of
deep concern are rare, that quiescence is common, and that, in general, the
congressman can count upon stereotyped reactions rather than persistent,
organized pursuit of material interests on the part of most constituents.[12]

4. Policies severely denying resources to large numbers of people can be
pursued indefinitely without serious controversy.

The silver purchase policy, the farm policy, and a great many other subsidies are obvious examples. The antitrust laws, utility regulations, and other
statutes ostensibly intended to protect the small operator or the consumer are
less obvious examples, though there is ample evidence, some of it cited below,
that these usually support the proposition as well.

The federal income tax law offers a rather neat illustration of the divergence between a widely publicized symbol and actual resource allocation
patterns. The historic constitutional struggle leading up to the Sixteenth
Amendment, the warm defenses of the principle of ability to pay, and the frequent attacks upon the principle through such widely discussed proposals as
that for a 25 per cent limit on rates have made the federal tax law a major
symbol of justice. While the fervent rhetoric from both sides turns upon the
symbol of a progressive tax and bolsters the assumption that the system is
highly progressive, the bite of the law into people's resources depends upon
quite other provisions and activities that are little publicized and that often
seriously qualify its progressive character. Special tax treatments arise from
such devices as family partnerships, gifts inter vivos, income-splitting, multiple trusts, percentage depletion, and deferred compensation.

---

[10]Truman, *op. cit.*, pp. 439–446; Earl Latham, *The Group Basis of Politics* (Ithaca,
N.Y., 1952), Chap. 1.

[11]I have explored this effect in labor legislation in "Interest Representation and
Labor Law Administration," *Labor Law Journal*, Vol. 9 (1958), pp. 218–226.

[12]See Lewis A. Dexter, "Candidates Must Make the Issues and Give Them Meaning," *Public Opinion Quarterly*, Vol. 10 (1955–56), pp. 408–414.

Tax evasion alone goes far toward making the symbol of "ability to pay" hollow semantically though potent symbolically. While 95 per cent of income from wages and salaries is taxed as provided by law, taxes are actually collected on only 67 per cent of taxable income from interest, dividends, and fiduciary investments and on only about 36 per cent of taxable farm income.[13] By and large, the recipients of larger incomes can most easily benefit from exemptions, avoidance, and evasions. This may or may not be desirable public policy, but it certainly marks a disparity between symbol and effect upon resources.

II

These phenomena are significant for the study of the political process for two reasons. First, there is a substantial degree of consistency in the group interest patterns associated with policies on highly diverse subject matters. Second, they suggest that nonrational reaction to symbols among people sharing a common governmental interest is a key element in the process. The disciplines of sociology, social psychology, and semantics have produced some pertinent data on the second point, which will now be investigated.

Harold Lasswell wrote three decades ago that "Politics is the process by which the irrational bases of society are brought out into the open." He marshaled some support in case studies for several propositions that have since been confirmed with richer and more direct experimental evidence. "The rational and dialectical phases of politics," he said, "are subsidiary to the process of redefining an emotional consensus." He argued that "widespread and disturbing changes in the life-situation of many members of society" produce adjustment problems which are resolved largely through symbolization, and he suggested that "Political demands probably bear but a limited relevance to social needs."[14]

The frame of reference suggested by these statements is sometimes accepted by political scientists today when they study voting behavior and when they analyze the legislative process. Its bearing on policy formation in the administrative process is not so widely recognized. It is true that cognition and rationality are central to administrative procedures to a degree not true of legislation or voting. But this is not the same thing as saying that administrative policies or administrative politics are necessarily insulated from the "process of redefining an emotional consensus."

Let us consider now some experimental findings and conclusions specifying conditions under which groups or personality types are prone to respond strongly to symbolic appeals and to distort or ignore reality in a fashion that can be politically significant.

---

[13]Randolph E. Paul, "Erosion of the Tax Base and Rate Structure," in Joint Committee on the Economic Report, *Federal Tax Policy for Economic Growth and Stability*, 84th Congress, 1st Session, 1955, pp. 123–138.

[14]*Psychopathology and Politics* (New York, 1960), pp. 184, 185.

1. People read their own meanings into situations that are unclear or provocative of emotion. As phrased by Fensterheim, "The less well defined the stimulus situation, or the more emotionally laden, the greater will be the contribution of the perceiver."[15] This proposition is no longer doubted by psychologists. It is the justification for so-called projective techniques and is supported by a great deal of experimental evidence.

Now it is precisely in emotionally laden and poorly defined situations that the most widely and loudly publicized public regulatory policies are launched and administered. If, as we have every reason to suppose, there is little cognitive familiarity with issues, the "interest" of most of the public is likely to be a function of other sociopsychological factors. What these other factors are is suggested by certain additional findings.

2. It is characteristic of large numbers of people in our society that they see and think in terms of stereotypes, personalization, and oversimplifications, that they cannot recognize or tolerate ambiguous and complex situations, and that they accordingly respond chiefly to symbols that oversimplify and distort. This form of behavior (together with other characteristics less relevant to the political process) is especially likely to occur where there is insecurity occasioned by failure to adjust to real or perceived problems.[16] Frenkel-Brunswik has noted that "such objective factors as economic conditions" may contribute to the appearance of the syndrome, and hence to its importance as a widespread group phenomenon attending the formulation of public policy.[17] Such behavior is sufficiently persistent and widespread to be politically significant only when

---

[15]Herbert Fensterheim, "The Influence of Value Systems on the Perception of People," *Journal of Abnormal and Social Psychology,* Vol. 48 (1953), p. 93. Fensterheim cites the following studies in support of the proposition: D. Krech and R. S. Crutchfield, *Theory and Problems of Social Psychology* (New York, 1948); A. S. Luchins, "An Evaluation of Some Current Criticisms of Gestalt Psychological Work on Perception," *Psychological Review,* Vol. 58 (1951), pp. 69–95; J. S. Bruner, "One Kind of Perception: A Reply to Professor Luchins," *Psychological Review,* Vol. 58 (1951), pp. 306–312; and the chapters by Bruner, Frenkel-Brunswik, and Klein in R. R. Blake and G. V. Ramsey, *Perception: An Approach to Personality* (New York, 1951). See also Charles Osgood, Percy Tannenbaum, and George Suci, *The Measurement of Meaning* (Urbana, Ill., 1957).

[16]Among the leading general and experimental studies dealing with the phenomenon are: M. Rokeach, "Generalized Mental Rigidity as a Factor in Ethnocentrism," *Journal of Abnormal and Social Psychology,* Vol. 43 (1948), pp. 259–277; R. R. Canning and J. M. Baker, "Effect of the Group on Authoritarian and Non-authoritarian Persons," *American Journal of Sociology,* Vol. 64 (1959), pp. 579–581; A. H. Maslow, "The Authoritarian Character Structure," *Journal of Social Psychology,* Vol. 18 (1943), p. 403; T. W. Adorno and others, *The Authoritarian Personality* (New York, 1950); Gerhart Saenger, *The Psychology of Prejudice* (New York, 1953), pp. 123–138; Erich Fromm, *Escape from Freedom* (New York, 1941); R. K. Merton, *Mass Persuasion* (New York, 1950).

[17]Else Frenkel-Brunswik, "Interaction of Psychological and Sociological Factors in Political Behavior," *The American Political Science Review,* Vol. 46 (1952), pp. 44–65.

there is social reinforcement of faith in the symbol. When insecurity is individual, without communication and reinforcement from others, there is little correlation with ethnocentricity or its characteristics.[18]

A different kind of study suggests the extent to which reality can become irrelevant for persons very strongly committed to an emotion-satisfying symbol. Festinger and his associates, as participant-observers, studied a group of fifteen persons who were persuaded that the world would come to an end on a particular day in 1956 and that they as believers would be carried away in a flying saucer. With few exceptions the participants refused to give up their belief even after the appointed day had passed. The Festinger study concludes that commitment to a belief is likely to be strengthened and reaffirmed in the face of clear disproof of its validity where there is a strong prior commitment (many of the individuals involved had actually given away their worldly goods) and where there is continuing social support of the commitment by others (two members who lost faith lived where they had no further contact with fellow members of the group; those who retained their faith had continued to see each other). What we know of previous messianic movements of this sort supports this hypothesis.[19]

3. Emotional commitment to a symbol is associated with contentment and quiescence regarding problems that would otherwise arouse concern.

It is a striking fact that this effect has been noticed and stressed by careful observers in a number of disparate fields, using quite different data and methods. Adorno reports it as an important finding in *The Authoritarian Personality:* "Since political and economic events make themselves felt apparently down to the most private and intimate realms of the individual, there is reliance upon stereotype and similar avoidance of reality to alleviate psychologically the feeling of anxiety and uncertainty and provide the individual with the illusion of some kind of intellectual security."[20]

In addition to the support it gets from psychological experiment, the phenomenon has been remarked by scholars in the fields of semantics, organizational theory, and political science. Albert Salomon points out that "Manipulation of social images makes it possible for members of society to believe that they live not in a jungle, but in a well organized and good society."[21] Harold Lasswell put it as follows:

> It should not be hastily assumed that because a particular set of controversies passes out of the public mind that the implied problems were solved in any fundamental sense. Quite often a solution is a magical solution which changes nothing in the conditions affecting the tension level of the commu-

---

[18]Adorno and others, *op. cit.*

[19]Leon Festinger, Henry Riecken, and Stanley Schachter, *When Prophecy Fails* (Minneapolis, 1956).

[20]Adorno and others, *op. cit.,* p. 665.

[21]Albert Salomon, "Symbols and Images in the Constitution of Society," in L. Bryson, L. Finkelstein, H. Hoagland, and R. M. MacIver (eds.), *Symbols and Society* (New York, 1955), p. 110.

nity, and which merely permits the community to distract its attention to another set of equally irrelevant symbols. The number of statutes which pass the legislature, or the number of decrees which are handed down by the executive, but which change nothing in the permanent practices of society, is a rough index of the role of magic in politics. . . . Political symbolization has its catharsis function. . . .[22]

Chester Barnard, an uncommonly astute analyst of his own long experience as an executive, concluded that "Neither authority nor cooperative disposition . . . will stand much overt division on formal issues in the present stage of human development. Most laws, executive orders, decisions, etc., are in effect formal notice that all is well—there is agreement, authority is not questioned."[23]

Kenneth Burke makes much the same point. Designating political rhetoric as "secular prayer," he declares that its function is "to sharpen up the pointless and blunt the too sharply pointed."[24] Elsewhere, he points out that laws themselves serve this function, alleging that positive law is *itself* "the test of a judgment's judiciousness."[25]

4. An active demand for increased economic resources or fewer political restrictions on action is not always operative. It is, rather, a function of comparison and contrast with reference groups, usually those not far removed in socioeconomic status.

This is, of course, one of the most firmly established propositions about social dynamics; one that has been supported by macrosociological analysis,[26] by psychological experiment,[27] and by observation of the political process, particularly through contrast between political quiescence and protest or revolutionary activity.[28]

The proposition helps explain failure to demand additional resources where such behavior is socially sanctioned and supported. It also helps explain the insatiability of the demand by some organized groups for additional resources (i.e., the absence of quiescence) where there is competition for such resources among rival organizations and where it is acquisitiveness that is socially supported. This behavior is more fully analyzed in Chapter 8.

5. The phenomena discussed above (the supplying of meaning in vague situations, stereotypes, oversimplification, political quiescence) are in

---

[22]Lasswell, *op. cit.,* p. 195.

[23]Chester I. Barnard, *The Functions of the Executive* (Cambridge, Mass., 1938), p. 226.

[24]Kenneth Burke, *A Grammar of Motives* (New York, 1945), p. 393.

[25]*Ibid.,* p. 362.

[26]Mead, *op. cit.;* Ernst Cassirer, *An Essay on Man.*

[27]See James G. March and Herbert A. Simon, *Organizations* (New York, 1958), pp. 65–81, and studies cited there.

[28]See, e.g., Murray Edelman, "Causes of Fluctuations in Popular Support for the Italian Communist Party Since 1946," *Journal of Politics,* Vol. 20 (1958), pp. 547–550; Arthur M. Ross, *Trade Union Wage Policy* (Berkeley and Los Angeles, 1948).

large measure associated with social, economic, or cultural factors affecting large segments of the population. They acquire political meaning as group phenomena.

Even among the psychologists, some of whom have been notably insensitive to socialization and environment as explanations and phases of the individual traits they identify, there are impressive experimental findings to support the proposition. In analyzing the interview material of his *authoritarian personality* study, Adorno concluded that "our general cultural climate" is basic in political ideology and in stereotyped political thinking, and he catalogued some standardizing aspects of that climate.[29] His finding, quoted above, regarding the relation of symbols to quiescence is also phrased to emphasize its social character. Lindesmith and Strauss make a similar point, emphasizing the association between symbols and the reference groups to which people adhere.[30]

Another type of research has demonstrated that because interests are typically bound up with people's social situation, attitudes are not typically changed by ex parte appeals. The function of propaganda is rather to activate socially rooted interests. One empirical study which arrives at this conclusion sums up the thesis as follows: "Political writers have the task of providing 'rational' men with good and acceptable reasons to dress up the choice which is more effectively determined by underlying social affiliations."[31]

George Herbert Mead makes the fundamental point that symbolization itself has no meaning apart from social activity: "Symbolization constitutes objects . . . which would not exist except for the context of social relationships wherein symbolization occurs."[32]

III

These studies offer a basis for understanding more clearly what it is that different types of groups expect from government and under what circumstances they are likely to be satisfied or restive about what is forthcoming. Two broad patterns of group interest activity vis-à-vis public regulatory policy are evidently

---

[29] Adorno and others, *op. cit.,* p. 655.

[30] Alfred R. Lindesmith and Anselm L. Strauss, *Social Psychology* (New York, 1956), pp. 253–255. For a report of another psychological experiment demonstrating that attitudes are a function of group norms, see I. Sarnoff, D. Katz, and C. McClintock, "Attitude-Change Procedures and Motivating Patterns," in Daniel Katz and others (eds.), *Public Opinion and Propaganda* (New York, 1954), pp. 308–309; also Festinger, Riecken, and Shachter, *op. cit.*

[31] Paul F. Lazarsfeld, Bernard Berelson, and Hazel Gaudet, *The People's Choice* (New York, 1944), p. 83. For an account of an experiment reaching the same conclusion see S. M. Lipset, "Opinion Formation in a Crisis Situation," *Public Opinion Quarterly,* Vol. 17 (1953), pp. 20–46.

[32] Mead, *op. cit.,* p. 78.

identifiable on the basis of these various modes of observing the social scene. The two patterns may be summarized in the following shorthand fashion:

1. Pattern A: a relatively high degree of organization—rational, cognitive procedures—precise information—an effective interest in specifically identified, tangible resources—a favorably perceived strategic position with respect to reference groups—relatively small numbers.
2. Pattern B: shared interest in improvement of status through protest activity—an unfavorably perceived strategic position with respect to reference groups—distorted, stereotyped, inexact information and perception—response to symbols connoting suppression of threats— relative ineffectiveness in securing tangible resources through political activity—little organization for purposeful action—quiescence— relatively large numbers.

It is very likely misleading to assume that some of these observations can be regarded as causes or consequences of others. That they often occur together is both a more accurate observation and more significant. It is also evident that each of the patterns is realized in different degrees at different times.

While political scientists and students of organizational theory have gone far toward a sophisticated description and analysis of Pattern A, there is far less agreement and precision in describing and analyzing Pattern B and in explaining how it intermeshes with Pattern A.

The most common explanation of the relative inability of large numbers of people to realize their economic aspirations in public policy is in terms of invisibility. The explanation is usually implicit rather than explicit, but it evidently assumes that public regulatory policy facilitating the exploitation of resources by knowledgeable organized groups (usually the "regulated") at the expense of taxpayers, consumers, or other unorganized groups is possible only because the latter do not know it is happening. What is invisible to them does not arouse interest or political sanctions.

On a superficial level of explanation this assumption is no doubt valid. But it is an example of the danger to the social scientist of failure to inquire transactionally: of assuming, in this instance, (1) that an answer to a questioner, or a questionnaire, about what an individual "knows" of a regulatory policy at any point in time is in any sense equivalent to specification of a group political interest; and (2) that the sum of many individual knowings (or not knowings) as reported to a questioner is a *cause* of effective (or ineffective) organization, rather than a consequence of it, or simply a concomitant phase of the same environment. If one is interested in policy formation, what count are the assumptions of legislators and administrators about the determinants of future political disaffection and political sanctions. Observable political behavior, as well as psychological findings, reveal something of these assumptions.

There is, in fact, persuasive evidence of the reality of a political interest in continuing assurances of protection against economic forces understood as powerful and threatening. The most relevant evidence lies in the continuing utility of old political issues in campaigns. Monopoly and economic concentration, antitrust policy, public utility regulation, banking controls, and curbs on management and labor are themes that party professionals regard as good for votes in one campaign after another, and doubtless with good reason. They know that these are areas in which concern is easily stirred. In evaluating allegations that the public has lost "interest" in these policies the politician has only to ask himself how much apathy would remain if an effort were made formally to repeal the antitrust, public utility, banking, or labor laws. The answers and the point become clear at once.

The laws may be repealed in effect by administrative policy, budgetary starvation, or other little publicized means; but the laws as symbols must stand because they satisfy interests that are very strong indeed: interests that politicians fear will be expressed actively if a large number of voters are led to believe that their shield against a threat has been removed.

More than that, it is largely as symbols of this sort that these statutes have utility to most of the voters. If they function as reassurances that threats in the economic environment are under control, their indirect effect is to permit greater claims upon tangible resources by the organized groups concerned than would be possible if the legal symbols were absent.

To say this is not to assume that everyone objectively affected by a policy is simply quiescent rather than apathetic or even completely unaware of the issue. It is to say that those who are potentially able and willing to apply political sanctions constitute the politically significant group. It is to suggest as well that incumbent or aspiring congressmen are less concerned with individual constituents' familiarity or unfamiliarity with an issue as of any given moment than with the possibility that the interest of a substantial number of them *could* be aroused and organized if he should cast a potentially unpopular vote on a bill or if a change in their economic situation should occur. The shrewder and more effective politicians probably appreciate intuitively the validity of the psychological finding noted earlier: that where public understanding is vague and information rare, interests in reassurance will be all the more potent and all the more susceptible to manipulation by political symbols.

We have already noted that it is one of the demonstrable functions of symbolization that it induces a feeling of well-being: the resolution of tension. Not only is this a major function of widely publicized regulatory statutes, but it is also a major function of their administration. Some of the most widely publicized administrative activities can most confidently be expected to convey a sense of well-being to the onlooker because they suggest vigorous activity while in fact signifying inactivity or protection of the "regulated."

One form this phenomenon takes is noisy attacks on trivia. The Federal Trade Commission, for example, has long been noted for its hit-and-miss attacks on many relatively small firms involved in deceptive advertising or unfair trade practices while it continues to overlook much of the really significant activity it is ostensibly established to regulate: monopoly, interlocking directorates, and so on.[33]

Another form it takes is prolonged, repeated, well-publicized attention to a significant problem which is never solved. A notable example is the approach of the Federal Communications Commission to surveillance of program content in general and to discussions of public issues on the air in particular. In the postwar period we have had the Blue Book, the Mayflower Policy, the abolition of the Mayflower Policy, and the announcement of a substitute policy; but the radio or television licensee is in practice perfectly free, as he has been all along, to editorialize, with or without opportunity for opposing views to be heard, or to avoid serious discussion of public affairs entirely.

The most obvious kinds of dissemination of symbolic satisfactions are to be found in administrative dicta accompanying decisions and orders, in press releases, and in annual reports. It is not uncommon to give the rhetoric to one side and the decision to the other. Nowhere does the FCC wax so emphatic in emphasizing public service responsibility, for example, as in decisions permitting greater concentration of control in an area, condoning license transfers at inflated prices, refusing to impose sanctions for flagrantly sacrificing program quality to profits, and so on.[34]

The integral connection is apparent between symbolic satisfaction of the disorganized, on the one hand, and the success of the organized, on the other, in using governmental instrumentalities as aids in securing the tangible resources they claim.

Public policy may usefully be understood as the resultant of the interplay among groups.[35] But the political and sociopsychological processes discussed here mean that groups which present claims upon resources may be rendered quiescent by their success in securing nontangible values. Far from representing an obstacle to organized producers and sellers, they become defenders of the very system of law which permits the organized to pursue their interests effectively.

Thurman Arnold has pointed out how the antitrust laws perform precisely this function:

> The actual result of the antitrust laws was to promote the growth of great industrial organizations by deflecting the attack on them into purely moral and ceremonial channels . . . every scheme for direct control broke to pieces on the great protective rock of the antitrust laws. . . .
>
> The antitrust laws remained as a most important symbol. Whenever anyone demanded practical regulation, they formed an effective moral obstacle, since all the liberals would answer with a demand that the antitrust laws be

---

[33]Cf. Wilcox, *op. cit.,* pp. 281, 252–255.

[34]Many examples may be found in the writer's study entitled *The Licensing of Radio Services in the United States, 1927 to 1947* (Urbana, Ill., 1950).

[35]For discussions of the utility of this view to social scientists, see Arthur F. Bentley, *The Process of Government* (1908; New York, reprint 1949); Truman, *op. cit.*

enforced. Men like Senator Borah founded political careers on the continuance of such crusades, which were entirely futile but enormously picturesque, and which paid big dividends in terms of personal prestige.[36]

Arnold's subsequent career as chief of the antitrust division of the Department of Justice did as much to prove his point as his writings. For a five-year period he instilled unprecedented vigor into the division, and his efforts were widely publicized. He thereby unquestionably made the laws a more important symbol of the protection of the public; but despite his impressive intentions and talents, monopoly, concentration of capital, and restraint of trade were not seriously threatened or affected.

This is not to suggest that signs or symbols in themselves have any magical force as narcotics. They are, rather, the only means by which groups not in a position to analyze a complex situation rationally may adjust themselves to it, through stereotypization, oversimplification, and reassurance.

There have, of course, been many instances of effective administration and enforcement of regulatory statutes. In each such instance it will be found that organized groups have had an informed interest in effective administration. Sometimes the existence of these groups is explicable as a holdover from the campaign for legislative enactment of the basic statute; and often the initial administrative appointees are informed, dedicated adherents of these interests. They are thus in a position to secure pertinent data and to act strategically, helping furnish "organization" to the groups they represent. Sometimes the resources involved are such that there is organization on both sides; or the more effective organization may be on the "reform" side. The securities exchange legislation is an illuminating example, for after Richard Whitney's conviction for embezzlement, key officials of the New York Stock Exchange recognized their own interest in supporting controls over less scrupulous elements. This interest configuration doubtless explains the relative popularity of the SEC in the thirties both with regulated groups and with organized liberal groups.

IV

The evidence considered here suggests that we can make an encouraging start toward defining the conditions in which myth and symbolic reassurance become key elements in the governmental process. The conditions[37] are present in substantial degree in many policy areas other than business regulation. They may well be maximal in the foreign policy area, and a similar approach to the study of foreign policy formation would doubtless be revealing.

Because the requisite conditions are always present in some degree, every instance of policy formulation involves a "mix" of symbolic effect and rational reflection of interests in resources, though one or the other may be

---

[36] *The Folklore of Capitalism* (New Haven, Conn., 1937), pp. 212, 215–216.
[37] They are listed above under "Pattern B."

dominant in any particular case. One type of mix is exemplified by such governmental programs outside the business regulation field as public education and social security. There can be no doubt that these programs do confer important tangible benefits upon a very wide public, very much as they promise to do. They do so for the reasons suggested earlier. Business organizations, labor organizations, teachers' organizations, and other organized groups benefit from these programs and have historically served to focus public attention upon the resources to be gained or lost. Their task has been all the easier because the techniques for achieving the benefits are fairly readily recognizable.

But the financing of these same programs involves public policies of a different order. Here the symbol of "free" education and other benefits, the complexity of the revenue and administrative structure, and the absence of organization have facilitated the emergence of highly regressive payroll, property, and head taxes as the major sources of revenue. Thus, business organizations, which by and large support the public schools that provide their trained personnel and the social security programs that minimize the costs of industrial pensions, pay relatively little for these services, while the direct beneficiaries of the "free" programs pay a relatively high proportion of the costs. Careful analysis of the "mix" in particular programs should prove illuminating.

If the conditions facilitating symbolic reassurance are correctly specified, there is reason to question some common assumptions about strategic variables in policy formulation and reason also to devise some more imaginative models in designing research In this area. The theory discussed here suggests, for example, a tie between the emergence of conditions promoting interests in symbolic reassurance and widened freedom of policy maneuver for the organized. It implies that the number of adherents of a political interest may have more to do with whether the political benefit offered is tangible or symbolic than with the quantity or quality of tangible resources allocated. It suggests that the factors that explain voting behavior can be quite different from the factors that explain resource allocations through government. The fact that large numbers of people are objectively affected by a governmental program may actually serve in some contexts to weaken their capacity to exert a political claim upon tangible values.

A number of recent writers, to take another example, have suggested that it is the "independence" of the independent regulatory commissions which chiefly accounts for their tendency to become tools of the groups they regulate. The hypotheses suggested here apply to regulatory programs administered in cabinet departments as well; and their operation is discernible in some of these programs when the specified conditions are present. The grazing service and the antitrust division are examples.

In terms of research design, the implications of the analysis probably lie chiefly in the direction of emphasizing an integral tie of political behavior to underlying and extensive social interaction. Analysts of political dynamics must have a theory of relevance; but the directly relevant may run farther afield than has sometimes been assumed. Political activities of all kinds require the most exhaustive scrutiny to ascertain whether their chief function is symbolic or substantive. The "what" of Lasswell's famous definition of politics is a complex universe in itself.

Review Questions

1. In what ways, if any, does current American political rhetoric reflect George Orwell's concept of political speech? What are current day examples of political speech being used "in defense of the indefensible"?
2. What does Daniel Boorstin mean by "pseudo-events"? Can you offer some recent examples of them at both the local and national level of politics?
3. How have political leaders used symbols to manipulate and lead their publics throughout history? Can you offer examples of mayors, governors and presidents using symbols to advance their public policies?

Chapter 11

Policy Analysis

Policy analysis is ubiquitous. You can hardly go through the day without bumping into it. You wake up to a talk radio show spewing vitriolic opinions on a new presidential proposal. As you eat breakfast reading the local morning newspaper, you are exposed to more analysis on regional issues such as school taxes and crime rates. At work your officemates freely give you their analyses of the behavior of a political leader caught in the latest financial or sex scandal. Returning home from work you review your mail and find more analyses in the magazines to which you subscribe and in the unsolicited junk mail from public interest groups and political parties. Finally, you conclude your day by falling asleep watching even more analyses on television news and talk shows. It seems that almost everybody is constantly complaining or explaining about something.

If journalism represents the first rough draft of history, it is also the first policy analysis that most people will hear or read on a new issue. The powers that be make policy but it is then reported and explained to the public by the journalistic media. All the major news organizations, both print and television, have reporters that specialize in various policy areas. Thus there are White House, congressional, Supreme Court, education, medical, consumer, and financial correspondents among others. It is these specialists that are almost always the first analysts to tackle a new policy issue. Scholarly analysis is usually years behind—unless, of course, it is done by the relatively small group of academics who also write for journalistic sources. The op-ed pages are full of college professors and think tank denizens telling the public what the implications are of any new policy.

All this—from the current buzz at work to the weekly news magazines—is informal policy analysis. These "quick and dirty" critiques of current issues are both widespread and essential to a flourishing democracy. While they may be made with style, wit, and true depth of feeling, they tend to lack the methodological rigor of a formal policy analysis.

Formal policy analysis uses a set of techniques that seeks to answer the question of what the probable effects of a policy will be before they actually occur. A policy analysis undertaken on a program that is already in effect is more properly called a program evaluation. Nevertheless, policy analysis is used by many to refer to both before- and after-the-fact analyses of public policies. All policy analysis involves the application of systematic research techniques (drawn largely from the social sciences and based on measurements of program effectiveness, quality, cost, and impact) to the formulation, execution, and evaluation of public policy to create a more rational or optimal administrative system. It was Jeremy Bentham's (see Chapter I) desire to see this kind of formal, methodologically rigorous analysis applied to all policy issues.

To the extent that we make judgments on governmental policies from affirmative action to zoning variances, we all do policy analysis. Any judgment on a policy issue requires an analysis however superficial. Policy analysis can be viewed as a continuum from crude judgments made in a snap ("The governor is an idiot and all his policies are stupid!") to the most sophisticated analysis using complicated methodologies ("I have just administered an I.Q. test to the governor and he really is an idiot.").

In 1854 Abraham Lincoln wrote this:

> The legitimate object of government is to do for a community of people whatever they need to have done, but cannot do, at all, or can not so well do, for themselves—in their separate and individual capacities.
>
> In all that the people can individually do as well for themselves, government ought not to interfere.

What Lincoln was calling for, though he didn't use the term, was a cost-benefit approach to ascertain whether goods and/or services should be provided collectively rather than individually. This is the test that James M. Buchanan and Gordon Tullock proposed for all public policies in their classic analysis, *The Calculus of Consent* (1962). They ask: "When will a society composed of free and rational utility-maximizing individuals choose to undertake action collectively rather than privately?" The answer is that the rational person takes collective action to obtain a collective good, anything of value (such as clean air, safe streets or tax loopholes) that cannot be denied to a group member.

A group can vary from all of society to any subset of it. Economist Mancur Olson in *The Logic of Collective Action* (1965) found that small groups are better at obtaining collective goods. The larger the potential group, the less likely it is that most will contribute to obtain the "good." Just as in military strategy concentration is the key. Thus a particular industry is better able to obtain tax loopholes for itself than the general public is able to obtain overall tax equity (fairness and justice in how taxes are assessed and administered).

The problem with collectively provided goods, those paid for by tax dollars, is that the demand will always exceed what can be supplied. After all, if something appears to be both desirable and "free," demand for it will only continue to rise. This leads to budget deficits and the kind of destruction illustrated by Garrett Hardin, in his article, "The Tragedy of the Commons," *Science* (December 13, 1968), reprinted here. This shows that the principle that the maximization of private gain will not result in the maximization of social benefit.

Garrett asks you to "picture a pasture open to all. It is to be expected that each herdsman will try to keep as many cattle as possible on the commons. Such an arrangement may work reasonably satisfactorily for centuries because tribal wars, poaching and disease keep the numbers . . . below the carrying capacity of the land." Eventually there "comes the day of reckoning, that is, the day when the long-desired goal of social stability becomes a reality. At this point, the inherent logic of the commons remorselessly generates tragedy." Because then each herdsman seeks to maximize his gain. . . . The rational herdsman concludes that the only sensible course for him to pursue is to add another animal to his herd. And another, and another . . . But this is the conclusion reached by each and every rational herdsman sharing a commons." When herdsmen sought to maximize individual gain by adding more and more cattle to a common pasture, the common was overgrazed. The resulting tragedy was that no one was able to effectively use the common for grazing. "Ruin is the destination toward which all men rush, each pursuing his own best interest in a society that believes in the freedom of the commons. Freedom in a commons brings ruin to all." The concepts involved with the tragedy of the commons apply to societal problems, such as pollution and overpopulation.

Neutral competence is a long-standing concept in public administration. It historically refers to a continuous, politically uncommitted cadre of bureaucrats at the disposal of elected or appointed political executives. This ethic of neutrality has now been borrowed by the policy analyst.

Policy analysts should be unbiased when they initially approach a problem. An open mind is essential for the systematic compilation and interpretation of facts. But once the analytical task of the analyst is complete, he or she may be transformed by his or her conclusions and attendant circumstances from an analyst to an advocate. This is dangerous. Presently policy analysis allows the analyst to pose as a neutral nonpartisan, disinterested professional. But prescribing public policy on the basis of an analysis takes the analyst into the realm of politics. The advocate may then become a lobby and risk his or her reputation for objectivity.

Just as there are best ways to undertake a policy analysis, there are also ways not to do it—paths that should not be taken. In 1976 Arnold J. Meltsner published *Policy Analysts in the Bureaucracy*. When he produced a revised edition in 1986 he included a new section on "The Seven Deadly Sins of Policy Analysts." These distilled "sins" are organized into the following seven categories, which Meltsner warns "are not mutually exclusive; they bleed into each other."

1. *Channeled advice:* Here "both analyst and client ignore that circumstances have changed or that constraints exist." In consequence, "the advice is in a rut, groove, or furrow."

2. *Distant advice:* This is a distance grounded in ignorance. "Policy analysts all too often come up with general solutions for very specific conditions." An example is "advice cooked up in Washington [that] does not square with the reality of San Antonio."

3. *Late advice:* Better late than never does not apply here. "An analyst may be late to his or her wedding but must be on time when advice is wanted."

4. *Superficial advice:* Beware of advice that "is too quick, too off-the-cuff, and not based on enough digging into the roots of the problem." Superficial efforts "interfere with appropriate diagnosis and the hard work necessary to achieve sensible policies."

5. *Topical advice:* This occurs when "the demand for advice stems from some sort of crisis." This too often "leads to a kind of firehouse mentality, advice on the run. Then the analyst is likely to provide superficial and distant advice."

6. *Capricious advice:* This refers to change for change's sake. "We lack enough incentives in policymaking to say just leave it alone."

7. *Apolitical advice:* This occurs when "political advice is not appropriately linked or integrated with the substantive advice of policy."

Meltsner offers this final bit of advice on his "sins." "Knowing what is wrong will not tell us what is good. But it is a start." To summarize we can put a positive perspective on Meltsner's "seven deadly sins" by asserting that policy recommendations should be unique to the circumstances, fitted to the specific condition, on time, based on solid research, not developed in a crisis atmosphere, only offered if true change is needed, and fully in keeping with the political environment. Of course, real life seldom offers ideal circumstances for public policy analysis. Thus policy analysts often find themselves in an inherently "sinful" occupation.

Some people have a gift for administration. We have all met such natural administrators. They are not only perpetually organized but have a knack for getting people to harmoniously work together. The administrative art is judgment, panache, and common sense. But the artist is useless without tools—without the technical skills (the science) that allow for the digestion and transference of information. Nothing is more pointless than to argue whether the practice of public administration is more art or science. It is inherently both. Of course, the more science you have, the better artist you'll be. But "book learnin'" won't make you an artist if you don't possess an element of the gift in the first place.

Aaron B. Wildavsky (1930–1993), one of the preeminent scholars in public administration, was well aware of the art versus science question in public administration. After he became the founding dean of the Graduate School of Public Policy at the University of California, Berkeley, he began to grapple with this same art versus science problem within the context of policy analysis. Reprinted here is "The Art of Policy Analyses" from his 1979 *Speaking Truth to Power*.

Of course all art includes a large degree of technique or science. Thus aspiring artists in public policy and policy analysis would be wise to study the experiences of other policy artists and would-be artists. In this way both the successes and failures of the past can be instructive. These studies traditionally take the form of case studies— in-depth analyses of a single subject. It is a history that offers an understanding of dynamic, constantly moving and changing, processes over time. Most traditional news stories use the case study approach. Note that aspiring journalists are taught that a story should contain all the essential elements of a case study: "who, what, why, when, where and how."

The first case studies examined battles and wars. Thucydides's *History of the Peloponnesian War* (404 B.C.E.) (discussed in Chapter 10) is the progenitor of these military case studies. Military colleges—and general staffs—have long used the case study method to review battles and study generalship. This same technique is now widely used in a civilian context to examine how policy proposals become law, how programs are implemented and how special interests affect policy development.

College courses in public policy and administration often use a case study approach. An entire course may consist of case studies of policy development and implementation. The goal is to artificially inculcate experience. Any policy analyst rich with years of experience will have had the opportunity to live through a lifetime of "cases." By having students study many cases, each of which may have extended over many years, the case study course compresses both time and experience. The relatively young student should then have the insight and wisdom of those who have had hundreds of years of experience. In theory this makes them so wise beyond their years that employers will eagerly seek them out.

41

The Tragedy of the Commons (1968)

Garrett Hardin

At the end of a thoughtful article on the future of nuclear war, J.B. Wiesner and H.F. York concluded that: "Both sides in the arms race are . . . confronted by the dilemma of steadily increasing military power and steadily decreasing national security. *It is our considered professional judgement that this dilemma has no technical solution.* If the great powers continue to look for solutions in the area of science and technology only, the result will be to worsen the situation."[1]

I would like to focus your attention not on the subject of the article (national security in a nuclear world) but on the kind of conclusion they reached, namely that there is no technical solution to the problem. An implicit and almost universal assumption of discussions published in professional and semipopular scientific journals is that the problem under discussion has a technical solution. A technical solution may be defined as one that requires a change only in the techniques of the natural sciences, demanding little or nothing in the way of change in human values or ideas of morality.

In our day (though not in earlier times) technical solutions are always welcome. Because of previous failures in prophecy, it takes courage to assert that a desired technical solution is not possible. Wiesner and York exhibited this courage; publishing in a science journal, they insisted that the solution to the problem was not to be found in the natural sciences. They cautiously qualified their statement with the phrase, "It is our considered professional judgment. . . ." Whether they were right or not is not the concern of the present article. Rather, the concern here is with the important concept of a class of human problems which can be called "no technical solution problems," and more specifically, with the identification and discussion of one of these.

It is easy to show that the class is not a null class. Recall the game of tick-tack-toe. Consider the problem, "How can I win the game of tick-tack-toe?" It is well known that I cannot, if I assume (in keeping with the conventions of game

Source: Garrett Hardin, "The Tragedy of the Commons." Reprinted with permission from *Science*, 162, (December 1968): 1243–1248. Copyright © 1968 American Association for the Advancement of Science.

theory) that my opponent understands the game perfectly. Put another way, there is no "technical solution" to the problem. I can win only by giving a radical meaning to the word "win." I can hit my opponent over the head; or I can falsify the records. Every way in which I "win" involves, in some sense, an abandonment of the game, as we intuitively understand it. (I can also, of course, openly abandon the game—refuse to play it. This is what most adults do.)

The class of "no technical solution problems" has members. My thesis is that the "population problem," as conventionally conceived, is a member of this class. How it is conventionally conceived needs some comment. It is fair to say that most people who anguish over the population problem are trying to find a way to avoid the evils of overpopulation without relinquishing any of the privileges they now enjoy. They think that farming the seas or developing new strains of wheat will solve the problem—technologically. I try to show here that the solution they seek cannot be found. The population problem cannot be solved in a technical way, any more than can the problem of winning the game of tick-tack-toe.

What Shall We Maximize?

Population, as Malthus said, naturally tends to grow "geometrically," or, as we would now say, exponentially. In a finite world this means that the per-capita share of the world's goods must decrease. Is ours a finite world?

A fair defense can be put forward for the view that the world is infinite or that we do not know that it is not. But, in terms of the practical problems that we must face in the next few generations with the foreseeable technology, it is clear that we will greatly increase human misery if we do not, during the immediate future, assume that the world available to the terrestrial human population is finite. "Space" is no escape.[2]

A finite world can support only a finite population; therefore, population growth must eventually equal zero. (The case of perpetual wide fluctuations above and below zero is a trivial variant that need not be discussed.) When this condition is met, what will be the situation of mankind? Specifically, can Bentham's goal of "the greatest good for the greatest number" be realized?

No—for two reasons, each sufficient by itself. The first is a theoretical one. It is not mathematically possible to maximize for two (or more) variables at the same time. This was clearly stated by von Neumann and Morgenstern,[3] but the principle is implicit in the theory of partial differential equations, dating back at least to D'Alembert (1717–1783).

The second reason springs directly from biological facts. To live, any organism must have a source of energy (for example, food). This energy is utilized for two purposes: mere maintenance and work. For man maintenance of life requires about 1600 kilocalories a day ("maintenance calories"). Anything that he does over and above merely staying alive will be defined as work, and is supported by "work calories" which he takes in. Work calories are used not only for what we call work in common speech; they are also required for all forms of enjoyment, from swimming and automobile racing to playing music and writing poetry. If our goal is to maximize population it is obvious what we must do: We must make the work calories per person approach as close to zero as possible. No gourmet meals, no vacations, no sports, no music, no literature, no art . . . I think that everyone will grant, without argument or proof, that maximizing population does not maximize goods. Bentham's goal is impossible.

In reaching this conclusion I have made the usual assumption that it is the acquisition of energy that is the problem. The appearance of atomic energy has led some to question this assumption. However, given an infinite source of energy, population growth still produces an inescapable problem. The problem of the acquisition of energy is replaced by the problem of its dissipation, as J. H. Fremlin has so wittily shown.[4] The arithmetic signs in the analysis are, as it were, reversed; but Bentham's goal is unobtainable.

The optimum population is, then, less than the maximum. The difficulty of defining the optimum is enormous; so far as I know, no one has seriously tackled this problem. Reaching an acceptable and stable solution will surely require more than one generation of hard analytical work—and much persuasion.

We want the maximum good per person; but what is good? To one person it is wilderness, to another it is ski lodges for thousands. To one it is estuaries to nourish ducks for hunters to shoot; to another it is factory land. Comparing one good with another is, we usually say, impossible because goods are incommensurable. Incommensurables cannot be compared.

Theoretically this may be true; but in real life incommensurables *are* commensurable. Only a criterion of judgment and a system of weighting are needed. In nature the criterion is survival. Is it better for a species to be small and hideable, or large and powerful? Natural selection commensurates the incommensurables. The compromise achieved depends on a natural weighting of the values of the variables.

Man must imitate this process. There is no doubt that in fact he already does, but unconsciously. It is when the hidden decisions are made explicit that the arguments begin. The problem for the years ahead is to work out an acceptable theory of weighting. Synergistic effects, nonlinear variation, and difficulties in discounting the future make the intellectual problem difficult, but not (in principle) insoluble.

Has any cultural group solved this practical problem at the present time, even on an intuitive level? One simple fact proves that none has: there is no prosperous population in the world today that has, and has had for some time, a growth rate of zero. Any people that has intuitively identified its optimum point will soon reach it, after which its growth rate becomes and remains zero.

Of course, a positive growth rate might be taken as evidence that a population is below its optimum. However, by any reasonable standards, the most rapidly growing populations on earth today are (in general) the most miserable. This association (which need not be invariable) casts doubt on the optimistic assumption that the positive growth rate of a population is evidence that it has yet to reach its optimum.

We can make little progress in working toward optimum population size until we explicitly exorcise the spirit of Adam Smith in the field of practical demography. In economic affairs, *The Wealth of Nations* (1776) popularized the "invisible hand," the idea that an individual who "intends only his own gain," is, as it were, "led by an invisible hand to promote . . . the public interest."[5] Adam Smith did not assert that this was invariably true, and perhaps neither did any of his followers. But he contributed to a dominant tendency of thought that has ever since interfered with positive action based on rational analysis, namely, the tendency to assume that decisions reached individually will, in fact, be the best decisions for an entire society. If this assumption is correct it justifies the continuance of our present policy of *laissez faire* in reproduction. If it is correct we can assume that men will control their individual fecundity so as to produce the optimum population. If the assumption is not correct, we need to reexamine our individual freedoms to see which ones are defensible.

Tragedy of Freedom in a Commons

The rebuttal to the invisible hand in population control is to be found in a scenario first sketched in a little-known Pamphlet in 1833 by a mathematical amateur named William Forster Lloyd (1794–1852).[6] We may well call it "the tragedy of the commons," using the word "tragedy" as the philosopher Whitehead used it[7]: "The essence of dramatic tragedy is not unhappiness. It resides in the solemnity of the remorseless working of things." He then goes on to say, "This inevitableness of destiny can only be illustrated in terms of human life by incidents which in fact involve unhappiness. For it is only by them that the futility of escape can be made evident in the drama."

The tragedy of the commons develops in this way. Picture a pasture open to all. It is to be expected that each herdsman will try to keep as many cattle as possible on the commons. Such an arrangement may work reasonably satisfactorily for centuries because tribal wars, poaching, and disease keep the numbers of both man and beast well below the carrying capacity of the land. Finally, however, comes the day of reckoning, that is, the day when the long-desired goal of social stability becomes a reality. At this point, the inherent logic of the commons remorselessly generates tragedy.

As a rational being, each herdsman seeks to maximize his gain. Explicitly or implicitly, more or less consciously, he asks, "What is the utility *to me* of adding one more animal to my herd?" This utility has one negative and one positive component.

1. The positive component is a function of the increment of one animal. Since the herdsman receives all the proceeds from the sale of the additional animal, the positive utility is nearly $+1$.
2. The negative component is a function of the additional overgrazing created by one more animal. Since, however, the effects of overgrazing are

shared by all the herdsmen, the negative utility for any particular decisionmaking herdsman is only a fraction of -1.

Adding together the component partial utilities, the rational herdsman concludes that the only sensible course for him to pursue is to add another animal to his herd. And another. . . . But this is the conclusion reached by each and every rational herdsman sharing a commons. Therein is the tragedy. Each man is locked into a system that compels him to increase his herd without limit—in a world that is limited. Ruin is the destination toward which all men rush, each pursuing his own best interest in a society that believes in the freedom of the commons. Freedom in a commons brings ruin to all.

Some would say that this is a platitude. Would that it were! In a sense, it was learned thousands of years ago, but natural selection favors the forces of psychological denial.[8] The individual benefits as an individual from his ability to deny the truth even though society as a whole, of which he is a part, suffers. Education can counteract the natural tendency to do the wrong thing, but the inexorable succession of generations requires that the basis for this knowledge be constantly refreshed.

A simple incident that occurred a few years ago in Leominster, Massachusetts shows how perishable the knowledge is. During the Christmas shopping season the parking meters downtown were covered with plastic bags that bore tags reading: "Do not open until after Christmas. Free parking courtesy of the mayor and city council." In other words, facing the prospect of an increased demand for already scarce space, the city fathers reinstituted the system of the commons. (Cynically, we suspect that they gained more votes than they lost by this retrogressive act.)

In an approximate way, the logic of the commons has been understood for a long time, perhaps since the discovery of agriculture or the invention of private property in real estate. But it is understood mostly only in special cases which are not sufficiently generalized. Even at this late date, cattlemen leasing national land on the Western ranges demonstrate no more than an ambivalent understanding, in constantly pressuring federal authorities to increase the head count to the point where overgrazing produces erosion and weed-dominance. Likewise, the oceans of the world continue to suffer from the survival of the philosophy of the commons. Maritime nations still respond automatically to the shibboleth of the "freedom of the seas." Professing to believe in the "inexhaustible resources of the oceans," they bring species after species of fish and whales closer to extinction.[9]

The National Parks present another instance of the working out of the tragedy of the commons. At present, they are open to all, without limit. The parks themselves are limited in extent—there is only one Yosemite Valley—whereas population seems to grow without limit. The values that visitors seek in the parks are steadily eroded. Plainly, we must soon cease to treat the parks as commons or they will be of no value to anyone.

What shall we do? We have several options. We might sell them off as private property. We might keep them as public property, but allocate the right to enter them. The allocation might be on the basis of wealth, by the use of an auction system. It might be on the basis of merit, as defined by some agreedupon standards. It might be by lottery. Or it might be on a first-come, first-served basis, administered to long queues. These, I think, are all objectionable. But we must choose—or acquiesce in the destruction of the commons that we call our National Parks.

Pollution

In a reverse way, the tragedy of the commons reappears in problems of pollution. Here it is not a question of taking something out of the commons, but of putting something in—sewage, or chemical, radioactive, and heat wastes into water; noxious and dangerous fumes into the air; and distracting and unpleasant advertising signs into the line of sight. The calculations of utility are much the same as before. The rational man finds that his share of the cost of the wastes he discharges into the commons is less than the cost of purifying his wastes before releasing them. Since this is true for everyone, we are locked into a system of "fouling our own nest," so long as we behave only as independent, rational, free enterprisers.

The tragedy of the commons as a food basket is averted by private property, or something formally like it. But the air and waters surrounding us cannot readily be fenced, and so the tragedy of the commons as a cesspool must be prevented by different means, by coercive laws or taxing devices that make it cheaper for the polluter to treat his pollutants than to discharge them untreated. We have not progressed as far with the solution of this problem as we have with the first. Indeed, our particular concept of private property, which deters us from exhausting the positive resources of the earth, favors pollution. The owner of a factory on the bank of a stream—whose property extends to the middle of the stream—often has difficulty seeing why it is not his natural right to muddy the waters flowing past his door. The law, always behind the times, requires elaborate stitching and fitting to adapt it to this newly perceived aspect of the commons.

The pollution problem is a consequence of population. It did not much matter how a lonely American frontiersman disposed of his waste. "Flowing water purifies itself every ten miles," my grandfather used to say, and the myth was near enough to the truth when he was a boy, for there were not too many people. But as population became denser, the natural chemical and biological recycling processes became overloaded, calling for a redefinition of property rights.

How to Legislate Temperance?

Analysis of the pollution problem as a function of population density uncovers a not generally recognized principle of morality, namely: *the morality of an act is a function of the state of the system at the time it is performed.*[10] Using the commons as a cesspool does not harm the general public under frontier conditions, because there is no public; the same behavior in a metropolis is unbearable. A hundred and fifty years ago a plainsman could kill an American bison, cut out only the tongue for his dinner, and discard the rest of the animal. He was not in any important sense being wasteful. Today, with only a few thousand bison left, we would be appalled at such behavior.

In passing, it is worth noting that the morality of an act cannot be determined from a photograph. One does not know whether a man killing an elephant or setting fire to the grassland is harming others until one knows the total system in which his act appears. "One picture is worth a thousand words," said an ancient Chinese; but it may take ten thousand words to validate it. It is as tempting to ecologists as it is to reformers in general to try to persuade others by way of the photographic shortcut. But the essence of an argument cannot be photographed: it must be presented rationally—in words.

That morality is system-sensitive escaped the attention of most codifiers of ethics in the past. "Thou shalt not . . ." is the form of traditional ethical directives which make no allowance for particular circumstances. The laws of our society follow the pattern of ancient ethics, and therefore are poorly suited to governing a complex, crowded, changeable world. Our epicyclic solution is to augment statutory law with administrative law. Since it is practically impossible to spell out all the conditions under which it is safe to burn trash in the back yard or to run an automobile without smogcontrol, by law we delegate the details to bureaus. The result is administrative law, which is rightly feared for an ancient reason—*Quis custodies ipsos custodes?*—Who shall watch the watchers themselves? John Adams said that we must have a "government of laws and not men." Bureau administrators, trying to evaluate the morality of acts in the total system, are singularly liable to corruption, producing a government by men, not laws.

Prohibition is easy to legislate (though not necessarily to enforce); but how do we legislate temperance? Experience indicates that it can be accomplished best through the mediation of administrative law. We limit possibilities unnecessarily if we suppose that the sentiment of *Quis custodiet* denies us the use of administrative law. We should rather retain the phrase as a perpetual reminder of fearful dangers we cannot avoid. The great challenge facing us now is to invent the corrective feedbacks that are needed to keep custodians honest. We must find ways to legitimate the needed authority of both the custodians and the corrective feedbacks.

Freedom to Breed Is Intolerable

The tragedy of the commons is involved in population problems in another way. In a world governed solely by the principle of "dog eat dog"—if indeed there ever was such a world—how many children a family had would not be a matter of public concern. Parents who bred too exuberantly would leave fewer descendants, not more, because they would be unable to care adequately for their children. David Lack and others have found that such a negative feedback demonstrably controls the fecundity of birds.[11] But men are not birds, and have not acted like them for millenniums, at least.

If each human family were dependent only on its own resources; *if* the children of improvident parents starved to death; *if* thus, over breeding brought its own "punishment" to the germ line—*then* there would be no public interest in controlling the breeding of families. But our society is deeply committed to the welfare state,[12] and hence is confronted with another aspect of the tragedy of the commons.

In a welfare state, how shall we deal with the family, the religion, the race, or the class (or indeed any distinguishable and cohesive group) that adopts over breeding as a policy to secure its own aggrandizement?[13] To couple the concept of freedom to breed with the belief that everyone born has an equal right to the commons is to lock the world into a tragic course of action.

Unfortunately this is just the course of action that is being pursued by the United Nations. In late 1967, some thirty nations agreed to the following: "The Universal Declaration of Human Rights describes the family as the natural and fundamental unit of society. It follows that any choice and decision with regard to the size of the family must irrevocably rest with the family itself, and cannot be made by anyone else."[14]

It is painful to have to deny categorically the validity of this right; denying it, one feels as uncomfortable as a resident of Salem, Massachusetts, who denied the reality of witches in the seventeenth century. At the present time, in liberal quarters, something like a taboo acts to inhibit criticism of the United Nations. There is a feeling that the United Nations is "our last and best hope," that we shouldn't find fault with it; we shouldn't play into the hands of the archconservatives. However, let us not forget what Robert Louis Stevenson said: "The truth that is suppressed by friends is the readiest weapon of the enemy." If we love the truth we must openly deny the validity of the Universal Declaration of Human Rights, even though it is promoted by the United Nations. We should also join with Kingsley Davis[15] in attempting to get Planned Parenthood-World Population to see the error of its ways in embracing the same tragic ideal.

Conscience Is Self-Eliminating

It is a mistake to think that we can control the breeding of mankind in the long run by an appeal to conscience. Charles Galton Darwin made this point when he spoke on the centennial of the publication of his grandfather's great book. The argument is straightforward and Darwinian.

People vary. Confronted with appeals to limit breeding, some people will undoubtedly respond to the plea more than others. Those who have more children will produce a larger fraction of the next generation than those with more susceptible consciences. The differences will be accentuated, generation by generation.

In C. G. Darwin's words: "It may well be that it would take hundreds of generations for the progenitive instinct to develop in this way, but if it should do so, nature would have taken her revenge, and the variety *Homo contracipiens* would become extinct and would be replaced by the variety *Homo progenitivus*.[16]

The argument assumes that conscience or the desire for children (no matter which) is hereditary—but hereditary only in the most general formal sense. The result will be the same whether the attitude is transmitted through germ cells, or exosomatically, to use A. J. Lotka's term. (If one denies the latter possibility as well as the former, then what's the point of education?) The argument has here been stated in the context of the population problem, but it applies equally well to any instance in which society appeals to an individual exploiting a commons to restrain himself for the general good—by means of his conscience. To make such an appeal is to set up a selective system that works toward the elimination of conscience from the race.

Pathogenic Effects of Conscience

The long-term disadvantage of an appeal to conscience should be enough to condemn it; but it has serious short-term disadvantages as well. If we ask a man who is exploiting a commons to desist "in the name of conscience," what are we saying to him? What does he hear?—not only at the moment but also in the wee small hours of the night when, half asleep, he remembers not merely the words we used but also the nonverbal communication cues we gave him unawares? Sooner or later, consciously or subconsciously, he senses that he has received two communications, and that they are contradictory: 1. (intended communication) "If you don't do as we ask, we will openly condemn you for not acting like a responsible citizen"; 2. (the unintended communication) "If you *do* behave as we ask, we will secretly condemn you for a simpleton who can be shamed into standing aside while the rest of us exploit the commons."

Every man then is caught in what Bateson has called a "double bind." Bateson and his co-workers have made a plausible case for viewing the double bind as an important causative factor in the genesis of schizophrenia.[17] The double bind may not always be so damaging, but it always endangers the mental health of anyone to whom it is applied. "A bad conscience," said Nietzsche, "is a kind of illness."

To conjure up a conscience in others is tempting to anyone who wishes to extend his control beyond the legal limits. Leaders at the highest level succumb to this temptation. Has any president during the past generation failed to call on labor unions to moderate voluntarily their demands for higher wages, or to steel companies to honor voluntary guidelines on prices? I can recall none. The rhetoric used on such occasions is designed to produce feelings of guilt in noncooperators.

For centuries it was assumed without proof that guilt was a valuable, per-haps even an indispensable, ingredient of the civilized life. Now, in this post-Freudian world, we doubt it.

Paul Goodman speaks from the modern point of view when he says: "No good has ever come from feeling guilty, neither intelligence, policy, nor compassion. The guilty do not pay attention to the object but only to themselves, and not even to their own interests, which might make sense, but to their anxieties."[18]

One does not have to be a professional psychiatrist to see the conse-quences of anxiety. We in the Western world are just emerging from a dreadful two centuries-long Dark Ages of Eros that was sustained partly by prohibition laws, but perhaps more effectively by the anxiety-generating mechanisms of education. Alex Comfort has told the story well in *The Anxiety Makers;*[19] it is not a pretty one.

Since proof is difficult, we may even concede that the results of anxiety may sometimes, from certain points of view, be desirable. The larger question we should ask is whether, as a matter of policy, we should ever encourage the use of a technique the tendency (if not the intention) of which is psychologi-cally pathogenic. We hear much talk these days of responsible parenthood; the coupled words are incorporated into the titles of some organizations devoted to birth control. Some people have proposed massive propaganda campaigns to instill responsibility into the nation's (or the world's) breeders. But what is the meaning of the word conscience? When we use the word responsibility in the absence of substantial sanctions are we not trying to brow-beat a free man in a commons into acting against his own interest? Responsi-bility is a verbal counterfeit for a substantial quid pro quo. It is an attempt to get something for nothing.

If the word responsibility is to be used at all, I suggest that it be in the sense Charles Frankel uses it.[20] "Responsibility," says this philosopher, "is the product of definite social arrangements." Notice that Frankel calls for social arrangements—not propaganda.

Mutual Coercion Mutually Agreed Upon

The social arrangements that produce responsibility are arrangements that create coercion, of some sort. Consider bank robbing. The man who takes money from a bank acts as if the bank were a commons. How do we prevent such action? Certainly not by trying to control his behavior solely by a verbal appeal to his sense of responsibility. Rather than rely on propaganda we follow Frankel's lead and insist that a bank is not a commons; we seek the definite social arrange-ments that will keep it from becoming a commons. That we thereby infringe on the freedom of would-be robbers we neither deny nor regret.

The morality of bank robbing is particularly easy to understand because we accept complete prohibition of this activity. We are willing to say "Thou shalt not rob banks," without providing for exceptions. But temperance also can be created by coercion. Taxing is a good coercive device. To keep downtown shoppers temperate in their use of parking space we introduce parking meters for short periods, and traffic fines for longer ones. We need not actually forbid a citizen to park as long as he wants to; we need merely make it increasingly expensive for him to do so. Not prohibition, but carefully biased options are what we offer him. A Madison Avenue man might call this persuasion; I prefer the greater candor of the word coercion.

Coercion is a dirty word to most liberals now, but it need not forever be so. As with the four-letter words, its dirtiness can be cleansed away by exposure to the light, by saying it over and over without apology or embarrassment. To many, the word coercion implies arbitrary decisions of distant and irresponsible bureaucrats; but this is not a necessary part of its meaning. The only kind of coercion I recommend is mutual coercion, mutually agreed upon by the majority of the people affected.

To say that we mutually agree to coercion is not to say that we are required to enjoy it, or even to pretend we enjoy it. Who enjoys taxes? We all grumble about them. But we accept compulsory taxes because we recognize that voluntary taxes would favor the conscienceless. We institute and (grumblingly) support taxes and other coercive devices to escape the horror of the commons.

An alternative to the commons need not be perfectly just to be preferable. With real estate and other material goods, the alternative we have chosen is the institution of private property coupled with legal inheritance. Is this system perfectly just? As a genetically trained biologist I deny that it is. It seems to me that, if there are to be differences in individual inheritance, legal possession should be perfectly correlated with biological inheritance—that those who are biologically more fit to be the custodians of property and power should legally inherit more. But genetic recombination continually makes a mockery of the doctrine of "like father, like son" implicit in our laws of legal inheritance. An idiot can inherit millions, and a trust fund can keep his estate intact. We must admit that our legal system of private property plus inheritance is unjust—but we put up with it because we are not convinced, at the moment, that anyone has invented a better system. The alternative of the commons is too horrifying to contemplate. Injustice is preferable to total ruin.

It is one of the peculiarities of the warfare between reform and the status quo that it is thoughtlessly governed by a double standard. Whenever a reform measure is proposed it is often defeated when its opponents triumphantly discover a flaw in it. As Kingsley Davis has pointed out,[21] worshipers of the status quo sometimes imply that no reform is possible without unanimous agreement, an implication contrary to historical fact. As nearly as I can make out, automatic rejection of proposed reforms is based on one of two unconscious assumptions: (1) that the status quo is perfect; or (2) that the choice we face is between reform and no action; if the proposed reform is imperfect, we presumably should take no action at all, while we wait for a perfect proposal.

But we can never do nothing. That which we have done for thousands of years is also action. It also produces evils. Once we are aware that the status quo is action, we can then compare its discoverable advantages and disadvantages with the predicted advantages and disadvantages of the proposed reform, discounting as best we can for our lack of experience. On the basis of such a comparison, we can make a rational decision which will not involve the unworkable assumption that only perfect systems are tolerable.

Recognition of Necessity

Perhaps the simplest summary of this analysis of man's population problems is this: the commons, if justifiable at all, is justifiable only under conditions of low-population density. As the human population has increased, the commons has had to be abandoned in one aspect after another.

First we abandoned the commons in food gathering, enclosing farm land and restricting pastures and hunting and fishing areas. These restrictions are still not complete throughout the world.

Somewhat later we saw that the commons as a place for waste disposal would also have to be abandoned. Restrictions on the disposal of domestic sewage are widely accepted in the Western world; we are still struggling to close the commons to pollution by automobiles, factories, insecticide sprayers, fertilizing operations, and atomic energy installations.

In a still more embryonic state is our recognition of the evils of the commons in matters of pleasure. There is almost no restriction on the propagation of sound waves in the public medium. The shopping public is assaulted with mindless music, without its consent. Our government has paid out billions of dollars to create a supersonic transport which would disturb 50,000 people for every one person whisked from coast to coast 3 hours faster. Advertisers muddy the airwaves of radio and television and pollute the view of travelers. We are a long way from outlawing the commons in matters of pleasure. Is this because our Puritan inheritance makes us view pleasure as something of a sin, and pain (that is, the pollution of advertising) as the sign of virtue?

Every new enclosure of the commons involves the infringement of somebody's personal liberty. Infringements made in the distant past are accepted because no contemporary complains of a loss. It is the newly proposed infringements that we vigorously oppose; cries of "rights" and "freedom" fill the air. But what does "freedom" mean? When men mutually agreed to pass laws against robbing, mankind became more free, not less so. Individuals locked into the logic of the commons are free only to bring on universal ruin; once they see the necessity of mutual coercion, they become free to pursue other goals. I believe it was Hegel who said, "Freedom is the recognition of necessity."

The most important aspect of necessity that we must now recognize, is the necessity of abandoning the commons in breeding. No technical solution can rescue us from the misery of overpopulation. Freedom to breed will bring ruin to all. At the moment, to avoid hard decisions many of us are tempted to propagandize for conscience and responsible parenthood. The temptation must be resisted, because an appeal to independently acting consciences selects for the disappearance of all conscience in the long run, and an increase in anxiety in the short.

The only way we can preserve and nurture other and more precious freedoms is by relinquishing the freedom to breed, and that very soon. "Freedom is the recognition of necessity"—and it is the role of education to reveal to all the necessity of abandoning the freedom to breed. Only so, can we put an end to this aspect of the tragedy of the commons.

NOTES

1. J. B. Wiesner and H. F. York, *Scientific American* 211 (No. 4), 27 (1964).

2. G. Hardin, *Journal of Heredity* 50, 68 (1959), S. von Hoernor, *Science* 137, 18, (1962).

3. J. von Neumann and O. Morgenstern, *Theory of Games and Economic Behavior* (Princeton University Press, Princeton, N.J., 1947), p. 11.

4. J. H. Fremlin, *New Scientist,* No. 415 (1964), p. 285.

5. A. Smith, *The Wealth of Nations* (Modern Library, New York, 1937), p. 423.

6. W. F. Lloyd, *Two Lectures on the Checks to Population* (Oxford University Press, Oxford, England, 1833).

7. A. N. Whitehead, *Science and the Modern World* (Mentor, New York, 1948), p. 17.

8. G. Hardin, Ed., *Population, Evolution, and Birth Control* (Freeman, San Francisco, 1964), p. 56.

9. S. McVay, *Scientific American* 216 (No. 8), 13 (1966).

10. J. Fletcher, *Situation Ethics* (Westminster, Philadelphia, 1966).

11. D. Lack, *The Natural Regulation of Animal Numbers* (Clarendon Press, Oxford, England, 1954).

12. H. Girvetz, *From Wealth to Welfare* (Stanford University Press, Stanford, Calif, 1950).

13. G. Hardin, *Perspectives in Biology and Medicine* 6, 366 (1963).

14. U Thant, *International Planned Parenthood News,* No. 168 (February 1968), p. 3.

15. K. Davis, *Science* 158, 730 (1967).

16. S. Tax, Ed., *Evolution After Darwin* (University of Chicago Press, Chicago, 1960), vol. 2, p. 469.

17. G. Bateson, D. D. Jackson, J. Haley, J. Weakland, *Behavioral Science* 1, 251 (1956).

18. P. Goodman, *New York Review of Books* 10 (8), 22 (23 May 1968).

19. A. Comfort, *The Anxiety Makers* (Nelson, London, 1967).

20. C. Frankel, *The Case for Modern Man* (Harper & Row, New York, 1955), p. 203.

21. J. D. Roslansky, *Genetics and the Future of Man* (Appleton-Century-Crofts, New York, 1966), p. 177.

42

The Seven Deadly Sins of Policy Analysts (1976)

Arnold J. Meltsner

Over the years I have noticed that the process of policy advising often suffers from a set of recurring problems. We sometimes think of these problems as problems of quality. If only the client had better analysts, then he or she would make better decisions. If the prime minister had a policy analysis office, then Great Britain's economy would be in better shape. Whatever the problem, good advice or some structure to give good advice would be the solution. Particularly in America, we love to tinker with our structures and institutions to achieve improved information, decisions, and outcomes. Seldom do we recognize the difficulty in doing so. Indeed, the incentives encourage us not to recognize the difficulties and push us instead to adopt the latest management gimmick. Management of Objectives, Zero-based Budgeting, or the holy acronym that will solve all: IAC, Improved Advice of Clients.

Before we can design an IAC, we have to recognize what is wrong. Of course knowing what is wrong will not tell us what is good. But it is a start. So I have developed a list of seven deadly sins. Sinful policy analysis is: channeled, distant, late, superficial, topical, capricious, and apolitical. These sins or categories are not mutually exclusive: they bleed into each other. One can try to fix one with the result of committing another. Advice that is too late for a decision, for example, has to be made more relevant, but if it is too relevant, it may also be too topical, too concerned with short-term events and payoffs. Nor is there anything so special about my list; those of us who are trained to find fault could easily add to the list or shift my examples to illustrate other sins. Despite these reservations, it is a list of sins that deserves attention because at one time or another we, as policy analysts, have committed them.

Being in a Rut

The sin of channeled advice means that the advice is in a rut, groove, or furrow. Locked into a solution, both analyst and client ignore that circumstances have changed or that constraints exist. Sometimes the advice stays in a rut because of bureaucratic routines, such as the military using field manuals from World War II to plan present actions and future contingencies. A client can also contribute to the channeling by insisting on inappropriate goals and beliefs. Secretary of Defense Robert S. McNamara thought he could save money on procurement and operating expenses by buying a common plane for the services. While the belief in commonality is probably appropriate to automobile production and procurement, it was inappropriate for what turned out to be the expensive and less than satisfactory TFX (F-111). Yet McNamara stayed in his rut while the Air Force and Navy stayed in theirs, insisting on their individual requirements and following through on their procurement folkways.

Sometimes the sin of channeled advice comes about because of the political and intellectual climate. That was certainly the case in the decade following the passage of Medicare and Medicaid. The majority of health experts, inside and outside of government, pushed for some form of national health insurance as a natural extension of previous legislation. Their efforts focused on which form of national health insurance, in terms of coverage, financing, and administration; few questioned the assumptions that the country needed some form of national insurance. Both analysts and clients stayed comfortably in their channel until the reality of rapidly escalating health costs caught up with them and their thinking.

Too Far Away

The sin of distant advice is that it is based on ignorance. Distant advice is not grounded in reality. The analyst does not have to be a utopian to commit the sin—just far away enough from immediate reality not to have an audience or to misjudge the application of his or her advice. Policy analysts all too often come up with general solutions for very specific conditions. Our training in the social sciences seems to encourage a bit too much confidence in the power of theory and data analysis. It is not surprising that the analysis of aggregate data does not always fit the conditions and individuals at the point a policy is applied. Yet we are continually amazed that the advice cooked up in Washington does not square with the reality of San Antonio, Texas. Surely by now, we ought to recognize the complexity that sheer geography creates in our federal system.

The sin of distant advice is not only caused by geography. Policy advising can be distant in a number of senses: the theory and underlying conceptions of causation can be too global or too refined; the chosen variables may make for neat statistical explanations but not be linked to actual policy levers or to immediate policy issues. At the very least the client should be informed as to whether the situation or problem is susceptible to his or her intervention. Instead of close and manipulatable causation that should be inherent in policy advice, the client is likely to get distant advice, advice that is likely to result in implementation problems, or in displacing the problem on the some other client, or in making it appear that something can be done when it cannot.

I recall a policy analyst who was evaluating several social programs, and thought it was appropriate to offer recommendations based solely on available performance numbers without going to the field. He thought it was a waste of his time to examine the actual operation of the programs. Obviously in foreign policy situations, where reliable information is hard to obtain, the analyst may inadvertently commit this sin, but what is the excuse of the domestic policy analyst who can easily find out the facts but does not want to do so?

Forget the Policy Process

Figuring out what to do, the policy process, makes harsh requirements on its participants. An analyst may be late to his or her wedding but must be on time when advice is wanted. Yet so much advice is simply too late to be used. Late advice is truly a sin because of the waste. It is information that no one at the time wants. Like advice that is too early, late advice floats around hoping for someone to use it.

The tyro is usually cautioned to be on time and to make sure that his or her work fits the timing requirements of the policy process. While developing good work habits can do much to alleviate the problem, it is not the whole story. Sometimes the analyst, in wanting to get one more fact or in checking one number, decides to risk being late to pursue being precisely right. Who can argue with such dedication? Is not accuracy and truth a virtue?

To make an appropriate decision as to the balance between accuracy and being on time, the analyst needs to understand the situation that confronts the client. Is it the kind of situation in which it is essential to have some rough insights early in the process or some carefully considered reflections later on? Is there some play in the timing of the decision? The sin of late advice frequently comes about when the analyst is ill-informed about the client's situation and the client has not taken sufficient steps to correct the analyst's perceptions. Somehow consumers and producers of advice get unhinged and separated. Neither seem to appreciate the situation of the other.

Typically one client asks for some advice and then is replaced by another client who has no need for it. No doubt many contracted studies are wasted simply because of the game of musical chairs that goes on in public and private organizations. A visible, and sometimes embarrassing, example occurs when the advisor is a presidential commission that is appointed by one president but submits its report to another. That was the case when President Nixon received the message that pornography was not as bad as he and his supporters thought. Perhaps President Johnson would not have liked the message either, but since the Commission on Obscenity and Pornography was not one of Nixon's offspring, it was easier for President Nixon to separate himself from its findings.

Know Too Little

Sometimes the advice is too quick, too off-the-cuff, and not based on enough digging into the roots of the problem, and that is when the sin of superficial advice is committed. I once worked for a person who had the reputation of being the best superficial mind in Washington. There is a hint of criticism in such a remark, but there is also a kind of admiration that testifies to the prevailing incentives of the policy process. Unfortunately acceptance of advice for both clients and analysts is much more important than the appropriate selection, definition, and analysis of a problem.

All too often clients and analysts are inclined to fire the head of a department as if that action alone will fix what is wrong with the organization. Let the new boss find out what is wrong is the motto of busy clients and their analysts. After all they will not be around to discover that the organizational problems persist and seem to be independent of the person who is supposed to be in charge. Most reorganization studies suffer from superficial analysis. The client wants to reorganize so the analysts shuffle boxes without much motivation to discover the costs of the reorganization or to ascertain whether the shuffling will enhance productivity and the capability to perform. President Carter, for numerous reasons, wanted to have a separate department of education, and so with effort it came to pass. Now President Reagan does not want a separate department and would like to change things back again. Both of these clients and their analysts cloaked these changes in the garments of efficiency. But this is nonsense because the same action and its reverse cannot both be efficient.

What annoys me about the sin of superficiality in the case of reorganization studies is that they deflect the attention of the client and they displace the effort of the analyst. Superficial solutions interfere with appropriate diagnosis and the hard work necessary to achieve sensible policies. Certainly we want to enhance the learning and potential of our children. We want to know how to do better at the mystery of teaching. The relationship of a federal reorganization to local school performance is at best tangential if not non-existent. The road to unintended consequences and high employment for policy analysts is paved with superficial advice.

Excessive Reactions

The fifth deadly sin is topical advice. All too often the demand for advice stems from some sort of crisis or manufactured crisis—an airplane crashes, DNA experimentation may be out of control, masses of people may die of swine flu. The crisis leads to a kind of a fire-house mentality, advice on the run. Then the analyst is likely to provide superficial and distant advice. Analysts may do this without the excuse of a crisis, but a crisis makes it acceptable. Putting aside these sins, there are still problems with topical advice. When clients and analysts keep reacting to perceived crises, they are likely to lose control of their agenda. How often is it said in foreign policy that the president is just reacting to external events and does not have a policy?

An organization that relies only on reacting may lose its future. Without some measure of anticipation a business, for example, can be preempted from an important emerging market. Topical advice concentrates on the salient and palpable, and so it should. We want our clients to be responsive to relevant events, and we want them to have the necessary information to do so. But we do not want them to do only that because we expect to live in the future as well as today. Therefore we want them to pay attention to the less visible problems and issues. We do not want analysts to ignore some issue just because it is less visible and has not assumed crisis proportions.

Thus the main trouble with topical advice is that it crowds out other less pressing advice. The client is too busy dealing with the daily crisis, and the analyst has to help. A wise client and analyst, therefore, will correct this defect in decision making, not by appointing a useless advanced planning unit, but by selecting some future issues for immediate attention. A mayor, for example, could point out that past years of neglect of sewers and roads has created a "crisis" in public works that will affect public health and safety unless something is done. That too few public officials have done so is confirmed by the invisibility of a major capital replacement problem in this country. Evidently these officials are too busy dealing with present problems and topical advice.

Change for Its Own Sake

The sin of capricious advice is not quite the same as the topical one. What I have in mind is the bias in advice to change things. We lack enough incentives in policymaking to say just leave it alone. Both analysts and their clients keep looking for changes. I realize that much of the organizational context of the client and analyst is devoted to maintaining routines and the way things are. But in trying to counteract this organizational inertia, we may not let things gel enough so we can learn something. It is difficult to evaluate a program if we do not let it operate for a while.

Consider our primary and secondary schools. Probably I am telescoping things, but I cannot remember a time when someone was not criticizing them and someone else was not suggesting a panacea. Not knowing the relationship of what we do to what we want to see happen, schools have been subjected to all sorts of teaching fads and methods. Just when the schools are about to return to some sort of equilibrium, they are confronted with one more commission report and one more change in direction. It is not just money that teachers need, we also have to stop hassling them and undermining their mental health with capricious advice.

Of course clients can not spend their entire time in office being content. Some policymaking activity is essential for maintaining support and approval.

Advisors for their part have to suggest something in order to keep their jobs or to advance; they cannot just keep saying leave it alone. Despite the incentives for change, clients and analysts have to be sensitive to the consequences of capricious advice and head off the gross foolishness before it starts.

Advice without Politics

The final sin is apolitical advice. By this I mean that political advice is not appropriately linked or integrated with the substantive advice of policy. Clients, particularly those who have just gone through an election, insist on being told what is right and want to leave the political judgment to themselves. Advisors, particularly technicians, for their part, insist that there are correct answers and have been educated to believe that politics is irrational, something outside the boundaries of expert discourse. Thus a peculiar division of labor arises in which we have experts who give policy advice and different experts who give political advice. Sometimes the client can integrate these two sources of information, but more often than not the client lands up being embarrassed.

A case in point is when President Carter wanted to have his analysts reform the welfare system without paying attention to political constraints. His idea was that welfare could be reformed without spending additional money, and his analysts worked very hard to give him what he wanted knowing full well that what he wanted was not politically viable. The proposed reform never got anywhere and became one more example of Carter's inability to function in the Oval Office.

Often rulers and clients are surrounded by analysts who suggest policies that cannot stand the test of legislative approval and executive implementation. What good does it do for the analyst to suggest, for example, deregulation of natural gas if the analyst has not thought of a practical way of doing so? Worse yet is the analyst who believes that anyone can give political advice and offers ready opinions without any investigation or testing of the prevailing political wisdom.

Maintaining a political perspective in policy advising, by both client and analyst, is essential, otherwise important opportunities may be lost. A few years ago in Zambia, the citizens beat up a village chief because the population of crocodiles was increasing and attacking the citizens almost daily. The citizens wanted the chief to get the government to do something about the problem. At the same time, the government in Lusaka was considering breeding crocodiles so the skins could be sold for foreign exchange. The problem for Lusaka was to get crocodiles off the endangered species list and then to establish breeding farms; the problem at the village level was to get rid of the crocodiles or at least control the growth of its population. I do not know what happened, but here was an excellent political opportunity.

If the government could have incorporated the local village's need for crocodile control in their foreign exchange plans, it would have earned the support and allegiance of the local citizens and contributed to the stability of the political system. The example may be a bit farfetched, but consider for a moment how our own general attitudes about the performance of government are conditioned by the efficiency, or lack of it, of daily mail delivery. Rulers have to consider not only the immediate operational aspects of a policy—whether the solution meets the requirements of the specific problem—but the broader significance of the policy as well. To do so requires that political understanding be integrated with policy substance, not just from rulers but also from their advisors.

In Western countries we have elevated the separation of knowledge and power to a matter of high principle. We create civil service systems, illusions of governance, fictions that uninformed political masters direct and control neutral experts. We say our civil servants should be apolitical. We teach our experts that science and politics do not mix. We do all these things and then wonder why clients and their analysts make policy blunders. We are so afraid that the analyst will usurp the client's function that we ignore that the client needs help in determining whether a policy is appropriate for governmental action, in developing a consensus and understanding of political feasibility, and in addressing the enduring matters of the maintenance of the state and its public philosophy.

43

The Art of Policy Analysis (1979)

Aaron Wildavsky

Policy analysis is an art. Its subjects are public problems that must be solved at least tentatively to be understood. Piet Hein put this thought-twister,[1] "Art is the solving of problems that cannot be expressed until they are solved." Policy analysis must create problems that decision-makers are able to handle with the

Source: Aaron Wildavsky, from *Speaking Truth to Power: The Art and Craft of Policy Analysis.* Copyright © 1987 by Transaction Publishers. Reprinted by permission of the publisher.

variables under their control and in the time available. Only by specifying a desired relationship between manipulable means and obtainable objectives can analysts make the essential distinction—between a puzzle that can be solved definitively, once all the pieces are put in place, and a problem for which there may not be a programmatic solution.

The technical base of policy analysis is weak. In part its limitations are those of social science: innumerable discrete propositions, of varying validity and uncertain applicability, occasionally touching but not necessarily related, like beads on a string. Its strengths lie in the ability to make a little knowledge go a long way by combining an understanding of the constraints of the situation with the ability to explore the environment constructively. Unlike social science, however, policy analysis must be prescriptive; arguments about correct policy, which deal with the future, cannot help but be willful and therefore political.

Analysis is imagination. Making believe the future has happened in the past, analysts try to examine events as if those actions already had occurred. They are strongly committed to "thought experiments," in which they imagine what might have been in order to improve what may come to pass. Theories are discarded instead of people. Naturally, this is risky. Often we do not know where we have been, let alone where we would like to go or how to get there. Retrodiction ("predicting the past") may be as much in dispute as prediction. Because what our past should have been, as well as what our future ought to be, is defined by differing values, one person's analytic meat may be poison to another. Following the practices of the analytic craft—norms for disciplining private imagination by making it more publicly assessable—can reduce but cannot eliminate disagreement over future consequences that no one has yet experienced.

Policies should be considered not as eternal truths but as hypotheses subject to modification and replacement by better ones until these in turn are discarded. Dogma is deleterious; skepticism is sound. Yet dogma is indispensable; without taking some things for granted some of the time, everything is in flux so that nothing comes amenable to examination. Drawing the balance is not easy: how much dogma versus how much skepticism?

The good organization is devoted to correcting errors, but is subject to exhaustion itself if it does not reject a high proportion of the allegations against its current practices. Anyone who knows contemporary education will acknowledge that. Error correction itself has to be traded off against error recognition, for the very visibility of error, which facilitates detection, is correlated with large size, which makes correction difficult. The widely acknowledged error in indexing social security against both wages and prices is easy to spot because its cost is huge, but difficult to end because so many millions benefit. Whether errors are recognized or eliminated depends on the interests of the people who participate in producing policy.

People make problems. How are they to be encouraged to do the right thing? How does one individual know what is right for others? What gives anyone the right to decide for others? How are preferences shaped and expressed? One way of shaping and expressing is to ask people, and another is to tell them. "Asking" means setting up institutions, such as voting for public office and bargaining over prices, to help people evolve preferences. "Telling" means deciding intellectually what is good for people and moving them in a predetermined sequence toward a preselected destination. Asking (which we will call social interaction or just plain politics) and telling (intellectual cogitation or just plain planning) both belong in policy analysis. When things go wrong, analysts, at least in a democracy, play politics. By altering the franchise or by imposing a cost constraint or by making monopoly less likely, analysts seek to adjust institutional interaction so as to secure better behavior. Planning is preferable when interaction is not feasible, because people can't get together, or when it is undesirable, because people might make morally impermissible choices. The highest form of analysis is using intellect to aid interaction between people.

Policy analysis, then, is about relationships between people. When we like the results of interaction between doctors and patients or teachers and students, we reinforce our approval of the institutional arrangements under which such persons come together. When we don't approve, we try to alter these relationships. Major changes take place when we shift the pattern of relationships (by paying doctors through government, or giving parents vouchers enabling them to choose public schools) so that outcomes change. Thinking about analysis as relations between people much like us—not as strange symbols or desiccated dollar signs—is not only more humane but also more accurate.

Policy analysis, to be brief, is an activity creating problems that can be solved. Every policy is fashioned of tension between resources and objectives, planning and politics, skepticism and dogma. Solving problems involves temporarily resolving these tensions.

But, if tensions do not have an end, they must have a beginning: what social forces do they reflect? Objectives may be infinite but resources are not; scarcity of resources is ubiquitous. Objectives, therefore, must be limited by resources; what one tries to do depends on what one has to do it with. But this does not always mean that resources are always good, so to speak, because they exist and objectives are bad, because they exceed what is available. On the contrary, objectives may demand too little so that resources flow in the wrong direction.

How dogmatic and how skeptical one is about policies and the way they are produced—who gets what and why, as Lasswell said—is a measure of trust in social relations. What one likes may depend on how one does. A record of success in economic markets would naturally increase confidence in that form of encounter. Cogitation may appeal more to groups that gain less from interaction. The tensions about which we talk, then, are social as well as intellectual; they are about power in society as well as analysis of policy.

The list of the goals one is not attempting to reach is necessarily much larger than those one does try for. I make no pretense of writing a "how-to-do-it" book, other than by illustrating forms analysis can take. This book is comparative in that I compare a wide range of American domestic policies, but it is not exhaustive (by no means does it include all or most policies) or international (I do not discuss experiences abroad). My impression is that west European nations are no more successful than we are in most of domestic policy; the big difference is that America publicizes its failures and most of these other nations do not. Defense policy is not covered because the scope of this book is already too broad. My purpose is not to cover everything, a task best left to an encyclopedia, but to exemplify the main characteristics of the art and craft of analyzing policy. The book is organized so that readers who wish to consider the main lines of policy development can go straight through, skipping the last section, which pursues policies in depth, to get to the conclusion on craftsmanship.

Policy Analysis is about the realm of rationality and responsibility where resources are related to objectives. Rationality resides in connecting what you want with what you can do, and responsibility in being accountable for making that connection.

Policy Analysis is also about calculation and culture: What combination of social interaction and intellectual cogitation, planning and politics, leads us to figure out what we should want to do and how to do it? In the course or relating resources to objectives culture is created by shifting patterns of social relationships. Analysis teaches us not only how to get what we want, because that may be unobtainable or undesirable, but what we ought to want compared to what others are to give us in return for what we are prepared to give them. Calculation comes in deciding whether and which decisions will be made by bidding and bargaining or by central command.

Always there is a tension between dogma and skepticism, where analysis embodies skepticism but can't get along with dogma. When results do not live up to our expectations, or we think we can do better, which is most of the time, the question of error detection and error correction comes to the fore. Nothing is ultimately sacrosanct, of course, but at any given time a proper degree of doubt—how much will remain unchallenged if not unchallengeable—is essential but difficult to determine.

These, then, are the tasks and tensions of policy analysis: relating resources to objectives by balancing social interaction against intellectual cogitation so as to learn to draw the line between skepticism and dogma.

My life is spent reading, talking and writing about public affairs. Yet I cannot keep up. And, though I have more time than most people, I cannot satisfy the endless demands for participation. Somehow we must be able to make sense out of public affairs without being consumed by them. How to help ourselves gain access to public life without becoming politicians is the challenge, for it means not only sporadic influence over policy but continuous participation as part of policy (as patients, postal patrons, donators to charities) as it is played out. Analysts are paid to spend full time on public affairs; citizens must relate time spent on their public activities to their private interests. I argue that citizens can act as analysts by becoming part of public policies through which they can determine what they are getting for what they give, by learning to perfect their preferences, and by exercising their autonomy so as to enhance reciprocity by taking others into account. Above all, policy analysis is about improvement, about improving citizen preferences for the policies they—the people—ought to prefer.

NOTES

1. As quoted by R. K. Merton in *The Sociology of Science in Europe,* R. K. Merton and Jerry Gaston, eds. (Carbondale: Southern Illinois University Press, 1977), p. 3.

Review Questions

1. What was Garrett Hardin's explanation for the cause of the "tragedy of the commons"? Can you apply Hardin's "tragedy" to a contemporary environmental problem?

2. What are the "seven deadly sins" that Arnold Meltsner asserts all policy analysts should avoid? Why is it so important that professional policy analysts offer advice that is in the best interests of their clients—as opposed to advice that is politically or ideologically biased?

3. Has Aaron Wildavsky been able to resolve the question of whether policy analysis is an art or a science? How does art complement science in the eternal debate over whether policy analysis (as well as public administration) is more one than the other?